INTRODUCING PERSONAL FINANCE

INTRODUCING PERSONAL FINANCE

WALT J. WOERHEIDE
The American College

JOHN WILEY & SONS, INC.

Acquisitions Editor	Leslie Kraham
Production Management	Jeanine Furino
Production Editor	Sandra Russell
Marketing Manager	Charity Robey
Senior Designer	Karin Kincheloe
Production Management Services	Argosy Publishing Services
Cover	Guy Crittenden/Stock Illustration Source

The paper in this book was manufactured by a mill whose forest management programs include sustained yield harvesting of its timberlands. Sustained yield harvesting principles ensure that the number of trees cut each year does not exceed the amount of new growth.

This book is printed on acid-free paper.

Library of Congress Cataloging in Publications Data:
Woerheide, Walter J.
    Personal finance / Walt Woerheide.
       p. cm.
    Includes index.
    ISBN 0-471-37059-2 (pbk. : alk. Paper)
    1. Finance, Personal. I. Title.

HG179.W563 2001
332.024--dc21

                                    2001045306

10 9 8 7 6 5 4 3 2 1

This book is dedicated to my wife, Pat.
Her support of my efforts far exceeds my
ability to show all the appreciation she deserves.

PREFACE

Web Link: www.wiley.com/college/woerheide

The field of personal finance is undergoing a major change as a result of three trends that occurred during the nineties. The first was the proliferation of Internet sites and the increasing ease of creating them. The second was a maturing of the technology that allows access to the Internet. The third was the emergence of a large population of people who can access the Internet easily and cheaply and who have enough education to do useful things with it. Put simply, there is a large and growing number of educated people with Internet access at home who are trying to figure out how the Internet can help them with personal financial decision-making.

A great quantity of the material on the Internet is aimed at selling products to the individual, but this is not what we mean by personal finance. Personal finance on the Internet is the material that offers information, answers, and even solutions to individuals' personal finance problems and questions. Some sites are provided in the hope that users will be so pleased with the information available that said users will buy the services or products of the site sponsors or site advertisers. Some sites, however, are offered by groups whose goal is simply to share information. These providers include governmental entities, educational institutions, and nonprofit and not-for-profit organizations.

The goal of this book is to provide a structural framework of personal finance so people will know what questions to ask and why, and to suggest Internet sites that will answer those questions. Over the years, the addresses of critical sites will change. Some sites will disappear. Others will come into existence. This book is not intended to be a permanent resource book. It is intended to prepare the student to use the Internet to answer his or her own questions and to solve problems. Once you are familiar with the field of personal finance and comfortable and knowledgeable about using the Internet to deal with personal financial issues, this book should cease to be of necessity to you.

What Are Web Links?

In this book, you will encounter many, many references to **web links.** References to web links recommend or require that you visit that web link. The number before the period in the reference indicates the chapter in which the web link is found. The second number in the web link is the unique reference for that chapter. The second numbers are mostly sequential. The web page where the web link may be found is listed on the first page of each chapter, as shown above.

Some web links, identified by the expression "(WSJ)" inserted between the words *Web Link* and the numerical reference, go to the *Wall Street Journal*'s interactive site. Everyone who buys a new copy of this book receives a subscription to this web site. Those who buy a used edition will need to acquire access to this site. You can subscribe to just the *Wall Street Journal* web site, or you can subscribe to the *Journal* itself and receive a free web site subscription.

The addresses shown at the web links are the actual addresses of the linked pages. Viewing the actual address can often give you valuable information about the provider of the site. There are certain common features of web addresses, technically known as **URLs** or Uniform Resource Locators. A URL consists of three parts. The first is a code identifying the transfer protocol to be used. This is expressed as *http://.* When you enter a web page address in a browser, it is not necessary to enter this part of the address as the browser identifies the transfer protocol automatically.

The second part of the address, also called the root name, identifies the server, the actual machine somewhere in the world, on which the file resides. The last section of the server address tells something about the provider of that web address. The most common suffix is .com, which identifies a commercial provider. The three other common suffixes are .org, .gov, and .edu. These indicate the sponsors are not-for-profit or nonprofit organizations, governmental entities, and educational institutions. Sites originating in countries other than the United States have a two-letter country code as the last part of the server address. Most country codes are easily decipherable.

The third part of the address is the full pathname, or file name locating the specific **Web Link Intro.1**   file on that server. For additional information on URLs, see **Web Link Intro.1.**

What Is Link Rot and How Can You Deal with It?

Link rot is when an address no longer works. One cause of link rot is that the linked web site or server no longer exists. If after you enter an address the browser displays an error message that it is unable to locate the server and/or that the server does not have a DNS entry, then the address is useless. As an example of a useless address, try *www.whatthe.com.*

The people who construct and maintain web pages are usually called **web masters.** Web masters sometimes change the configuration of their web sites: they may move pages to a different location (a different pathname) or simply remove them. When this happens, some sites will invite you to use a site map or a search calculator to find the location of a missing page. Other sites will transfer you to the site's **home page.** The home page is the page you would reach if you entered the machine's address and provided no file name.

If you are using a long URL with multiple paths associated with it (new paths are introduced by a slash) and the browser fails to find the desired page, deleting parts of the address may help you. Start by deleting the last listed path- or file name and reenter the address. Thus, if you started with *www.whatthe.com/firstpath/secondpath/thirdpath/ file.html,* and received the message that the desired page no longer existed, lop off *file.html* and try the address again. Then delete *thirdpath* and try again. Keep deleting pathnames until you are back at the machine address (or root name). When you obtain an address that brings up a real web page, look for links that might take you to the desired web page. An alternative approach is to delete all of the URL except for the home page or root name, and look for the appropriate link from there.

What Is a Search Engine?

Web Link Intro.2

Between the time when this book was written and the associated web pages constructed and the time when you are using it, link rot will wipe out some of the links. Although it is our intention to replace rotted links with new links on a regular basis, replacement cannot occur on a daily basis and may not always be possible. When the strategy above fails to work, you might need to use a **search engine** to locate the desired web page. A search engine is a web page that will provide the addresses of (and links to) web pages that the user may be seeking. Browsers usually come with one or more search engines built into them. A list of several search engines is also provided at **Web Link Intro.2.**

What Is a "Pointer Site," and What Are Some?

Web Link Intro.3

A **pointer site** exclusively or primarily provides links to other sites. The more links offered, and the better organized they are, the better the quality of the pointer site. A well-constructed pointer site may be more efficient for locating particular web pages than a search engine. Some comprehensive pointer sites in the personal finance area are provided at **Web Link Intro.3.**

How Is This Book Organized?

In the first chapter, we will consider the personal financial planning model and the miscues of life. The components of this model and the types of miscues define much of the field of personal finance. Part I of the book addresses basic issues that are associated with many of the other topics in the book. Thus, this part covers not only the personal financial planning model, but also the basics of financial planning and budgeting, taxes, the use of time value of money, and the management of liquid assets.

Part II covers the acquisition of assets and the use of debt to pay for these assets. Chapters 6 and 7 focus on open account credit such as credit cards and on longer-term debt such as installment loans. Chapter 8 looks at how one might go about buying the two major consumer assets that most people buy: houses and cars. Chapter 9 then considers how to pay for these two acquisitions.

Part III covers the various forms of insurance. Insurance is critical because it is the most efficient way to manage many of the risks an individual faces. The four major types of insurance covered are homeowner's, auto, life, and health.

Part IV provides an introduction to investments. Many students take a personal finance course because they want to know more about investing. Investing is a major element of personal finance, but it is not the only element. The material in these four chapters will serve as an introduction to someone with no experience in investments.

Part V deals with the last period of most people's lives, namely, retirement and then death. Retirement planning starts with a basic model for determining the income one would need in retirement. The next step is to review the four sources of retirement income, which are Social Security, pensions, tax-favored programs, and personal savings. The key finance elements associated with dying, wills, trusts, and gift and estate taxes, are especially important for those who have parents who need to prepare financially for death, or who care how their own assets are distributed among their beneficiaries.

ARE THERE ANY SPECIAL FEATURES OF THIS BOOK?

There are two special features of this book. As indicated above, one of its objectives is to encourage people to learn what questions they should be asking with regard to personal finance. Hence, instead of subtitles, questions are used to introduce each new section. Moving away from an encyclopedic style of presentation of material, with its steady diet of factual and descriptive statements, I have rather used a Socratic approach, in which the material is presented in a question and answer format. The emphasis of this book is on solving problems rather than on just defining terms and concepts.

The second special feature of this book is that it is meant to be read in conjunction with the Internet. Thus, there is a noticeable lack of pretty figures and elaborate charts in the book itself; the pretty figures and charts are found on the Internet, not in the textbook. Most of the figures provided are solely to give the reader an indication of what the Internet page they are looking for should look like. Whether you literally sit at your computer while reading this book in order to look up the web sites, or read the book first and then go to the Internet to look up the sites, depends on your own individual learning style. But if you read the book without going to the Internet, then you are missing the entire purpose of why the book was written.

Finally, some of the web links are discussed within the text, and the purpose of visiting the web link is stated. Other web links are shown in the margin with no explicit discussion as to what you would find there. I have attempted to place the web link references in the margins next to the lines to which they pertain. Such links usually provide nothing more than additional discussion of the topic being addressed on that particular line.

Acknowledgments

This book would not exist today without the encouragement and support of the many students who have taken the personal finance course from me in recent years. My thinking on this topic started in about 1995 when an investments student asked why we didn't examine the Internet in the course. I suddenly realized that if I didn't start incorporating the Internet into my courses, my students would be shortchanged.

I made it a point to start learning about useful personal finance sites and incorporating such sites into my courses. I also added to my personal finance course a term project in which the students were required to construct their own web pages that posed personal finance questions and identified links that would answer them. What I found most fascinating was that even though I never gave one word of instruction on how to construct a web page, and such knowledge was not a prerequisite for the course, everyone successfully completed this project. This demonstrated to me that it was time to build a course around the web. I therefore want to thank all the students in my personal finance courses since 1995 who have responded so enthusiastically to my attempts to incorporate the Internet into the course.

I also thank several colleagues and acquaintances who gave me strong encouragement for this book, including Tom Eyssel, Don Holdren, Dede Pahl, and Kathryn Ioaniddes, as well as the early reviewers of sample chapters: Carlene Creviston, Kyle Mattson, and Barbara Poole. I particularly thank Karen Lahey and Michael J. Woodworth for reading the entire manuscript and making many substantive changes thereto.

Finally, thank you to the Rochester Institute of Technology for granting a sabbatical for the winter quarter of 1997–1998, which allowed me to really get started on this project.

Walt J. Woerheide
Bryn Mawr, Pennsylvania
August 17, 2001

CONTENTS

PART IV
INVESTMENTS

ABOUT THE AUTHOR

Walt J. Woerheide is the Vice-President of Academic Affairs at The American College in Bryn Mawr, Pennsylvania. Prior to that, he held faculty and administrative positions at the Rochester Institute of Technology, University of Michigan – Flint, and the University of Illinois at Chicago, and served as a Visiting Scholar with the Federal Home Loan Bank Board in Washington, D.C. He has published in a wide variety of journals, including *Journal of Financial and Quantitative Analysis, Financial Services Review, Financial Counseling and Planning, Journal of Consumer Affairs, Journal of Financial Planning, Journal of Retail Banking, Journal of Institute of Certified Financial Planners,* and *Real Estate Issues.* He has served as President of the Academy of Financial Services and the Midwest Finance Association. Dr. Woerheide's undergraduate degree is in mathematical-economics from Brown University, and both his M.B.A. and Ph.D. with concentrations in finance are from Washington University in St. Louis.

PART 1

BASIC ISSUES IN
FINANCIAL PLANNING

UNDERSTANDING THE FINANCIAL PLANNING PROCESS

LEARNING OBJECTIVES

- Define the six steps of the personal financial planning process
- Describe the five strategies to managing one's finances
- Identify the various types of financial planners and how they are compensated
- Define human capital
- Describe how to select a job or a career
- Find a job using the Internet
- Decide among job offers based on both salary and location

Web Link: www.wiley.com/college/woerheide

INTRODUCTION

Many students entering a personal finance course think that personal finance is about how to save money. Although personal finance is sometimes promoted as a series of money-saving ideas, that is not what it is about. What ultimately gives people pleasure in life is not making lots of money (although that is nice), not accumulating a huge hoard of wealth (although that can be nice also), but using their money the best way for them. Personal finance is about the management, protection, and ultimate use of wealth. Personal financial management is best accomplished through a six-step model.

WHAT ARE THE SIX BASIC STEPS OF THE FINANCIAL PLANNING PROCESS?

Web Link 1.1

The financial planning process may appear as a bizarre collection of indecipherable symbols. But when you break this complex process into its elements, it can be more easily understood. Effective personal financial planning involves six steps. They are

1. Define your current situation.
2. Define where you want to go.
3. Identify the barriers to getting where you want to go.
4. Develop a written plan.
5. Implement the plan.

Web Link 1.2

6. Regularly review and revise the plan.

3

How Do I Define My Current Situation?

The first step in reading any map is to ascertain where you are on that map. Publicly displayed maps always have a big sign that says, "You are here." In our personal finances, financial statements (a balance sheet and income statement) define where we are. Chapter 2 covers financial statements.

How Do I Define Where I Want to Go?

Usually people turn to serious financial planning when they sense that they are not moving toward where they want to go. Financial planning goals are not just monetary goals, although such goals are obvious and appropriate. Goals can be short term, intermediate term, and long term. Short-term goals are for the coming 12 months. What do you want your personal balance sheet to look like in 12 months? What would you like to do during the coming year: where would you like to vacation; how much would you like to spend on the vacation? What assets, such as a new computer or a new car, would you like to acquire?

Intermediate goals are usually more financial in nature and less specific in terms of activities and acquisitions. As you think further into the future, you care more about having the financial ability to do things and less about the details of what you will do. For example, it would be somewhat silly to ask a recent college grad about what activities he or she plans to do upon retirement but reasonable to ask about how much wealth he or she hopes to accumulate by retirement. Most intermediate goals would likely include more than just wealth targets. For example, a recent college graduate may target a date for buying his or her first home. Intermediate goals often address where one wants to be in five or twenty years.

For most people, long-term goals include their date of retirement and their accumulated wealth at retirement. What sort of personal balance sheet do they want to have at retirement? Chapters 17 through 19, on retirement planning, are critical to helping people set these long-term goals.

What Are the Problems in Getting from Here to There?

The first barrier to achieving goals is usually a monetary one. That is, most people have a list of acquisitions they want to make over the years, as well as targets that involve ever-higher values of wealth accumulation. These acquisitions and targets usually require saving a specific amount each year, as well as getting a specified rate of return on investments. Meeting the savings target for each year is a key reason people should do cash budgeting. Cash budgeting is addressed in Chapter 2. Managing investments to achieve certain rates of return is covered in Chapters 13 through 16.

A second and very important barrier in getting from "here" to "there" is the element of risk. In this context, risk is anything that might cause you to fail to meet your financial planning objectives. The sources of risk might be called the **miscues of life.**

The last three steps of the financial planning process, developing and writing down a plan, implementing it, and regularly reviewing and revising the plan are all self-explanatory.

What Are the Miscues of Life? The miscues of life include premature death, divorce, health problems, unemployment, casualty and theft losses,[1] being sued, and significant investment losses. Note that death itself is not a miscue of life. We will all die eventually. Preparing for our eventual death is part of setting our long-term goals. Thus, for everyone who has engaged in appropriate financial planning, death is not a problem; dying substantially earlier (or in some cases later) than we expect to die may create a financial problem. Students often ask to add bankruptcy to this list of the miscues of life. Personal bankruptcy usually occurs when someone has suffered one or more of the miscues listed above, therefore bankruptcy is a result of miscues rather than a miscue itself.

Effective personal financial planning involves taking steps to minimize the impact of these miscues. Let's consider each in turn.

The first and foremost tool in mitigating the financial effects of premature death is always life insurance, to which Chapter 11 is dedicated. There are other tools to reduce the financial impact of premature death. One example is the accumulation of wealth. Someone like Bill Gates, whose wealth is measured in the billions of dollars, has no need for life insurance, since his accumulated wealth would probably be sufficient to take care of all of his dependents if he died prematurely. Another example is having a spouse who works or at least maintains job skills.

Divorce is more difficult to prepare for. Premarital agreements are about the only tool for attempting to isolate the financial impact of a divorce. It is noteworthy that only the wealthiest of individuals tend to ask prospective mates to sign premarital agreements. There is something clearly unromantic in planning to marry, conditional on a mutually satisfactory premarital agreement. In addition, premarital agreements cannot protect one from certain basic responsibilities embedded in state laws. Premarital agreements are really a legal issue, so they are not addressed in this book.

Health problems, casualty and theft losses, and being sued can all be effectively covered by insurance. Hence, Chapter 10 covers property and casualty insurance as well as umbrella insurance policies and Chapter 12 will address health plans as well as health and disability income insurance.

There is no easy way to protect against unemployment, but there are several half steps. Most people are covered by state unemployment policies, but such policies do not provide full protection and they do not provide protection to everyone without a job. The major strategy for protecting against unemployment would be to invest in skills and expertise that are salable. The greater a person's skills and expertise, the more likely that person is to find another source of income in the event he or she becomes unemployed. The process of developing one's human capital and selling it in the marketplace (i.e., finding a job) is the focal point of the second part of this chapter.

The final major miscue in life is significant investment losses. The number-one protection from significant investment losses is extensive diversification in one's investment portfolio. The second form of protection against significant investment losses is to hold some of one's investment assets in low-risk securities. Diversification and the degree of securities investment risk are covered in Chapters 13 through 16, which deal with investments.

---

[1] A casualty loss is a loss due to the destruction of an asset. A casualty loss could result from a natural event such as a fire or storm or from a man-made event such as a car accident.

Develop, Implement, and Review a Plan

The remaining three steps of the personal financial planning process are the "guts" of this book.

WHAT ARE THE FIVE BASIC STRATEGIES OF FINANCIAL PLANNING?

The five basic strategies of financial planning range from extreme conservatism to wild profligacy. To better understand these strategies, let's define three terms. Let C_t equal the amount a person spends each year. Let Y_t represent that person's income each year. Finally, let N be the number of years this person expects to live. The first strategy can be represented by the expression

$$C_t < Y_t \text{ for all values of t from } t = 1 \text{ to } t = N.$$

In words, this expression says that the person spends less money each year than he or she takes in as income. Thus, this person is an **annual net saver.** This is the type of strategy utilized by a person who wants to die *"owning* a million dollars." Popular strategies for how to become rich almost always include the axiom **pay yourself first.** What this expression means is that the first action each pay period is to transfer a fixed, regular amount to some sort of savings program.[2] If this person then limits his or her spending to what is left of each paycheck after this contribution to savings, then the above strategy will be achieved. We call this strategy the annual saver strategy. Some people might call it the Scrooge strategy!

The second strategy could be called the **lifetime saver** strategy. In notational form, this strategy would be expressed as

$$C_1 + C_2 + \dots + C_N < Y_1 + Y_2 + \dots + Y_N.$$

This strategy differs from the first in that there is no relationship between income and spending in any one year. Thus, in the first year, spending could be greater than income (i.e., $C_1 > Y_1$). All that counts is that over this person's projected lifetime, the combined total of expected spending is less than the combined total of expected income. This person would also be expected to die wealthy, although probably not as wealthy as the annual saver.

The third strategy could be called the **annual balanced** strategy. In notational form, this strategy would be expressed as

$$C_t = Y_t \text{ for all values of t from } t = 1 \text{ to } t = N.$$

The person with this strategy has no safety margin in his or her life. A dramatic drop in income would produce an immediate reduction in this person's standard of living. Many people follow this strategy. During their working years, they live comfortably. During their retirement years, life becomes less fun.

---

[2]As a practical matter, most people do deposit some of each paycheck into savings, in the form of contributions to pensions and other retirement programs.

The fourth strategy could be called the **lifetime balanced** strategy. In notational form, this strategy would be expressed as

$$C_1 + C_2 + ... + C_N = Y_1 + Y_2 + ... + Y_N.$$

As with the lifetime savings strategy, there is no relation between spending and income in any given year. This person intends to leave no inheritance. As noted in Chapter 19, one of the shortest wills on record states, "Being of sound mind, I spent it all." This would be the sentiment of someone targeting a lifetime balanced strategy.

The fifth and final strategy would be called the **lifetime spending** strategy. In notational form, this strategy would be expressed as

$$C_1 + C_2 + ... + C_N > Y_1 + Y_2 + ... + Y_N.$$

Although this person may save in one or more years, and may be balanced in one or more years, his or her goal is to spend more than he or she earns. One could say that this person wants to die *"owing* a million dollars." The creditors, of course, would be unhappy to see this person die. Sometimes when we see continued large purchases by our friends and neighbors, we think, how can they afford that? In some cases, the answer is that they can't! They have just been able to find someone willing to lend them the money to make their purchases. It is not necessarily their intent to repay the loans before dying.

Which Strategy Is Optimal?

There is no one correct strategy to choose. When I ask a class "how many of you want your parents to die owning a million dollars," virtually every hand goes up. When I ask this same group how many want to die leaving their own children a million dollars, only a few hands (if any) go up. Naturally, people often change strategies at different points in their lives. Note that the strategies refer to what you want to accomplish between now and your death. A single person graduating from college may opt for the aggressive or lifetime balanced strategy. Marriage and the birth of children start many people thinking more conservatively, even though it may be financially more difficult to follow a more conservative strategy. Retired people tend to fall into two groups. Some people truly want to leave their children (and grandchildren) a substantial inheritance. Others believe that the prospect of a large inheritance will only cause their children to lose the desire to earn their own way in the world or miss the satisfaction of that endeavor. Again, there is no one correct way to think about financial planning. The purpose of effective financial planning is to help a person get the most out of whichever strategy he or she chooses.

Isn't the Quality of My Life Defined by My Wealth? There is a strong propensity to associate wealth or standard of living with quality of life. Wealth is normally defined of assets owned less any outstanding debts. Standard of living is measured in terms of annual income. For some people, wealth or standard of living may be the correct measure of their quality of life. For many, that is not the case. Two observations demonstrate this point.

Many people give away substantial amounts of wealth during their lifetimes. They give to their places of worship, they give to charities, and they give to not-for-profit organizations (such as their alma maters). Some may claim that people make these gifts solely for the purpose of saving taxes. However, as we will see in Chapter 3 when we discuss taxes, if I give $10,000 to United Way, I might save $3,000 on my taxes. Thus, the gift still costs me $7,000. A person seeking strictly to maximize his or her wealth will not give away $10,000 to save $3,000 in taxes! The tax impact of the gift reduces the true cost of the gift; it never makes giving the gift a profitable activity. People give gifts because they derive pleasure from it or because they have a sense of obligation.

The second observation is that many people hold jobs noted for low pay. For example, most people in religious professions (such as priests and ministers) earn extremely low pay compared with what their level of educational training could earn them in other professions. Many people pass up lucrative corporate incomes in order to be self-employed. The lure of being one's own boss is worth a lower income to some people. Perhaps the self-employed hope that their business will some day make them wealthy, but that is rarely the case.[3] Some people seek jobs with no pay. Full-time, stay-at-home parents are examples of people who accept unpaid jobs based on the benefits they perceive from managing the household.

Obviously, many people regularly make choices that are not wealth- or income-maximizing, and these choices are perfectly rational and important to their lives. A person with $50,000 in wealth and $25,000 in income may have a substantially better quality of life than another person with $500,000 in wealth and $250,000 in income. **Proper financial planning seeks only to help people make the most of their wealth and income given the non-pecuniary choices they make in their lives, not just maximize their wealth and income.**

CAN I DO MY OWN FINANCIAL PLANNING OR DO I NEED A FINANCIAL PLANNER?

Web Link 1.3
Web Link 1.4

A basic premise of this book is that most people can do their own financial planning. The resources now available on the Internet allow most people intent on serious financial planning to do their own planning and manage their own situations. The wealthy, and those with complex personal and financial situations, will always need professional financial planners. Doing one's own financial planning does not preclude using financial professionals for special situations. Lawyers who are familiar with a state's laws and practices should draw up most wills. Some people are more comfortable having a stockbroker manage their investments than taking on that task themselves. People with complicated tax situations might find that a tax professional could save them more on their tax returns than the price of his or her fee.

Anyone undertaking his or her own financial planning will naturally seek many sources for financial advice. No source of competent financial advice is truly free (even this book has a price tag on it!). When seeking out financial advice, one should avoid or use with extreme caution advisors with a **conflict of interest.** A conflict of interest exists when the person providing the advice may personally benefit from the advice he or she is providing. A broker who calls you to convince you to buy a stock would of course benefit

---

[3]A casual reading of the bankruptcy filings in the local paper would show that nearly all such bankruptcies are among small firms that consist of little more than a self-employed person or couple.

from the commission. However, this broker may also already own some shares of this stock and may benefit in other ways from your purchase.

Who Is a Financial Planner?

A financial planner can be anyone who hangs up a plaque and claims to be one! No state has created licensing requirements for financial planners. Thus, anyone seeking the help of a financial planner needs to be quite careful that the individual has legitimate credentials, and there are many legitimate credentials.

Web Link 1.5

An organization called the **CFP Board** administers nationwide exams in the field of financial planning. Those who pass the exam are permitted to identify themselves as **Certified Financial Planners**® (CFPs). To construct the exam, the CFP Board regularly studies the skills and working knowledge of effective financial planners. The Board then constructs exams to test whether applicants have this knowledge and skill set. Many peo-

Web Link 1.6

ple are never able to pass this exam.

If someone claims to be a CFP®, or if you are interested in obtaining the names of practicing, licensed CFPs® located in your area, the CFP Board has a simple license check. Consider the following example:

> *Sam Weese is a recent college graduate. He has been working for a few years, and realizes that his life is a financial mess. After graduation, Sam got a good-paying job. The money seemed so good, in fact, that Sam felt financial planning was not necessary for him. He had more money than he knew what to do with. Now, a few years later, Sam realizes he has accomplished nothing more with his newfound wealth than to fritter away the cash as fast or faster than it has come in. He knows he needs to get serious about financial planning. Sam would like to talk to a financial planner who holds a CFP® certification. If Sam lives in the Syracuse, New York, area, how many planners could he contact?*

Web Link 1.7

To answer this question, go to and enter Syracuse and New York for the city and state for which you are searching. At the time of writing, this search produced a list of 34 people, of whom 28 are practicing.

An alternative certification that represents additional training beyond that necessary to obtain the CFP® is the **Chartered Financial Consultant** (ChFC). The ChFC is awarded

Web Link 1.8

by The American College.

There are many other types of people who are highly qualified to render financial planning advice, but who do not hold a CFP® license or a ChFC certification. These people usually hold other licenses or certifications. For example, a **Certified Public Accountant** (CPA) may specialize in taxes or financial planning or both. The CPA license is awarded by the state based on a rigorous accounting exam. There are no licenses for specialty areas. Thus, just as anyone with an MD may claim expertise in a specialty, so anyone with a CPA may claim to be a specialist in an area.

A practicing lawyer must also be licensed by the state, and to be licensed requires passing what is known as the state bar exam. There are no specialty exams, and any lawyer may claim to specialize in financial planning. Lawyers who are financial planners tend to focus on wills and trusts.

Insurance agents are also licensed after passing a state exam. Insurance agents may pursue professional certifications. An agent specializing in life insurance may become a

Web Link 1.9

CLU, or **Chartered Life Underwriter,** a credential also awarded by The American College. Insurance agents who represent themselves as financial planners tend to recommend plans that focus on the purchase of life insurance policies.

Finally, some stockbrokers will also pitch themselves as financial planners. Stockbrokers must pass a licensing exam, although the exan is industry sponsored. Again, there is no special exam to show expertise in the broad area of financial planning. Stockbrokers who advertise themselves as financial planners tend to focus on managing investments.

Web Link 1.10

Nothing prevents one person from collecting a combination of certifications and licenses. A financial planning professional will almost certainly belong to one or more professional associations. On January 1, 2000, the Institute of Certified Financial Planners (ICFP) and the International Association of Financial Planners (IAFP) merged to become the **Financial Planning Association.** To verify that someone is a member of this organization, you should view its web site.

Web Link 1.11

How Are Financial Planners Paid?

Financial planners tend to fall into three categories with regard to compensation. The first category includes fee-only planners. Fee-only planners provide advice and plans, but do not execute any plans. The consumer must go to separate professionals to obtain services and products. Commission-only planners form the second category. The commission-only planner's advice is free, but the individual is expected to buy the necessary services and products from the planner. The planner earns his or her income from the commission on the products sold, whether they are legal services, insurance policies, or equities. The third category of planners takes from both ends; they charge fees and sell products and services on commission.

If we follow the advice rendered earlier in this chapter to be on the lookout for conflicts of interest, then we must be wary of planners who sell products and/or services as part of the plan. This does not mean they cannot give good advice or sell good products. Both the advice and products might be excellent. But it certainly would be easy for commission-based planners to let the nature of their commission income influence the advice they give.

If one is approached by two financial planners, and one offers to prepare a plan for free while the other asks for a $1,000 fee it clearly goes against human nature to choose to pay a fee.. Nonetheless, there is a greater chance for unbiased advice with a fee-only planner.

Some financial planners take control of the consumer's assets, and then charge an annual fee on the value of the total assets. Such an arrangement may appear to be fee based, but it functions for all practical purposes like a commission-based arrangement.

Finally, the type of planner you seek may depend on your needs. People who are just getting started and have few assets may find it more effective to use a commission-based planner, while people with substantial assets and more complex needs may find a fee-based planner a better deal.

How Do I Select a Prospective Planner?   Selecting a financial planner is no different than selecting a family doctor, dentist, lawyer, or stockbroker. There is no sure-fire way to ensure you have selected the best person available. You can start by asking family,

friends, and acquaintances for recommendations. As with any other professional you hire, there are several questions you should ask this person to increase your comfort level about his or her ability and what he or she will do for you. These are[4]

- What experience do you have?
- What are your qualifications?
- What services do you offer?
- What is your approach to financial planning?
- Will you be the only person working with me?
- How will I pay for your services?
- How much do you typically charge?
- Could anyone besides me benefit from your recommendations?
- Have you ever been publicly disciplined for any unlawful or unethical actions in your professional career?
- Can I have it in writing?

A few comments on these questions are in order. Most everyone likes to work with experienced professionals. However, if all clients worked only with experienced professionals, how would new planners get started in the business? It is not completely inappropriate to work with someone who is new in the business, but it is best if the person has a particular strength that offsets the lack of work experience.

The financial planner's approach is particularly important. It must match what the prospective client is seeking. Consider your willingness to work with the planner's assistant. Some financial planners take on a new client, and then all subsequent client contact is through an assistant. In fact, the assistant may do much of the work.

If the planner sells policies or services for a particular provider, then someone besides you may benefit from the planner's recommendations. Again, be wary of potential conflicts of interest. If a planner has been publicly disciplined for unlawful or unethical actions, he or she may be unlikely to confess to a prospective client. It never hurts to run some quick checks on a planner. Phone numbers of various watchdog agencies and organizations may be found at the bottom of any of the sites listed in **Web Link 1.12.**

Web Link 1.12

WHAT IS HUMAN CAPITAL?

Web Link 1.13

The largest single asset most people have is **human capital.** Human capital refers to our individual ability to generate income from work-related endeavors.

Although some of us are born with natural human capital (singers, actors, and athletes, for example), most of us have to acquire our human capital through an investment in education. Investment in education consistently provides one of the highest rates of return of any type of asset.

---

[4]These questions are obtained from the web sites listed at **Web Link 1.12.**

How Do I Go About Getting Information on Higher Education Opportunities?

Obtaining information about both undergraduate and graduate programs is pretty much the same. Web sites that deal in both undergraduate and graduate programs are provided in **Web Link 1.14.** Some sites that deal exclusively with graduate programs are listed at **Web Link 1.15.** Accreditation by a professional association is even more important for graduate schools than for undergraduate programs. If you are considering a master's of business administration (MBA) or a master's of science (MS) in any of the business disciplines, then you should seriously consider schools accredited by the Association for the Advancement of Collegiate Schools of Business (AACSB). One might obtain a good education at a non-accredited program, but accreditation offers an external validation of the ingredients believed to provide a quality education.

Web Link 1.14
Web Link 1.15

Web Link 1.16

WHERE CAN I GET INFORMATION ON VARIOUS CAREERS?

An important part of selecting a college is to decide what sort of career the prospective student is interested in. Many of us know little about what most careers entail. Asking relatives and friends about their jobs gives us only a limited sample. Thus, access to job descriptions would be quite helpful. Some people know their strengths, weaknesses, and interests well enough that a detailed job description will help them to identify their career preferences. Other people may need to start at a more elementary level.

Web Link 1.17

This more elementary level of career interest or aptitude assessment includes personality tests and career interest quizzes. Many of these tests and quizzes are fun, and some of them may be quite helpful in determining a job path.

Web Link 1.18

What Are the Key Trends in Employment Opportunities?

For many people, more than one type of job or career opportunity may seem intriguing. Some seek jobs offering the best economic potential. Expanding fields offer more career advancement potential, more job mobility, and the prospect of more rapid salary increases. It is difficult to state which fields will have the greatest growth over the next ten years. However, there are several web sites willing to speculate.

Web Link 1.19

What Do Salaries Look Like for a Particular Job or Career?

An important aspect of any job or career is the typical salary paid to people in that field. Salary surveys are suspect because some data isn't available to the public and because income in many professions comprises bonuses and commissions that may vary substantially from year to year. Nonetheless, surveys can offer some general insight.

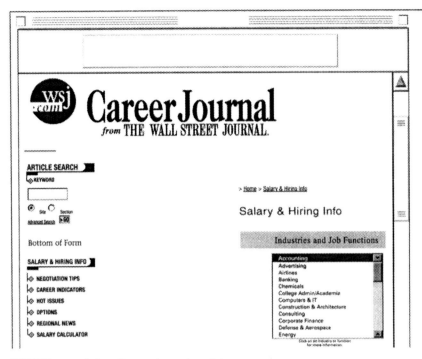

FIGURE 1-1 Salary figures for various jobs

**Web Link
(WSJ) 1.20**

A screen print of this web page is provided in Figure 1.1.
  Consider the following example:

> *Juanita Piccione is considering a career in the trust department of a bank. She is interested in the salaries for the top trust officers of a bank.*

At **Web Link (WSJ) 1.21,** Juanita would first click on banking, then on banking executives, and scroll down until she finds the title "top trust." At the time of writing, the median salary is $107,500, and the median total cash compensation is $152,602.

HOW CAN I FIND JOB OPPORTUNITIES ON THE INTERNET?

One approach to finding a job is to decide the company for which you might like to work. Many companies and organizations have job opportunity information on their home page. The address for most companies is usually of the form www.*companyname*.com. If that address does not work, then you might try entering the company name in a search engine, or using a major pointer site. Remember, if the organization you are interested in working for is an educational institution, a governmental entity, or a not-for-profit or non-profit organization, the extensions would be edu, gov, and org.

Consider the following example:

Juanita Piccione has decided she would like to be a stockbroker. She would like to see what job opportunities currently exist at some of the leading full-service broker-age firms. What are some brokerage firms she might try?

Web Link 1.22

If Juanita were to go to **Web Link 1.20,** she would find links to 268 full-service broker-age firms (at the time of writing).

Web Link (WSJ) 1.23

Another approach is to visit the many sites, such as **Web Link (WSJ) 1.23,** that function much like classified ads in the newspaper. A copy of the *Wall Street Journal* page is shown in Figure 1.2. Consider the following example:

Juanita now decides she would like to work in the field of accounting in New Mexico. Based on the Wall Street Journal *Job Seek, how many openings are listed?*

At the time of writing, three such jobs were identified. These were for an Assistant Controller–Taxation, a Senior Auditor, and a Senior Tax Manager.

Many of these sites at **Web Link (WSJ) 1.23** have job lists that often run into the tens of thousands. In addition to sites that provide job listings, there are also a large number of pointer sites that don't display job listings themselves, but point to other sites with

Web Link 1.24

Web Link 1.25

such listings.

For some folks, working abroad holds a particular attraction.

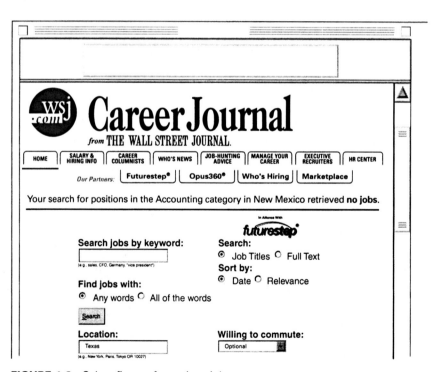

FIGURE 1-2   Salary figures for various jobs

When and Where Will Career Fairs Be Held?

A useful technique for locating job opportunities is to attend career fairs where a large number of employers set up booths to provide information to job seekers. Because these career fairs are constantly changing, it is not possible to list web site addresses for each one, though there are sites that identify upcoming career fairs.

Web Link 1.26

How Can I Advertise Myself on the Internet?

So far, the focus has been on using the Internet to find job opportunities. An alternative approach is to post your own resume and hope a job recruiter finds you. A substantial number of sites provide this opportunity, all at no charge. The problem with this approach is that you leave yourself open to harassment from people who abuse such sites.[5] In addition, if you are already employed, you might be concerned about your current employer finding out that you are looking for a job.

Web Link 1.27

Web Link 1.28

Where Can I Get Help in Putting Together My Resume?   A typical recruiter allocates no more than 10 seconds to reviewing each resume received for the first cut. So you (actually, your resume) have a maximum of 10 seconds to convince this person you merit further consideration. The quality of the construction of your resume will thus be a

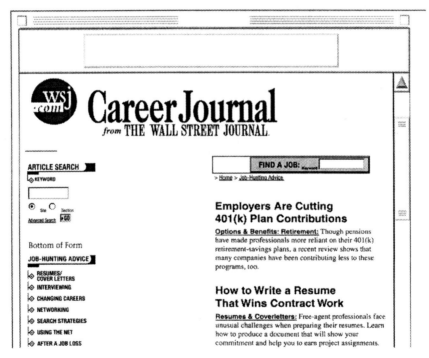

FIGURE 1-3   Job hunting advice

[5]This author's resume is permanently posted on the Internet, but not to seek a job offer. Nonetheless, I receive several calls each year from recruiters who have found my resume and want to bring a job opportunity to my attention.

Web Link 1.29

major determinant of the number of employers giving your application serious consideration. The content of your resume is important, but if two resumes have the same content, the one that presents the content better will receive greater consideration. **Web Link 1.29** lists sites that offer suggestions, hints, and ideas for developing an effective resume.

Web Link
(WSJ) 1.30

Where Can I Get Help Composing a Cover Letter? A cover letter may be just as important as a resume when it comes to that initial contact with a prospective employer. Cover letters can be tailored for a particular employer. If you are applying to 30 companies for a job, it is unlikely you will develop 30 versions of your resume, one that targets each company, but you may well be able to tailor a cover letter for each company. The *Wall Street Journal* link is shown in Figure 1.3.

Web Link
(WSJ) 1.31

Where Can I Get Help for the Job Interview Process? If the style and content of your resume are attractive to an employer, you may be invited for an interview. Although it is critical that you are honest, open, yourself at a job interview, there are certain "dos and don'ts" of interviewing (see Figure 1.3).

Web Link
(WSJ) 1.32

Where Can I Get Help in Negotiating a Salary? If the job interview goes well, you may receive a job offer, and you may have an opportunity to negotiate on the salary. Be prepared with a good idea as to what a fair and reasonable salary might be. We discussed earlier the process of ascertaining what the current salary numbers are for various jobs and careers. That information can be critical in deciding what job to accept (see Figure 1.3).

HOW DO I DECIDE WHETHER TO ACCEPT A JOB, OR WHICH JOB TO ACCEPT?

If you receive only one offer in your job search, then your choice is to accept that offer or to keep looking. If you are fortunate enough to receive multiple offers, then you must choose among them or keep looking. The first issue in deciding to accept a job is, of course, whether the job interests you. If the job interests you,[6] then the second issue is compensation. The primary component of compensation is, obviously, the salary or wage rate, but it is a mistake to focus strictly on salary. If your job offers are in two different cities, then you need to consider the quality of life and the cost of living in each location. Finally, you need to consider all the other components of compensation. These include the quality and cost of the company's health care plan, the rules and contribution rates for the pension plan, and the other perquisites associated with a job.

Where Can I Obtain Information on Cost-of-Living Comparisons?

The purchasing power of a salary varies among cities. A $40,000 salary in one city may go further than a $50,000 salary in another city. Taxes may be one reason. Federal taxes are the same regardless of where one lives. Remember, however, that part of the difference

---

[6]If you are destitute, then any job that pays a salary probably matches your interests!

between a higher-paying job and a lower-paying job is taken up by federal income taxes. In addition, there are substantial variations in state taxation. Some states have no state income taxes, and others impose fairly stiff income taxes.

Cost of housing is another reason purchasing power differs between cities. The price of real estate varies substantially among cities. High real estate prices produce high rental rates, so even if you plan to rent rather than buy, you will need to consider the cost of housing. Consider the following example:

> *Juanita Piccione has just received her MBA from Syracuse University. After an active job search, she has received two job offers. The first is in Buffalo, New York, and has a salary of $45,000. The second is in Houston, Texas, and has a salary of $40,000. In terms of purchasing power, which salary is the better deal?*

Web Link 1.33

At the time of writing, one calculator indicates that a $45,000 salary in Buffalo offers the same buying power as a $42,433.63 salary in Houston. A second calculator indicates that for someone who owns a home, a salary of $100,000 in Buffalo has an equivalency of $96,164 in Houston. Applying this ratio to the $45,000 salary in Buffalo would produce a salary equivalent of $43,274 (= $45,000 × $96,164 / $100,000) in Houston. Thus, although the two calculators do not agree down to the nearest dollar, they are consistent that on the basis of salary alone, the Buffalo job is the better offer even though it costs slightly more to live in Buffalo than Houston.

Salary comparison calculators are sometimes used by people who are currently employed and are negotiating a salary offer with a potential employer for a job in another city. They may also be used when you have received a job offer elsewhere and your current employer is attempting to keep you with a matching salary offer. Naturally, if the cost of living is lower where you are currently living, then there is probably no value to the calculator. But if you receive a job offer in an area where the cost of living is lower, then the calculator may help you to negotiate an even higher salary to stay in a high cost-of-living area.[7]

How Can I Compare the Quality of Life in Two Different Cities? In addition to comparing salary differences between cities, you may also want to think about the differences in leisure opportunities and the quality of life. There is no right answer in terms of which city a person should prefer. A characteristic one person likes (such as high snowfall, which allows for a long ski season) might be considered a negative attribute by another. Many cities have their own home pages, which can be a major source of information.

**Web Link
(WSJ) 1.34**

How Can I Get an Internship or Coop?

Job advertisements frequently request people with experience. This means that without experience, it is difficult to obtain experience. One way to get experience is though a **coop** or **internship.** A coop job offers some form of compensation that approximates entry-level wages. In an internship the employee works primarily or exclusively for the experience. Many employers use coops or internships as an inexpensive way to get an extended look at a potential employee without the commitment to hire that person.

Web Link 1.35

---

[7]One of the author's former students added about $10,000 to his salary from just such a negotiation.

How Can I Start My Own Company?

An alternative to seeking a job is to hire yourself! Many people aspire to being self-employed. A budding entrepreneur should keep in mind one sobering statistic: more than 95 percent of all new businesses fail within three years, and most fail within the first year. It is not easy to start a new company. You must have a solid business plan. In addition, you need to be truly competent in the business you are undertaking. Being an excellent cook is not enough to succeed in your own restaurant or bakery.

Web Link 1.36

SUMMARY

➤ The six steps of the personal financial planning process are to define one's current situation, to define where one wants to go in life, to identify the problems in getting there, to develop a written plan, to implement that plan, and to review and revise that plan regularly.

➤ The five strategies to managing one's finances are: annual saver, lifetime saver, annual balanced, lifetime balanced, and lifetime spending.

➤ Anyone can claim to be a financial planner. Planners who have a Certified Financial Planner® or Chartered Financial Consultant designation are more likely to be well qualified. Lawyers, accountants, stockbrokers, and insurance agents also act as financial planners. Planners may be compensated on a fee-only basis, commission-only basis, or a combination.

➤ Human capital is the skills and knowledge a person has that enable him or her to earn wage or salary income.

➤ Selecting an optimal job depends on one's interests and aptitudes, as well as knowledge of particular types of jobs. Tests of one's interests and job descriptions of various types are readily available on the Internet. Trends in employment opportunities and even salary information for various jobs are also provided on the Internet.

➤ Finding job openings is easy on the Internet, with a large number of sites from which to choose.

➤ Finally, those lucky enough to have two or more job offers may have to consider not only the salary they are offered, but also the cost of living and quality of life in different areas.

KEY TERMS

annual balanced	annual net saver	Certified Financial Planner®
Certified Public Accountant	CFP Board	Chartered Financial Consultant
Chartered Life Underwriter	conflict of interest	coop
Financial Planning Association	human capital	internship
lifetime balanced	lifetime saver	lifetime spending
miscues of life	pay yourself first	

PROBLEMS

1. What are the six steps of the personal financial planning process?

2. On the Internet, find three job openings to which you might apply upon graduation.

3. How many active CFP® licensees are there in Denver, Colorado?

4. Compare a starting salary of $30,000 in your community with the same salary in any city of your choice.

5. List three dos and three don'ts for a job interview.

6. Provide the name, date, and location of two career fairs that will be held near you in the next few months.

REFERENCES

Web Link 1.37 Advise on common financial mistakes people make /general advice
Web Link 1.38 Glossary of financial planning terms

WALL STREET JOURNAL RESOURCES

Web Link (WSJ) 1.39 Recent articles on financial planning
Web Link (WSJ) 1.40 Recent articles on college planning
Web Link (WSJ) 1.41 Current articles and information on starting one's own company
Web Link (WSJ) 1.42 "Web Sites Simplify Job-Hunting, So Forget Searching the Classifieds," *The Wall Street Journal Interactive Edition*, November 7, 1999
Web Link (WSJ) 1.43 "Internet Service Offers Some Nobel Advice on Personal Finances," *The Wall Street Journal Interactive Edition*, August 12, 1999
Web Link (WSJ) 1.44 "Methods Our Readers Employ To Make and Save Money," *The Wall Street Journal Interactive Edition*, February 2, 1999
Web Link (WSJ) 1.45 "With These Three Strategies, Saving Money Isn't So Hard," *The Wall Street Journal Interactive Edition*, August 25, 1998
Web Link (WSJ) 1.46 "Financial Success Requires Saving, Spending Discipline," *The Wall Street Journal Interactive Edition*, May 5, 1998

For information that has changed since the book was written, for new information that pertains to this topic, and for some new web sites that pertain to the topic of this chapter, see **Web Link 1.47.**

CHAPTER 2

FINANCIAL PLANNING AND BUDGETING

LEARNING OBJECTIVES

- Construct a personal financial balance sheet and income statement
- Compute financial ratios and explain their meaning and purpose
- Distinguish between an income statement and a cash budget
- Define and compute hidden expenses
- Evaluate whether it is worth having a two-income household
- Estimate the cost of having a child

Web Link: **www.wiley.com/college/woerheide**

INTRODUCTION

The balance sheet, the income statement, and the cash budget are the heart of the financial planning process. All three of these statements require time and record keeping. Prior to the development of the Internet and various software packages, the time and effort required to develop these three statements was enough to keep most people from a serious effort to control their finances. With computer assistance, record keeping is a little simpler and the time needed to organize data and create financial statements is greatly diminished.

These statements play a role in three of the six steps of the financial planning process described in Chapter 1. First, financial statements can define your current situation. Second, they can define your goals. Third, they help to measure how well you are achieving those goals. If you are serious in wanting to set and meet goals, regular construction of financial statements is critical. For example, if a person wants to purchase a new car and is debating whether to do so now or to wait a year, then knowing where he or she is relative to his or her goals will help in making that decision. However, if this person buys the new car today regardless of where he or she is relative to his or her goals, then it would be pointless to construct financial statements. In other words, if you are not willing to let information about your progress toward financial goals influence your purchase and investment decisions, then you shouldn't bother to define these goals. In this chapter, we will consider the case of Ron and Pat Meller as they try to make some sense out of their financial situation.

WHAT IS A PERSONAL BALANCE SHEET?

A **balance sheet** has three sections. The first is a statement of assets. Assets are things that one owns. The second section is a statement of liabilities, that is, a list of one's debts. The third section is called net worth. It is the difference between one's assets and one's liabilities. Businesses regularly construct balance sheets following a rigorous set of accounting rules. Personal balance sheets are constructed much less formally, although they should follow some of the same general rules incorporated into business balance sheets.

A personal financial balance sheet is a financial snapshot of you at a single point in time. Each day your balance sheet changes somewhat. Because the day-to-day changes in a personal balance sheet are usually trivial, there is no value in computing a balance sheet on a daily basis, much less a weekly or monthly basis. In most cases, constructing a personal balance sheet on an annual basis is sufficient. To be consistent, you should probably construct your balance sheet at the same time each year. New Year's Day is usually a convenient time for several reasons. First, most people use the calendar year as their tax year. Because the preparation of a balance sheet involves reviewing the same documents that are to be reviewed to prepare taxes, little incremental effort is involved in preparing a balance sheet at this time. Second, a great deal of financial information is available to individuals at the close of business on the last business day of December. There is no other day of the year when you can get as many statements about your various financial positions. Finally, many people like to use New Year's Day to think about where they are going and how to improve their lives.

What Are the Assets on a Personal Balance Sheet?

The assets on a personal balance sheet may be placed in any order that make sense to you. After all, it is *your* personal balance sheet, intended primarily for *your* personal use. The most common practice is to list assets in descending order of **liquidity.** Liquidity refers to an asset's ability to be converted to cash quickly with little or no loss in value. This means that the asset usually listed first is cash. Don't count the cash in your pocket or your piggy bank (unless it is a significant portion of your wealth). Cash in this case refers to money in accounts such as checking accounts, savings accounts, money market accounts, money market mutual funds, and certificates of deposit with a maturity of less than one year.[1] The management of cash and near-cash assets will be discussed in detail in Chapter 5.

The second category of assets listed is known as fixed assets, fixed-principal assets, fixed-return assets, or debt instruments. This category includes investment that represents a loan made by you to someone else. A loan is characterized primarily by the promise to repay the principal on a specific date. Most loans are also characterized by the promise to pay fixed amounts of interest at specified points in time. Fixed-return assets are primarily corporate and government bonds, but may also be mortgages held (i.e., where you have loaned someone money to buy real estate), mutual funds that invest primarily in bonds,

---

[1]The cash category also includes assets known as **money market instruments.** Money market instruments, discussed in Chapter 5, include Treasury bills, negotiable certificates of deposit, commercial paper, and bankers' acceptances. Because the minimum price to purchase most money market instruments directly is $100,000, and the common trading unit is $1 million, these instruments are owned by few individuals.

fixed annuities, and any other monies owed to you. Fixed-return investments will be discussed in detail in Chapter 13.

The third category of assets listed is usually equity investments. An equity investment represents an ownership interest. The most common equity investment is common stock. If you own common stock in a firm, you are an owner of that firm. Other examples of equity investments include mutual funds that hold mostly common stock, variable annuities, and partnerships.

The fourth category of assets is the value of pensions and other retirement accounts, including IRAs, Keogh accounts, and 403(b) and 401(k) accounts.

The last category of assets is usually personal or tangible assets, also known as **real assets.** This category includes assets bought primarily for comforts, like your home, car, furniture, clothing, jewelry, and any other personal articles with a resale value. In listing personal assets on a personal financial statement, remember to question the asset's **materiality.** Materiality means that the personal asset in question is of sufficient monetary value to make a meaningful difference in the evaluation of the balance sheet. "Small ticket" items are not worth tracking. A sweater you bought three years ago for $50 may have a resale value of 50 cents in a garage sale. It is not worth your time to track such an item.

How Should Assets Be Valued?   Assets should be listed on the balance sheet at their market value. However, determining market value can sometimes be tricky. Some assets have a clear and precise value. For example, the amount of money in your checking account on a specific date is defined down to the penny (assuming your checkbook is properly reconciled with the bank's statement). For other assets, the market value may be vague. For example, a stamp or coin collection may be quite valuable, but trading activity for many items may be so slow that any values assigned to the whole collection would be uncertain at best. For other assets, the market value may be reasonably certain, but there may be substantial costs in the form of taxes or transaction fees to convert these assets to cash. Consider the following three examples:

> *Ron and Pat Meller own 100 shares of stock in Eastman Kodak. They bought the stock five years ago for $20 per share. The stock recently closed at $50 per share, and the price appreciation is classified a long-term capital gain. The tax rate on long-term capital gains is 20 percent. At what value should they list this stock on their personal balance sheet?*

It would be tempting to list the stock at $5,000 (100 shares × $50 price per share), which is the product of the number of shares they own and the most recent closing price per share. However, if they actually had to sell the stock, they would have to declare a $3,000 long-term capital gain based on the fact that they have a gain of $30 per share ($50 current price – $20 original cost) and they have owned the stock for at least one year. As the tax rate on long-term capital gains is 20 percent, they would owe $600 in taxes ($30 gain per share × 100 shares × 20% tax rate) if they sold this stock today. Thus, this stock could not be converted into $5,000 cash. It could be converted into $4,400 cash ($5,000 market value – $600 in taxes).

A second problem in valuing assets is demonstrated with the following example:

> *Ron and Pat Meller own a home that is similar to many other homes in the neighborhood. Several of these similar homes have sold recently for $200,000. Thus, they*

believe they also could obtain a price of $200,000 for their house. At what value
should they list their home on their personal balance sheet?

The answer to this question would appear to be $200,000, but almost all real estate trans-actions carry a high *transaction fee*. For example, suppose the Mellers believe that to obtain the best price for their home they would have to list it with a realtor who charges a 6 percent commission. Thus, even if someone bids $200,000 for the house, the Mellers would have to pay a $12,000 commission ($200,000 price × 6% commission) and would receive only $188,000 ($200,000 price – $12,000 commission). They would also owe other fees and probably the expense of a lawyer to handle the sale. After all the transaction fees were paid, they might net $185,000 on the sale of their home.

A third problem in valuing assets is demonstrated with another example:

> *The Mellers, who are both in their late 30s, have Individual Retirement Accounts*
> *(IRAs). Ron's IRA is worth $28,000 and Pat's IRA is worth $12,000. At what value*
> *should they list their IRAs on their personal balance sheet? Assume a 30 percent*
> *income tax rate.*

If the Mellers withdraw any money from their IRAs in the current year, they would have to treat the withdrawal as taxable income and have to pay a 10 percent tax penalty for early withdrawal. Thus, although the market value of the IRAs is clearly $40,000 ($28,000 + $12,000), converting them to cash in the current year could result in income taxes and penalties amounting to 40 percent (30% income tax rate + 10% penalty) of the withdrawal. In other words, were the Mellers to cash out their IRAs immediately, they would end up with only $24,000 ($40,000 × [1 – .40]), not the $40,000 face value in cash. If the IRAs are left untouched until retirement, then their true value is much closer to $40,000. The value of the IRAs depends on when they are actually cashed out. The $24,000 valuation figure would be the most conservative. IRAs are discussed further in Chapter 17.

Pension plans can pose even more valuation problems. There are two primary types of pension plans. Defined contribution plans can usually be valued at any point in time, similar to valuing an IRA. Defined benefit plans, however, are extremely difficult to value at a point in time. You may get a liquidation benefit if you drop out of a defined benefit pension program, but the liquidation value is usually far less than the value of the pension if you were to stay in the program and draw benefits upon retirement. Thus, pension plans should be valued based on the individual's intended cash-out date and on how long the employee intends to continue with the same employer.

Everyone would like to see the total value of his or her assets as high as possible. It is pleasant to think that your house is worth $200,000 rather than $185,000. It is more fun to value IRAs as worth $40,000 rather than $24,000. We are inclined to ignore transaction fees, taxes, and ambiguities in valuing personal assets. There is nothing wrong with such overstatements in value, as long as you are aware you are making these simplifications.

What Are the Liabilities on a Personal Balance Sheet?

Liabilities are debts that you currently owe. They are normally listed in order of increas-ing maturity. Thus, a credit card bill that is due in a few days would be listed before a mortgage on which you owe payments for the next 28 years. In general, debts should be listed at the amount you would owe if you were to pay the debt off today. Do not include any prepayment penalties.

Some debts may be worth much less than the principal owed. For example, assume you have 20 years left to pay on your mortgage and the interest rate on your mortgage is 6 percent. Assume that the current rate on new mortgages is 9 percent. The fact that your mortgage has an interest rate substantially lower than the going rate on new mortgages would make the intrinsic value of this mortgage less than the principal owed. It would be tempting but inappropriate to adjust the value of this loan to reflect the lower rate. First, you cannot "cash out" this difference between the value of the mortgage and the principal owed. Second, there is always uncertainty about when a mortgage will be paid off. If you have to move and sell your house next year, you will have to pay off the full amount of the mortgage owed at that time. Thus, even debts with very low interest rates should be listed according to the principal owed and not according to an imputed intrinsic value.

One source of confusion in computing the liabilities on a balance sheet is how to treat monthly payments. For example, if you are computing your balance sheet as of December 31, and you have a car loan payment due January 3 and a utility bill due January 5, should these items be listed as liabilities? The answer is no. Part of the car loan payment is implicit in the principal owed on the car loan balance listed for December 31. Listing a nearly due car loan payment separately would be partially double counting. Of course, you could compute the accrued interest on the loan at the time of the valuation date and list that as a liability without double counting, but consider whether the effort is worth the materiality of the result.

The utility bill would not be listed because it is a future expense. Future income is not an asset and future expenses should not be listed as liabilities. If any bill is overdue, then it should be listed as a liability.

What Is the Net Worth on a Personal Balance Sheet?

The **net worth** on a balance sheet is the difference between the total value of assets owned and the total amount of liabilities owed. Net worth is the measure of a person's financial wealth. When individuals are setting long-range goals, which is step 2 in the financial planning process, one of the goals should always be projected net worth at various points in time. In particular, you should specify your desired net worth at the time of retirement. Consider the following:

> Ron and Pat Meller own a home they believe to be worth $200,000. The current balance on their mortgage is $150,000. There is $2,000 in their checking account. They own 100 shares of Eastman Kodak stock worth $50 per share. They both have Individual Retirement Accounts (IRAs). Ron's IRA is worth $28,000 and Pat's IRA is worth $12,000. They have $20,000 invested in a bond mutual fund. They own two automobiles, worth a combined value of $25,000. They have one car loan outstanding on which the current principal owed is $8,000. Ron has a pension at work that is currently worth $62,000. What is the Mellers net worth? Ignore taxes and transaction fees in considering the value of the assets.

**Web Link
(WSJ) 2.1**

The balance sheet form from the *Wall Street Journal* site is shown in Figure 2.1.

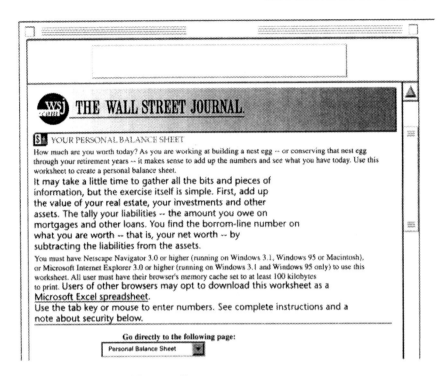

FIGURE 2-1 Personal Balance Sheet

Regardless of which web page is used, the balance sheet should look something like the following:

Assets:		Liabilities:	
Checking Account	$2,000	Auto Loan	$8,000
Bond Mutual Fund	20,000	Mortgage	150,000
Stock	50,000	Total Liabilities	158,000
IRAs	40,000		
Pension	62,000		
House	200,000		
Autos	25,000	Net Worth:	$241,000
Total Assets	$399,000	Total Liabilities and Net Worth:	$399,000

In developing a personal balance sheet, it would appear that in cases where a loan is pledged against a specific asset, the presentation could be simplified by showing the asset at the **net equity value.** Net equity value is the value of an asset less the current balance of any loans against it. In the above example, the net equity value of the house is $50,000 and the net equity value of the autos is $17,000. Note that showing assets at net equity value does not affect the computation of net worth.

Despite the implied simplicity, assets should not be shown at net equity value because this distorts how one's assets are allocated. In the above example, approximately one-half of the Mellers wealth is invested in their house. If assets were shown at net equity value, then it would appear that the Mellers have only $50,000 invested in their house, not the full $200,000. Suppose the value of the Mellers' house dropped by 10 percent. In the above balance sheet, it is easy to see that this decline in value would mean a reduction in net worth of $20,000. Were the house shown at net equity value, the impact of a potential 10 percent drop in the value of their home would not be as apparent.

WHAT IS AN INCOME STATEMENT?

Where the personal financial balance sheet is like a snapshot of your net worth *at a particular point in time*, an **income statement** is a statement of income and expenses *over a period of time*. The time frame is usually the past year. You could prepare a forecast of your income statement, but the objectives for so doing would usually be better met by a cash budget. The purpose of an income statement is to answer the question that perplexes most people: where did all my money go? Because there is some similarity between an income statement and a tax return, it makes sense to prepare an income statement for the prior year at the same time you prepare your tax return. An income statement consists of three sections.

The first section of an income statement is the income. Income includes wages and salaries, income from investments such as bonds, stocks, certificates of deposit, and rental property, and distributions from retirement accounts. Such accounts would include pension funds, IRAs, Keoghs, 403(b)s, 401(k)s, and annuities. Income does not include the liquidation of assets. If you sell some securities and use the cash to purchase an asset like a car, or even to meet your daily living expenses, you are *not* receiving income. Rather, the transaction would be treated as negative savings.[2] Income also does *not* include employer contributions to your pension accounts, or dividends, interest, and price appreciation in any retirement account such as a pension, IRA, etc. These monies are not available to you for personal use.

The second section is a statement of expenses. Expenses are usually listed in order of magnitude, with the basic necessities being listed first. Thus, housing, food, and transportation are typically at the top of the list. Expenses are also grouped by similarity. Thus, you would list insurance premiums as a general category, and then include life insurance, auto insurance, health insurance, homeowner's or renter's insurance, disability insurance, and any other insurance premiums you pay under this general category. The acquisition of personal assets is also treated as an expense. If you buy a car, the cost of the car is an expense. The car would then appear on the next balance sheet as an asset. Purchases of financial assets are not treated as expenses. The interest on loan payments is an expense, but not the repayment of principal.

The third section is a summary that represents the **contribution to savings.** Contribution to savings is the difference between the total of income in the first section and the total of expenses in the second section. In equation form:

$$\text{Contribution to Savings} = \text{Total Income} - \text{Total Expenses}.$$

---

[2]Some people find it counterintuitive that the liquidation of financial assets is not treated as income. Liquidating a financial asset is, obviously, a cash inflow, but not all cash inflows are income.

If the contribution is positive, you need to reconcile where the savings went. If the net contribution was negative, you need to determine where the savings were absorbed. A positive contribution to savings would normally show up in the purchase of investments, a reduction in debt, or some combination of the two. A negative contribution to savings shows up in the liquidation of assets, an increase in debt, or some combination of the two. Consider the following example:

> *Ron and Pat Meller had income from all sources last year of $88,000. Their total expenses were $80,000. They added $5,000 to their investment portfolio and paid off $3,000 on their car loan. What was their contribution to savings and resulting change in net worth?*

In this example the Mellers had a contribution to savings of $8,000 ($88,000 – $80,000). Of this $8,000, they invested $5,000 and used the remaining $3,000 to pay down loans. Hence, their assets increased by $5,000 and their liabilities decreased by $3,000. Whether the contribution to savings is invested or used to pay down loans, net worth increases by the same amount. Thus, regardless of what portion of their contribution to savings the Mellers had invested and what portion they had used to pay off loans, their net worth would have increased by $8,000.

WHAT ARE THE PERSONAL FINANCIAL RATIOS?

Once you have finished your personal balance sheet and income statement, it is time to consider what these two statements can tell you. The net worth number is significant in and of itself, since the larger the net worth, the better off a person is financially, but these two statements contain even more useful information you should consider. The traditional approach for analyzing financial statements is through the use of what are known as **financial ratios.** Financial ratios combine two or more numbers from the financial statements to measure a specific aspect of your personal financial situation. Financial ratios are used (1) to measure changes in the quality of your financial situation over time, (2) to measure the absolute quality of your current financial situation, and (3) as guidelines for how to improve your financial situation.[3]

When it comes to using financial ratios to evaluate a business, many well-known ratios are used, for which there are well-established optimal values. Few personal financial ratios are popularly known and used, however, and the optimal values are not well defined. Let us consider some ratios for household use. We will group the ratios into the following eight categories: liquidity, solvency, savings, asset allocation, inflation protection, tax burden, housing expenses, and insolvency/credit.

The first category, *liquidity*, is analyzed to better understand the likelihood a household will have problems paying its bills. Several ratios are used to measure liquidity. Three of these measures (labeled L_1, L_2, and L_3 for convenience) include the following:

[3]This description as well as some of the material to follow is drawn from "The Usefulness of Financial Ratios as Predictors of Household Insolvency: Two Perspectives," by Sharon DeVaney, *Financial Counseling and Planning*, Vol. 5 (1994), pp. 5–24, and "Ratios and Benchmarks for Measuring the Financial Well-Being of Families and Individuals," by Sue A. Greninger, Vickie L. Hampton, Karrol A. Kitt, and Joseph A. Achacoso, *Financial Services Review*, Vol. 5, No. 1 (1996), pp. 57–70.

L_1 = ratio of liquid assets to monthly expenses

L_2 = ratio of liquid assets to monthly disposable income

L_3 = ratio of liquid assets to current debt

Liquid assets are defined as cash and cash equivalents. Current debts are all loan payments and other borrowings due within one year. If your income were to suddenly stop, the first two ratios tell you how many months of living expenses you could pay out of current liquid assets and how many months of income you could replace. The third ratio tells you how many years (or fraction thereof) worth of debt payments you could make out of current liquid assets.

One of the issues of personal financial planning is how many months of living expenses one should keep on hand. Most discussions of this issue suggest three to six months' worth of living expenses.[4] We will discuss this issue in more detail in Chapter 5, but note that both excessively high and excessively low values of the liquidity ratio indicate problems. If the ratio is too high, then you may be keeping too many assets in liquid form. Liquid assets usually provide rates of return substantially lower than on less liquid assets. Thus, excessive holdings of liquid assets represent potentially huge opportunity losses of investment income. If your liquidity ratio is too low and there is a disruption to your income, then you will likely have some difficulty meeting daily living expenses. There are, of course, exceptions. If you believe that the stock market is going to drop substantially in the near future, you would likely want to have a substantial portion of your assets in a liquid form. If you feel there is a high probability of losing your job in the near future, then you would also want high liquidity ratios.

Note that if monthly expenses approximately equal monthly disposable income, then there is no significant difference between the first two measures of liquidity. This author prefers the first two ratios (L_1 or L_2) to the third (L_3). With the third ratio, current debt might have little to do with either income or expenses. If, for example, someone is effectively living from paycheck to paycheck on a cash-only basis, they may have little or no current debt. They will have a high ratio of liquid assets to current debt but not a healthy amount of liquidity.

A complement to any measure of liquidity is the **solvency ratio.** This ratio equals total assets divided by total liabilities:

$$\text{Solvency Ratio} = \text{Total Assets/Total Liabilities}$$

A value of less than one means that total liabilities exceed total assets, and therefore net worth is negative. A negative net worth means a household is technically insolvent, but does not mean a household must declare bankruptcy. For example, individuals graduating from college with outstanding student loans frequently have negative net worth, but if they have a good-paying job then they will likely be able to start paying down their loans and begin moving the balance sheet to a positive net worth. If a family whose primary income producer is nearing retirement has a solvency ratio of less than one, this family may face

Web Link 2.2

[4]Although most financial planners talk about holding a specific amount of liquid assets as a safety measure, and define this amount of assets in terms of current income or expenses, there is an alternative approach. One alternative approach, as shown in Web Link 2.2, is to compute actual dollar values that you might need for specific emergencies and to set this amount aside.

a substantial risk of having to declare bankruptcy in the near future. In general, the higher the ratio of assets to liabilities, the better off a person is. Under the U.S. tax code, however, mortgage interest expenses and interest expenses on loans that finance the purchase of investments can be used as deductions against taxable income. Because of this, aggressive investors find that the acquisition of some debt can actually lead to a faster and larger accumulation of wealth over time.

The solvency ratio is sometimes computed as the ratio of net worth to total assets or total assets to net worth, instead of total assets to total liabilities. All of these definitions are perfectly acceptable. This author prefers the assets to liabilities definition because it provides a simple guideline that higher values are usually better, and it avoids awkward values that would be associated with negative net worths.

The third area of ratio analysis is the **savings rate** of a household. The savings rate is the percentage of income that is being saved:

Savings Rate = Contribution to Savings/Income

The savings rate may be measured as a percentage of gross income or as a percentage of net income. Most personal finance professionals feel a household savings rate should be in excess of 10 percent.[5] The ideal value of this ratio would clearly have to be adjusted for different household situations. If the primary income earner were unemployed, then the household should not be focusing on growing its savings. A newly married double-income couple planning on starting a family may want to consider a substantially higher savings rate. A retired widow or widower in his or her later years may want to consume savings rather than add to savings. That is, his or her goal may be to start disposing of his or her assets, so the ideal savings ratio may actually be negative.

The fourth area of ratio analysis is **asset allocation,** which is addressed in Chapter 13. There are three asset allocation ratios (labeled below as A_1, A_2, and A_3) of importance in a financial analysis. These include:

A_1 = the ratio of liquid assets to net worth

A_2 = the ratio of financial assets to net worth

A_3 = the ratio of foreign investments to total investments

Although A_1 may look like a liquidity measure, it is more. Liquid assets are held for two reasons. The first is a precautionary motive and the second is that liquid assets may be a normal part of your investment portfolio. Holding liquid assets in an investment portfolio reduces the riskiness of that portfolio, and allows you take advantage of downturns in the financial markets. The optimal quantity of liquid assets will vary with the size of your investment portfolio and age. Financial planning professionals usually recommend that this ratio be at least 15 percent. More conservative investors would likely want a higher ratio, and more aggressive investors would likely want a lower ratio. One of the miscues in life discussed in Chapter 1 is a collapse of financial markets. One way to protect against this particular miscue is to hold higher levels of liquid assets.

---

[5]The ideal savings ratio recommended by personal finance professionals appears to be the same, regardless of whether the savings ratio is based on the gross income or net income definitions! Clearly, it is more challenging to save 10 percent of gross income than of net income.

The ratio of financial assets to net worth (A_2) indicates how much of your net worth is represented by financial assets. Financial assets are those assets acquired for sake of liquidity and/or for the financial returns they might provide. Whether something is a financial asset or a real asset sometimes depends on intent. Some assets, such as a valuable stamp collection, could be difficult to classify. Ultimately, the creature comfort joys of life come from owning real assets, not financial assets.

The third ratio of this category (A_3), the ratio of foreign investments to total investments, is an indication of the importance attached to investments overseas. The most fundamental principle of investments is diversification. The growth in the sophistication of the world's financial markets in recent years has allowed individuals to easily acquire and monitor foreign assets. Foreign assets offer a highly efficient method of diversification.

The fifth category of ratios focuses on the magnitude of one's protection against **inflation.** These ratios (labeled I_1, I_2, and I_3) include:

I_1 = the percentage change in net worth divided by the rate of inflation

I_2 = the percentage change in investment assets divided by the rate of inflation

I_3 = the amount of equity investments divided by the amount of total investment assets

The concept and measurement of the rate of inflation is discussed in Chapter 4. The rate of inflation represents the decline in the purchasing power of the dollar. Thus, if the rate of inflation were 4 percent in a given year, then at the end of the year, it would take $1.04 to buy what $1.00 bought at the start of the year. One cannot control the rate of inflation. The only way for an individual to deal with the resulting loss of purchasing power is to grow his or her wealth at a faster rate. In general, financial planning professionals recommend that one try to grow one's net worth and/or investments (I_1 and I_2) at a rate of at least twice the rate of inflation.

For the first two ratios, note that there is no specific time period covered by them. Thus, one can use whatever time period is deemed most relevant. What is critical is that the percentage change in net worth or in investment assets be computed over the same time period as the rate of inflation is computed. Consider the following example:

> Over the last year, Ron and Pat Meller note that their net worth has grown by 8 percent while the rate of inflation for that period was 2 percent. However, looking back over the last five years, their net worth for the five-year period has grown 30 percent while the rate of inflation for the same five-year period was 15 percent. How well have the Mellers protected themselves against inflation?

For the last year, the value of I_1 was 4 (8% / 2%). For the last five years, the value of I_1 has been 2 (30% / 15%). Thus, they have overcome the harm done by inflation for the last five years, but they have been particularly successful over the last year.

The third ratio is an indirect measure of inflation protection. Equities have historically had the highest rate of return among investments made by most households. Thus, as long as a sufficient portion of your investments are in equities, it is likely that your investments will grow over time at a rate substantially in excess of the inflation rate.

The sixth category of ratios measures your **tax burden.** The two ratios used to measure the tax burden are the income tax burden (T_1) and the total tax burden (T_2). These are defined as

T_1 = federal, state, and local income taxes and social security taxes/gross income

T_2 = all taxes/gross income

All taxes include the income and social security taxes from the first ratio, as well as real estate taxes, sales taxes, and any personal property taxes. Because of the progressive nature of our federal tax system and the fact that most state and local tax codes are also progressive, the recommended level for this ratio is a function of your income level and the city and state in which you live.[6] In general, even at higher levels of income, a comprehensive tax ratio in excess of 35 percent would represent a substantial tax burden.

The seventh category of financial ratios involves **housing expenses.** Housing is the largest single monthly expense of most people. It is difficult and often expensive to change the amount of one's monthly housing expenses once one has committed to a certain form of housing (by either buying a home or signing a lease). The first housing ratio (H_1) is

H_1 = renter's expenses/gross income

A renter's expenses include rent, renter's insurance, and utilities. Financial planning experts suggest the renter's expense ratio not exceed 30 percent.

The second housing ratio (H_2) is

H_2 = homeowner's expenses/gross income

Homeowner's expenses include **PITI,** homeowner's association fees (if any), utilities, maintenance, and repairs. PITI stands for the principal and interest payment on a mortgage loan, property taxes, and homeowner's insurance. The principal and interest payments on a mortgage loan together constitute the mortgage payment. Financial planning professionals recommend the homeowner's expense ratio not exceed 35 percent.

When a prospective homebuyer applies for a mortgage to facilitate the purchase of the home, the mortgage lender looks at two additional housing-related ratios. The first is the ratio of PITI to gross income. This ratio must not exceed 28 percent, and would ideally not exceed 25 percent. The second key ratio used by mortgage lenders is the ratio of PITI plus all other debt payments that continue longer than six months to gross income. This ratio should not exceed 36 percent.

The eighth and final category of ratios is the insolvency/credit ratios. These ratios (labeled C_1, C_2, and C_3) include:

C_1 = nonmortgage debt payments/after-tax income

C_2 = total debt payment/after-tax income

C_3 = total expenses/after-tax income

Financial planners have found that when these ratios become too high, bankruptcy is usually imminent. The value of the non-mortgage debt payments in ratio C_1 is the sum of the consumer debt payments that represent fixed monthly payments. If you pay your credit

---

[6]All of these taxes will be discussed in later chapters. A progressive income tax means that a higher tax rate is applied to higher levels of income. An example of a progressive tax rate structure would be if the tax rate were 10 percent on the first $20,000 of taxable income, and then 25 percent on income above that. Thus, if you earned $30,000 in taxable income, you would pay $2,000 in taxes on the first $20,000 of income, and $2,500 in taxes on the last $10,000 of taxable income.

card in full each month, you are not making a consumer debt payment. You are simply using the credit card to pay for expenses that could otherwise have been paid with cash. If you pay less than the full amount of the credit card balance each month, then part of your payment becomes a de facto installment loan and would be included in the numerator. Other examples of consumer debt payments include the monthly installments on car loans, home improvement loans, and line of credit loans. A final example would be installment payments for services. For example, if a child needs orthodontia work, the orthodontist may propose monthly installment payments for the next two years. Although this is not a formal loan, it has the same effect as payments on any other loan you have taken out. Commitments on fixed monthly payments reduce the amount of your disposable income available for other uses, such as food, housing, and transportation. Once these fixed commitments reach a certain level, you simply don't have enough income left over to meet other obligations. Financial planning experts usually suggest that the ratio of non-mortgage debt payments to after-tax income not exceed 10 percent. A value of 20 percent or greater for this ratio is a sign of significant financial difficulties.

The second ratio (C_2) uses the numerator of the first ratio, and adds to it the value of the monthly mortgage payment. The target value for this ratio is around 35 percent and a value of 45 percent or more is considered a sign of serious financial distress.

The final ratio in this category (C_3) is the complement of the savings rate. Since the savings rate should be about 10 percent (with many exceptions noted), ratio C_3 should be about 90 percent.

WHAT IS A CASH BUDGET?

The most critical tool of the three financial statements is the **cash budget.** The cash budget is where you specify how you want to spend your money over some period in the future. A cash budget differs from an income statement in that income statements are typically historical in nature and serve as a measure of success in contributing to one's savings during the year. An income statement is a summary for the year. A cash budget is a forward-looking detailed plan, meant to be a control tool or a warning device. As an example, wages and salaries for the entire year are listed as a single number on the income statement, but cash budgets break this number down, usually into monthly intervals. Another critical difference is that income statements do not include elements of saving. A cash budget would include the actual amount of savings planned each month, and what form those savings would take. To further emphasize the difference between an income statement and a cash budget, consider the following example.

> *The Mellers take out a one-year $1,000 loan on December 31. The loan has a 12 percent interest rate and calls for monthly payments on the last day of each month. The monthly payment is $88.85. How will this loan show up on the income statement for the year, and how will it show up on a cash budget?*

On the cash budget, the loan will show up as a payment of $88.85 each month. Over the course of twelve months, the Mellers will pay $1,066.20 ($88.85 × 12 months). Of this, $66.20 represents the payment of interest and $1,000 represents the repayment of the principal. Thus, on the income statement, the Mellers would report the $66.20 in interest payments as an expense, and the $1,000 in principal payments as part of the contribution to savings. The Mellers' change in net worth will be augmented by $1,000 because they started the year with a $ 1,000 loan as a liability, and by the end of the year the loan was gone. Remember, a reduction of a liability will mean an increase in net worth.

Creating a cash budget is easy. Doing something with it after you have created it is the difficult part. During or at the end of the budget period, you have to be willing to let the numbers in the budget analysis guide your spending. For example, if you discover you are overspending on entertainment, you would have to be willing to give up some evenings out until your expenditures get back in line with your budget. If you are not willing to do this, then there is no point in attempting to maintain a budget. The *Wall Street Journal* budget page is shown in Figure 2.2.

Web Link (WSJ) 2.3

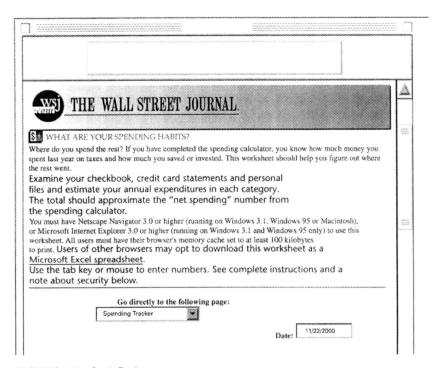

FIGURE 2-2 Cash Budget

Sometimes the failure to stick to a budget reflects a lack of understanding of the monetary benefits. It is easy to say, for example, that if you ate out one less time per month you could save $50 per month, but what's $50 per month over the long term? The value of these types of savings can be easily computed. The mathematics and concepts behind such computations will be presented in Chapter 4. For now, consider the following example:

> *Ron and Pat Meller have reviewed their budget and concluded they could eat out one less time per month. This would save them $50 per month. Ron is 40 years old and plans to retire at age 65. The Mellers believe they could invest (or save) this money at a rate of 6 percent. If their combined marginal federal and state tax rate is 35 percent, how much could they accumulate after 10 years on a before- and after-tax basis? How much could they accumulate by retirement on a before- and after-tax basis?*

Web Link 2.4 In this example, the savings turn out to be

Savings after 10 years:
    Before taxes $8,163
    After taxes $7,253

Value at retirement:
    Tax *deferred* $33,979
    Taxable $24,548

After looking at these numbers, eating out one extra dinner per month starts to look pretty expensive!

WHAT ARE HIDDEN EXPENSES?

In constructing a budget, **hidden expenses** are those expenses that do not occur every month. It is in identifying the hidden expenses that a cash budget can really help a person who wants to control his or her finances. For example, if your take-home pay is $2,000 every month and your fixed expenses are exactly the same every month, say $1,500, then you know each month that you have $500 to spend on optional expenses. A fixed expense is an expense one either is legally liable for or cannot avoid. Fixed expenses include rent or mortgage payments, food, telephone, utilities, loans, and transportation. Optional expenses include entertainment, cable bills, and hobbies. Because hidden expenses occur as rarely as once a year or as frequently as every other month, they can easily create problems for anyone living from paycheck to paycheck. The solution to handling hidden expenses is simple. First, you must figure out the monthly equivalent of the annual hidden expenses. Next, you set aside this amount of money each month, just as if these were fixed, monthly expenses. You could literally set up a special savings account or checking account just for this purpose. Then, as each hidden expense comes due, you pay it out of this special account. Consider the following example:

> *Ron and Pat Meller are attempting to identify their hidden expenses so that they can determine the amount of money they need to set aside each month to meet these expenses. They pay $700 on auto insurance every six months, $500 on homeowner's insurance once a year, and $1,000 on life insurance once a year. They would like to spend $3,000 on their vacation this year. They will spend about $500 on various presents over the course of the year, and another $500 on all of their Christmas presents. They will spend about $1,000 on auto maintenance on their two cars over the year, and another $1,000 on maintenance on their home. Their property taxes will be $2,500, payable in two installments. What are their monthly hidden expenses?*

Web Link 2.5 **Web Link 2.5** provides a calculator to facilitate this exercise. The expenses in this example total $11,400. The monthly set-aside should be $950 ($11,400 / 12 months).

IS IT WORTH IT TO HAVE A DOUBLE-INCOME HOUSEHOLD?

After preparing a cash budget, many people discover that their projected cash outflows exceed their projected cash inflows. There are always only two solutions. The first is to cut back on projected cash outflows and the other is to increase projected inflows. Both are simple to say, neither is simple to do. For an individual, or for a couple in which only one of the partners works, one solution is to take on a second job. It is easy to look at the gross paycheck of the second job and to think of that as the incremental cash inflow. However, the cash inflow from a second job must be reduced by the additional income taxes that would have to be paid on that income. In addition to the income taxes, there would likely also be additional deductions such as the mandatory cost of health insurance and other employee benefits.[7] There is still one more set of Reductions. When a second job is taken on, either by the primary income earner or by a non-working spouse, new expenses usually develop. These could include incremental childcare expenses, transportation costs, housekeeping expenses, and additional meals out. Consider the following situation:

> *Ron and Pat Meller have developed their cash budget for the coming year. Their cash outflows exceed their cash inflows by $15,000. Pat currently does not work, so she proposed to take a job to provide the additional cash inflow. Pat thought that a $1,500 monthly salary should do the trick. The Mellers marginal federal and state tax rates are 28 percent and 6 percent. Pat would be employed as opposed to self-employed and would owe Social Security taxes. The kids would have to be placed in childcare for about two hours each day, which would cost about $200 per month. Driving their second car to work increases the auto insurance premium by $10 per month, and the gas, oil, and additional maintenance will cost $50 per month. Pat would need a housekeeper biweekly, and this would cost $150 per month. Finally, the reduction in leisure time for Pat would necessitate eating out one day per week more than would normally be the case. This would cost about $100 per month. What is the actual value of Pat taking a job?*

Web Link 2.6

It turns out that that the $1,500 gross paycheck will provide monthly net cash inflow to the household of $365. The rest of the paycheck is spent as follows: employment taxes $115, income taxes $510, and extra expenses $510. From this, Pat concludes that she would either have to obtain a substantially higher paying job or give up the idea of her working and look for ways to reduce planned expenses.

Web Link (WSJ) 2.7

HOW MUCH WILL A CHILD COST ME?

Until this century, a significant motive of many couples for having children was retirement planning! Many parents planned to move in with a child when they became too old to live independently, take care of themselves, or support themselves.[8] Few people today have children as part of their retirement planning. The decision to have children is usually an

---

[7]Some employers offer a cash bonus to employees opting out of health insurance. If the primary jobholder has adequate family health insurance, then a cash rebate for opting out of health insurance increases the income from the second job.

[8]In many of the poorer countries today, retirement planning is still a significant motive for having children.

emotional one. It is not the intent of this chapter to encourage or discourage anyone from having children. However, it is important in financial planning for a couple to fully understand the costs of having and raising a child.

Some of the expenses of a child are obvious and direct. These would include such items as childcare, food, clothing, and babysitting. However, there are also many indirect expenses. For example, people with children buy bigger homes. A bigger home costs more to buy and to maintain. People with children also buy bigger cars, take more elaborate vacations, and incur extra insurance bills. The total dollar cost of a child up to age 18 can easily exceed one-quarter of a million dollars. Consider the following example:

> *Ron and Pat Meller are considering having an additional child. They project the following average annual expenses for the following age ranges for the child: Day care from ages 2 to 12 at $2,000 per year; additional groceries from birth to age 18 at $1,000 per year; furnishings from birth to age 18 at $500 per year; babysitting from ages 0 to 12 at $250 per year; family vacations from ages 4 to 18 at $1,000 per year; a bigger home from ages 4 to 18 at an incremental cost of $2,000 per year; dental bills from ages 6 to 18 at $300 per year; a bigger car from ages 4 to 18 at $1,000 per year; extra insurance for the family from ages 0 to 18 at $1,000 per year; education from ages 6 to 18 at $500 per year; medical bills from ages 0 to 18 at $500 per year; children's activities from ages 2 to 18 at $500 per year; and miscellaneous from ages 0 to 18 at $3,000 per year. What is the total projected cost of this child?*

Web Link 2.8   The total cost in the above example turns out to be $202,400. This number is before funding a college education.

SUMMARY

> There are three key documents in the financial planning process: the personal balance sheet, the income statement, and the cash budget. The personal balance sheet shows one's assets, liabilities, and net worth. Net worth is the difference between assets and liabilities. Assets should be listed at market value and net of taxes and transaction fees incurred at sale, although most people list them at gross value. Liabilities should be listed at the cost of paying off each debt today.

> An analysis of financial statements can be done with various ratios. There are eight categories of these ratios: liquidity, solvency, savings, asset allocation, inflation protection, tax burden, housing expenses, and insolvency/credit. Ratios can serve as both targets for financial planning and measures of progress.

> The control part of financial planning comes from setting up a cash budget and using it to make choices. This differs from an income statement, which is historical.

> Hidden expenses are those that do not occur every month.

> Families desiring to grow their net worth at a faster rate may consider the primary wage earner taking a second job, or a nonworking spouse going to work. It is easy to overestimate the contribution to savings that such a job will bring in because of the incremental taxes due and the incremental household expenses that are incurred.

> Finally, having children is usually an extremely heavy financial burden.

KEY TERMS

asset allocation	balance sheet	cash budget
contribution to savings	deferred	financial ratios
hidden expenses	housing expenses	income statement
inflation	liquidity	materiality
money market instruments	net equity value	net worth
PITI	real assets	savings rate
solvency ratio	tax burden	

PROBLEMS

2.1. You own some land that you bought five years ago for $10,000. You recently received an offer for the land of $20,000 that you turned down. Comparable land in the area has sold recently for $25,000. If you sold the land, you would have to pay a realtor a 5 percent commission. You would also owe a capital gains tax. The capital gains tax rate is 20 percent and is based on profit net of transaction fees. What are the minimum and maximum values at which you might show this land on your personal balance sheet?

2.2. You bought your home 20 years ago for $100,000 and took out a mortgage for $80,000. Today, you still owe $45,000 on that mortgage. Because the interest rate on your mortgage is 5 percent and current market interest rates are 10 percent, your lender recently sent you a letter offering to let you pay off the mortgage in full for $40,000. The offer is good for 30 days. At what value should you list your mortgage on your balance sheet?

2.3. You are reviewing your financial situation, and find that as of January 1, 2002, you have the following assets and liabilities:

Checking account	$1,212	Stocks	23,519
Mutual funds (stock)	18,742	Home	160,000
Money market funds	8,577	IRA–Roth	6,488
IRA–traditional	15,579	Pension (DC)	48,599
Car #1	15,000	Car #2	4,000
Margin loan	1,588	Mortgage	122,541
Auto loan	9,553	Cash value of life insurance	5,518

What is your net worth? What is your solvency ratio? What is your ratio of liquid assets to net worth (A1)?

2.4. Jake and Patty DiMartino have developed their cash budget for the coming year. Their cash outflows exceed their cash inflows by $15,000. Jake currently does not work, so he proposed to take a job to provide the additional cash inflow. Jake thought that a $1,500 monthly salary should do the trick. The DiMartino's marginal state tax rate is 5 percent, and their marginal federal tax rate is 31 percent. Jake would be employed as opposed to self-employed, and would owe Social

Security taxes. The kids would have to be placed in childcare for about two hours each day, which would cost about $500 per month. Driving their second car to work will increase the auto insurance premium by $20 per month, and the gas, oil, and additional maintenance will cost $50 per month. Jake would need a housekeeper biweekly, which would cost $100 per month. Finally, the reduction in leisure time for Jake would necessitate eating out one day per week more than would normally be the case. This would cost about $200 per month. What is the actual value of Jake taking a job?

2.5. Ron and Pat Meller are considering having an additional child. They project the following average annual expenses for the following age ranges for the child: day care from ages 2 to 12 at $4,000 per year; additional groceries from birth to age 18 at $2,000 per year; furnishings from ages 0 to 18 at $800 per year; babysitting from ages 0 to 12 at $400 per year; family vacations from ages 4 to 18 at $1,500 per year; a bigger home from ages 4 to 18 at an incremental cost of $3,000 per year; dental bills from ages 6 to 18 at $200 per year; a bigger car from ages 4 to 18 at $2,000 per year; extra insurance for the family from ages 0 to 18 at $500 per year; education from ages 6 to 18 at $500 per year; medical bills from ages 0 to 18 at $1,000 per year; children's activities from ages 2 to 18 at $500 per year; and miscellaneous from ages 0 to 18 at $4,000 per year. What is the total cost of this child?

2.6. Construct your own personal balance sheet and income statement. Next, compute the ratios described in this chapter as they apply to you. Identify those ratios you would most like to improve, and project target values for each of these ratios.

REFERENCES

Web Link 2.9 Software for preparing personal financial statements
Web Link 2.10 Pointer sites and miscellaneous sites on the budgeting process

WALL STREET JOURNAL RESOURCES

Web Link (WSJ) 2.11 WSJ discussion on household budgets
Web Link (WSJ) 2.12 How much money are you setting aside?
Web Link (WSJ) 2.13 How much you must save to meet your financial goals?

For information that has changed since the book was written, for new information that pertains to this topic, and for some new web sites that pertain to the topic of this chapter, see **Web Link 2.14.**

CHAPTER 3

MANAGING YOUR TAXES

LEARNING OBJECTIVES

- Describe the basic federal income tax model
- Distinguish between adjustments to income and itemized deductions
- Determine the impact of itemized deductions on taxable income
- Determine a person's marginal tax rate
- Decide how much in federal taxes you will withhold on your paycheck
- Determine the tax impact of a capital gain or a capital loss
- Discuss some of the differences in taxation among the various states
- Understand the likelihood of having your tax return audited
- Know how to do your own research on a tax question

Web Link: www.wiley.com/college/woerheide

INTRODUCTION

The primary revenue source for any government is taxes. Most people agree that many of the things our federal, state, and local governments do are good and beneficial. Most people accept that these government activities need to be funded. Most people appear to feel they pay more than their fair shares of taxes.

Regardless of what your fair share of taxes should be, taxes are a critical part of our financial lives. Even if you hire a professional tax preparer, you need to understand the structure of our tax system. A better knowledge of our tax system allows you to make better personal financial decisions and to be a more knowledgeable voter when it is time to choose between political candidates with different opinions about how our tax system should be structured.

What follows is a single chapter on taxes in a book that is dedicated to the broad topic of personal financial decision making. It is not intended to make you an expert on taxes. But when you finish reading this chapter, you should be able to converse intelligently about the basics of our tax system. In this chapter, we will focus on Roberta Klein, a woman who is caught up in preparing her taxes and making some financial decisions that have significant tax implications.

WHAT IS THE BASIC FEDERAL INCOME TAX MODEL?

The largest single tax that most people pay is the federal income tax. Federal income tax forms (as well as most state income tax forms) appear incredibly complicated—and they are! Keep in mind, however, that the forms are just an elaborate construction to help you determine your tax bill under what might be called a basic equation or tax model.

The basic tax model has not changed significantly since the first modern tax return form was distributed in 1913. Most of the changes have been the addition of detail. Over the years Congress has opted to use the tax system to encourage and discourage certain economic activity. One of the perennial issues in Congress is the appropriateness of using our tax code to achieve social and economic objectives that are politically desirable.

Web Link (WSJ) 3.1

The following discussion on the tax return is based on the assumption that the student is able to obtain a copy of IRS Form 1040.[1] The basic federal income model is as follows (the line numbers shown refer to Form 1040 for 2000):

> Total Income (line 22)
>
> − Adjustments to Gross Income (line 32)
>
> = Adjusted Gross Income or AGI (line 33)
>
> − Standard Deduction or Itemized Deductions (whichever is larger) (line 36)
>
> − Personal Exemptions (line 38)
>
> = Taxable Income (line 39)

Based on your taxable income, you can determine your tax liability according to what is referred to as your filing status. Then, the following formula is applied:

> Tax liability (line 40)
>
> − Credits (line 50)
>
> + Other taxes owed
>
> = Total taxes for the year (line 57)
>
> − Taxes paid to date (line 65)
>
> = Tax refund or payment due (lines 66 or 69)

WHAT IS TOTAL INCOME?

The various sources of gross income are listed on lines 7–21, with their sum listed on line 22.[2] The reader should obtain a copy of the current Form 1040 to review the 15 components of

---

[1]Although the IRS site will likely always be the best source for federal tax forms, a multitude of other sites also offer them. Some of these alternative sites provide only links to the federal forms, but others provide their own original forms. Links to some of these sites may be found at **Web Link 3.1a**.

[2]These line numbers are based on the 2000 tax forms. **Web Link (WSJ) 3.1** will always bring up the most current version of Form 1040. Because some of the line numbers may change from year to year, it is possible that a line number reference in the text may be slightly off. The author asks the reader to be tolerant of such miscues.

total income. Some of the more significant components of total income are wages, salaries, taxable interest, ordinary dividends, business income (or loss), capital gain (or loss), the taxable portion of total pensions and annuities, alimony received, and taxable portion of Social Security benefits.

What Are Adjustments to Total Income?

The second part of the federal income tax model is the **adjustments to total income.** These adjustments are reductions of your total income. On Form 1040, the adjustments are listed on lines 23 through 31a, with the sum listed on line 32. The more significant adjustments include IRA deduction, student loan interest deduction, moving expenses (when they qualify), Keogh and self-employed SEP and SIMPLE plans deductions, and alimony paid. The **adjusted gross income** (or AGI) is then computed on line 33 as the difference between total income (line 22) and the adjustments (line 32). The AGI is the key figure used in completing other parts of the tax return. For purposes of computing your tax liability, the AGI is a vastly more important number than is your total income. If you have no adjustments to your total income (as is the case for many people), then your AGI will be the same as your total income.

What Are Deductions?

After computing your adjusted gross income (line 33), you have completed the first page of Form 1040. You then go to the second page, and on the first line of the second page (line 34), you reenter the adjusted gross income figure.

The next step is to compute and subtract the **deductions** to which you are entitled. You are always entitled to the larger of either a designated standard deduction or the sum of your itemized deductions.

The **standard deduction** is specified each year and is adjusted for inflation. The amount of the standard deduction is based on your filing status. There are five filing statuses: single, head of household, married filing jointly, married filing separately, and surviving spouse. All of these categories are clear, except for perhaps the head of household category. To be eligible for head of household status, you must be single and able to claim someone else as a dependent. For further information on the head of household status, the reader should consult an IRS publication such as **Publication 17,** which provides a comprehensive overview of the tax code. To be eligible for surviving spouse status, your spouse must have died during the tax year. A person may claim surviving spouse status only once for each spouse he or she has survived. For 2000, the standard deductions for each of these filing statuses were

Single	$4,400
Head of household	6,450
Married filing jointly	7,350
Married filing separately	3,675
Surviving spouse	7,350

Web Link 3.2

The standard deductions for the current year are listed on page 2 of Form 1040. Current and recent standard deduction values may also be found at **Web Link 3.2.**

Web Link 3.3

You should compute your **itemized deductions** if there is any chance the total is greater than your standard deduction. Itemized deductions are shown on Schedule A of Form 1040. There are seven categories of itemized deductions. They include the following (the line numbers refer to the Schedule A for the year 2000):

1. Medical and dental expenses (only to the extent they exceed 7.5% of AGI) (line 4)

2. Taxes (line 9) *(Property & Mstate PIT)*

3. Interest expenses (line 14) *(Mortgage)*

4. Gifts to charity (not to exceed 50% of AGI) (line 18)

5. Casualty and theft losses (reduced by $100 per event, and only to the extent they exceed 10% of AGI) (line 19)

6. Job-related expenses and most miscellaneous deductions (only to the extent they exceed 2% of your AGI) (line 26)

7. Miscellaneous deductions (line 27)

Medical expenses include services; prescriptions; medical insurance premiums; health insurance costs for self-employed people; transportation, meals, and lodging to obtain medical services; and medical expenses of a deceased spouse or dependent. These expenses used to be fully deductible, but are now deductible only to the extent they exceed 7.5 percent of your AGI. Consider the following example:

> Roberta Klein had $5,000 in unreimbursed medical expenses last year, including doctors' bills and prescriptions. What would be her allowable itemized deduction for medical expenses if her AGI were $50,000?

If her AGI were $50,000, the 7.5 percent would be $3,750 and her allowable deduction would be $1,250 ($5,000 – $3,750).

The itemized deduction for taxes includes primarily state and local income taxes, real estate taxes, and personal property taxes. Sales taxes used to be deductible, but as part of one of its simplification acts, Congress eliminated this deduction.

Interest expenses include the interest on mortgage and home-equity loans and interest expenses on loans used to finance the purchase of taxable investments. It is easy to see why so many homeowners itemize. For most homeowners, the sum of their property taxes and the interest on their mortgage each year usually provides itemized deductions well in excess of what their standard deduction would be.

not student loans?

Gifts to charity include contributions to your church or other religious organization, as well as most charities. Any contributions in excess of $250 to any one organization may require documentation. Note that if you give $10 each week at church, the IRS counts it as 52 contributions of $10, and not one contribution of $520, and thus, these contributions would not normally require special documentation. Many people have noted that one could claim a $5 or $10 cash contribution to church each week, and it would be nearly impossible for anyone to prove otherwise. Research into taxpayer compliance finds that few people intentionally cheat on the income taxes with these types of fibs.

Charitable contributions may be made with cash or in the form of assets. Contributing assets may earn the donor substantially more tax savings. We will discuss this point again later. The charitable contribution deduction cannot exceed 50 percent of AGI. One of the most misunderstood aspects of the charitable contribution deduction is the purchase of tickets or other goods or services from a charity. In such a case, you are entitled to a deduction only to the extent that the price exceeds the fair market value of what you buy. Thus, if you were to pay $100 to play in a charitable golf tournament and the entry entitles you to play 18 holes, use a golf cart, and participate in an open bar and a dinner, then you must determine the fair market value of these items. Let us say the fair market value is $60. Then your itemized deduction is limited to $40, the difference between the $100 you paid for the ticket and the fair market value of what you received.

It should be noted that not all organizations claiming to be charities are so recognized by the IRS. A contribution to an organization not recognized by the IRS as a legitimate charity is not deductible. Consider the following example:

The United States Olympic Committee of Colorado Springs, Colorado, has approached Roberta Klein for a contribution. Roberta would like to contribute, but she wants to make sure that if the IRS audits her, this contribution would not be disallowed. Is this a legitimate charity for tax itemization purposes?

Web Link 3.4

You should be able to find out from at least one of the sites listed in **Web Link 3.4** that this organization does in fact qualify as a legitimate charity for tax purposes.

Casualty and theft losses have one of the more complicated formulas for determining an allowable itemization. First, any insurance or other compensation you receive offsets your deduction. Second, each deduction must be reduced by $100. Third, you can deduct only the amount of losses in excess of 10 percent of your AGI. Consider the following example:

Roberta Klein had two losses last year. In the first, she totaled her car when she hit a tree. As she had no collision coverage, she sustained the full $5,200 value of the loss. In the second, she had a fire in her basement that destroyed several items of property. The total value of the loss was $15,000, but her insurance covered $13,000. If her AGI were $50,000, how much of these losses could she deduct? Suppose her AGI were $30,000?

The first step to determine her itemization is to deduct $100 from her net loss on each item. In the case of the car, this would leave her with a $5,100 loss. In the case of the fire, the insurance reimbursement reduces her loss to $2,000, and the $100 offset reduces the potential deduction to $1,900. The combination of these two net losses is $7,000 ($5,100 + $1,900). If her AGI were $50,000, she could only take an itemization for the amount in excess of $5,000, namely $2,000. If her AGI were $30,000, then the 10 percent hurdle equals $3,000, and she would be entitled to an itemization of $4,000.

Job-related and most other miscellaneous expenses are the next itemization category. These deductions are allowable only to the extent they collectively exceed 2 percent of AGI. Naturally, only expenses not reimbursed by one's employer qualify.

Other miscellaneous deductions are the final itemization category. These deductions are different than the previous category in that there is no threshold that you must exceed before you would be allowed the deduction. It should be noted that not many items qualify for this category.

Many of the questions people have about the standard deduction, itemized deductions, and even taxable income may be answered at the IRS Tax Trails and other web sites.

What Is the Impact of Itemized Deductions on Taxable Income?

Once you have computed the total allowable itemizations for each of the seven categories, you then total these and compare that amount to the standard deduction for your filing status. Itemized deductions have value only to the extent they exceed the standard deduction. Consider the following example:

> For 2000, Roberta Klein has $1,500 in medical and dental expenses, $2,000 in state income taxes, and $1,500 in property taxes. She paid $8,000 in mortgage interest and gave $1,000 to legitimate charities during the year. She had $500 in unreimbursed casualty losses, $200 in unreimbursed job-related expenses, and no deductions that qualified as miscellaneous deductions. She is single and has $50,000 in adjusted gross income. What is the value of her itemized deductions?

To start with, Roberta's medical and dental expenses, casualty loss, and job-related expenses do not exceed the thresholds required to qualify as itemized deductions. This leaves her with only the state income taxes, property taxes, mortgage interest, and charitable contributions as her itemized deductions. These deductions total $12,500.

Roberta's standard deduction as a single person for 2000 is $4,400. Itemizing her deductions will actually reduce her taxable income by only $8,100.

Note that each dollar of itemized deductions beyond the standardized deduction reduces Roberta's taxable income by one dollar. Thus, if she had opted in 2000 to give another $100 to a charity at the end of the year, she would have reduced her taxable income by the full $100 because she is beyond the standard deduction threshold.

As is usually the case with taxes, there is one qualification to the previous discussion. Itemized deductions are reduced once your AGI exceeds a threshold limit that is adjusted for inflation each year. For the year 2000 this threshold limit is $128,950 ($64,475 if married filing separately). The reduction is 3 percent of the amount by which your AGI exceeds the upper threshold limit. The upper threshold for your AGI before you must start reducing your otherwise allowable itemized deductions is indicated in line 28 at the bottom of Schedule A. The threshold limits for current and recent years may also be found at **Web Link 3.2.** Consider the following example:

> Roberta's AGI in 2000 is $140,000. Her itemized deductions are $20,000. How much in net itemized deductions can she actually claim?

In this case, Roberta's AGI exceeds the threshold limit for 2000 by $11,050 ($140,000 − $128,950). Three percent of this difference is $331.50 ($11,050 × 3%), so the itemized deductions that she can claim are $19,668.50 ($20,000 − $331.50).

What Are My Exemptions?

After determining whether your itemized deductions or your standard deduction is larger, you next compute the value of what are known as **exemptions.** An exemption is a reduction against taxable income, similar in nature to the standard deduction. The difference is that a taxpayer can opt for itemized deductions over the standard deduction, but there is no choice with regard to an exemption.

Everyone receives an exemption. A husband and wife filing jointly receive two exemptions. You are also entitled to an exemption for each dependent you declare on your tax return. For someone to qualify as a dependent he or she must live with you and you must provide at least one-half of his or her support. Thus, if you have children living with you and you are the sole source of their support, these children clearly qualify as dependents. In divorce situations, the parents must resolve which of them will claim each child as a dependent. Both cannot simultaneously claim the same child. **Web Link (WSJ) 3.5a** provides a discussion of dependents, and part of this web page is reproduced in Figure 3.1.

Web Link (WSJ) 3.5a

FIGURE 3-1 Dependency Tests

Since 1987, the IRS has required that each filer list the names of all dependents, and provide their social security numbers if the dependents are more than two years old. Amazingly, the number of dependents claimed on tax returns in 1987 dropped to 70 million from 77 million the year before! Either there were a lot of children missing that year, or the change in rules eliminated a method of cheating for a large group of taxpayers. The value of an exemption is adjusted for inflation each year. For 2000, an exemption is worth $2,800 unless your income exceeds the upper limit threshold. For 2000, personal exemptions begin to be phased out once the AGI of a married couple filing jointly exceeds $193,400, and once a single person's AGI exceeds $127,950.

Web Link 3.2

Roberta has $50,000 in AGI in 2000. She is divorced and has two children living with her. She is the sole source of their support. If she files as head of household and takes the standard deduction, what will her taxable income be after deductions and exemptions?

The standard deduction for head of household for 2000 was $6,450. She is entitled to three exemptions. If the exemptions were worth $2,800 each, her taxable income would be $35,150 ($50,000 – $6,450 – [3 × $2,800]).

WHAT IS MY TAX LIABILITY?

Web Link 3.6

After determining your taxable income, you then ascertain what is known as your tax liability. Actually, this number should be known as your **preliminary tax liability** because once you determine its value, you will then adjust it for any credits or additional taxes owed. The 2000 tax schedule for people whose filing status is single is shown in Table 3.1. For single taxpayers, all taxable income up to $26,250 is taxed at a rate of 15 percent. If the taxpayer's income is exactly $26,250, then the tax liability is $3,937.50 ($26,250 × 15%). If the taxpayer's income is more than $26,250 but less than $63,550, then the tax liability is $3,937.50 plus 28 percent of the amount over $26,250. In other words, for a taxpayer with a taxable income of $40,000, the first $26,250 is taxed at 15 percent, and the next $13,750 ($40,000 – $26,250) is taxed at 28 percent. The rate at which the last dollar of taxable income is taxed is known as one's **marginal tax rate** or MTR.

The different rows in Table 3.1 are referred to as **tax brackets.** Note that the income in each higher bracket is taxed at a higher rate. The higher marginal tax rates for the higher income brackets is known as a **progressive tax system.** For many years, there have been calls for a flat tax system. In a flat tax system, there would be only one bracket and all income in excess of the deductions and exemptions allowed to a person or family would be taxed at a single rate. In contrast, some people believe that our tax system should be

Table 3.1

Tax Schedule for Taxpayers Filing as Single for the Year 2000

Schedule X—Use if your filing status is Single

If the amount on Form 1040, line 39, is: over —	but not over —	enter on Form 1040, line 40		of the amount over —
$0	$26,250		15%	$0
26,250	63,550	$3,937.50 +	28%	26,250
63,550	132,600	14,381.50 +	31%	63,550
132,600	288,350	35,787.00 +	36%	132,600
288,350		91,857.50 +	39.6%	288,350

Web Link
(WSJ) 3.7a

Web Link 3.7

more progressive in the sense that higher income levels should be taxed at marginal rates substantially higher than the marginal rates applied to the lower tax brackets.

Because it is quite easy to make an arithmetic error if you use the tax schedule to compute your tax liability, the IRS provides tax tables for taxpayers with taxable income less than 100,000. Consider the following example:

> Roberta has taxable income of $38,657. According to the tax tables, what is her tax liability for the year 2000? Her filing status is head of household.

On the tax table you would first click on the line to show that the taxable income is between $35,000 and $40,000. Next, you would scroll down and click on the line to indicate the taxable income is between $38,600 and $38,800. Then you would look at the row that indicates the taxable income is between $38,650 and $38,700. Under the head of household column, the tax liability shown for 2000 is $6,416.

To understand the impact that your filing status has on your tax liability, you simply have to look at the tax liability for the other three filing statuses. If Roberta filed as a single person with the same taxable income for 2000, she would owe $7,534. If her status were married filing jointly or married filing separately, she would owe $5,801 or $8,076, respectively. Filing status matters a lot!

What Are the Tax Credit and Additional Taxes Due?

Tax credits include credits for child and dependent care expenses, adoption expenses, and foreign taxes paid. In 1998, Congress introduced a tax credit, currently $500, for each child under the age of 17 at the end of the year. This tax credit begins to be phased out when your AGI exceeds $110,000 for a married couple filing jointly or $75,000 for a single person or head of household. The Additional Other Taxes Owed category includes the self-employment tax (Social Security for self-employed individuals, discussed in Chapter 17), the alternative minimum tax, and household employment taxes.

Congress created the **alternative minimum tax** (AMT) in response to cases where some high-income individuals were paying little or no income taxes. There were no accusations of fraud or tax cheating; high-income taxpayers were taking advantage of the tax code, which legitimately allowed them to report little or no taxable income. In other words, the AMT was created so that if a taxpayer takes advantage of too many tax-saving features of the tax code, he or she is penalized with some additional taxes.

When the AMT was initially created, few taxpayers were required to compute or pay an AMT. But as income levels for most taxpayers have risen in recent years, a large and growing number of taxpayers are finding that they owe an AMT.

Can Educational Expenses Be Taken as Credits or Deductions?

Educational expenses can be taken as an itemized deduction or as credits under certain circumstances. Let's first consider the situation in which such expenses might qualify as deductions. Educational expenses are included in the job-related expenses category. The tax code has always *disallowed* educational expenses that qualify a person for a new job. Any education expenses incurred to meet the minimum educational requirements of a trade or business do not qualify. Even if you have already been hired into that trade or business, the deduction of expenses to acquire entry-level skills would be the equivalent of allowing the deduction of expenses to qualify for a new job. To qualify as a deduction, educational expenses must be required by the employer to keep a person's job, salary, or status. If the educational expenses are not required by the employer to retain one's job, they may still be deductible if they improve one's job skills without qualifying one for a new job. As an example, if a bookkeeper were to enroll in courses that prepared him or her to take the CPA exam, such expenses would be qualifying the bookkeeper for a new job and would not be allowable. If you have educational expenses that qualify, they would be reported on Form 2106, and then on Schedule A as part of job-related expenses. Remember that only job-related expenses that exceed 2 percent of AGI qualify as itemized deductions.

Educational expenses may also qualify as credits. Tax credits are, obviously, substantially more valuable than deductions as a tax credit of one dollar saves one dollar in taxes and one dollar in deductions saves only a fraction of a dollar in taxes. There are two types of credits for educational expenses: the **Hope credit** and the **lifetime learning credit.** Neither credit can be taken in a given year if a student has a tax-free withdrawal from an educational IRA. Also, the two credits cannot be claimed simultaneously for the same student, although a family may claim a Hope credit for one person and a lifetime learning credit for another person. The educational expenses are based on qualified tuition and related expenses you pay for yourself, your spouse, and any dependents you claim on your tax return. The qualified expenses must be paid in the tax year for a term beginning in the same tax year.

A Hope credit of up to $1,500 per year can be claimed for each eligible student. A Hope credit can be claimed for no more than two years for any one student. To be eligible for the Hope credit, a student must meet four criteria. They are

1. The student has not completed the first two years of secondary education.

2. The student is enrolled in a program that leads to a degree, certificate, or other recognized educational credential.

3. The student is taking at least half of the normal full-time work load.

4. The student has no felony conviction for possessing or distributing a controlled substance.

The first $1,000 of educational expenses qualifies for a Hope credit, and the next $1,000 qualifies for a credit at the rate of 50 percent.

The lifetime learning credit is 20 percent of qualified expenses up to a maximum of $1,000 for all students claimed in a family. The lifetime learning credit is not subject to a workload requirement, it is not limited to the first two years of post-secondary education, and there is no limit on the number of years in which a person my claim a lifetime learning credit.

There are other limits on the Hope and the lifetime learning credits. If a person's AGI exceeds $100,000 if married filing jointly, or $50,000 if filing single, then that person is not eligible to claim either of these credits. The credit is prorated if a person's AGI exceeds $80,000 ($40,000 if filing single). Also, the amount of education expense credit is reduced by any credits taken for child and dependent care expenses and any credits for the elderly or disabled.

Web Link 3.7b

To claim a tax credit for any educational expenses, one has to file Form 8863.

WHY IS MY MARGINAL TAX RATE IMPORTANT?

Your marginal tax rate is the one number from your tax return that you need to remember during the entire year. Your marginal tax rate tells you how much tax you will pay on incremental income or how much tax savings you will receive from decisions that reduce your taxable income. Consider the following example:

> *Now that Roberta knows that the United States Olympic Committee is a legitimate charity for tax purposes, she is considering contributing $500. How much will this save her in taxes if her marginal tax rate is 28 percent?*

If Roberta is already itemizing her deductions for the year, then the $500 contribution increases her itemized deductions by this same amount. If her AGI does not exceed the upper limit for taking the full amount of itemized deductions, then her taxable income will decline by an additional $500 if she makes the contribution. With a 28 percent marginal tax rate, her tax liability will decline by $140 ($500 × 28%). Hence, the contribution really costs Roberta $360 ($500 gift – $140 tax savings).

Assume in the above example that Roberta must take the standard deduction rather than being able to itemize, and that her other expenses that could be itemized are minimal. In this case, the $500 contribution will have no effect on her deductions, and thus would produce no tax savings. Now the contribution costs Roberta the full $500.

A final case would be that Roberta's other deductions that could be itemized are just short of the standard deduction. In this case, the $500 contribution could cause her itemized deductions to exceed her standard deduction. Consider the following example:

> *Late in December, Roberta is adding up her likely itemized deductions for the year. She is crestfallen to note that they will total only $4,100. Roberta remembers that she had been thinking about contributing $500 to a charitable program promoted by her employer. How much would this contribution actually cost her if she makes it before the end of the year? (Assume the standard deduction for Roberta would be $4,400 and that her marginal tax rate is 28 percent.)*

If Roberta makes this contribution, her itemized deductions would rise to $4,600. She receives economic benefit only from the amount in excess of the standard deduction of $4,400, which in this case would be $200. The tax savings on this $200 would be $56 ($200 × 28%). Thus, the true cost of the contribution would be $444 ($500 gift – $56 tax savings).

HOW AND WHY DO I PAY TAXES DURING THE YEAR?

Witholding

Beardsley Ruml, chairman of both Macy's department store and the New York Federal Reserve Bank, moved Congress in 1943 to pass legislation creating the withholding of federal taxes from paychecks. Prior to that time, everyone paid his or her taxes in the spring. A large tax liability created problems for anyone who had not set aside money during the previous year to pay the taxes owed.

Web Link 3.8

When you start a job, you are now required to fill out a W-4 form. You may file an amended form W-4 at any time you believe your circumstances have changed. This form allows the employer to figure out the appropriate amount of taxes to withhold from each paycheck. On a W-4 form, you must declare your filing status, declare the number of allowances you want to claim, and indicate any additional monies you would like withheld from each paycheck.

The allowances you want to declare are based on the number of exemptions and the magnitude of the itemized deductions you plan to claim when you file your tax return. A worksheet is provided with the W-4 to help you convert the magnitude of your itemized deductions into a specific number of allowances.

Web Link 3.9

The more allowances you claim, the less tax withheld from your paycheck. A similar procedure is normally followed for the withholding of state income taxes. The W-4 form also allows you to request an additional cash amount to be withheld. If you believe you will not owe any income taxes for the year, the form allows you to have nothing withheld.

Should I Claim More or Fewer Withholding Allowances?   Suppose that you fill out form W-4 and ascertain you should claim seven withholding allowances on your W-4 form if you want to end the year having your actual withholding almost equal to your projected tax liability. Nonetheless, you might want to consider the strategy of claiming more allowances than seven, and the strategy of claiming fewer allowances than seven.

The least number of allowances you might claim is zero. With zero allowances, the maximum amount of taxes will be taken out of your paycheck. This means that when you file your tax return for the year, you will receive a substantial refund. Deliberately over-withholding in order to receive a substantial refund is a form of **forced savings.** That is, you are lending money to the federal government at a zero rate of interest via over-withholding, so that you can accumulate some savings. From an economic perspective, this is foolish. After all, you could withhold the correct amount and put what would have been the additional withholding into a savings account paying interest. The problem is that some people do not have the self-discipline to save out of every paycheck. If you lack the discipline to save on your own, then the real issue is whether you are better off saving through a forced savings program or not saving at all. This is a question only you can answer.

Note that over-withholding is an extremely popular practice. On average, about 70 percent of all tax returns filed claim refunds. In 2000, the average refund claimed was about $1,700. This works out to slightly less than $150 per month. Put simply, would you rather have an extra $150 per month this year in take-home pay, or would you rather receive a lump sum payment of about $1,700 in early spring of the next year. The majority of taxpayers opt for the latter!

The other strategy is that you might claim more allowances than you technically are entitled to claim. There are several problems with this strategy. First, when you submit the withholding form, you must sign a statement stating, "under penalty of perjury, I certify that I am entitled to the number of withholding allowances claimed on this certificate, or I am entitled to claim tax exempt status." Thus, deliberately under-withholding is a violation of the law.

The second problem is that if you end up under-withholding, then you may owe additional taxes when you file your tax return and you may be subject to an under-withholding penalty. The penalty is avoided as long as your withholding and other payments equal or exceed your last year's tax liability, or they equal at least 90 percent of this year's actual tax liability.

What Are Quarterly Installments?

If you discover you are under-withholding during the year, you are deliberately under-withholding, or you need to pay additional taxes, you may want to pay estimated quarterly installments directly to the Treasury. Some people set their withholding taxes to equal their tax liability if they have no other income during the year. They then make quarterly installments at such time as they receive other income. For example, a person may not know at the start of the year the magnitude of the capital gains he or she will have to report for the year. It would seem foolish to set one's withholding to match a speculative estimate of capital gains. It makes much more sense to just make quarterly installments at the end of each quarter depending on the amount of capital gains one had taken during each quarter.

Some people, such as retirees, have no wage income from which to pay withholding taxes. Generally, if these people expect to owe more than $1,000 in federal income taxes for 2001, they would need to pay installments throughout the year or have the providers of the non-wage income take out taxes if that is possible. Clearly, people with substantial non-wage income have to be much more careful in their tax planning.

Web Link 3.10

The form used to pay estimated taxes is Form 1040ES. Installments are due April 15, June 15, and September 15 of the tax year, and January 15 of the following year. If you pay insufficient taxes during the year, then the amount of your penalty will depend on how much you had paid in each quarter of the year. The penalty is relatively small if the underpayment of taxes is due to a problem in the last quarter of the year. The penalty is substantially larger if the underpayment goes back to the first quarter of the year.

Must I File Form 1040?

Everyone need not file Form 1040. Some people may not even need to file a tax return. For example, if your income is less than the sum of your standard deduction and your exemptions, then it is not required that you file a return. You may nonetheless want to file a return. One reason would be if you had taxes withheld from your paycheck, and you would like to obtain a refund of those taxes. If you are unsure whether you need to file, the IRS provides a questionnaire to help answer this question. An overview about whether you need to file may be found at **Web Link (WSJ) 3.13**. This web page is also reproduced in Figure 3.1 (page 45).

Web Link 3.12
Web Link (WSJ) 3.13

Many people may be able to file a simplified version of Form 1040. For example, you may file Form 1040A if your income is from only a limited number of sources, you take the standard deduction, and your income is less than $50,000. To ascertain whether you are eligible to file Form 1040A, obtain a copy of this form and its instructions.

Web Link 3.14

Even more restrictive is Form 1040EZ. You must meet eight requirements to file this form. Some of these requirements include that your income must be only from a limited number of sources, you (and your spouse if filing jointly) must be under age 65 and not blind, your income must be less than $50,000, and you must not have any dependents.

Web Link 3.15
Web Link 3.16

Visit **Web Link 3.16** for some clear guidelines on which 1040 form to use.

Are There Other Ways to Do a Tax Return? There are a multitude of ways to do a tax return other than the process outlined so far in this chapter.

First, there are web sites that offer worksheets for doing tax returns. These sites will crunch the numbers, indicate your tax liability and your refund or additional taxes owed, and provide line-by-line data for actually filling out your tax return. Some of these online worksheets are for informational purposes only (they serve as advertising for the site sponsor). Other online worksheets give you the ability not only to prepare your taxes online, but even to file them electronically from the site. There is, of course, usually a fee for this service.

Web Link 3.17

A second procedure is to buy one of the commercial software packages for doing the federal tax return. The two most popular packages are *Intuit's Turbo Tax* and *Kiplinger's Tax Return*. These programs take you through a series of questions and then provide you with a completed copy of your tax return. They will also perform audits to identify possible errors in your return, and even suggest ways to save money on your tax return. These programs also include a dialup process that allows you to check with the producer for any corrections to the software before you start using it. Because Congress sometimes does not finalize all of the tax rules until late in the year, and because of the urgency of getting these software packages distributed rapidly, there are sometimes minor bugs and errors in these programs.

Web Link 3.18

A third method is to go to a professional tax preparer. There are many to choose from. First, always be aware that anyone can be a paid tax preparer! There are no minimum qualifications or licensing requirements for selling one's services to prepare tax returns. If you want to consult with someone who is well trained in taxation, you should consult either an **enrolled agent** (EA), a CPA specializing in taxes (known as a **tax accountant**), or a lawyer specializing in taxation (known as a **tax lawyer**). These three are listed in increasing order of cost. Generally, one does not go to a tax lawyer unless one has extremely complicated and extensive tax problems. Many individual tax preparers have their own web sites. It is not the intention of this book to promote individual commercial operations. These listings are *not* endorsements. Each firm listed is either a national firm with offices throughout the country or a directory for local firms.

Web Link 3.19

What Happens If I Can't Get My Return Prepared by April 15?

If filing a tax return by April 15 of each year is a problem, then you might consider electing as your tax year a period of time other than the calendar year. Each year, there are many people who just can't get all the paperwork together by the April 15 deadline. For such people, the IRS has created Form 4797. This form requests an automatic four-month extension for filing the paperwork. The extension does not allow a delay in actually paying the taxes. The form requires a taxpayer to estimate his or her total tax liability, provides credit for the withholdings and installment payments, and asks the taxpayer to send in the balance due. If there is any uncertainty about the amount of taxable income, deductions, or credits the taxpayer will have, then it is better to overestimate on this final payment than to underestimate. The formal return is due no later than August 15. This can be described as pay now, show and tell later.

It is conceivable the taxpayer may not be able to file the formal return even by August 15. An additional extension is still possible, but it is not automatic, and the taxpayer must provide a legitimate reason for the continued delay.

Where Do I Get the Figures to Fill Out My Tax Return?

By January 31 of each year, individuals are supposed to be informed of various relevant tax information for the preceding year. For example, all of your employers during the prior year are supposed to provide you with a Form W-2. A Form W-2 is a summary of information from your paychecks. It includes your gross pay for the year, as well as how much you paid in federal, state, local, and Social Security taxes. Your employer also files a copy of this form with the IRS. The IRS then attempts to match these forms with people's individual tax returns, and looks for discrepancies. If your W-2 form overstates your income, you have all the incentive in the world to contact your employer immediately to correct any error. If your W-2 form understates your income, you still need to contact your employer to correct the error. The reason is that it is likely this form will eventually be corrected and the corrected information sent to the IRS. Even though the error may have been your employer's error, you would still be obligated to pay any interest and penalties due to the understating of income on your tax return.

The other most common form people receive is the 1099 form, which has many versions. For example, 1099-INT reports any interest income you received during the year on accounts such as interest-bearing checking accounts or savings accounts. This form is also used to advise you of any interest you paid during the year. If you have a mortgage, the mortgage lender must provide you with a statement indicating the amount of mortgage interest you have paid. A payer is obligated to provide this form only if the interest paid to you exceeds $10 for the year. Even if you do not receive this form, you are still obligated to declare this income. Form 1099-DIV reports any dividend income you received during the year. Yet another 1099 form reports the total of all proceeds from the sale of securities during the year. The IRS then checks your tax return to verify that the combined sales of securities reported by you matches the amount indicated to them. Like Form W-2, a copy of each Form 1099 is also sent to the IRS.

HOW ARE CAPITAL GAINS AND CAPITAL LOSSES TAXED?

When investors buy and sell securities such as stocks and bonds, they create **capital gains and capital losses.** The tax treatment of these gains and losses has fluctuated in recent years, but appears to have settled down. When you buy a security, you establish a **cost basis** for that security. The cost basis is what you paid for that asset, including the commission. Thus, if you buy 100 shares of Xerox for $60 a share and pay a $20 commission, your cost basis is $6,020 ($60 price × 100 shares + $20 commission). When you then sell the security, you compute the net proceeds of the sale. Thus, if you sell the Xerox holdings for $80 a share and pay another $20 commission, then your net proceeds would be $7,980 ($80 price × 100 shares − $20 commission). In this case, you would have a capital gain of $1,960 ($7,980 − $6,020). Had you sold the stock for $40 per share with a $20 commission, you would have incurred a $2,040 capital loss ($3,980 − $6,020).

After determining whether you have a capital gain or capital loss, you next determine the length of time you held the stock. If you held it more than one year, then your holding period is considered long term. If you held it exactly one year or less, then your holding period is considered short term. As you can see, the result of buying and selling a security will be classified into one of four categories: long-term capital gain (LTCG), long-term capital loss (LTCL), short-term capital gain (STCG), and short-term capital loss (STCL). Let us consider the tax treatment if you have only one transaction for the year to report. If your only transaction is an STCG, the STCG will be added to your other income in determining total income and it will be taxed the same as any other income. If your marginal tax rate is 28 percent, then you will pay a tax of 28 percent on your gain. If your only transaction is a LTCG, the total is again added to your other income to determine your total income. The LTCG will be taxed at a lower rate than an STCG. If your marginal tax rate is 15 percent, then the tax on your LTCG is 10 percent. If your marginal tax rate is 28 percent or higher, then the tax on your LTCG is 20 percent. If your only transaction is an STCL or an LTCL, you will use the loss to reduce your total income, up to a limit of $3,000 per year ($1,500 per year if you are married filing separately). For example, if you have an STCL for the year of $5,000, then you would use $3,000 of the loss to reduce your total income, and the remaining $2,000 STCL would be listed as a carry forward. You would carry this loss forward to the next year's tax return, and treat it as if you had a $2,000 STCL in that year. The same treatment would apply if you incurred a $5,000 LTCL.

Capital gains and losses are reported on Schedule D of Form 1040.

Web Link 3.21
Web Link 3.22

How Are Car and Home Sales Taxed?

Your home and your car are considered personal assets rather than capital assets. The tax code rules that losses on personal assets are not deductible. There is no tax benefit if you lose money on the sale of a home or a car. The tax code also rules that gains on the sale of personal assets are treated as capital gains. If you sell your car for more than you paid for it, you will owe taxes on your capital gain.[3] Special rules apply to the sale of a home. As with capital gains, these rules have changed in recent years. The current rule on the sale of a home is that the first $250,000 of gain is exempt from taxation, as long as you have lived in the home for at least two of the past five years and you have owned the home for two of the past five years. If you are married filing jointly and both spouses meet the ownership and occupancy tests, then the exemption is increased to $500,000.

Web Link 3.23

Are There Tax Benefits to Donating Securities to a Charity?

Many charities encourage people to donate securities or other assets as well as cash. Contributing assets to a charity gets special tax treatment. Specifically, you are allowed to treat the current market value of the asset as the value of your contribution. If the asset

---

[3]If a person has a business on the side that involves the purchase and sale of vehicles, then a gain on such a transaction would be part of business income reported on Schedule C.

contributed has appreciated substantially from the date of purchase, you avoid paying taxes on that capital gain. Consider the following example:

Roberta has some stock that she bought 20 years ago for $1,000. Today, that stock is worth $5,000. What are the cash consequences if she donates the stock directly to a charity, and what are the cash consequences if she sells the stock first and then donates the cash to charity? Roberta is in the 28 percent marginal tax bracket.

If she donates the stock directly, Roberta will save $1,400 ($5,000 × 28%) on her taxes. That is, she will give $5,000 worth of stock to the charity and add this amount to her itemized deductions. The increase in itemized deductions times her marginal tax rate produces the $1,400 tax savings. For all practical purposes, Roberta has actually donated $3,600 to the charity on an after-tax basis, but both she and the charity can think of her donation as worth $5,000.

If Roberta sells the stock first, then she has an LTCG of $4,000. Because she is in the 28 percent bracket, this gain will be taxed at 20 percent and she will owe $800 in taxes. If she sets aside from the sale the cash to pay her taxes, she will be able to donate only $4,200 to the charity. This donation reduces her taxes by $1,176 ($4,200 × 28%). In this case, she has again given up $5,000 worth of stock, but the charity will receive only $4,200, and the contribution has effectively cost her $3,824 ($5,000 – $1,176). If she sells the stock first, the contribution will cost her $224 ($1,400 tax savings for a direct contribution – $1,176 tax savings of selling first) more, and the charity will receive $800 less than it otherwise would have received.

If you want to donate to a charity or church, it makes much more sense to give appreciated securities than to sell the securities and give cash, or even to just give cash. This is true even if you think the securities will continue to appreciate. If you think the securities are still an excellent investment opportunity, donate the securities, then take the cash you would have given and buy back the same holding. In this way, you also boost your cost basis in the stock so that you will owe substantially less capital gains tax when you do sell it. The repurchase must be delayed at least 31 days from the time you donated the stock. The sale and repurchase of the security within 30 days is treated as a **wash sale,** which the IRS disallows. Finally, if you wish to fund a charitable contribution with a stock that has gone down in value, *sell* the stock first to benefit from the capital loss, then donate the proceeds to the charity.

Is It Likely That My Return Will Be Audited?

The IRS selects a relatively small number of returns each year for a **tax audit.** Only a few people know the formula that the IRS uses to select returns for auditing, but some of its features are widely known. Your chances of being audited are higher under the following conditions:

- If your income is high
- If you are self-employed
- If your deductions in a certain category exceed guideline amounts

- If your job is in one of the job categories where people have a propensity to under-report (the most common are jobs where most of the income is in the form of tips)
- If you live in a sparsely populated state

The honest taxpayer need not fear an audit. An audit means the IRS would like to see additional verification for the income and deductions claimed in your return. There are some web sites with information that would be helpful with an audit.

Web Link 3.26

The IRS does have an appeal process if you have been audited and you feel the result is inaccurate or unfair.

Web Link 3.27

What Is "Bunching of Deductions"?

People whose itemized deductions just fall short of the standard deduction every year may want to try one common method for cutting taxes. Bunching deductions is moving some itemized deductions to an every-other-year basis. Consider the following example:

> A few months into the year, Roberta projected her itemized deductions to be $4,000 for the year, just short of her standard deduction of $4,300. She noted that $1,000 of her itemizations was charitable contributions, so she decided to postpone these contributions for this year, and then donate the full $1,000 on January 2 of the following year. Another $800 of her itemized deductions is property taxes. The taxes are due by January 31 of the following year. She plans to hold off on this payment until its due date. How will these actions affect her taxes for this year and the next?

The postponement of the contribution and tax payment will have no effect on this year's taxes, since Roberta will have to take the standard deduction either way. However, the postponement will increase her itemized deductions for the following year by $1,800 ($1,000 gift + $800 property taxes). If her itemizations for the following year would otherwise have been $4,000 again, she will now have $5,800 in itemizations in the second year, allowing for a reduction in her taxable income of approximately $1,500 ($5,800 – $4,300). This process is known as the **bunching of deductions.**

In theory, most itemized deductions are subject to time shifting. You could make an extra mortgage payment toward the end of the year to ensure you pay accrued interest in the current year rather than at the start of the next year. If you have enough uninsured medical bills to claim a medical expense deduction, you could arrange to make payments timed to maximize your deductions. You might also consider scheduling any elective medical procedures with an eye on the tax implications. You could make a substantial payment on your state income taxes, even if you don't actually owe the taxes. The only problem with this last strategy is that it will result in additional taxable income in the form of a taxable state income tax refund the following year.

Web Link 3.28

There are several strategies for reducing one's tax liability.

HOW CAN I DO MY OWN RESEARCH ON TAX QUESTIONS?

With the Internet, a substantial amount of tax research may be accomplished easily and quickly. The first source is Publication 17, which is a basic summary of the information

Web Link 3.30 you need to answer most tax questions. It is accessible over the Internet and from the IRS upon request. It includes many examples and, because it is a government publication, may be copied freely. In fact, some companies make a practice of taking Publication 17, doing some minor editing, and selling it during the tax season!

Web Link 3.31   All of the sites at **Web Link 3.31** provide a full copy of the IRS Code along with the ability to search for specific phrases or words.

HOW DO STATE INCOME TAXES WORK?

Web Link 3.24 States' rules for income taxes vary. Some states do not have state income taxes. Most states model their tax returns on the federal return, require you to use the same numbers as on your federal return, and ask you to submit copies of pages from your federal return. It is really not possible to provide a detailed description of a general state return because most Web Link 3.25 state tax returns are unique. **Web Link 3.25** shows each state's: (1) lowest and highest marginal tax rates, (2) number of tax brackets, (3) income level for the lowest and highest brackets, (4) personal exemption values for a single person, married couple, and each child, and the (5) ruling on whether your federal income tax payments are tax deductible on the state return.

A few observations from **Web Link 3.25** include the following.[4] First, there are no state income taxes in Alaska, Florida, Nevada, South Dakota, Texas, Washington, and Wyoming. New Hampshire and Tennessee limit the state income tax to taxation of interest and dividend income only. Rhode Island and Vermont set the state income tax at a fixed percentage of one's federal tax liability; 25.5 percent and 24 percent, respectively. Montana has the highest state marginal tax rate at 12 percent of taxable income over $50,000. Connecticut has the highest personal exemptions at $12,000 for a single person and $24,000 for a married couple, but these are phased out at higher income levels. Several states share the highest exemption for a child, at $2,750, and Connecticut has the lowest exemption per child at zero.

A **municipal bond** is one issued by any state or local government or agency thereof. On federal tax returns, the interest income from municipal bonds is exempt from taxation. State governments, however, may tax the interest income paid on municipal bonds issued within their own state, and they usually tax the interest income on municipal bonds issued in other states. In practice, though, most states do not tax the interest income on bonds issued by their own state and local governments. Thus, if you live in New York and own a municipal bond from Pennsylvania, you would pay New York state income tax on the interest income from that bond. If you owned a municipal bond from New York, you would be exempt from both federal and state income tax on the interest from that bond. In other words, municipal bonds from your own state are double tax exempt. This is why municipal bond mutual funds and municipal money market mutual funds exist for such states as New York and California. They are especially designed for taxpayers in those two states who wish to minimize both their federal and state income tax liabilities.

Interest income from bonds issued by the federal government is exempt from state and local taxation, but not from federal taxation. So we can say that municipal bonds are

---

[4]These observations are made for 2001. State rules, like federal rules, are subject to change every year.

exempt from federal taxation, and federal bonds are exempt from state and local taxation, but because the federal tax liability is usually so much greater than the state and local tax liability, we refer to municipal bonds as being tax exempt, and to federal bonds as taxable.

How Are Itemized Deductions Affected by State Income Taxes?

In cases where a state recognizes the same itemized deductions recognized on a federal tax return, there are additional tax savings for incremental itemizations. However, the tax savings are not additive. The reason they are not additive is that an additional itemization on a state return reduces the state income tax itemization on the federal return. Consider the following example:

> *It is the end of a good year, and Roberta is feeling charitable. There has been a local disaster and she would like to donate $1,000 to the local Red Cross. If she has a 28 percent marginal federal tax bracket and an 8 percent marginal state tax bracket, how much will the cash contribution cost her on an after-tax basis if she lives in a state that allows this as an itemized deduction?*

As we saw earlier, the contribution will directly save her $280 ($1,000 × 28%) on her federal tax return. It will also save her $80 on her state tax return ($1,000 × 8%). However, because her state taxes are now reduced by $80, she will have $80 more in taxable income on her federal tax return. This incremental $80 will result in additional federal taxes of $22.40. Thus, her net federal tax savings is not $280, but $257.60 ($280 – $22.40). Her combined tax savings is thus equal to $337.60 ($257.60 + $80). So on an after-tax basis, the contribution costs Roberta $662.40 ($1,000 – $337.60).

Simply adding the two marginal tax brackets together would suggest a combined marginal tax bracket of 36 percent (28% + 8%). If Roberta thought in terms of just the combined brackets, she would estimate the net cost of the contribution at $640 ($1,000 × [1 – 36%]).

In summary, if you don't itemize state income taxes on your federal tax return, then your effective combined marginal tax rate is for expenses that can be itemized on both returns:

$$MTR_{combined} = MTR_{federal} + MTR_{state}.$$

But if you do itemize your state taxes on your federal return, then your effective combined marginal tax rate for expenses that can be itemized on both returns is

$$MTR_{combined} = MTR_{federal} + MTR_{state} \times (1 - MTR_{federal}).$$

This distinction in the effective marginal tax rate is extremely important when you use Internet-based calculators. Some calculators assume the effective combined MTR is based on the first formula and others assume it is based on the second formula. The value of the combined effective MTR obviously affects the final answer of any calculation in which it plays a role, so use caution when entering marginal tax rate numbers to ensure the combined tax rate used in the calculator reflects your actual tax situation.

SUMMARY

➢ The basic federal tax model computes total income then reduces it by adjustments to income to obtain adjusted gross income. Adjusted gross income (AGI) is then reduced by the larger of the standard deduction or itemized deductions and exemptions to obtain taxable income. Taxable income and filing status determine tax liability. The tax liability is then adjusted for any credit or additional taxes due. The total tax liability is compared to the sum of taxes withheld and additional payments to determine the tax or refund due.

➢ Everyone is entitled to any adjustments to income incurred. A taxpayer will benefit from an itemized deduction only if the sum of itemized deductions exceeds the standard deduction for that taxpayer's filing status.

➢ A person's marginal tax rate is the rate at which incremental income would be taxed.

➢ Itemized deductions reduce taxable income only to the extent they exceed the standard deduction.

➢ A taxpayer may arrange to have too much, too little, or exactly the correct amount withheld from his or her paycheck. The correct choice depends upon the desire for forced savings.

➢ Long-term capital gains are taxed differently than ordinary income, and capital losses may be deducted directly from ordinary income.

➢ State taxes vary substantially. Some states have no state income taxes and a few tax only interest and dividend income, while some have substantial state income taxes.

➢ The likelihood of being audited depends on a variety of factors. Taxpayers who have lower incomes and average itemized deductions have little likelihood of being audited.

➢ The Internet provides substantial opportunities for tax research, particularly as the IRS moves to place Publication 17 on line in a user-friendly format.

KEY TERMS

adjusted gross income	adjustments to total income	allowance
alternative minimum tax	bunching of deductions	capital gain/capital loss
carry forward	cost basis	deduction
exemption	enrolled agent	filing status
forced savings	Hope credit	itemized deduction
lifetime learning credit	marginal tax rate	municipal bond
preliminary tax liability	progressive tax system	Publication 17
standard deduction	tax accountant	tax audit
tax bracket	tax lawyer	wash sale

PROBLEMS

3.1. Jill reports the following for the year 2000: wages $20,000, taxable interest $1,322, tax-exempt interest $477, ordinary dividends $874, taxable refunds $369, business income $37,415, deductible IRA contribution $2,000, self-employment tax $165, Keogh contributions $4,000. Her filing status is single, she has no dependents, and she takes the standard deduction. What is her taxable income?

3.2. Alice reports the following expenses during the year 2000: medical and dental $10,000, state income taxes $3,519, property taxes $4,550, mortgage interest $8,712, interest on investment loans $919, interest on an auto loan $1,582, contributions to her church $1,000, United Way contributions $250, casualty losses of $2,200 and $1,500 and theft losses of $8,000 (her insurance covers 50 percent of all losses), and job-related expenses $748. Alice's AGI is $70,000 and her filing status is single.

   a.   What is the total of Alice's itemized deductions?

   b.   Should Alice take the itemized deductions or the standard deductions?

   c.   If Alice's marginal tax rate is 28 percent, what are the tax savings of her itemizations?

   d.   If only federal income taxes are considered, how much would an additional charitable gift of $1,000 during the year have cost Alice (to the nearest penny) on an after-tax basis?

   e.   Suppose Alice has a 28 percent marginal federal tax rate and a 6 percent marginal state tax rate, and that charitable gifts are deductible on her state taxes. How much would an additional charitable gift of $1,000 during the year have cost her (to the nearest penny) on an after-tax basis?

3.3. Jeannie has an AGI of $55,000 and uses the standard deduction. Compute her tax liability for 2000 if she is (a) single (no children), (b) married filing a joint return (two children), (c) married filing a separate return (no children), and (d) head of household (two children). She is entitled to a personal exemption for herself and each child and her husband where relevant.

3.4. Carol anticipates her filing status for 2000 will be single. If she believes she will have itemized deductions of $15,000 and an AGI of $65,000, how many allowances (or exemptions) should she claim if she wants to have the exact appropriate amount withheld from her paycheck?

3.5. For 2001, what would be the tax impact of each of the following securities transactions for a person in the 28 percent marginal tax bracket:

	Date Bought	Date Sold	Cost Basis	Proceeds
Transaction 1	1/18/75	7/14/01	$1,547	$3,962
Transaction 2	4/15/88	10/12/01	$5,742	$1,488
Transaction 3	3/17/01	3/25/01	$8,422	$1,573
Transaction 4	3/26/01	8/14/01	$1,943	$2,577

3.6. Ann Marie owns $10,000 worth of stock for which she originally paid $1,000. She is thinking about donating the stock to her alma mater. She has a 28 percent marginal federal tax rate, a 6 percent marginal state tax rate, and charitable contributions are deductible on her state return.

    a. What would be the after-tax cost of her donation if she sells the stock and donates the after-tax proceeds to the school?

    b. What would be the after-tax cost of her donation if she gives the stock directly to the school?

3.7. John is single and has $50,000 in taxable income (after deductions but before exemptions). How much state income tax would he owe for 2000 if he lived in the following states: Florida, Colorado, Illinois, and Connecticut?

3.8. Raina is eligible for head of household status, is claiming three exemptions for 2000. She has a salary of $50,000, federal tax withholdings of $4,000, state tax withholdings of $3,000, and Social Security payments of $3,825. She had $100 in taxable interest, $300 in dividends, and $2,000 in long-term capital gains. She paid $3,000 in real estate taxes, $5,000 in home mortgage interest, and gave $3,000 to charity. What is her tax liability? Does she owe taxes or is she entitled to a refund? How much?

REFERENCES

Web Link 3.33 Description of sales taxes for each state
Web Link 3.34 Miscellaneous taxation sites
Web Link 3.35 Pointer sites for taxation
Web Link 3.36 Glossaries
Web Link 3.37 Sites with FAQs

WALL STREET JOURNAL RESOURCES

Web Link (WSJ) 3.32 Recent articles on personal taxation
Web Link (WSJ) 3.38 "Form 1040: Mirror to Your Finances," *The Wall Street Journal Interactive Edition*, April 11, 2000
Web Link (WSJ) 3.39 "Many Filers Miss Key Credits When Filling Out Tax Returns," *The Wall Street Journal Interactive Edition*, March 19, 2000
Web Link (WSJ) 3.40 "Filing Taxes Electronically May Mean Fewer Mistakes," *The Wall Street Journal Interactive Edition*, February 6, 2000
Web Link (WSJ) 3.41 "Getting Rid of Losing Investments Can Prove a Winning Tax Strategy," *The Wall Street Journal Interactive Edition*, November 28, 1999
Web Link (WSJ) 3.42 "Tax-Law Revisions Meant to Aid 'Innocent Spouse,'" *The Wall Street Journal Interactive Edition*, July 15, 1998

For information that has changed since the book was written, for new information that pertains to this topic, and for some new web sites that pertain to the topic of this chapter, see **Web Link 3.43.**

CHAPTER 4

TIME VALUE OF MONEY

LEARNING OBJECTIVES

- Compute the future value of an investment
- Compute the present value of a future cash requirement or benefit
- Explain how to select an interest rate for a present value of money problem
- Describe an annuity
- Compute the future and present value of an annuity
- Compute the future and present value of a growing annuity
- Explain how to adjust a problem when compounding is more than once per year
- Compute an effective annual rate
- Compute an inflation rate
- Compute an after-tax rate of return

Web Link: www.wiley.com/college/woerheide

INTRODUCTION

Many decisions in personal finance involve comparing the value of money at different points in time. For example:

1. You buy for $1,000 today an investment that promises to pay you back $1,500 in five years. Is this a good investment?

2. You are considering two five-year life insurance policies with the same death benefit. The first policy charges you a flat premium of $500 per year for five years. The second policy charges you a $400 premium for the first year and then increases the premium by $60 per year for each of the remaining four years. Which policy would cost you less?

3. You are looking at two apartments to rent. The first charges a flat rate of $900 per month for a three-year lease. The second charges $850 per month for a one-year lease. If you expect the rate to increase by 6 percent at the end of each of the next two years, which lease is the better deal over the three-year period?

Any time you have to compare the value of money at two different points in time, you are working a **time value of money** problem. These problems can be quite complex and may sometimes require the attention of someone with extensive training. Luckily, a substantial number of Internet calculators offer solutions to many time value of money problems. The real trick is to find the correct calculator for the particular problem you are attempting to solve, so thus, it is critically important to make sure that you understand the nature of the problem.

The primary objective of this chapter is to familiarize you with the basic time value of money problems so that you have a good chance of using the correct calculator for a particular problem. We won't overload you with mathematical notation.

WHAT IS A FUTURE VALUE CALCULATION?

The most basic time value of money problem is a one-period, future value calculation. Let us assume you have $100 to invest. You go to the bank and invest your money in a one-year certificate of deposit that pays 5.5 percent. How much money will you have at the end of the year? The money you will have at the end of the year (the future value) may be computed as the product of the amount you invested and an interest factor equal to one plus the interest rate:

$$\$100 \times (1 + .055) = \$105.50 \tag{4.1}$$

We can generalize this computation as follows:

$$V_0 \times (1 + r) = V_1 \tag{4.2}$$

where

V_0 = the initial cash you have to invest

r = the interest rate at which you invest the cash

V_1 = the ending value of your investment

The problem just described is an investment problem because you start with some cash on hand today and you invest it so that you will have more cash in the future. A borrowing problem is similar. Suppose you borrow $100 today and promise to pay the lender back in one year, at an interest rate of 5.5 percent. How much would you owe? The solution is the same as that shown in equation 4.1, although in this problem, the person lending you the money is the investor. What the lender will receive is the same as what you will owe. In other words, equation 4.1 and the more general equation 4.2 can be used to compute the future value of either a one-period investment or a one-period loan.

Now suppose you deposit money in a savings account for two years at an interest rate of 5.5 percent. How much will you have at the end of two years, if you let the interest earned in the first year remain in the account? Because equation 4.1 already provides the answer for the value of the account at the end of the first year, we need to solve only for the value of the account at the end of the second year. In this case:

$$\$105.50 \times (1 + .055) = \$111.30 \tag{4.3}$$

The actual answer is \$111.3025, but because the penny is the smallest coin in our currency, it is appropriate to round our results to the nearest penny. This equation can be generalized as follows:

$$V_1 \times (1 + r) = V_2 \qquad \text{equation 4.4}$$

where

$$V_2 = \text{the value of your cash at the end of the second time period.}$$

If we substitute the value of V_1 in equation 4.2 into equation 4.4, we obtain the following statement:

$$V_0 \times (1 + r)^2 = V_2 \qquad \text{equation 4.4a}$$

This last equation can be extended to any number of time periods by replacing the number 2 with the letter N. In other words, the general case for future value is written as

$$V_0 \times (1 + r)^N = V_N \qquad \text{equation 4.5}$$

The second term in equation 4.5, $(1 + r)^N$, is referred to by several names. Some of these include the **future value interest factor** (FVIF), the future value factor, the compound value interest factor, the compound value factor, and, in cases where the meaning is clear, the interest factor. Because this calculation is so important in financial decision making, a table showing the future value factor for various combinations of interest rate and time periods is provided in Appendix A.1. Let's solve a problem using Appendix A.1.

Stan Hoi has just borrowed \$1,000 from his parents. He has promised to pay them all principal and interest in six years. The interest rate is set at 5 percent (his parents view the low interest rate as a gift). How much will he owe in six years?

We can use equation 4.5 to solve this problem. The value of V_0 is \$1,000. The interest factor of $(1 + r)^N$ can be found in Appendix A.1, and is 1.3401. The product of these two numbers, \$1,340.10, is our answer (i.e., V_N).

Solving time value of money problems by hand, or even with the use of a table like Appendix A.1, can be tedious work. For this reason, most people use calculators, financial calculators, or Internet financial calculators. Let's consider how to solve the problem shown above using one of the calculators on the Internet. Specific instructions for using each calculator will vary slightly. In general, to solve this problem, set the present or current value at \$1,000. If a future value cell is shown, leave it blank; this is the number for which we are solving. The number of periods (or payment periods) is six. If a payment amount is requested, set it at zero (we will discuss this one later). Finally, enter 5 percent for the interest rate. Then click on the appropriate *calculate* button, and the answer will be \$1,340.10. In some calculators, the answer will be negative. This is because some calculators are constructed to compute the present value as either a cash inflow (positive) or a cash outflow (negative) and to deliver the future value as the opposite (outflow or inflow). Consider the following examples involving future value calculations:

(a) Stan Hoi puts \$1,000 into a savings account that pays interest of 7 percent. He plans to leave the interest and principal in the account for 10 years. How much will he have in his account at the end of the 10-year period?

Web Link 4.1

(b) Stan has just taken a new job paying an annual salary of $30,000. He projects that the inflation rate will average 3 percent over his working career. What would his salary be in 40 years if he just matches the inflation rate?

(c) Stan was daydreaming one day that his great, great grandfather, upon arrival in this country 150 years ago, had put $10 into a savings program that paid an interest rate of 4 percent. If Stan were to find the paperwork that allowed him to claim this account, how much would it be worth today?

The answer to problem (a) is $1,967.15. It would be computed as

$$\$1,000 \times (1 + .07)^{10} = \$1,967.15$$

The answers to (b) and (c) would similarly be computed as

$$\$30,000 \times (1 + .03)^{40} = \$97,861.13$$

$$\$10 \times (1 + .04)^{150} = \$3,589.23$$

The second problem is neither an investment nor a lending problem; it is a growth problem. A growth problem is similar to an investment problem. Just think of the value of a savings account at the end of each year as equal to the salary for that year.

Another variation of a future value problem involves the computation of price increases. The inflation rate in a price increase problem is no different than the interest rate we used in growth or investment problems. Rather than being the rate at which money in a savings account grows (an interest rate problem), we are looking at the rate at which a price grows (an inflation rate problem). Consider the following problem:

Stan Hoi is looking at an SUV he would like to buy. The vehicle costs $30,000 today. Stan realizes he has to deal with some other financial issues before he can really afford the SUV. He projects that he will have to wait five years to make the purchase. He believes the price of the vehicle will increase at the annual rate of 3 percent per year during this period. What will the SUV cost five years from today if Stan's projection is correct?

Web Link (WSJ) 4.1a

The solution to this may be found using the calculator at **Web Link (WSJ) 4.1a**. The future price will be $34,778.

WHAT IS A PRESENT VALUE CALCULATION?

Future value calculations are intuitive to most people, while present value calculations strike most people as difficult and backward. In truth, present value is simply future value worked in reverse.

Consider again equation 4.2, shown below.

$$V_0 \times (1 + r) = V_1 \tag{4.2}$$

This equation says that the value in one year of money that is saved today equals the amount saved today times one plus the interest rate. Let us now assume that V_1 is known and we want to solve for V_0. If we solve this equation for V_0, the result is shown below in equation 4.6.

$$V_1 \times \frac{1}{(1 + r)} = V_0 \tag{4.6}$$

Thus, if you were expecting to receive $100 in one year and you believe you can invest any money you had today at 10 percent, then we would say that $100 in one year is worth $90.91 today, as shown in equation 4.6a.

$$\$100 \times \frac{1}{(1 + .10)} = \$90.91 \tag{4.6a}$$

This is easy to verify by going back to equation 4.2 and noting that if you had $90.91 today and invested it at 10 percent, you would end up with $100 in one year.

Just as we generalized equation 4.2 from a one-year time horizon to a time horizon of N years in equation 4.5, so we can generalize our present value from a one-year time horizon to an N-year time horizon. The general equation for present value is

$$V_N \times \frac{1}{(1 + r)^N} = V_0 \tag{4.7}$$

Consider the following problem:

Stan Hoi's grandmother tells him that he is her favorite grandson and that she will leave him $10,000 in her will. Stan offers thanks for the gift. To show appropriate appreciation, not too much and not too little, he needs to ascertain how much the gift is worth today.

Stan needs to know two things before he can determine how much the gift is worth today. First, he needs to know when he should expect to receive this inheritance. He can ascertain this by consulting a mortality table to look up how long his grandmother is expected to live.[1] Let us assume that the table indicates she is expected to live another 10 years. Second, he needs to know the rate of return at which he could invest that money today if he had it. Let us assume he believes he could invest at a rate of 8 percent.

We can now use equation 4.7 to solve the valuation problem faced by Stan. The value today of Stan's $10,000 inheritance in 10 years is

$$\$10,000 \times \frac{1}{(1 + .08)^{10}} = \$4.632$$

The expression $1/(1+r)^N$ is known by several names, including **present value interest factor** (PVIF), present value factor, discount factor, discount interest factor, or even capitalization factor. Where the context is clear, it is simply referred to as the interest factor.

Web Link 4.2 Present value interest factors for various combinations of time periods and interest rates can be found in Appendix A.2. Consider the following examples involving present value calculations:

(a) Stan Hoi would like to have $1,000,000 on the day he retires. He plans to retire in 30 years and believes he can earn a 10 percent rate of return on his money. How much would he have to set aside today to achieve his goal?

(b) Stan's daughter plans to attend college in 10 years. Stan would like to have $50,000 cash on hand when his daughter first enrolls in college. How much would he have to set aside today to achieve this goal if he believes he can invest his money at 8 percent? 10 percent?

---

[1]Mortality tables indicate the probability of a person dying next year, and the average life expectancy for each age. They are discussed in Chapter 11.

(c) Stan plans to buy a house in five years. He will need a down payment of $20,000. If he can invest his money at 6 percent, how much would he need to set aside today to achieve this goal?

In problem (a), the correct answer is $57,308.55. This would be computed as

$$\$1,000,000 \times \frac{1}{(1 + .10)^{30}} = \$57,308.55$$

In order to send his daughter to college in problem (b), Stan needs to set aside $23,159.67 if the interest rate is 8 percent. However, if he can earn 10 percent on his money, he would need to set aside only $19,277.16. Finally, to fund the down payment on his house in problem (c), Stan would need to set aside $14,945.16. Use one of the Internet calculators in **Web Link 4.2** to verify each of the above answers.

How Does One Determine the Interest Rate in a Present Value Problem?

In any present value problem, think of the interest rate as an **opportunity rate of return.** An opportunity rate (or discount rate) is what you think you could earn if you in fact had the present value of the money in your hands today. You won't use the same interest rate for all present value problems. A major principle of financial theory is that the discount rate must reflect the degree of risk in the cash that is being discounted. Thus, if you are virtually certain you will receive $10,000 in five years, then you would use as your discount rate the rate of return you could achieve on investments that were extremely safe, such as Treasury bonds or a bank certificate of deposit. You might go to your local bank and ascertain what interest rate they are paying on certificates of deposit that mature in five years. You would use that interest rate to discount the perfectly certain $10,000 you would receive in five years.

In the case of the three problems in Example 4.4, Stan is certain of the amounts he wants to save, but his commitment to each goal might vary. The greater his degree of commitment to achieving a goal, the safer the investment Stan should use to achieve it and thus the lower the discount rate he should use in planning.

As demonstrated by problem (b), using a higher discount rate means Stan will have to set aside less cash today than if he were willing to accept more risk. If Stan wants perfect certainty in achieving all three goals in the previous example, he will have to set aside a lot of money. For example, suppose that 5 percent was considered a perfectly safe rate of return in today's markets. If we rework each problem in the previous example using 5 percent as the discount rate, the present value of each future cash flow would be $231,377, $30,695, and $15,670, or a total of $277,742. This compares to the total of $95,413 ($57,308.55 + $23,159.67 + $14,945.16) computed in the solution (using the 8 percent discount rate in problem [b]). Obviously, this is a substantial difference.

Stan will have to decide how much certainty he wants in achieving each of his goals. If he is willing to allow more uncertainty in his retirement goal, then he might be willing to invest this money in more speculative investments such as common stocks rather than Treasury bonds or bank certificates of deposit. On average, stocks provide higher rates of return than Treasury bonds or bank certificates, but they also increase the risk that the savings target will not be achieved. Thus, a critical part of any present value problem is to decide how much certainty you want in achieving a particular goal.

Finally, not all present value calculations necessarily mean that you will be setting aside money today. Consider the following:

> Stan and his wife are shopping for some furniture. They find an identical set of couches at two different furniture stores. The first store sells all products on a cash-only basis, and they want $2,000 for the couches. The second store is running a promotion that allows Stan and his wife to pay in two years. This store charges a price of $2,400. Which store has a better deal?

To answer this question, Stan needs to decide how much certainty he would like to have in meeting the $2,400 payment in two years. Suppose he decides he can handle a relatively aggressive position on this decision, and opts for a 10 percent discount rate. In this case, the couches with the delayed payment have a present value cost of $1,983.47 ($2,400 × [1 / (1 + .10)^2]), making them slightly cheaper than the couches that are being sold for $2,000 cash. This decision does not mean that Stan would actually set aside $1,983 today in an account earmarked to pay for the couches in two years. Stan may well decide to spend the $1,983 he would have earmarked for the couches on a vacation. He would then plan to pay the $2,400 in two years from his income at that time. Whether he earmarks the cash to pay for the couches or spends it—or if he doesn't have the cash on hand—the deferred payment remains a slightly better deal. Suppose, however, that Stan worries about whether he would have the money to pay for the couches in two years. Or, suppose he really dislikes the thought of carrying debt. In either of these cases, he would use a lower (less risky) discount rate. If he opted to use a discount rate of 5 percent, then the present value of the deferred payment is $2,176.87 ($2,400 / (1 + .05)^2).

ANNUITIES

Annuity problems come up frequently in financial decision making. An annuity is a finite series of equal, consecutive payments.

What Is the Future Value of an Annuity?

Many people do their saving for retirement through set-asides in the form of an annuity. That is, they make equal, consecutive contributions to a savings program. Consider the following example:

> Stan has recently heard about the Roth IRAs discussed in Chapter 18 and has decided that he will invest $2,000 per year for the next 40 years into such an account. He believes that he can earn an average rate of return of 9 percent on the investments in this account. How much will his Roth IRA be worth in 40 years, assuming he makes each contribution at the end of the year and leaves all profits in the account?

It is possible to work this problem as a collection of future value problems. If Stan makes his first deposit at the end of the first year, that deposit will have 39 years in which to accumulate returns. The second deposit will have 38 years in which to accumulate returns. The last deposit is contributed at the same time that the account reaches its evaluation date and will therefore not accumulate returns. After computing the future value of each of the 40 separate deposits, one can add them all for a final future value. That is a lot of work!

To simplify a future value of annuity problem, the interest factor, known as the **future value interest factor of an annuity** (FVIFA), can be computed in advance. Then one need only multiply the annual deposit by this interest factor. In equation form:

$$\text{Annual Deposit} \times \text{FVIFA}_{r,N} = \text{FVA} \qquad \text{equation 4.8}$$

where

$\text{FVIFA}_{r,N}$ = future value interest factor of an annuity where the interest rate is r

and the number of time periods is N

FVA = future value of an annuity

In Example 4.6, the FVIFA can be found in several ways. One way is to compute it directly. The formula for the FVIFA is

$$\text{FVIFA}_{r,N} = \frac{(1+r)^N - 1}{r}$$

To compute this value for the problem in Example 4.6, we substitute appropriate values:

$$\text{FVIFA}_{09,40} = \frac{(1+.09)^{40} - 1}{.09} = 337.882$$

Another way is to go to Appendix A.3 and look up the FVIFA for 40 years at 9 percent. The value is the same as we just calculated. The final computation for Example 4.6 is $2,000 \times 337.882$, or $675,764.

Web Link 4.3   A third way to solve this problem is to go to a web site with a calculator for future value of annuity problems. General instructions for using a web calculator to solve this problem are as follows. Enter zero in the present value cell (if there is one) because this problem involves no cash on hand at the start of the savings program. Leave the future value cell blank as this is the value for which we are solving. For the number of payment periods and payment amount, enter 40 and $2,000, respectively. Finally, enter 9 percent as the interest rate and then click on the appropriate *calculate* button. Any of the calculators should provide the correct answer of $675,764.89. Remember, some of the calculators will show the answer as a negative number if the annual contribution is entered as a positive number.

To understand the importance of the interest rate in time value of money problems, rework the problem in the previous example using an interest rate of 10 percent. The future value of the annuity now becomes $885,185.11. Note that a 1 percent increase in the rate of return increases the final value of the annuity by approximately $210,000.

In the preceding future value of annuity problems, the objective was to compute the final amount of money that would be saved. In the problems below, we are given the final savings goal, and must determine one of the other elements in the future value of an annuity calculation. The calculators at **Web Link 4.3** allow one to enter all but one of the elements of a future value of annuity problem (except the interest rate) and solve for the remaining factor.

(a) Stan wants to accumulate $1,000,000 by the time he retires in 40 years. He believes he can achieve a 10 percent rate of return on his investments. How much money must he set aside at the end of each year in order to reach his goal?

(b) Stan wants to accumulate $1,000,000 by the time he retires. He believes he can earn 8 percent on his investments and he plans to set aside $3,000 per year toward this goal. How many years will he have to save in order to reach his goal?

(c) Stan wants to accumulate $1,000,000 by the time he plans to retire in 40 years. He is prepared to set aside $2,500 at the end of each year to achieve this goal. What is the minimum rate of return he has to earn on his investments?

Using a web calculator, the answers to the above three problems are (a) $2,259.43, (b) 43.14 years, and (c) 9.627%. The first two answers can be directly computed. The answer to problem (c) requires some trial and error. Enter the annual contribution of $2,500 (be sure to give it a negative value), a present value of zero, 40 time periods, and an estimated interest rate. Then click on the button to compute the future value. If your interest rate estimate was 9 percent, the future value would be $844,706.11, much lower than Stan's goal of $1,000,000. Try again with a higher interest rate, and adjust the interest rate until you get a future value of approximately $1,000,000. This occurs at about 9.627 percent.

The problems in the previous example may also be solved using the FVIFA table at the back of this book. In problem (a), we can look up the FVIFA because we know both the number of time periods and the interest rate. For 40 years and 10 percent, the FVIFA is 442.59. If we plug this value and the FVA value into equation 4.8, we have the following:

$$\text{Annual Deposit} \times 442.59 = \$1,000,000$$

The annual deposit must equal $2,259.43 ($1,000,000 / 442.59).

In problem (b), we know the annual deposit and the FVA, but we don't know one of the components that allows us to look up the FVIFA. So we solve for the FVIFA using the equation

$$\$3,000 \times \text{FVIFA} = \$1,000,000$$

The FVIFA equals 333.33 ($1,000,000 / $3,000). We then go to the FVIFA table and look in the column associated with an 8 percent interest rate to see which row has the value closest to 333.33. In this case, the row with the closest value is that associated with 45 years.

For problem (c), where the deposit is $2,500 and the ending value is $1,000,000, we solve

$$\$2,500 \times \text{FVIFA} = \$1,000,000$$

to determine that FVIFA equals 400 ($1,000,000 / $2,500). We then go to the FVIFA table and look across the row corresponding to 40 years until we come to the FVIFA of 400 (or the closest value to it). In this case, the closest value is in the column for 10 percent.

How Do I Combine Future Value and Future Value of Annuity Problems?
It is possible that one might have occasion to combine a future value problem with a future value of annuity problem. Consider the following example:

Stan is now 40 years old. He has accumulated $80,000 toward his retirement. He would like to retire in 25 years. If he is able to save $5,000 per year at the end of each year between now and his retirement date, how much will he have saved upon retirement? Assume an interest rate of 8 percent.

This problem can be worked using the future value and future value of annuity tables at the back of the book. It is a two-step process in which the future value of the current savings and the future value of the annuity are figured separately and the two numbers are added together. In equation form:

$$(\$80,000 \times [1 + .08]^{25}) + (\$5,000 \times FVIFA_{.08,25}) = \text{Future Value} \qquad (4.9)$$

In this case, the future value factor of $(1 + .08)^{25}$ equals 6.8485 and the FVIFA factor is 73.1059. This produces a combined future value of $913,408.

Web Link 4.4

This problem can also be solved using any of the calculators at **Web Link 4.4.** Generally, the entries would be $80,000 for present value, the future value would be left blank, the number of payments would be 25, the payment amount would be $5,000, and the interest rate would be 8 percent. The answer is again that Stan will have accumulated $913,408.

A person planning his or her retirement may actually want to work the above problem in the reverse. He or she may have a specific savings goal and know how much has already been set aside. The problem is to ascertain how much he or she needs to save each year. Let's change the above problem to reflect this change in perspective.

Stan is now 40 years old. He has accumulated $80,000 toward his retirement. He would like to retire in 25 years. If he would like to have accumulated $1,000,000 at the time of retirement, how much would he have to set aside at the end of each year between now and his retirement date? Assume an interest rate of 8 percent.

This changes equation 4.9 to the following:

$$(\$80,000 \times [1 + .08]^{25}) + (\text{Annual Deposit} \times FVIFA_{8\%,25}) = \$1,000,000 \qquad (4.10)$$

Web Link 4.5

The solution may be found using **Web Link 4.6** or by using the time value of money tables at the back of the book. Using the tables, find both interest factors and plug them into equation 4.10, then solve for the annual deposit. These steps produce the following:

$$(\$80,000 \times 6.8485) + (\text{Annual Deposit} \times 73.106) = \$1,000,000$$

$$\frac{\$1,000,000 - (\$80,000 \times 6.8485)}{73.106} = \$6,184.44$$

How Does One Compute the Present Value of an Annuity?

We have now discussed three time value of money problems: future value, present value, and future value of an annuity. The astute reader will surmise that there is one more type of problem to be discussed—the present value of an annuity. A primary example of a present value of annuity problem is one in which an individual has some money saved up today and wants to make steady withdrawals from this savings over a period of time. Consider the following example:

In planning his retirement, Stan Hoi has decided that he would like to fund an annuity for himself from which he could draw $40,000 at the end of each year of retirement. Stan expects to live no more than 25 years after retirement. He plans to keep this money invested at a rate of 6 percent. How much money would he need upon retirement to fund this annuity?

Although it is tempting to solve this problem by multiplying the $40,000 by 25 years and to conclude that Stan would need an initial investment of $1,000,000, it is also incorrect. The savings continue to grow at the investment rate of return. Think of the problem this way: each withdrawal must be funded separately, so each withdrawal has a separate present value computation. The sum of these present values is the initial investment that Stan needs. The mathematics of the process, although complex, allows us to do all of the present value calculations with only one computation. In equation form, we have that the

$$\text{Annual Withdrawal} \times \text{PVIFA}_{r,N} = \text{Initial Investment} \qquad (4.11)$$

where

$\text{PVIFA}_{r,N}$ = **present value interest factor of an annuity** where the interest rate is r and the number of time periods is N.

PVIFA values for various combinations of interest rates and time periods are shown in Appendix A.4. In the above example, the interest rate is 6 percent and the number of time periods is 25. Appendix A.4 indicates that the PVIFA is 12.7834, so the initial investment needed is

$$\$40,000 \times 12.7834 = \$511,336$$

If you had solved this problem by multiplying the $40,000 withdrawals by the 25 years, the $1,000,000 answer is roughly double what is actually needed!

As with FVIFA, the PVIFA can be explicitly computed. The formula behind the term is

$$\text{PVIFA}_{r,N} = \frac{1}{r} - \frac{1}{r \times (1+r)^N}$$

Thus, for the above problem, the direct calculation of this factor is

$$\text{PVIFA}_{6\%,25} = \frac{1}{.06} - \frac{1}{.06 \times (1+.06)^{25}} = 12.7834$$

Web Link 4.6

Using any of the calculators at **Web Link 4.6,** enter zero for the future value, 25 for the number of periods, $40,000 for the payment amount, and 6 percent for the interest rate. The answer will be $511,334.25.

A common variation on this problem is that you know the initial amount of money on hand, and you would like to compute the annual withdrawals that can be generated. Consider the following:

Stan Hoi has achieved his goal of accumulating $1,000,000 upon retirement. Stan expects to live no more than 25 years. He plans to keep this money invested at a rate of 6 percent. If he wants to withdraw equal dollar amounts from his savings at the end of each year for the next 25 years, how much can he withdraw?

In this case, we can compute the PVIFA and we know the initial investment, so we can set up equation 4.11 as follows:

Annual Withdrawals × 12.7834 = $1,000,000

Division reveals the answer to be $78,226.45 ($1,000,000 / 12.7834). At **Web Link 4.6,** you would solve this problem by entering $1,000,000 as the present value, zero as the future value, 25 as the number of payment periods, and 6 percent as the interest rate per period. The payment amount would be left blank and when the appropriate *calculate* button is clicked, the answer displayed should be $78,226.72.

   Installment loans are another form of a present value of annuity problem. In an installment loan, the borrower agrees to make an equal number of payments to a lender for a fixed number of time periods. The two most common installment loans are car loans and mortgages. The concept behind an installment loan is the same as the concept behind the withdrawal program just discussed: the sum of the present values of each payment you make in the future will total the amount you are borrowing today. For example, suppose you take out a loan in which you agree to repay $100 per year for three years, and the interest rate on the loan is 10 percent. The present values of the three payments are $90.91, $82.64, and $75.13. The sum of the three present values, or the face amount of the loan, is $248.68. Consider the following example:

> *Stan takes out a $10,000 loan for five years at 8 percent. He will make annual payments. What will his annual payment be?*

Let us solve this using equation 4.11, except we substitute the term payment for annual withdrawal and the term loan for initial investment.

$$\text{Payment} \times \text{PVIFA}_{r,N} = \text{Loan}$$

The payment is then equal to

$$\text{Payment} = \text{Loan}/\text{PVIFA}_{r,N}$$

To solve the above problem, we look up the PVIFA in Appendix A.4 for 8 percent and five years. The value is 3.9927. Thus, the annual loan payment is

$$\$10,000/3.9927 = \$2,504.57$$

WHAT ARE GROWING ANNUITIES?

Some of the most important problems in personal finance decision making involve **growing annuities** or escalating series. A growing annuity is one in which each payment (or receipt) is larger than the previous one by a fixed percentage amount. Consider the following example:

> *Stan Hoi plans to retire at the age of 65. He is confident he will live no longer than 30 years past retirement. Stan would like to make annual withdrawals from his portfolio at the end of each year. To compensate for inflation, he would like to assure that each withdrawal is 3 percent greater than the previous withdrawal. If he wants his first withdrawal to be $30,000 and if he believes he can earn an average rate of*

return of 8 percent on his portfolio, what should be the value of his portfolio on the day he retires?

This problem is known as a present value of a growing annuity. It is a present value problem because Stan wants to know the value of his portfolio before he starts making withdrawals. It is a growing annuity because each withdrawal will be 3 percent greater than the previous withdrawal. The formula for ascertaining this present value is

$$V_0 = \text{Payment}_1 \times [\frac{1}{r-g} - \frac{1}{r-g} \times \frac{(1+g)^N}{(1+r)^N}]$$

where $\text{Payment}_1 =$ the first payment, or withdrawal, at the end of the first year

$r =$ expected rate of return on the portfolio

$g =$ rate at which payments will grow

$N =$ the total number of payments (or withdrawals) that are planned

For the above problem, we would compute the present value as

$$V_0 = \$30,000 \times [\frac{1}{.08-.03} - \frac{1}{.08-.03} \times \frac{(1+.03)^{30}}{(1+.08)^{30}}] = \$455,271.08$$

In Example 4.12, each payment can be expressed as a function of the previous payment

$$\text{Payment}_t \times (1+g) = \text{Payment}_{t+1}$$

or each payment can be expressed as a function of the first payment

$$\text{Payment}_t = \text{Payment}_1 \times (1+g)^{t-1} \qquad \text{where } 1 < t \leq N$$

A similar problem occurs when someone wants to accumulate money over time, but rather than making equal annual payments, they want their payments to grow at a constant rate. Consider the following problem:

Stan wants to accumulate $1,000,000 by the time he retires. He believes he can earn 10 percent on his investment portfolio. However, he wants the pain of his contributions to be spread evenly over his working career. He expects his annual salary will grow at the average annual rate of 4 percent and he will keep his contribution program at a fixed percent of salary. If he expects to work 35 years before retiring and he makes the contribution at the end of each year, what should be the value of his first contribution?

This is a basic example of what is known as a future value of a growing annuity problem. It is a future value because Stan is accumulating money over time and we are interested in his final accumulation. It is a growing annuity because each payment will be 4 percent greater than the previous payment (because his contributions are tied to his salary and his salary is expected to grow at a 4 percent rate). The formula for solving this problem is

$$V_N = \text{Payment}_1 \times [\frac{(1+r)^N - (1+g)^N}{r-g}]$$

If we substitute the values from Stan's situation, we find that Stan's first payment needs to be

$$\$1,000,000 = \text{Payment}_1 \times [\frac{(1 + .10)^{35} - (1 + .04)^{35}}{.10 - .04}] = \text{Payment}_1 \times 402.6056$$

$$\text{Payment}_1 = \$1,000,000 / 402.6056 = \$2,483.82$$

Note that in a future value of growing annuity problem, just as in a present value of growing annuity problem, the relationship among the payments can be described as either

$$\text{Payment}_t \times (1 + g) = \text{Payment}_{t+1}$$

or

$$\text{Payment}_t = \text{Payment}_1 \times (1 + g)^{t-1} \qquad \text{where } 1 < t \leq N$$

HOW DOES COMPOUNDING INTEREST MORE THAN ONCE PER YEAR AFFECT TIME VALUE OF MONEY PROBLEMS?

In the discussion so far, we have assumed that interest is compounded (paid or earned) once per year. In fact, interest is often compounded more than once per year. The most common alternative compounding frequency is monthly, although interest can be compounded over any interval, including semiannually, quarterly, weekly, and even daily. Compounding frequency affects all time value of money problems.

Let's start with how future values are affected. In the case of a future value calculation, you must first ascertain the number of times compounding occurs per year. In the case of monthly compounding, it is 12 times per year. If compounding were quarterly, it would be 4 times per year. You then make two adjustments in the computation. First, the interest rate is divided by the number of times compounding occurs per year. Second, the number of years is multiplied by the compounding frequency per year.

> *Stan Hoi has put $200 into a two-year certificate of deposit at his credit union. The account pays interest at the rate of 6 percent per year, compounded monthly. How much will Stan's deposit be worth at the end of two years?*

The first step is to divide the 6 percent interest rate by 12. The effective interest rate in this case is not 6 percent per year, but .5 percent per month. Second, multiply two years by 12: the number of time periods is not two years, but 24 months. Thus, Stan has deposited his money at a rate of .5 percent per month for 24 months. To solve this problem, go to **Web Link 4.1.** Where the calculator asks you to enter the number of years, enter 24. Where the calculator asks for the interest rate, enter .5 percent. The correct answer of $225.43 should then be displayed. In equation form, this problem would appear as follows:

$$\$200 \times (1 + .06/12)^{(2 \times 12)} = \$225.43$$

For all of the other time value of money problems (present value, future value of annuity, present value of annuity, and growing annuity), the adjustment process for compounding more than once per year is the same. Let us look at some examples:

> *(a) Stan would like to have $5,000 in five years. His local bank offers a CD that pays 8 percent, compounded quarterly. How much would he have to deposit today to assure he reaches his goal?*

> *(b) Stan plans to deposit $100 every six months into a savings account that pays 4 percent interest, compounded semiannually. At the end of three years, how much will his savings have grown to?*

> *(c) Stan is looking to buy a car. The bank offers him a $10,000 five-year installment loan at 12 percent, with monthly payments. What would his monthly payment be?*

In problem (a), the quarterly compounding frequency means that compounding occurs four times per year. Thus, before doing any calculations, we would have to adjust the interest rate to 2 percent and the number of time periods to 20. In equation form the solution would appear as

$$\$5,000 \times \frac{1}{(1 + .08 / 4)^{(5 \times 4)}} = \$3,364.86$$

This answer may also be obtained at **Web Link 4.2** by entering $5,000 for the future value amount, 2 percent for the interest rate, and 20 for the number of years.

In problem (b), the semiannual compounding frequency means that interest is compounded twice per year. The adjustments require dividing the interest rate by two and multiplying the number of years by two to determine the number of time periods. In other words, depositing $100 every six months for three years into an account that pays interest at 4 percent compounded semiannually is the same as depositing $100 at the end of every year for six years into an account that pays 2 percent compounded annually. The final value will be $630.81. This result may be verified at **Web Link 4.3.** Enter $100 as the investment, six as the number of years, annual for the frequency of compounding, and 2 percent as the annual percentage yield.

In problem (c), the monthly compounding frequency means that interest is compounded 12 times per year. Divide the interest rate by 12 and multiply the number of years by 12. In this case, the $10,000 loan for five years at 12 percent compounded monthly is the same as a $10,000 loan for 60 years at 1 percent compounded annually.

These adjustments in problem (6) may be unnecessary, however. Virtually all web pages on loan computations assume that payments are made on a monthly basis, so you

Web Link 4.7 can usually use annual data without adjustments. For example, in **Web Link 4.7**, if you enter the $10,000 as the loan amount, 5 as the number of years of the loan (unless the calculator explicitly asks for the number of months), and 12 as the annual percentage yield, you will ascertain that the monthly payment is $222.44. See Chapter 6 for more information about Internet calculators that compute the monthly payments of a loan.

WHAT IS THE DIFFERENCE BETWEEN NOMINAL AND EFFECTIVE ANNUAL RATES?

In the previous section, we discussed how having interest compounded more than once per year requires adjustments in the interest rate and the number of time periods before a problem can be solved. Adjusting the interest rate creates a distinction between what is known as the **nominal** (or stated) **interest rate** and the **effective annual rate.** The effective annual rate is the true annual interest rate in a problem. Solving a problem using the effective annual interest rate is easier than solving a problem involving compounding more than once per year.

The adjustment process to determine an effective annual interest rate is the same as the adjustment process when compounding is more than once per year. Think of the interest rate as being for a one-year loan or investment. Divide the nominal interest rate by the number of times per year compounding occurs and add this to one. Take this sum to the power of m and subtract one from the result. The formula for this is

$$r_{ear} = (1 + \frac{r_{nom}}{m})^m - 1$$

where r_{ear} = effective annual interest rate

$\qquad r_{nom}$ = stated nominal annual interest rate

$\qquad m$ = number of times per year compounding occurs

As an example, you look at your credit card statement and note that the interest rate is 18 percent. Interest on credit cards is charged each month on the unpaid balance, so the interest is compounded monthly or 12 times per year. The effective annual rate would then be computed as

$$r_{ear} = (1 + .18/12)^{12} - 1 = .1956 \text{ or } 19.56\%$$

Stan is considering two different banks for his savings account. The first bank pays 4 percent compounded daily, and the second bank pays 4$\frac{1}{4}$ percent compounded annually. Which bank offers the higher effective annual rate?

No adjustment is necessary for the bank that pays interest compounded annually. Any interest rate compounded annually is automatically stated as an effective annual rate. To adjust the interest rate at the second bank, which compounds daily, we start by noting that daily compounding means 365 times per year. We can thus compute the effective annual rate for the second bank as

$$r_{ear} = (1 + .04/365)^{365} - 1 = .0408 \text{ or } 4.08\%$$

This makes it clear that the bank offering 4$\frac{1}{4}$ percent compounded annually offers a better interest rate.

HOW DO I COMPUTE RATE OF INFLATION?

When people think about time value of money problems, they also must sometimes think about the rate of inflation. The **inflation rate** is the rate at which prices are rising. A lot of problems could be simplified if we knew what the future rate of inflation was going to be. For example, you plan to retire in 20 years, and you would like to know the extent of inflation between now and then to make sure that your income would be sufficient to achieve the standard of living you desire during retirement. It is not sufficient to say, If I had $60,000 of income I could retire comfortably. What you probably mean is, If I had an income that was sufficient to buy what $60,000 could buy today, I could retire comfortably.

Inflation rates can be computed only on a historical basis. In truth, there are a lot of different inflation rates, of which the most commonly cited is based on the **Consumer Price Index** or CPI. To compute the CPI, the U.S. Bureau of Labor Statistics (BLS) first defines what is known as a market basket of goods and services regularly purchased by a traditional family of four living in an urban area. Each month, the BLS then ascertains via various types of surveys what the goods and services in this market basket actually cost. For example, to learn the current level of food prices for specific foods, they may go into supermarkets and look at the prices of the foods on the shelf. The BLS then computes the total value or cost of this hypothetical market basket of goods and services. Although it could report the actual dollar cost of this basket, the BLS instead standardizes the cost to a common basis. The common base period currently used is 1982–84. Thus, the BLS divides the cost of the market basket of goods and services at the current month's prices by the cost of the same basket during the base period. The BLS then multiplies this ratio by 100 to provide the current level of the index. In equation form

$$\text{Current Value of the Index} = \frac{\text{Value of the Basket in the Current Month}}{\text{Value of the Basket in the Base Period Month}} \times 100$$

To see the current values of the Consumer Price Index, click on **Web Link 4.8,** which displays a large menu of different price indices one might examine. The one of most interest is the first: U.S. All items, 1982–84=100. If you select this index and scroll down to identify the number of years for which you want data and the format in which you would like to view the data, you can then click on *Retrieve Data*. A copy of this web page is provided in Table 4.1.

Web Link 4.8

Table 4.1
Example of Consumer Price Index—All Urban Consumers

Year	Jan	Feb	Mar	Apr	May	Jun	Jul	Aug	Sep	Oct	Nov	Dec
1997	159.1	159.6	160.0	160.2	160.1	160.3	160.5	160.8	161.2	161.6	161.5	161.3
1998	161.6	161.9	162.2	162.5	162.8	163.0	163.2	163.4	163.6	164.0	164.0	163.9
1999	164.3	164.5	165.0	166.2	166.2	166.2	166.7	167.1	167.9	168.2	168.3	168.3
2000	168.8	169.8	171.2	171.3	171.5	172.4	172.8	172.8	173.7	174.0	174.1	174.8
2001	175.1	175.8	176.2	160.2								

Source: ftp://ftp.bls.gov/pub/special.requests/cpi/cpiai.txt, May 15, 2001.

As an example of how to use this table, note that the CPI for August 2000 was 172.8. For August of 1999, the CPI was 167.1. We can now estimate the rate of inflation over this twelve-month period as:

$$\text{Rate of Inflation} = \frac{\text{CPI}_{\text{AUG. '00}} - \text{CPI}_{\text{AUG. '99}}}{\text{CPI}_{\text{AUG. '99}}} = \frac{172.8 - 167.1}{167.1} = .034 \text{ or } 3.4\%$$

Anyone using CPI numbers should be aware of several problems associated with the CPI computations. First, it is difficult to incorporate quality changes into the CPI. For example, would you prefer to visit a physician who has available the current state of knowledge of medicine in 2002, or one whose knowledge is based on what was known in 1986? The answer is clearly the 2002 physician. This being the case, the fact that the 2002 physician charges more than the 1986 physician cannot be attributed entirely to inflation. Some of the price difference reflects the improvement in the knowledge and skills of the physician.

A second major problem is that most people do not qualify as a traditional family, and thus do not all buy the same basket of goods and services. A bachelor likely buys a different set of goods and services over the course of a year than does a family with two parents and four children. Both of these households probably also differ from that of a newlywed couple. Because the rates of price changes on individual components of the market basket are not all equal and not everyone buys the same basket, different families will experience different rates of inflation. In fact, over periods of time, the prices of some goods and services actually go down. If your typical purchases include a disproportionately large number of these items, you may actually experience deflation (i.e., a decline in your cost of living) when others are experiencing inflation.

How Might I Use the Inflation Rate in Planning Decisions?

One way to incorporate the inflation rate into planning decisions is to recognize that if you are saving to make a major purchase, the price of the product you want to buy will probably be increasing. For example, you may decide you would like to buy a new car in three years. You can go out today and price the type of car you would like to buy, but saving exactly that amount of money over the next three years does not guarantee you will have enough cash to buy the car in three years. The incorporation of an inflation rate into prices adds an extra step to problem solving.

In our car purchase example, the first step is to figure out what the car will cost when you are ready to buy it. This is nothing more than a future value calculation where the interest rate is replaced by the projected inflation rate.

> *Stan plans to buy a house in five years. If he were buying it today, he would need $20,000 as a down payment. He believes the price of the house (and thus his down payment required) will grow at the rate of 3 percent per year. If he believes he can earn 8 percent on his investments, how much should he set aside today to achieve his goal?*

The first step is to ascertain exactly how much money Stan will need when he is ready to make the down payment. In this case, we want to figure the future value of $20,000 that is growing at the rate of 3 percent per year for five years. If we use **Web Link 4.1,** we can compute the answer as $23,185.48. The second step is then to find the present value of this $23,185 by discounting it at 8 percent for five years. This can be done at **Web Link 4.3.** The answer is $15,780.

Another way to incorporate inflation into financial decision making is to consider the true purchasing power of your savings objective.

Stan has $20,000 set aside as part of his savings program. He believes that over time he will average at least an 8 percent rate of return. If he saves for the next 30 years, how much will he have accumulated? If the inflation rate averages 3 percent, what will be the purchasing power in terms of today's dollars of this accumulated savings?

Web Link 4.9   **Web Link 4.9** shows that the future value of the savings program will be $201,253 (= $20,000 \times [1 + .08]^{30}$). This sounds impressive. However, the calculator also shows that the purchasing value of this money in terms of today's dollars is only $82,914 (= $201,253 / [1 + .03]^{30}$). This is still a lot of money, but not quite as much as the $201,253 initially sounded.

HOW DOES ONE COMPUTE AFTER-TAX RATES OF RETURN?

In all our saving and investing discussion, we have not mentioned taxes. Since investment income is subject to taxation, we must consider how to incorporate taxes into the time value of money computations. As we saw in Chapter 3, the impact of taxation is through the individual's marginal tax rate. If your marginal tax rate is 28 percent and you are saving money, you will pay in taxes 28 percent of whatever you save. If you earn 10 percent on your money, you will actually keep only 7.2 percent of what you earn. Your money will actually grow at a rate of only 7.2 percent, rather than the 10 percent you initially identified. When doing the various time value of money calculations, use an after-tax rate of return. The after-tax rate of return can be computed as

$$r_{after-tax} = r_{pretax} \times (1 - \text{marginal tax rate})$$

where $r_{after-tax}$ = after-tax rate of return and

r_{pretax} = pretax rate of return

SUMMARY

➤ The most intuitive time value of money problem is a future value problem in which a fixed amount of money is invested today at a known or expected rate of return, and the investor wants to know how much money he or she will end up with.

➤ A more common problem is the reverse, in which an investor tries to ascertain the value today of a specified amount of money in the future.

➤ For present value problems, the interest rate used to discount the future cash values is based on the opportunity cost of an investment whose risk is the same as the risk of the future cash flows.

➤ An annuity is a finite number of fixed, consecutive payments. The future value of an annuity is the accumulations from annuity contributions and accrued investment income.

➤ A slightly more complex savings problem than a future value or a future annuity involves combining an immediate cash contribution with a set of annuity contributions.

➤ The payments for an installment loan represent an annuity, and the loan is the present value of this annuity.

➤ Many investors would do well to approach savings accumulation and wealth distribution problems not as annuities but as growing annuities. A growing annuity is a fixed number of payments that grow at a fixed percentage rate each period. It would make more sense for investors to save using a growing annuity to figure each year's contribution. It would also make more sense for investors to think about drawing retirement cash in the form of a growing annuity rather than a regular annuity.

➤ An effective annual interest rate can be computed once the nominal interest rate and frequency of compounding are known. The formula is

$$r_{ear} = (1 + \frac{r_{nom}}{m})^m - 1$$

➤ Investors usually need to incorporate some estimate of inflation into their retirement planning calculations. Estimating the recent annual rate of inflation and projecting the future inflation rate to be the same may provide a reasonable approximation of the future inflation rate.

➤ An after-tax rate of return can be computed based on a pre-tax rate and a marginal tax rate. The formula is

$$r_{after-tax} = r_{pre-tax} \times (1 - \text{marginal tax rate})$$

KEY TERMS

annuity	Consumer Price Index	effective annual rate
future value interest factor	future value interest factor of an annuity	growing annuity
inflation rate	nominal interest rate	opportunity rate of return
present value interest factor	present value interest factor of an annuity	time value of money

PROBLEMS

4.1. You want to save $1,000,000 for retirement, which will be 40 years from today. How much would you have to set aside to fund the retirement if you make a single deposit today? Assume interest rates of 6, 8, 10, and 12 percent.

4.2. A broker approaches you to manage your stock account. He promises that if you deposit $20,000 in assets with him today, in 20 years time he will grow your account to $100,000, assuming you leave all cash in the account over that time period. What rate of return is he promising to achieve? Should you be impressed by this promise?

4.3. You want to save $1,000,000 for retirement, which will be 40 years from today. How much would you have to set aside each year to fund the retirement if you made 40 equal annual deposits beginning one year from today? Assume interest rates of 6, 8, 10, and 12 percent.

4.4. You want to accumulate $30,000. You can set aside $300 per month and invest the money at an annual rate of 8 percent. How many months will it take you to accumulate the money?

4.5. You have sold your house, and in the process have taken a second mortgage from the buyer. The buyer will pay you $500 a month for the next six years. A private investor approaches you and offers to buy this mortgage from you for $27,000. What rate of return is the private investor expecting to receive if the buyer makes all of the payments on schedule?

4.6. You just received your notice to pay your life insurance premium. You can pay a one-time premium today of $600, or you can pay one-twelfth of the premium each month, but must add a $3 service fee to each monthly payment. The first payment is one month from today. What is the effective interest rate you are being charged to spread out the payments?

4.7. You want to leave your children $1,000,000 each. You expect to live 50 more years, and you believe you could earn an average of 10 percent on your investments. If you wanted to fund each inheritance with a single payment today, how much would you have to set aside for each child?

4.8. You are planning for your child's college education. You believe that tuition will be $20,000 the first year and will grow at a rate of 4 percent per year. If your child attends college for four years, how much will you need to have at the start of your child's college career to fully fund his or her education if you can earn a 10 percent rate of return?

4.9. You want to accumulate $1,000,000 by the time you retire. However, you want the pain of your contributions to be spread evenly over your working career. You have decided to contribute $2,000 to an investment program at the end of the first year. You expect this contribution to grow at the same rate as your annual salary, 4 percent per year. If you expect to work 35 years before retiring, you make the contribution at the end of each year, and you earn an 8 percent rate of return, will you achieve your goal of $1,000,000?

4.10. The current value of the CPI is 200. What is the annual inflation rate if the CPI was 195 twelve months ago?

4.11. You are saving to buy a home in five years. The home you would like to buy costs $150,000 today. You would like to make a 20 percent down payment and you anticipate an annual inflation rate of 3 percent over the next five years. How much would the home cost in five years, and what would be the amount of your down payment?

4.12. You have $50,000 invested in certificates of deposit at your local bank. You are earning a rate of 8 percent compounded quarterly. You feel pretty good about this investment until your tax accountant reminds you that even though you are allowing the interest to accumulate on the certificate, you are still paying taxes on that income. Your marginal tax rate is 30 percent. What is your effective annual pretax rate of return on the CD? What is your after-tax effective annual rate of return?

4.13. Having just turned 50 years old, you decide that now is the time to start seriously saving toward retirement. Your portfolio is worth $150,000. You plan to contribute $5,000 per year for the next 15 years to this account, and you believe you can average at least a 9 percent rate of return. Given these assumptions, how much would your portfolio be worth at the end of 15 years?

REFERENCES

Web Link 4.10 Tutorials on time value of money

Web Link 4.11 Instructions on using financial calculators

WALL STREET JOURNAL RESOURCES

Web Link (WSJ) 4.12 "Financial Success Requires Saving, Spending Discipline," *The Wall Street Journal Interactive Edition*, May 5, 1998. Compute the future value that derives from using some of the saving suggestions.

Web Link (WSJ) 4.13 "Calculating Retirement? It's No Simple Equation," *The Wall Street Journal Interactive Edition*, February 7, 2000

For information that has changed since the book was written, for new information that pertains to this topic, and for some new web sites that pertain to the topic of this chapter, see **Web Link 4.14.**

CHAPTER 5

MANAGING LIQUID ASSETS

LEARNING OBJECTIVES

- Discuss the issues in deciding how much liquidity to hold
- Name the various depository institutions and explain how they differ
- Discuss the features of a checking account
- Describe the different types of checks
- Discuss the effect of different endorsements on a check
- Describe the process for resolving a bad check
- Discuss online banking
- Describe the ways interest is paid on savings accounts
- Describe a money market deposit account
- Discuss various aspects of deposit insurance
- Describe savings bonds, Treasury instruments, and money market assets

Web Link: www.wiley.com/college/woerheide

INTRODUCTION

Cash is absolutely critical in our lives for convenience, but it has major drawbacks. Cash can be lost or stolen and it does not provide a rate of return. Cash is part of a larger concern—liquidity. In Chapter 2, we defined liquidity as the ability to convert an asset to cash quickly and with little or no loss in value. We listed assets on a balance sheet in decreasing order of liquidity. In this chapter, we focus on liquid assets. Liquid assets have a degree of liquidity so high that they are considered as perfect or near-perfect substitutes for cash. Liquid assets include checking accounts, savings accounts, certificates of deposit, money market deposit accounts, Treasury bills, money market mutual funds, and even cash management accounts. In this chapter, we will consider the situation of Oscar Pena, a young man dealing with issues involving liquidity.

How Much Liquidity Should I Hold?

In Chapter 2 we discussed several ratios for measuring liquidity. These included the ratios of liquid assets to monthly expenses, liquid assets to monthly disposable income, and liquid assets to current debt. The first two ratios indicated how many months of living expenses you could pay out of current liquid assets or how many months of income you could replace if you were to lose your job. Good financial planning requires not just that you know how much liquidity you have, but that you decide how much liquidity you *should* have.

Most financial planning professionals indicate you should have three to six months of income in the form of liquid assets. Let us consider the validity of this range. The primary purpose of holding liquid assets is to assure that you have cash to meet daily expenses in the event of job loss or an unexpected major expense. Liquid assets are normally an unattractive type of asset to hold because they provide a rate of return much lower than expected rates of return on less liquid investments. If one of your goals in life is to accrue wealth, then excessive investing in liquid assets will do harm. For each person, there is some optimal amount of liquid assets to hold.

There are several things to think about in setting this optimal amount of liquidity. First, if you lose your job, you may be willing to reduce your standard of living until such time as you find a new job. This might include such activities as postponing any major expenses such as a vacation or a new car for which you were saving, eliminating further contributions to your savings programs, eating out less often, and working to cut your daily living expenses. The more willing you are to adjust your standard of living, the less liquidity you would need.

Second, if you have little or no debt outstanding, then you have the ability to borrow money. In this case, we are not talking about debt such as mortgages or automobile loans. We are talking about debts such as the credit limits on your credit cards, unused lines of credit at your bank, loans against any securities you own, and loans against your life insurance policies. For example, suppose you have a $12,000 line of credit on your credit card and you charge an average of $2,000 per month on it. You would be able to go approximately six months making charges and paying only the minimum monthly payment before you hit your credit limit. As we will see in the next chapter, the interest rate on these credit card loans can be quite expensive. However, if you believe you would be able to pay off those credit card loans relatively quickly once your need for liquidity is over, then the absolute cost of these loans may be relatively minor.

Think about it this way. John McFadden holds as his liquidity reserve $50,000 in a passbook savings account paying 4 percent. Connie Fontaine holds as her liquidity reserve $5,000 in her passbook savings account, and puts the other $45,000 into investments that pay an average of 8 percent. Over the course of one year, Connie will have earned $1,800 ([8% − 4%] × $45,000) in investment income more than John. If that continues for five years, Connie will have accumulated more than $9,000 in additional investment income. In five years both people lose their jobs. John has a large amount of liquid assets to fall back on and should be in good shape for many months. Connie will most likely have to borrow money or sell some less-than-liquid assets to obtain the cash to carry her until she finds a new job. The issue now is whether the extra $9,000 in income over the years will cover the extra cost of obtaining the cash she needs to live on during this time period.

The above example illustrates several key points about the optimal amount of liquidity. First, the longer it might take you to find a new job, the more liquidity you need. Second, the more frequent the events when you need to use your liquidity, the more liquidity you need. Third, the greater your resources in borrowing or otherwise obtaining cash, the fewer liquid assets you would need.

Let's consider two examples. A recent college graduate starting a new job may need a substantial amount of liquidity. A new hire is always at risk of being the first to be let go if the company hits hard times. The new graduate may have relatively small credit limits on his or her credit cards. He or she may also be laboring under student loans and possibly even a loan to buy a car. Finally, he or she may have little in the way of nonliquid assets to borrow against or to sell.

Contrast this recent graduate with someone who has been in the labor force for 20 years. This second person has several credit cards with combined credit limits approaching $20,000. He or she also owns $50,000 worth of stock with no loans against the stock, and he or she owns two autos worth a combined value of $25,000. This person has a $50,000 life insurance policy against which $5,000 could be borrowed automatically. Finally, this person has no loans outstanding except for a mortgage. The mortgage has been paid down enough that he or she has an unused $10,000 home equity line of credit against the house. This person has little in the way of immediate liquid assets, but more important, this person has the ability to borrow and otherwise obtain substantial amounts of cash. The bottom line is that this second person has substantially less need for liquid assets than the first person.

The major point here is that the amount of liquidity you need should not be considered separately from all other assets and resources. Simplistic rules about optimal liquidity run the risk of being highly inaccurate. Finally, the wealthier you are in terms of assets and resources, the less immediate liquidity you need to keep on hand.

WHAT ARE THE DEPOSITORY INSTITUTIONS THAT PROVIDE LIQUIDITY?

Most of the financial institutions that provide liquidity are referred to as depository institutions, because they accept deposits in the form of checking and savings accounts.

The primary depository institution is the **commercial bank.** Commercial banks are stockholder-owned corporations. They may be federally chartered or state chartered, although the nature of their charter has no real impact on the individual using the bank's services. Commercial banks are typically full-service organizations, which means they have the authority to offer almost any type of financial service, and may be community banks or chain banks. Community banks function primarily in one community. Chain banks have branches throughout a state, a region, or even the country.

Two closely related types of depository institutions are **savings and loans** and **savings banks.** To the ordinary consumer, these two may look and act much like a commercial bank, but there are some key differences. First, some savings and loans and savings banks are mutuals rather than stockholder-owned companies. In this case, mutual means that the depositors technically own the institution, although most depositors at mutuals are oblivious to the fact. This is because the depositors do not share in the profits of the mutual as the stockholders would share in the profits of a stockholder-owned corporation. No special benefits accrue to the depositors because they are technically owners. The terms of an account at a mutual institution are defined just like the terms of an account at any other depository institution. The second major way savings and loans and savings banks differ from commercial banks is that commercial banks typically make business loans their primary assets. Savings and loans and savings banks typically hold mortgages as their primary assets. Savings and loans and savings banks, like commercial banks, may be federally or state chartered.

The other type of depository institution is the **credit union.** All credit unions are mutual organizations. When a credit union is created, it must define a **field of membership.** This field of membership is typically work-related or geographically based. In fact, many large companies have their own credit unions, where the employer pays some or even most of the operating expenses of the credit union. This is because some companies see the credit union as a perk to its employees. A member of the credit union is anyone who is within the field of membership and who holds a savings account there. Only members can borrow from a credit union. Small credit unions may offer relatively limited services to members, while many larger credit unions' offerings are virtually indistinguishable from those of the other depository institutions. Like the other depository institutions, credit unions may also have a federal or a state charter. The type of charter it holds defines some of the operating features of a credit union, but has little impact on the depositor. The financial statements of any credit union are readily available over the Internet.

> *Oscar Pena is thinking about moving from Philadelphia taking a job with the post office in Rochester, New York. Several of the employees have indicated that one of the benefits of working there is the strong service provided by the credit union. Oscar would like to learn a little more about this credit union.*

Web Link 5.1   Oscar must first go to the National Credit Union Association web site. As Oscar knows only that the credit union is located in Rochester, he needs to obtain its charter number. He does this by entering Rochester and New York in the search calculator, and then clicking on the *find* button. The results tell him that the charter number is 63210. He then returns to the first page, enters this charter number, and again clicks on the appropriate *find* button. At this point, Oscar learns basic information about the credit union and can choose from a menu of financial statements for additional study.

WHAT ARE CHECKING ACCOUNTS?

The most basic liquid asset other than cash itself is a checking account. A checking account is also referred to as a demand deposit account since funds in a checking account are available literally upon demand. Years ago, a checking account at one bank operated almost exactly like a checking account at another bank. It was illegal to pay interest on money held in a checking account, and only banks could offer checking accounts. As a result of financial deregulation in the 1980s, depository institutions can now offer variations of checking accounts. Traditional checking accounts still exist. They are characterized by the lack of payment of interest. The most common variation since the 1980s is known as a *negotiable order of withdrawal* or NOW account. Credit unions offer share draft accounts. Most banks offer both checking accounts and NOW accounts. Because of the lack of significant differences among these accounts, we will simply refer to all such accounts that allow you to write an unlimited number of checks per month as checking accounts.

The key to selecting a checking account is to find the one with the best combination of terms. There are many features to consider, including minimum balance requirements, transaction limits, fees, and interest rates. Most financial institutions offer a menu of checking accounts, and the features of accounts at one institution may have little to do with the features of accounts at another institution. Probably the most important thing to know about any checking account is how to avoid any monthly fee or per-check charges. You can usually avoid monthly fees and per-check charges by having your paycheck or Social Security check direct deposited or by maintaining a minimum balance. Other features are also important. These would include the charge per overdraft, and whether there are any fees to open or close the account. To better understand the complexity of the decision, review the following.

> *Oscar Pena would like to open a checking account at one of the local banks in Philadelphia, Pennsylvania. A branch of Bank of America is located nearby. Oscar knows that this bank has branches in many states, which would provide convenience when he travels. He is not sure which checking account to open.*

Web Link 5.2
Web Link 5.2 shows that in Pennsylvania Bank of America offers four checking accounts: These are Bank of America Advantage™, Regular Checking, Bank of America Express Account™, and Student Checking. The Advantage account has substantial free benefits and services, but also requires the account holder to keep a substantial amount on deposit, or have a substantial amount of bank loans outstanding in order to avoid a large monthly fee. If Oscar would meet these requirements anyway, then this would be a good account for him. If Oscar would not meet the requirements but places a substantive value on the free services and benefits, then he might consider making the additional deposits in order to qualify for this particular account. If Oscar would not meet the deposit requirements naturally and does not particularly value the services offered as part of the package, then he should consider one of the other types of checking accounts or consider a different bank's offering.

> *Oscar goes into The Fictional National Bank and sees that it offers a premier checking account. The account provides a free safe deposit box (normally a $50 annual fee), free checks (which would normally cost Oscar about $20 per year), and free traveler's checks (which would normally cost Oscar about $30 per year). In the past, Oscar has kept about $2,000 in his checking and savings accounts at the banks he has used. To qualify for this account, Oscar must keep a combined total of $5,000 in these accounts; otherwise he will have to pay a $10 monthly fee. Should Oscar consider opening this account?*

If Oscar deposits an additional $3,000 ($5,000 requirement – $2,000 normal deposit total), he will save $100 ($50 safe deposit box + $30 traveler's check fees + $20 check expenses) per year. As a "rate of return," this earns Oscar about 3.33 percent ($100 / $3,000). These are, of course, after-tax dollars. Thus, Oscar needs to convert this to a pretax rate by dividing the rate of return by one minus his effective marginal tax rate. If his effective marginal tax rate were 33 percent, then the pretax equivalent of these benefits is 4.975 percent (3.33 / [1 – .33]). What Oscar should do depends on how attractive he views this perfectly safe rate of return and what his alternatives are.

The distinction between **minimum balance** and **minimum average daily balance** can have an impact on your analysis of a checking account. A minimum balance requirement usually means that your balance cannot fall below the minimum at any time during the month or you would be subject to the specified fees. A minimum average daily balance usually means that the balance on any given day does not matter; what counts is the average of the daily balances. Thus, if your account had balances over a three-day period of $800, $300, and $400, your average daily minimum balance would be $500 ([$800 + $300 + $400]/3). While this account would meet a $500 minimum average daily balance requirement, it would not meet a $500 minimum balance requirement because at least one of the daily balances is less than $500.

Another important feature is how long a bank waits to make funds available to your account. If you deposit cash into your account, the cash is always immediately available, but most people deposit checks rather than cash. The Federal Reserve has regulations on the maximum amount of time a bank can take to make funds available. The maximum time depends on whether your deposit is to open an account or is adding to an existing account, as well as whether your deposit is from a local or out of town bank and whether the issuer of the deposited check is the U.S. Treasury, another bank, or an individual or company. If not enough funds are available when a check you have written is presented to your bank for collection, the check may be returned and your account charged an insufficient funds fee.

Some banks use a practice known as **truncation,** which means that the bank keeps your cancelled checks. The main advantage of truncation is that it saves you from having to store several years' worth of cancelled checks. Banks offering truncation will provide photocopies of any specific checks you request. The main disadvantage of truncation is that it takes time to recover photocopies of cancelled checks.

Finally, many checking accounts pay interest. Interest rates are quite visible, but their value may be misleading. An account with a high interest rate and substantial fees may be a worse deal than an account with a lower rate and much lower fees.

To see examples of attractive checking account programs around the country, visit Web Link 5.3.

Web Link 5.3

What Are the Different Types of Checks?

There are certain types of checks that have special status. The first is a **certified check.** A certified check is guaranteed by your bank. To obtain a certified check, you write your check as you normally would. Before you present it for payment, you take this check to your bank. The bank stamps the word *certified* on the front of the check and places cash from your checking account to pay for the check in a special account until the check is presented for payment. The bank has certified that the check is payable.

A **cashier's check** or **bank check** is a check issued by the bank itself. To obtain a bank or cashier's check, you write a check payable to the bank and the bank then drafts its own check payable to whomever it is you actually wish to pay. Once again, the bank's guarantee of the check has replaced your personal guarantee of the check. In most cases where the payee requires a special guarantee for a check, a certified check or a cashier's check are equally acceptable. Some banks charge different fees for different types of checks. It is always worthwhile to check ahead to verify which form of payment is acceptable. Some examples of situations where you might be required to pay with a certified check or a cashier's check are the closings when you buy a house or a car. In both cases, the seller is transferring the title of the property to you at the closing, and naturally wants as much certainty as possible that the payment you are making is good.

Another form of a check is a traveler's check. The American Express Company first issued traveler's checks in 1891, as the product of an extended trip by the president of the company, James Fargo. Fargo had become frustrated by all the paperwork necessary to obtain currency overseas. Traveler's checks simplify the process. When you buy traveler's checks, you pay the issuer an amount of money. The issuer then gives you traveler's checks, in a range of denominations, equivalent to the amount you paid (usually less a transaction fee). In the issuer's presence, you sign the face of each check. When you are ready to use one of the checks, you sign it again in the presence of the person to whom you are giving the check. The double signature is the primary form of protection on the account. Traveler's checks are issued in a variety of currencies; the currencies American Express offers are found at **Web Link 5.24.**

Web Link 5.24

The last type of check is a **money order,** issued by the post office and most financial institutions. A money order is similar to a cashier's check in that you pay the issuer the amount of the check (plus a small fee usually), and the check is then issued to you. You enter the payee's name. Money orders are generally used for small amounts of money, by individuals who do not have checking accounts.

What Are the Different Types of Endorsements on a Check?

When you deposit or cash a check, you must endorse it. Only the person to whom a check is payable may endorse that check. An endorsement is placed on the back of the check. There are several types of endorsements; we will review the most common. The first is a **blank endorsement.** A blank endorsement is the signature of the person to whom the check is payable with no other wording added. A check with a blank endorsement is equivalent to cash.

The second type of endorsement is a **special endorsement.** This specifies a new person or organization to whom the check is payable (different from the person to whom the check was originally made payable). This person or organization must then endorse the check in turn before the check may be further negotiated. For example, suppose Oscar Pena has received a check made out to him for $20 from Kevin Douglass. He signs the back of the check and adds the words "payable to Greg Tobey." The check cannot be cashed or deposited until Greg Tobey adds his endorsement. Once Greg endorses the check, he can cash or deposit or even sign it over to someone else.

A **restrictive endorsement** is a special endorsement with the word only added. In our above example, if Oscar endorses the check with his name and adds "payable to Greg Tobey only," then Greg cannot endorse the check to someone else. The most common use of a restrictive endorsement is when you intend to deposit a check in your own account you endorse the check as "for deposit only."

A **qualified endorsement** means the person endorsing the check assumes no responsibility whatsoever for the check. For example, if Kevin writes a $20 check payable to Oscar and Oscar endorses the check and adds "payable to Greg Tobey without recourse" then Greg has no subsequent claim on Oscar if the check is bad. Avoid accepting checks with qualified endorsements.

What Happens If I Write a Bad Check?

There are two reasons for a check to be "bad." The most common is insufficient funds in the account to pay the check when it is presented to the bank for payment. Insufficient funds can be the result of a simple error on your part or possibly (but rarely) the bank's part. Resolving this error can be as simple as paying any overdraft fees and putting more cash in your account.

The other reason for a check to be bad is knowingly engaging in fraud. Currently, about $8 billion in bad checks are written every year. Fraudulent checks often share certain common characteristics. The most common feature of bad checks is that the check number is between 101 and 499. Fraudulent checks also tend to have four smooth edges, as opposed to having one perforated edge. If you receive some hassle in attempting to pay by check, it may be that your check has one of these common characteristics.

Sometimes people make mistakes when writing checks. The three most common check-writing errors are having the amount in numbers and the amount in words differ, not entering a date or entering an incorrect date, and not signing a check. If the amount of the check in numbers differs from the amount in words, the amount in words is the binding amount. If you forget to date a check, then the person receiving it may enter an appropriate date, or the check may be processed without a date. It is technically illegal to predate or postdate a check. If you forget to sign a check, the person depositing it may proceed with the deposit and if your bank does not protest, the check will clear. However, the person receiving your check certainly has the right to return your unsigned check for a signature. If there is a critical date for the check to have been received, the receiver has the right to treat the legal receipt as when the signed check was received.

Most states have a statutory period during which you have a grace period to make good on a bad check. This period ranges from two days in Massachusetts to 15 days in each of several states. Failure to make good on a check is effectively nonpayment. Each state has its own penalty if the check is not made good. The most common penalty is that the merchant may sue in small claims court for the original amount of the check plus three times the amount of the check as a penalty, with a minimum penalty of $100 and a maximum of $500. The intent is obviously to make it worth the effort of the merchant to go to court.

Web Link 5.39

Web Link 5.38

ELECTRONIC BANKING

Web Link 5.1a

Initially, most online banking was accomplished by banks partnering with software companies so that customers buying the particular software could have direct access to their accounts and other services at the bank. More recently, the trend has been for banks either to develop their own software or to provide direct access over the Internet.

Dedicated software programs, whether it be a bank's proprietary software or something like MS Money or Quicken, not only allow you to access your account at the bank, but they also typically provide cash budgeting programs, financial statement programs, and other personal finance information. Since the biggest time-consuming element in cash budgeting programs is always data entry, the opportunity to have the bank enter some of the basic information is quite attractive.

Internet access to your checking account has also opened up the ability to make direct payments from your checking account. Some banks have had this service available via the telephone for many years. Direct payments give you greater control over when your money is disbursed and may save you a substantial amount in postage over the course of a year. Many banks charge for direct payments while others offer it as a free service to certain types of accounts.

The major advantages of direct Internet access checking accounts over software-based access are ease of use, low costs, and portability—you can use any machine with Internet access. If you want to access your checking account from work you don't have to install your bank's software on your employer's computer.[1]

In recent years, we have seen the appearance of banks that serve their customers only

Web Link 5.37 through the Internet. Some Internet-based banks may not have fraud insurance.

What Is EFTS?

EFTS stands for **electronic funds transfer system,** the process through which funds can be automatically deposited to or automatically paid out of your account. For example, many employers can directly deposit paychecks into designated accounts. The federal government has long offered direct deposits on Social Security checks.

You may also arrange for certain bills to be paid through direct debits. Many mortgage lenders like to debit your checking account directly for your monthly mortgage payment. Utilities such as phone, gas, and electric companies also typically offer plans to directly debit your checking account. Some companies, such as the American Association for Retired Persons (AARP), actually offer a discount to customers willing to authorize this service. Authorization of a direct debit usually requires you to sign a statement approving it and provide the vendor a cancelled or voided check to establish the account. EFTs

Web Link 5.40 are processed through automated clearinghouses or ACHs.

Bill presentment is another electronic bill payment method. In a direct debit, your account is charged the designated amount and you receive the bill in the mail separately. With bill presentment you receive the bill itself through your checking account. Bill presentment can occur only for those who have some form of Internet banking. The difference between bill presentment and direct debit is that bill presentment does not involve automatic payment of the bill. Once the bill is received, the consumer then designates how much of the bill should be paid. The consumer may also ask any questions about the bill

Web Link 5.41 to the vendor through the presentment process.

What Is an ATM?   ATM stands for automated teller machine. When you open a checking account (or even a passbook savings account) with a financial institution, you can usually obtain an ATM card. This card allows you to go to any of that bank's ATMs to conduct business, usually without a fee. The two primary transactions conducted at ATMs are cash withdrawals and deposits.

An exchange network allows you to use the ATMs of other banks for cash withdrawals, but there is a catch when you use another bank's ATMs. The other bank will charge you a fee and your own bank may also charge you a fee. If you use another bank's ATM on a regular basis, these fees can become exorbitant. This raises the question of where to find the closest ATM machine, whether it's your bank's or that of another finan-

Web Link 5.35 cial institution.

---

[1]This is especially important if your employer monitors your computer usage for abuse of company resources.

HOW IS SAVINGS ACCOUNT INTEREST DETERMINED?

The most basic type of savings account is a passbook savings account. A passbook savings account has little or no constraints upon it in terms of when you can take the money out. The key features to consider for a savings account are usually the nominal interest rate, the frequency of compounding, and the method of determining the balance on which interest is paid. The relationship between the nominal interest rate and the frequency of compounding was developed in Chapter 4, but is repeated below. Specifically,

$$r_{ear} = (1 + r_{nom}/m)^m - 1$$

where

$$r_{ear} = \text{effective annual interest rate}$$

$$r_{nom} = \text{stated nominal annual interest rate}$$

$$m = \text{number of times per year compounding occurs}$$

For example, if a savings account pays 5 percent interest compounded quarterly, then the effective annual rate would be 5.09 percent ($[1 + .05/4]^4 - 1$).

There are a number of methods to determine the balance on which interest is paid. The simplest and most favorable for the bank is the low balance method. The bank finds the lowest balance in the account during the compounding period and pays interest on that amount. The most favorable method for the depositor is the average daily balance. There are a number of other variations, most of which fall someplace in between low balance and average daily balance in terms of desirability to a depositor. Although depository institutions are usually quite explicit in advertising the interest rate on an account, most say little to nothing (unless asked) about how they determine the balance on which interest is paid.

What Are Certificates of Deposit?

A **certificate of deposit** (CD) differs from a passbook savings account in that a CD has a time commitment to it. Typical time commitments include three months, six months, one year, and two years. The maturities may go out as far as 10 years, and may be as short as 30 days. The interest rate paid on a CD is higher than that paid on a passbook savings account, to give depositors incentive to guarantee that their money will remain on deposit for the term specified. You can withdraw from a CD before the maturity date, but you will pay a penalty. This penalty for early withdrawal will be the loss of all interest for a specified period of time. There usually are exceptions for obtaining a waiver of these penalties, but one would normally hope not to qualify for one of these exceptions. They include the death or legal mental incompetence of the depositor. Any early withdrawal penalty paid is included as an adjustment to income on your federal tax return but since the penalty would also have been included in your interest income, your taxable income isn't really reduced. The adjustment is only recognition that you did not actually receive the interest income that was deducted as a penalty.

Because there is usually no cash inflow or outflow associated with a CD, except for the accumulation of interest, the balance of a CD doesn't fluctuate. For that reason there

Web Link 5.5

is no concern about how the bank determines the balance on which interest is paid. There are usually minimum balance requirements to buy a CD, however, and these may vary from one depository institution to another.

The really critical variable on a CD is the interest rate. The amount of money you are going to deposit and the time horizon you desire should affect the amount of time you spend selecting the depository institution. If you want to deposit $500 for three months, then the place where you normally do most of your banking would probably be satisfactory. If you were depositing $10,000 for five years, then you would certainly want to do some research to obtain the best interest rate possible. A good place to start would be by viewing the national averages for the maturity of CD you wish to purchase.

Web Link (WSJ) 5.6

Web Link (WSJ) 5.7

WHAT ARE MONEY MARKET DEPOSIT ACCOUNTS?

Web Link (WSJ) 5.6

Web Link (WSJ) 5.7a

Money market deposit accounts (MMDAs) were authorized in 1982 to allow depository institutions to compete with money market mutual funds (which will be discussed later). MMDAs tie the interest rate on the account to market rates (unlike passbook savings accounts and CDs, which have fixed rates). These accounts usually carry limited check-writing privileges. As in the case of CDs, national averages and rates offered on MMDAs by particular depository institutions can be found at **Web Links (WSJ) 5.6** and **5.7.**

WHAT IS DEPOSIT INSURANCE?

All of the accounts described so far, checking, passbook savings, CDs, and MMDAs, are usually covered by deposit insurance. The primary deposit insurer is the **Federal Deposit Insurance Corporation,** or FDIC. The FDIC is an agency of the federal government[2] that insures accounts at commercial banks, savings and loans, and savings banks through two funds, the **Bank Insurance Fund** (BIF) and the **Savings Association Insurance Fund** (SAIF).

The FDIC currently insures depositors for $100,000,[3] but special kinds of accounts may be insured for more. If you have money on deposit in a bank that is covered by the FDIC and that bank fails, you are guaranteed to receive back at least the first $100,000 of your money on deposit. All other financial products sold by banks, including mutual funds, Treasury securities, and annuities, are NOT covered by deposit insurance. Deposit insurance does not cover the contents of your safe deposit box and it does not provide coverage in the event of a bank robbery, fire, or other destruction of the bank. Banks normally carry other types of insurance to protect against these losses.

The FDIC earns its primary income by charging each bank and savings and loan association it insures a premium based on the amount of deposits it carries. Because the FDIC has operated at a substantial profit over the years, it has built up a large reserve. In

---

[2]For detailed and or current information about the FDIC, the reader is referred to **Web Link 5.8.**

[3]The $100,000 limit for depositors was established in 1980. Prior to that, the limit had been $40,000. When deposit insurance was first created in the 1930s, the insurance limit was $2,000 per depositor.

1997, the FDIC earned a net income of $1.44 billion. These profits are transferred into the BIF and SAIF.

As a depositor you do not really have to worry whether the reserves of the FDIC are large enough to cover the losses if your particular bank or savings and loan goes under, for several reasons. The first is that the FDIC usually tries to arrange a merger of any failing financial institution. The merger process frequently allows the FDIC to avoid most or all of the costs of covering the deposits of failed institutions. The second reason is that the FDIC has the authority to borrow money from the U.S. Treasury to cover losses. The third reason is that Congress is absolutely dedicated to assuring that this country never incurs another **bank panic.** A bank panic happens when there is widespread loss of confidence in banks, causing people to withdraw their money from these institutions. Although any one person can always withdraw all of his or her money from a bank, if all of a bank's customers tried to do this simultaneously, the bank would fold no matter what its financial condition. Most economists believe that Congress will do whatever is necessary to sustain the confidence of the public in the FDIC's ability to insure accounts.

Deposit insurance is based on the names on the accounts, not the accounts. This means that if you have both a checking and a savings account in your name, then your deposit insurance coverage is $100,000 for both accounts combined, not $100,000 on each account. If you have enough money on deposit that this limitation creates a problem, there are several ways to bypass it. If you are married, you could have one account in your name, one account in your spouse's name, and one account as a joint account so that between you and your spouse you would have $300,000 in account coverage. If you have a child, then the combinations of single and joint accounts could increase your deposit coverage substantially.

Web Link 5.9

The FDIC has a calculator, found at **Web Link 5.9**, that will indicate the insurance status for any institution you name. If you are unsure of the name, you can enter the city and state of the institution to check its deposit insurance coverage. Be careful if you search by city and state because the banks are listed by the community where their home office is located, so even if a bank has a branch in your community, you may not find it listed under insured banks in your community. Other, broader methods of searching for a particular bank may be found at **Web Link 5.10.**

Web Link 5.10

Is the FDIC the Only Agency Providing Deposit Insurance?

There is one other agency that provides deposit insurance. **The National Credit Union Share Insurance Fund** (NCUSIF) is the federal fund created by Congress in 1970 to insure member's deposits in credit unions. By law, federally insured credit unions maintain one percent of their deposits in the NCUSIF. The NCUA Board, which overseas the NCUSIF, can levy a premium if necessary for additional revenue to cover its operating expenses or costs of closing failed institutions. The NCUA Board has charged only one premium in its history, when three large New England credit unions failed in 1992.

Web Link 5.11
Web Link 5.12

ARE THERE OTHER SAFE SAVINGS VEHICLES?

There are several ways to save money safely other than in accounts covered by deposit insurance. The three primary alternative investments are

1. Savings bonds
2. Treasury bills, notes, and bonds
3. Money market mutual funds

Although none of these three savings vehicles carry deposit insurance, the first two are actually safer than insured deposits and the risk of loss in the third is so remote that it is virtually impossible to envision.

WHAT ARE SAVINGS BONDS?

A bond is a piece of paper that represents the basic terms of a loan. The par value or face value of the bond is the principal that will be repaid at the maturity of the loan. It also usually represents the amount of money that was originally paid (i.e., lent) when the bond was sold by the issuer to the investor. Most bonds stipulate an interest rate, also known as a coupon rate, and pay this interest each year. Some bonds are sold at a price substantially lower than the par value. The interest on such bonds is paid in the appreciation of the price of the bond, which will equal the par value at maturity.

Savings bonds are sold by the U.S. Treasury to help pay for the cost of running the government. The traditional savings bonds, Series E bonds, were issued from May 1941 through June 30, 1980. Many investors still hold Series E bonds since the bonds have continued to accrue interest past their original maturity date. They were issued at 75 percent of face amount, and face values range from $25 to $10,000. On the back of a Series E bond is a schedule showing the amount you would receive back if you redeemed the bond on or after various dates. The increases in redemption values represent the accrual of interest that is being paid to the bond investor. The bonds are redeemable at nearly all commercial banks and at Federal Reserve Banks. Several calculators on the Internet will compute the current redemption value for these bonds.

It is February 2001. Oscar is looking through some old papers in his parents' house and finds a Series E Savings Bond with a $100 face value that was bought in his name in January 1975. He would like to know the current redemption value.

Web Link 5.13 As of February 2001, this bond could be redeemed for $449.16. Clearly this is a nice find for Oscar.

Series E bonds were replaced with Series EE bonds in July 1980. The purchase price of EE bonds is one-half the face value and face values range from $50 to $10,000. These bonds may be held for up to 30 years. You are limited to buying no more than $30,000 per year in face value of these bonds.

For both Series E and EE bonds, the interest may be reported on one's income taxes annually based on the increase in redemption value or at the time of final redemption (even if that includes the maturity of any HH bonds into which the EE bonds may be exchanged).

The interest rate paid by Series EE bonds is adjusted on May 1 and November 1 of each year, and is currently 90 percent of the average yields on five-year Treasury securities for the preceding six months. The redemption value is adjusted at six-month intervals. To ascertain the redemption value, consider the following example:

Web Link 5.16

> *Years ago Oscar purchased a $500 face value Series EE bond issued in March 1990. He had put it in his safe deposit box, and had forgotten about it until now. He is curious as to what the bond is currently worth (as of February 2001) and how much interest income he would have to declare if he cashed in the bond.*

Web Link 5.14

The redemption value as of February 2001 was $465.20. The purchase price of the bond, one-half of face value, was $250. If Oscar cashed in the bond on the above date, he would have to declare $215.15 (= $465.20 redemption value – $250 cost basis) in interest income.

In 1990, the Treasury Department introduced the Education Bond Program. This program allows the interest on Series E or EE bonds to be completely or partially excluded from federal income tax when the bond owner pays qualified higher education expenses to an eligible institution or a state tuition plan in the same calendar year the bonds are redeemed.[4]

Series H bonds were first offered on June 1, 1952. They differed from Series E bonds in that they were bought at face value in denominations of $500 to $10,000 and paid interest semi-annually. Series H bonds were replaced by Series HH bonds on January 1, 1980, but Series H bonds issued between February 1957 and December 1979 were granted extended maturities for up to 30 years. So the last of the Series H bonds sold could be good through December 2009. Series H interest payments are taxable in the year received. Series H bonds can be redeemed only at Federal Reserve Banks.

Series HH bonds are not much different than Series H bonds. They are current-income securities that are bought at face values ranging from $500 to $10,000 with interest paid semiannually by a direct deposit to your checking or savings account. One difference between Series H and HH bonds is that the latter can be bought only by exchanging Series EE, Series E, savings notes, or matured Series H bonds. HH bonds pay interest at a fixed rate set on the day you buy the bond; the current rate of 4 percent has been in effect since March 1, 1993. Interest rates are reset on the 10th anniversary of the HH bonds' issue date if you continue to hold the bonds.

The most recent savings bond offering is the Series I bond, radically different from the Series EE or HH. The Series I interest rate has two components. The first is a fixed rate that provides a real rate of return, and which is set afresh on every new bond issue. The second is an inflation adjustment factor, which is reset every May and November. The Treasury declared that if prices actually go down during any period (if the inflation rate is negative) by an amount greater than the fixed rate component, then the interest rate will be set to zero. The interest accrues monthly and is compounded semiannually. You can cash in Series I bonds at any time and receive interest up through the most recent month. If you cash Series E/EE or H/HH bonds early, you receive interest only through the last interest payment date, so to cash these bonds one day before an interest payment or accrual date

---

[4]There are income limits to this program. In 1999, the exemption was not available for taxpayers filing singly with modified AGIs of more than $68,100 or for married taxpayers filing jointly with modified AGIs of more than $109,650. The current limits are provided at **Web Link 5.15.**

would cost you almost six months worth of interest. The Series I bonds may be held for up to 30 years.

Series I bonds are nonredeemable for six months, and there is a redemption penalty of three months' worth of interest if they are redeemed in the first five years. To compute the inflation rate for setting the interest rate on this bond the Treasury uses the Consumer Price Index for All Urban Consumers: U.S. City Average for All Items (CPI-U). The current rate on new Series I bonds may be found at **Web Link 5.16.**

Web Link 5.16

WHAT ARE TREASURY BILLS, NOTES, AND BONDS?

Treasury bills, notes, and bonds are marketable securities issued by the Treasury to finance government operations. They are nothing more than simple IOUs issued by the federal government. At the time of writing, the current debt of the federal government is $5,653,380,479,214.62. The current debt is posted daily by the Bureau of Public Debt and can be found at **Web Link 5.17.** The public debt randomly fluctuates up and down and can change by $30 or $40 billion in a single day. Because the federal government is currently running surpluses (meaning it is taking in more in the form of revenues—including income taxes—than it is spending on its programs and operations), the total amount of debt is more likely to go down than up in the next few years. It is this debt that is financed by Treasury bills, notes, and bonds, as well as the savings bonds discussed previously.

Web Link 5.17

Treasury bills are substantially different than notes and bonds. Upon issuance, Treasury bills have a maturity of no more than one year and most have a maturity of no more than 13 weeks. At the time of writing, there was $725,517,000,000 worth of Treasury bills outstanding with an average interest yield of 4.702 percent.

Web Link 5.18

Treasury bills are pure discount instruments. This means that they are sold at a price less than par. Par is $10,000. At maturity, the owner of a Treasury bill receives back par. The difference between the purchase price of a Treasury bill and what it is sold for or matures at is treated as interest income for tax purposes. Capital gains do not exist for Treasury bills, because all price change is by definition interest income.

Because of their short maturity and the perception that the U.S. government is financially the strongest and safest in the world, Treasury bills are considered the essence of a risk-free investment. The only risk associated with investing in Treasury bills is the loss of purchasing power that is referred to as inflation risk. However, in this period of low inflation and because of the relatively short maturity of these securities, this risk is currently negligible.

Treasury notes and bonds pay interest semiannually. The primary difference between a Treasury note and a Treasury bond is their term to maturity. Notes generally have a term to maturity of 1 to 10 years and bonds 10 to 30 years. The par value on a note or bond may be $1,000, $5,000, or $10,000. In general, notes and bonds are considered investment assets rather than liquid assets because of their term to maturity. Despite the original term to maturity on a note or bond, as a liquid asset there is no significant difference between a Treasury note or bond with less than one year to maturity and a Treasury bill with a comparable maturity.

How Do I Find Current Market Prices on Treasury Bills, Notes, and Bonds?

Quotes on Treasury bills, notes, and bonds may be found at **Web Link (WSJ) 5.19.** The quotations are in order of increasing maturity, so finding the most recent quote for a particular security may be somewhat difficult. Also, Treasury bills are quoted in a slightly different manner than notes and bonds.

In the table found at **Web Link (WSJ) 5.19,** the two important columns for Treasury bills are the bid yield column and the ask yield column. Treasury bills are quoted using an approximation formula for their yield to maturity. To determine the actual dollar price of a Treasury bill, you must convert the yield price into dollars via the formula. The ask yield column represents the price you would have to pay if you wanted to buy that particular Treasury bill. The bid yield column represents the price you would receive if you wanted to sell that particular security. The bid yield always translates into a lower dollar price than the ask yield.

For Treasury notes and bonds, the two most important columns are the bid price and the ask price column. The numbers in these columns are quoted as a percentage of par value. As with Treasury bills, the ask price is the price you would pay for the notes or bonds, and the bid price is the price you would receive if you sold your notes or bonds.

> Oscar would like to buy $20,000 worth of par value of the Treasury bonds that mature February 15, 2004. What are the current bid and ask prices for this bond?

At the time of writing, the bid price is 103.1484 and the ask price is 103.2109. Oscar wants to buy bonds, so he will pay the ask price. Because the price is quoted as a percentage of par, we need to multiply the ask price by the par value amount he wants to buy. In this case, the bonds would cost Oscar $20,642.18 ($20,000 × 103.2109%).

Approximate yields to maturity on various Treasury securities may be found at **Web Link 5.23.**[5] In this table, which displays yields on many different securities, the yields on Treasury bills, notes, and bonds are shown in the format known as constant maturities. With constant maturity, a bill, note, or bond of that specific maturity may not actually exist on the date of release, but the yield shown is what the yield of such a security would likely be if such a security existed. The estimated yield is based on the actual yields of securities whose maturities are immediately before and after the designated date. For example, the yield for a 10-year Treasury bond on April 23, 1999, was shown as 5.26 percent. A Treasury bond with exactly 10 years to maturity may not have existed on that day, but if it had, its yield would have been approximately 5.26 percent.

How Do I Buy Treasury Securities?

There are two ways to buy Treasury securities. One is through a stockbroker. In fact, many of the Internet-based brokerage services allow you to enter orders online for various Treasury securities. The one drawback is that the online menu of Treasury securities you can buy is usually limited. If you telephone an order, you can choose any security to buy.

The other way to buy Treasury securities is by opening an account with a Federal Reserve Bank to buy new securities when they are auctioned off. Each time the Treasury

---

[5]The concept of yield to maturity will be discussed in Chapter 13.

needs to raise additional monies, it sells a new bond issue through an auction process. Anyone may place a bid at the auction. There are two types of bids: competitive and noncompetitive. In a competitive bid, you are bidding a specific price for a specific face value amount of bonds. Competitive bids may be only on paper. In a noncompetitive bid, you indicate you are willing to pay the same price as the average winning competitive bid. Noncompetitive bids may be placed over the Internet, by phone, or on paper. For each issue, the Treasury totals the face value amounts of noncompetitive bids, which determines how much of the issue will be sold via competitive bids. It then rank orders the competitive bids starting with the highest dollar bid per bond. The competitive bids are accepted until the issue has been fully distributed. For example, assume the Treasury brings out an issue for $500,000,000 in face value. If the Treasury receives noncompetitive bids totaling $300,000,000, then it would look to the competitive bids for the first $200,000,000 with the highest dollar prices per bond. Based on the prices from the competitive bids, the price for the noncompetitive bids is then set.

Web Link 5.20
Web Link 5.21

If you wish to buy Treasury securities via noncompetitive bids, the easiest way is to open a **Treasury Direct account.** This is an account with the Treasury from which new purchases can be made, and into which maturities are deposited. Currently, you are charged for holding this account only if you have more than $100,000 worth of par of securities in the account. In this case, a $25 annual fee is imposed. Since even one such purchase through most stockbrokers would usually require a commission of at least this much, it is quite a bargain. If your account has less than $100,000 in Treasury securities, there is no fee.

Web Link 5.22

WHAT ARE MONEY MARKET MUTUAL FUNDS?

A **money market mutual fund** (MMMF) is just one in the broad category of investments known as investment companies. Although Chapter 15 is devoted to a discussion of investment companies, it is appropriate to discuss this specific form here. The basic idea behind any investment company is that many investors pool their money and then the money is used to buy various securities. The investors hold shares in investment companies, and the investment companies hold the securities. Before opening an account in an MMMF, an investor should read carefully the prospectus for that fund.

Web Link 5.34

What separates MMMFs from other investment companies is that MMMFs invest only in **money market instruments.** The most common money market instrument is the Treasury bill. The other major money market instruments include **commercial paper, negotiable CDs, banker's acceptances,** and **repurchase agreements.**

When you buy shares in an MMMF, you are buying a claim on a portfolio that owns only money market instruments. Indirectly, you own a small share of these money market instruments. Money market instruments are characterized as having a large denomination; with the exception of Treasury bills, most money market instruments have a par value of anywhere from $100,000 to $1,000,000. Only the richest individual investors could afford to purchase these securities directly. Money market instruments are highly safe short-term debt instruments. As mentioned before, Treasury bills are considered the safest investment in the world; other money market instruments are just one short step behind Treasury bills in terms of safety. The maturities of money market instruments are no more than one year and frequently no more than six months. Finally, most money market instruments trade in highly liquid markets.

Web Link
(WSJ) 5.31

The current yields on major money market instruments are provided at **Web Link (WSJ) 5.31.** A copy of this web page for August 1, 2001 is provided in Figure 5.1.

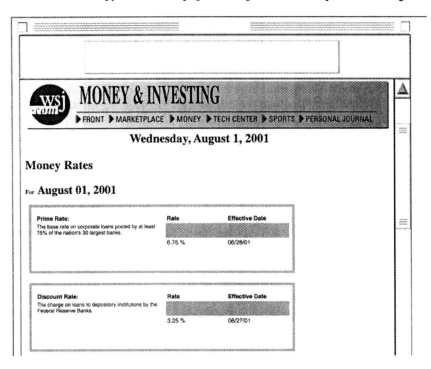

FIGURE 5-1 Money market rates

Commercial paper is a short-term IOU issued by the largest and safest corporations in the country. If General Motors needed $100,000,000 for the next six months, the company might raise the money by selling six-month commercial paper. The well-known corporate name combined with the perception of a high degree of safety would make selling the commercial paper a relatively simple operation. The maximum maturity on commercial paper is 270 days, and the average maturity is 30 days.[6] Commercial paper comes in denominations ranging from $100,000 to $1,000,000. It is most commonly sold on a discount basis just like Treasury bills, but is occasionally sold at par "with interest to follow." If the reputation of the issuer of the commercial paper is anything less than superb, the issuer will obtain a letter of credit from a major bank guaranteeing that the bank will provide the funds to pay off the commercial paper if necessary. The risk of default is incredibly small on commercial paper.

Web Link 5.25
Web Link 5.26

---

[6]If the maximum maturity were longer than 270 days than the issuer of the commercial paper would incur substantial registration costs because the Securities and Exchange Commission would classify the paper as a long-term debt instrument.

Web Link 5.27

Negotiable CDs differ from the regular or nonnegotiable CDs discussed earlier in this chapter in that negotiable CDs usually have a par value of $1,000,000. If you want your money back early with a nonnegotiable CD, you can cash in the CD at the bank and pay the early withdrawal penalty. With a negotiable CD, you can sell the instrument to another investor at current market price.

Banker's acceptances (BAs) are more complex instruments than the other money market securities. BAs are normally created in conjunction with international trade. Suppose Joe's Import Company wishes to buy some hats from Jose's Export Company in Argentina. Joe is hesitant to send Jose the money before he receives the hats, and Jose is hesitant to ship until he sees proof of payment. So, when Joe receives documentation that the hats have been sent, he sends paperwork to his bank, which then stamps the invoice as accepted. In a specified number of days, the bank agrees to pay the face amount of the invoice to Jose. Joe agrees to pay his bank. The invoice marked accepted is then sold in the secondary market and becomes known as a banker's acceptance. Because the BA has both the guarantees of Joe and his bank, it is known as two-signature paper and is considered incredibly safe as an investment.

Web Link 5.28
Web Link 5.29

The last popular money market instrument is the repurchase agreement, or repo. In a repurchase agreement, a person sells some securities to a second party with an agreement that the first party will buy the securities back at a specified date and a specified price. The securities sold are usually money market instruments. The loan is extremely safe because the securities that were sold to the second party serve as collateral. As long as the market value of the securities sold exceeds the amount of the loan, it is virtually impossible for the second party to lose any money.

Web Link 5.30

As indicated above, an MMMF is distinguished from other investment companies in that it holds in its portfolio primarily the five money market instruments just described. To keep the accounting process simple, an MMMF declares dividends daily on its portfolio. It is then able to maintain its daily share price at exactly $1. So in an MMMF, there is no distinction between the number of shares you own in the fund and the dollar value of those shares. If you have 5,325.27 shares, then your investment is worth exactly $5,325.27. The interest is normally credited to your account on a monthly basis. The monthly interest is paid in the form of additional shares if you have the interest accrued in your account and it is sent as a check if you are having the cash distributed. MMMFs provide a check-writing feature with their accounts, usually with a minimum amount required for each check. Other than this minimum amount requirement, an MMMF can work much like a checking account for an individual.

Web Link 5.32
Web Link 5.33

Banks and the other depository institutions are always quick to point out that money deposited with them is insured and cash in an MMMF is not insured. This is true. However, the degree of safety in the securities held in the MMMFs' portfolios is so strong that the need for insurance is moot.

SUMMARY

> ➤ The amount of liquidity a person should hold depends on a multitude of issues, including job security, alternative sources of income, and availability of loans from other sources.

> ➤ The primary financial institutions that provide liquidity are commercial banks, savings banks, savings and loans, credit unions, and money market mutual funds.

> ➤ Checks come in a variety of forms, including certified checks, cashier's or bank checks, money orders, and even traveler's checks.

> ➤ Most people use blank endorsements or restrictive endorsements, but other endorsement forms are appropriate at times.

> ➤ The growth in online banking will change the nature of banking for many, whether it is done with proprietary software or through web sites.

> ➤ Consumers need to be aware how interest is calculated on various accounts and how the balance on which interest is paid is computed.

> ➤ Deposit insurance coverage is based on the name or names on an account and not on a per-account basis.

> ➤ Deposit insurance provided by the FDIC and NCUASIF undoubtedly provides comfort to many.

> ➤ There are many other investments that are as safe as insured deposits. These include Treasury bills, notes, and bonds, which are various forms of debt issued by the U.S. Treasury.

> ➤ The current forms of savings bonds sold to the public are Series EE, HH, and I savings bonds. These differ from Treasury bonds in that they can only be redeemed, not sold.

KEY TERMS

bank check	Bank Insurance Fund	bank panic
banker's acceptance	blank endorsement	cashier's check
certificate of deposit	certified check	commercial bank
commercial paper	credit union	electronic funds transfer system
Federal Deposit Insurance Corporation	field of membership	liquidity
minimum average daily balance	minimum balance	money market deposit account
money market instrument	money market mutual fund	money order
National Credit Union Share Insurance Fund	negotiable CD	qualified endorsement
repurchase agreement	restrictive endorsement	savings and loan
Savings Association Insurance Fund	savings bank	special endorsement
Treasury Direct account	truncation	

PROBLEMS

5.1 If Adam received a $100 Series EE savings bonds for each of his first three birthdays (he was born March 24, 1981), how much cash did he receive if he redeemed them in December of 2000?

5.2 John is purchasing $10,000 worth of par value at Treasury bonds that will mature April 15, 2006. If the bid price is 105.1240 and the ask price is 105.6321, how much money does John need to purchase the bonds?

5.3 What is the difference between a NOW account and a checking account?

5.4 If you have 13,156 shares in a money market mutual fund (MMMF), how much is your investment worth?

REFERENCES

Web Link 5.47 Deposit insurance in other countries
Web Link 5.48 Deposit insurance reform

WALL STREET JOURNAL RESOURCES

Web Link (WSJ) 5.42 "Banks Cater to Young Savers," *The Wall Street Journal Interactive Edition*, October 31, 1999

Web Link (WSJ) 5.43 "Traveler's Checks Lose Their Luster," *The Wall Street Journal Interactive Edition*, August 20, 1999

Web Link (WSJ) 5.44 "Plan Ahead and Shop Around to Avoid a String of Bank Fees," *The Wall Street Journal Interactive Edition*, September 19, 1999

Web Link (WSJ) 5.45 "Credit Unions Have an Edge Over Banks on Basic Service," *The Wall Street Journal Interactive Edition*, March 2, 1998

Web Link (WSJ) 5.46 "Use of On-Line Banking Grows as Banks Offer New Features," *The Wall Street Journal Interactive Edition*, February 2, 1998

For information that has changed since the book was written, for new information that pertains to this topic, and for some new web sites that pertain to the topic of this chapter, see **Web Link 5.49.**

PART II

BUYING ASSETS AND TAKING ON DEBT

CHAPTER 6

BORROWING ON OPEN ACCOUNT

LEARNING OBJECTIVES

- Discuss the pros and cons of using credit
- Describe credit cards and analyze their features
- Describe how debit cards and secured credit cards work
- List the protections a consumer has with credit cards
- Compute whether a home equity line of credit is beneficial
- Compute how large a home equity line of credit can be obtained
- Describe the difference between a credit counselor and a credit "doctor"
- Describe a FICO score and how it is computed
- Discuss the role of the credit bureaus

Web Link: www.wiley.com/college/woerheide

INTRODUCTION

Borrowing on open account is any credit account from which money is borrowed only as needed and which offers flexibility in the repayment of the loan. Credit cards are the most obvious example of open credit. You do not borrow any money until you make a purchase with a credit card. When you receive the monthly statement, you usually have the choice to pay the entire amount owed, a minimum payment, or some amount in between. There are several types of credit cards. Most are bank credit cards, which include Visa, Master-Card, and Discover. A credit card can be used with any merchant who accepts that particular type of card.

A second example of open credit is a travel and entertainment, or T&E, card. The best-known examples of these cards are American Express and Diners Club. T&E cards do not charge interest, since they require payment in full every month. They do, however, charge late fees. If these late fees were treated as interest charges, they would represent a rather high rate of interest.

A third form of open credit is a charge card. Charge cards are the credit cards issued by a merchant for use only in its own stores. Examples of these include any of the gasoline company cards and department store cards such as Sears and JC Penney. A home equity line of credit is another form of open credit.

Web Link 6.1

In this chapter we will explore the various types of open credit, including debit cards. We will also consider some of the common decisions people make in selecting and using credit cards. Because credit cards have a heavy impact on people who get into financial difficulty and/or must declare bankruptcy, we will also look at the process of getting credit in this chapter. A short quiz to analyze your ability to effectively handle credit is provided in **Web Link 6.1.**

USING CREDIT CARDS

Web Link 6.2

Using credit carries substantial advantages over paying cash or writing a check. First, the Fair Credit Billing Act gives you a lot of protections you would not have if you paid cash. Second, cash is usually unrecoverable if lost or stolen but a credit card may limit your loss to a maximum of $50. If you are able to report the loss quickly enough, there may be no loss whatsoever. Third, if you charge $500 every month and pay it off every month, then using your credit card is like getting a one-time free $500 loan. The first month you use the card, you avoid $500 in upfront payments. In the second month you use the card, you pay your bill from the first month, but postpone payment on the second month's bill until the third month.

The major disadvantage to using a credit card is the possibility that it may induce you to make purchases you cannot afford. A sign of this problem is the inability to pay your credit card bill in full every month. Many credit cards have effective annual rates as high as 19 percent. If you fail to pay your bill in full every month, you could end up borrowing money at an incredibly high rate. Credit cards are also useful because some businesses, such as airlines and hotels, will not provide services if you do not have a credit card.

What Are Bank Credit Cards? The bank credit card is the primary type of credit card. Bank credit cards include Visa, MasterCard, Optima, and Discover. Each bank issues its own credit card under one of these program names and selects its own customers, so the credit account is with the bank itself, and not with the credit card corporation. Any one bank can offer more than one type of bank credit card, although each bank may opt to promote one type of credit card over the others.

Banks make money in three ways from credit cards. First, they charge the vendor a small percentage for processing the credit card payment. A typical vendor fee is one to two percent of the charges. Second, the banks charge interest whenever the balance is not paid in full. Third, they sometimes charge an annual fee. The biggest expense to the bank is that of loan defaults. Thus, the most desirable customers for a bank to issue a credit card to are those who use their cards extensively, and have sufficient assets and income that they are unlikely to default on any unpaid balances.

The credit card business has been so profitable in recent years that banks are constantly seeking new customers. The average person between the ages of 20 and 65 receives well over 20 credit card solicitations per year, and that number keeps going up. To encourage people to respond to these credit card offers, banks offer a multitude of attractive features.

How Does a Credit Card Work?

The key feature to how a credit card works is the magnetic strip on the back of each credit card. This strip contains information about your account. For example, on a MasterCard card there are two tracks. The first contains your name, the card's expiration date, card type, and data such as your PIN and credit limit. The second track contains your account number, start date, and other discretionary data.

Account numbers are 16 digits. The first six digits identify the company that issued the card. The next four digits indicate region and branch information for the issuer. The next five digits are your unique account numbers. The last digit is a check digit for extra security. If the check digit is not consistent with a formula that uses the first 15 digits, then the card company knows the account number is either reported in error or fraudulent.

All cards carry expiration dates, which range from 12 to 36 months from the time of issue. A new card is issued about 30 days before the expiration date if there are no problems with the account. More and more cards now contain a holographic image, which is invisible to the naked eye but which can be seen under an ultraviolet lamp. A quick scan of this image can be used to verify a card's authenticity.

Is the Annual Fee Negotiable?

Credit cards have many features and characteristics that can vary widely. It is difficult to say which feature or characteristic is most important because the relative importance depends on how a card is utilized. One feature that is always important is the annual fee charged on the card. Annual fees range from zero to $50 or more. Some credit card companies will waive the annual fee if you ask them. Other companies will waive the fee if you charge enough on your card over the course of the year to make you a valuable customer. If you are going to ask for a waiver, do it before the anniversary date on which the annual fee is charged. At that time you can threaten to cancel your card and take your business elsewhere. After the fee is formally charged, you have less bargaining power.

Web Link 6.4

How Important Is a Credit Card's Interest Rate?

A feature that can be important is the interest rate charged on balances carried over from one billing period to the next. For people who pay their bill in full every month, the interest rate is irrelevant. For people who carry substantial balances from one month to the next, the interest rate may be extremely important.

Dan Tessoni recently saw on TV that some credit cards charge outrageous interest rates. Dan had never given much thought to the interest rate on his card. He was attracted to his current card because it has no annual fee. Dan currently has an outstanding balance on his card of $5,000. He charges an average of $500 per month and makes payments of $600 per month. The interest rate is 18 percent (or 1.5 percent per month). Dan wants to know how much impact the interest rate is having on the amount of time it takes him to pay off his balance.

Web Link 6.5

The solution may be found using any of the calculators at **Web Link 6.5.** At an 18 percent interest rate, it will take Dan approximately 95 months (almost 8 years) to pay off his outstanding balance. Dan's monthly statement includes a $75 interest charge. This interest charge equals the $5,000 outstanding balance Dan owes times the 1.5 percent monthly interest rate on the loan.[2] Dan is paying only an extra $100 per month toward reducing his outstanding balance, leaving only $25 to go toward a reduction of the loan. The calculator also shows via a graph that if the interest rate on the credit card were 12 percent, Dan could pay off the loan in 70 months (almost 6 years), and at a 7 percent rate, the loan could be paid off in 60 months (5 years).

If Dan wants to improve his financial situation, there are two things he could consider. The first would be to find a card with a lower rate or take out a bank loan at a lower rate and use the loan proceeds to pay off the credit card loan. The other action Dan could take is to increase his monthly payments.

> *Dan owes $5,000 on his credit card and anticipates future monthly charges of $500. He had planned to make monthly payments of $600, but now that he has found out how long it will take to pay off his loan, he has decided to increase his monthly payment to $700. His goal is to pay off his loan within 24 months. Dan anticipates no changes in the current interest rate of 18 percent. There is no annual fee with his card. Will this strategy of paying an extra $200 per month help him achieve his 24-month goal? If not, how much extra will he have to pay per month to achieve his goal?*

Web Link 6.6

To pay off the loan in 24 months, Dan would actually have to make payments of $751 per month. If he sticks to $700 per month, it will take him 32 months to pay off the loan.

Some cards come with what are known as **teaser rates.** A teaser rate is an unusually low initial interest rate on balances transferred from other cards. Teaser rates are marketing ploys to attract the attention of potential cardholders. Teaser rates probably also help convince people that it is worth the effort to apply for the new card with the teaser rate and to transfer the balances. If the only rates credit card companies charged were teaser rates, they would go out of business quite quickly, so the ongoing offerings of teaser rates suggest that most people do not pay off the balances during the introductory period. Even if you don't pay off the balance during the introductory period, there may be value to teaser rates. Suppose your current interest rate is 18 percent (or 1.5 percent per month). If you have a $5,000 balance on your credit card and another company offers you a teaser rate of 6 percent (or .5 percent per month) for three months before reverting to an 18 percent annual rate, how much would this teaser rate be worth? First, the teaser rate is saving you 1 percent per month (1.5% − .5%). If we assume there is no significant change in the balance you owe, then one percent per month on $5,000 translates into a monthly saving of $50. For three months, that would be savings of $150.

> *Dan Tessoni is thinking about a new credit card. He currently has a balance outstanding of $3,000. He plans future monthly payments of $500, but anticipates average future monthly charges of $400. He is considering two credit cards, both of which have lower rates than his current card. The first card has a regular rate of 12 percent and an annual fee of $35. It also comes with a teaser introductory rate of 4 percent that will be good for the next three months. The second card has no annual*

---

[2]Credit cards differ in how the balance on which interest is charged is determined.

fee, but has a regular rate of 14 percent. It too comes with a teaser rate, but this rate is 6 percent and is good for four months. Which card is the better deal for him over the next three years?

Web Link 6.7

The solution may be found using any of the calculators at **Web Link 6.7.** The calculators indicate that over the next three years, the card with the annual fee will save Dan a total of $16. In other words, there is really not much difference between the two cards. One way to think about the problem is ignore the teaser rates and focus on the fact that Dan is initially saving 2 percent per year with the lower interest rate (14% − 12% = 2%). On an initial balance of $3,000, this produces annual interest savings of $60. It makes sense to spend a $35 annual fee to achieve a $60 savings. In the above problem, however, Dan is slowly paying off his balance over time since he pays $100 more each month than what is represented by his new charges. As his loan balance goes down, the value of the interest savings diminishes. The chart on the web calculator that is labeled "Cumulative cost over time" shows that for up to 39 months the card with the annual fee is the cheaper card, but that after 39 months, the card *without* the annual fee becomes the cheaper card. At that point the annual fee can no longer be justified in terms of the interest savings because the interest payment is small since the balance owed is smaller. The final solution is that Dan should take out the card with the fee for 38 months and then close that card and move his business to the card without the fee.

Another attractive feature in credit cards is airline mileage. Many banks offer a bonus in airline miles for signing up for their card, and often offer one-frequent-flyer-mile credit for every dollar charged on the card. There are sometimes limits on the amount of mileage that can be earned in any one year and usually a high annual fee and/or a high interest rate. The trick to deciding if one of these cards is worthwhile is to estimate how many frequent flyer miles you will earn in a year, how many miles will be used in applying for a particular flight, and what the cost of that flight might have been.

> *Dan has decided that he would like to compare a flight mileage card to a low-rate card. Neither card offers an introductory rate. The flight card charges 18 percent on unpaid balances, and the low-rate card charges 12 percent. The flight card carries a $50 annual fee and the low-rate card carries a $35 annual fee. Dan currently has a balance on his credit card of $5,000. He expects to charge an average of $500 per month in the future and to make monthly payments of $600. The flight card pays 1 frequent flyer mile per dollar charged on the card, and provides a 2,000-mile bonus for activating the card. A maximum of 60,000 in frequent flyer miles per year can be earned. The airline that the card is associated with charges 20,000 miles for the particular flight Dan would like to take. Normally the airline ticket would cost Dan $700. Which card should Dan take out if he plans to use this card for at least three years?*

Web Link 6.8

The low-rate card will cost Dan $316 less over the three-year period. The basic elements of the analysis are fairly simple. If Dan is charging $500 per month in new charges, he is charging $6,000 per year ($500 × 12) and earning 6,000 frequent flyer miles per year. With the activation bonus, he will earn his first free trip in exactly three years. But thereafter, it will take him three years and four months to earn another trip worth $700. The incremental annual fee costs Dan $15 per year and $45 over the next three years. This comparison clearly favors the flight card. But because Dan is carrying more than $5,000 in credit card debt, choosing the flight card will cost him almost $300 in extra interest the first year. If Dan were transferring no balances to the new card and would pay his bill in full each month, then the flight card would cost Dan $655 less ($700 free flight every 3 years – 45 incremental fees every 3 years) over the three-year period. Dan should stick with a low-rate card until he gets his balances paid down sufficiently, and then switch to the flight card.

Other credit cards offer a cash rebate at the end of the year, credit with a particular vendor at the end of the year, or an immediate discount on purchases with a particular vendor. If it is certain that you will spend the credit with the merchant, then there is no difference between a cash rebate and merchant credit.

> *Dan is trying to choose between a rebate card and a card with a low-interest rate. Neither card has an introductory rate. The rebate card has an interest rate of 18 percent and the low-rate card has a rate of 12 percent. The rebate card carries an annual fee of $25 and the low-rate card has an annual fee of $35. Dan has a current credit card balance of $5,000, which he would transfer to the new card. He expects to charge an average of $500 per month on the card and to pay an average of $700 per month. The rebate card provides a 1 percent rebate on all purchases and a 5 percent rebate at Wegmans Grocery Store. Dan spends about $100 per month at Wegmans. The maximum rebate is $1,000 per year but there is no lifetime limit on the rebate. The rebate would be paid to Dan in cash each year. Which card is the better deal for Dan over the next three years?*

Web Link 6.9

Dan would save approximately $208 with the low-rate card over the next three years. The major factor is again the interest on the outstanding balance. The interest on the rebate card will cost Dan nearly $300 more than the low-rate card in the first year. If Dan charges $500 per month on the rebate card, he will spend $6,000 per year and the 1 percent rebate will deliver only $60 in cash back. The 5 percent rebate on the purchases at Wegmans will contribute another $60 per year ($100 × 12 × 5%). Finally, the rebate card will save Dan $10 in annual fees. The combined benefits total approximately $130. This is nowhere near the interest saving of nearly $300 on the low-interest-rate card. If the outstanding balance were eliminated from the problem, then the rebate card unquestionably becomes the card of choice.

In the above example, the cash rebate described is a fixed percentage of all purchases. Many times the cash rebate is structured as a step function. For example, a card that advertises cash rebates "up to 1 percent" may provide rebates as follows: $\frac{1}{4}$ percent on the first $1,000 of purchases during a 12-month period, $\frac{1}{2}$ percent on the second $1,000 of purchases during the period, $\frac{3}{4}$ percent on the next $1,000 of purchases during the period, and then a full 1 percent on all purchases over $3,000 during the period. Let's see how this works for someone charging an average of $500 per month, or $6,000 per year. In this case, this person would receive the following cash rebate:

$$\frac{1}{4}\% \times \$1,000 = \$2.50$$
$$\frac{1}{2}\% \times \$1,000 = 5.00$$
$$\frac{3}{4}\% \times \$1,000 = 7.50$$
$$1\% \times \$3,000 = \underline{30.00}$$
$$\$45.00$$

A cash rebate of $45 on total annual purchases in this case actually works out to $\frac{3}{4}$ of 1 percent ($45 rebate/ $6,000 total charges). A true 1 percent rebate would be $60 in this example. If one were using the rebate calculator at **Web Link 6.9** to compare a low-interest-rate card to this rebate card, one would use $\frac{3}{4}$ of 1 percent as the cash rebate figure, not the full 1 percent.

Still other credit cards offer "gold" card or "platinum" card features. Gold and platinum cards offer substantially higher credit limits and usually provide extra services and insurance benefits. Examples of services and benefits include collision damage waiver on auto rentals, travel insurance, extended warranty on purchases, and roadside assistance. A big selling point of these cards is that they carry prestige. The interest rate on these cards may be as much as 1 percent lower than on the regular card, but the annual fee is usually higher. When bank credit cards first became popular in the fifties and sixties, there was only one card with one set of terms per issuer, but not all customers were equally desirable.

Credit card issuers eventually found that to obtain the most desirable customers, they had to offer terms more attractive than their standard credit cards, so they created gold and platinum cards. To qualify, the prospective card user must have higher assets and income than the typical applicant for the regular credit card.

Web Link 6.10

Some credit cards are issued as affinity cards. The issuer of an **affinity card** agrees to turn a small percentage of the user's total charges over to a specific group. For example, some universities give alumni lists to a credit card company to solicit an affinity card that provides payments to the university. The card provider might pay the university $\frac{1}{2}$ percent of all purchases made on the card. If knowing you are sending money to your affinity group makes you feel good, then there might be some value in obtaining such a card. But all cards should be evaluated primarily in terms of what they do for you. Are the annual fee, the interest rate, the grace period, and the other characteristics the best deal you can obtain? If not, you should go with another card. If you still want to do something for your affinity group, then take some or all of the money you save with a cheaper credit card and donate it directly to the affinity organization. The direct donation is tax deductible if you itemize. An indirect donation through an affinity credit card is *not* a tax-deductible contribution.

Is the Cheaper Rate Always the Better Deal?   As obvious as the above question may seem, the answer is no. There is more to the computation of your interest charge than just the interest rate. There is also the computation of the debt balance to which the interest rate is applied. The most common method of determining the debt balance is the **average daily balance,** in which each month's daily balances are added together, then divided by the number of days in the month. Some card issuers will use the average daily balance from the previous month. Others will add the new charges from the current month to determine the average daily balance. Most card issuers use only the last billing cycle to compute the average daily balance. Some card issuers compute average daily balance based on the last two billing cycles. The best deal is usually the card that calculates daily balances based on the most recent cycle only and excludes new purchases.

Two other methods of computing the balance on which interest is charged are the **previous balance** method and the **adjusted balance** method. In the former, the loan balance is based on the amount owed at the end of the previous billing period. In the latter, all payments during the month are subtracted from the balance owed at the end of the previous month.

The **grace period** can also be important on a card. The grace period is the amount of time a lender allows before charging interest on any balance due. Most card companies use a grace period of 25 days from the date of the bill. Some companies have no grace period. This means that interest starts accruing from the date of the purchase.

It is important to note that credit card companies use approximately the same billing date each month for a customer. If you plan a major purchase and make it on the day after your billing date, you could postpone your payment to nearly two months from the date of purchase without incurring interest charges. That is, you would have almost a full month from the date of purchase to the next billing date, and then another 25 days for the grace period.

Some card issuers will charge you an **overlimit fee.** If you exceed the credit limit for your account, they might not only put a freeze on your account but also charge you. Overlimit fees usually run $20 to $25. Card issuers may also impose a **late fee** if your payment arrives after the grace period. These late fees can reach $25.

Some card issuers also charge a **transaction fee** for a cash advance. A cash advance is a loan taken through the credit card. Interest is charged from the day of the loan. Cash advance fees may be fixed in dollar terms (e.g., $2), fixed in percentage terms (e.g., 1% to 2% of the cash advance), or even some combination of both. The transaction fee is in addition to the interest that is charged you on the cash advance balance. The interest rate on cash advances is usually, but not always, the same interest rate as on purchases. If the two interest rates differ, make sure when you make payments above the minimum that the excess funds are directed toward the balance with the higher interest rate.

Other fees that have popped up in recent years include a lack of use fee, a fee for closing an account, and a fee for paying off your balance in full each month over the course of a year. A **lack of use fee** might be imposed for failure to use a card over as little as a six-month period.

When you use your credit card in a foreign country, some card companies will add a currency conversion fee of from 1 percent to 4 percent.

Another recent trend among credit card companies is to change their contracts to allow them to raise your interest rate if you have late payments to any creditors. If you are late making a monthly payment to a department store on a store charge card, your bank could raise your credit card rate. The credit card companies contend this policy better matches the interest rate on each account with the risk of default potential of that account.

Finally, if you plan to make less than full payment at times, you may want to consider how the credit card company computes the minimum payment. Most companies require a minimum of the greater of 2 percent of the balance due or a nominal payment such as $20 or $25.

Web Link 6.11

What Are Floating-Rate or Variable-Rate Credit Cards?

All credit cards have variable rates in the sense that the credit card companies can change the rates at any time with appropriate notice to the cardholders. In fact, a credit card company is free to change *any* feature of the credit card contract with appropriate notice to the cardholders. A cardholder has the right to cancel his or her credit card if he or she does not like the new terms. A floating-rate or variable-rate credit card is one in which the interest rate charged on balances is tied to some market interest rate such as the yield on Treasury bills.

How Do I Decide Which Card Is Best for Me?

There are many issues to consider in selecting a credit card. There are the APR and the annual fee. If rewards and rebates are offered, then you must evaluate their potential value. The method used to calculate the outstanding balance and how the interest charge is computed are also important. Next, there are all the potential fees, including fees for late payments, overlimit charges, and cash advances. Finally, there is the length of the grace period. Selecting the best credit card is something that can probably be done only in hindsight. But careful selection should help you to obtain a card that works well for you. For some additional suggestions about what to look for or what to avoid in a credit card, see **Web Link 6.12.**

Web Link 6.12

How Do I Obtain a Credit Card with the Particular Features I Want?

To obtain the particular features you want on a credit card, you can sit back and wait until such a card is offered to you or you can actively seek it out. There are several web sites that facilitate locating cards with particular features. These sites typically group the cards by their dominant features.

Web Link 6.14

Many credit card companies are more than happy to have you apply for a credit card over the Internet. In most cases, the company's web address is based on the company's name. Some common card company addresses are provided in **Web Link 6.28.**

Web Link 6.28

What Are Debit Cards?

Debit cards come in two forms: online and offline. Online debit cards are commonly known as ATM cards. When you use an online debit card, you are transferring money immediately from your checking account to the vendor's account. Using an offline debit card is like writing a check: it will take one to three days for the funds to be transferred from your checking account to the vendor's account. Offline debit cards are also known as **check cards.** Some of the better-known check cards include Visa Check™ and Master-Money™. They are accepted at all locations that accept Visa or MasterCard credit cards. The easiest way to recognize when you are using an online debit card is that you must enter a PIN (personal identification number) when you make the charge. With an offline card you sign for the charge just as with a credit card.

From the perspective of cash management, a debit card would seem foolhardy. The use of a credit card typically gives you anywhere from 30 to 60 days from the time you use the credit card until you have to pay the monthly statement. Nonetheless, many debit card users feel debit cards help them manage their personal finances. They see debit cards as substitutes for cash or as a technique for keeping credit card bills in line. Debit cards provide a form of spending constraint because the user knows that if the money is not in the checking account the debit will not work.

Another rationale for using debit cards is to have immediate access to review how much is being spent. A parent might give a child a debit card rather than a credit card when the child is being given access to credit for the first time.

Web Link 6.16

What Are Secured Credit Cards?

Secured credit cards might be an option for people with no credit or damaged credit. Secured cards require a deposit into a special savings account to serve as collateral for the credit line. Some issuers will actually pay interest on these deposits. The physical appearance of a secured card and a conventional (unsecured) credit card are the same. Only the cardholder and card issuer are aware the card is secured. Interest rates and annual fees on secured cards are normally higher than for conventional cards, and the issuer may charge application, processing, and set-up fees. Despite these costs, secured cards may be worthwhile for people unable to obtain conventional cards. Credit cards can be used as a form of identification and are often required on such occasions as checking into a hotel (even if you don't intend to pay with the credit card).

Web Link 6.17

What Legal Protection Do I Have with a Credit Card?

Web Link 6.18

There are four basic rights associated with a credit card. The first right is that of cancellation. If you notify the card company in writing within 40 days of being billed an annual fee you can close the account and nullify the fee.

Your second right is that the most you can be held responsible for is $50 worth of purchases if your card is lost or stolen. Even if the thief goes on a shopping spree, you're free of responsibility for anything over $50. (Liability will be less than $50 if you notify the card issuer before the unauthorized user incurs $50 of charges.) If your cards are lost or stolen, you are responsible for contacting the companies that issued them as soon as possible. If you have given someone else, such as a girlfriend, a child, or even your spouse, permission to use your account and this person is not jointly liable on your account, then you are liable for any and all debts they might charge on the account. If someone steals your account number, as opposed to stealing and using your card, you have no obligation for any of the fraudulent charges.

Web Link 6.19

Your third right is that, under the **Fair Credit Reporting Act,** when you make your complaint in writing, you may dispute a bill up to 60 days after the card issuer sends a bill with an error. The Fair Credit Reporting Act protects your rights *only* if you make your claims in writing. You may also dispute a bill even after you have paid it. If you dispute a charge before paying for it, the issuer must investigate your complaint and provide proof that the charge is correct. During this protest period, you are not obligated to pay any disputed bills or any interest charges that might arise from this deferral. If the charge proves to be correct, however, you are legally responsible for any accrued interest on unpaid balances if the issuer opts to charge you. This authority to charge interest if a dispute is resolved in favor of the credit card company is clearly intended to prevent consumers from abusing the right to dispute charges on their monthly bills. The law also protects you from an unfavorable credit report about an unpaid charge while you dispute the charge.

Your fourth right is to refuse to pay for any defective merchandise that costs more than $50 if you are unable to resolve the problem with the merchant and the purchase was made within your home state or within 100 miles of your mailing address.

How Can I Prevent Unauthorized or Fraudulent Use of My Credit Card?

You can never be absolutely certain that someone will not make unauthorized or fraudulent use of your credit card or credit card number, but there are several things you can do to minimize the chances of this happening: If you have not initiated a phone call do not give your credit card number during that call. Always sign new credit cards immediately upon receipt. Keep a list of your credit card numbers and the phone numbers you need to contact if your cards are lost or stolen. Keep this list in a place different from where you keep your cards. Although a safe deposit box may sound appropriate as a place to store the list, remember that your cards might be stolen on the weekend just after your bank closes. Storage at work or in a secure spot at home are the recommended locations. Many credit card companies offer to store your credit card numbers and notify the appropriate companies if any card is lost or stolen, but you can easily do it yourself.

An additional step to prevent abuse of your credit card number is to destroy elsewhere any carbon paper if it is used as part of the credit card slip. Always draw a line through any empty spaces on a charge slip, never sign a blank charge slip, and ask for the ruined copy if a salesperson has to rewrite a charge slip.

HOW CAN YOU DEAL WITH EXCESSIVE CREDIT CARD DEBT?

Some people end up with credit card bills they can't pay. In some cases, people with good financial resources who are reasonable users of credit encounter unforeseen problems such as the loss of a job or uninsured medical expenses. In other cases, card users are borderline credit risks and irresponsible with their credit card use. In still other cases, people obtain credit with the intention of abusing it.

If you find yourself overextended and want to work out your debts, there are several steps you can take. The first is to approach your lenders and ask them about the possibility of restructuring your debt to extend the maturity of your loan.

> *Dan took out an auto loan for $12,000 earlier this year. The loan was for three years at a rate of 10 percent. The current balance of the loan is $11,000, and Dan's current monthly payment is $387.21. Dan has suffered a reduction in income. To help avoid problems until he can rebuild his income, he has approached the lender about restructuring his loan to a five-year maturity. What is Dan's monthly payment if he keeps the same interest rate and extends the loan to five years? What will his payment be if the lender raised the rate to 12 percent?*

Web Link 6.20

If the loan is at the same rate, the monthly payment falls to $233.72. If the rate is increased to 12 percent, the monthly payment becomes $244.69. If he keeps the same rate Dan could reduce his monthly payment on this loan by $154. Even with the higher interest rate, Dan's monthly payment is lower by $143. It is true that either of these two new loans will force Dan to pay substantially more interest, measured in dollars, over the next few years than he would have paid with the old loan. Dan's primary motivation, however, is not to minimize his total interest expense, but to keep from having to use more drastic methods to deal with his financial problems. The higher interest expense can just be viewed as one of the costs of working through Dan's financial problems.

Restructuring debt will be discussed further in Chapter 7.

What Are Debt Consolidation and Home Equity Loans?

An alternative to negotiating extensions in various debts separately is a **debt consolidation loan** or a home equity loan. In a debt consolidation loan a new, larger loan is used to repay most or all of one's current debts. Thus, one smaller monthly payment replaces what had been many monthly payments. A home equity loan can be used as a debt consolidation loan. The primary differences are that the home equity loan has higher upfront costs and that the interest is an itemized deduction because it is a type of mortgage.

A debt consolidation loan provides the money to pay off some of the more expensive loans that cannot be renegotiated. There are usually two objectives in a debt consolidation process. The first is to reduce the monthly payment to a level that can be handled without undue stress. The second is to get out from under the highest interest rate loans. For a debt consolidation loan to achieve its objectives, at least one of three conditions must be met: The new loan must have a substantially longer maturity than at least some of the existing loans; the new loan must have a lower interest rate than some of the existing loans; the interest on the new loan must be tax deductible where the interest on the old loan was not.

Dan feels he has gotten in over his head on his debts. He has the following loans and debts on which he is currently paying:

Loan	Monthly Payment	Amount Owed	Months Left
Auto Loan #1	$387.21	$11,000	33
Auto Loan #2	451.99	7,526	18
Education Loan	446.00	22,000	60

Debt	Amount Owed	Interest Rate
Credit Card #1	$16,000	18%
Credit Card #2	12,000	15

(Note: This problem statement is keyed to the Internet calculator.)

Dan can take out a home equity loan at 10 percent for 10 years (120 months). There is a $375 upfront fee for the loan. Dan's combined federal and state income tax rate is 34 percent and he can earn 10 percent on any savings. How would the consolidation loan affect Dan's initial monthly payment and what are the long-term costs to this loan?

Web Link 6.21

The solution to this problem may be found using any of the calculators on **Web Link 6.21.** These calculators estimate the monthly payment on loans under Dan's current debt structure is costing him $1,346.[3] The consolidation loan will cost him $907 per month. The consolidation loan will save Dan $439 per month in immediate cash flow. Thus, if Dan's primary goal is to conserve his cash flow, the consolidation loan meets this objective.

[3]The calculators at this web link compute a monthly payment for each credit card. However, they do not indicate what assumptions they are using to calculate the current monthly payment.

Overall, the consolidation loan will cost Dan $4,114 over the next 120 months. This is because the other loans would all have been paid off much sooner than the consolidation loan. This extra cost reflects both additional interest payments and the benefit that the interest on the debt consolidation loan may be an itemized deduction on Dan's taxes. The interest on a home equity loan is treated the same in the federal tax code as interest on a mortgage loan.

Dan now needs to decide if the immediate relief on the monthly cash payments is worth the additional costs that he will incur over the next 10 years. A drawback to debt consolidation loans not indicated in this example is that sometimes they include stiff prepayment penalties.

A separate step in dealing with being overextended is to work with a nonprofit **credit counselor.** These counselors usually charge reasonable fees and can help you work out ways to handle your debts by carefully examining your budget situation. Actions recommended by credit counselors might include extending loan maturities and obtaining a debt consolidation loan.

Web Link 6.22

How Large a Line of Credit Can I Obtain?

If you are planning to obtain a **home equity line of credit** (HELOC) to replace several loans, you should know in advance how much you would be able to borrow on the line of credit. As with all loans, the individual lender ultimately decides whether to make or reject a particular loan, but there are certain guidelines all lenders tend to follow. In the case of a HELOC, you are taking out a second mortgage against your home. The most common rule that lenders use in this case is that the total of all your mortgages (i.e., first and second mortgages) should not exceed 80 percent of the appraised value of your home. The sum of the balance due on all of the mortgages associated with a home, divided by the market value of that home, is known as the loan-to-value ratio. If the amount of the HELOC for which you are applying is within this limit, the lender will analyze whether your income is sufficient to afford your mortgages and all other debts after taking out the HELOC.

> *Dan Tessoni believes his house would appraise at $150,000. His first mortgage is down to $99,500. If a lender approves HELOCs up to an 80 percent loan to value ratio, what is the maximum HELOC he could take out?*

Web Link 6.23

The first step is to compute 80 percent of the appraised value. In this case, 80 percent of $150,000 is $120,000. The sum of Dan's mortgages cannot exceed $120,000. Since his first mortgage is $99,500, the maximum HELOC Dan could take out is the difference, or $20,500 ($120,000 maximum loan – $99,500 existing loans). This does not mean that Dan will automatically receive a HELOC for this amount; his income must also allow him to qualify for this loan.

What Is the Best Interest Rate Deal on a HELOC?

Lenders advertise the rates they charge on HELOCs just as they advertise any other loan rate so you can call several lenders (including any of the depository institutions discussed earlier) and ask for the current HELOC interest rate. The rate may depend on the size of the loan, with larger loans carrying a lower rate. As with other loans, the cheaper interest rate loan is not always the best deal. A critical part of a HELOC is the appraisal process, for which you may be charged a fee. There are other fees to this loan, including the cost of a credit check and the fees to record the mortgage with the appropriate government unit (e.g., a county or township office). There may also be a processing fee. Asking a lender what the interest rate is without inquiring about fees will get you only part of the story.

HELOC interest rates are usually variable because HELOCs are typically open-ended loan approvals. You might open a HELOC today and not take out a loan for several years. A lender cannot afford to risk being locked into a fixed interest rate forever. To find the current national average rate on HELOCs, see **Web Link 6.24.**

Web Link 6.24

"Credit Doctor" or Credit Counselor?

A "**credit doctor**" is a person or business that claims to resurrect your credit. A credit counselor helps you work out your credit problems. A credit doctor will try to make your credit problems disappear. Credit doctors are usually expensive and sometimes suggest fraudulent schemes. Credit doctors usually do three things. The first is to guarantee they will obtain a credit card for you. This guaranteed credit card is, of course, a secured card that you could obtain on your own. The second is to attempt to get your credit cleaned and reestablished quickly. This involves protesting every negative piece of information in your credit file. The credit bureau is obligated to reconfirm protested information with vendors. Since reconfirmation requires work with no direct compensation, some vendors will not take the time to reconfirm. The third action is to try to negotiate a reduction in the amount owed to various creditors. Creditors typically do not simply accept debt reductions. They might renegotiate the term of the loan, but they typically do not agree to just reduce the amount owed.

Credit doctors may also ask you to turn over a fixed payment to them each month in lieu of your payments to your creditors. This may sound like a debt consolidation loan, but it is not. The credit doctors are simply taking your money and distributing it among your creditors, after taking out a fee for themselves. This is something you could do yourself without having to pay a fee.

Because of abuses by credit repair organizations, Congress passed the **Credit Repair Organization Act** that took effect April 1, 1977. The basic provisions are that credit repair companies can no longer claim they can "fix" credit records by removing accurate credit information to cover up past payment problems. The law requires that these companies give customers written disclosure of the customers' legal rights before contracts are signed. It also prohibits them from taking payment from customers before services are carried out, and prevents them from providing any services until a three-day waiting period has elapsed. In general, credit doctors take advantage of people having financial difficulties. They do not actually solve any problems or do anything you cannot do yourself with a little knowledge and effort.

Web Link 6.25

Web Link 6.26
Web Link 6.27

HOW IS MY CREDIT RATING DETERMINED?

When you apply for a credit card or any type of credit the prospective lender will evaluate the quality of your credit. The approach used in evaluating your creditworthiness is known as the four Cs. The four Cs stand for **character, capacity, capital,** and **collateral.** Character refers to the borrower's intent and willingness to repay a loan. Capacity alludes to the borrower's income relative to the loan amount. Capital addresses the wealth of the individual relative to the loan amount. Collateral is self-explanatory.

Of these, character easily dominates the other three. All lenders would prefer to lend to someone who makes repayment a matter of pride—even if the borrower's income and wealth are not quite at desirable levels—rather than someone who doesn't really care about repayment. The world is full of wealthy deadbeats and it is also full of poor people who have perfect credit histories.

The problem the lender faces is that collecting and verifying data on capacity, capital, and collateral are relatively simple. Collecting data on character is difficult at best. One of the best signs of character is a record of having made all required payments on all loans and other debts in a timely manner. A person who has borrowed often but repaid all loans in full in a timely manner has a much better credit standing than a person who has never taken out a loan in his or her life. The former has a legitimate credit record and the latter is an unknown quantity.

The first step in obtaining a loan or credit is to fill out a loan or credit application. Among other things, you will be asked to provide your social security number. The prospective lender uses this number to obtain your credit record from one of the three major credit bureaus. The lender then cross checks your credit report with your application. If you have neglected to mention that you have eight credit cards currently in use and are behind in payments on six of them, it is unlikely you will be approved.

Most lenders compute a credit score for each applicant. Researchers Bill Fair and Earl Isaac originally developed the idea of credit scoring at Stanford University in the 1950s. The company they set up to market their scoring scheme was Fair, Isaac & Co., and their scoring scheme became known as **FICO.** Now, almost any scoring scheme is referred to as a FICO.[4] The original FICO score ranges from 350 to 900. The higher the FICO score, the more likely the applicant is to receive credit. Each prospective lender is free to use the FICO as it sees fit. Thus, even if two lenders have the same FICO score for you, one could turn down your credit application and the other could approve it. The FICO score itself does not determine acceptance or rejection of your application; it is the lender's interpretation of the FICO score that determines the acceptance or rejection.

Some standards are common among lenders. A FICO score above 700 is considered so stellar that many lenders may automatically grant approval without the need for further verification of information. A score above 650 is considered excellent and will usually assure that you receive credit. A score of less than 620 will usually put the borrower at substantial risk of not having the loan approved. You are certainly entitled to ask a lender what your FICO score is after he or she has processed your application, but the lender is not legally obligated to provide it to you. Your credit report shows the primary elements affecting your score. **Web Link 6.31** offers tables showing the relationship between credit scores and the quality of credit for mortgage borrowers.

Web Link 6.31

FICO scores are beginning to turn up in places other than credit offices. Many employers, as well as prospective landlords run credit checks on job or rental applicants. Some insurers use FICO scores to set premiums for auto and homeowner insurance

---

[4]Fico is still the name of the scoring scheme used at Experion (formerly TRW). Equifax uses a model known as Beacon, and TransUnion uses a model known as Empirica. For additional descriptions of these models see **Web Link 6.29.**

policies. Health care providers sometimes obtain these scores to decide whether to grant a patient credit or require payment up front. Cellular phone companies also run credit checks. Even the Internal Revenue Service uses FICO scores as part of its decision process in selecting taxpayers to audit. Anyone running a credit check is supposed to obtain your permission, but some vendors do so without your permission—a car dealer deciding whether to let you test drive a car, for example.

Because there are a variety of FICO models (and any lender can create its own FICO), there are no universal rules about FICO scores.[5] However, most FICOs have several common elements. If you have filled out a standard credit or loan application, you can probably figure out most of these common elements just from the questions asked. The key points in establishing your FICO include how long you've lived at your current address, how long you've worked at your current job, the nature of your job, and whether you own or rent your home. Other factors include the amount of credit you have outstanding, the amount of credit you are using, and the number of late payments you have had over a period of time. Scoring models will sometimes include such items as whether you have a savings account and your marital status.

The length of time you have been at your residence and at your job and the nature of your job are used to establish your stability. An ideal applicant will have lived at his or her current and previous address for at least six years each and will have worked at his or her current job for at least four years. People in professions that require substantial qualifications and are difficult to relocate, such as physicians, lawyers, and engineers, are rated highly. People in jobs that can be quickly and easily relocated, such as barbers, waiters, and writers, are rated lower.

Lenders consider the number of accounts you have opened in the past 12 months, along with the number of times someone has requested a copy of your credit record. A large number of requests for your credit record will cause lenders concern that you are having difficulty obtaining credit.[6] You cannot, of course, control who requests your credit record. Anyone who has your Social Security number and belongs to a credit bureau may run a credit check on you. A good example of this problem became public when a former top official of the first Bush administration was turned down for a Toys R Us rebate credit card despite an annual salary of $123,100 and a clean credit record. In the previous year, this individual had refinanced his mortgage, moved a home equity loan from one bank to another, and applied for one credit card. All of these actions required credit checks and each in turn created greater concern for the next lender. Some lenders will give you an opportunity to explain why particular requests were made. The good news is that the credit card company did eventually reverse its decision and approve the credit card.

Web Link 6.32

To help understand how the quality of your credit is evaluated, consider the following example:

---

[5]For additional information at this point, see **Web Link 6.30.**

[6]Credit checks are classified as **internal** or **external credit checks.** A credit check by a creditor you have an account with is considered an internal credit check. An external credit check is by someone who would be a new creditor for you. Internal credit checks are considered a normal part of business by that creditor and are not reported to anyone else. The only one who may ascertain what internal credit checks have been run on you is you.

Dan Tessoni is applying for a mortgage to buy a house. On the home he has just sold, Dan had one late mortgage payment within the past 12 months. He had never had a mortgage before. He did file for bankruptcy six years ago but has no bankruptcy proceedings in process. He has had no collections, judgements, tax liens, charge-offs, or delinquent property within the past two years. The condition of the property he is buying is good. His total mortgage payment will be $800. His installment and other revolving debt payments each month total $500. His monthly income before taxes is $4,000. The last time Dan saw a credit report on himself, his FICO score was 610. He has had credit with about ten vendors for at least one year, and with seven for at least two years. Dan has had only one 30-day late auto loan payment within the last two years. How good is the quality of his credit?

Web Link 6.33

The credit calculator (at **Web Link 6.33**) indicates Dan has a primary credit quality of B+, and a secondary credit quality of A. The major blemish on his record is the 30-day late mortgage payment within the past 12 months.

How Can I Improve My FICO?

Over time, good personal finance practices will lead to an improved FICO score. If you stick at the same job, buy a home and live at that home for an extended time, make all minimum payments when due, and obtain new credit accounts on an occasional basis, your FICO score will rise. There are some actions that can have an immediate impact. You should close out credit cards that you do not use or do not need. Keep the number of active credit cards to a handful, and try to have those be the ones where you have had the account the longest. If you are struggling to make payments on your credit cards or if you have missed a payment in the past 12 months, consider a consolidation loan to get the monthly payment down to what you are absolutely certain you can handle. If you are concerned that the consolidation loan would only tempt you to charge new things that you otherwise would not buy, put the credit cards in your safe deposit box to protect yourself from buying on whim or splurging. Avoid any actions that would cause someone to run a credit check on you. This means that you should not acquire a cellular phone, should avoid any test drives at an auto dealership, should not apply for any new credit cards, and should not apply for any increases in your credit limits.

Web Link 6.34
Web Link 6.35

How Will a Divorce Affect My Credit Rating?   Any credit that you and your spouse undertake jointly when you are married will remain an obligation to both of you even if you divorce. There are several good reasons for this. First, a lender is counting on the income and financial resources of both spouses when considering whether to make the loan. If you and your spouse really want only the income and financial resources of one of you to be considered, then that partner should be the only one applying for the credit. If a lender had known in advance that only one of the spouses would be taking responsibility for repayment of a particular loan, it might not have approved that loan. If in the divorce decree you and your spouse agree that your spouse will take responsibility for a particular loan, then you should contact that creditor individually to seek the creditor's legal binding release of your obligation. A creditor is not obligated to release you, but may do so if it believes your spouse could have obtained the same credit in his or her name alone.

Web Link 6.36

How Long Will Negative Information Stay in My Credit File?

In general, negative information will stay in your file for seven years provided that it is believed to be accurate. There are several noteworthy exceptions. Some information has no time limitation, including information reported because of an application for a job with a salary of more than $75,000 or because of an application for more than $150,000 worth of credit or life insurance. Bankruptcy information can be reported for 10 years. Information about a lawsuit or a judgment against you can be reported for seven years or until the statute of limitations runs out, whichever is longer. Default information concerning U.S. government insured or guaranteed student loans can be reported for seven years after certain guarantor actions.

WHAT IS A CREDIT BUREAU?

Web Link 6.37

A credit bureau is an organization that collects and sells credit information on consumers. Currently there are three major credit bureaus: **Experion** (formerly TRW), **Equifax,** and **TransUnion Corp.** Companies who receive information from these credit bureaus also provide them with information on their own customers. In addition, the credit bureaus collect information from court documents and other public sources of information.

How May I Validate My Credit Report?

Some states have passed legislation that allows you to obtain free copies of your credit report. In all states, if you are turned down for credit based on information in your credit report you are entitled to a free copy of that report within 60 days. You are also entitled to one free report a year if you can prove that you're unemployed and plan to look for a job within 60 days, that you're on welfare, or that your report is inaccurate because of fraud.

Web Link 6.38

Under the **Equal Credit Opportunity Act,** a creditor must give you a specific reason if you are turned down for credit. It is not sufficient to say your FICO score was too low. You may challenge any information in your report and you are entitled to enter brief statements in your report regarding negative information. Thus, if a merchant lists you as not paying a particular bill and the reason is that the product was defective and you could not reach an accommodation with the merchant, you may note this in your record.

When you contact a credit bureau you should be prepared to provide the following information: full name, birthdate, current address, former addresses in past five years, photocopy of driver's license showing your current address, and a photocopy of your Social Security card.

If you would like to validate the quality of your credit but are not interested in paying the fee, a simple way to make sure your credit is acceptable is to apply for credit from a vendor. You do not want to do this too often, because the large number of credit cards you would accumulate would be a negative on your record, but do it at least every few years. Be sure when you open a new credit account that you close out an old one.

If you are checking your credit record, you should check it with all three credit bureaus. The three bureaus do not share information with each other. In fact, they all collect their information independently. So it is possible that you might get a strong FICO from one bureau and a weak FICO from another.

Web Link 6.39
Web Link 6.40
Web Link 6.41

You may order your report over the phone from each company through its toll-free telephone number (see **Web Link 6.39**) or you may order over the Internet (see **Web Link 6.40**). A list of the fees charged by the three bureaus in the various states as well as a list of the states that allow you to obtain a free report appears in **Web Link 6.41.** There are also services available that will alert you when someone runs a credit check on you and inform you who this person or business is.

SUMMARY

➤ The advantages of using credit cards rather than cash are certain legal protections, the limitations of loss in the event of theft, and the ability to postpone payment. The major disadvantage is that credit cards allow people who cannot control their spending impulses to get into financial trouble.

➤ Credit cards vary in terms of the interest rates on balances and cash advances, how interest is computed, when payments are due, how late payments are treated, and when special benefits (such as cash rebates or frequent flyer miles) are offered.

➤ Credit card users have four basic rights: cancellation, limit of losses on a stolen card to $50, the right to dispute a bill, and the right to refuse defective merchandise under certain conditions.

➤ A home equity line of credit may be the most attractive form of open credit as the interest is an itemized deduction.

➤ Credit counselors help people deal with debt problems. Credit doctors claim to fix these problems.

➤ Lenders usually compute a FICO score for an individual seeking credit, and base the awarding of credit on this score.

➤ Credit bureaus collect information on each of us and provide this data to customers who pay to have access to this information.

KEY TERMS

adjusted balance	affinity card	average daily balance
capacity	capital	character
check card	collateral	credit counselor
credit doctor	Credit Repair Organization Act	debt consolidation loan
Equal Credit Opportunity Act	Equifax	Experion
external credit check	Fair Credit Reporting Act	FICO
grace period	home equity line of credit	internal credit check
lack of use fee	late fee	overlimit fee
previous balance	teaser rate	transaction fee
TransUnion Corp.		

PROBLEMS

6.1 Ralph currently has a $3,000 balance on his credit card. The interest rate is 18 percent. He will charge an average of $200 per month in the future and will pay an average of $500 per month. How long will it take him to pay off his card? If he could cut his interest rate to 12 percent, how many months sooner could he pay off his card balances?

6.2 Earl owes $12,000 on his credit card. He anticipates future monthly charges of $1,000 and planned to make monthly payments of $1,200. He is planning to buy a house in three years and would like to have his card balances cleaned up by then. He thinks that if he increases his monthly payment to $1,300 he will achieve this goal. If the interest rate on his card is 16 percent, will he achieve his goal?

6.3 Tess Harper has come to the conclusion she is getting ripped off by her current credit card company. She has a balance outstanding of $6,000. She plans future monthly payments of $500, but anticipates average future monthly charges of $400. On the Internet, she has found two credit cards that look attractive, both of which have lower rates than her current card. The first card has a regular rate of 10 percent and an annual fee of $50. It also comes with a teaser introductory rate of 4 percent that will be good for the next three months. The second card has a $20 annual fee and a regular rate of 14 percent. It too comes with a teaser rate, but this rate is 6 percent and is good for four months. Which card is the better deal for Tess over the next three years?

6.4 Jennifer has decided that she would like to compare a flight mileage card to a low-rate card. The flight mileage card has an introductory rate, 2.9 percent for four months. The flight card charges 16 percent on unpaid balances, and the low-rate card charges 10 percent. The flight card carries a $50 annual fee and the low-rate card carries a $25 annual fee. Jenn currently has a balance on her credit card of $8,000. She expects to charge an average of $800 per month in the future and to make monthly payments of $1,000. The flight card pays two frequent flyer miles per dollar charged on the card and provides a 5,000-mile bonus for activating the card. A maximum of 60,000 in frequent flyer miles per year can be earned. The particular airline that the card is associated with charges 20,000 miles for domestic flights—the ones Jenn is most likely to use. A typical flight would cost Jenn about $500. Which card should Jenn take out if she plans to use this card for at least five years?

6.5 Cindy has just received two credit card solicitations. One card offers a rebate and the other offers a particularly attractive interest rate. The rebate card has an introductory rate of 3 percent for three months. The rebate card has an interest rate of 18 percent and the low-rate card has a rate of 12 percent. The rebate card has an annual fee of $25 and the low-rate card has an annual fee of $50. Cindy has a current credit card balance of $9,000, which she would transfer to the new card. She expects to charge an average of $900 per month, and to pay an average of $1,200 per month. The rebate card provides a 1 percent rebate on all purchases and a 5 percent rebate at Goldies Specialty Store. Cindy spends about $50 per month at Goldies. The maximum rebate is $1,000 per year, but there is no lifetime limit on the rebate. The 1 percent rebate would be paid to Cindy in the form of cash each year. Which card is better for Cindy over the next five years?

6.6 Susie is considering a cash rebate card. The card carries a $50 annual fee. She expects to charge $8,000 per year on her card. The rebate schedule is $1/4$ percent on the first $1,000 in annual charges, $1/2$ percent on the next $2,000, $3/4$ percent on the next $2,000, and 1 percent on all additional charges in an annual period. What rebate could Susie expect from the card, net of the annual fee?

6.7 Identify some of the main features of the following acts: Fair Credit Reporting Act, Credit Repair Organization Act, and the Equal Credit Opportunity Act.

6.8 What is the current national average interest rate charged on HELOCs? What is the rate currently being charged at three different banks in your community or state?

6.9 Evaluate your own credit record using one of the credit evaluation calculators at **Web Link 6.33.**

6.10 Jim and Julie's home has a current market value of $150,000, although they originally bought the home for $125,000. Their current mortgage balance is $90,000, down from an initial balance of $100,000. What is the maximum home equity line of credit they could arrange today if the lender approved a loan to value ratio of 80 percent?

6.11 Jerry would like a little relief from the cash flow pinch in which he finds himself. He has the following loans and debts on which he is currently paying:

Loan	Monthly Payment	Amount Owed	Months Left
Auto Loan #1	$457.26	$15,500	40
Auto Loan #2	587.11	8,300	18
Education Loan	283.87	14,000	60

Debt	Amount Owed	Interest Rate
Credit Card #1	$ 6,000	18%
Credit Card #2	12,000	15

Jerry can take out a home equity loan at 9 percent for 10 years (120 months). There is a $400 upfront fee for the loan. Jerry's combined federal and state income tax rate is 34 percent. Assume that the rate earned on any savings (i.e., Jerry's opportunity cost of money) is 8 percent. How would the consolidation loan affect Jerry's initial monthly payment, and what are the long-term costs to this loan?

REFERENCES

Web Link 6.42 Glossaries for terms related to open account credit
Web Link 6.43 FAQs about open account credit
Web Link 6.44 Pointer sites

WALL STREET JOURNAL RESOURCES

Web Link (WSJ) 6.45 "Credit-Card Issuers Hoping to Have a Green Christmas," *The Wall Street Journal Interactive Edition*, December 15, 1998

For information that has changed since the book was written, for new information that pertains to this topic, and for some new web sites that pertain to the topic of this chapter, see **Web Link 6.45.**

ACQUIRING CONSUMER LOANS

LEARNING OBJECTIVES

- ▦ Describe the different types of installment loans
- ▦ Compute the monthly payment for an installment loan
- ▦ Discuss amortization and construct a loan amortization table
- ▦ Show the impact on an amortization table of adding extra principal to a payment
- ▦ Describe an add-on rate loan
- ▦ Identify the lenders who most commonly provide installment loans and determine current rates
- ▦ Evaluate whether it is better to take out an auto loan or a home equity loan to buy an auto
- ▦ Discuss what happens when you default on a loan with collateral
- ▦ List the protections a consumer has from a debt collector
- ▦ Discuss the two primary methods for declaring bankruptcy: Chapters 7 and 13

Web Link: www.wiley.com/college/woerheide

INTRODUCTION

In Chapter 6 we looked at the topic of open-ended credit, credit obtained before borrowing, such as takes place with the use of credit cards. The other type of consumer credit is the **installment loan.** An installment loan is for a specific amount, negotiated at the time the loan is made, with a fixed repayment schedule. Installment loans play a major role in our economy. Many people buy cars with installment loans. Student loans are a form of installment loan. Home equity loans are installment loans. Motorcycles, boats, snowmobiles, washers and dryers, and freezers are all examples of items frequently bought with installment loans. In short, without installment loans consumer spending for big-ticket items would decline dramatically as everyone would have to save up the cash to make these purchases.

In this chapter, we look at the different types of installment loans. We also consider different institutions to which a person would go for an installment loan.

WHAT ARE THE TYPES OF INSTALLMENT LOANS?

Installment loans are classified according to the purpose of the loan and/or the collateral pledged for the loan. Frequently, the purpose of the loan is to buy the asset that will become the collateral. The most common consumer installment loan is the automobile loan. There are two categories of automobile loan: new and used. Because a lender assumes more risk in a used automobile loan, many lenders charge higher rates on a used automobile loan than they charge for a new automobile loan.

Another category of installment loan is the home improvement loan. If the home itself is pledged as collateral on this loan, then this loan is effectively a second mortgage. A marine loan would be used to purchase a new or used boat. A camper or recreational vehicle loan would be used to buy one of those two types of equipment.

Many installment loans are personal loans. An unsecured personal loan is sometimes referred to as a **signature loan** because the only collateral is the good word of the borrower that he or she will repay the loan when it is due. Only the signature of the borrower backs a signature loan. Among installment loans, signature loans usually have the lowest limits on loan size.

A **secured personal loan** usually means that a nontraditional personal asset is pledged as collateral. A nontraditional personal asset might be something like a coin collection or artwork. Most lenders will not accept used household goods as collateral because of the questionable resale value of such items.

Some borrowers will pledge a certificate of deposit (CD) as collateral on a loan. Although this might seem a little eccentric at first, there are some practical reasons to do this. One is that the borrower may have a marginal credit record. One way to build or rebuild a good credit record is to establish a track record of successfully repaying installment loans. This creates a Catch 22 problem. If an established credit record is built on successful repayments of loans, then how does a person establish a credit record to obtain the loan in the first place? One solution to this problem is the CD-secured loan.

A second reason for a CD-secured loan is that it is a form of **forced savings.** As discussed in Chapter 3, forced savings is any arrangement wherein a consumer accepts a lower rate of return on an investment, or a higher interest rate on a loan, than otherwise would be the case because he or she will be forced to save money.

> *Andy Van Fleet has $5,000 in cash. He would like to buy a computer and a few things for his house that cost about $5,000. He can spend the $5,000 he has for the items or he can put the $5,000 in a three-year CD paying 6 percent and take out a three-year, CD-secured loan that costs him 8 percent. What are the advantages and disadvantages of each approach?*

Spending the $5,000 cash directly has the advantage that the opportunity cost of the money is only 6 percent. Placing the money in the CD and obtaining a CD-secured loan has the disadvantage that Andy is paying the bank 2 percent per year for the privilege of using his own money. However, the CD-secured loan has the advantage that Andy now has a legal obligation to make monthly payments to repay the loan. At the end of the three years, his credit record will be stronger. He also knows he will still have his $5,000 at the end of the three years, plus he will have the accrued interest. If he spends the cash directly, he will have to rebuild the $5,000 in savings from scratch through a voluntary savings program. Many people think or know they cannot trust themselves to resave the money, so they would rather leave untouched any cash they have accumulated and borrow for their purchases.

Web Link 7.1

For examples of the various types of installment loans, and a description of some of the details of the loan, see **Web Link 7.1.**

What Is a Single Payment Loan?   A **single payment loan** has literally only one payment due. This payment will include both the repayment of principal and the payment of interest on the loan. Single payment loans are usually taken out when the borrower is expecting a specific source of cash that will enable him or her to repay the loan. One of the best examples of a single payment loan would be when someone is anticipating a tax refund. If you are filing a tax return with a $2,000 refund claim, then many lenders will extend you a single payment loan for approximately $2,000 with the agreement that you will pay off the loan when the refund arrives.

How Much Will My Monthly Payment Be?

A traditional installment loan is the perfect example of a present value of annuity problem. You take out a loan today, and you agree to make equal payments over a fixed number of consecutive periods (usually months) in the future. By definition, the present value of those payments must equal what has been borrowed, where the payments are discounted at the interest rate of the loan. Recall that in Chapter 4 we presented the mathematical solution to a present value of annuity problem as

$$\text{Payment} \times \text{PVIFA} = \text{Loan Amount} \tag{7.1}$$

where

Payment = the payment made each period

PVIFA = the present value interest factor for the annuity based on the number of payments and the interest rate of the loan

Loan Amount = the amount initially borrowed

In most cases, borrowers know the amount they want to borrow and they know the length of time over which the loan will be repaid as well as the interest rate on the loan. This means the only unknown is the payment amount on the loan. Hence, equation 7.1 is frequently written as

$$\text{Payment} = \text{Loan Amount/PVIFA} \tag{7.2}$$

As indicated in Chapter 4, you can look up the value of the PVIFA in Appendix A.3 or compute it using equation 4.12.[1] It is even easier to compute the payment using one of the Internet calculators.

> *Andy wants to take out a $10,000 home improvement loan. His local bank indicates he can have a five-year loan at an 8 percent interest rate with* annual *payments. What would his* annual *payment be?*

[1]Don't forget that if the loan is based on monthly payments, then the annual rate on the loan must be converted to a monthly rate before looking up the value of the PVIFA.

Web Link 7.2

Using one of the calculators at **Web Link 7.2,** we would enter $10,000 as the present value, zero as the future value, 5 as the number of payments, and 8 percent as the interest rate. We would leave the payment amount blank and click on the *calculate* button. This should provide the answer of $2,504.56.

Most installment loans call for monthly payments rather than annual payments. We can use the same calculators in **Web Link 7.2,** but we first have to adjust the interest rate and the number of time periods to reflect payments on a monthly rather than annual basis. Let's reconsider:

> *Andy wants to take out a $10,000 home improvement loan. His local bank indicates he can have a five-year loan at an 8 percent interest rate with monthly payments. What would his monthly payment be?*

Using the financial calculators, we again enter $10,000 as the present value and zero as the future value. However, we enter 60 (5 years × 12 months per year) as the number of payment periods, and .6667 (8% / 12 months per year) as the interest rate per period. The monthly payment turns out to be $202.77.

Web Link 7.3

There are many calculators on the Internet that build in the assumption of a monthly payment. Examples of these are provided at **Web Link 7.3.** In some of the calculators, you enter the term of the loan as five years. In the rest, you enter the term as 60 months. All the calculators will give the correct answer of $202.77.

Why Isn't the Monthly Payment One-Twelfth the Annual Payment?

In the above two examples, the monthly payment of $202.76 is slightly less than one-twelfth the annual payment. The annual payment for the above five-year loan example is $2,501.88, and one-twelfth of this is $208.49. These two numbers differ because each payment you make consists partly of principal and partly of interest. So when you make monthly payments, each payment contributes toward a reduction in the principal of the loan. Because the principal goes down with each payment, the interest that you owe on the principal also goes down over time. This declining interest means that monthly payments can be smaller than annual payments. To better understand this process, let's consider a loan amortization table.

WHAT IS AN AMORTIZATION TABLE?

Amortization refers to the reduction in the amount of principal owed that occurs with each payment in an installment loan. A **loan amortization table** shows the portion of each payment that is interest and the portion that is repayment of principal. This table is important for two reasons. First, it clarifies how much would be owed if a loan were paid off early. Second, because the interest portion of a loan payment may be tax deductible, it is essential to know how much interest is paid each year.

> *Andy Van Fleet wants to take out a one-year (i.e., 12-month), $1,000 home equity installment loan with monthly payments. The loan is to pay for the balance he owes on his federal income taxes. The interest rate for the loan is 12 percent. As Andy is particularly concerned about his tax position for the coming year, he wants to know how much interest he will pay on this loan during the calendar year. Also, there is a good chance that by next January 1 Andy will be able to pay the loan off in full. If*

today is April 1, how much interest will Andy pay for the current calendar year, and what will be the outstanding loan balance on January 1?

The amortization for this loan is shown in Table 7.1. Five numbers are provided for each month. The first one is the balance owed at the start of each month. The second is the payment for each month, which is normally the same for all months or all but the last month. The third and fourth numbers are the portions of each payment that are interest and principal repayment. The fifth number is the balance due at the end of the month and this will be the same number as the first number for the next month. Let us consider how these numbers are calculated.

Table 7.1
Simple Interest, Monthly Installment

Loan Amortization Table

Month	Beginning of Month Balance	Monthly Payment	Interest Portion	Repayment of Principal	End of Month Balance
April	$1,000,00	$88.85	$10.00	$78.85	$921.15
May	$921.15	$88.85	$9.21	$79.64	$841.51
June	$841.51	$88.85	$8.42	$80.43	$761.08
July	$761.08	$88.85	$7.61	$81.24	$679.84
August	$679.84	$88.85	$6.80	$82.05	$597.79
September	$597.79	$88.85	$5.98	$82.87	$514.91
October	$514.91	$88.85	$5.15	$83.70	$431.21
November	$431.21	$88.85	$4.31	$84.54	$346.67
December	$346.67	$88.85	$3.47	$85.38	$261.29
January	$261.29	$88.85	$2.61	$86.24	$175.05
February	$175.05	$88.85	$1.75	$87.10	$87.96
March	$87.96	$88.83	$0.88	$87.95	$0.00

The computation of the monthly payment of $88.85 was discussed in the previous section. The key number in the amortization table is the portion of the payment that is interest. The interest portion is computed by multiplying the *monthly* interest rate by the amount of the loan owed at the start of that month. The monthly interest rate in this example is 1 percent, which is the 12 percent annual rate divided by 12 months. The amount owed at the start of the first month is the original loan amount of $1,000. The interest portion of the first month's payment is $10, or $1,000 × 1 percent. The portion of the payment that goes toward repayment of principal is the difference between the $88.85 total payment and the $10.00 of interest, or $78.85. Finally, the amount of principal owed at the end of the first month equals the difference between the original loan and the portion of the first month's payment that was principal, or $921.15 ($1,000 – $78.85). The interest and principal portions of each subsequent month's payment are figured the same way. However, because the amount owed at the start of each subsequent month is less, less of each payment is interest and more is principal.

There are several calculators on the Internet that prepare loan amortization tables. The exact format will tend to differ from calculator to calculator, so it is difficult to generalize about the details of such a table. These calculators are shown at **Web Link 7.4.**

Web Link 7.4

How Do the Interest Rate and Maturity of the Loan Affect the Size of the Payment?

A borrower often is more interested in the size of the monthly payment than in the interest rate on the loan or the maturity of the loan. If a person's goal is to maximize his or her wealth, then the most important variable is *always* the overall cost of the loan, but maximization of wealth is not necessarily every person's goal. There may be more satisfaction derived from purchasing goods or services today than from postponing the purchase because the cost of borrowing the money to make the purchase is too high. Furthermore, the consumer may face such a tight budget constraint that the only way to make the purchase is to minimize the monthly payment.

In most cases, the interest rate on a loan will have relatively little impact on the monthly payment. It is the maturity that significantly alters the size of a monthly payment.

> *Andy is considering a $5,000 loan to be paid back over three years. He can obtain the loan at a rate of 8 percent. He wonders how much his monthly payments would change if the rate were 6, 7, 9, and 10 percent. Also, if he does take out the loan at 8 percent, he wonders what the monthly payment would be for maturities ranging from one to five years.*

Using a calculator from **Web Link 7.3,** we can construct the following table:

3-Year Maturity		8-Percent Interest Rate	
Interest Rate	**Monthly Payment**	**Maturity**	**Monthly Payment**
6%	$152.11	1 Year	$434.94
7	154.39	2 Years	226.14
8	156.68	3 Years	156.68
9	159.00	4 Years	122.06
10	161.34	5 Years	101.38

It is easy to see from this table that the interest rate has relatively little impact on the monthly payment while the maturity of the loan has a dramatic effect.

What Happens If I Add Additional Cash to My First Payment?

Some installment loans have a prepayment penalty that can make it cost prohibitive to add cash to a payment or to consider paying the loan off early. If there is no prepayment penalty, then adding cash to a loan payment may be worthwhile. Let us consider again the example in which Andy borrows $1,000 for one year at 12 percent and makes monthly payments. The monthly payment is $88.85. Suppose Andy adds $100 to the first payment only. The interest calculation for the first payment is not altered, it is still $10.00, but the payment of principal rises from $78.85 to $178.85. The amount of principal owed at the end of the first month will fall from $921.15 to $821.15. These adjusted numbers are shown in Table 7.2. The real difference takes place in the interest computations that occur in the subsequent months.

Table 7.2

Installment Loan Amortization Table

with Additional Cash Added to the First Payment

Month	Beginning of Month Balance	Monthly Payment	Interest Portion	Repayment of Principal	End of Month Balance
April	$1,000,00	$188.85	$10.00	$178.85	$821.15
May	$821.15	$88.85	$8.21	$80.64	$740.51
June	$740.51	$88.85	$7.41	$81.44	$659.07
July	$659.07	$88.85	$6.59	$82.26	$576.81
August	$576.81	$88.85	$5.77	$83.08	$493.73
September	$493.73	$88.85	$4.94	$83.91	$409.81
October	$409.81	$88.85	$4.10	$84.75	$325.06
November	$325.06	$88.85	$3.25	$85.60	$239.46
December	$239.46	$88.85	$2.39	$86.46	$153.01
January	$153.01	$88.85	$1.53	$87.32	$65.69
February	$65.69	$66.34	$0.66	$65.68	$0.00
March	—	—	—	—	—

The amount of interest owed in the second month now becomes $8.21 rather than $9.21. For each subsequent month, the interest is lower than it would have been and the principal portions of the payments are higher. Note that the eleventh payment is only $66.35, and the twelfth payment is eliminated.

The mechanics of how the extra cash affects the loan amortization are straightforward. The more interesting question is whether it is a good idea actually to do this. The answer revolves around one simple fact. By paying extra cash on a loan, you are effectively investing your money at the loan's interest rate for the maturity of the loan. In this case, the extra $100 Andy pays in has effectively been invested for 11 months at a 12 percent interest rate. Whether this is a good idea depends primarily on the rate Andy would invest his money at if he does not pay down the loan. If he could invest it at a rate of greater than 12 percent, then this prepayment may not be such a good idea. If he could invest it only at a rate less than 12 percent, the prepayment seems like a terrific idea. Bear in mind that the payment toward the loan is a *risk-free* investment. That is, Andy knows with certainty that his cash is earning 12 percent. Even if he can earn more elsewhere, if a higher rate of return involves risk, the perfectly certain 12 percent rate might still be a good deal.

There are two more issues to be considered here. Once Andy pays the $100 toward the loan, he cannot get that money back. If Andy invests the money elsewhere in something that allows him to get his money back, he has more liquidity. Also, the sooner Andy gets this loan paid off, the larger the amount he would be able to borrow elsewhere. Let's say Andy was getting ready to purchase a car. His paying off this loan early will only increase the size of the subsequent car loan he would be able to take out.

Are Mortgage Loans Different from Other Installment Loans?

With regard to the basic mathematics, mortgages are fundamentally no different than any other installment loan. Discussed in detail in Chapter 9, mortgages are distinguished from other loans by two basic features. First, they are normally for a large amount of money. A small mortgage might be for $50,000 and a large mortgage might be for $500,000. Even the small mortgage is larger than the typical installment loan used by consumers. Second, the most common maturity on a mortgage loan is 30 years. Shorter mortgages are for terms of at least 15 years. Thus, even a short mortgage loan has a substantially longer maturity that the typical installment loan used by consumers.

Web Link (WSJ) 7.24

A substantial number of Internet calculators will compute a monthly mortgage payment; several are provided at **Web Link (WSJ) 7.24.** The breakdown of each month's payment into principal and interest is even more important for mortgages than for regular installment loans because the interest on a mortgage is an itemized deduction. A multitude of amortization tables will break down a mortgage payment; several are found at **Web**

Web Link 7.25

Link 7.25. A shortcut formula will determine the tax savings. The formula is

$$\text{Tax Savings} = \text{Principal} \times \text{Interest Rate} \times \text{Marginal Tax Rate}$$

where

$$\text{Tax Savings} = \text{the reduction in your taxes attributable to the mortgage}$$
$$\text{interest deduction}$$

$$\text{Principal} = \text{the principal amount of the mortgage due at the start of the year}$$

$$\text{Interest Rate} = \text{the interest rate on the mortgage and}$$

$$\text{Marginal Tax Rate} = \text{your combined marginal federal and state income tax rate}$$

> *Andy wants a quick estimate of how much he will save annually on his taxes as a result of taking out a $120,000 mortgage at 8 percent. His combined marginal federal and state income tax rate is 35 percent.*

Using the shortcut formula, the tax savings is approximately equal to

$$\text{Tax Savings} = \$120,000 \times .08 \times .35 = \$3,360$$

This approximation assumes that the loan is outstanding for the full year. If the loan were taken out on August 1, the tax savings should be prorated. To prorate, multiply $3,360 times .4167, since 41.67 percent (5/12) of the year remains. This indicates approximate tax savings of $1,400.11. Remember, the correct answer is always slightly less than the approximation because the approximation does not reflect the reduction in principal that

Web Link 7.26
Web Link 7.27

occurs with each mortgage payment.[2] A calculator for determining this tax savings is available at **Web Link 7.27,** but it provides the annual tax savings only in 12-month intervals.

---

[2]The actual tax savings will be $1,398.11. However, this assumes that Andy has enough deductions to itemize and that the total of itemizations exceeds the standard deduction by the mortgage interest expense. If not, the true tax savings will be less.

Because mortgages have long maturities, changes in a mortgage's maturity have relatively little effect on the monthly payment. Consider a mortgage for $120,000 with an 8 percent rate and maturities of 15, 20, 25, and 30 years.[3] Using any of the links at **Web Link (WSJ) 7.24,** you can find the following numbers for monthly payments:

Maturity (years)	Monthly Payment	Monthly Payment as a % of the 30-Year Monthly Payment
30	$ 880.52	—
25	926.18	105.2%
20	1,003.73	114.0
15	1,146.78	130.2

Notice that the 15-year maturity does not result in a payment double the payment associated with the 30-year maturity. The 15-year payment is only 30.2 percent greater than the 30-year payment. The reason the differences in monthly payments are relatively small (at least compared to what most people would expect), is that most of the initial payments in the life of a mortgage go toward interest, little goes toward principal. The amount of interest due the first month is the same regardless of the life of the mortgage.

In our example, if the interest rate is 8 percent and the loan is for $120,000, then the first month's interest payment will be $800 regardless of the maturity of the loan. So the amount of the first payment that goes toward principal is the difference between $800 and the actual payment. With the 30-year mortgage, $80.52 of the first month's payment goes toward repayment of principal. With the 15-year mortgage, $346.78 of the first month's payment goes toward repayment of principal. The maturity of the mortgage significantly affects the amount of the payment that goes toward repayment of principal.

Are Car Loans Different from Other Installment Loans?

Car loans, like mortgages, don't differ in the basics from any other installment loan. However, there is one issue that is somewhat unique to auto loans. We saw earlier in the chapter that increasing the maturity of an installment loan reduces the monthly payment. It also slows the amortization process. Thus, if a car buyer were having difficulty fitting the installment payments on a car loan into his or her budget, it would seem to make sense to simply increase the maturity of the installment loan until the car payments are low enough to fit into the budget. The problem with this strategy has to do with the interaction between the car loan payments and the market value of the car. The decline in the market value of a car over time is known as depreciation and is attributable to two factors. One is that the car steadily wears out with time. The other is that a car loses style over time and people are simply less interested in owning a less than stylish car.

A car's depreciation process is typically the reverse of the loan amortization process. The amortization of an installment loan proceeds slowly initially, and then accelerates as

---

[3]A mortgage with maturity of less than 30 years will usually have a lower interest rate than a 30-year mortgage. However, the point of this discussion is to show the impact of maturity on the monthly payment, not to suggest that the interest rate would be unaffected by the maturity.

Web Link 7.28

the end of the loan is approached. A new car has a huge depreciation in the first year and then each year's depreciation tends to be less. To estimate the depreciation on a car, use **Web Link 7.28.**

Andy has just bought a new car for $20,000. He would like to know the approximate market value of the car after one, two, and three years. His model car has an average depreciation rate.

Using **Web Link 7.28,** the cumulative depreciation figures are found to be $5,000, $6,800, and $8,384. Thus, the market value of Andy's car will be $15,000, $13,200, and $11,616.

Now let's consider the interaction between the depreciation process and the amortization of the loan.

Andy is looking into buying a new car that costs $20,000. He intends to put down 10 percent and to borrow the remaining $18,000 with a 10 percent 5-year installation loan. He believes the car will incur normal depreciation. What will his equity in the car be at the end of each of the next three years?

Web Link 7.29

The equity in a car equals the market value of the car less the amount of any loan used to buy the car. For an average depreciation schedule, we can use the one in **Web Link 7.28.** To determine the amount owed on the installment loan at the end of each of the next three years, we can use **Web Link 7.29.** The resulting market values of the car and the loan balances at the end of each of the next three years are shown in Table 7.3. The equity is minus $691 at the end of the first year. By the end of the second year the equity is barely positive at $53. By the end of the third year the equity will be up to a more reasonable $1,282.

Table 7.3
Schedule of Equity Value

Year	Car Value BOY	Car Value EOY	Loan BOY	Loan EOY	Net Equity
1	$20,000	$15,000	$18,000	$15,691	–$691
2	15,000	13,200	15,691	13,147	53
3	13,200	11,616	13,147	10,334	1,282

Note: BOY = Beginning of the Year, and EOY = End of the Year.

In other words, if the installment loan for a car has a sufficiently large maturity, then a period of negative equity will exist. If the car owner keeps the car for the entire period of the loan, there is no problem. If the car owner decides or is forced to sell the car during the time in which a negative equity exists, a problem arises. The car owner will have to come up with enough cash to pay off the negative equity. If the car owner is trading in the old car to buy a newer one, there is a strong temptation to roll the negative equity into the new financing deal, which may simply start the process of digging a huge hole of debt. If a particular car purchase would result in a period of negative equity, the car buyer should either come up with more cash to reduce the amount of the loan or consider buying a car with a smaller price tag.

Although a longer-term car loan creates the potential for negative equity, it may be less expensive in present value terms. Consider the following:

> *Andy is looking into financing a new car purchase. He can choose a 36-month loan or a 60-month loan. Both loans carry an interest rate of 6 percent. Andy invests his money aggressively and thus earns an average rate of return of 10 percent. His marginal tax rate is 20 percent. Which loan is the better deal?*

In this case, the longer loan is probably the better deal. The shorter loan will have a higher monthly payment than the longer loan. If he takes the longer loan, he could invest the difference between the two payments to earn his average rate of return. After adjusting for taxes, this provides a return of 8 percent (10% × [1 − .20]). Thus, even though the interest on the auto loan is nondeductible and the yield on his investments is taxable, he would still come out ahead. If the after-tax return on his investments were lower than the rate on the auto loan, then the shorter loan would be a better deal.

Let's change this last example to allow the shorter loan to have a lower interest rate. Now the decision of which loan is better becomes quite complex. The longer loan allows Andy to invest more money at a rate higher than the cost of the loan. However, the shorter loan means Andy will pay less interest on the money he has borrowed.

> *Andy has signed to buy a car for $20,000. He will put down $2,000 down and borrow the rest. His bank has offered a 24-month loan at 6 percent or a 48-month loan at 7 percent. Andy's rate of return on his savings is 10 percent, and his marginal tax rate is 20 percent. Which maturity should he select?*

Web Link 7.30

The answer may be found using any of the calculators at **Web Link 7.30.** The shorter loan costs Andy less on a present value basis by $12. In other words, the investment benefit just about exactly offsets the benefit of the lower interest rate on the loan.

Should I Take Out a Home Equity Loan or an Auto Loan?   At one time, all personal interest expenses were itemized deductions. It didn't matter whether you took out an automobile loan or a home equity loan to buy a car; the interest was an itemized deduction. As part of the reform of our federal tax structure in the 1980s, the type of interest that was deductible was severely restricted. To be deductible, interest expense must be associated with a loan that has real estate or investments as collateral; interest expense on an automobile loan is not deductible. Many people have found it worth the effort to take out a home equity loan and use the cash to buy a car, even if an auto loan is cheaper.

> *Andy Van Fleet is considering buying a new car. After shopping around for deals on loans, the best rate he found was 8 percent on a 48-month loan. He noted that his credit union was currently offering home equity loans at a rate of 9 percent for 48 months. There would be no change in the rate over the life of the loan. They also wanted a $200 application fee. The car would cost $20,000, but Andy is putting $2,000 down and will borrow the rest. Andy lives in Texas so he pays no state income tax, but his federal tax rate is 28 percent. Any money Andy saves could be invested to earn a rate of return of 8 percent. Which loan should Andy take out?*

Web Link 7.10

The answer can be found at **Web Link 7.10.** The home equity loan will cost Andy $315 less than the automobile loan in present value terms. In other words, choosing the home equity loan gives Andy the equivalent in after-tax dollars of having the same payments he would have had if he had chosen the auto loan but received a cash gift of $315. The home equity loan has the drawbacks of an immediate $200 fee to pay and $8 more in each monthly payment. The advantage of the home equity loan is that Andy will save money on his taxes from the deductibility of the interest payments. The present value of the tax savings exceeds the incremental costs of the fee and the higher monthly payments by a value of $315 in today's after-tax dollars.

To better understand the role of taxes, suppose that instead of living in a state with no state income taxes, Andy lives in a state where he pays a marginal state tax rate of 10 percent. His combined state and federal tax rate is 38 percent. If we rerun the calculator, we find that the advantage to the home equity loan is now $641.

There are some disadvantages to the home equity loan relative to the auto loan that cannot be quantified. First, there is always the possibility that Andy might want to pay off the loan early. One of the outputs of the calculator shows the costs of each loan as a function of time. The auto loan is cheaper for about the first one and one-half years. After that, the home equity loan becomes cheaper with each passing month, reaching a maximum differential at 48 months. Thus, if there is a reasonable chance that Andy might pay off the loan within one and one-half years, the auto loan might be the better deal.

The second disadvantage of the home equity loan is the risk of what happens if you default on your loan. The worst-case scenario with the automobile loan is that your car is repossessed. With a home equity loan, the worst-case scenario is that you could lose your home! Losing a home or an auto is a serious matter; losing a home would probably be more serious.

WHAT IS AN ADD-ON RATE LOAN?

So far, we have discussed simple interest installment loans. A simple interest loan means that interest is charged only against the balance owed at a particular point in time. Some lenders provide another type of loan known as an **add-on rate loan.** An add-on rate loan is characterized by a unique method of computing the total interest for a loan and for determining the interest and principal allocations within each monthly payment. The interest for an add-on rate loan is computed as if the entire loan balance were owed for the full loan period. The allocation of each payment into interest and repayment of principal is independent of any time value of money considerations. The process is best shown with an example.

Let's assume Andy contacts his local credit union for a one-year signature installment loan for $1,000. The credit union indicates it offers such loans at a 6 percent add-on rate. What is Andy's monthly payment, what does his loan amortization table look like, and what is the effective annual rate on this loan? Figuring the monthly payment for an add-on rate loan is a two-step procedure. The first step is to determine the total interest that will be paid on the loan. For an add-on rate loan, the total interest that will be owed equals the amount borrowed times the add-on rate times the length of the loan in years. In equation form:

Total Interest Due = Amount Borrowed × Add-on Rate × Maturity in Years

In our example, the total interest would be $60, computed as $1,000 × 6% × 1 year.

The second step is to add together the amount borrowed and the loan interest and then divide this sum by the number of months in the loan. In equation form:

Monthly Payment = (Amount Borrowed + Interest) / Maturity in Months

In our example, the monthly payment would be $88.33, computed as ($1,000 + $60)/12.

Allocating principal repayment and interest for each monthly payment is complex. The process follows the **Rule of 78ths.** The Rule of 78ths is simply an arbitrary way to make these allocations; it isn't a rational procedure like simple interest loans. The first step in the Rule of 78ths is to add together the digits associated with the monthly payments! In our example, the digits associated with the monthly payments run from 1 for the first payment to 12 for the last payment. The sum of these 12 numbers is 78 (hence the name of the rule).[4] The second step is that the interest portion of each payment is the product of the total interest charge multiplied by the ratio of the number of payments remaining (including the current one) to the sum of the digits. In our example, the interest portion of the first payment would be computed as

$$\text{Interest Portion of Payment} = \text{Total Interest Due} \times \frac{Q}{S}$$

where

Q = the number of remaining payments including the current one and

S = the sum of the digits

The interest for the first month would be $9.23 ($60 × [12 / 78]). The principal repayment portion is the difference between the monthly payment and the interest. For the first month the principal repayment would be $79.10, computed as $88.33 − $9.23. The interest portion of the second payment would be $8.46 ($60 × [11 / 78]). The full amortization table for this loan is provided in Table 7.4.

Table 7.4
Add-on Rate Installment Loan

Amortization Table

Month	Beginning of Balance	Monthly Payment	Interest Portion	Repayment of Principal	End of Month Balance
1	$1,000.00	$88.33	$9.23	$79.10	$920.90
2	$920.90	$88.33	$8.46	$79.87	$841.03
3	$841.03	$88.33	$7.69	$80.64	$760.39
4	$760.39	$88.33	$6.92	$81.41	$678.99
5	$678.99	$88.33	$6.15	$82.18	$596.81
6	$596.81	$88.33	$5.38	$82.95	$513.87
7	$513.87	$88.33	$4.62	$83.71	$430.15
8	$430.15	$88.33	$3.85	$84.48	$345.67
9	$345.67	$88.33	$3.08	$85.25	$260.41
10	$260.41	$88.33	$2.31	$86.02	$174.39
11	$174.39	$88.33	$1.54	$86.79	$87.60
12	$87.60	$88.37	$0.77	$87.60	$0.00

[4]The digits add up to 78 if the maturity of the loan is one year. If the maturity is two, three, or four years, the digits will add up to 300, 666, and 1,176.

If you look closely at Table 7.1, which is for a 12 percent simple interest rate loan and Table 7.4, which is for a 6 percent add-on rate loan, both for $1,000 to be repaid over 12 months, you will note they are quite similar! The monthly payment of the simple interest loan is $88.55 and that of the add-on rate loan is $88.33, a difference of only 22 cents. If the monthly payments are similar, and the loan amount and term are identical, then the effective interest rates must also be approximately the same. They are. The effective annual interest rate on an add-on rate loan is almost double the stated rate.

Web Link 7.6
There are a number of calculators on the Internet that calculate the effective annual interest rate on an installment loan, several of which are provided at **Web Link 7.6.** In the case of our add-on rate loan example, go to any of these calculators and insert the loan amount of $1,000, the monthly payment amount of $88.33, and the term of the loan as 1 year or 12 months. The answer you get back for the effective annual rate should be 10.89 percent.

An oddity with add-on rate loans occurs whenever the stated rate is high and the term of the loan is relatively long.

Andy is considering taking out a $10,000 add-on rate loan at an interest rate of 12 percent for 10 years (120 months). Despite the long maturity of the loan, he believes he might be able to pay off the loan at the end of the first year. How much would he owe?

Web Link 7.5
Using the calculator at **Web Link 7.5,** we find that the monthly payment would be $183.33. The amortization table shows that at the end of one year, he would owe $10,071.12. This is more than he originally borrowed! The interest portion of each of the first 12 payments exceeds the monthly payment. For the first month, the interest portion is $198.35, which exceeds the monthly payment of $183.33 by $15.02. Whenever the interest due exceeds the payment, the difference is added to the loan amount. This process is called **negative amortization.** In this example, negative amortization occurs through the first 10 months. The loan balance due if Andy wants to pay off the loan early does not fall below the original loan amount until 20 months into the loan.

As mentioned above, add-on rate loans can be deceptive in that the stated rate is slightly less than half the effective annual rate. Add-on rate loans can also give a sense of unfairness if you incur negative amortization. In addition, prepayment of any principal does not reduce the interest portion of subsequent payments. For these reasons, one should avoid taking an add-on rate loan. Nonetheless, there might be circumstances under which an add-on rate loan might be desirable. For example, if a consumer were offered a 5 percent add-on rate loan and a simple interest installment loan at 12 percent, then the add-on rate loan has the lower effective annual rate and would probably be the better deal.

HOW DO I OBTAIN AN INSTALLMENT LOAN?

The list of lenders of installment loans starts with the same institutions that offer checking or savings accounts. The major lenders are commercial banks, mutual savings banks, savings and loans, and credit unions. Commercial banks hold the largest dollar amount of installment loans, but installment loans are not necessarily a major part of their business. Savings and loans used to be restricted to holding only mortgages, but in the early 1980s they were granted the authority to place a limited amount of their assets in the form of consumer installment loans.

Credit unions have always focused their business on consumer installment loans. Automobile loans have particularly been a major component of their loan portfolios. In recent years, credit unions have been moved into mortgages, but consumer installment loans are still their bread and butter.

Another major lender of consumer installment loans is the consumer finance company. Some examples of consumer finance companies are provided in **Web Link 7.7.**

Web Link 7.7

What Are the Current Interest Rates on Installment Loans?

The interest rates on installment loans vary with the type and maturity of the loan, as well as the creditworthiness of the borrower. The interest rates advertised may be misleading if there are any special fees or costs associated with any given loan. Nonetheless, for someone looking for an installment loan, it's good to start with a sense of average rates. Some national averages for certain installment loans may be found at **Web Link 7.8,** and state averages are located at **Web Link 7.9.** At the time of writing, the national average rates were reported as follows:[5]

Web Link 7.8
Web Link 7.9

Type of Loan	Rate
36-month new car loan	7.89%
48-month new car loan	8.01
60-month new car loan	8.03
36-month used car loan	8.77
personal loan	14.83
home equity	8.48

These rates are typical in the following three respects. First, new auto loan rates are the cheapest because the quality of the collateral is excellent and the market is highly competitive. Second, personal loans have the highest rates because no collateral is associated with personal loans. Third, the longer the maturity of a car loan, the higher the interest rate.

WHAT HAPPENS IF I DEFAULT ON MY LOAN?

If a borrower is unable to make the required payments on a loan, he or she should first attempt to negotiate an accommodation directly with the lender. If no accommodation can be reached, then the loan is eventually declared to be in default. The necessary conditions for this declaration would be found in the documentation signed at the time the loan was extended. Once the loan is declared to be in default, the lender may then foreclose on or seize the property pledged as collateral and assume ownership. For example, a car owner who is in default on his car loan may wake up in the morning and find that his or her car appears to have been stolen. In fact, it may have been reclaimed during the night by the lender.

[5]Source: http://www.bankrate.com/brm/rate/avg_natl.asp, July 27, 2001.

When a lender forecloses on property, it will attempt to sell the property in the most expeditious manner. Lenders have no desire to hold on to foreclosed properties. If the lender is able to sell the property for more than the outstanding loan, the accumulated interest and fees, and any out-of-pocket costs, then it would return to the borrower any left-over cash. If the lender is unable to recoup what is owed, it will usually hold the borrower liable for the difference. As a practical matter, lenders will not pursue borrowers they believe to be destitute.

What Do I Do When a Debt Collector Is After Me?

Web Link 7.11

A creditor usually turns over an excessively overdue account to a debt collection agency or a debt collector. When a debt collector contacts you, you have certain rights as defined under the **Fair Debt Collection Practices Act.** Under the act, debt collectors may contact you only between 8 a.m. and 9 p.m. They may not contact you at work if they know your employer disapproves. They may not harass, oppress, or abuse you and they may not lie when collecting debts, such as falsely implying that you have committed a crime. They may not add unauthorized charges to your bill. Debt collectors must identify themselves to you on the phone. Finally, debt collectors must stop contacting you if you ask them in writing to do so. Also, they may not contact your family or friends in an attempt to collect.

When Should I Consider Declaring Bankruptcy?

If you are so in debt that you are overwhelmed, you certainly might consider bankruptcy. However, there are several steps you should consider first.[6] The first is to make your lifestyle as spartan as possible and use every resource you have. You might sell any second car, second TV, or expensive adult toys such as boats. You could sell collections and heirlooms. You might also sell your house if you have any equity in it or at least take out a HELOC that takes full advantage of your equity. Of course, if you don't repay the HELOC you would lose your home. You might dip into your pension funds to the extent you can tap this money.

If this first step does not work, the second step is to attempt to negotiate directly with your creditors for loan reductions. This is neither a short nor easy task, nor is it often successful.

The third step is to consult a professional credit counselor (not a credit doctor) as discussed in Chapter 6. A credit counselor sets up a debt repayment plan similar to what you would arrange in a Chapter 13 bankruptcy proceeding. The fourth step is a Chapter 13 bankruptcy, and the fifth and most drastic step is a Chapter 7 bankruptcy.[7]

Chapter 7 is the liquidation chapter of the bankruptcy code.[8] If you are approved for Chapter 7 bankruptcy, you are required to sell certain assets you might have and in the

---

[6]Additional discussion on the steps leading up to bankruptcy may be found at **Web Link 7.12.**

[7]At the time of writing, attempts are being made to alter substantially the federal bankruptcy codes. As such legislation is often unsuccessful, none of the proposed changes will be presented or discussed herein. If the changes do go through, then the web links will be updated to reflect the new laws. For that reason, material in the web links may not match the discussion in the text.

[8]The bankruptcy code is Title 11 of the U.S. Code. The various chapters of bankruptcy are the chapters within Title 11. Title 11 may be found at **Web Link 7.13.**

end your debts are wiped clean. Several conditions must be met to qualify for Chapter 7 bankruptcy. The major condition is that you must not have been granted a Chapter 7 discharge or completed a Chapter 13 plan within the past six years.

Web Link 7.14

    For an extensive discussion of Chapter 7 of the bankruptcy code, see **Web Link 7.14. Chapter 13** is the reorganization chapter of bankruptcy. You are given protection from your creditors (and bill collectors) so that you can work out a plan to eventually pay off all or most of your debts. Filing for bankruptcy costs anywhere from about $500 to $2,000 in legal fees. Like with many other legal actions, however, a lawyer is not a legal requirement for filing for bankruptcy. An individual willing to learn the procedures can file his or her own bankruptcy paperwork.

    If your primary purpose in declaring bankruptcy is to cheat your creditors by voiding debts that you could eventually pay off without declaring bankruptcy, then declaring bankruptcy is morally and ethically wrong. If you took on debt in good faith and were honest in all applications for credit and loans but hit difficult times as a result of loss of a job or extended illness, then bankruptcy may well be an appropriate line of action. Remember, all creditors and lenders include a premium in their interest rates to cover losses associated with bankruptcy. If a lender charges 18 percent interest on a credit card, that 18 percent likely includes a 3 percent compensation for bankruptcy losses. If that lender fails to collect exactly 3 percent of its payments because of bankruptcy, then it has predicted well. If it loses 2 percent of its payments due to bankruptcy, the lender actually comes out ahead. However, if the lender loses 4 percent of its payments because of bankruptcy, it loses money because it underestimated the magnitude of bankruptcy among its borrowers.

    Although the federal bankruptcy code controls the primary rules of bankruptcy, each state has its own set of additional rules. We can discuss some of the common or general rules.

How Does Chapter 7 Bankruptcy Work?

In a Chapter 7 bankruptcy, property is categorized as **nonexempt** and **exempt.** The debtor must turn over all nonexempt property to the bankruptcy trustee, who converts this property to cash for distribution to the creditors. The debtor receives a discharge of all dischargeable debts. Exempt property includes the following: motor vehicles, reasonably necessary clothing, household furnishings and goods, appliances, jewelry (to a limit), personal effects, life insurance, pensions, and tools of one's trade or profession to a certain value. A more comprehensive list of what can be kept may be found at **Web Link 7.15.** Some items that are exempt in specific states include the family Bible and wedding and engagement rings in Virginia, one gun in Nevada, two guns in Texas as well as two horses, donkeys, or mules, 12 head of cattle, 60 head of other livestock, and 120 fowl. Also exempt are title to watercraft over 12 feet in Illinois, a church pew in South Dakota and Minnesota, and one sewing machine in New York. In some states, people have clearly attempted to take advantage of these exemptions. For example, Virginia allows you to keep one horse. One former multimillionaire bought a thoroughbred racehorse for over one-half million dollars just before declaring bankruptcy and attempted to retain the horse. After this event was publicized, the Virginia state legislature amended its bankruptcy code to limit retained animals to pets not kept or raised for sale or profit. Texas and Florida place no limit on the exemption for a primary home, so some people in these states purchase mansions before declaring bankruptcy.

Web Link 7.15

    Nonexempt property will automatically be seized and sold to pay debts. Some examples of nonexempt property include musical instruments (unless you're a professional musician), family heirlooms, cash, bank accounts, stocks, bonds, and other investments, and a second or vacation home.

Just as assets can be divided into exempt and nonexempt categories, a creditor's debts may be divided into dischargeable and nondischargeable. Virtually all debts can be discharged, with a few exceptions. Exceptions include back child support and alimony obligations, student loans (unless repayment would cause undue hardship), income taxes less than three years past due, and court judgments for injuries or death to someone arising from intoxicated driving. Some debts that would normally be dischargeable are nondischargeable if certain special situations apply. For example, debts incurred on the basis of fraud, such as lying on a credit application or writing a bad check cannot be discharged. Similarly, debts from willful or malicious injury to another's property cannot be voided. You can discharge debts acquired through divorce other than child support and alimony payments. For example, if your divorce decree calls for you to pay off an account at a certain department store, and that store has agreed to remove your spouse's name from the account, you could be discharged from that debt. Additional discussion of nondischargeable debts may be found at **Web Link 7.16.**

Web Link 7.16

After you file for a Chapter 7 bankruptcy, the discharge and disbursement process normally is completed within six months. A Chapter 7 bankruptcy stays on your credit record for 10 years, and may cause some creditors to automatically reject you for future credit. Some creditors, however, actually seek out people who have gone through Chapter 7 bankruptcy. Their reason is that someone who has undergone a Chapter 7 bankruptcy will have little in the way of debt and, if they have a job with sufficient income, they should be able to handle the new debt payments. In addition, anyone who declares bankruptcy cannot do so again for at least six years.

How Does Chapter 13 Bankruptcy Work?

The purpose of Chapter 13 bankruptcy is to allow you to keep as many of your assets as possible yet still pay off your creditors. Chapter 13 is available only to debtors who on the date of filing owe less than $250,000 in unsecured debt and $750,000 in secured debt. Chapter 13 is like a court-imposed debt consolidation loan. That is, the court arranges for your creditors to accept smaller payments. The amount you owe is not altered but the monthly payments are reduced. Clearly, you will take longer to pay off your loans than if you had not sought Chapter 13 protection. If your debts exceed the limits for Chapter 13, and you do not or cannot qualify for Chapter 7 treatment, then there is a third option, **Chapter 11.** Chapter 11 is normally used by businesses to protect them from creditors while they reorganize. But individuals can qualify for Chapter 11 under special circumstances.

Chapter 13 stays on your credit record for only seven years as opposed to 10 years for Chapter 7. It has the benefit of showing future creditors that you did not seek to avoid completely repayment of your debt, only that you needed court help to plan those payments. It is easier to reestablish credit after filing a Chapter 13 bankruptcy than after filing Chapter 7 bankruptcy.

The first step in Chapter 13 is that the court decides on a monthly payment it believes you can afford to pay on your unsecured debts and any arrearages on your secured debts, after accounting for living expenses and current monthly payments on your secured debts. The plan typically lasts for 36 months but can stretch as long as 60 months. Each month you turn over the set amount to a trustee. The trustee distributes it pro rata among your creditors. At the end of the plan period, you are discharged from all your unsecured, dischargeable debts and arrearages on your secured debt, even if you have not paid in full what is owed.

Web Link 7.17

It should be noted that courts extend no mercy for missing payments when you are in Chapter 13. As soon as you miss a payment, your protection from creditors under Chapter 13 is removed.

If I Plan to Declare Bankruptcy, Why Not Spend All the Way to the Court?
If you are already hopelessly in debt and plan to file for bankruptcy, it might be tempting to plan a spending spree in the last days or weeks before filing (if you have an ability to charge). This is unwise because the court would most likely declare that such a spending spree was a deliberate attempt to commit fraud because you had no intention to pay your bills. You would be unable to obtain relief under Chapter 7 for the bills associated with your spending spree and the spree might prevent you from filing for Chapter 13.

SUMMARY

> Installment loans include new and used auto loans, home improvement loans, debt consolidation loans, home equity loans, and signature loans.

> On a simple interest loan, the monthly payment is computed by dividing the loan amount by the present value interest factor for an annuity based on the monthly rate and the number of monthly payments to be made.

> A critical part of every installment loan is a loan amortization table. It shows the amount due to pay off the loan if all the payments have been made on time and the amount of interest paid during any period, which is critical if the interest is tax deductible.

> Adding additional cash to an installment payment is the equivalent of investing one's money risk-free at the interest rate on the loan.

> An add-on rate loan computes the interest owed as if the full principal were owed for the entire period. The monthly payment is the sum of the principal and interest divided by the number of payments. The amortization schedule is based on the Rule of 78ths, rather than a time value of money computation.

> The best sources for installment loans are commercial banks, savings and loans and savings banks, and credit unions, as well as consumer finance companies and sales finance companies. Internet pages usually show national averages, state averages, and rates for specific lenders.

> Because of our current tax structure, home equity loans may be substantially cheaper than most other types of installments loans since the interest may qualify as an itemized deduction. It may be cheaper to pay a higher interest rate on a home equity loan to buy a car than to take out an auto loan at a lower rate.

> When someone defaults on a loan that is collateralized, the lender may seize the collateral and sell it for cash to pay off the loan. If the cash raised is insufficient, the borrower is still liable for the balance due.

> Debt collectors are limited in when and where they may call a person. They may not harass, oppress, or abuse the indebted person; they must always identify themselves; and they must restrict themselves to written communication if requested.

> Chapter 7 of the bankruptcy code involves liquidation of assets to pay off debts and the eventual elimination of most debt. Chapter 13 gives individuals protection from creditors to allow time to reorganize and eventually repay debts.

KEY TERMS

add-on rate loan	Chapter 7	Chapter 11
Chapter 13	exempt	Fair Debt Collection Practices Act
forced savings	installment loan	loan amortization table
negative amortization	nonexempt	Rule of 78ths
secured personal loan	signature loan	single payment loan

PROBLEMS

7.1 Jerry Fisher wants to borrow $10,000 to do some work on his house. He would like to pay the loan back over a period of five years. The bank indicates the interest rate would be 9 percent.

   a. If he agrees to make five annual payments, what would his annual payment be?

   b. If he agrees to make 60 monthly payments, what would his monthly payment be?

   c. Why is the monthly payment less than one-twelfth of the annual payment?

7.2 Construct a loan amortization table for the simple interest installment loan with the monthly payments described in Problem 7.1

   a. How much would Jerry owe if he wanted to pay off the loan at the end of the first year?

   b. How much interest would Jerry pay the first year?

7.3 If Jerry adds an extra $100 to his first payment (see Problem 7.2) and asks the lender to apply this $100 to the principal, how will the interest portion of his second payment be affected?

7.4 Before he takes out his loan, Jerry visits his credit union and learns that they will make a 60-month, $10,000 loan at a 5 percent add-on rate. Jerry is really impressed at the lower interest rate.

   a. What will Jerry's monthly payment be with the credit union loan?

   b. How much will Jerry owe if he pays off this loan at the end of the first year?

   c. How much will Jerry pay in interest the first year?

7.5 The local bank points out to Jerry that if he takes a $10,000 loan in the form of a home equity loan rather than a home improvement loan, the interest on the loan could become an itemized deduction and save Jerry a substantial amount in taxes. The rate on the home equity loan is 10 percent, compared to 9 percent on the home improvement loan. Both loans are for five years with monthly payments. The home equity loan carries a $300 application fee. There is no fee to apply for the home improvement loan. Jerry's effective combined marginal tax rate is 35 percent. Which loan is the better deal for Jerry if the rate Jerry could earn on any savings is also 10 percent?

7.6 a. What are the current national averages and the current averages for your state for the following loans: 36-month new car loan, 48-month new car loan, 60-month new car loan, used car loan, personal loan, and home equity loan?

   b. See if you can find a better deal than the national average from one of your local lenders for at least three of the above loans.

REFERENCES

Web Link 7.18 Glossaries of loan terms
Web Link 7.19 FAQs about installment loans
Web Link 7.20 Pointer sites for loans
Web Link 7.21 Glossaries with terms pertinent to the bankruptcy process
Web Link 7.22 Additional information on bankruptcy

WALL STREET JOURNAL INTERACTIVE RESOURCES

Web Link (WSJ) 7.23 Types of loans

For information that has changed since the book was written, for new information that pertains to this topic, and for some new web sites that pertain to the topic of this chapter, see **Web Link 7.31.**

CHAPTER 8

BUYING AND SELLING PERSONAL ASSETS: HOUSES AND CARS

LEARNING OBJECTIVES

- Decide whether to buy or rent a home
- Obtain information on renting
- Obtain information about houses for sale
- Understand the benefits and costs of using a realtor to buy or sell a house
- Explain the common features of a bid to buy a home
- Discuss the strategies of setting an asking price and developing a bid price for a home
- Discuss the problems associated with the concept of square footage of living area
- Discuss how to select a home inspector
- Obtain estimates of the cost of moving
- Discuss the tax treatment of moving expenses
- Decide what type of car you should buy
- Obtain estimates of values of various cars
- Explain the relevance of MSRP and dealer's cost in buying a new car
- Discuss how to make an initial bid for a new car
- Explain how to locate and buy a car over the Internet

Web Link: www.wiley.com/college/woerheide

INTRODUCTION

For most people, the single biggest expense each year is the cost of housing, and housing decisions are rarely permanent. It is unlikely that you or anyone you know will live in the same residence their entire lives. Most people find that every few years they must make a new decision about housing as events such as a job transfer, marriage, divorce, the birth of children, and retirement make it clear that the current residence needs to be changed.

The most fundamental decision in the selection of housing is whether to buy or rent. Regardless of the answer, you must next decide what location and type of housing best serves your needs. Finally, if you decide to buy a house you start the complex process of negotiating a purchase.

The second single largest expense for most people is the purchase of a vehicle. Most of the issues that apply to housing also apply to transportation. That is, a buyer must decide on a new or used car, choose whether to buy or lease (rent), select a particular vehicle, make a bid, and negotiate financing.

In this chapter, we follow Steve and Sue Gold. Steve is being transferred from Boston, Massachusetts, to Charlotte, North Carolina. The Golds own their home in Boston. They are unsure whether to buy or rent in North Carolina as Steve is still waiting to receive some indication of how long he should expect to be in Charlotte before he is transferred again. The Golds will need to sell their home in Boston and to obtain housing in Charlotte. The Golds are also in the process of buying a vehicle.

SHOULD I BUY OR RENT A HOME?

Although most people can choose between buying and renting, some can not. What separates those who can choose from those who cannot is usually the **down payment** necessary to buy a house. The down payment is the cash you will pay for the house from your own resources. Unless you have enough cash that your down payment covers the full purchase price of a property, you will have to take out a **mortgage** for the balance of the purchase price. A mortgage is a loan used for buying real estate. The real estate purchased serves as collateral for that loan. Mortgages and down payments are discussed in greater detail in Chapter 9. The standard down payment is 20 percent of the purchase price. By taking out private mortgage insurance or obtaining an FHA or VA mortgage (see Chapter 9), a home buyer might be able to get the down payment down to as little as 5 percent of the purchase price. In addition to a down payment, there are other costs associated with the purchase of real estate. These other costs may add to the down payment as much as 2 percent of the cost of the house. Thus, if you want to buy a home for say, $100,000, you would need immediate cash of anywhere from $7,000 (5 percent down payment plus $2,000) to $22,000 (20 percent down payment plus $2,000).

Several traditional methods help prospective buyers overcome the lack of cash to make the standard 20 percent down payment. The first is to obtain the cash from relatives in the form of a gift.[1] A second is to take out a loan for the purpose of making a down payment. Any loans obtained to acquire cash for a down payment must be reported to the prospective mortgage lender. Such loans diminish the likelihood that the mortgage lender will provide the mortgage because of concern about the borrower's ability to make the payments on both the down payment loan and the mortgage loan. A third method of dealing with the lack of a down payment is to buy a cheaper house than you really want. Some people buy a **handyman's special.** A handyman's special is a house that is in deteriorated physical condition but could be fixed up. A homeowner able do this would then hope to resell this home at a substantially higher price. The profit on this sale could then serve as the down payment for the purchase of the type of house the homebuyer originally wanted. Profiting on improvements to a handyman's special is known as **sweat equity.**

Let us assume that you have sufficient cash on hand to make a down payment, so that the buy-versus-rent choice is a real one. Although the choice as to the type of housing you acquire is technically separate from the rent-versus-buy decision, they cannot always

---

[1]As will be discussed in Chapter 19, gifts to an individual in excess of $10,000 (or $20,000 if given jointly) are subject to gift taxes.

be kept separate. Consider the stock of rental housing and the stock of buyer-owned housing. The term *stock* refers to the quantity and quality of each type of housing. The stock of rental housing is not exactly the same as the stock of buyer-owned housing.

Housing comes in many forms. Although the most common form of housing is the single-family residence, other forms of housing exist: multiple-family residences (duplexes, triplexes, etc.), row houses, condominiums, town houses, and apartment buildings. Buyer-owned housing consists predominantly of single-family residences, condominiums, and town houses. Rental housing consists primarily of multiple-family residences and apartment buildings. Although single-family houses can be rented and a unit in a multiple-family residence can be purchased, the number of single-family houses that may be rented is extremely small compared to the number of those that may only be purchased. If you want a single-family residence, you have much greater choice if you can buy. If you want to live in a multiple-family residence, you have much greater choice if you are willing to rent. So, if you want a particular form of housing and you want to have substantive choice in the final selection, your buy-versus-rent decision may already be made for you. The difference between the stock of rental housing and the stock of buyer-owned housing also means that you can rarely make a buy-versus-rent decision considering comparable properties.

Several factors are crucial to the choice of the type of housing you seek. One factor is the size of your family and your desired lifestyle. Couples with children tend to want single-family residences and are thus more likely to buy. Single people tend to want freedom from home and lawn maintenance and thus are more likely to rent.

A second factor is how long you expect to live at the new residence. Buying and selling a residence usually involves substantial costs. So the shorter your expected occupancy, the more likely you should rent rather than buy. The higher the costs associated with buying and selling a residence, the more likely you are to rent.

A third factor is the rate at which you expect the price of housing to appreciate. Housing is one of the few **consumer durables** that has the potential to appreciate in value. A consumer durable is any expensive asset consumers buy that is expected to have a long life. Most consumer durables, such as cars, washing machines, dryers, and refrigerators, decline in value as they age. Housing is an asset that both satisfies a basic need and can be an investment. The higher the rate at which you expect housing prices to appreciate, the more likely you are to buy rather than rent.

A fourth factor is taxes. The two major expenses normally associated with the ownership of a home, property taxes and the interest portion of a mortgage payment, are itemized deductions. The higher your marginal tax bracket, the more likely you are to want to own. The lower your marginal tax bracket, the less valuable the tax deductions become, and the more likely you are to rent.

A fifth factor is the opportunity cost of money. The purchase of a house usually involves a substantial outlay of cash. The higher the rate of return at which you could invest this cash, the less attractive the purchase of a house becomes and the more likely you are to rent.

A sixth factor is the cost of the mortgage, including the cost of acquiring the mortgage (referred to as closing costs) and the interest rate on the mortgage. It is much easier to buy housing when mortgage interest rates are 6 to 8 percent than when they are 12 to 15 percent.

Web Link 8.1

Steve and Sue Gold are being transferred from Boston to Charlotte. They own their home in Boston and they are unsure how long they will be living in Charlotte, so they are unsure if they should buy or rent. They have found a nice apartment that rents for $900 a month. Renters' insurance would cost them $15 per month ($180 per year). The house they are looking at would cost about $150,000. They would make a down payment of 20 percent of the purchase price of the house (or $30,000). Closing costs would run about $2,000. The interest rate on a 30-year, fixed rate mortgage would be 8 percent. Their combined marginal federal and state income tax bracket is 35 percent. The annual real estate taxes on the house would cost about $2,000. Annual maintenance expenses would run about $1,000 per year and homeowner's insurance would cost $50 per month ($600 per year). They anticipate an inflation rate (i.e., the annual increase in rent) of 4 percent, but think housing will appreciate at the rate of only 3 percent per year. They anticipate that when they sell their Charlotte house, the realtor's commission and other closing costs would be 8 percent of the selling price. The opportunity cost of the money they put down on the house is 10 percent. If the apartment and house are reasonable substitutes in terms of lifestyle, is it economically worthwhile to buy the house?

Web Link 8.2

The critical variable in this example (and any buy-versus-rent problem) is how long the buyer will live in the acquired home. To resolve whether the Golds should buy or rent you can use a calculator to solve for the best fiscal choice by considering different periods of occupancy. Go to any of the calculators at **Web Link 8.2** and solve this problem assuming occupancy periods of one, two, three, and four years.

The calculator indicates that if the expected occupancy is one year, renting is cheaper by $9,477. If two years, renting is cheaper by $4,991. If three years, renting is cheaper by $545, and if four years, *owning* is cheaper by $3,858. These answers are in present value terms. If the Golds expect to live at their next residence for two years and had to make one single payment today to cover all of the costs for the next two years, the single payment for renting would be $4,991 cheaper than the single payment for owning. An alternative interpretation is that if the Golds decide to buy a house rather than rent for the next two years, their decision is equivalent to their making a single payment today of $4,991 and then making all of the payments they would have made if they had rented. This does not mean that the Golds must rent. They may in fact decide that the pleasure and satisfaction of owning their own home for the next two years are worth the additional expenses they will be incurring.

Web Link 8.3

There are other sites, found at **Web Link 8.3,** that provide insight to the buy-versus-rent decision. Most incorporate fewer variables than do any of the calculators at **Web Link 8.2.**

HOW DO I GO ABOUT RENTING A HOME?

If you have decided to rent, the next step is to obtain information on rental units. Rental information typically is only of local interest, so community web pages, such as those of the local newspaper or local realtors, will provide the best information, but some sites provide national coverage.

Steve and Sue have decided to rent when they move to Charlotte. They would like to get as much detailed information as possible on various apartment units they would consider renting. They would like a two-bedroom unit, and are willing to pay rent in the range of $900 per month.

Web Link 8.4 The sites at **Web Link 8.4** are able to identify a variety of choices, along with substantial details, floor plans, and pictures.

Web Link 8.5 Another way to obtain up-to-date information on apartments that are available is to use the classified ads of a local newspaper. Use **Web Link 8.5** to access those newspapers with classifieds on the Internet.

HOW DO I BUY A HOME?

If you have decided to buy, the next step is to find the optimal residence. The best way to do this is to start by deciding the characteristics of your ideal residence. Once the ideal is defined, then you need to find the residences on the market that are closest to this ideal. Finally, to inspect many of the residences on the market, you will need to work with a realtor.

How Do I Decide What Type of Home I Am Looking For?

The number of properties for sale in any market at any time can be huge. A successful search requires the prospective buyer to narrow the properties to be inspected to a manageable list that can be viewed in the time available.

Steve and Sue have set aside four days to travel to Charlotte to look for a house to buy. Before they arrive, they need to make as many specific decisions as possible about what they are seeking. They need some sort of checklist to help them focus their thoughts. They need to make sure in advance they are clear on what they each want, and they need to communicate these preferences as clearly as possible to their realtor.

Web Link 8.6 The sites at **Web Link 8.6** provide various checklists.

How Do I Find Out About the Various Communities in Which I Might Live?

Once you decide on the characteristics of the house you would like, you need to decide which particular community or communities are the most desirable. Most metropolitan areas tend to have a large number of suburbs. Realtors can provide some information on Web Link 8.7 the various communities in an area. You can find more information on the Internet.

One way to decide which communities you want to search in is to focus on communities offering the greatest choice of the type of house you want. For example, suppose you would like a four-bedroom house with a three-car garage costing about $200,000. You search each community in a particular metropolitan area and find that three communities each have more than 15 such homes on the market. Each of the rest of the communities have fewer than three such homes on the market. It is highly likely that you will end up living in one of these three communities.

How Do I Find Out What Is on the Market?

Once you decide on the characteristics of the residence you are seeking and the community or communities in which you wish to search, you next want to obtain information on all the residences that meet your criteria.

Steve and Sue have (after much effort) agreed on the major features of a single-family residence that they would like to own. They would like a home that has 2,500 square feet of living space, four bedrooms, and two and one-half baths and that is priced at about $150,000. They would like to be in Charlotte proper. Now they want to see homes on the market that meet these criteria.

Web Link 8.8

The major site for finding a home would be **Web Link 8.8.** Its home page is shown in Figure 8.1. At the time of writing, 573 properties were found that met the Gold's criteria in the above example. Clearly, the Golds need to refine their search criteria. The advantage of the site at **Web Link 8.8** is that it includes listings from *all* of the **multiple listing services** (MLSs). When someone wishing to sell a house signs a contract with a realtor to sell his or her home, one of the realtor's first steps is to put information about the house into the local MLS. Almost all the realtors serving that community subscribe to this service and will immediately receive the information about the new home for sale. The major advantage of the MLS to a seller is that any potential buyer working with a realtor will then have the information on the seller's home. In fact, with the growth of web sites dedicated to providing housing information, even buyers not working with realtors can access information on homes on the market.

Web Link 8.9

Many local and national brokerage firms also have their own web sites that are limited to listings only through those firms.

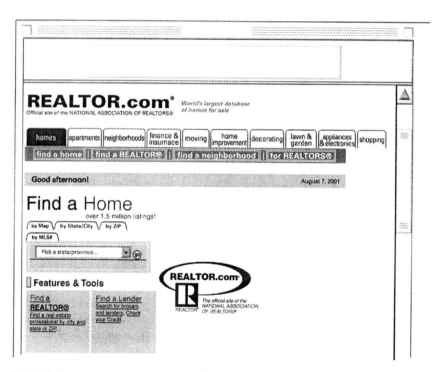

FIGURE 8-1 Home Page for www.realtor.com

How Can I Get a Listing of Repossessed Property?   Some homeowners run into misfortune and end up **defaulting** on their mortgages. Defaulting on a mortgage simply means a homeowner has ceased to make monthly payments on the mortgage. All mortgages have the provision that the lender may seize the property in order to sell it to satisfy the debt if the homeowner defaults. Such property is called **repossessed property.** If the lender sells the property for more than the loan amount and the cost of selling the property, the lender must return the excess cash to the borrower. In truth, the lender has no incentive to sell the property for more than what is due. In fact, any attempt to sell the property for more than what is due the lender may delay the sale and end up costing the lender more time, money, and effort. If the lender sells the property for less than what is due, most mortgage agreements allow the lender to seek the additional balance from the homeowner. If a homeowner believes he or she will default on a mortgage, he or she should attempt to sell the property for at least what is owed on the mortgage.

Web Link 8.10

From the buyer's perspective, repossessed property may represent a potential bargain. It is also a specialized area of the market fraught with danger.

Should I Use a Realtor to Help Me Buy a House?

A person must pass a state exam in order to be licensed as a realtor. There are many characteristics to consider in selecting a realtor. Some realtors obtain certifications beyond the minimal state license requirement. Some realtors work full-time and some part-time. Some have been in the business for 30 years and some have recently entered the business.

Buyers may hire realtors to work with them. In this case, the prospective buyer and the realtor negotiate a fee directly. Most buyers simply ask a realtor to work with them and let the seller pay the realtor's commission (this payment process is discussed in the next section). There are usually two realtors in every transaction. One is the realtor who has listed the property that is being sold (the **selling realtor**). The other is the realtor who brings in the buyer for the property (the **buying realtor**). It is absolutely clear that the selling realtor works as an **agent** of the seller. An agent is a person employed to represent the interests of the person who has hired them. The selling realtor is obligated to obtain the best possible deal for the seller.

The buying realtor may be an agent of the seller or an agent of the buyer. This varies by state. In the past five years, agency laws in all 50 states have been amended to require real estate agents to indicate who they represent when showing a property.[2] If the buying realtor is an agent of the seller, he or she is obligated to obtain the best possible deal for the seller, not the buyer. Potential buyers are sometimes confused after working with a buying realtor for several days, weeks, or even months and start to think of the buying realtor as their friend, helper, and agent. When it comes time to bid on a residence a buying realtor who is an agent of the seller will seek the best possible deal for the seller, not the buyer. If, in the realtor's presence, one spouse said to the other "let's bid $110,000 for the house, but I am certainly willing to pay as much as $120,000," the buying realtor would be obligated to relay that information to the seller.

---

[2]An awkward problem arises if the selling realtor also brings in the buyer for the property. The agent becomes a "dual agent" and may not be able to serve either party well.

Using the Internet, Steve and Sue have identified 30 properties they would like to see. Access to view these properties is only through a realtor. In addition, there are probably some properties not listed on any Internet site that a realtor might be able to bring to their attention. They would like to learn about the different realtors in their area.

Web Link 8.11   Steve and Sue will find information on realtors on **Web Link 8.11.**

How Do I Make a Bid on a Property?

When you have selected the residence you would like to purchase, you will make a bid on it. If you found the property through a realtor, that realtor should write up and present your bid. If you found the property on your own, then you could go to a lawyer or any realtor to write up the bid. If a realtor has listed the property, the full commission will be due regardless of who writes up the bid or how it is presented to the seller.

When the seller lists the house, an **asking price** is specified. The asking price represents the seller's ideal price of what he or she would like to receive for the house. Most of the time, homes sell for less than the asking price. However, when particular real estate markets get hot, anxious buyers may bid the asking price or even more than the asking price. The buyer must decide the price he or she is willing to bid. It is important to note that there are other elements to the bid besides the bid price.

One key bid element is the projected closing date and the date of possession. The closing date is the date on which the legal sale of the property (and the payment of the cash) will take place. The date of possession is the date the buyer is entitled to move in. A seller should never allow a buyer to move in before the date of closing. There is always a chance the deal will fall through. If it does, the seller then has the incredible problem of getting that buyer out of the house in order to start showing it to new prospective buyers. Having the date of possession after the date of closing can be just as much a problem for the buyer. In cases where possession is after closing, a daily rental rate is usually specified in the contract for the time from the closing date to the possession date, but several things can go wrong. First, the seller may not be able to physically get out of the house. Imagine pulling up with a moving van to take possession of your new home only to discover the seller is still in full occupancy with all of his or her furniture in place. The second problem is that the seller may damage the house in the process of moving out. Imagine moving into a home only to discover a huge gash in the wall where a piano used to be, especially if you had looked behind the piano when you first viewed the house and observed no such gash. The seller will likely argue that the gash had always been there. If possession is after closing and there is no security deposit, you really have no recourse except to repair the gash yourself. If possession is at the time of closing, then you can inspect the property on your way to the closing. You then have some leverage in discussing who should repair the gash in the wall. In practice, the date of possession is usually a matter of local custom.

The bid should also specify details about what is being purchased. For example, the bid might include such items as the seller's refrigerator, washer and dryer, lawnmower, and a beautiful grandfather clock in the living room. The bid should also include **contingencies.** A contingency is a condition that must be fulfilled before the deal can be finalized. The most critical contingency is that the buyer receives approval for a mortgage. Other common contingencies include a building inspection, a radon inspection, and an opportunity for the lawyers of both parties to review the contract.[3] A time limit must be specified for each contingency. If the buyer feels that any contingency has not been met, then he or she has the privilege of canceling or renegotiating the bid. For example, if a major structural defect in the house is found by the building inspector, the buyer may cancel the contract without fault, ask the seller to repair the defect, or present a new bid for the property.

Finally, the buyer attaches **earnest money** to the bid. Earnest money is provided to demonstrate the buyer's sincerity. The seller may keep the earnest money if the buyer reneges on the contract. If the buyer later finds a residence he likes better, he could simply tell the seller he is no longer interested in the property and cancel the contract, but he would forfeit the earnest money. The larger the earnest money, the more willing a seller should be to accept a bid, even if the other terms are not exactly to his liking.

Once the bid is presented to the seller, the seller has three choices. The seller may accept the bid, reject the bid, or make a counteroffer. For example, if the asking price is $150,000 and the bid price is $138,000, the seller may counter at $142,000. The seller may also remove or change some of the inclusions or contingencies in the bid. If the seller does not want to sell the grandfather clock, he or she crosses it off the bid. If the seller does not want to have a pest inspection, he or she crosses that off the bid.

A counteroffer legally invalidates the original offer. If a counteroffer is made, the buyer has the same three choices the seller had: accept, reject, or make a new counteroffer. It is possible that several counteroffers could be made before a deal is finalized.

If a buyer and a seller are close on a deal but cannot resolve a few small items, both should remember that there are usually four parties to any real estate deal, not two: the seller, the buyer, the buying realtor, and the selling realtor. If a deal is at an impasse over a small item, many realtors will offer to pay for something out of their commission to save a deal. If your realtors are hesitant to do this, it is okay to ask them directly. They have no legal obligation to do so, however.

What Should the First Bid Price Be? A buyer might be tempted to think that starting the negotiations at an unusually low price may cause the final price to be lower than it otherwise would be. This strategy carries two problems. First, if the initial bid is too low the seller may think the buyer is not serious and not budge from the asking price or budge by only a few dollars. Nothing will really be accomplished in the negotiations. Second, making a low initial offer may cause the negotiations to stretch out over time. It is possible that a third party may bid on the same property while a series of counteroffers is occurring. In fact, even if the third party comes in with a bid that is the same as the first buyer's initial bid, the seller may accept the third party's bid only because he or she has become so annoyed in dealing with the first bidder.

A buyer may find it useful to know the prices the desired home sold for in recent years, if there have in fact been any sales. A buyer may also like to know the prices of any other homes in the neighborhood. The price history of a particular home, all the homes on a particular street, or all the homes in a particular neighborhood is available at

Web Link 8.15a **Web Link 8.15a.**

---

[3]State laws usually require pest inspections. If not, however, then a pest inspection would be an appropriate contingency.

Should I Use a Realtor to Sell My House?

There is no law that requires sellers to use a realtor to sell their home. If your home has not been listed and someone approaches you about buying it, you may certainly negotiate to sell your property. You can sell your own home yourself just like you can sell your own auto or any other asset that you own. If you decide to market your own house formally, then your property is known as a **FSBO** or a "for sale by owner" property. There are some drawbacks to selling your house yourself. The first is that you must develop and pay for your own marketing. A realty firm is usually able to negotiate special deals on newspaper advertising and many participate in special publications that list homes for sale; such special rates or other outlets are not available to the individual. If your house is on the market for an extended amount of time, you may end up paying as much in marketing fees as you save in realtors' commissions. The growth of the Internet has helped FSBO sellers by allowing for the development of sites that list FSBO properties. Some of these sites focus on a relatively small geographic area such as a state or a region in a state, others are national in their scope. Some sites with national property listings may be found at **Web**

Web Link 8.15   **Link 8.15.**

If you decide to use a realtor, most experts advise that you interview at least three prospective realtors before selecting one. The most important question to ask is what specifically that realtor is going to do to help to sell your house. You should discuss how often the realtor will run ads on your home, what the size of the ads will be, and where the ads will be placed. Additional topics include how open houses will be handled. Some realtors send assistants to cover the open houses. Some realtors attempt to be present every time a prospective buyer is shown your property. Other realtors decline to be present.

If you choose a realtor to sell your home, you will sign a listing agreement, which is a contract detailing the legal relationship between you and the realtor. There are four key terms to the listing agreement. These are the provision for **exclusivity,** the length of the contract, the selling price, and the commission rate. Exclusivity means that the realtor earns his or her commission for the sale of the property regardless of who brings in the buyer. If you sign a listing agreement in the morning and that afternoon a colleague makes an offer for your house that you want to accept, the realtor would still earn the commission. One way to bypass this problem is to prepare a list of "exclusions." These are people who might be interested in buying your property but need an additional few days to think about it. If anyone named in the exclusion list buys the house, the realtor does not earn the commission. The realtor will want the exclusion list to have an expiration date—one that is relatively quick. It is also in your interest to set a relatively short time frame for exclusions as the realtor may not attempt to market the property aggressively until the expiration date of the exclusion list has passed. No realtor wants to spend time and money marketing a property only to see it sold to someone on the exclusion list.

The listing agreement will also have an expiration date. When the agreement expires, you can negotiate a new listing agreement with the realtor or look for another realtor if you believe the realtor has not made a sincere and worthwhile effort to sell the house. Realtors like a long time horizon for the listing agreement, typically at least three to six months. It is in your best interest to place as short a time horizon as possible on the contract so that the property can be placed with a new realtor if the current realtor is unsatisfactory. A realtor will also claim the right to the commission if the property is sold to anyone who saw the property during the time it was listed with him or her. This is a legitimate claim; it prevents a prospective buyer and seller from getting together, especially near the end of the listing agreement, and agreeing to a transaction immediately after the expiration of the listing agreement in order to eliminate the realtor's commission.

The listing contract will also specify the commission structure for the selling and buying realtors. For example, suppose you agree to pay a 6 percent commission. You then specify how the commission is to be split between the two realtors, such as each receiving 3 percent. If most commissions in your community are set at 6 percent and are split three and three, then an aggressive seller might offer to pay a 7 percent commission, with the buying realtor receiving 4 percent. All other things being equal, a realtor working with buyers is more likely to show a property offering the higher commission to the buying realtor.

It is also possible to negotiate a lower commission. If the lower commission is applied to the buying realtor, the property would likely receive little traffic from potential buyers. If the lower commission is applied to the selling realtor, the selling realtor might offset the lower rate with a smaller marketing effort.

All realtors work simultaneously as buying and selling realtors. A buying realtor will be inclined to show his or her own properties to prospective buyers because he or she is entitled to both shares of the commission.

Although the selling realtor should act in the best interest of the seller, he or she is required by law to advise prospective buyers of any known problems such as structural defects. The selling realtor is not obligated to reveal other information that could be just as important. For example, even if the seller of the home had been receiving death threats, the selling realtor is not required to reveal this information.

What Should Be the Initial Asking Price?   The first and most common problem

in selling a house is setting the asking price too high. A seller may hope that by setting a high asking price he or she can cause the final sale price to be higher than it would otherwise be. The first fault with this strategy is that an asking price out of line with a description of the property will cause many prospective buyers to pass over the property in search of ones priced more competitively. Similarly, many realtors, when given a choice of which houses to show, will opt to show houses with the most attractive asking prices as they have the best chance of actually selling. The second fault with this strategy is that if buyers get tired of extended negotiations caused by large differences between what they want to pay and the asking prices, they could decide to pursue an alternative property.

In setting the initial asking price, a seller should attempt to ascertain the most likely final selling price. One way to do this is to ask several local realtors. In fact, when a seller is interviewing realtors to select the one with whom the property will be listed, he or she should ask each prospective realtor what the listing price and likely sale price would be.

Some realtors engage in **highballing,** where they suggest prices that are unrealistically high. The hope is that the prospective seller will be so impressed at how much he or she could obtain for the house that the realtor will "win" the listing. When the house fails to sell and traffic is minimal, the realtor then suggests lowering the asking price to a more reasonable level. Although a seller might think there is little harm in asking a higher price for the house, there is a hidden cost. The longer a house is on the market, the more it becomes viewed as stale goods. Prospective buyers start to assume something must be wrong with the house if it has been on the market for a long time.

Some realtors engage in **lowballing,** where they encourage a seller to set a lower price than the property should actually bring. The idea here is that although the realtor may earn a slightly lower commission, a low asking price will draw lots of traffic and encourage a quick sale. The realtor is trading off a quick and near-certain commission for a delayed and less-certain commission.

In the end, it is the seller who tells the realtor the price at which to list the house. If the realtor believes the listing price is inappropriate, he or she has the right to refuse to accept the listing. It is best to list a home with a realtor who has similar beliefs about the value of the house as the seller.

A second method to setting the initial asking price is to keep an eye on what recent properties in the neighborhood have sold for. One way of valuing real estate is to figure the cost per square foot of living area for homes sold in the neighborhood. The seller then measures the square footage of his or her own home and multiplies this by the standardized cost per square foot. This number may need to be adjusted up or down for variations. For example, if most of the homes in the neighborhood have extensive finished basements and yours does not, then you would want to lower the cost per square foot by a small amount. If your lot is smaller than the others in the neighborhood or if you have an undesirable location such as a corner lot, then you also need to revise down the cost figure somewhat. Next, the seller needs to ascertain the ratio of selling price to asking price for recent sales in the area. The seller then divides the desired or expected selling price by this ratio to set a realistic asking price. Consider the following example:

> *The Golds are preparing to sell their house. In the past year, three homes on their block have sold. The first had 2,100 square feet of living area and sold for $176,400. The second had 2,150 square feet and it sold for $178,450. The third had 2,400 square feet and sold for $204,000. The Golds believe that the second house was the most comparable to theirs in terms of style. The ratios of final sales prices to initial asking prices for homes in their area have been averaging 95 percent. The home they are selling has 2,200 square feet. What would be a good asking price for their home?*

The prices per square foot of living area for the three homes were $84, $83, and $85. If the Golds believe that the second house was the most comparable to theirs, then $83 would be a legitimate cost per square foot. This figure is then multiplied by the actual square footage of the Golds' home to obtain a realistic selling price of $182,600. Finally, when we divide this number by the 95 percent ratio, we obtain a realistic asking price of $192,210. Most people like to list homes with asking prices just below an even multiple of $1,000, so the Golds might consider rounding this number down to $191,900.

One final consideration in setting an asking price is that many buyers look for a home in a specific price range bounded by increments of $10,000. In the case of the Golds, they are more likely to have their house compare well to the competition if people willing to spend up to $190,000 are looking at it. People who are willing to spend up to $200,000 likely will be looking at other homes that are somewhat nicer. So a final strategy is to set the house price just below some interval of $10,000. If the Golds are anxious to sell their home quickly, they might consider an initial asking price of $189,900.

The buyers are going through the same mathematics. They can ascertain the square footage of living area and selling prices of homes in an area to obtain a ballpark figure of what homes are selling for per square foot. Next, they can look up the ratios of the sales prices to the asking prices. So if a buyer observes that homes are going for an average of

$84 per square foot and he or she wants a home with about 2,000 square feet of living area, he or she should expect to negotiate a final price of about $168,000. If the ratio of selling price to asking price is 95 percent, the buyer should be looking at homes with asking prices in the $170,000 range. A serious initial bid in this case would be at least $160,000.

How Is the Square Footage of Living Area Measured?   Square feet of living area is not as precise a number as one might think. There is no absolute legal rule as to how it is determined. Some people measure based on the external walls of the house. Others measure from a point halfway between the outside of the exterior wall and the inside of the interior wall. Still others measure based only on the interior walls. For a single-story home, the square footage should be fairly easily measured under any of the above definitions. The square footage of a perfectly rectangular two-story home with no cathedral ceilings would be found by multiplying the length of the front of the house by the length of the side of the house and then multiplying by two.

How Should I Choose a Home Inspector?

Most bids for a home include the privilege to send a professional home inspector to the property within a specified time period (such as two weeks) and the right to withdraw or amend the bid based on the home inspector's report. A home inspection will typically cost the buyer $250 to $500 (unless the bid specifies that the seller is to pay for the cost of the inspection). If the seller objects to such an inspection, the prospective buyer should start looking for another property immediately.

Choosing a home inspector can be tricky. Most states have no licensing requirements for this job, so anyone can call himself or herself a home inspector. There are some certification societies. The National Association for Home Inspectors requires a provisional member only to send a notarized application form providing information on training, education, work experience, and home inspection history, along with a check for anywhere from $180 to $310, depending on the time of year the application is submitted. The American Society of Home Inspectors actually requires a prospective member to take an exam and perform supervised inspections. Once licensed, members must fulfill continuing education requirements. Information on these two organizations and their requirements to **Web Link 8.16** become a member and the names of inspectors certified may be found at **Web Link 8.16.**

As with hiring any professional, a prospective buyer should probably interview at least three building inspectors. You want someone whose primary occupation is inspection, not someone who inspects to fill time between activities on their "real" job. You want someone who inspects several homes a week and has done so for several years. The primary product of the home inspector is a written report, so you should also request a copy of a recently completed report produced by each inspector. A poor report will consist of a simple checklist. A good report will contain descriptive information, identify items that need to be fixed, indicate the cost of such repairs, and indicate the consequences of failing to make such repairs.

Note that home inspectors do not guarantee their inspection. Most will ask you to sign a disclaimer limiting their liability to the amount of the fee. Guarantees are not a realistic expectation, since if something critical is missed in the inspection, there is always the possibility that it was not observable at the time of the inspection.

Home inspectors can be found in the telephone book. In addition, most real estate lawyers and the buying realtor could also be sources of recommendations. There is a potential bias in any recommendations of the buying realtor. If a home inspector is able to identify all the flaws in a home, a prospective buyer might change his or her mind about the proposed purchase. Thus, a home inspector who is too thorough can potentially kill a deal.

Web Link 8.17

How Do I Find Help on Moving?

Web Link 8.12
Web Link 8.13
Web Link 8.14

Moving can be an expensive, exhaustive, and frustrating process, particularly if treasured possessions are broken or disappear. It is important to know up front approximately how much a move will cost. Consumer information and help with moving is widely available on the Internet.

What Are the Tax Consequences to Moving?

Anyone who moves because of a job transfer or a new job, even graduates moving to take their first job, may be eligible to use much of the moving expenses as an adjustment to their income.[4] You must pass two tests to use moving expenses as an adjustment. The first is the **mileage test.** The current provision is that the distance between your new primary job and your residence must be at least 50 miles greater than your previous commute (the distance between your old residence and your old job). Consider the following two examples:

> *(a) Steve currently drives 55 miles to work each day. He has found a new job that is 100 miles from his current residence. Steve is thinking about moving closer to his new job. Could this move be used as an adjustment to Steve's income?*

The difference between Steve's new commuting distance if he did not move (100 miles) and his current commuting distance (55 miles) is 45 miles. As this is less than the 50-mile requirement, there would be no tax break for Steve's move.

> *(b) As part of their move, Sue would change jobs. Sue currently has a 5-mile commute to work. She would likely take a new job that is approximately 100 miles from their current residence. Can the move now be used as an adjustment to income?*

The tax code requires only that at least one of the spouses meet the mileage test. As the mileage differential for Sue will be approximately 95 miles, it is likely that their moving expenses can be used as an adjustment. However, Sue has to be careful not to accept a new job that is less than 55 miles from her former residence!

The second test that you must pass to use moving expenses as an adjustment to your income is the **time test.** You must be employed and live in your new residence for at least 39 weeks during the first 12 months after the move. You need not necessarily be employed at the same job. Also, if your employer terminates your employment or your employer transfers you again, the 39-week rule is waived. If you are self-employed, you must maintain your employment for at least 78 weeks during the first 24 months at the new location.

---

[4]Recall from Chapter 3 that adjustments to income are not the same as deductions. A deduction is valuable only to the extent that one's total itemized deductions exceed the standard deduction for one's filing status. Adjustments to income are automatic reductions of taxable income; they reduce the value of one's AGI. A reduction in AGI could make other itemized deductions more valuable.

The intent here would appear to be to prevent people from moving to such places as a retirement home and using these moving expenses as an adjustment to income.

If you pass all of the above tests, then you are allowed to use three categories of expenses as adjustments. The first is the cost of packing, shipping, and insurance covering up to 30 days of temporary storage. The second is the cost of traveling once to your new home, including lodging (but not meals) and actual driving costs, or 10 cents a mile, whichever is greater. The third is the cost of utilities disconnection at your old home and hookups at the new home.

Web Link 8.18

WHAT TYPE OF CAR SHOULD I GET?

As mentioned earlier, a vehicle is usually the second most expensive item most people buy. They also buy vehicles more frequently than they buy homes. Thus, the cost of acquiring vehicles is clearly a major component of a person's expenditures. In addition, the annual cost of owning a vehicle is also high. The major expenditures associated with auto owner-ship include insurance, depreciation, maintenance, and of course the direct costs of gasoline and oil.

Web Link 8.19

The process of buying a car is similar to that of buying a house or any other major consumer durable. First, you need to decide what you want and need. For example, you may want a fancy sports car with a heavy-duty engine. Suppose, however, that you will use this car primarily driving to and from work and will probably drive an average number of miles per year (10,000 to 12,000 miles per year). Then perhaps you would be better off economically to buy a standard or economy car with a regular size engine.

Once you have decided what features you would like in a car, the second step is to identify cars that meet your criteria. The more cars that meet your criteria, the better your ability to bargain and otherwise seek out the best deal. Consider the following example:

Steve and Sue realize they need another car for their eldest son. They have no prefer-ences on the manufacturer, but they would like a 1999 economy car in the price range of $13,000 to $16,500. How many different cars meet these criteria?

Web Link 8.20

At the time of writing, **Web Link 8.20** provided a list of eight different makes and models that the Golds should investigate further. The many car search calculators on the Internet are not really comparable because each one focuses on somewhat different criteria, so it is worthwhile to use several of these search calculators until you find one that uses the exact criteria you have in mind.

Web Link 8.21

Should I Buy a New or a Used Car?

One of the first decisions all prospective car buyers must make is whether to buy a new or used car. Although a used car is cheaper to purchase, it is not always cheaper to own over long periods of time. When a new car is bought and held for 12 years, the distribution of expenses associated with ownership are as follows:[5]

Web Link 8.21a   [5]See Web Link 8.21a.

Depreciation and finance Charges	38%
Insurance	21
Gasoline and oil	19
Maintenance and repair work	13
Other	9
Total	100

Depreciation and financing charges make up the majority of the expenses of ownership. These charges will always be higher for a new car than a used car. Insurance, gasoline, and oil expenses will usually be comparable for a new and used car, although (as will be discussed in Chapter 10) there are some opportunities to reduce the cost of insurance on older cars. Only maintenance and repair work are likely to be higher for a used car.

> *Steve and Sue are looking at a new car and a three-year-old version of the same car. The new car costs $15,000. Whichever car they buy, they will make a $2,000 down payment. The interest rate on the new car loan will be 8 percent and the rate on the used car loan will be 9 percent, both for 36 months. The Golds plan to hold the car for four years. They project the average monthly maintenance to be $30 on the new car and $120 on the old car. Which car is cheaper to own over the four-year period?*

Web Link 8.21b

Any of the calculators at **Web Link 8.21b** will indicate that the used car will likely cost an average of $84 more per year. More important, if you click on the graph for this calculator, you will see the average annual cost of ownership as a function of time. In this example, the used car is the cheaper car to own for up to about three and one-half years. After that, the new car becomes the cheaper car to own.

One must always remember in calculations such as this that minimizing the cost of ownership is not necessarily the only objective. Many people derive substantial pleasure from owning a new car. In cases where the new car is more expensive to own than the used car, the prospective car buyer must ultimately decide if the incremental costs of owning a new car are worth the pleasures so derived. This is not a question that can be answered with dollars and cents, but it is a question in which dollars and cents play a role.

How Can I Learn About a Car's Current Price or Value?

Once you have identified various makes and models that fit your criteria, the next step is to learn more about them. The good news: there is a tremendous volume of information and opinions about cars on the Internet, including information on their pricing. Traditionally, the primary source of new and used car prices has been the **Kelley Blue Book.** Kelley Blue Book pricing is now available on the Internet.

> *Steve and Sue own a 1994 Pontiac Trans Sport SE Wagon with a V6 3.1 liter engine that is in good condition and has 70,000 miles on it. It is a 7-passenger vehicle with air conditioning; power steering, windows, and door locks; tilt wheel; cruise control; AM/FM stereo; cassette; and ABS. It has a roof rack, privacy glass, alloy wheels, and front-wheel drive. What might the Golds receive for this as a trade-in? What could they expect to pay for this car if they bought it from a dealer?*

Web Link 8.22

At the time of writing, the estimated values were $6,305 for trade-in and $10,315 for retail purchases. The difference represents the cost to the dealer of prepping the car for resale, selling expenses, and most likely providing a warranty of some sort, in addition to the dealer's profit margin. The spread between these two values suggests the potential value to the Golds of attempting to sell this car themselves rather than using it as a trade-in.

Web Link 8.23

Web Link 8.24

There are other sources of car prices, and it is worth the effort to check with several sources before settling on a particular value for a car. But there is more to a car than just its price, of course. There are quality issues. Several sites that provide opinions about particular vehicles may be found at **Web Link 8.24.**

What Is the Relationship Between the MSRP and the Dealer's Cost for New Cars?

A buyer must know two key numbers when preparing to buy a new car: the **MSRP,** or manufacturer's suggested retail price, and the **dealer's cost.** The MSRP is also known as the sticker price because it is usually posted on the car window with a breakdown of the price for each feature of the car, the transportation cost, and the sales tax. The dealer's cost is what the dealer paid the manufacturer for the car.

Cars are usually bought through a negotiation process (much like houses). Think of the MSRP as the asking price of a house. It is simply the starting point in the negotiation between the dealer and the prospective buyer. If you walk into a dealer's showroom and casually ask the price of a car, a sales person will usually quote you the MSRP. The dealer's cost is the real starting point in the negotiations for the prospective buyer. Because the car dealer has to make some profit on the sale of each car in order to stay in business, a prospective buyer knows he or she will have to pay something more than the dealer's cost. The issue is where the final price will fall in the range bounded by the dealer's cost and the MSRP.

How Do I Determine My Bid Price?   It is quite unlikely the dealer will show you his cost basis for any particular car. However, if you enter negotiations knowing the dealer's cost basis, then the dealer will be only too happy to show it to you as a sign of good faith. There are several organizations that will sell you an estimate of the dealer's cost.

Web Link 8.25

There are some, such as *Edmund's* and *Consumer Reports,* that provide this information in their publications. These publications are usually available at a local library.

To decide on a bid for a specific model, start with the dealer's cost. Next, add the invoice price for each option you are adding to the car. The third step is to deduct any

Web Link 8.27

rebates and/or incentives currently offered on that particular model.

The key point now is the percentage markup for the car. The absolute best a prospective buyer can hope to do is to obtain a car for $100 over dealer's cost. A more likely best price mark is $200 to $300 above a dealer's cost. At the upper end, one could expect to pay a 3 percent profit margin. Thus, a car that had a dealer's cost of $20,000 might require a bid of as much as $600 above the dealer's cost. These numbers are just guidelines. A major factor in determining the final price will be the current demand and supply situation for a car. If sales for a particular model are slow, a dealer is usually more willing to come down in price. If sales are doing well and a dealer is having a difficult time keeping a model in stock, the final price will be close to the MSRP. There are even times when a particular model is so hot that dealers are actually able to sell it for prices in excess of the MSRP! A buyer looking for a good deal in financial terms would do well to avoid models in very high demand.

A part of the price for a car is a collection of extras. Every car comes with a transportation charge. The transportation charge is usually nonnegotiable as the dealer pays it in full. Other charges are simply pass-throughs, including sales taxes, licensing, and registration fees. Because fees are mandated by state and local governments, there is, again, usually no opportunity to negotiate.

Finally, there will usually be a set of **dealer-added fees.** These may include such things as an advertising fee and a dealer preparation fee. There is no limit to the names and concepts a dealer may dream up to add to the price of the car. An advertising fee is usually a fee the dealer pays to other groups or organizations for generic advertising. A dealer preparation fee is the cost of cleaning the car for delivery to the buyer. All of these fees are fully negotiable. The more expenses a dealer is able to pass on to the buyer, the smaller the profit margin he needs on the sale itself.

There is an added quirk in the pricing process: the feature known as a **holdback.** A holdback is a percentage of the MSRP that the auto manufacturer gives to the dealer. The holdback is intended to cover the dealer's cost of financing a car for the first 90 days. When a dealer orders a car, he or she pays for the car at that time, usually financing the payment with a bank loan. Suppose a car carries an MSRP of $18,000 and the holdback is 3 percent. The manufacturer will pay to the dealer $540 (= 3% × $18,000) to cover the costs of financing and carrying the car for up to 90 days. If the dealer's actual costs are lower (if, for example, the car is sold only 10 days after arrival), he or she has made a larger profit on the car. If the dealer takes six months to sell a car, then he or she will probably end up losing money on that car. Although 3 percent is the standard holdback rate, holdbacks do vary by manu-

Web Link 8.28

facturer. When a car is special ordered, the holdback is almost pure profit for the dealer because he or she will not have to hold the car at all. Because the buyer has no knowledge of how long a dealer has held a car, the holdback is not something that can be negotiated, but the buyer should be aware that the dealer is probably making additional profit on a car

Web Link 8.29

above and beyond any profit margin that is directly negotiated in setting a price.

Can I Buy a Car Over the Internet?

As with most products nowadays, a great deal of the research and shopping for a car can be done over the Internet. Keep one caveat in mind: just because shopping for a car on the Internet is easy does not mean that you will necessarily obtain the best deal. Remember, not all dealers utilize the Internet. The web is only one method of advertising, promoting, and selling cars. It is easy to find dealers on the Internet.

Steve and Sue Gold have decided they would like to buy a Ford. Their ZIP code is 14450 and their address is 4 Chablis Dr. in Fairport, New York. What dealers are closest, and how far are they?

Web Link 8.30
Web Link 8.31

Based on the search calculator at **Web Link 8.30** at the time of writing, there were four nearby dealers. The closest one was 4.04 miles away.

How Long Should I Keep My New Car?

Once you purchase a new car, you then need to decide how long to keep the car before replacing it. Because the largest expense of car ownership is depreciation and the biggest portion of depreciation comes in the first year or two, keeping a car longer actually reduces the impact of depreciation. In addition, automobile insurance for an older car may be less (see Chapter 10). Older cars have higher maintenance expenses, however, as significant parts of the engine and other components have to be repaired or replaced. *One rule of thumb for how long to hold a car is to hold it until the necessary repairs exceed the market value of the car.* At that point, give the car to a charity and take a tax deduction if you are able to itemize.

A more logical approach to determine how long to hold a car uses one of the calculators found at **Web Link 8.31a.**

Web Link 8.31a

> *Steve and Sue have just bought a new car for $20,000 and paid a $2,000 down payment. They expect average depreciation on the car. They took out a 36-month loan at 8 percent. They believe their savings rate is 10 percent, and their marginal tax bracket is 34 percent. The sales tax on cars is 5 percent. They are trying to decide if they should hold the car for a long time (nine years) or a short time (three years). If they hold it for nine years, their average repairs will cost $600 per year, their auto insurance will average $500 per year, and their licensing fees will average $200 per year. If they hold it for three years, these costs will average $300, $700, and $400. In economic terms, which is the better holding period?*

The calculators indicate that the nine-year holding period costs $11,479 less in today's dollars than if the Golds were to hold three cars for three years each over that same time frame. The key is that over nine years the Golds would incur $15,301 in depreciation expenses with the one car and $25,152 in depreciation expenses with the three consecutive cars. If we change the rate of depreciation from average to low, then the savings from the long holding period drop to $6,542.

These calculations do not mean that the Golds have to hold their car for nine years! Everyone enjoys the beauty, comfort, and cleanliness of a newer car. These calculations only mean that if the Golds want the luxury of owning only newer cars, they should be aware of how much extra this luxury is costing them.

SUMMARY

➤ The buy-versus-rent decision involves many economic factors, including particularly the expected growth rate in the price of real estate and the opportunity cost of the down payment. Personal factors may cause a person to choose the more expensive option.

➤ Information on rentals, homes for sale, prospective communities, and even repossessed homes is available on the Internet.

➤ Realtors facilitate the buying and selling of homes but are not mandatory. Sellers may try to sell their property themselves.

➤ Making an initial bid on a property and negotiating the ultimate terms may be a complex process.

➤ The single most important task of someone selling property is to set a proper initial asking price.

➤ There is no universally accepted method to measure the square feet of living area of a home. Prospective buyers should treat such numbers with caution.

➤ One can choose from a wide variety of home inspectors. It is usually best to choose one who is highly qualified and inspects as their primary business activity.

➤ Moving expenses may qualify as an adjustment to gross income, provided such expenses are not reimbursed by an employer, and the move meets the mileage and time tests.

➤ The Internet makes available information on all makes and models of vehicles, including suggested market values for new and used vehicles.

➤ The final price a buyer bids for a vehicle should be between the MSRP and the dealer's cost.

➤ The Internet is not always the cheapest place to buy products, including vehicles. It is only a starting point in the search for a vehicle.

KEY TERMS

agent	asking price	buying realtor
consumer durables	contingencies	dealer-added fees
dealer's cost	defaulting	down payment
earnest money	exclusivity	FSBO
handyman's special	highballing	holdback
Kelley Blue Book	lowballing	mileage test
mortgage	MSRP	multiple listing service
repossessed property	selling realtor	sweat equity
time test		

PROBLEMS

8.1. Sally Henneman is pondering a move from Chicago, Illinois, to Flint, Michigan. She found a nice apartment that rents for $600 a month. Renter's insurance would cost her $15 per month ($180 per year). The house she is looking at would cost about $100,000. She would make a down payment of 20 percent of the purchase price of the house. Other closing costs would run about $1,500. The interest rate on a 30-year, fixed rate mortgage would be 7.5 percent. Her combined marginal federal and state income tax bracket is 35 percent and her filing status is single. The real estate taxes on the house would cost about $1,500. Annual maintenance expenses would run about $1,200 per year, and homeowner's insurance would cost $60 per month. She anticipates an inflation rate (i.e., an annual rent increase) of 2 percent, but thinks housing will appreciate at the rate of 5 percent per year. She anticipates that when she sells her house, the realtor's commission and other closing costs would be 7 percent of the selling price. The opportunity cost of the money she puts down on the house is 8 percent. She plans to live in Flint for about four years. If the apartment and house are considered reasonable substitutes in terms of lifestyle, is it economically worthwhile to buy the house?

8.2. Identify through the Internet three apartment rental options in Atlanta. Assume you are looking for a two-bedroom apartment and are willing to pay up to $1,000 per month.

8.3. You are interested in buying a three-bedroom single-family home in Dallas, Texas. You would like 2,200 square feet of living area and two full baths. If you are interested in spending about $150,000, how many homes do you have to choose from? Select three homes you would like to visit.

8.4. Ascertain if there are any repossessed homes for sale in your community.

REFERENCES

Web Link 8.33   Miscellaneous sites about buying a house
Web Link 8.34   Miscellaneous sites about renting
Web Link 8.35   Miscellaneous sites about buying a car
Web Link 8.35a Comprehensive sites about buying and selling real estate and vehicles

WALL STREET JOURNAL INTERACTIVE RESOURCES

Web Link (WSJ) 8.32   Recent articles on home and auto ownership
Web Link (WSJ) 8.36   "Car Buyers Find They Don't Always Get Great Deals Online," *The Wall Street Journal Interactive Edition*, November 23, 1999
Web Link (WSJ) 8.37   "Web Sites for Home Buyers Can Be Like a Cluttered Garage," *The Wall Street Journal Interactive Edition*, January 29, 1999
Web Link (WSJ) 8.38   "Homeowners Declare They Can Sell It Themselves," *The Wall Street Journal Interactive Edition*, July 10, 1998
Web Link (WSJ) 8.39   Learn the basics of home ownership targeted to your stage of life
Web Link (WSJ) 8.40   Buying a house
Web Link (WSJ) 8.41   Selling your home
Web Link (WSJ) 8.42   "Personal Wealth Is at the Front Door," *The Wall Street Journal Interactive Edition*, December 26, 1999

For information that has changed since the book was written, for new information that pertains to this topic, and for some new web sites that pertain to the topic of this chapter, see **Web Link 8.43.**

CHAPTER 9

FINANCING PERSONAL ASSETS: MORTGAGES, CAR LOANS, AND CAR LEASES

LEARNING OBJECTIVES

- Explain the advantages of prequalification
- Describe the different types of mortgages available
- Identify current mortgage interest rates
- Ascertain how much you could afford to pay for a house
- Decide how much of a down payment you would like to make
- Estimate your closing costs
- Decide on the appropriate mortgage for you
- Evaluate whether it would be profitable to refinance your current mortgage
- Describe the process by which property taxes are determined
- Evaluate automobile financing choices
- Analyze an auto lease proposal

Web Link: www.wiley.com/college/woerheide

INTRODUCTION

Not only is the purchase price of both a house and a car quite expensive, the cost of financing these purchases is also quite expensive. Some people pay more in interest on their mortgages than they pay for the house! Although the interest payments on a car loan will usually not exceed what was paid for the car, they can be a significant annual expense in owning the car. A savvy buyer should pay at least as much attention to the details of financing these purchases as to the price of the purchase.

There are lots of choices available when it comes to selecting a mortgage. The borrower has to decide the term of the loan, whether to pay points, how much of a down payment to make, whether to obtain an insured loan, and whether to take out a fixed or variable rate loan, among other things. Even after the loan has been taken out, the borrower must decide whether to add extra cash to each month's payment and whether to refinance the mortgage. Auto loans require some of these same decisions. In addition, car buyers usually have the choice nowadays of borrowing to buy versus leasing an auto.

Should I Get Prequalified or Preapproved?

After negotiating to purchase a home (or any real estate), the prospective buyer applies for a mortgage (unless the bid was an all-cash bid). A prudent buyer minimizes the chances of getting turned down for a mortgage *before* placing a bid on a property in one of three ways. One is to use Internet calculators that indicate the maximum mortgage for which the buyer could qualify. A second way is to become prequalified. The prequalification process is a quick review of the borrower's financial position relative to the size of the mortgage that the borrower is considering. Prequalification requires no documentation and really only gives the borrower an indication of where he or she would stand in seeking a mortgage. Some lenders will issue a **prequalified letter** to the prospective homebuyer. The third way is to become preapproved. Upon approval the lender will issue the prospective buyer a **preapproval letter.** A preapproval letter does not absolutely guarantee you will ultimately be approved for a mortgage. It only indicates that if the lender is able to verify your statements about your income and debts, and if the property appraises for a reasonable value relative to the purchase price, then the buyer will receive the mortgage. A preapproval letter is a stronger commitment from a lender than is a prequalified letter.

Once the buyer has a contract to buy a property, he or she is ready to make a formal mortgage application. Now the lender asks for proof as to income, wealth, job status, etc. The lender will ask for copies of recent tax returns, recent bank statements, evidence of current income, driver's license, and a copy of the purchase bid. The lender will run a credit check on the borrower and spouse or anyone else with whom the property is being bought. If everything checks out, the lender will issue a **mortgage commitment letter.** This letter is good for a fixed number of days and the borrower/buyer must ensure that the closing on the house occurs before the expiration of the commitment letter.

The number of mortgage application forms on the Internet is growing at a phenomenal rate. The Mortgage Bankers Association (MBA) estimates that by mid-1999 more than 3,000 lenders offered mortgages on the Web, up from only 60 in 1996. Although the actual number of mortgages originated online is small relative to the total number of mortgages originated each year, the MBA estimates that by the year 2003, approximately one out of every four loans will originate on the Internet.[1]

Web Link 9.1

Web Link 9.2

Web Link 9.3

WHAT ARE MY CHOICES FOR A MORTGAGE?

A large variety of mortgages are available today. The two most common terms to maturity on mortgages are 30 years and 15 years. The traditional and most common mortgage is a **fixed rate** 30-year mortgage. With this mortgage, the mortgage payments will be identical for the next 30 years or as long as the borrower owns the house.

The alternative to a fixed rate mortgage is an **adjustable rate mortgage** (ARM). The most common maturity term on an ARM is the 1-year adjustable. On a 1-year adjustable, the lender computes a new monthly mortgage payment once per year according to a formula specified in the mortgage loan agreement. In the adjustment process, the

---

[1] In view of the recent dramatic decline in viability of Internet-based companies, this estimate may be overly optimistic.

original maturity of the mortgage remains unaltered. Thus, the full amount of the change in the interest rate is reflected in the monthly payment.[2]

One variation on the 1-year adjustable is to make the adjustment period longer, such as 3 years or 5 years. A second variation is to make the first adjustment period a long one. Examples include 3/1, 5/1, and 7/1 ARMs. The interest rate on a 7/1 ARM is fixed for seven years; the mortgage becomes a 1-year adjustable starting on the seventh anniversary of the loan. A third variation is to adjust only once. Examples would be 7/23 and 5/25 ARMs. The interest rate on the 7/23 is fixed for the first seven years; on the seventh anniversary there is a one-time adjustment that fixes the rate for the remaining 23 years. All these adjustments are done in accordance with a formula specified in the mortgage contract.

Most mortgages have a monthly payment. Some lenders offer mortgages with a semimonthly or even a biweekly payment. Because the maturities of such mortgages are still 15 or 30 years, each payment on these mortgages is about one-half of what the monthly payment would have been.

The most common mortgage is also a **conventional** mortgage, which means it is not insured or guaranteed. An insured or guaranteed mortgage means that a third party (someone other than the borrower or the lender) is providing assurances to the lender that if the borrower defaults, the lender is protected from any loss on the mortgage loan. The most common insuring agency is the **Federal Housing Authority** (FHA). Borrowers may also obtain (or be required to obtain) **private mortgage insurance** (PMI) for their mortgage. There is a cost to the borrower for obtaining mortgage insurance. Insured mortgages generally take the same forms as discussed above, but the menu of insured mortgages is limited because the various insurers have not approved all forms of conventional mortgages.

Web Link
(WSJ) 9.7

Jumbo mortgages are mortgages with a high loan amount, currently any loan in excess of $252,700. Rates on jumbo mortgages are higher than rates on conventional mortgages because of the higher risk associated with such a large loan to a single borrower.

What Is the Current Mortgage Interest Rate?

At some time in the house-buying process the buyer needs to ascertain the general level of the mortgage interest rate to figure out how large a mortgage he or she may get. After a bid for a house has been accepted, the buyer wants to obtain the *cheapest* mortgage available.

There is no such thing as "the mortgage interest rate." Each mortgage carries different terms and bears different degrees of risk for the lender and the borrower. Mortgages differ by (1) maturity, (2) whether they have a fixed or adjustable rate and the nature of that adjustment, (3) insurance coverage, and (4) the amount of **points** charged (a point is one percent of the mortgage loan). Later in this chapter we will discuss the process of how one decides which mortgage to choose. At this point let us focus on how the prospective homebuyer obtains information on mortgage rates.

Stan and Ichiko Sato are thinking about buying a house. They will borrow less than $240,000, they live in New York, and they will be interested in a 30-year fixed rate mortgage. Before they can decide: (1) how much they can afford to bid, (2) what their monthly payment would be, and (3) which type of mortgage to get, they need to know what current mortgage rates are.

[2]Some ARM mortgages may not fully incorporate the change in the interest rate into the monthly payment. In this case, the homeowner may be hit with negative amortization on the mortgage!

Web Link 9.4

For planning purposes, Stan and Ichiko should start with an approximation of the national average rate on a 30-year fixed rate mortgage with zero points. At the time of writing, this national rate was 7.32 percent.

Web Link (WSJ) 9.6

The national average rate is a benchmark. The actual rate a borrower will be quoted will depend on the property, the credit risk of the borrower, and the features of the mortgage. A *Wall Street Journal* web page showing current rates is in Figure 9.1. At this site, rates are provided for 30-year fixed rate mortgages, 15-year fixed rate mortgages, and 1-year ARMs. Regional averages are also provided.

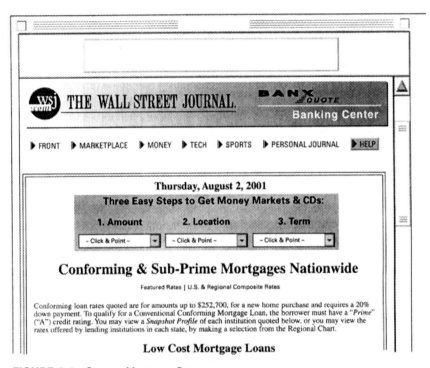

FIGURE 9-1 Current Mortgage Rates

Actual quotations for specific lenders include information about the **lock period** and the **application fee.** The most common lock period is 60 days, but it may range from as few as 10 days to as many as 90 days. A 60-day lock means that if a borrower applies today for a mortgage and that mortgage is approved, the rate is guaranteed for only 60 days from the day of application. At the end of the lock period, the lender may still grant the mortgage, but the lender has the right to update the mortgage rate. If mortgage rates have gone up since the original date of application, it is likely the lender will increase the rate.

Web Link 9.5

The application fee is simply a way for a lender to increase its profits. If the terms of a mortgage are particularly attractive, it might be worthwhile to pay a large application fee. Other things being equal, however, a borrower should seek out lenders with low or nonexistent application fees.

Suppose that the Satos are at the point that they would like to see what kind of deal they could get on an ARM. They would then visit **Web Link (WSJ) 9.6** and look at the choices for a 1-year ARM. An example of the type of information and terms that would be provided for a 1-Year Adjustable Mortgage would be a **teaser rate** of 5.00 percent, one-half point, a 30-day lock, no **convertibility**, a 2.75 percent **margin, caps** of 2 and 6 percent, and a 1-year Treasury bill **index.** Let us consider what each of these mean.

A **teaser rate** is a low rate offered for the initial time period of the mortgage. In this case, the teaser rate of 4.5 percent is good for one year. A point is a prepaid interest charge that equals 1 percent of the mortgage loan. Thus, one point means that when the loan is made, the borrower would have to pay the lender an advance interest charge of 1 percent of the amount borrowed. This particular mortgage is nonconvertible. A **convertible** mortgage could be converted automatically into a fixed rate mortgage at a later date.

The **margin, caps,** and index numbers mean that on each anniversary date (as specified in the mortgage agreement), the lender will ascertain the rate on a designated 1-year Treasury bill index. A 1-year Treasury bill **index** usually means the rate published by an entity such as the Federal Reserve Bank as an approximation of what one-year Treasury bills are yielding at that point in time. A Treasury bill with exactly one year to maturity may not actually exist at that time. The lender will then add 3 percent (the margin) to that rate to determine the new rate on the mortgage. The lender guarantees, however, that whatever the computation produces, the new rate each year will not differ by more than 2 percent (the annual cap) from the previous interest rate and that the new rate will never differ from the *original* interest rate by more than 6 percent (the lifetime cap).

Suppose the Satos take out the 1-year adjustable described in the previous paragraph. One year later, the 1-year Treasury bill index is at 5.00 percent. The lender adds 3 percent to obtain a new mortgage rate of 8.00 percent. Because the initial rate was 4.50 percent, the rate for the second year would be set at 6.50 percent because of the 2 percent annual cap. The highest rate that could ever be charged on the mortgage is 10.50 percent. Whenever the lifetime change cap exceeds the initial rate on the mortgage, such as in the example where the lifetime cap is 6 percent and the initial rate is 4.5 percent, the lowest rate that could ever be charged is usually the margin itself. In this case, the lowest rate would be 3 percent.

How Much Will My Mortgage Payment Be?

The mathematics of computing the payment on a loan was discussed in Chapter 7 and will not be repeated here.[3] Regardless of the type of mortgage one takes out (fixed rate mortgage, adjustable rate mortgage, balloon mortgage, etc.), the initial monthly payment is calculated treating the mortgage as if it were a fixed rate mortgage for the specified maturity of the mortgage.

> *Stan and Ichiko Sato plan to take out a $120,000 30-year adjustable rate mortgage. The mortgage is a 5/1, with a teaser rate of 8 percent. The Satos want to know what their initial monthly mortgage payment would be.*

Web Link (WSJ) 9.8

The correct answer of $880.52 may be found at any of the links in **Web Link (WSJ) 9.8.**

Every bit as important as the monthly payment is a description of how much of each payment is principal and how much is interest, which is known as the mortgage amortization table. The interest payment is important because the interest paid on a mortgage might be itemized on one's tax return. The principal payment is important because it determines

---

[3]Mathematical discussions of the calculations of a mortgage payment may be found at **Web Link 9.7a.**

the amount owed when the mortgage is paid off. The description of how this composition is determined is provided in Chapter 7.

HOW LARGE A MORTGAGE CAN I AFFORD?

In this book, we saw first how a person selects and buys a house before we began the financing discussion. In truth, the house-buying process works in the reverse order. After determining current mortgage interest rates, the prospective homebuyer should then determine how large of a mortgage he or she can afford or would like to have. The size of the mortgage combined with the down payment the buyer plans to make tells the buyer the price range he or she should be looking in, which drives the selection and purchase process.

The size of mortgage one can qualify for is not a well-defined number. Each lender is entitled to make its own decision as to how large a mortgage it will provide a particular borrower. The approving lender is referred to as the originating lender, or **originator.** Lenders have certain rules of thumb, called standards, that are successful in limiting mortgage defaults without unduly restricting the number of loans granted. In addition, many mortgage lenders resell a mortgage as soon as the loan has been made. The primary buyers are federal agencies, but other buyers include banks, savings and loans, pension funds, and insurance companies. When an originating lender plans to resell a mortgage, the lender uses the lending standards of the prospective mortgage buyer. Because many of the prospective buyers use the same standards, most originating lenders also use these standards.

The single most important number that lenders use to evaluate a prospective borrower is the ratio of principal, interest, taxes, and insurance (**PITI**) to gross income. Principal and interest together constitute the mortgage payment. Taxes in PITI represent property taxes, and insurance is the premium on the homeowner's insurance.[4] PITI and gross income may be calculated on either an annual or monthly basis. The monthly numbers are simply one-twelfth the annual numbers. For discussion purposes, let us focus on monthly numbers. Two common rules used by lenders to evaluate mortgage borrowers are that

1. the ratio of PITI to gross income not exceed 28 percent and
2. the ratio of the sum of PITI and other debt payments not exceed 36 percent of income

Some forms of the "other debt payments" indicated in rule 2 are fairly easy to define, such as the monthly payments on student loans and auto loans. Other forms are not so easy to define. For example, there is no universal agreement on what the monthly payment on a credit card balance should be. Some lenders may use an amount of 5 percent of the outstanding balance. For people who (1) pay their credit card bill in full every month, (2) have done so for years, and (3) use their credit card primarily to minimize the amount of cash they need to carry around, a credit card balance may not represent any burden whatsoever. In fact, many lenders would not count the credit card debt of such a person as part of his or her current debt payments.

---

[4]The lender evaluates the size of the property taxes and homeowner's insurance payment whether the payments are paid as part of the monthly payment and placed in escrow or are paid directly by the borrower.

Because of the variation in the rules lenders use when evaluating a loan application and because evaluation can be done at various levels of completeness, it is easy to see why some lenders will grant loans to applicants turned down by others. That is why a useful first step in the home-buying process is to visit a mortgage lender and ask it to prequalify you.

Let us consider an example of this problem of deciding how much mortgage a prospective buyer could afford.

> *Stan and Ichiko have a contract to buy a home for $150,000, with a stipulation they will apply for a $120,000 mortgage. They have a $60,000 annual income ($5,000 monthly income). They have $1,200 in other annual income ($100 a month). They currently pay $200 per month in installment loans. The current balance on their credit cards is $3,000, but they pay their credit card bill in full every month. The Satos expect their property taxes to run about $3,000 per year and their homeowner's insurance to be about $300. There will be no mortgage insurance. Between the net proceeds from the sale of their old house and additional savings, they expect to have as much as $50,000 for the down payment and the various closing costs. They will be taking out a 30-year, 8 percent fixed rate mortgage. How large of a mortgage can they afford to take out, and how much could they afford to pay for their house?*

Web Link 9.12

The solution to this problem may be found in **Web Link 9.12**. The results are also reproduced in Figure 9.2. The calculator tells us that under a conservative estimate with a 20 percent down payment, the Satos could afford to put down $42,282, borrow $169,128, and pay a total of $211,410 for a home. The conservative estimate is appropriate if the Satos have a less-than-perfect credit record. The calculator also indicates that if the Satos's credit record and their financial resources (i.e., wealth) are in good shape, then the Satos could put down as much as $52,708, borrow $210,831, and buy a house for $263,538. This answer involves a down payment greater than what the Satos believe they would have available. Nonetheless, this calculator gives the Satos an indication that if they plan on a 20 percent down payment, they could afford to bid something between $210,000 and $260,000 for a home. A more precise indication would require knowledge about their credit record and the current state of their finances.

A Conservative Estimate

	5% Down	10% Down	20% Down
Down Payment Amount	$7,685	$16,665	$42,282
Loan Amount	$146,024	$149,981	$169,128
Price of Home	$153,709	$166,645	$211,410
Your Future Monthly Payment:			
Principal and Interest	$1,071	$1,101	$1,241
Taxes and Insurance	$275	$275	$275
Mortgage Insurance	$82	$52	$0
Total Monthly Payment	$1,428	$1,428	$1,516

A graph available at **Web Link 9.12** shows the amount of mortgage the Satos would likely qualify for as a function of the monthly payments on other debts. The Satos are fine up to about $400 in monthly payments. After that, each $100 in monthly payments on other debt reduces dramatically the size of mortgage they could take out. This graph suggests that if a person is getting ready to buy a home, particularly if the purchase is a financial stretch, then taking on other debt at that time (such as an installment loan to buy a car) could make it difficult to qualify.

**Web Link
(WSJ) 9.13**

Most calculators for mortgage potential ask for slightly different input information, and virtually all compute a different answer as to how much of a mortgage the Satos could afford. This should not be surprising. As mentioned earlier, different lenders employ different qualification rules and different treatments for such items as credit card debt. If different lenders come up with different answers as to how much they will lend a person, the calculators sponsored by different lenders will also come up with different answers.

How Much Should I Put Down?

Some homebuyers have the luxury of a choice of how much money to put down on a real estate purchase. Lenders normally look for at least a 20 percent down payment. Down payments of less than 20 percent usually mean the lender will charge a higher interest rate. The lower down payment would almost certainly cause the lender to add a mortgage insurance requirement for the loan. Down payments of more than 20 percent normally do not lower the interest rate from what it would be if the down payment were exactly 20 percent.[5] If an increase in the down payment does not result in a lower interest rate, then the question of whether to make a larger down payment is simple. It depends on the rate at which the borrower could invest the additional monies not used for a down payment. If the investment rate is greater than the mortgage rate, then the borrower should seriously consider a lower down payment. If the investment rate is lower than the mortgage rate, then the borrower should almost certainly make the larger down payment.

A secondary issue involves liquidity. If the borrower makes the larger down payment and then later needs that money for something else, he or she cannot get it back. Of course, the borrower might be able to take out a home equity loan using the higher equity position in the home as collateral.[6] Such a process involves time and fees and the risk that the borrower may not qualify for the home equity loan, but it is not an overly burdensome process. However, making a lower down payment and investing the money in an easily liquidated investment (such as a mutual fund) means the money could be accessed with no paperwork or cost (other than capital gains taxes if the mutual fund has appreciated in value).

The problem is more complex if making a larger down payment results in a lower mortgage rate and the alternative investment rate is higher than the mortgage rate.

---

[5]An exception to this observation would be where the purchase price of the house was large enough that a 20 percent down payment might still leave the buyer needing a jumbo mortgage. Because jumbo mortgage rates are higher than conventional mortgage rates, a higher down payment that puts the borrower below the jumbo threshold would reduce the mortgage rate.

[6]Home equity loans are discussed in Chapter 7.

Although the Satos had planned to put down $30,000 (20 percent), they are now considering putting down $45,000 (30 percent). The higher down payment lowers their mortgage rate from 8¼ percent to 8 percent. Their marginal federal and state income tax rate is 35 percent and their investment rate is 10 percent. They expect to own the home for seven years. Should they make the lower down payment?

Web Link 9.14

The calculator shows that the higher down payment will produce savings with a present value of $74 over the seven years. In other words, the savings from the lower mortgage rate on the entire loan is slightly more attractive than the opportunity cost of investing the extra down payment money at a rate of return higher than the mortgage rate. The Satos would conclude that they should probably go with the higher down payment. There may be other factors to consider, however, such as the impact of the down payment on the degree of liquidity of their personal balance sheet. In other words, despite the mathematical solution favoring the higher down payment, the value of the savings may not be sufficient to offset the peace of mind from the incremental liquidity that is achieved from placing the cash elsewhere. In this situation, there is no simple answer.

What Will My Closing Costs Be?

A closing is the meeting in which the buyers, sellers, lawyers, and any other relevant parties get together to legally transfer the title to the property and make all the payments.[7] **Closing costs** are the monies you will have to pay when you go to the closing. The down payment (adjusted for the earnest money) is invariably the primary closing cost, but there are other items to be paid at closing. One major expense for the buyer might be **prepaid interest.** Prepaid interest arises because lenders prefer to charge the borrower immediately for the interest due at the end of the month in which a mortgage is taken out. This way there will be no mortgage payment due on the first day of the next month (or whichever day of the month the mortgage payment is due). The first full payment would be due the following month. Thus, if a borrower closes on July 27 and the first mortgage payment is due on September 1, the borrower would owe prepaid interest for four days. That is, the borrower would owe interest for July 28, 29, 30, and 31. The interest for August would be paid with the first mortgage payment due September 1.

A nearly universal mandatory purchase at closing is **title insurance.** Title insurance is a policy that pays in the event that problems subsequently develop with respect to the title of the property being purchased. The buyer normally buys the title insurance for the lender. However, this protects only the lender. The buyer may also buy a title insurance policy for himself. If a mortgage is being refinanced, the homeowner may use the original issuer of the title insurance and receive what may be a substantial credit from the first title insurance policy.[8]

If the lender requires the borrower to **escrow** the homeowner's insurance and property taxes, then the borrower may be required to make a contribution to assure there will be sufficient monies in the escrow account when the first insurance and property tax

---

[7]It is certainly possible that the sellers not attend the closing. The sellers have little paperwork to actually sign and can usually sign in advance. If the sellers are not present, their lawyer certainly should be. It is not mandatory that both parties to a deal use a lawyer, but in view of the quantity of money and the value of the property that is changing hands, using a lawyer seems a wise investment.

payments are due. Under escrow, the homeowner adds money to each mortgage payment that will go toward payment of the homeowner's insurance policy and the property taxes. Some lenders require escrow for these payments and others offer escrow as an option. The major drawback to the escrow process is that most lenders do not pay interest on escrowed money.[9] A minor drawback is that lenders like to assure that the money in the escrow account will exceed the payments when they come due, so the monthly escrow payment tends to exceed by a healthy margin what is normally necessary to be set aside.

Web Link 9.16

Finally, there are a host of miscellaneous closing costs. The buyer of the property pays some of these charges and the seller pays the rest. Who pays what is usually determined by local custom, but may be determined as part of the purchase negotiation process. For example, the buyer may include in the bid for the property that the seller pays for the survey. A nonexhaustive list of potential miscellaneous fees includes: origination fee, processing fee (also called a lender or document preparation fee), credit report charge, recording fee, escrow fee, transfer tax, appraisal report, survey fee, attorney's fees, flood certification fee, municipal lien certificate, tax service fee, and termite inspection report. An important guideline for a homebuyer (and seller) to remember is that at closing a large number of parties are attempting to put their hands in the pockets of the buyers and sellers. Both the buyer and seller should not hesitate to question and even debate the appropriateness and magnitude of any prospective closing costs.

If the loan involves points, the points are paid at closing. Let us consider an example:

> *The Satos are ready to proceed to the closing on the purchase of a house. They will be taking out a $120,000 mortgage to buy the house for $150,000. They have received notice of the following closing costs: one (discount) point on the mortgage, a 0.5 percent origination fee, a $200 lender fee, a $50 credit report charge, no escrow fee, a $420 title insurance premium, a $25 recording fee, no transfer taxes, $300 for the appraisal report, a $175 survey charge, and $50 for the termite inspection report. Their annual property taxes are estimated to be $3,000, and the annual premium on the homeowner's insurance policy is $600. What will their total closing costs be, exclusive of the down payment?*

Web Link 9.15

The answer to this question can be computed at **Web Link 9.15**. The escrow process will cause the **monthly payment** to be greater than the mortgage payment. Many people (even some mortgage lenders) inadvertently use the terms mortgage payment and monthly payment interchangeably. If taxes and insurance are not being escrowed, and if no other payments (such as mortgage insurance) are being made, then the monthly payment and the mortgage payment will be the same. Otherwise, the mortgage payment is only one element of the monthly payment.

How Can I Reduce My Mortgage Insurance Costs?

Borrowers are usually asked to take out private mortgage insurance (PMI) whenever their down payment is less than 20 percent.[10] The cost of mortgage insurance will vary according to the provider, but the larger the down payment, the lower the mortgage insurance. Taking out mortgage

---

[8]The reason there would be a credit is that the title insurance company would not have to research the title of the property back to its beginning, only back to when the current owner bought the property.

[9]Some states mandate the payment of interest and even the interest rate to be paid.

[10]For a thorough discussion of PMI, the reader is directed to **Web Link 9.16a**.

insurance is not necessarily a commitment for the life of the mortgage. At any time you can have your property appraised. If the current mortgage balance is less than or equals 80 percent of the most recent appraised value, you can usually drop the mortgage insurance. This event may occur through either or both the price of the house appreciating or the balance due on the mortgage declining.

> *The Satos are concerned about conserving their cash balances. They are considering a less than 20 percent down payment on their purchase of a house for $150,000. They would like to know what their mortgage insurance would be and how long they would have to pay it. They plan to occupy the house for approximately seven years. They do not expect the property to appreciate in value during this time. Assume a rate of 8 percent on a 30-year mortgage regardless of the down payment amount.*

Web Link 9.17

This site at **Web Link 9.17** indicates the following ranges of monthly insurance premiums, monthly payments, and the number of years to achieve an 80 percent loan-to-value ratio.

	Down Payment Percentage			
	5%	10%	15%	20%
Down Payment	$7,500	$15,000	$22,500	$30,000
Monthly Mortgage Insurance	80	47	34	0
Total Monthly Payment	1,125	1,037	969	880
# of Years	11.83	9.33	5.83	0

Note that if the down payment is 5 or even percent, the mortgage insurance will be owed for the entire seven years of expected occupancy. Higher down payments allow the possibility of terminating the mortgage insurance during the period of occupancy due to the decline in the mortgage loan balance.

The cost of mortgage insurance can be incredibly expensive. In the above example, consider the case of increasing the down payment from $22,500 (15%) to $30,000 (30%). This means coming up with an extra $7,500. This additional down payment would allow the buyer to save the monthly mortgage insurance premium. The premium in this example is $34 per month, or approximately $408 per year (12 × $34). The additional down payment is also saving the buyer 8 percent (the mortgage rate) per year on this money, or $600 (8% × $7,500). Combined, this results in a saving to the buyer of approximately $1,008 per year ($408 + $600) or 13.44 percent ($1,008 / $7,500)![11]

Web Link 9.18

Is VA or FHA Mortgage Insurance a Better Deal than Private Mortgage Insurance? A **VA-guaranteed** or a **FHA-insured** mortgage might be a better deal for some homebuyers than private mortgage insurance. Some people might be able to buy a home only with a VA or FHA mortgage. Let us consider the details of each of these programs.

---

[11]Of course, this return combines pretax and after-tax dollars because the interest expense would likely have been tax deductible but the mortgage insurance is paid with after-tax dollars.

After World War II, Congress created as a benefit to veterans the Veteran's Administration (VA) mortgage loan. Buying a home with a VA mortgage is much like the normal process, with two major differences. One is that the veteran obtains a certificate of eligibility from the local VA office. The other is that the appraisal must be ordered through the VA. The major benefit of a VA loan is that in most cases, no down payment is required.[12] The VA does, however, charge a funding fee. For most veterans, the funding fee is 2 percent of the loan. Down payments of 5 percent and 10 percent reduce this funding fee to 1.5 percent and 1.25 percent.

A VA loan cannot exceed the appraised value of the property, and there is currently an upper limit of $203,000 on the amount of the loan. The actual loan itself can be negotiated with any lender, at the best rate available. The loan may be a fixed rate loan or an adjustable rate loan. VA loans are assumable with the approval of the VA. An assumable mortgage means that at such time as the owner sells the home, the buyer may request that he or she be allowed to take responsibility for the existing mortgage. Assumption of a mortgage may provide a substantial portion of the financing for the house. In situations where the interest rate on an assumable mortgage is substantially below current mortgage rates, the assumption feature of a mortgage may make a house much easier to sell or allow a home to sell for a higher price than would otherwise be the case.

Web Link 9.19

The Federal Housing Administration (FHA), a federal agency within the U.S Department of Housing and Urban Development (HUD), insures FHA loans. FHA's primary objective is to assist in providing housing opportunities for low-to-moderate-income families. FHA has both single-family (1- to 4-unit homes) and multifamily (5 or more units) mortgage lending programs. The agency does not generally provide the funds for the mortgages, but rather insures home mortgage loans made by the private industry lenders. FHA loans have lower and upper limits. The general guideline limits are adjusted for specific high-cost living areas. As of August 2001 the standard limit for single-family residences was $115,200 and the limit for high-cost areas was $208,800.

Web Link 9.20

Stan and Ichiko Sato are considering an FHA-insured loan. They are looking at buying a home in Erie County, New York, in the Buffalo–Niagara Falls metropolitan area. What is the maximum FHA loan they can obtain for a single-family residence?

Web Link 9.21

As of August 2001, the maximum loan amount in this county was $127,500 because it falls into one of the high-cost areas of the country.

An FHA mortgage is desirable from a borrower's perspective because the borrower can put down as little as 3 percent of the purchase price and borrow up to 97 percent of the purchase price (provided this does not exceed the limit for the particular location). There is a cost, however, to obtaining this mortgage. Most of the time, the borrower must pay a 2.25 percent premium at the time of the closing. This premium may be rolled into the mortgage loan itself. In addition, the borrower must pay an annual premium of 0.50 percent of the loan, pro-rated into monthly payments. Both of these premiums are for the insurance coverage. Each borrower of an FHA mortgage is put into an insurance pool. Insurance premiums are collected for each borrower in each pool. These premiums are used to pay off the lenders when there are defaults. If not all of the money in a pool is used to cover

---

[12]This discussion focuses on the veteran who is using a VA loan for the first time. The rules change slightly with repeat uses.

defaults, then each borrower in the pool is entitled to a refund on his or her share of the premiums when that particular pool is liquidated. The average refund works out to nearly $700. To qualify for a refund, the homeowner would have had to pay on the mortgage for at least seven years and the mortgage must have been paid off.

Web Link 9.22

WHICH MORTGAGE SHOULD I CHOOSE?

Looking at the menu of mortgages discussed earlier, the casual observer might think it foolish to take out any mortgage other than a fixed rate 30-year mortgage. Consider the following, however. First, the interest rate on alternative mortgages (particularly the ARMs) can be substantially cheaper in the first year or first few years. Second, the average life of a mortgage is about seven years. Mortgages must be paid off when the house is sold unless the mortgage is assumable, and most are not assumable. Also, whenever interest rates drop, some people find an opportunity to refinance their mortgage at a lower interest rate. It is extremely unlikely a homebuyer will actually pay on the original mortgage for the entire 30 years. In fact, it is highly likely a homebuyer will pay off or refinance the initial mortgage within 10 years. Thus, a mortgage that has a cheaper interest rate in the early years may be a substantially better deal than one that has a fixed rate for 30 years. There are several decisions a homebuyer needs to make with regard to selecting a mortgage. Let us consider some of these. Note that there is never an absolutely correct answer as to which mortgage is best for an individual, except with hindsight.

Which Is Better: Fixed or Adjustable?

The teaser rates on ARMs are virtually always lower than the interest rate on fixed rate mortgages. Thus, if one expects to live in a house a relatively short period of time (no more than three years), then it is highly likely an ARM provides a better deal.

It is true that the monthly payments on an ARM can go up or down. Selection of an ARM exposes the homeowner to uncertainty with respect to future mortgage payments. If such uncertainty creates great anxiety for a homeowner, then he or she should choose the certainty of the fixed rate mortgage. Also, if there is a risk of decline in the homeowner's income, then a fixed rate mortgage becomes more attractive. Finally, the homeowner may have an expectation of the future direction of interest rates. If he or she believes interest rates will rise over the life of the mortgage, then he or she should almost certainly choose a fixed rate mortgage. If he or she believes interest rates will stay the same or decline over the life of a mortgage, then he or she should choose an ARM. Let the reader be forewarned, however, that even market professionals cannot predict interest rate movements over long time periods. (In fact, it would appear most market professionals cannot consistently predict interest rate movements over short time periods!)

The Satos are looking at a 30-year, 8 percent fixed rate mortgage for $120,000. Suppose they inquire about an ARM and the loan officer indicates that a one-year adjustable is available. The initial rate is 6 percent; the caps are 2 percent (annual) and 6 percent (lifetime). The rate on the ARM cannot go below the initial rate. Assume that they expect to live in the home for seven years. What is the breakeven point for the two mortgages under a worst-case scenario?

Web Link 9.23

The answer, which can be computed at **Web Link 9.23,** is approximately 36 months, or three years. This calculator shows the first monthly payments will be $880.52 and $719.46 under the two mortgages. The Satos will save nearly $2,000 during the first year, and during the second year, the payments on the two mortgages would be the same under the worst-case scenario.

Web Link
(WSJ) 9.24

Should I Pay Points to Lower My Rate?

Web Link 9.25a

Lenders charge a lower interest rate in exchange for the payment of points. A point is equal to 1 percent of the mortgage loan. Thus, on a $120,000 loan, one point would represent a payment at closing of $1,200. The mortgage interest rate usually goes down one-quarter of 1 percent per point paid. Hence, a mortgage lender may offer the following choices for 30-year fixed rate mortgages:

Rate	Points
8.00%	0
7.75	1
7.50	2
7.25	3

Is the payment of points a good deal? It depends. First, if your employer is paying the points as part of your moving expenses, then it is a good deal, and the more points paid the better! Second, the value of paying points depends on the life of the mortgage. For example, suppose you are considering the 8 percent mortgage with no points and the 7.75 percent mortgage with one point. The payment of one point will save you one-quarter of 1 percent on your mortgage rate, so it will take you at least four years to recoup the cost of the point you paid. This ignores the time value of money and the tax impact. Points are normally tax-deductible, but the interest payments on a mortgage are also normally tax deductible. A rule of thumb is it is probably worthwhile to pay points if you are absolutely sure you will be owning the property for five years or more. If you expect to own the property for less than five years, the payment of points is almost certainly *not* a good deal. If the spread in interest rates and points were something other than a $1/4$ percent interest for each point, then the above rule would have to be modified.

> In further conversations with the mortgage loan officer, Stan and Ichiko decide to focus on paying either no points or a lot of points. They reason that if paying one point is a good deal, then paying three points must be an even better deal. So they want to choose between an 8 percent mortgage with no points and a 7.25 percent mortgage and 3 points. Assume their marginal federal and state tax rate is 35 percent, they plan to own the house for seven years, and their opportunity cost of money is 6 percent. Which mortgage is the better deal?

Web Link 9.25

Using the calculators at **Web Link 9.25** shows that paying the points results in a present value saving over the seven years of $1,137.

One other feature of paying points is that the lower interest rate mortgage causes the principal due to decline at a slightly faster rate. At the end of seven years, this difference in principal due will amount to $1,177. **Web Link 9.25** also provides a graph that indicates the break-even point between the two mortgages. The break-even point is about four years

Web Link
(WSJ) 9.26

and five months. One problem with paying points to obtain a lower rate is that homeowners always have the option to refinance their mortgages at any time. The higher one's mortgage interest rate, the more likely one would find it attractive to refinance in the future. In other words, it may be cheaper to not pay points today and to use that money to refinance the mortgage at a lower rate in the future.

Which Is Better: A 15-Year Term or 30-Year Term?

The 15-year mortgage often appeals to prospective homebuyers with the idea of owning a home free and clear of all debt after only 15 years. What is attractive, however, is also deceptive. Let's assume a homebuyer is choosing between a 15-year and a 30-year fixed rate mortgage. If the interest rates on both mortgages are the same, the 15-year mortgage has a higher monthly payment. The homeowner could take out a 30-year mortgage and make payments equal to what the payments on the 15-year mortgage would have been. The advantage of this is that if the homeowner becomes strapped for cash, he or she can always withhold the supplemental payment. This strategy gives homeowners more flexibility in managing their money.

It is more common for the 15-year mortgage to have an interest rate that is lower by one-quarter to one-half of a percentage point. A rate differential makes choosing between the two maturities much more interesting. The shorter mortgage allows the homeowner to pay off the mortgage sooner and save some interest expense to boot. The concept of opportunity cost is missing from this line of thinking. Suppose the owner computes the difference in the monthly payments and invests that amount each month at a rate greater than the interest rate on the mortgage. Then, when the homeowner is ready to pay off the mortgage, he or she sells the other investment and uses the proceeds to pay off the mortgage. Depending on how long the homeowner has held the mortgage and the rate of return on the investments, the homeowner could have money left over.

The Satos are choosing between a 15-year mortgage at 7.75 percent and a 30-year mortgage at 8 percent. In both cases, the loan would be for $100,000. Their combined marginal federal and state tax rate is 35 percent. They plan to sell the property in seven years. They believe they can invest their money at 9 percent. Which mortgage should they take out?

Web Link 9.27

In this example, the 15-year mortgage is cheaper in present value terms by $559. In other words, the interest savings on the loan from the lower mortgage rate more than offsets the incremental investment income derived from investing the difference between the two mortgage payments.

Is It Worthwhile to Add Money to Each Payment or to Make Extra Payments Each Year?

Most homeowners like the idea of adding money to each monthly payment to accelerate the payoff of their mortgages. Some people add an extra $100 to each payment. Other people make an extra mortgage payment each year. Is either strategy worthwhile? The answer to this question involves several issues. First, making extra principal payments is the same as investing one's money at the current mortgage rate. If the mortgage rate is 8 percent, then adding $100 to each monthly mortgage payment is the same as investing the $100 at

8 percent. A nice feature about this process is that this investment is risk-free if the homeowner has a fixed rate mortgage. With a variable rate mortgage, there is some uncertainty as to the future returns.

> *The Satos bought their house 12 months ago for $150,000. They took out an 8 percent, 30-year fixed rate mortgage for $120,000. They are considering adding $100 to each monthly payment to accelerate the payoff. If they continue to do this over the life of the mortgage, how many months sooner will the mortgage be paid off, and how much interest will the Satos save over the life of the mortgage?*

Web Link 9.28

The life of the mortgage will be shortened by 98 months (8 years and 2 months) and the total amount of interest saved will be $62,062.

The numbers in this last example would sound good to anyone, but they are highly misleading. Remember that an alternative to the extra payments is to invest that money elsewhere, such as a mutual fund. If the return on the mutual fund is greater than the mortgage rate, then the homeowner is actually better off not prepaying. The catch is that the alternative investments likely involve risk. So, the question facing the homeowner is this: would the homeowner rather invest extra money at an expected return greater than 8 percent that is risky or at an 8 percent return that is perfectly safe?

The decision of whether to make extra payments toward the mortgage comes down to comparing a risky, higher expected return to a risk-free, lower rate of return. A side issue is the ability to access money for emergencies or other uses.

> *The Satos bought their house 12 months ago for $150,000. They took out an 8 percent, 30-year fixed rate mortgage for $120,000. Their mortgage balance is now $118,997.56 and they are considering adding $100 to each monthly payment to accelerate the payoff. Their marginal federal and state tax rate is 35 percent. They could invest their money at a rate of 10 percent in a tax-deferred investment. Is making the extra payments a good idea?*

Web Link 9.29

If $100 were added to each payment, then the mortgage balance would be down to $202.64 in 249 months.[13] Alternatively, if the $100 had been invested at 10 percent, the investments would have grown to $109,776.40 over the same period. The mortgage balance at that time would be down to $63,658.91. At that time, the alternative investment could be liquidated and the mortgage paid off, and $46,117.49 ($109,776.40 – $63,658.91) would be left over. These numbers surely sound better than the numbers in the previous example.

SHOULD I REFINANCE MY MORTGAGE?

Web Link 9.31

Whenever mortgage rates fall below the interest rate on their current mortgage, homeowners need to consider whether to refinance their mortgage. To refinance a mortgage means to pay off a mortgage by taking out a new mortgage. The most common motive for refinancing

---

[13]In the prior example, it was indicated that adding payments would result in the mortgage being paid off 98 months early. That would mean 262 months (= 360 months – 98 months) from when the mortgage was taken out. This example indicates that adding the extra payments will mean 249 more payments. This calculator does not allow for one last payment to take care of the $202 balance as the other one did. Adding the extra payment for the final balance, and adding the 12 months that have already elapsed, this calculator also shows that adding $100 to each payment will terminate the mortgage 262 months from its start.

a mortgage is to obtain a lower interest rate. The new mortgage is usually for approximately the same amount as the old mortgage, although some people will use the refinancing opportunity to take out a larger or smaller mortgage loan. The larger mortgage loan would be obtained if they wanted to cash out some of the equity in their home, and the small loan would be obtained if they wanted to substantially reduce their monthly payment.

A popular rule of thumb is that a homeowner should refinance if the interest rate on the mortgage can be reduced by at least 1½ percent (a reduction from 8 percent to 6.5 percent, for example). Research has demonstrated, however, that this rule of thumb often leads to an incorrect decision, since much smaller reductions in the rate may also make it economically profitable to refinance. The three key variables in the decision to refinance are the closing costs to refinance, the amount of additional time the homeowner expects to own the property, and the amount of reduction in the interest rate. Although a present value analysis is the correct methodology for analyzing the refinancing decision, a payback analysis provides a rough guideline to the correct answer and is much simpler. A payback analysis looks at the money saved each month by refinancing and divides it into the cost of refinancing. The calculation shows how many months are required to justify the refinancing in terms of recouping costs. Because payback ignores the time value of money it always shows a slightly shorter period of ownership is necessary to justify refinancing than what is indicated by present value analysis. If the payback period were two years, a present value analysis would probably suggest that one would need to own the property at least two years and three months to justify the refinancing economically.

> *Five years ago the Satos took out a 30-year fixed rate mortgage at 8 percent. Their current monthly payment is $880.52. They recently noted that new 30-year, fixed rate mortgages have a 7 percent rate. Their original mortgage was for $120,000. After exactly five years of payments the principal due is $114,083.83. The costs to refinance would include a 1 percent origination fee and $1,000 in other fees. The Satos would refinance exactly the existing balance on their current mortgage. Is it economically profitable to refinance?*

Web Link 9.30

Web Link (WSJ) 9.30a

The new monthly payment will work out to be $759, or $122 cheaper than the current monthly payment. The value today of refinancing is $2,021. Thus, it would be profitable to refinance today.

One final point on the refinancing decision is that even though refinancing may be profitable, it may not be optimal. This is because interest rates may drop in the near future and it might be even more profitable to wait and refinance at a better interest rate a few months later. Unfortunately there is no way to know if waiting to refinance will be worth it.

HOW ARE PROPERTY TAXES COMPUTED?

Property taxes are imposed on property owners for the purpose of providing the primary funding for local governments, school districts, and other agencies with governmental powers such as park districts and library districts. The process for determining and collecting property taxes varies from state to state, but there are some common elements.

The first step in the determination of property taxes is the determination of what is known as **assessed valuation.** A local assessor assigns a value to each property. Many people confuse assessed value with market value or appraised value. The market or appraised value is the price at which a home would be expected to sell for in a reasonable amount of time on the market. The market value is what a home is truly worth, the assessed value is a contrived number created by a tax assessor. In some areas, the assessor may attempt to set the assessed value equal to the market value. The objective of most assessors is to assess all properties to the same base. For example, in one township, the assessed value is what the assessor thinks the property would have been sold for in 1962. Thus, the assessed value is quite low relative to market value. The second step in determining property taxes is for each tax district to set a **millage rate.** A millage rate is the tax per $1,000 of assessed valuation. So an area with low assessed valuations will have a high millage rate per $1,000 of assessed valuation. An area with high assessed valuations will have a low millage rate per $1,000 of assessed valuation. The property tax is the product of the assessed valuation of the property and the millage rate applied to that property.

SHOULD I FINANCE OR PAY CASH TO BUY A CAR?

Let us now turn from financing a home purchase to financing a car purchase. Up until the mid-1980s, the interest paid on car loans was allowed as an itemized deduction. It no longer is, so the decision to borrow and buy versus pay cash is now a simple comparison between the interest rate on the car loan and the after-tax savings rate that is available. If the interest rate on the car loan is more than the after-tax savings rate, the car buyer should pay cash. If it is less, borrow and buy.

> Stan and Ichiko have decided to buy a car that costs $20,000. They have the cash available, but they have no objection to taking out a loan to buy the car if they can obtain a good deal. At their credit union, they are offered a four-year loan at 7.5 percent if they make a $2,000 down payment. They feel they could invest any monies at 10 percent and they plan to own the car for seven years. Their combined federal and state marginal tax rate is 35 percent. Should they pay cash or take out the loan?

In this case, the Satos after-tax savings rate is 6.5 percent (10% × [1 − .35]). Because this is less than the loan rate, it would be more economical for the Satos to pay cash for the car. Taking out a loan would cost them an extra $254 over the next seven years. However, despite the expected economic value of paying cash, there is the intangible consideration of liquidity that could motivate the Satos to keep the cash and take the loan.

Web Link 9.36

Is a Rebate or a Low Interest Rate the Better Deal?

One of the gimmicks used nowadays to facilitate the sale of cars is for car dealers to offer the buyer a choice between a rebate and a low-interest-rate loan. The best way to look at this choice is to think of the price less the rebate as the true price of the car. By forgoing the rebate (i.e., paying the dealer a one-time fee), the buyer can obtain a more attractive financing package. If the rebate given up is small enough and the reduction in interest rate large enough, then it may make sense to take out the low-rate loan. Some dealers don't offer the rebate choice and simply advertise low-rate loans. They are building the cost of this financing into the price of the car. A consumer who wants the choice between a rebate and a special financing deal should find another dealer who negotiates strictly on price.

This way, the car buyer can now consider the price differential as the rebate and compare this de facto rebate to the special financing.

> *Stan and Ichiko have picked a car that will cost $20,000. The dealer is offering a special loan rate of 2 percent for 36 months. Another dealer will sell them the same car for $18,500. They would make a $2,000 down payment regardless of which dealer they buy the car from. If they buy from the second dealer, they can obtain a 36-month loan from their credit union at a rate of 8 percent. Their savings rate is 8 percent and their combined federal and state marginal tax rate is 35 percent. Which is the better deal?*

Web Link 9.37

The low rate is the better deal by $49. By looking at the graph that shows the extra cost as a function of the loan rate, it is clear that the decision of which deal to take is quite sensitive to the term of the loan. A three-year loan is about the break-even point. A shorter maturity favors the rebate and a longer maturity favors the low-rate loan.

How Much Should I Put Down to Buy My Car?

So far in our examples, we have consistently used 10 percent as a down payment amount. Does this amount make sense? The answer is actually quite simple. Let's consider first the case in which the interest rate on the loan is unaffected by the down payment amount. In this case, the optimal down payment depends on the interest rate on the loan compared to the after-tax rate of return that could be used on the monies not used for a down payment.

> *Stan and Ichiko are considering two down payments for the car they are buying for $15,000. They must make a minimum down payment of $1,500, but they could put down as much as $5,000. Regardless of how much they put down, they will take out a 24-month loan at 8 percent to finance the purchase. If they went with the minimum down payment, they could invest the extra $3,500 ($5,000 – $1,500) at 10 percent. Their combined tax rate is 20 percent. Which is the better down payment?*

Web Link 9.39

The answer is that it makes no difference as to which down payment is made. The after-tax return the Satos can achieve from investing the extra cash is 8 percent (10% × [1 – .20]), the same as the interest rate on the loan. Taking out less of a loan at 8 percent is the same as investing at 8 percent.

Let's assume that the higher down payment enables the Satos to reduce their interest rate to 7.75 percent from 8 percent. This one change makes the higher down payment loan more attractive in present value terms by $25. Suppose their savings rate is 11 percent rather than 10 percent. In this case, the fact that the after-tax return on savings is higher than the loan rates favors the lower down payment, but the lower loan rate on the higher down payment loan favors that down payment. **Web Link 9.39** shows that the tradeoffs in this example are now about equal as the lower down payment is favored by a present value of $3.

HOW DO I LEASE AN AUTO?

Web Link 9.42

In 1985, about 5 percent of new cars were acquired through leases. Currently, about 33 percent of all new cars are acquired through leases. Leases are particularly designed for people who

1. drive less than the common 10,000 to 12,000 miles per year

2. have a strong preference for driving new cars

3. seek to minimize their monthly payments and cash down payments

4. don't like to haggle over the prices of cars when buying and selling them

Every lease can be a specialized arrangement. Leases may be classified as either closed-end or open-end. The majority of consumer leases are closed-end. In both types of leases, there is an estimate of what the market value of the vehicle will be at the end of the lease. This is referred to as the **residual value.** With a closed-end lease, if the residual value is less than the projected residual value, the dealer absorbs the loss. With an open-end lease, if the residual value is less than the projected residual value, the consumer is obligated to make up the difference. There is clearly more risk in an open-end lease. Regardless of which type of lease the consumer obtains, the individual has the option to buy the car at the residual value or to return it.

How Is a Lease Rate Computed?

Web Link 9.40

Car dealers may set whatever monthly lease payment they want to charge, but they generally follow a formula. A general way of computing a lease rate is as follows, based on the example presented in **Web Link 9.40.** The dealer starts with the capitalized cost, which is the price the car would actually sell for, and a predicted value of the vehicle at the end of the lease term, which is a percentage of the MSRP (manufacturer's suggested retail price). The dealer next multiplies the sum of these two numbers by a "money factor." The money factor is usually computed by dividing an annual interest rate by 24, regardless of the term of the lease. This product is then summed with a monthly depreciation charge and any relevant taxes or fees. If you are interested in a popular model, the lease rate may be a little lower because the dealer is confident of the resale value of the car. If your choice of car is a slow-moving model, then your lease rate will be somewhat higher. Let's consider some actual numbers.

Assume the car you want has an MSRP of $25,000, you want a three-year lease, and the fair market price (i.e., capitalized cost) is $23,000. Add in a destination charge of $400, an acquisition fee of $450, and a security deposit of $500. Security deposits should be refunded at the end of the lease. The destination fee and the acquisition fee together are called a **capitalized cost reduction.** The total payment due at the lease signing would then be the capitalized cost reduction plus the security deposit, or $1,350 ($400 + $450 + $500). Next, let's assume that the dealer is using a residual value of 55 percent of the MSRP for three-year leases. So in this case, the residual value would be $13,750. The difference between the capitalized cost of $23,000 and the residual value of $13,750 is the term depreciation of $9,250. To compute the money factor, let's assume an interest rate of 8 percent. The money factor is 8 percent divided by 24, or .003333. The next step is to multiply the money factor by the sum of the capitalized cost and the residual value. This product, which in our case equals $122.49 (.003333 × [$23,000 + $13,750]), is the monthly lease rate. But this is not the end of the calculations.

Next, the **monthly depreciation** is computed. Monthly depreciation is the term depreciation divided by the length of the lease contract. In our example, the term depreciation is $9,250, and the length of the lease is 36 months, so the monthly depreciation is

Web Link
(WSJ) 9.41

$256.94 ($9,250 / 36). The monthly payment is the sum of the monthly lease rate, the monthly depreciation, and any relevant sales tax. In our example, let's assume a sales tax rate of 5 percent. The sum of the monthly depreciation and monthly lease rate is $379.43 ($122.49 + $256.94). A 5 percent sales tax on this total is $18.97 ($379.43 × .05). Thus, the monthly payment is $398.40 ($379.43 + $18.97).

Should I Borrow and Buy or Lease a Car?

In general, leasing will always produce lower monthly payments than borrowing and buying a car. This statement assumes that the negotiated price of the car is the same in both cases, and that there is no special low dealer rate provided for the loan. The reason that leasing produces a lower monthly payment is that the consumer is paying only for the use of the car during a period and not buying the car. If you take out a three-year lease, at the end of the three years you have nothing to show for three years' worth of payments except an option to buy a car at a price that may be above the current market value of the car. If you take out a three-year loan, at the end of the three years you own the car outright.

> *Stan and Ichiko have negotiated a price on a car of $23,000. They are prepared to put down $2,300 as a down payment and to borrow the rest at 8 percent on a 36-month loan. The state sales tax is 5 percent. They expect the car they are buying to have an average depreciation schedule. At the last minute, the salesperson asks them if they would like to consider a lease. The lease is $400 per month for 36 months, with a $500 security deposit and an $850 down payment. Which is the better deal?*

Web Link 9.44

Using the calculators at **Web Link 9.44,** the borrow-and-buy option costs an average of $4,515 per year. The leasing option costs an average of $4,818 per year. Thus, borrowing and buying is cheaper by approximately $303 per year. The monthly payment on the installment loan is $648, which is substantially more than the $400 monthly payment on the leasing contract. In addition, the money paid at closing is less with the lease, and the lease has the refund of the security deposit (if all goes well). However, the analysis must factor in the value of the car at the end of the three-year period. In this example, that value is enough to offset the lower monthly payment of the lease. As proof of this point, reconsider the above example and change the expected depreciation rate from average to high. When this happens, the annual cost of leasing remains unchanged at $4,818. But the annual cost of borrowing and buying rises to $5,422. Now, the lease contract is a better deal by more than $600 per year.

Web Link 9.45

SUMMARY

➢ Prequalification allows one to focus on the correct price range and minimize the risk of being rejected for a mortgage.

➢ Mortgages can be conventional or insured, can be fixed or variable rate, and range in maturity from 15 to 30 years.

➢ Current mortgage rates may be found on the Internet, including on the *Wall Street Journal* site.

➢ Internet calculators allow one to ascertain an economically affordable price of a home.

➢ Closing costs are the expenses paid at the closing session when the house is bought and paid for.

➤ The appropriate mortgage depends on the expected period of ownership, the opportunity cost of funds, and the homeowner's willingness to accept risk.

➤ The economic worth of refinancing a mortgage depends on the expected period of occupancy, the interest rate reduction, and the closing costs.

➤ Property taxes are determined through a combination of assessed valuation and the rate per $1,000 of assessed valuation.

➤ Autos may be financed with term loans of varying maturity or with an open-end or closed-end lease arrangement.

➤ It is not always clear whether it is cheaper to borrow and buy or to lease an auto. Many factors come into play, including the opportunity cost of funds.

KEY TERMS

adjustable rate mortgage	application fee	assessed valuation
capitalized cost reduction	caps	closing
closing costs	conventional	convertibility
convertible	escrow	Federal Housing Authority
FHA-insured	fixed rate mortgage	index
jumbo mortgage	lock period	margin
millage rate	monthly depreciation	monthly payment
mortgage amortization table	mortgage commitment letter	originator
points	PITI	prepaid interest
preapproval letter	prequalified letter	private mortgage insurance
residual value	teaser rate	title insurance
VA-guaranteed		

PROBLEMS

9.1. What is the best rate you can find today for each of the following mortgages: 30-year fixed rate, 15-year fixed rate, 1-year adjustable (with a 30-year maturity), and a 5/1 ARM (with a 30-year maturity)?

9.2. Ascertain the monthly payment for the following mortgages: 30-year fixed rate at 6 percent, 15-year fixed rate at 6 percent, 1-year adjustable (with a 30-year maturity) at 6 percent.

9.3 Compute the monthly payment for a 10 percent fixed rate mortgage for $100,000 with the following maturities: 15 years, 20 years, 25 years, 30 years, 35 years, and 40 years. What are the actual dollar and percentage reductions in the monthly payment with each 5-year extension in maturity?

9.4. Your wage income is $40,000 per year. You could obtain a 30-year fixed rate mortgage with an interest rate of 7 percent. Closing costs would run 2 percent of the mortgage balance. You have $2,400 in other annual income. You pay $300 per month on an auto loan. You have $15,000 cash on hand. Homes in your area have a property tax rate of 3 percent of the home's value, and homeowner's insurance runs .5 percent. How large of a home could you afford to buy with a 20 percent down payment? With a 10 percent down payment?

9.5. Bob Mason is looking at a 30-year, 6 percent fixed rate mortgage for $200,000. He is also thinking about a one-year ARM (with a 30-year maturity). The initial rate is 4.5 percent, the caps are 2 percent (annual) and 5 percent (lifetime). The adjusted rate each year is the index value plus a 1 percent margin. The current value of the index is 5 percent. Let us assume that Bob is interested in a pessimistic scenario. He wants to know what would happen to his monthly payments if the index rate changed once per year, and it went up .2 percent on each change. Bob believes that the differences in monthly payments would be invested at a rate of 10 percent. Finally, assume that Bob expects to live in the home for five years and his combined federal and state marginal tax rate is 35 percent. Which mortgage would you recommend he take out? Why?

9.6. Judy Ferrari wants to take out a 30-year, $100,000 mortgage. She is considering taking a mortgage at 7 percent with no points, or paying two points to obtain a rate of 6.5 percent. Her opportunity cost (savings rate) is 10 percent. If her combined marginal state and federal income tax rate is 33 percent and if she plans to live in the home for five years, which mortgage is the better deal?

9.7. Kathleen Atchinson is attempting to choose between a 15-year mortgage at 6.5 percent and a 30-year mortgage at 6.75 percent. Her combined marginal state and federal income tax rate is 33 percent, and she plans to live in the home for five years. She needs a mortgage for $100,000. If she could invest her money at 10 percent rate, which mortgage should she take out?

9.8. Five years ago the Warths took out a 30-year fixed rate mortgage for $90,000 at 10 percent. They recently noted that new 30-year, fixed rate mortgages have a 9.25 percent rate. If their closing costs on refinancing were $3,000, would it be economically profitable to refinance?

REFERENCES

Web Link 9.47   Glossaries with mortgage terms
Web Link 9.47a   Miscellaneous sites for mortgages
Web Link 9.48   Sites providing mortgage FAQs
Web Link 9.49   Pointer sites for mortgages
Web Link 9.50   Glossaries with auto financing terms
Web Link 9.51   Sites with auto financing FAQs
Web Link 9.52   Pointer sites for auto financing
Web Link 9.53   A quiz on leasing

WALL STREET JOURNAL INTERACTIVE RESOURCES

Web Link (WSJ) 9.46   Recent articles on home and auto ownership
Web Link (WSJ) 9.54   "Paying Extra Mortgage Principal Has Merit for Some Homeowners," *The Wall Street Journal Interactive Edition*, November 28, 1999
Web Link (WSJ) 9.55   "Criticism Aimed at High Fees for Biweekly-Mortgage Plans," *The Wall Street Journal Interactive Edition*, December 29, 1998
Web Link (WSJ) 9.56   "Low Interest Rates Prompt a Cash-Out, Refinance Dance," *The Wall Street Journal Interactive Edition*, October 12, 1998

Web Link (WSJ) 9.57 "Making a Home Sweet Refinanced Home," *The Wall Street Journal Interactive Edition*, January 14, 1998

Web Link (WSJ) 9.58 "Interest-Only Mortgage Is a Good Risk for Some," *The Wall Street Journal Interactive Edition*, November 28, 1997

Web Link (WSJ) 9.59 "When to Question Your Mortgage Insurance," *The Wall Street Journal Interactive Edition*, January 16, 1997

For information that has changed since the book was written, for new information that pertains to this topic, and for some new web sites that pertain to the topic of this chapter, see **Web Link 9.60.**

PART III

RISK AND INSURANCE

CHAPTER 10

RISK MANAGEMENT AND PROPERTY AND CASUALTY INSURANCE: AUTOMOBILE AND HOMEOWNER'S POLICIES

LEARNING OBJECTIVES

- Identify the types of risks for which insurance coverage is appropriate
- Describe the basic principles of insurance and how an insurance premium is determined
- Describe the basic coverages of an automobile insurance policy
- Calculate an optimal amount of auto coverage for the minimum premium
- Obtain insurance premium quotes on the Internet
- Describe forms of homeowner's insurance
- Explain the advantages of full replacement value coverage
- Describe the appropriate coverages for condominium apartment owners, renters, and college students
- Calculate an optimal amount of homeowner's coverage for the minimum premium
- Discuss strategies for working with agents and representatives
- Research an insurance company's rating and complaint record
- Explain the role of an umbrella insurance policy

Web Link: www.wiley.com/college/woerheide

INTRODUCTION

A critical part of financial planning is preparing for the misfortunes that will occur in life—those with serious financial consequences, such as a house being burnt, as well as those with primarily emotional consequences, such as a romance falling apart. Chapters 10–12 focus on the first category of misfortunes, in which the first objective is always to minimize the financial impact of potentially large losses.

Costly misfortunes are usually divided into three broad categories: premature death, expensive health problems, and property and casualty misfortunes, the subject of this chapter. Life and health insurance are covered in Chapters 11 and 12.

Property and casualty misfortunes include not only loss or destruction of property, but also lawsuits. Thus, one buys automobile insurance not only to cover the cost of the car being stolen or destroyed in an accident, but also to protect oneself against lawsuits incurred as a result of an accident. In this chapter, we will consider the example of Dan Joseph, as he considers his options when evaluating property and casualty insurance.

WHEN SHOULD INSURANCE BE CONSIDERED?

When choosing insurance, part of anyone's financial planning, follow one simple principle: *insurance should be bought to protect against catastrophic disasters, not to protect against commonplace events.* Although this statement sounds simple and obvious, as we will see in this and the next two chapters, it has implications that many find objectionable. Consider the following two situations: a person is held responsible for an auto accident that causes hundreds of thousands of dollars worth of injury and damage, while another person loses a textbook (such as this one). Both events could be considered disasters (especially if the book is lost right before an exam). However, the former has serious financial implications and the latter relatively minor ones. Because the former would be classified as a catastrophic disaster and the latter as a commonplace event, insurance is clearly appropriate in the first case and not even worth considering in the second. The premium for textbook insurance is likely equal to the cost of a new book, and no lives could conceivably be ruined by a need to replace it. When buying an insurance policy, apply such tests to each element of the policy to determine whether the policy provides protection from catastrophic or merely commonplace events.

WHAT ARE THE BASIC PRINCIPLES OF INSURANCE?

All insurance companies follow certain basic principles. When a buyer pays an insurance premium and a company issues a contract, referred to as a policy, the buyer is insured by the company. The insurance company calculates premiums and payments through **underwriting,** which has two elements. First, the company chooses which risks it will cover. Second, it determines what rates to charge for each policy issued.

Web Link 10.1

Insurance companies only issue policies for what are called **insurable risks.** Six conditions must exist for a risk to be insurable:

1. The loss must be fortuitous. This means that only chance events can be insured against. Insurance is not sold to cover the gradual loss of value of one's car, because all cars deteriorate over time, whereas theft insurance is sold, because theft of a car is always a chance event.

2. The loss must be well defined. This means one cannot insure against feeling blue, a difficult condition to define precisely. The monetary loss associated with such events is not easily computed.

3. The loss must be predictable in aggregate. This means that the insurer must be able to predict approximately how many people out of a large group will be affected by this loss, as well as what the average value of each loss would be.

4. The loss must be personal. This means that one or a few people are affected each time a loss occurs. Hence, losses associated with wars or even meteors hitting are either not covered or have limited coverages. No insurance company could risk all or even many of its policyholders making a claim on the same event.

5. A large number of policies with similar risk exposure must be available. This limits the chance of only those people who expect to incur a particular loss applying for a policy.

6. The loss exposures must be widely distributed. This means that an insurance company does not want many people with identical risk exposure applying for the same coverage. For example, a homeowner's insurance company that sold a large portion of its policies in one community could fail if some natural disaster hit that community. Such a company would need to assure that its policies were sold in geographically diverse communities.

Because they are only insuring against a loss, insurance policies either explicitly or implicitly seek only to **indemnify.** Indemnification means "to make whole again." Thus, insurance policies seek only to reimburse a person for his or her loss.

Insurance policy buyers must demonstrate a clear element of **insurable interest.** In other words, the insured will sustain clear economic loss if a misfortune strikes whatever is being insured. Thus, you cannot buy an automobile insurance policy on your friend's car because you would sustain no loss if the car were destroyed, and you cannot buy homeowner's insurance on your neighbor's house. This would look particularly bad if shortly thereafter a fire of mysterious origins destroyed your neighbor's house! Most importantly, you cannot take out a life insurance policy on your professor! Unless, of course, you are related to the professor and depend on the income that person earns. For additional discussion of insurable interest, see **Web Link 10.2.**

Web Link 10.2

HOW ARE INSURANCE
PREMIUMS DETERMINED?

Insurance premiums (the amount paid by the buyer of insurance) have two components: the **basic premium** and the **loadings.** The basic premium is the amount the insurance company must charge to assure that the expected claims can all be paid. Basic premiums are determined by using **actuarial tables.** For example, the life insurance industry uses tables that indicate the numbers of people in each age group that are expected to die each year. For a randomly selected group of 20-year-old males, approximately 1.9 people per thousand will die within one year. Therefore, if the insurance company sells insurance policies to 10,000 such people, it can expect 19 claims to be made in the coming year. It just doesn't know which 19 policies will be making claims! If the company sells each 20-year-old male a policy that pays $10,000 in the event of death, it can expect to pay $190,000 in death benefits to this group in the coming year. If the $190,000 in expected death benefits were then divided by the 10,000 policies sold, the basic premium would be $19. If fewer than 19 people from this group die in the coming year, then the insurance company is said to earn an underwriting profit. Loadings are what the insurance company charges to cover its operating expenses and to ensure that it profits on the policy.

All companies operate under the same expectations of losses. Thus, all insurance companies must charge the same basic premium for the same risk exposure. Differences in premiums arise from the varying ability of companies to control costs and from their desire to compete for business. Hence, one can save a lot of money by comparison shopping on insurance policies—not only when a policy is initially purchased, but every time the policy comes up for renewal.

Two factors allow substantial savings on insurance premiums: **deductibles** and **coinsurance.** A deductible is the amount which the insured agrees to pay himself or herself on any claim. Coinsurance means that the insured agrees to split the total claim with the insurance company. Both of these features will be described later in the context of how they apply to specific types of policies. Deductibles and coinsurance are tools that allow the insurance company to pay smaller claims; they also keep the insured person more motivated to take steps to avoid making a claim. Consider the following example:

> *Dan Joseph just bought a new car. He has some business in a rather dangerous part of town. When he arrives, he has two choices of where he may park. He can pay $5 to park in a lot with an attendant, or he can use a vacant lot farther down the street. Which is he likely to choose?*

If Dan carried, say, a $1,000 deductible in the event of theft, then he is more likely to pay the $5 to avoid having to pay $1,000 in the event his car is stolen. If Dan has full coverage in the event of theft, then he is more likely to choose the free, unmonitored parking, because the insurance company would pay in full if his car were stolen.

WHAT ARE THE BASIC FEATURES OF AUTOMOBILE INSURANCE?

An automobile insurance policy covers the insured against four basic risks:

1. property damage to the insured's car
2. physical injury to the insured and any occupants of the insured's car
3. legal liability for damage to the property of others
4. legal liability for injury to others

Web Link 10.3   The standard automobile insurance policy covers not only the insured but also any of the insured's family members who might be driving the car. The standard policy also covers the insured and the insured's family members when they are driving someone else's car with that person's permission. It also covers anyone else driving the insured's car with permission. Consider the following example:

> *Dan Joseph is on vacation in New Orleans. He would like to rent a car to visit some of the more famous antebellum homes in the area. He shows up at the rental agency to sign the papers, at the agreed-upon price, and the agent encourages him to take out a short-term insurance policy to cover the period of the lease. The agent notes that the policy only costs an extra $20 and could save Dan a lot of grief later. Is this a good deal?*

As Dan is paying for the rental, he is clearly driving the rental car with the permission of the owner. Hence, Dan's policy on his own car would apply to this rental car. Dan might be interested in the policy only under a few limited circumstances. For example, if Dan were renting the car in a foreign country where his policy did not extend coverage, then such a purchase would be crucial. Second, if Dan felt his own coverage were inadequate, then he might desire the supplemental insurance coverage. Of course, this would also suggest that the moment Dan gets back home he should look into increasing his own coverage to eliminate the need to buy extra policies such as the rental car company's.

What Is Covered Under Physical Injury and Legal Liability for Injury to Others?

The expenses covered under personal liability include not only the actual settlement that must be paid but also the insured's legal defense costs (i.e., the expense of a lawyer and any associated court costs) and the cost of bail bonds. The one exception to legal defense costs is if the insurance company agrees to a settlement and the insured wants to take the case to court. Settlement expenses would include property damages, loss of services, bodily injury, medical services, loss of income, and death.

An auto insurance policy typically defines the extent of injury and legal liability for injury coverage by using two numbers. For example, a typical policy might provide coverage of "100/300." Both numbers are stated in thousands of dollars, the first number representing the coverage per person, the second total coverage for all persons combined. Thus, with 100/300 coverage the insured is covered for up to $100,000 for each person injured in an accident, and the combined coverage for all people injured may not exceed $300,000. Consider the following example:

> Dan Joseph has coverage of 50/150. Dan made a mistake driving to work the other day, resulting in an accident that caused a car carrying four women to hit a tree. The first woman had serious neck injuries, the second woman lost the use of an arm, the third woman suffered two broken legs, and the fourth woman suffered from whiplash. The claims included ambulance charges, hospital and surgeon charges, and rehabilitation expenses, as well as lost income. The first woman claimed $40,000 in injuries, the second claimed $30,000, the third claimed $90,000, and the last $45,000. How well is Dan protected by his policy?

The claims of the first two women and the last woman fall under the $50,000 limitation for individual claims under Dan's policy. Only the first $50,000 of the claims of the third woman is satisfied under Dan's policy. Thus, Dan can be held personally liable for the remaining $40,000 of her claim. In addition, the four claims combined total $165,000 (counting the $50,000 of the third claim that is covered). That total exceeds the aggregate claim limit of $150,000. Thus, Dan is also personally responsible for another $15,000 of the claims. In summary, Dan could be held personally liable for $55,000 of claims ($40,000 + $15,000).

What Is Covered Under Legal Liability for Property Damage?

Coverage for property damage is fairly straightforward. Property damage is usually included in the description of the policy limits as a third number, for example, 100/300/100. The first two numbers relating to liability for injury were discussed in the previous section; the third number represents the property damage limitation in thousands of dollars. Consider the following example:

In the same accident described in the previous example, Dan's car spins out of control and hits a third car, causing $15,000 in damage. The car Dan hit crashes into a building, causing $30,000 in damage. How well is Dan protected by his policy?

In this case, Dan is fully protected by his policy, as the sum of the damage of $45,000 ($15,000 + $30,000) is well under his policy limit of $100,000.

What Is Covered Under Medical Payments?

Medical payments covers emergency medical treatment for the insured, covered passengers, and covered family members. Note that it does not cover the emergency medical treatment of others. In the preceding example, the emergency medical treatment to the injured women is paid strictly out of the personal liability protection. Medical payments are **first party coverage,** applying only to the person who buys the policy. Personal liability coverage is **third party coverage** because it covers people not included in the policy.[1] Medical payments cover just about everything covered by regular medical insurance coverage (e.g., physicians, hospital expenses, ambulance fees, surgery, and X-rays), and also covers items such as funeral expenses.

What Is Covered Under Underinsured/Uninsured Motorists Coverage?

State laws govern underinsured/uninsured motorist coverage and differ as to what must be covered. However, in most states this component of an auto insurance policy covers the insured for both bodily injury and property damage caused by a motorist who has inadequate or no auto insurance. Note that this would also provide coverage in the case of a hit and run accident, when, for all practical purposes, there is no known insurance coverage on the offender. Like medical payments, underinsured/uninsured motorist coverage is first party coverage, applying only to the insured, the insured's passengers, and family members. The injury coverage includes bodily injury as well as disease, sickness, and death.

What Is Covered Under Collision and Comprehensive Protection?

Both **collision coverage** and **comprehensive coverage** are also first party coverages. Collision coverage protects the insured's car in the event it is damaged in any sort of collision, including moving objects (e.g., another car) and stationary objects (e.g., a fire hydrant). It can be considered a collision even if one were to hit a curb and flip one's car. In situations where the collision object is another car, the insured obtains compensation from his or her own insurance company, which then seeks reimbursement from the other party (or his or her insurance company) if the other party is at fault.

Comprehensive coverage is the catchall category for protection from events not covered by collision. It includes damage from falling objects (e.g., a tree limb), fire, theft, vandalism, and even natural disasters such as explosions and earthquakes.

---

[1]The second party in insurance is the insurance company itself.

The maximum coverage under collision and comprehensive is **replacement value.** Many policies will reimburse only up to the **actual cash value** of the vehicle—the amount for which the car could be sold in the used car market, analogous to the wholesale price of the car. Replacement value is analogous to the retail value, or what you would have to pay to obtain a car like the one damaged or destroyed.

If a car is totally destroyed, its market value becomes speculative, as it cannot be inspected. Auto insurers must base their settlement on average values defined in various publications (sources which were discussed in Chapter 8). Unfortunately, even if your car was in immaculate condition, had unusually low mileage, and was worth over a thousand dollars more than the average market value, the insurance company would still offer a settlement based on the market averages.

Insurance companies will sometimes declare a car **totaled** even when it is still usable. Totaled only means that the cost of repairing the car to normal condition exceeds the market value of the car. Some cars that have been "totaled" can still be driven, occasionally even without the appropriate repairs having been made! When a car has been totaled, the insurance company usually seeks to provide a replacement car of similar make, age, and mileage, although a cash settlement is certainly possible. Replacement cars are frequently cheaper for insurance companies, because they can buy them at wholesale prices.

Comprehensive coverages frequently have limitations and exclusions. Installed items such as audio systems are not covered under most policies.

How Much Auto Insurance Should a Person Have?

You should review your auto policies at least annually to determine not only if your premium is reasonable, but also to ensure that your coverage is adequate. The single most important item in your auto insurance policy is the liability coverage. In theory, you could be sued for an unlimited amount of money, but as a rule your coverage should roughly match your personal wealth. People with few assets do not really need a substantial amount of insurance coverage. Lawsuits are based on the ability to collect money, and the poorer you are the less likely anyone is to sue you! Another essential factor in determining the amount of liability coverage you need is the option of obtaining additional liability coverage through an umbrella policy separate from your auto insurance policy. Umbrella policies will be discussed later. All states have a minimum amount of liability coverage that everyone must carry. Incremental amounts of liability are relatively inexpensive, considering how much protection you receive in return. If it is at all affordable, most people should obtain the maximum amount of liability coverage their insurer will provide. Certainly coverage of 250/500 or more is not unreasonable.

Your policy's medical payments insurance should be primarily a function of your health insurance coverage. A person with good health insurance really needs little, if any, medical payments insurance. Remember, this is first party coverage, which means it is only covering the medical expenses of you and your family. The only real risk occurs if occupants of your car who are injured do not have adequate medical insurance. If you have no health insurance coverage or have a substantial deductible, then consider substantial medical payments coverage as part of your auto policy. Coverage up to $5,000 or more may be reasonable.

As discussed above, uninsured and underinsured coverage is mandatory in most states, although the mandated amount is usually relatively low. In some places, injury to your car from an underinsured/underinsured motorist would be covered under collision, and so the primary benefit of this coverage would be for physical injury. Many experts argue that if you have good health insurance coverage, then there is no need for underinsured/uninsured coverage. The only problem with this argument is that one can claim pain and suffering under this coverage, and one cannot claim pain and suffering on a health insurance claim. Also, underinsured/uninsured claims are higher in areas (either states or communities) with high concentrations of low-income individuals. Thus, anyone using a car regularly in low-income areas would be more likely to consider higher underinsured/uninsured coverage.

Your collision and comprehensive coverages offer opportunities for substantial insurance savings because you specify the amount not of coverage but of the deductible. When most people buy new cars, they usually buy policies with a relatively small deductible, as they would certainly repair any and all damage to their new cars. However, as the car gets older and as dents and rust start to appear, new physical damage becomes less and less likely to be repaired. Consider the following example:

> *Dan Joseph is reviewing his auto insurance policy. The current market value of his car is about $5,000 (at best). Rust and scratches can be seen over the entire car. Dan has carried a $50 comprehensive deductible since he bought the car new. His insurance agent points out that if he raised his deductible to $500, he would save $112.50 a year in insurance premiums. Is this a good deal?*

Several factors come into play in this analysis. First, Dan has to assess his own driving record. In the above scenario, Dan already has a $50 exposure every time he makes a claim on his comprehensive. So increasing his deductible to $500 is increasing his risk exposure by only $450 ($500 − $50). This increased risk exposure represents four years worth of incremental premiums ($450 / $112.50). Thus, if Dan expects to have a comprehensive claim less frequently than once every four years, he is clearly better off taking the larger deductible. If he expects a claim more frequently than once every four years, he *might* stick with the lower deductible. The word *might* is emphasized for two reasons. First, all property and casualty insurers become nervous about customers who make frequent claims. Thus, if Dan has a claim of $100 that would provide a $50 reimbursement under the lower deductible, he might elect not to make the claim just to keep his record clear, in order to facilitate the renewal of his policy at a reasonable rate. Second, Dan would have to ask himself whether the incremental $450 deductible meets the condition of catastrophic loss. Most people could handle occasionally paying an extra $450 on a claim without destroying their finances.

Finally, Dan might also consider actually dropping his comprehensive altogether if his car becomes old and/or dilapidated enough that he could replace it on an out-of-pocket basis. For example, suppose Dan were planning to buy a new car next year anyway. If the car were destroyed and he no longer carried comprehensive, his only real cost would be **Web Link 10.4** slightly earlier replacement of the vehicle.

Should One Buy Towing Insurance?

Most insurance companies will add **towing insurance** to the policy, in which case towing expenses are reimbursed, up to a limit. Depending on the premium for this feature, it could be a good deal, although one could argue that this is insuring for the commonplace and not the catastrophic. Furthermore, towing is available through other sources such as automobile clubs. If one belongs to such a club or would like to consider belonging to such a club, then towing services could be obtained through the club and skipped on the insurance policy.

What Factors Determine Auto Insurance Premiums?

As described earlier, an auto insurance premium includes the basic premium and the loadings. The basic premium is based on the likelihood both that the insured will be in an accident and that an outside claim will involve the car. Insurance companies, who do a great deal of research to calculate the probabilities of a particular insured driver making a claim, have found certain categories of people to be more frequently involved in accidents. Women are in fewer accidents, as are people over age 25, and people who are married. In addition, those with clean driving histories and defensive driver or driver education courses have fewer accidents. Finally, people who commute to work daily and/or use their car for work have more accidents, as do those who live in urban areas.

Features of the car can also have a major impact on the insurance premium. Sports cars and high-performance vehicles are charged higher rates, as are cars that cost more to repair. However, having some safety features such as air bags and anti-lock brakes will lower premiums.

Finally, many insurance companies lower their premiums when more than one car is insured with them, and if other insurance policies (such as a homeowner's or umbrella policy) are purchased from the same company. Some companies also offer discounts if premium payments come directly from a savings account, checking account, or even a payroll deduction plan. In fact, payroll deduction plans for insurance premiums will probably be one of the most rapidly spreading perks for employees over the next few years.

Web Link 10.5

What Are Strategies for Reducing One's Auto Insurance Premiums?

The best way to reduce your auto insurance premium is to maximize deductibles and minimize or eliminate coverage you have elsewhere (such as medical payments or towing insurance). Because premiums can differ substantially among particular models and features of cars, it may be worthwhile to contact an insurance agent to learn how each model and feature you are considering would affect the annual insurance premium. For example, auto insurers regularly conduct surveys to determine which cars are most frequently involved in claims and which are frequently stolen. At the time of this writing, the vehicle with the most claims is the Jeep Wrangler, and the vehicle most often stolen is the Honda Accord. Taking a driver education or defensive driving course may also provide more than enough savings to justify the time and cost of such a course.

Web Link 10.6
Web Link 10.6a
Web Link 10.6b

It is extremely important to keep your driving record as clean as possible. Thus, if you should be ticketed, it is financially worthwhile to fight the ticket or at least attempt to have the level of the charge reduced. The expense of an attorney may turn out to be less than the cost of the even more expensive auto premiums you will pay over the next several years. The easiest way to keep a clean driving record is simply to drive safely at all times. Consider the following example:

> *Dan Joseph was recently ticketed for speeding (doing more than 20 mph above the speed limit). Dan's lawyer has advised him that with legal representation, Dan could get the charge substantially reduced. The legal fees would be $500. The benefit of the reduction is that Dan's fine would be reduced from $150 to $75, and without the reduction Dan's auto insurance premiums would rise by $150 per year for the next five years. If Dan's opportunity cost is 10 percent, is it worthwhile to hire the lawyer?*

By spending $500 today, Dan would save $75 in fines today. He would also save $150 per year for four years. The present value of this annuity is $568.62 ($PVIFA_{5 \text{ yrs}, 10\%} \times \$150 = 3.7908 \times \$150$). Thus, between the immediate savings in the amount of fine and the insurance premium savings, Dan would save a total of $643.62 ($75 + $568.62). Hence, by hiring the lawyer Dan would achieve an expected savings of $143.62 ($643.62 − $500). Of course, Dan could have saved $500 had he not been speeding in the first place!

Web Link 10.7

How Much Might Auto Insurance Cost?

Web Link 10.7a

As should be clear from the previous discussions, auto insurance premiums will vary substantially, so it pays to shop around extensively.

WHAT PROTECTIONS DOES HOMEOWNER'S INSURANCE PROVIDE?

Homeowner's insurance is quite similar to automobile insurance in terms of the four basic coverages it provides. A homeowner's insurance policy covers four basic risks:

1. property damage to the insured's home, its contents, and related personal property
2. physical injury to the insured's guests
3. legal liability for damage if the insured causes damage to the property of others
4. legal liability if the insured causes injury to others

What Are the Different Forms of Homeowner's Insurance?

Web Link 10.8

Homeowner's insurance policies, standardized for use in all of the states, come in many forms, five of which apply to owner-occupied, single-family homes: HO-1, HO-2, HO-3, HO-5, and HO-8. The HO-1 provides the least coverage, insuring against only 11 named perils. A peril is the cause of a possible loss, such as fire, windstorm, theft, explosion, or riot. **Named peril coverage** means that protection is provided only for the misfortunes that have been specifically named. HO-2 provides more protection, covering 18 named perils. The most popular form of homeowner's insurance is HO-3, which provides **comprehensive coverage** on your home and coverage against many perils on your contents. Comprehensive coverage means you are protected against all sources of loss, except for exclusions specifically named. Most homeowners should consider purchasing an HO-3 policy.

Some companies provide the HO-5 policy—comprehensive coverage on both your home and its contents. HO-5 is not offered everywhere, and the resultant premium can be quite expensive. Finally, HO-8 is for older homes, where the market value of the home is substantially less than the replacement cost.

What Does the HO-3 Form Consist of?

The HO-3 policy is divided into two general sections. Section I Coverage is divided into Coverages A, B, C, and D, and provides the property protection. Section II is divided into Coverages E and F, and provides the liability protection.

Coverage A is for the dwelling itself and defines the value of the policy. The maximum insurance specified under Coverage A would be the cost to replace the home. We will discuss this in more detail later.

Coverage B extends to detached structures such as storage sheds or detached garages. The standard limit for Coverage B is 10 percent of the value specified in Coverage A, although an insured may amend the policy for a higher coverage amount. Coverages A and B are comprehensive coverages.

Coverage C is for the personal property of the insured. The standard limit is 50 percent of Coverage A. An important feature of Coverage C is that personal property is covered, even when not on the premises of the insured home. This coverage is named peril, and is usually based on **actual cash value** as opposed to **replacement value,** two terms that will be discussed shortly. **Internal limits**—maximum amount of protection for certain items, regardless of the total limits of coverage—are always specified on certain types of property. Some typical internal limits would include the following:

- firearms: $1,000
- jewelry (including furs, precious and semiprecious stones): anywhere from $1,000 to $2,500
- cash (including medals and precious metals): $100
- passports (including securities, stamp collections, and tickets): $1,000
- watercraft (including equipment, motor, and trailer): $1,000

These limits are rather restrictive, and in many cases might provide coverage that is only a fraction of the loss.

It should be pointed out that Coverage C provides reimbursement for many items that most people would not normally assume to be covered. For example, under Coverage C homeowners can obtain reimbursement for losses involving credit cards, forgery, and counterfeit money.

Coverage D pays for temporary living expenses while the home specified in Coverage A is being restored to a normal living condition, and is normally 20 percent of Coverage A.

Coverage E, the first part of the Section II coverage, provides liability protection if a claim is made or suit is brought against an insured because of bodily injury sustained on the insured's property or as a result of actions by the insured. It also provides coverage for damage to the property of others caused by the insured. As with automobile liability coverage, protection extends not only to the insured but also to the insured's family. The standard amount of protection is $100,000 per occurrence. Naturally, a higher limit may be obtained for an additional annual premium. In addition to paying any settlement against the insured, Coverage E also pays for such expenses as legal costs, provision of first aid to others, damage to property of others, and loss assessment charges. There are usually internal limits on some of these supplemental protections.

The last of the six basic coverages is **Coverage F.** This provides for necessary medical expenses for bodily injury of others in accidents on the insured's premises. However, it also applies to accidents the insured might cause elsewhere. The standard coverage has a basic limit of $1,000 per person, but as is always the case, the policyholder may select higher limits.

To summarize the above discussion, consider the following example:

> *Dan Joseph is in the process of buying a home. As part of the closing process, he must present a receipt for the purchase of a homeowner's insurance policy for his new home. If Dan believes the cost to replace the house to be $200,000, what would be the normal and customary protections in a HO-3 policy?*

Web Link 10.9

If rebuilding the house would cost $200,000, Dan should ask the insurance agent for $200,000 of protection in Coverage A. Coverages B, C, and D would automatically be defined at $20,000 (10%), $100,000 (50%), and $40,000 (20%). Coverage E would be set at $100,000, and Coverage F would start at $1,000.

What Are Common Homeowner's Policy Endorsements?

Standardized policies can be tailored to your needs by means of **endorsements,** additions to the original contract. The first endorsement you might consider is automatic inflation adjustment for Coverage A (and thus implicitly for Coverages B, C, and D). However, not all home prices go up at the rate of inflation. Some home prices go up faster than the inflation rate, some go up slower, and the prices of some homes actually decline. Thus, a homeowner may do better to review the policy limits each year at renewal rather than to build in automatic increases. Another possible endorsement is earthquake coverage, usually excluded in Section I of the HO-3 policy. Also, as mentioned above, homeowners who have valuable detached structures on the covered property would certainly want to increase the limit for Coverage B through an endorsement.

If the internal limits in Coverage C are severely constraining for a homeowner, property coverages could also be extended with one or more endorsements. These are known as scheduled property items, and the homeowner may specify the desired amount for each item insured. However, a homeowner may always take out separate policies to cover specific personal property of substantive value. Because the most cost-effective way to obtain the incremental insurance is not clear in advance, both routes should be explored.

Web Link 10.10

A final endorsement to consider is one for personal property replacement cost. The standard provision in a policy is that the property loss settlements under the homeowner's policy are made on an actual cash value basis. When the replacement cost endorsement is added, the loss settlement payment is sufficient to replace the item for the cost at the time of loss without deductions for depreciation.

How Much Homeowner's Insurance Should Be Purchased?

Coverage A in your policy should contain only enough insurance to rebuild the house—an amount not necessarily equal to the market value of the house. When you buy a home, you are buying real estate, which includes the land on which the property is located and all of the permanent structures on that land (the house, driveway, landscaping, and detached structures). However, you do not need to insure the land, which will not normally be destroyed by the perils included in your policy. A nuclear explosion might be the exception, but policies normally do not cover nuclear explosions. Similarly, the perils that would normally destroy the home would also not destroy the foundation. Thus, the value for which one insures a home is likely to be less or substantially less than the market price that was paid for the home. It could be substantially less if the home is located in a community where the land is extremely expensive. For example, a home that might sell for $100,000 in Flint, Michigan, could easily sell for $500,000 if it were located in a major market in California or the New York City metropolitan area. The cost of building this home would not differ substantially in any of these communities. The difference in the price primarily reflects the cost of the land. A homebuyer in California could conceivably end up insuring his or her home for $80,000 or so, despite having paid $500,000 or more for it.

You can learn the cost of rebuilding your home in several ways. One is to ask a few builders in the area what the average cost per square foot of living area is, then multiply this amount by the square footage of living area in the home. Note that these calculations do not include such items as a garage, a finished basement, or a deck. Separate valuations must be made for these supplements to a house.

A second way to ascertain the cost to rebuild a home is to ask the insurance agent. Each insurance company uses a formula to estimate the cost of rebuilding a home in that area. Hence, when you contact an agent about a homeowner's policy, he or she will ask such questions as how much square footage of living area you have, how many bedrooms, bathrooms, and fireplaces the house has, whether the chimneys are on the interior or exterior of the home, and how big the garage is. The agent then inputs this information into the company's formula to ascertain the amount of insurance recommended. You will quickly discover that no two companies will come up with the same calculation. For reasons to be explained shortly, it is critical that you be comfortable with the amount of insurance recommended for Coverage A. In this case, comfortable means confident that the house can in fact be rebuilt for the suggested amount.

As discussed above, the amount you choose for Coverage A will determine the other amounts in Section I of the HO-3 policy, unless you add endorsements for specific alternative coverages. Next, determine the amounts of coverage for Section II. The standard coverage amounts are $100,000 and $1,000. As is the case with auto insurance, both of these amounts can and usually should be endorsed to higher amounts, particularly as the value of the home or the wealth of the homeowner grows. The incremental premiums for increasing these coverages are typically relatively small for the amount of protection you receive. As with auto insurance, the cost of increasing these coverages can be potentially offset by opting for the largest deductibles possible on Coverage A or any of the Section II coverages.

Web Link 10.10a

What Happens If a Person Buys Less Than Full Replacement Value?

It is certainly possible to buy less than 100 percent replacement value. The consequences of doing so will depend on how much less you purchase. Eighty percent is a key number. As long as a homeowner has at least 80 percent coverage, any Section I claim would be settled with the lesser of the claim or face amount of the policy. Consider the following example:

> *Dan Joseph just bought a home for $200,000. He assesses the land, foundation, and driveway to be worth $50,000. His own calculations and those of the insurance agent show a cost to rebuild of $150,000. Nonetheless, Dan buys Coverage A insurance for only $120,000. If a fire destroys part of his home, how much insurance coverage would he receive if the damage totaled $100,000? $125,000? $150,000?*

If the damage totals $100,000, Dan would receive the full $100,000 reimbursement, as he is considered fully covered with at least 80 percent coverage. However, if the fire creates $125,000 or the full $150,000 in damage, Dan will still receive only the maximum of $120,000 in coverage.

If Dan has less than 80 percent coverage, then his claim would be based on the greater of either of two values. The first is actual cash value. Actual cash value is the replacement cost of an item less the estimated depreciation. The alternative method of valuing the loss when there is less than 80 percent coverage is to determine the percent of 80 percent coverage that a person has, and multiply this percentage by the amount of the claim. Consider the following example:

> *Dan Joseph has a home with a replacement cost of $100,000. His Coverage A is $70,000. The useful life of this home when new was 40 years, but the home is now 10 years old. A hailstorm produces $10,000 in damage. How much reimbursement would he receive?*

Under the actual cash value method, the home would be considered one-quarter depreciated (10 years / 40 years). Thus, the $10,000 claim would produce an actual cash value settlement of

$$\text{Actual Cash Value} = \$10,000 \times (1 - .25) = \$7,500.$$

The formula approach would be computed as

$$\text{Formula} = \frac{\$70,000}{\$100,00x.80} \times \$10,000 = \$8,750.$$

The greater of the two would be $8,750, and this would be Dan's settlement.

Does a Person Who Lives in a Condominium or Who Rents Need Homeowner's Insurance?

As we have seen, homeowner's insurance covers much more than just damage to one's house. It also covers damage and loss of personal property and it provides protection against personal legal liability. For example, if a guest slips on an ice cube, falls, and does serious damage to his or her person, then a condominium owner or renter could need both personal liability and medical payments protection. It is true that condominium owners are usually protected by a policy paid for by the condominium association. When one is renting, the property would be protected by an insurance policy held by the landlord.

Web Link 10.11
Web Link 10.12

For condominiums, the insurance industry uses Form HO-6. A renter may purchase Form HO-4. These two policies are quite similar, but obviously not identical. Both policies cover losses from 17 named perils. These 17 perils are loss from or damage due to

- fire or lightning
- windstorm or hail
- explosion
- riot or civil commotion
- aircraft
- vehicles
- smoke
- vandalism or malicious mischief
- theft
- glass or safety-glazing material that is part of a building
- volcanic eruption
- falling objects
- weight of ice, snow, or sleet
- water-related damage from home utilities
- electrical surge damage

Note that floods and earthquakes are not on this list. Hence, people living in areas prone to either of these natural disasters should obtain separate coverages for these perils.

Some states, such as Texas, have approved two forms of renter's insurance, the Broad Form (HO-BT) and the Comprehensive Form (HO-CT). The Broad Form is a named peril coverage, and the Comprehensive Form covers everything not specifically excluded by the policy.

Does a College Student Need Renter's Insurance?

College students occupy a special situation for renter's insurance, because they are normally covered under their parents' homeowners' policies. The parents of some college students may not have a homeowner's insurance policy, or some may have policies that exclude college students. Thus, before going off to college, prospective students should check with their parents' insurance agents to verify coverage and ascertain if any additional renter's insurance coverage is needed. In particular, students may want to verify that any

Web Link 10.13

high-priced possessions such as computers are fully covered.

Do I Need Earthquake, Flood, and/or Hurricane Insurance?

Coverages for earthquakes, floods, and hurricanes are normally excluded from homeowner's policies. Policies for these disasters are sold separately. Clearly, only people exposed to these risks need to consider these policies. The largest market for earthquake insurance is, not surprisingly, California. In fact, the state has a law that any insurance company selling fire insurance to a consumer must also make available an earthquake policy. Because of the staggering losses from the 1994 Northridge earthquake, many insurance companies opted not to sell earthquake insurance; to avoid this, they had to cease selling fire insurance also! Information on earthquake insurance, most of it related to the California and Washington markets, may be found at **Web Link 10.14.**

Web Link 10.14

While areas for earthquakes and hurricanes are common, flooding is a more universal phenomenon. Any home located in a **Special Flood Hazard Area** (SFHA) should purchase flood insurance. However, approximately one-third of the homes damaged by flood insurance lie outside of SFHAs. The Federal Emergency Management Agency (FEMA) sponsors the **National Flood Insurance Program** (NFIP), which offers three standard flood insurance policy forms. The first is the Dwelling policy, which insures residential structures and their contents. The General Property policy covers other residential and non-residential structures and their contents. Finally, the Residential Condominium Building Association Policy form is available for purchase by the condominium associations.

Web Link 10.15

How Much Might Homeowner's Insurance Cost?

The key to the cost of a homeowner's insurance policy is, of course, the size of the deductibles. A policy with all deductibles set at $1,000 might cost half as much as the same policy with no deductibles. Every homeowner should get a premium quote with no deductibles and maximum deductibles, and then divide this difference into the size of the deductible to see if the payback and the risk exposure are worth taking the deductibles. Consider the following example:

> Dan Joseph just bought a home for $200,000. When he contacted his insurance agent, Dan obtained a quote of $850 with no deductibles and $550 with $1,000 deductibles. Which policy should Dan take?

In this case, Dan would divide the $1,000 by the difference in premiums, or $300 ($850 – $550). The answer is $3\frac{1}{3}$ years ($1,000 / $300). Hence, if Dan expects to make claims less frequently than once every $3\frac{1}{3}$ years, he should clearly take the deductibles—so long as he can handle the $1,000 deductible if a claim should arise.

Web Link 10.16

How Can I Reduce the Cost of Homeowner's Insurance Premiums?

Many insurance companies give premium discounts for certain attributes of the home or the homeowner. We have already talked about the substantial discounts associated with deductibles. Younger homes (one to ten years old) receive lower rates. A discount is usually available if more than one insurance policy is purchased through the same company. In addition, many companies will give discounts for homes that have smoke detectors on all floors, deadbolt locks on all doors, and burglar and fire alarms that report to a central service. Some companies will also give discounts to senior citizens or those who are retired, to nonsmokers, and to nondrinkers.

Web Link 10.17

How Can I Get Auto or Homeowner Insurance Quotes Over the Internet?

Many web sites will readily provide quotes on auto insurance, homeowner's insurance, and both. Studies have shown that although the Internet certainly allows ample opportunity for price shopping, the best prices are not necessarily found through the Internet. Thus, the best strategy would be to shop on the Internet for the best deal, and then call several local agents or representatives to see if they can beat that deal.

Web Link 10.18
Web Link 10.19

What Information Is Normally Requested in a Policy Application?

To receive a quote on a homeowner's insurance policy or actually apply for coverage, you must share several pieces of information. These include the complete address, a basic description of the house (e.g., construction material, the number of stories and rooms, and square footage), the age of the house, the distance from the nearest fire department and fire hydrant, security devices, the coverages desired, and the limits and deductibles wanted. An applicant also needs to certify whether the home will be owner-occupied, and if it is the primary home or a vacation home. Companies will also likely want to know the number of claims made on any other homeowner's policies within recent years.

Web Link 10.20

Should I Buy Insurance from an Agent or a Representative?

Insurance is sold through either agents or representatives. An **agent** is a person who sells policies for multiple insurance companies. A **representative** is a person employed by a particular insurance company to sell the policies of that company. For example, the Allstate Insurance Company sells through representatives. Thus, you can only buy a policy with Allstate through an Allstate representative. An agent can sell you a homeowner's policy from one company and an auto insurance policy from a different company. In theory, agents seek to place their customers with the company offering the best combination of terms and premiums at that moment in time. Agents cannot, obviously, sell policies for the companies that employ representatives. It is fairly easy to tell an agent from a representative. A representative works in an office that uses that name of his employer. An agent works in an office that goes by the name of the agent or some general descriptive term. Some representatives refer to themselves as agents, but in reality they are representatives and not agents.

Debate exists about whether to buy from an agent or a representative. For example, some people argue that an agent is more interested in the welfare of the customer and the representative is more interested in the welfare of the insurance company. However, premiums tend to be lower at companies that use representatives rather than agents. It is quite easy to obtain the names of both agents and representatives over the Internet, and several

Web Link 10.21
Web Link 10.22

examples of sites that do this are provided at **Web Links 10.21** and **10.22**. The former is for representatives and the latter is for agents.

How Can I Find a Specific Company?

It is certainly possible that a person might want to start a search for insurance by contacting a particular company that he or she has heard about, used before, or has received a recommendation for. Links to a large number of insurance companies are provided at **Web Link 10.22**.

How Is a Particular Insurance Company Rated?

Buying insurance is unlike purchasing most other products. For most products, if you discover after purchasing them that they are unsatisfactory or inappropriate for your needs, you can usually return the product and obtain a refund. With an insurance policy, you are buying the right to make a claim. You will never know whether you are satisfied with your policy and company until you have to make a claim. If you are unsatisfied with your company's response to your claim, it is too late to demand a refund of your premium and attempt to switch your premium and claim to another company.

Web Link 10.23
Web Link 10.24

Consumers can obtain protection in two ways. One is to avoid purchasing a policy with a company in financial difficulty. The other is to research consumer complaints against that particular company. An example of consumer complaints regarding auto insurance as catalogued by the Texas State Department of Insurance is provided in **Web Link 10.24**.

What Is an Umbrella Insurance Policy?

An **umbrella insurance policy** provides liability protection beyond the coverage in the basic homeowner's and auto insurance policies. All umbrella policies require that the basic policies carry liability coverage for at least a specified amount. For example, an umbrella policy may require that the insured have auto policy liability limits of $100,000/$300,000 or higher. Homeowner's policy liability limits (Coverage E) can be $300,000 or higher, and renter's insurance liability limits $100,000 or higher. Some insurance companies actually insist on being the provider of the primary liability policies, while others will simply accept proof that the primary policies exist and have the appropriate minimum limits.

How Much Coverage Should I Obtain Under an Umbrella Insurance Policy?

Umbrella policy coverages typically come in increments of $1,000,000. Thus, the choices would typically be $1 million, $2 million, and so on. Remember, an umbrella does not provide protection until and unless the liability limits on a primary policy are exceeded. Thus, if an insured has a $1 million liability on his or her auto and homeowner's policies, then the purchase of a $1 million umbrella policy actually gives the insured $2 million in coverage.

Umbrella policies are a perfect example of the central principle of this chapter: insurance should be bought to protect oneself against catastrophic events, not commonplace events. Umbrella policies are relatively inexpensive for the quantity of coverage obtained—a premium of $135 for a $1 million policy on one home and two cars would not be out of line.

As with other liability insurance coverages, a key to the amount of coverage needed is the personal wealth of the insured. The wealthier a person is, the more liability coverage needed. A third party injured through actions of the insured will expect the insured to be able to pay more. Hence, a successful surgeon or lawyer would need substantial coverage under an umbrella policy, whereas someone earning minimum wage or on the verge of bankruptcy would probably not need an umbrella policy at all.

Web Link 10.25

SUMMARY

➤ Insurance should be bought to protect against catastrophic disasters, not to protect against commonplace events.

➤ The basic principles of insurance are that losses must be fortuitous, well-defined, predictable in aggregate, personal, and that a large number of risk exposures must be available and those exposures widely distributed. The two components of an insurance premium are the basic premium and the loadings.

➤ Standard auto insurance policies provide for liability coverage on a per person and per accident basis. They cover other property and the insured's property.

➤ Car owners should normally seek to have the highest liability and property protections that can be obtained. Taking the maximum deductibles can finance this.

➤ Homeowner's insurance (HO-3) comes in two sections and six coverages. These coverages include both liability and property protection.

➤ Homeowners need to make sure their policies cover the full replacement cost of their properties, keeping in mind that features such as the land, driveway, and foundations would not normally be destroyed in any catastrophe.

➤ People seeking insurance should choose either an agent or a representative, and they should investigate the insurance company from whom they are buying the policy.

➤ Most people would need to supplement their auto and homeowner's or renter's policies with an umbrella policy of $1 million or more in coverage.

KEY TERMS

actual cash value	actuarial tables	agent
basic premium	coinsurance	collision coverage
comprehensive coverage	Coverage A	Coverage B
Coverage C	Coverage D	Coverage E
Coverage F	deductibles	endorsements
first party coverage	indemnify	insurable interest

insurable risks	internal limits	loadings
named peril coverage	National Flood Insurance Program	replacement value
representative	Special Flood Hazard Area	third party coverage
totaled	towing insurance	umbrella insurance policy
underwriting		

PROBLEMS

10.1 Obtain a copy of an auto insurance policy and determine how much you can lower the premium by increasing various coverages and increasing all deductibles to the maximum. If the policy already has maximum deductibles, determine what the increase in the premium would be if the deductibles were lowered.

10.2 Elaine Mae noted on her auto insurance policy that she could obtain a $1,000 deductible on her comprehensive coverage. She had been carrying a $200 deductible. The increase in the deductible would lower her annual insurance premium by $250. How long would Elaine Mae have to go without an accident to profit by increasing the deductible?

10.3 John Walker was driving home one night and at the same time talking on his cell phone. He did not notice that the car in front of him had stopped. John rear-ended the other car, a brand-new luxury car, which was totaled. Physical injuries to three people in the car were extensive and John was sued John for $80,000, $50,000, and $30,000. The cost of replacing the car is $60,000. If John's insurance coverage is 50/100/50, how much will John be held personally liable for?

10.4 Jake Sawyer owns a home he believes he could sell for $150,000. He assesses the land, foundation, and driveway to be worth $25,000. His own calculations and those of the insurance agent set the cost to rebuild at $125,000. Nonetheless, Dan buys Coverage A insurance for only $100,000. If a fire destroys part of his home, how much insurance coverage would he receive if the damage totaled $50,000? $100,000? $125,000?

10.5 Alice Gare has a home with a replacement cost of $150,000. Her Coverage A is $100,000. The useful life of this home when new was 40 years, but the home is now 20 years old. A hailstorm causes $10,000 in damage. How much reimbursement would she receive?

REFERENCES

Web Link 10.26 Miscellaneous sites for insurance
Web Link 10.27 Miscellaneous sites for auto insurance
Web Link 10.28 Miscellaneous sites for homeowner's insurance
Web Link 10.29 Practice quizzes on auto insurance
Web Link 10.30 Practice quizzes on homeowner's insurance
Web Link 10.31 FAQ sites for auto insurance
Web Link 10.32 FAQ sites for homeowner's insurance
Web Link 10.33 Glossaries for property and casualty insurance

WALL STREET JOURNAL RESOURCES

Web Link (WSJ) 10.34   Overview of Homeowner's Insurance

Web Link (WSJ) 10.35   "As Children Leave the Nest, It's Time to Rethink Insurance," *The Wall Street Journal Interactive Edition*, September 12, 1999

Web Link (WSJ) 10.36   "Homeowner's Insurance: Don't Overlook the Details," *The Wall Street Journal Interactive Edition*, February 13, 1998

For information that has changed since the book was written, for new information that pertains to this topic, and for some new web sites that pertain to the topic of this chapter, see **Web Link 10.37.**

CHAPTER 11

INSURING YOUR LIFE

LEARNING OBJECTIVES

- Describe when a person should and should not have life insurance
- Describe the basic differences between a term and a cash value policy
- Describe the variations of cash value policies
- Discuss the appropriateness of borrowing against a whole life policy
- Describe participating policies, riders, and viatical settlements
- Compute the value associated with buying term and investing the difference
- Compute how much life insurance a person should have
- Discuss whether a survivor should pay off a mortgage
- Obtain quotes on various term policies
- Describe the way a life insurance company rates a person
- Describe how to locate a nearby agent or a company's web page
- Describe how insurance agents are compensated and how this might influence their recommendations
- Discuss when insurance coverage should be reviewed

Web Link: www.wiley.com/college/woerheide

INTRODUCTION

There is a saying among life insurance agents that life insurance is sold, not bought. The idea is that although individuals might decide on their own to buy a new car or computer, they typically do not initiate the purchase of life insurance. It is up to the insurance agent to make people aware they need life insurance and to help them address that need. The primary reason you need life insurance is if a dependent is counting on you for financial support. Once you decide to buy life insurance, you have several additional choices. The first is how much—too little can be devastating for one's dependents, while too much means wasted premium dollars. You also need to decide what type of life insurance policy to get. Selection of the wrong type of policy could be harmful enough to render meaningless a correct decision on how much insurance to buy.

Life insurance, like any other product, should be reevaluated on a regular basis. Every few years, anyone with life insurance should ask himself or herself three questions. First, do I still need life insurance? If so, how much? Finally, is my current policy the best one for my needs? In the last few decades the life insurance industry has undergone a major revolution. It is certainly possible that the best type of policy for a person today might be inferior to a new policy developed several years from now. It is also possible that changed circumstances might cause a person to reconsider a policy that originally fit his or her needs.

In this chapter, we will consider the situation of Charlie and Rene Brucker. Charlie has decided he needs life insurance. Rene is thinking about it. They are then confronted with the questions of how much, what type of policy, and from whom should they buy the policy.

Web Link 11.1

WHY SHOULD A PERSON BUY LIFE INSURANCE?

As described in Chapter 10, insurance should protect against the catastrophic, not the commonplace. Although we each view our own death as catastrophic, our own deaths are also certain. Thus, you buy life insurance not because you will die, but because you might die prematurely. *The primary motivation for the purchase of life insurance is always the fact that a person has dependents counting on financial support from income the insured would earn.* Usually, dependents are children and a nonworking spouse. Other dependents could include parents and any incapacitated relatives or friends whom one has agreed to support. Someone old with no dependents (or who is dependent on someone else) would have little need for life insurance.

Because you buy insurance for the benefit of your dependents, you only need to insure that income lost by one's death. Consider the following example:

> *Charlie and Rene Brucker are considering life insurance for themselves. Charlie's salary is $100,000 per year. He has investment income from his stock and bond portfolio of $20,000. Rene devotes herself full time to taking care of the children and the house. Do both Charlie and Rene need life insurance?*

It is highly likely that Charlie would need life insurance to replace his salary if he were to die. The investment income will presumably continue after Charlie's death, so long as Charlie willed the investment assets to Rene upon his death so Rene would continue to receive the $20,000 per year in investment income.

A more interesting question is whether Rene needs life insurance. Rene currently provides her dependents no support of a strictly financial nature. Thus, Rene's death would not cost her family lost income, although it would naturally cause them great emotional distress.

It is often argued that this scenario is overly simplistic. For example, Rene provides services to the household that would be costly to replace. If Rene died, Charlie might have to place his children in day care and pay for housecleaning. The list of items that Charlie might have to pay for if Rene passed away could be quite long.

These are fair observations, but are not complete. First, Rene's services to the household are not truly free. Rene consumes a certain amount of the household budget for her own food, clothing, entertainment, and transportation. If the family has two cars, one could be sold and the cost of maintaining it saved. Second, some of Rene's responsibilities might be replaced at no cost if, for example, Charlie opted to do the housecleaning himself. Also, Charlie might have a lower standard of household cleanliness and let some of the cleaning go undone.

The real issue for insurance coverage for Rene is whether the expenses that she saves the household are greater or less than the costs she adds to the household. If she adds more costs to the household than savings, then from a financial perspective it is unnecessary for her to buy life insurance. If she saves more for the household than she consumes, and these net savings are considered critical and essential to replace, then Rene's life ought to be insured in an amount to cover this net difference.

WHEN SHOULD A PERSON
NOT BUY LIFE INSURANCE?

If you have no dependents, your need for life insurance is diminished or eliminated. A prime example of a person in this situation is an unmarried college student. Another example is **DINKS** (couples with **D**ouble **I**ncome and **N**o **K**id**S**). If each spouse could live comfortably independently of the other's income, then insuring that income is needless. After all, leaving a large death benefit to a spouse who does not need it only makes that spouse more attractive to future suitors. Who wants to sacrifice today to create a nest egg for the surviving spouse to enjoy with someone else?

Generally, children also do not need life insurance, unless they earn a substantial income and the parents are dependent on them. Some argue that children need life insurance coverage against funeral expenses. In reality, however, funeral expenses usually can be managed, even if it means taking out a loan and repaying it with the money that would have been spent on the child had he or she survived. Others argue that by buying an insurance policy today, the parents could be locking in extremely low rates for their child for life. Although this is true, keep in mind that the most expensive things to buy are things you truly don't need. It is not economically efficient to purchase a life insurance policy just to save on the premiums later. The present value of what the parents will pay in premiums will easily exceed the present value of what the child would ultimately save once he or she is ready to actually take out a policy.

A final example of someone who does not need life insurance is a retired person. By definition, being retired means having no wage income. Hence, no wage income is lost by the death of a retired person. An obvious exception would be elderly parents who care for a handicapped child. The appropriate plan would be for the parents to accumulate sufficient wealth in a trust over their lifetime to take care of the child after their deaths. If no such trust exists or if the assets are insufficient and the dependent survives on the Social Security and pension income of the parents, then a life insurance policy might be quite appropriate.

Sometimes parents will take out large insurance policies so that their children or other dependents will be financially well off when the parents die. There is nothing wrong with wanting to improve the situation of one's children. However, one's children should not be financially better off by a parent's death than if the parent doesn't die. Life insurance is to prevent your dependents from suffering financial hardships due to your premature death, not to materially improve their lives by your death!

The purchase of life insurance always involves a trade-off. When you buy life insurance, you are paying a premium (sometimes a large one) that could have been spent on other things. Few people would live an impoverished life just to ensure that their dependents will be rich when they die. Life is about both doing things today with your dependents (such as your children and spouse) and making financial plans for the possibility of your premature death.

To sum up, you want to have enough life insurance to prevent your dependents from being financially harmed by your death, but not so much that your current standard of living suffers.

Web Link 11.2

WHAT IS THE DIFFERENCE BETWEEN POLICY OWNER AND INSURED?

Normally, a policy owner and the insured are one and the same person. However, a person can take out a policy on someone else's life, although you need the permission of the insured to do so. For example, a wife could take out a policy on her husband's life. Ownership of a policy can also be transferred. It is quite common for policy owners to transfer ownership of their policies later in life to a spouse or to children to minimize estate taxation. If the insured is also the policy owner and the insured dies, the death benefit is counted as part of the estate regardless of who the beneficiary is. If the estate is large enough, increased estate taxes could result. If the policy is owned by someone other than the insured, then the death benefit passes outside of the estate and there are no estate tax consequences.

Signing over a policy to a beneficiary may make great sense from a tax perspective, but it can have undesired consequences. The new owner is free to change the beneficiaries, take out a policy loan (to be discussed shortly), or even to cancel the policy and take any cash surrender value that might be associated with it. Imagine turning over a policy to your spouse, only to have the spouse later file for divorce, allowing him or her and his or her new spouse to live comfortably on the proceeds of your death benefit! Obviously, transfer of ownership should not be undertaken lightly.

WHAT ARE THE TWO BASIC TYPES OF LIFE INSURANCE POLICIES?

There are basically two types of life insurance policies: term and cash value. A **term policy** insures you for a specific number of years. The simplest policy a person could buy would be a one-year term policy. If you die during the year, your beneficiary receives the death benefit. If you are alive at the end of the year, you are presumably happy to be alive but poorer by the amount of the premium. A **cash value policy** guarantees to cover you for your entire life. A whole life policy is the simplest example of a cash value policy. As long as you pay the premium, you will have a policy in effect when you die.

What Are the Variations on Term Policies?

The most common variation on a term policy is to lengthen the period of coverage. Examples include 5-year, 10-year, 20-year, to age 65, or even to age 90 policies. Another variation is **decreasing term,** in which you buy a policy for a time period such as 20 years and the death benefit declines each year. This type of policy is also known as a **mortgage insurance** policy because it is frequently purchased when people take out a mortgage. The declining death benefit is intended to parallel the declining balance on the mortgage.

If a person's dependents consist of his or her children, and if those children are expected to be on their own within about 20 years, then the purchase of a 20-year term policy makes a lot of sense. Furthermore, if the amount of insurance coverage needed is expected to decline as the children grow older, a decreasing 20-year term policy makes even more sense.

Web Link 11.3

HOW DO WHOLE LIFE POLICIES WORK?

When you buy a basic **whole life policy,** you are receiving a fixed death benefit and agreeing to pay premiums until you die or reach age 100, whichever comes first. In a simple policy, the premiums are fixed for the life of the policy. This policy differs from term in that the insurance company credits the policy with a cash value that increases over time.

To fully understand all cash value policies, you must understand why this cash value is created. Because a whole life policy can remain in effect until a person dies, the insurance company has to assure that it builds enough assets to pay the death benefit. Although the premium on a whole life policy is fixed for life, at the time the policy is purchased the premium is substantially higher than, say, the premium on a five-year renewable term policy with the same death benefit. The lower premium on the term policy reflects the lower probability that you will die during the next five years. The higher premium on the whole life policy reflects the much higher probability that you will die eventually. Thus, the premium on the five-year term policy reflects what might be called the true cost of insurance for the next five years. The difference in the two premiums is then invested to build the cash value of the policy. After five years, had you bought the term policy and then wanted to maintain your coverage of the same death benefit, your premium would be higher. The difference between the new term premium and the ongoing whole life premium will be smaller. This difference is still used to further build the cash value of the policy. If you keep renewing the five-year term policy, the premium will eventually be higher than the ongoing premium on your whole life policy. Nonetheless, the cash value of the whole life policy will continue to grow because of the value of the accumulated assets to that date.

At any time, the insured may cancel the whole life policy and receive the cash value. The fine print of this cancellation privilege must be noted. First, although the premium of the whole life policy is fixed for life, the cost of the insurance coverage is constantly going down. Consider the following example:

> *Charlie has a $100,000 whole life insurance policy. The current cash surrender value of the policy is $40,000. Charlie pays $1,000 per year in premiums. What is his true cost of insurance?*

If Charlie cashed in the policy today, he would receive $40,000. Thus, his true insurance coverage is only $60,000. In other words, he is paying $1,000 in an annual premium for what is effectively $60,000 worth of insurance coverage. In addition, although the cash value is earning a rate of return, it is certainly possible that this rate of return could be less than what Charlie could be earning if he had that money in his control.[1] Thus, although Charlie's annual premium stays the same, his premium per $1,000 of true insurance coverage goes up each year because the cash value grows each year.

Second, rates of return can be deceiving. It is always tempting to think about whole life policies as an investment. The policy owner pays premiums over the years, and then cashes in the policy for the cash surrender value for a rate of return which can be computed. Consider the following example:

> Charlie has a $100,000 life insurance policy. The policy does not pay a dividend. Charlie is currently 35. He has owned the policy for 10 years, and he expects to live to age 80 (45 more years). His marginal federal and state tax income rates are 28 percent and 6 percent. Charlie plans to retire at age 65 and cash the policy in then. The insurance company has guaranteed a $47,100 cash surrender value at that time, while the current cash surrender value is $5,800. Charlie pays a premium of $808 once a year. What is his rate of return on this policy from inception to date, to age 65, and to age 80?

Web Link 11.3a   In this example, Charlie's rates of return are –6 percent, 1 percent, and 3 percent. If Charlie were to cash in the policy today, he would receive the full $5,800 cash surrender value, an amount less than the premiums paid to date and thus with no tax consequences. If Charlie were to cash in the policy at age 65, he would receive $41,075 before taxes because the cash surrender value will exceed the premiums paid, creating taxable income. Upon Charlie's death at age 80, his beneficiaries would receive the full $100,000.[2] These are lousy rates of return!

However, remember that a whole life policy provides two things: a death benefit from the day the policy is sold and the cash surrender value. The death benefit is not a freebie. A *true calculation* of the return on the policy should be based only on the portion of the premium that goes to the cash value, not the portion that goes to pay for the death benefit. Alas, such a number is not available for a whole life policy. Thus, any attempt to ascertain a rate of return on a whole life policy will appear to provide weak rates of return. Such a calculation should really be used only when comparing whole life policies with each other and not when comparing a whole life policy with another form of insurance.

Should a Person Borrow Against a Whole Life Policy?

With whole life policies, the insured may also borrow against the cash value at an interest rate specified in the policy. The exact rate charged on this loan will vary among companies

---

[1]The opportunity cost associated with the cash value is more complicated than the above description would indicate. The growth in cash value is potentially tax-free, and if the policy were canceled and the cash value directly invested, then Charlie would have to choose between taxable, tax-deferred, and tax-exempt investments.

[2]If the ownership of the policy has been transferred to Charlie's beneficiaries by the time of his death, then the tax-free status of the policy is certain. If Charlie were still the owner of the policy, then the $100,000 death benefit would be considered part of his estate and could be subject to estate taxation.

and policies. This loan option may create some interesting investment strategies. Consider the following example:

> *Charlie has a $100,000 life insurance policy with a current cash surrender value of $40,000. His policy allows him to borrow up to 95 percent of the cash surrender value at 5 percent. There is no specific timetable for repaying this loan, as long as the interest payments are made when due.[3] If Charlie dies before repaying the loan, the loan balance and any accrued interest is deducted from the death benefit of the policy. Would borrowing against this cash value be a good idea if Charlie: (1) could invest the money at 8 percent, (2) would give the money to his beneficiary, or (3) would use the money to make some major household purchases?*

If Charlie could earn 8 percent on money for which he pays 5 percent, then this is a good deal. Consider that 95 percent of $40,000 is $38,000. If he earns 8 percent on this money, that is an income of $3,040 (8% × $38,000) per year. If he pays interest at the rate of 5 percent, then the money costs him $1,900 (5% × $38,000). In other words, he can increase his annual income by $1,140. If the money is in fact used for investments, the interest on the loan can be used as an itemized deduction. There may be additional tax benefits depending on how the money is invested. One common criticism of this strategy is that the money would not be there for the beneficiary when Charlie dies. However, if Charlie includes in his will that the assets acquired through this transaction be left to the same person who would have been the beneficiary of the life insurance policy, then no harm is done.[4]

The second use of this money could be to give the cash to the beneficiary now. The problem here is that the death benefit is intended to provide income to the beneficiary when the insured dies. If the beneficiary invests the money appropriately (say at 8 percent), then the beneficiary would actually be better off having received the cash benefit early. If the beneficiary uses the cash to support fun and games today, then the insured will not have met his or her obligation to take care of his or her beneficiaries upon death. Of course, one could argue that if the beneficiary receives part of what would have been the death benefit and uses up the money on frivolous items now, then the beneficiary would probably do the same later.

The third use of the cash value is in purchases that benefit Charlie's household today. If such a purchase truly weakens the death benefit that Charlie's beneficiaries would need if he died tomorrow, then it is clearly inappropriate. If the money is spent on items the beneficiaries would have bought anyway, then it is not clear that the money has been poorly used.

Finally, always keep in mind that insurance needs decline as one gets older. If Charlie's needed death benefit has declined by at least $40,000, then there is no harm in taking the $40,000 out of the policy and using it any way he sees fit. In fact, if Charlie's needed death benefit has declined by at least $100,000, Charlie could consider canceling the policy and taking the full $40,000 as the cash surrender value.[5]

Web Link 11.4
Web Link
(WSJ) 11.5

---

[3]If Charlie misses all or part of an interest payment, the loan balance is increased by the amount of interest that was not paid. This adding of interest to the loan value is automatic as long as the current loan outstanding is less than the maximum amount that can be borrowed by at least the amount of missed interest.

[4]In fact, because assets that are inherited acquire as a cost basis their market value at the time of death, a substantial amount of taxes may be completely avoided on the growth in the value of these assets over time.

[5]The amount by which the cash surrender value exceeds the cumulated premiums paid to date is taxable income. For traditional whole life policies, this is not a likely event. For more complex policies, discussed later, this is a real possibility.

WHAT IS A PARTICIPATING POLICY?

The insurance industry is made up of two types of companies: stock and mutual. A stock company is owned by its stockholders. A mutual company is technically owned by its policyholders. Mutual companies sell policies called participating policies. At the end of each year, a mutual company reviews its profitability for the prior year and declares dividends payable to policyholders who own participating policies.

From a tax perspective, such dividends are considered a refund of part of the premium and thus not taxable income. The policyholder should also consider the dividends a rebate of the premium, rather than any sort of profit on an investment. These dividends make it difficult to compare a participating policy with a nonparticipating policy. The whole life policy described in the previous sections is a nonparticipating policy, as are most policies.

The premiums on participating policies tend to be set high to assure that the company will be able to cover its expenses, including the death benefits it will owe. Because of this conservative approach, it is likely that dividends will be paid on participating policies. When these policies are sold, the company always predicts dividends to show the prospective buyer what the projected net premium (gross premium less the projected dividend) will be.

The problem, of course, is that the dividends are only guesses, not guarantees. If the company's investment income is less than anticipated or its expenses greater than anticipated, then the dividends will be less than projected. Some debate exists about whether the dividends on participating policies have been consistently overestimated. The dividends can be applied to reducing the premium as described above, to buying additional paid-up insurance to increase the death benefit, or to increasing the cash value of the policy.

Web Link 11.5a

WHAT ARE RIDERS?

Along with your insurance policy, you may purchase **riders,** attachments that add a specific privilege or coverage to the policy. A rider may be free or may require additional payment. Some riders may be attached only to term policies and others only to whole life policies. Some riders can be attached to any type of policy.

A common rider for a term policy is what is known as a conversion feature. Conversion allows the policy owner to exchange the term policy for a cash value policy. The death benefit is normally the same, although some riders allow the death benefit to be increased by specific multiples of the current death benefit. The premium on the cash value policy would be based on the insured's age at the time of conversion. The major advantage of conversion is that a health exam is not required. To understand the full value of this benefit, consider the following:

> *Charlie took out a five-year convertible $100,000 term insurance policy four and one-half years ago. The policy allows Charlie to increase the death benefit by multiples of $100,000 up to $500,000 maximum upon conversion. Charlie has just been diagnosed with cancer that may be terminal.*

In this case, Charlie is extremely fortunate to have both convertible and renewable (see below) features of the policy. At this point, Charlie absolutely would not want to submit to another health exam for a life insurance policy, as it is a near certainty he would be denied. Charlie should probably notify his agent that he wants to convert his policy at a time when he can lock in the lowest rate on a whole life policy, no later than the expiration date on his term policy. Charlie would also want to give serious consideration to increasing his death benefit, perhaps to the maximum, given the high probability of his premature death. Many term policies include the conversion feature in the policy itself and not as a rider.

Another feature common to term policies, sometimes added as a rider, is to have the policy be renewable. Renewability is useful, but has two drawbacks. First, future premiums are not guaranteed. Thus, if you take out a five-year R&C (renewable and convertible) policy, you are guaranteed the privilege of renewing the policy after five years, but the premium will be whatever that company is charging to people of your age at that time for that policy. Also, if you find the current company's premium exorbitant and want to switch to a different company, you will absolutely have to undergo a new health exam.

A traditional rider for life insurance policies is a **double indemnity** clause. This clause means that the death benefit is doubled in the event of a death caused by an accident as opposed to a natural death due to illness, disease, or old age. Like almost all riders, the advantage of this rider is that it is inexpensive. Also attractive is the potential for your beneficiaries to come into a lot of extra money. The double indemnity rider has some drawbacks as well. If the initial amount of death benefit is considered optimal, then having the death benefit doubled represents needless insurance coverage. Second, the needs of the beneficiaries are the same regardless of how the insured dies. That is, the spouse and children have the same financial needs whether the insured dies of pneumonia or a car accident.[6] Finally, it is unwise to use double indemnity to buy half of the death benefit you actually need. Such a strategy could put the beneficiaries into a terrifying financial situation if death is in fact from natural causes.

Other common rider provisions include a disability waiver of premium and an accelerated death benefit. The **disability waiver** allows the premium to be waived if the insured becomes disabled. This same coverage can be acquired through a disability income policy (see Chapter 12). Thus, you should check whether it will be cheaper and more convenient to guarantee having cash to pay the premium through a disability waiver rider or to increase the disability income policy by an appropriate amount. The **accelerated death benefits** (ADB) rider is relatively new, having been introduced in the late 1980s. By 1998, nearly 40 million policies contained this provision, up from half that amount in 1994. An ADB rider allows death benefits to be paid prior to death in certain situations, such as diagnosis of a terminal illness or physical condition within a specific time period (usually six or twelve months), occurrence of a life-threatening medical condition that would require extraordinary medical treatment, the need for extended long-term care in an institution or at home, or permanent confinement to a nursing home.

Web Link 11.6
Web Link 11.6a

---

[6]Lingering death from illness could create medical bills that would not occur in case of a sudden accidental death, but such potential expenses should be covered by health insurance. (See Chapter 12.) Buying additional life insurance to cover the contingency of medical bills is improper financial planning.

WHAT IS A VIATICAL SETTLEMENT?

A **viatical settlement** is similar to an accelerated death benefit. The difference is that in a viatical settlement the insured sells the policy to an outside party at a discount to face value. As the new owner, the buyer is responsible for all subsequent premiums, and will name himself as the beneficiary. A viatical settlement is the only way an insured could cash in an insurance policy for more than the cash surrender value when ADB coverage is not available. A viatical settlement may have important financial consequences. It may affect the viator's eligibility for benefits from Supplemental Security Income (SSI), Medicaid, Aid to Families with Dependent Children (AFDC), and Drug Assistance Programs. In addition, payments received under a viatical settlement may be subject to collection by a viator's creditors.

Because each viatical settlement is a unique transaction, amounts of settlement offered by various companies vary greatly, depending on such factors as the current cash value of the policy and the life expectancy of the insured.

Web Link 11.7

WHAT ARE SOME OF THE VARIATIONS ON WHOLE LIFE INSURANCE?

There are many kinds of whole life policies. One such variation is a **modified premium** or **graded premium** policy. Some companies particularly emphasize this product for college students. It is characterized either by low premiums for a few years, followed by typical premiums for a whole life, or by rising premiums for the life of the policy. The appeal here is that students may be hesitant to take on a large premium when they first enter the working world, so such policies can be easily handled before the student is ready to take on a larger obligation. An alternative to a modified premium policy is to take out a term policy that is convertible, and then convert it when you are ready to take on the higher premiums. As discussed earlier, however, most college students don't need life insurance coverage.

Another variation on whole life is a **limited pay** whole life. On this type of policy, the premiums are paid over a fixed number of years (e.g., 10 or 20 years), and then the policy remains in force until it is canceled or the insured dies. The idea behind this policy is to reduce the burden of the life insurance premium in later years. It also accelerates the build-up of the cash flow. However, this strategy may not make a lot of sense. Consider the fact that for most people, both nominal and real income goes up during their working lives. Thus, it may be easier for a 40-year-old to handle a large life insurance premium than a 30-year-old.

The ultimate in a limited pay policy is to have a **single premium policy.** In this case, the person taking out the policy is making just one premium payment, and then the policy becomes a fully paid-up policy requiring no further payments.

Another variation on whole life is an **endowment policy.** An endowment policy has a specific maturity date such as 10 or 20 years from its inception, or an age such as age 65, if the insured is still alive.[7] Not only are this policy's premiums higher than in a whole life, they are set so that the cash value equals the death benefit at the maturity of the policy.

[7]For an example of an endowment policy, see **Web Link 11.8.**

Thus, if the insured dies before the maturity date, the beneficiaries receive the death benefit. If the insured survives to the maturity date, the insured receives the death benefit. The idea behind this policy is really to use it as a retirement savings program.

Endowment policies have two drawbacks. First, the rates of return typically are quite low compared to what you could receive in a more traditional retirement savings program. Thus, as a retirement savings program, it is an expensive one. The second drawback is that it is easy to forget about the impact of inflation in such a program. Consider the following example:

> Charlie is 25 years old. He is considering taking out a $100,000 endowment policy that would pay off at age 65. What is the purchasing power of this payoff in terms of today's dollars if the inflation rate averages 3 percent, 4 percent, and 5 percent over the next 40 years?

Web Link 11.9

The solution to this problem is to take the present value of $100,000 for 40 years, discounted at each of the interest rates. At inflation rates of 3, 4, and 5 percent, the present values are $30,656, $20,829, and $14,205. In other words, what might sound like a generous retirement nest egg today could be devastated by inflation during a person's working career.

Another type of whole life policy is a **joint and survivorship** or **second to die** policy. This policy is based on two people, usually a husband and wife, and it pays when the second person dies. Such a policy is usually intended to pay for estate taxes (see Chapter 18). The idea is that when the first spouse dies, the deceased leaves all or most of his or her share of the couple's assets to the other spouse. When the second spouse dies, there is a greater likelihood that there will be a substantial estate tax due before the assets can be **Web Link 11.10**   passed to the couple's children.

WHAT IS MEANT BY "BUY TERM AND INVEST THE DIFFERENCE"?

Because cash value policies are a combination of life insurance and a savings program, there is legitimacy to comparing the purchase of a whole life policy to the purchase of term insurance combined with a self-directed investment program. Such a comparison would require the sum of the term premium and money invested each year equal the whole life premium. This purchase of term insurance combined with an investment program is referred to as "buy term and invest the difference." If this comparison is made with the assumption that the death benefit is kept the same as the whole life death benefit, then the premiums on the term insurance policies will become prohibitively expensive in later years. However, a true "buy term and invest the difference" strategy requires that the death benefit on the term policy be reduced at each renewal date by an amount equal to the growth in value of the investment portfolio. Thus, although the premium per $1,000 of insurance coverage goes up each renewal date under term, the amount of coverage purchased goes down. The actual premium owed on the term policies may actually go down rather than up! Let's consider an example:

> Charlie is 25 years old and a nonsmoker. He has contacted an insurance company about buying a $100,000 whole life policy. The annual premium is $808. Charlie has

*heard about the benefits of buying term and investing the difference. He obtains
quotes on a five-year renewable and convertible term policy for $100,000. By how
much would Charlie come out ahead if he undertakes a strategy of buying term and
investing the difference, assuming that he is able to stick to it and that the projected
figures turn out to be accurate?*

The annual premiums, the death benefit, and the cash surrender value at five-year intervals
of a whole life policy are shown in Table 11-1. At an annual cost of $808 for a $100,000
death benefit, the cost to Charlie is $8.08 per $1,000 of death benefit. Note that if Charlie
terminates the policy at age 65, he would receive $47,410 as the cash surrender value.
Some of this cash would be taxable income, because the total exceeds the premiums Charlie would have paid on the policy. The total premiums Charlie would have paid would
equal $32,320 ($808 × 40).

Table 11-1
Premiums and Cash Surrender Values for a Level Premium, Whole Life Policy

Age	Premium	Cash Value, EOY	Death Benefit
26	$808	$ 0	$100,000
30	808	1,500	100,000
35	808	5,800	100,000
40	808	10,800	100,000
45	808	16,700	100,000
50	808	23,300	100,000
55	808	30,700	100,000
60	808	28,700	100,000
65	808	47,410	100,000

The current and projected quotes for the five-year renewable and convertible term
policy are shown for five-year intervals in Table 11-2. Note that although the premium per
$1,000 of death benefit goes up on each renewal date, it does not exceed the premium on
the whole life until age 56, when the cost per $1,000 of death benefit jumps to $8.48. Keep
in mind that the premiums for the first five years of a five-year renewable and convertible
policy are certain. The premiums for the renewals thereafter are speculative.

Table 11-2
Premiums for a Five-Year Renewable and Convertible Term Insurance Policy

Age	Premium/$1,000 coverage
26–30	$1.63
31–35	1.76
36–40	1.90
41–45	2.37
46–50	3.32
51–55	4.68
56–60	8.48
61–65	15.75

Table 11-3 shows the mathematics of the "buy term and invest the difference" strategy. For the first five years of the policy, the insured would have a death benefit of $100,000 (same as under the whole life policy). The term premium is $163. The difference is $645 ($808 – $645).

Table 11-3

Buy Term and Invest the Difference Benefits

Ages	Whole Life Premium	Term Death Benefit	Term Premium	Difference	Cumulative Savings Invested at 8%
26–30	$808	$100,000	$163	$645	$ 4,087
31–35	808	95,913	169	639	10,055
36–40	808	89,945	171	637	18,810
41–45	808	81,190	192	616	31,538
46–50	808	68,462	227	581	50,018
51–55	808	49,982	234	574	77,128
56–60	808	22,872	194	614	117,215
61–65	808	—	—	808	177,343

If this $645 is set aside at the start of each year when the premium is paid and invested at a rate of return of 8 percent, then at the end of 5 years it will have built up to $4,087. Because of the investment savings of $4,087, Charlie no longer needs to purchase the full $100,000 in death benefit. He actually only needs $95,913 in death benefit ($100,000 – $4,087). The new premium rate for Charlie for ages 31–35, is $1.76 per $1,000 of death benefit. However, because he only needs $95,913 in death benefit, his total premium would be $169 ($1.76 × 95.913). The difference between this premium and the $808 premium on the whole life is $639. If Charlie invests this $639 at the start of each year at the same 8 percent rate, and the accumulated investment from the first five years continues to grow at an 8 percent rate, he will have saved $10,054. Specifically, the additional premium savings and the interest on those savings will contribute $4,049 to Charlie's savings. The $4,087 savings from the first five years will have grown to $6,005. The sum of these two numbers is the $10,054 accumulated savings. Thus, when Charlie goes to renew his policy at age 36, he now only needs $89,946 in death benefit.

Because this savings process permits a reduction in the necessary death benefit, the total dollar premium at ages 56 to 60 is actually lower than for ages 51–55 even though the cost per $1,000 has gone up. By age 60, Charlie's accumulated savings total $117,219. Thus, for ages 60–65, Charlie does not even need to purchase any more term and is able to save the entire $808 per year. At age 65, Charlie has an accumulated savings of $177,349, compared to a cash surrender value on the whole life policy of $47,410. He has also never had less than $100,000 in death benefits through the combination of his term policy and his savings.

The most obvious flaw in this example is that if the 8 percent rate of return used is a pre-tax number, then the example overstates the benefits of "buy term and invest the difference" by omitting all of the taxes that would have been due on the savings. The appropriate tax treatment for these savings depends on the type of investment or investments made with the savings. So rather than debate the effective tax rate on these investments, let's just focus on what the final numbers would be if the return figure represented the effective after-tax return. Table 11-4 shows the accumulated savings at age 65 for various effective after-tax savings rates. If the differences in premiums are invested at an after-tax rate of 3 percent, then the policyholder is better off buying the whole life policy. But as soon as the after-tax rate of return jumps to 4 percent, the term strategy becomes more beneficial by $6,315.

Table 11-4
The Ending Value Advantage of Buying Term and Investing the Difference

Interest Rate	Ending Value Under Term Policy	Ending Value Under Whole Life	Difference
3%	$ 39,559	$47,410	($7,851)
4	53,725	47,410	6,315
5	72,751	47,410	25,341
6	98,325	47,410	50,915
7	132,742	47,410	85,332
8	177,343	47,410	129,993

The common response of the insurance industry to this strategy is that although the numbers are technically correct, in practice consumers will not engage in such a savings program and will instead spend the money. Thus, as they approach their retirement years, the increases in the term premiums become prohibitively expensive for them.

There are, of course, rebuttals to this response. For example, as people approach retirement and they become empty nesters, their need for life insurance coverage decreases. Thus, even if they have failed to save the difference, they do not need as large a policy as they would have needed in earlier years. So although the premium per $1,000 would be higher, the smaller death benefit would help to keep the dollar value of the premium down.

Web Link 11.11

WHAT ARE VARIABLE LIFE, UNIVERSAL LIFE, AND VARIABLE UNIVERSAL LIFE POLICIES?

The attractiveness of buying term and investing the difference has not gone unnoticed by the insurance industry, particularly as more and more investors opt for this practice. To respond to this shift by consumers, the industry developed policies that are themselves variations of the same practice!

The first such policy was variable life. Variable life provides a death benefit that varies with the performance of an underlying portfolio of investments. The policy owner chooses an allocation of premiums among a variety of investments provided by the insurance company. These typically offer varying degrees of risk and expected return. The policy owner is allowed to change this selection of investments. The cash value of the policy at any point in time depends on the performance of the underlying portfolio. The cash value is not guaranteed, and the policy owner bears the risk. Like all the other policies discussed so far, variable life does not allow the premium to vary, does not allow the policy owner to simply withdraw cash from the policy, but does allow loans against the cash value. Although the death benefit will vary with the investment performance of the policy, the policy owner cannot on his or her own change the death benefit. There is one major drawback to a variable life policy. If the investments do extremely poorly, the policy owner might be required to come up with additional cash in order to keep the policy intact.

Universal life insurance policies are another form of insurance that mimics the "buy term and invest the difference" process. Universal life insurance policies allow the policy owner, after the initial payment, to pay premiums at any time in virtually any amount, within certain limits. The policy owner directs how the premiums will be allocated. They can be used to increase the death benefit (although if increased beyond the original amount of the policy, an additional health exam would probably be required). The portion of the premium that goes above the amount necessary to pay any policy expense charges is invested. Unlike with variable life, the excess premiums are invested in what is essentially a money market account. Once the cash value becomes large enough, the policy owner may use it to pay the premiums rather than paying additional cash into the policy. The major drawback on a universal life policy is that if the rates of return do not work out as expected, the policyholder could end up paying a lot more in premiums in the long run. However, if the policy owner voluntarily pays extra premiums, the cash value of the policy will grow even faster. Remember, within the policy itself, investment returns are tax-free. Also, if loans are taken out against the cash value, the loans are tax-free. Taxes are due only when a policy is canceled and the cash surrender value exceeds the total premiums paid, a difference that is taxable income. In such a case, extensive surrender penalties might also be costly.

Once the insurance industry had introduced variable life and universal life policies, it did not take long for someone to think of combining them into variable universal life (VUL) policies. Basically, VUL policies combine the features of variable life and universal life, bringing the policy owner as close as possible to an application of "buy term and invest the difference." The term component of a VUL policy usually means that the policy provides permanent protection only to age 95. (Other than to pay estate taxes, one wonders why a 95-year-old would need life insurance!) In addition, because the policy owner can pay part of the premiums with the investment's cash value, which is tax-free income, a portion of premiums can be paid with pre-tax dollars. A VUL policy's variable life features include the option to select how your cash value is invested or to move your money around without incurring taxes when your portfolio objectives change. A VUL policy's universal life features include the option to pay more than the designated premium amount to increase the cash value (within the limits of certain IRS restrictions) and to increase your death benefit (with a health exam perhaps required). Like a universal life policy, a VUL policy also allows you to either withdraw some of your cash value or to take out a policy loan. Again, if withdrawals exceed the policy owner's premium payments, they then become taxable income. However, you can still use your VUL policy as retirement income by taking withdrawals until such time as they would become taxable, and then taking the cash in the form of loans. The cash value of a VUL policy can serve as collateral for loans from other lenders and is usually not accessible by creditors. Finally, a VUL policy's death benefit is not subject to probate (discussed in Chapter 18).

Web Link 11.12

Web Link 11.13

Web Link 11.14
Web Link 11.15

WHAT IS GROUP LIFE INSURANCE?

Group life insurance is sold to large groups of people through some common organization, such as an employer. When you leave an employer—whether you quit, retire, or are fired, laid off, or downsized—you automatically lose your group life insurance coverage unless you have opted to continue the policy on your own, usually at substantially higher rates. Group coverage tends to have an upper limit, which varies according to company policy. Generally, such coverage will be excessive for those with little or no insurance needs (e.g., DINKS) and inadequate for those with substantial needs (e.g., a married couple with one incomeless and several small children). Nonetheless, for those who need substantial coverage, group life insurance represents a good base around which to build coverage.

HOW MUCH LIFE INSURANCE SHOULD A PERSON HAVE?

So far, we have focused on who should and should not buy insurance, and what types of policies are available. However, probably the most important question of all is how large a death benefit a person should buy.

There are four general approaches to determining how much life insurance one should carry:

1. the appropriate size premium approach
2. the human life value approach
3. the multiple of earnings approach
4. the needs approach

The appropriate size premium is the least appropriate of these methods. Using this approach, the insured decides how much he or she wants to pay each year in insurance premiums, and then obtains a policy with a premium equal that amount. Rules of thumb suggest anywhere from 5 to 10 percent of the family budget. As we saw earlier, because of the different types of policies available, vastly different death benefits can be obtained for the same premium dollar. Hence, this rule is of little value.

The **human life value** (HLV) approach starts by estimating the future wage and salary income of the insured. Next, the portion of that income that is spent on the insured is deducted. The remainder is then discounted. Consider the following example:

> *Charlie Brucker has a current annual earned income of $100,000. The estimated annual value of his employee benefits is $10,000. Charlie is 35 and plans to retire when he is 65. Charlie's personal maintenance expenses (i.e., the portion of income he spends on himself) are 15 percent. Charlie estimates that his salary will grow at an average annual rate of 3 percent between now and retirement. He believes an appropriate discount rate would be 8 percent, and his average federal and state income tax rate is 36 percent. How much insurance should he have under an HLV approach?*

Based on **Web Link 11.19**, Charlie's HLV is $967,011.

Web Link 11.17

Web Link 11.18

Web Link 11.19

Although the HLV approach has a certain sense of reasonableness to it, it also has deficiencies. For example, Charlie's wife may earn twice as much as he. In this case, Charlie's insurance needs are greatly diminished or nonexistent. Notice that the HLV is the same regardless if Charlie is childless, has three children in diapers, or has two children almost ready to go off to college. Does this mean that the HLV calculation is useless? Not really. It provides an *upper limit* on the amount of life insurance a person should have. Simply put, it makes no sense to have a person be worth more to his or her family dead than alive! In the above example, suppose Charlie bought $2,000,000 in insurance despite an HLV calculation of $967,000. If Charlie were then to die, his family's economic situation would not simply be maintained but vastly improved. Meanwhile, Charlie's insurance premiums are at least twice as high as they need to be. One suspects that Charlie's family would much rather spend the extra insurance premium money on things they could enjoy as a family today, rather than sacrificing to pay extra premium so that they could be much richer if Charlie were to die prematurely. Therefore, calculating HLV can help you avoid spending too much on life insurance.

The **multiple of earnings** approach follows on the HLV approach by assuming that the ratio of the life insurance needed under the HLV formula to the individual's current income will be roughly the same for people within certain age ranges. You use the multiple of earnings approach by locating your age range and income level in a publication of these ratios. An example from the *Wall Street Journal Interactive Edition*, is shown in Figure 11.1.

Web Link (WSJ) 11.20

The final of the four, the **needs** approach, is the most complex. The needs approach ignores the current income of the insured, focusing instead on the expenses necessary to

THE WALL STREET JOURNAL.

ROUGHING OUT YOUR LIFE INSURANCE NEEDS
To estimate the amount of coverage you need to replace 75% of your take-home pay for the years you would have been working, multiply your salary by the number in the box where the columns for your salary and current age intersect. For example, if your salary is $60,000 and you're 40, that number is 9.*

Annual pay (before taxes)	Current age of person insured						
	25	30	35	40	45	50	55
$20,000	14	13	12	10	9	7	6
$30,000	14	13	12	10	9	7	5
$40,000	13	12	11	10	9	7	5
$60,000	12	12	11	9	8	6	5
$80,000	12	11	10	9	8	6	4

FIGURE 11-1 Multiple of Earnings Approach

allow the survivors to achieve desired lifestyles. In an ideal world, the HLV and needs approaches would both produce virtually the same calculation of how much life insurance a person should carry—that is, what you would like your survivors to have would equal exactly what they would receive had you lived. In practice, however, these two methods usually produce different amounts, the needs approach usually demonstrating a higher life insurance need. The disparity occurs because the needs approach allows the insured to dream about what he or she would like his or her family to have in their future. The HLV approach sticks strictly to financial considerations of what income the insured would have generated, without accounting for subjective estimations of what the insured's family might need. For example, if you cannot afford to send your children away for several weeks of overnight summer camp, you still might envision this opportunity as a true need that you would like to allow for in the event of your premature death. If so, under the needs approach you would add the present value of the cost of the summer camps into your life insurance needs.

A needs approach divides the future into several time periods and computes the amount of death benefits necessary to fund all of these time periods. The first time period is the immediate needs. Immediate needs include financial costs and legal expenses. They might also include money to pay off outstanding bills, including the mortgage. Immediate needs are also sometimes categorized as the **final expenses.** These will be discussed in more detail in the next section. Some financial advisors recommend paying off the mortgage, while others do not. We will discuss this point later. Finally, immediate needs might even include a cash reserve. The immediate needs time period lasts about two months.

The second stage is the grief period. During this period, the survivors are dealing emotionally with the death of their loved one and may not be quite ready to make significant lifestyle changes. This period can last as long as two years. By the end of this period, the survivors should have planned the adjustments they must make as a result of the loss.

The third stage involves enacting the appropriate lifestyle changes, which may include moving to a more modest home and reducing some of the luxuries to which they had become accustomed. It might include the surviving spouse taking a part-time or full-time job.

The fourth and subsequent stages account for the onset of adulthood for each minor child. If the children's college has been financed separately, then the fourth and subsequent stages occur as each child leaves for college. The departure of each child reduces the costs of maintaining the household.

The next-to-last stage is when the last child leaves the household. At this point, the surviving spouse enters what is known as the "empty nester" period. The surviving spouse can then work full-time if he or she was not so doing before. He or she can greatly reduce his or her living expenses. In general, less support is probably necessary at this stage of life.

The final stage is retirement, when the surviving spouse retires and the wage income of the deceased would no longer have been relevant. Some support may be needed during this period, as the survivor's retirement income may be substantially smaller than what it would have been if the deceased had lived to retirement age.

In the needs approach to life insurance, the monthly (or annual) expenses that would be necessary for each stage are determined, along with the amount of income that would be available. The differences are then computed. Presumably, the projected expenses exceed the projected income for each stage. These differences are referred to as the financing needs of each period. Finally, the present values of these financing needs are computed for each stage other than the first stage. As the first stage involves immediate expenses, no time value adjustment is necessary. The present values of the financing needs are then added together, along with the immediate needs, and this sum represents the total estate needs.

The last step is to compute what resources are already available. The first available resource is existing insurance coverage such as group life insurance. The next available resource includes the liquid assets and financial assets the family already owns. Thus, if a family computed that the sum of the present value of their financing needs plus their immediate needs totals $750,000, and they have $500,000 in financial assets and another $500,000 in existing insurance coverage, then this family would actually be over-insured.

Web Link 11.21

Web Link 11.23

You must formulate many assumptions to work out an extensive needs calculation. Each calculation may result in a different answer to the question of how much insurance coverage you need, because each underlying model is built on different assumptions. The assumptions of some models are quite simple (shown in **Web Link 11.21**), while others (such as the one in **Web Link 11.22**) are quite complex.

Web Link 11.22

Web Link 11.24

For younger families with small children, the total amount necessary to fund all the expenses under a needs approach is usually quite a large number! The willingness of the surviving spouse to reenter or expand his or her job activity can make a big difference in how much insurance coverage is needed today.

SHOULD THE SURVIVORS PAY OFF THE MORTGAGE?

In figuring out how much the survivors will need, a critical factor (if the family owns a home) is whether to pay off the mortgage with the insurance proceeds. If so, the amount of the mortgage should be included in the category of immediate expenses. Paying off the mortgage would also mean that the projected family expenses over the years could be reduced by the amount of the mortgage payment. Is this a good idea? The answer is not clear-cut, and depends on the same issues discussed in the section of Chapter 9 on paying down the mortgage early. If the survivors use some of the death benefit to pay off the mortgage, then they are essentially investing this money at the mortgage rate. So the primary determinant of whether to pay off the mortgage is whether the money could be invested elsewhere at a higher rate. A second issue is that paying off the mortgage provides a risk-free rate of return at the mortgage rate.

WHAT ARE SOCIAL SECURITY SURVIVORSHIP BENEFITS?

Chapter 17 describes how easy it is to obtain via the Internet a statement from the Social Security Administration listing the current and projected levels of one's Social Security benefits. Although most people think about Social Security as retirement benefits, a major component of the program is survivorship benefits.

Web Link 11.26

The full description of who can get survivor's benefits is somewhat lengthy, and may be found at **Web Link 11.26**. Most important, a widow or widower can receive full benefits at age 65 or older, and reduced benefits as early as age 60. A disabled widow or widower can get benefits from ages 50 to 60. A widow or widower at any age can obtain survivor's benefits if she or he takes care of any of the deceased's children who are under 16 or disabled. Unmarried children under 18 or up to age 19 if they are attending elementary or secondary school full time are entitled to benefits. Children of the deceased can get benefits at any age if they were disabled before age 22 and remained disabled.

Divorced spouses are also eligible for survivor's benefits if the marriage lasted 10 years or more. In fact, the ex-spouse does not have to meet the length-of-marriage rule if she or he is caring for any children of the deceased who are under 16 or disabled and who are also getting Social Security benefits. Note that the benefits paid to a surviving divorced spouse who is age 60 or older (50–60 if disabled) do not affect the benefit rates available for any other survivors.

Once you establish that the survivors are in fact covered under Social Security's rules, then you must determine the amount of the benefit. The easiest way to obtain this estimate is to request a PEBES (Personal Earnings and Benefit Estimate Statement) from **Web Link 11.27** Social Security.

HOW MUCH SHOULD I SET ASIDE FOR MY CHILDREN'S COLLEGE EDUCATION?

An element of projected life insurance needs for many people is how much to set aside to fund a college education for each of their children. Two factors are involved. First, what does a college education cost? Second, given the time value of money, how much should be set aside now so that an adequate amount will be available when the children are old enough to attend college?

The cost of a college education is not a simple number to estimate. Location and type of institution must be considered. Today, the tuition of many public community colleges ranges from $1,000 to $2,500 per year. Prestigious private four-year colleges have tuitions that exceed $30,000 per year. Room, board, books, and other supplies add to the cost. Nonetheless, several sources can help you make broad estimates of the cost of attending **Web Link 11.29** college. The simplest way to determine the figure is to call the college (or type of colleges) you think your children might attend and ask them for their current cost figures. These current estimates of the cost of college can then be translated into future estimates and back **Web Link 11.30** into present value terms with the calculators at **Web Link 11.30** and **11.31.** Many of these **Web Link 11.31** calculators have built-in estimates of what a college education will cost.

HOW MUCH WILL LIFE INSURANCE COST ME?

Life insurance costs depend on the type of policy purchased. A one-year term policy is the cheapest, while policies that emphasize rapid building of cash values are the most expensive. The two fundamental factors in setting the premium for a policy, the basic premium and the loadings, were discussed at the start of Chapter 10. Because of variations in the loadings it can really pay to shop around when buying a life insurance policy. However, this does not necessarily mean you should buy the cheapest policy. You must consider other issues, such as a company's service quality and financial soundness. Nonetheless, one should start one's search for insurance coverage by identifying the lowest-priced policies. Consider the following example:

> *Charlie and Rene have decided to purchase $500,000 in life insurance on Charlie. They now wish to identify the companies offering the best prices. Charlie is a 50-year-old male, born on March 17, 1949, who does not smoke. The Bruckers live in Pennsylvania. They wish to pay their insurance premium annually, and would like to buy a 20-year term policy. What companies should they investigate further, and how much will an insurance policy potentially cost them?*

Web Link 11.33

Price quotations for life insurance on the Internet seem to be restricted to term insurance policies. All of the links found at **Web Link 11.33** were checked for quotes on policies of various terms. No one company had all of the best quotes, although only one company had all of the highest quotes for the various policies. The maximum and minimum quotes for the policies considered were

Policy Term	Minimum Premium	Maximum Premium
1-Year Term	$ 650	—
5-Year Term	810	$1,065
10-Year Term	970	1,270
15-Year Term	1,225	1,630
20-Year Term	1,298	2,680

Web Link 11.34

For the 20-year term policy, Charlie would clearly want to give serious consideration to the policy charging $1,298 per year.

HOW WILL AN INSURANCE COMPANY RATE ME?

If you tried to obtain quotes using the above links, you probably encountered health questions. All life insurance companies price their policies from the same **actuarial table.** Actuarial tables are constructed by the insurance industry and provide the life expectancy for a person of any age. However, each insurance company tries to obtain an edge by selling the best-priced policies to the customers with the best chances of living longer than expected, and selling higher priced policies to those people whose life expectancy is lower. To divide their prospective policyholders into groups according to risk, they usually give a simple physical exam. The thoroughness of the exam depends on the age of the individual and the size of the policy being requested. Thus, an individual under the age of 40 applying for a policy for less than $100,000 in death benefit may not even be asked to undergo an exam. An individual over 50 applying for a death benefit of $1,000,000 would most likely be given a thorough medical exam, including a treadmill EKG. In most cases, the medical exam includes only a few tests, such as blood pressure, blood sample, urine specimen, height and weight measurements, and perhaps even a cardiogram. The insurance company also may attempt to obtain a copy of a person's medical history from the Medical Information Bureau (MIB) where that is available. A crucial factor in all life insurance policies is whether the person is a smoker.

Web Link 11.35
Web Link 11.35a

WHAT IS THE ADDRESS OF A NEARBY AGENT?

Web Link 11.36
Web Link 11.37

Although you can easily obtain quotes and apply for term life insurance over the Internet, you might want to buy a cash value type of policy, or perhaps you would prefer to deal with an agent face-to-face. Some companies have directories for finding the nearest agent.

HOW GOOD IS THE COMPANY
I AM BUYING THE POLICY FROM?

Web Link 11.38

Each state's department of insurance regulates insurance companies to prevent policy-holders from suffering in the event of a company's financial collapse. So long as the regulatory bodies are doing their job, you need not be too concerned about the quality of the company you are buying a policy from, which must be legally registered to do business in your state. Various state insurance departments communicate with each other, primarily through the **National Association of Insurance Commissioners** (NAIC). At NAIC's home page, click on *Insurance Regulators* and then select a state on the map to visit the home page of almost any state's department of insurance. At the Illinois State Department of Insurance's home page, for example, you'll find a place to: (1) file a complaint, or (2) view the companies that have had ten or more complaints per 10,000 policies filed during the most recent year.

Web Link 11.39
Web Link 11.40

You will certainly experience less anxiety and potentially less inconvenience if your insurance company is in good financial shape. Organizations that rate insurance companies, such as A.M. Best, rank companies on a scale from A++ (superior) to S (rating suspended).

HOW ARE LIFE INSURANCE
SALESPEOPLE COMPENSATED?

Most insurance salespeople are compensated with commission. For life insurance, the commission is usually a large percentage of the first year's premium, sometimes as high as 95 percent or more. Salespeople then receive a small percentage of each year's subsequent premium (perhaps 5 percent) in order to assure their interest in servicing the policies they have sold. The net effect of this compensation schedule is that agents have an overriding interest in selling new policies rather than primarily servicing existing policies. Furthermore, agents have a strong interest in selling cash value policies rather than term policies.

WHEN SHOULD A PERSON REVIEW
HIS OR HER INSURANCE COVERAGE?

Although you might think that an annual review of life insurance coverage would be appropriate, it is really not necessary. You should review coverage whenever you experience major changes in your personal situation. The birth of a child is probably the single most important time to review one's policy. In truth, however, the actual birth is probably a little late for such a review. As soon as you know your family is expecting a new member, you should increase your coverage. To go a step further, it might be time to increase coverage as soon as you decide to add another child to the family. Occasionally, a husband will die after his wife conceives but before the couple knows that conception has occurred. It is much easier to cancel unnecessary coverage than to try to add coverage later—especially if the husband has already died!

Other good times to review coverage include marriage, divorce, and the death of a spouse or of any dependents. If your salary substantially increases and your dependents become accustomed to a higher standard of living, than a review would be appropriate. Also, after any significant round of inflation, you should reconsider the purchasing power of your policy's death benefits.

If none of the above events have occurred, then life insurance coverage should probably be reviewed at least once every four to five years just to make sure the policyholder is comfortable with the arrangements that would result upon the death of the insured. Additional discussion of when to review one's life insurance coverage may be found at **Web Link 11.41.**

Web Link 11.41

SUMMARY

> Anyone whose dependents rely on his or her income should have life insurance. If no one else is dependent on your income, life insurance is unnecessary.

> A term policy lasts a specific period of time. A cash value policy remains in place until one dies, as long as all the premiums are paid in a timely manner.

> Cash value policies include whole life, limited pay life, endowment life, variable life, universal life, and variable universal life (VUL).

> Borrowing against the cash value of a whole life policy may be financially prudent, so long as the intended death benefit is not compromised.

> A participating policy may pay dividends, a rider is an attachment to a policy, and a viatical settlement is when a terminally ill person sells his or her policy to another.

> Buying term and investing the difference requires that the savings in premiums be invested, and that the future death benefits of the term policies be reduced by the value of the investments.

> The four general approaches to determining how much life insurance you should carry are (1) the appropriate size premium approach, (2) the human life value approach, (3) the multiple of earnings approach, and (4) the needs approach.

> The decision to pay off the mortgage if the breadwinner dies depends on the opportunity cost of doing so, as well as whether it would create a liquidity problem.

> Quotes on life insurance policies, as well as information about insurance agents, may be readily obtained over the Internet.

> Insurance companies rate prospective policyholders based on their health, hobbies, profession, and so on.

> Insurance agents are frequently paid commission out of the first year's premium, which often leads them to promote cash value policies over term policies.

> Life insurance coverage should be reviewed on an occasional basis, but always at the time of an important life event such as a marriage, a divorce, or the birth of a child.

KEY TERMS

accelerated death benefits	actuarial table	agents
cash value policy	decreasing term	DINKS
disability waiver	double indemnity	endowment policy
final expenses	graded premium	group life
human life value	joint and survivorship	limited pay
modified premium	mortgage insurance	multiple of earnings
National Association of Insurance Commissioners	needs	representatives
riders	second to die	single premium policy
term policy	viatical settlement	whole life policy

PROBLEMS

11.1 Using one of the human life value calculators, compute the amount of insurance you need. Make up whatever assumptions you need, using the following information:

- Your current annual earned income is $50,000.
- The estimated annual value of your employee benefits is $10,000.
- You are 25 years old.
- You plan to retire at age 65.
- 20 percent of your income is spent on yourself.
- You expect your annual rate of increase in income to be 4 percent.
- You believe your dependents can earn an average of 8 percent on investments.
- Your combined federal and state tax bracket is 33 percent.

11.2 Using one of the needs-based calculators, compute your optimal life insurance coverage. Make up whatever assumptions you need using the following information:

- Funeral expenses of $7,500
- $20,000 in outstanding debts to be liquidated
- $6,000 to cover three months worth of bills
- a mortgage of $120,000 to be paid off at your death
- you have three children, ages 10, 10, and 12, each of whom will attend 4-year public institutions
- your estate will be worth $1,000,000, all of which would go to your surviving spouse
- none of your estate will go through probate, and you believe your estate will be of moderate complexity
- you will have no financial obligations after your death
- you want a $20,000 emergency fund
- you are married and your spouse is 40 years old, and does not work outside the home
- your family's monthly income needs without you are $8,000, and there is no other annual income

- during retirement, your spouse will have no other income, and her monthly income needs would be $6,000
- during retirement, your spouse will receive $40,000 per year from retirement plans, but will have no other annual income
- you believe the long-term inflation rate would be 3 percent, and your spouse will be able to earn an average return of 8 percent

11.3 Assume that you conclude you need $500,000 in life insurance coverage. You are 30 years old and live in New York. Obtain three estimates of the cost of a 10-year term policy. Make sure your quote guarantees that the premiums are fixed for the entire 10-year period.

11.4 Using one or more of the glossaries available on the Internet, provide definitions for the following terms:

conditional receipt	flat extra premium	proceeds
re-entry option	replacement	elimination period
LOB	load	redlining

REFERENCES

Web Link 11.42 Glossary of life insurance terms
Web Link 11.43 Some FAQ sites
Web Link 11.44 Miscellaneous sites

WALL STREET JOURNAL RESOURCES

Web Link (WSJ) 11.45   Overview of life insurance

For information that has changed since the book was written, for new information that pertains to this topic, and for some new web sites that pertain to the topic of this chapter, see **Web Link 11.46.**

CHAPTER 12

INSURING YOUR HEALTH

LEARNING OBJECTIVES

- Name the basic types of medical insurance policies and describe their features
- Describe the different types of managed care programs
- Identify the six choices available under Medicare
- Distinguish between Medicaid and Medicare
- Analyze the advantages and disadvantages of long-term care insurance
- Describe the key features of disability income insurance
- Discuss how Social Security disability benefits and worker's compensation affect the amount of disability income insurance you need

Web Link: **www.wiley.com/college/woerheide**

INTRODUCTION

Health insurance is the one area of personal finance where many people actually have no decisions to make. That is, they usually are covered by a single policy provided through their employer and seek no other coverage. However, some people have decisions to make about health insurance when their employers offer a menu of health insurance plans, when no health insurance coverage is provided by their employers, or if they are unemployed or retired. In addition, many people have to make health insurance decisions for others such as their parents who may be retired and/or are incapable of making their own decisions. In this chapter, we will consider the case of Larry Barker as he deals with some of the issues involved in health care insurance.

WHAT ARE THE BASIC TYPES OF MEDICAL INSURANCE POLICIES?

Medical insurance policies can be grouped into six broad categories: a basic policy, a major medical policy, an indemnity policy, a Medigap policy, a long-term care policy, and a group policy. A basic policy is sometimes referred to as a **first dollar coverage** policy. That is, it is intended to cover initial expenses, but has upper limits on what is covered. An example of a basic policy is a hospital-surgical policy. First dollar coverage policies may or may not contain deductibles, but they also contain coinsurance provisions (discussed in the following pages). The second type of medical insurance is a **major medical policy,** which is designed to pick up where basic policies leave off. Basic and major medical policies should always be purchased in tandem.

Basic and major medical policies are known as fee-for service policies. The alternative to fee-for-service is a managed care plan. Although fee-for-service and managed care plans differ in important ways, they both usually cover an array of medical, surgical, and hospital expenses, and provide for prescription drugs. Both fee-for-service and managed care plans will sometimes include coverage for dentists and other providers of medical services.

The third of the six types of policies is an indemnity or limited policy, which covers only specific events and/or illnesses. Examples would be a hospital indemnity policy and specific disease policies. The most common specific disease policies cover cancer.

The next two categories are the **Medigap policies** and the **long-term care policies.** The Medigap policies are designed for people who are covered by Medicare but wish to fill in some of its many holes. Long-term care policies protect buyers against the high cost of care if they are institutionalized in their old age. The final type of policy is the group policy, which is usually provided by employers.

Web Link 12.1

WHAT IS A FEE-FOR-SERVICE POLICY?

Unlike in managed care, fee-for-service coverage generally assumes that the medical provider (usually a doctor or hospital) will be paid a fee for each service rendered that is covered by the policy. With fee-for-service insurance, the patient goes to the doctor of his or her choice and the patient, doctor, or hospital submits a claim to the insurance company for reimbursement. Reimbursement is provided only for "covered" medical expenses, which are those listed in a benefits summary statement.

Fee-for-service policies almost always include coinsurance and deductibles. The amount paid by the insurance company is based on the **reasonable and customary charges** in a given geographic area. With **coinsurance,** the insurer pays a fixed percentage of the reasonable and customary charges. A policy's **deductible** is the amount that the insured must pay out-of-pocket each year before the insurance company provides any reimbursement. Consider the following example:

> *Larry Barker recently had to undergo some minor surgery. The bill for the surgical procedure was $2,500. The insurance company defines the reasonable and customary charge for this procedure to be $2,100. This is Larry's first claim of the calendar year. His fee-for-service policy has a 20 percent coinsurance provision, and a $300 deductible. How much will Larry have to pay out of his own pocket?*

If the coinsurance rate is 20 percent, then the insurance company will pay 80 percent of the reasonable and customary charge of $2,100. This comes to $1,680 ($2,100 × 20%). However, as this is Larry's first claim, the reimbursement is reduced by the deductible of $300. So the insurance company will pay for $1,380 of the cost of the surgery, leaving Larry with a surgery bill of $1,120 ($2,500 − $1,380). Some physicians and hospitals will waive charges that are in excess of the reasonable and customary charge used by the insurance company to figure its share of the cost.

Deductibles usually range from $100 to $300 per year per individual, and $500 or more per family. Generally, the higher the deductible, the lower the premiums. In fact, many companies actually offer the consumer a menu of choices as to the sizes of deductibles and premiums. Consider the following example:

Larry Barker is offered a fee-for-service policy through his employer. He must pay part of the annual premium out of his paycheck. Larry has the following choices:

Deductible	Annual Premium
$100	$2,400
300	2,250
500	2,100

Which deductible and premium should Larry choose?

If Larry ends up with no claims against the policy for the year, then the $500 deductible is the cheapest policy, as he would only have paid $2,100 in premium. However, if Larry has extensive claims and pays the full $500 of deductible expenses, then that same policy is the most expensive, as he will have paid a total of $2,600 ($500 deductible and $2,100 premium). With extensive claims, the cheapest would have been the $100 deductible, wherein Larry's out-of-pocket costs would run a total of $2,500 ($100 deductible and $2,400 premium). Thus, there is no clear answer. Larry really has to forecast the likelihood of incurring medical expenses.

Most fee-for-service policies have an out-of-pocket maximum. This means that once the patient's expenses reach a certain amount in a given calendar year, the reimbursements for the reasonable and customary charges for covered benefits are paid in full. However, the fees in excess of the reasonable and customary charge would still have to be paid by the insured. Finally, most fee-for-service policies also have lifetime limits on benefits paid under the policy. It is generally recommended that consumers only consider those policies with lifetime limits of at least $1,000,000.

WHAT ARE THE BASIC FEATURES OF HOSPITAL-SURGICAL POLICIES?

A hospital-surgical policy covers most of the expenses associated with hospitalization and normally provides first dollar coverage. These include room and board (remember, staying at a hospital is a little like staying at a hotel), and the standard group of hospital services that would include surgery, nonsurgical services performed at the hospital, X-ray, laboratory expense, and room and board in an extended care facility. The benefits are most commonly stated in terms of the hospital's daily rate for a semiprivate room. Surgery expenses may be covered under a schedule that defines the reimbursement for each type of surgical procedure, or they may be covered according to the reasonable and customary charges in one's community.

Web Link 12.2

WHAT IS MANAGED CARE?

There are three major types of managed care plans: **health maintenance organizations (HMOs)**, **preferred provider organizations (PPOs)**, and **point-of-service plans (POSs)**. Managed care plans are not traditional insurance programs. In a managed care plan, the member (or the employer, or someone else) pays a monthly fee to the health care organization. The fee is analogous to an insurance premium. However, it is more of a pre-paid share of the projected health care costs for the participants in the plan. Thus, participants, physicians, and hospitals do not file claims for payment or reimbursement. The costs of all services rendered have effectively been pre-paid.

A traditional argument in favor of a managed care plan is that the health care organization has tremendous incentive to keep its patients healthy. The healthier the patients, the fewer the health problems that must be treated, and the more financially successful the organization, since its earnings are based on projected expenses. In a traditional health insurance plan, the more health problems the members have, the larger the revenue of the health care provider organization. A counter argument to this point is that in a managed care system once a patient becomes seriously ill, it is cheaper to reduce his or her treatment rather than to make extensive and expensive efforts to keep the patient alive! A traditional health care provider could generate much revenue by keeping a seriously ill patient alive as long as possible.

The most common type of managed care program is the HMO. An HMO can be organized in several ways. Some HMOs are structured so that patients go to a specified medical facility to see a doctor. This arrangement is known as an **exclusive HMO.** Such plans provide no out-of-network care except in emergencies and special cases, have no annual deductible, and allow members to pay a flat co-payment rather than a percentage of the allowed charge. A **primary care physician (PCP)** coordinates the patient's care and determines how, when, and where the patient will be treated. The PCP also determines the specialists and hospitals to which the patient will be referred.

An alternative structure is a network of individual practitioners. In these **individual practice association HMOs (IPA-HMOs)**, the patient goes to the office of a particular physician, who does not work in a facility run by the HMO. One physician is designated as the PCP. Physicians participating in IPA-HMOs may also operate their regular practice out of their office at the same time. In an exclusive HMO, the physician is an employee of the HMO and does not run a separate practice.

Regardless of whether you are in an HMO or an IPA-HMO, your primary care physician is usually selected according to your needs, and could be a family practice doctor, an internist, a pediatrician, and so on. The PCP is responsible for referring the patient to a specialist when this is deemed appropriate. Normally, the specialist is a participating provider in the HMO. However, if the HMO does not have that type of specialist, then the patient would be referred to providers outside the HMO network and the HMO covers the expense.

Some HMOs require a co-payment for such basic services as an office visit or a prescription. These co-payments may serve either or both of two functions. First, they clearly help to generate revenue to cover the cost of operations. Second, they help prevent abuse of medical services. When people see any good or service as free, they will use substantially more of it. If HMOs had no co-payments, patients might perceive the cost of incremental medical services as free; over time, the cost of those services would rise for everyone. Over short periods of time patients would not normally observe these costs. Thus, co-payments create a real monetary cost to using medical services, causing patients to limit their use of the HMO.

WHAT IS THE DIFFERENCE BETWEEN A PPO AND A POS PLAN?

A PPO (preferred provider organization) is a fee-for-service plan, but the covered person must use a physician, hospital and healthcare provider from the plan's preferred provider list. PPOs do not usually assign a PCP. The idea is that the PPO contracts provide significantly better benefits in exchange for the policyholder's agreement to stick to the preferred providers. Using out-of-network providers would cost more and some services may not be covered. PPOs, like HMOs, have contracts with doctors, hospitals, and other providers, with whom they have negotiated fees. As long as you get your care from these providers, then you would pay only your normal co-payment. Unlike in an HMO, referrals to specialists are not needed in a PPO.

A POS (point-of-service) organization usually provides each member with a PCP who coordinates patient care. The POS plan negotiates discounted fees with the doctors in the network. The patient is subject to both deductibles and co-payments. If the patient chooses to use in-network providers, a flat co-payment applies. If the patient opts for out-of-network care without a referral from the PCP, then the patient pays for a higher percentage of the cost.

Typically, PPO and POS plans offer more flexibility to a patient than a traditional HMO, but their premiums also tend to be higher. In both PPO and POS plans, the patient receives some reimbursement if he or she receives a covered service from a provider who

Web Link 12.3 is not in the plan.

WHAT ARE INDEMNITY POLICIES?

Web Link 12.4 Indemnity policies do not explicitly cover your expenses but pay you directly when medical expenses arise. For example, a **hospital indemnity policy** pays a specific amount of cash for each day a person is in the hospital. Naturally, all such policies contain an upper limit on the number of days that can be reimbursed. In theory, if one entered a "low cost" hospital, one could potentially make a profit on this type of policy if the cash payment per diem exceeded the cost of the hospital stay. In practice, the daily cash payment is invariably below what a daily hospital stay costs. If it were higher than the actual cost of a stay in the hospital, people might seek reasons to be checked into hospitals in order to profit from these policies. However, when other policies already cover some or all of the hospital expenses, a hospital indemnity policy just provides extra cash to the insured.

A specific disease policy is usually an indemnity type of policy. The most common types of specific disease policies are cancer and heart disease. Thus, if you are hospitalized for the disease named in the policy, cash payments are provided, independent of your costs and other policy coverages.

It would be a sad mistake to build your health insurance protection around a series of specific disease policies. Imagine if you owned policies for the 15 most common diseases and contracted some expensive-to-treat obscure disease for which you are not covered. In fact, if you have adequate coverage through a fee-for-service or managed care plan, then you do not need an indemnity policy. In this case an indemnity policy becomes analogous to a speculative investment.

Web Link 12.5

WHAT IS MEDICARE?

Web Link 12.7

Medicare is a health insurance program managed by the **Health Care Financing Administration (HCFA)**. This agency also administers Medicaid and the State Children's Health Insurance Program (SCHIP). Medicare is a component of the Social Security program (see Chapter 17).

As the result of a provision in the Balanced Budget Act of 1997, people eligible to enroll in Medicare may now choose from among six plans.[1] Not all of the plans are available in all parts of the country. The six plans are

- Original Medicare Plan (OMP)
- Original Medicare Plan with a Supplemental Insurance Policy
- Medicare Managed Care Plan
- Private Fee-for-Service Plan
- Medicare Medical Savings Account Plan (MSA)
- Religious Fraternal Benefit Society Plan (RFB)

The Original Medicare Plan, available to everyone, will be the focus of most of our discussion. The other five plans are difficult to understand until you grasp the basics of the OMP. An interesting detail common to the other five plans is that they do not accept anyone with end-stage renal disease (i.e., kidney failure). They also are limited to specific geographic areas.

The OMP includes hospital insurance (Part A) and medical insurance (Part B). Hospital insurance, including care in hospitals, skilled nursing facilities, a hospice, and some home health care, is provided automatically to anyone aged 65 or over who is receiving retirement benefits from Social Security. Part B, medical insurance, includes coverage for medically necessary services, laboratory and diagnostic services, durable medical equipment, outpatient hospital care, ambulatory surgical services, physical therapy, and certain outpatient drugs. Physical and occupational therapists and some health services are also covered. Individuals must enroll in the Part B program, unlike Part A, in which enrollment is automatic.

Web Link 12.7a

---

[1]Prior to 1997, the only program offered was the Original Medicare Plan. At that time it was known simply as Medicare because there were no alternatives.

What Does Medicare Not Cover?

Although Medicare's Part A and B coverage may seem extensive, many expenses are not covered, such as outpatient prescription drugs, nursing home care, dental and vision care, care provided outside the United States, or care provided by nontraditional providers. To cover such items, you should consider at least some combination of the following policies:

Web Link 12.7b

- Medicare Managed Care
- Medicare Select
- Medicaid
- Medigap
- Retiree health benefits
- Long-term care insurance

Whom Does Medicare Cover?

Medicare currently covers approximately 39 million people. Medicare is primarily for people age 65 years and older. However, it also covers some younger people with disabilities who have been disabled for more than two years, as well as people with permanent kidney failure who require dialysis or a transplant. To be eligible for Medicare, a person must have worked at least 10 years in Medicare-covered employment. If you are paying Social Security taxes, you have Medicare-covered employment. Spouses of covered workers are also covered. The rules of coverage are discussed in Chapter 17.

Web Link 12.8

How Much Does Medicare Cost?

Part A coverage of Medicare is free to those who automatically qualify for it. At present, this protects over 90 percent of the people receiving Medicare coverage. Seniors who have fewer than 30 quarters of Medicare-covered employment and disabled individuals under 65 who lost disability benefits because of work and earnings must pay for Part A coverage. The full monthly premium for Part A coverage in 2001 was $300. Beneficiaries age 65 or older who have from 30 to 40 quarters of Medicare-covered employment pay a monthly premium of $165. Quarters of coverage are discussed in Chapter 17.

For the year 2001 the premium for Part B jumped about 10 percent, up to $50 from $45.50 per month in both 1999 and 2000. The Part B premium is deducted directly from a person's Social Security retirement check. Nearly everyone who subscribes to Part A also obtains Part B coverage.

Web Link 12.9

Even if you participate in one of the alternative plans to the OMP, you must pay the Part B premium if you want to subscribe to this service.

What Are the Co-payments and Deductibles with Medicare?

The Medicare Part A deductible in 2001 for inpatient hospital care was $792. The deductible is a beneficiary's only cost for the first 60 days of inpatient care. The cost to beneficiaries for hospital stays between 60 and 90 days is $198 per day. For over 90 days the daily co-payment is $396 per day. The skilled nursing facility deductible, which kicks in after the first 20 days, is $99 per day. Stays at skilled nursing facilities are covered only up to 100 days, following a three-day hospitalization. There is no cost sharing for medically necessary home health care, but there is a 20 percent coinsurance for durable medical equipment. Hospice expenses are covered as long as the patient's doctor certifies the need for them. There is cost sharing for outpatient drugs and inpatient respite care.

Part B expenses have a $100 deductible. Confirmation of these numbers and some additional cost numbers are provided at **Web Link 12.9**. The principles of Medicare reimbursement may be found at **Web Link 12.9a**.

Web Link 12.9a

What Is the Original Medicare Plan with a Supplemental Insurance Policy?

Although the OMP is an attractive policy (particularly as Part A is free upon retirement and Part B's premium is reasonable),[2] it is not comprehensive. Many participants should therefore consider buying Medicare supplemental insurance from a private company. Such insurance is known as a Medigap policy. Medigap policies have become sufficiently standardized that most states approve 10 Medigap variations, known as Forms A through J. Medigap policies may be purchased by anyone who has enrolled in Medicare Part B coverage. If the Medigap policy is purchased within six months of when the Medicare Part B coverage is obtained, then the insured cannot be rejected for any pre-existing conditions.

Web Link 12.6

How Do Medicare Managed Care Plans Work?

Medicare Managed Care Plans (MCPs) are relatively new on the health care scene. Although they are available only in some areas of the country, about 15 percent of people in Medicare are enrolled in these programs. They function like HMOs. A Medicare Managed Care Plan may be provided through four different organizational structures:

- Health Maintenance Organization (HMO)
- HMOs with Point of Service Option (POS)
- Provider Sponsored Organization (PSO)
- Preferred Provider Organization (PPO)

All Medicare MCPs must cover everything provided in Parts A and B of the OMP. For most of these plans, the insured can only go to doctors, specialists, or hospitals that are part of that plan. Anyone enrolled in a Medicare-contracting HMO continues to pay the Part B monthly premium of Medicare. In some cases, the consumer may have to make co-payments for each visit and/or pay an additional monthly premium to the HMO. These plans then provide at a minimum all the hospital and medical benefits covered under the OMP. In some cases, additional coverage may also be provided.

---

[2] In truth, Part A is not actually a free insurance policy. The insured pays the premiums for this policy as part of his or her Social Security taxes over his or her entire working life.

Although these co-payments and the additional premium may sound more expensive, a Medigap policy is not necessary for anyone in a Medicare-contracting HMO. If someone who is covered under the OMP and decides to join a Medicare-contracting HMO, then this person ought to be sure he or she can reacquire the Medigap policy if he or she later drops out of the Medicare-contracting HMO. In the ideal scenario, departure from the HMO coverage should allow one to purchase the Medigap policy regardless of his or her age or health status at that time. Your ability to do this will depend on the company selling the policy as well as on state law. Some companies that run Medicare-managed HMOs (at the time of writing) may be found at **Web Link 12.11.**

Web Link 12.10

Web Link 12.11

Web Link 12.12

How Do Private Fee-for-Service Plans Work?

Private fee-for-service plans are a new Medicare health care choice in some areas of the country. As Medicare-approved private insurance, these plans cover all Medicare Part A and Part B benefits. Like the managed care plans, they frequently provide benefits not provided under the OMP. Medicare simply pays these plans a monthly fee for each Medicare patient enrolled in the plan. The major advantage of the private fee-for-service plans is that one may go to any doctor, specialist, or hospital.

Web Link 12.13

What Is a Medicare Medical Savings Account Plan?

A Medicare Medical Savings Account (MSA) plan is a health insurance policy with a large annual deductible. Currently, this is being operated as a test program for up to 390,000 Medicare beneficiaries. The participant chooses a Medicare MSA plan, which is a health insurance policy with a high deductible. Medicare pays the premium for the Medicare MSA plan and makes a deposit to a Medicare MSA established by the participant. The participant then uses the money deposited in his or her Medicare MSA to pay for medical expenses. Unused cash is carried forward to the next year. Cash may be withdrawn from the MSA plan for non-medical uses, if declared as taxable income. Depending on the Medicare MSA plan you choose, you could either go to any doctor or hospital or perhaps be limited to a network of providers. Medicare MSA plans first became available in November 1998.

Medicare MSA plans have the advantage that they frequently pay for some things not covered in the OMP. However, the payments don't kick in until the insured has met the annual deductible. Thus, whether Medicare MSA plans are a good deal depends on the insured's ultimate needs.

Web Link 12.14

What Is a Religious Fraternal Benefit Society Plan?

A Fraternal Benefit Society (FBS) plan is health insurance offered by a society only to its members. Each such society must meet both IRS guidelines and Medicare requirements to qualify. Because of their unique nature and limited role, there is no need for further discussion of these plans.

Web Link 12.15

WHAT IS MEDICAID?

Web Link 12.18
Medicaid is a jointly funded, federal/state health insurance program designed to serve low-income and needy people. Medicaid was authorized under Title XIX of the Social Security Act in 1965, initially as a program for people eligible for Aid to Families with Dependent Children (AFDC).[3] Over a period of three decades, Congress transformed Medicaid into a large, complex program that currently covers nearly 36 million individuals, including children, the elderly, blind, disabled, and those eligible for federally assisted income maintenance payments. Medicaid recipients are entitled to both federally mandated benefits and benefits added by each state. In order to receive federal matching funds, each state must provide a certain core set of services and cover eligible groups of individuals. In addition, some states provide further coverage and extended eligibility to their Medicaid programs.

Web Link 12.16
Web Link 12.16a

The federal contribution to the cost of each state's program varies by state and is based primarily on how a state's median income level compares to that of other states. The poorest states (in terms of the income of residents) receive a larger percentage share of federal matching funds.

Web Link 12.17

Medicaid coverage includes: in-patient hospital services, out-patient hospital services, laboratory and X-ray services, skilled nursing home services, physicians' services, physical therapy, hospice care, and rehabilitative services. Choice is restricted under Medicaid programs. Each state maintains a list of approved physicians and other providers of medical care. Even then, many approved physicians limit the number of Medicaid patients they see because they are not fully reimbursed for their services by Medicaid.

States are prohibited from reducing the welfare benefits of anyone who becomes eligible for Medicaid. In addition, states may not impose restrictions regarding U.S. citizenship or residency (other than that an applicant must be a resident of that state). Neither the age of applicants nor the fact that they work may disqualify them from receiving Medicaid.

Medicaid has had extensive problems with fraud since its inception. In 1996, Congress passed a law that made people criminally liable if they fraudulently misrepresent themselves in order to become eligible for medical assistance.

HOW DO GROUP PLANS WORK?

In a **group plan** a person is automatically covered under a health insurance plan just by being a member of a particular group. Group plans are most commonly provided through employment. Before a new employee is enrolled in a group plan, it is not uncommon to have a waiting period, which may be as short as one month. Group plans may also have a limited enrollment period, requiring that new employees enroll within a certain number of days of being hired or forgo the benefit of enrollment until the next **open enrollment period.** Employers allow employees to add, change, or drop various benefits such as a group health insurance plan when certain events occur (such as a marriage, a divorce, or the birth of a child) or during an annual open enrollment period, which lasts for a limited number of days.

---

[3]The AFDC program is now referred to as the Temporary Assistance for Needy Families (TANF) program.

The cost of a group plan is frequently split between the employer and the employee. In some cases an employer may pick up the entire cost of a group plan. However, as medical costs continue to grow, this has become less common.

A group plan may actually consist of a menu of different health insurance packages, in which the cost to the employee varies with the plan selected. Some employers even allow an employee to opt out of health insurance coverage; they may pay those who do so a small bonus. Opting out makes sense when both spouses work and both are covered by group plans. For a single person or a family with only one worker, forgoing health insurance just to obtain the bonus could easily be an incredibly expensive mistake.

Web Link 12.19

HOW DO I ACQUIRE TEMPORARY HEALTH INSURANCE COVERAGE?

If your health insurance is provided under a group plan at work, you could be at risk of losing your coverage if you quit, move to a new job where there is a waiting period for health insurance coverage, get fired or laid off, or retire. By law, group health insurance plans must allow former group members to continue their health insurance coverage by paying the premium directly. Unfortunately, this usually results in a substantial jump in the cost of health insurance, particularly if the employer was paying the entire premium. However, such a continuation is often highly desirable, because virtually all health insurance policies deny coverage to **pre-existing conditions**—illnesses or health problems known to exist when the health insurance policy is initially acquired. Even group plans will deny coverage for pre-existing conditions. Many plans, however, will eventually cover pre-existing conditions once a person has been covered in the plan for one or two years.

An alternative to continuing the group plan on a personal basis is to simply approach various insurance agents about buying a policy. The drawback is, again, that these policies are extremely expensive when purchased on an individual basis. The insurance agent receives a generous commission on personal health insurance policies, so it is usually not difficult to find an agent anxious to sell you one.

Web Link 12.20

WHAT IS LONG-TERM CARE INSURANCE?

Long-term care insurance covers the costs of living in a nursing home. It is fairly easy to buy when you are younger and in good health, but after being diagnosed with AIDS or any of the serious ailments of old age, such as Alzheimer's, multiple sclerosis, Parkinson's, degenerative nerve diseases, cancer, or emphysema, you would be much less likely to acquire such insurance. Long-term care policies always have upper limits on the amount of reimbursement, which include both daily maximums and lifetime maximums.

The cost of the premium is influenced by age, the length of the benefit period, the maximum amount of benefit, the **elimination period,** as well as any special features of the policy, such as a **cost-of-living adjustment** (COLA) option and the option to cover both home care and facility care. The elimination period is the amount of time one must wait before collecting benefits. Naturally, the younger you are when the policy is purchased, the lower the annual premium, but this does not necessarily mean that you should buy a long-term care policy when you are younger. Financial planners generally recommend doing so sometime between the ages of 55 and 65. Consider the following example:

*Larry Barker is 55 years old. His insurance agent recommends he buy a long-term care insurance policy. The policy would cost $900 per year, payable at the end of each year. The policy would pay a daily maximum of $100 for a period of three years, after a 100-day **elimination period**. Based on family history, Larry would not expect to be placed in a nursing home until age 80. If Larry believes he could earn an 8 percent rate of return on his money, is this policy a good deal?*

The solution to this problem involves applying the time value of money to two different annuities. First, we would need to figure the future value of a 25-year annuity (i.e., the future value of the premiums), and then we would need to figure the present value of the three years' worth of benefits (i.e., the present value of the benefits).

At an 8 percent interest rate, the future value of premiums equals the annual premium times the future value interest factor of an annuity. Using Appendix A.3, we find that this works out to $900 \times \text{FVIFA}_{8\%, 25 \text{ years}} = \$900 \times 73.1059 = \$65,795.31$. In other words, this total is the money Larry could accumulate on the day he was admitted to the home care facility if he were to invest his money for 25 years rather than buying the insurance policy.

To find the present value of the insurance benefits, we must adjust the discount rate to a daily rate. This can be approximated by dividing the annual rate of 8 percent by 365 to obtain a daily rate of .0002191 (.08 / 365). Because this interest rate is not shown in the back of the book, we will need to compute the interest factor directly. The present value of the benefits on the day Larry would be admitted would be equal to $100 \times \text{PVIFA}_{.02191\%, 1095 \text{ days}} = \$97,345.60$, where 1,095 is the number of days in three years. In this case, the purchase of the long-term care policy turns out to be a pretty good deal, as Larry would be better off by $31,550.29 ($97,345.60 – $65,795.31) on the day of admission to the nursing home.

If, however, Larry believes he could earn 11 percent on his money rather than 8 percent, then our answer changes. The present value of his benefits drops to $93,254.36, but the future value of his premiums grows to $114,413.30 ($100 × 114.4133). Thus, Larry would be worse off by $21,158.94 ($93,254.36 – $114,413.30).

To this problem must be added all of the uncertainties of the benefits. First, Larry might die before reaching the age of 80. Second, he may not be placed in a nursing home until after age 80. If admission to the nursing home is delayed until age 85 or later, then the future value of the premiums easily overwhelms the benefits of the policy. Third, Larry may not stay in the nursing home for the full three years. He might either die or recover sufficiently to move out before the three years is up. In other words, although comparing the future value of the premiums to the present value of the projected benefits of a long-term care policy can be useful, it cannot provide a definitive answer as to whether the purchase is a good deal.

Web Link 12.22 The annual premiums escalate rapidly the longer one waits to purchase such a policy. However, as the last example demonstrated, there is a significant time value of money to the relationship between the premium and when one might have to file a claim on this type of policy. See Figure 12.1 for a table comparing premiums on long-term care policies.

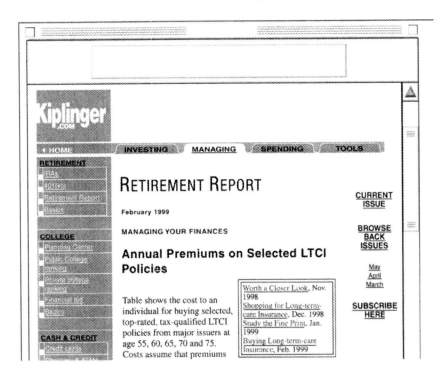

FIGURE 12-1 Quotations for Long-Term Care Insurance

Web Link 12.21

Finally, long-term care policies could well change over time. What appears to be a good policy today may be of little value in 25 or 30 years when you need its benefits.

What Features Should I Look for in a Long-Term Care Policy?

Web Link 12.23

Due to the unpredictable nature of long-term care policies, you should investigate the features of any policy more carefully. First, make sure that the daily benefit is sufficient to cover all or most of the average daily nursing home cost in your state. Average daily costs for most states are between $90 and $150, with Alaska a standout at $413. Next, look for an annual inflation rider. A generous inflation rider would increase the benefits by 5 percent per year. Third, as the average nursing home stay is three years, make sure the benefit period is at least three years and consider a benefit period of four years.

Fourth, look for a policy that generously defines when you would qualify for nursing home care. Fifth, a policy should also provide coverage for assisted living facilities and home health care, as well as for custodial, skilled, and intermediate care. Finally, the policy should be renewable for life and the premiums should be waived if you become insti-

Web Link 12.24

tutionalized.

Now that you know what features make a policy desirable, how can you save on its cost? The first and foremost method of saving on the cost of a long-term care policy is the same way you save on any consumer purchase: shop around. Second, some companies offer a couple's discount. Third, some companies offer a discount if you can demonstrate you are in good health. Fourth, stretching the **elimination period** (provided one has the resources to cover the costs incurred during that time) usually produces substantial savings. Finally, if you are single, you may want to eliminate the home care benefit portion of the policy, which pays only for part-time services. If full-time service were required, you would probably need to make other plans to be taken care of.

Web Link 12.25

WHAT IS DISABILITY INCOME INSURANCE?

Although disability income insurance is not a health insurance product, it is nonetheless part of a health insurance program. Disability income insurance provides income when you are unable to work. The income could be used to pay medical expenses, but the primary purpose of such policies is to replace wages or salary lost as a result of the insured not being able to work.

Several decisions come into play in the selection of a policy. The first is how much income to replace. Naturally, you cannot buy a policy to replace more than your current income—any insurance company selling such a policy would soon go broke from a stampede of claims! In fact, most policies set an upper limit on the percentage of your income you can replace. These limits, called **replacement ratios,** generally run from 50 to 70 percent. The lower the percentage of income replaced, the lower the premium. Policies specify an exact dollar payment to be paid in the event of a disability, with a maximum figured as a percentage of income. Consider the following example:

Larry Barker earns $60,000 a year. He is looking into a disability income insurance policy that will pay 50 percent per year. What would the face value of the policy be?

At a 50 percent benefit rate, the policy would provide for $30,000 per year. It would likely be described as $2,500 per month.

The second decision in selecting a policy is how much time you will wait between the onset of the disability and the start of benefits, otherwise known as the elimination period. The shortest elimination period is usually about two weeks, the longest about six months. The longer the elimination period before the benefits are paid, the lower the premium charged on the policy.

The third decision is how long the benefits should last. Disability income insurance policies are usually divided into short-term and long-term. Short-term policies last up to two years and usually have relatively short elimination periods. Long-term policies will last up to age 65, but usually have relatively long elimination periods.

In addition to the regular policy, you can buy a **residual rider,** which will provide partial disability payments if you are able to return to your job only on a part-time basis.

If your salary grows over time, then what was once an adequate disability income policy may prove to be inadequate in terms of the income replacement ratio. Policies vary as to when they allow you to increase coverage and by what percentage without undergoing a new physical exam. Of course, you could always buy an additional policy, but it would require you to pass a new physical exam. Thus, the more lenient a policy is toward the augmentation of coverage, the better the policy. Most policies will allow the insured to increase coverage annually for the first two to four years for up to 10 percent without getting a new physical. Naturally, any increase in coverage will add to a policy's premium.

If the policy includes **guaranteed future insurability,** then you may increase the policy every time you receive a raise. Many policies have COLA rider, which allows you to increase coverage (commensurate with the rate of inflation) with no additional physicals.

Policies that are guaranteed renewable and are noncancelable are strongly preferred. If a policy is not guaranteed renewable, then the insurance company could refuse to renew it at some point in the future. Guaranteed renewable means that the only circumstance under which the insurance company could decline to renew the policy would be nonpayment of the premium. While drawing benefits under a policy, you need not worry about losing those benefits just because the policy comes up for renewal; benefits will continue to be paid according to the contractual agreement in the existing policy. However, if the disability is temporary and you are likely to return to work, then you would certainly want the disability income policy to remain in place for future disabilities. The noncancelable clause means that the premium rate stated on the policy can never be raised.

A final provision of a disability income insurance policy is the definition of disability. The least favorable definition for an insured person is one that defines disability as a condition that prevents a person from doing any meaningful form of employment, while the most favorable defines disability as a condition that prevents a person from performing in a job for which the insured is trained and qualified. To understand the difference, consider a surgeon who loses one eye. The surgeon would no longer be able to perform surgery, and would thus probably lose a significant portion of his or her income. Under the least favorable definition, the surgeon could still perform many jobs and would not be considered disabled. Under the most favorable definition, the surgeon is permanently disabled.

It is not uncommon for someone to obtain two disability income policies. The first one would be a short-term disability policy, set to cover a fairly large percentage of his or her income, starting with an elimination period of two weeks to a month at most, and lasting no more than two years. Most disabilities are resolved within two years, but in the event that the person is still disabled after two years, the disability may well be permanent; by that time, the individual may be able to start making lifestyle adjustments allowing him or her to get by on a lower income than what he or she had been used to. Second, the long-term disability income policy would kick in once the first policy terminated its payments. Hence, it would have an extremely long elimination period. It would be for a lower percentage of income, but would have that income last until what would have been the normal retirement age. At that point in time, the person's originally intended retirement benefits would then be available.

Web Link 12.26

DO I REALLY NEED DISABILITY INCOME INSURANCE?

When most people think about their insurance needs, disability income is not one that immediately comes to mind. Auto insurance and homeowner's insurance are policies that people most readily buy, probably because auto insurance is required by law of all drivers, and proof of homeowner's insurance is required by all mortgage lenders. Life insurance is usually next on people's lists, particularly if they know someone who died young leaving children economically vulnerable. Nonetheless, the chances of becoming disabled for 90 days or longer before you retire are approximately one in three—a much higher probability than that of dying during your working years.

As with any type of insurance policy, disability income insurance is only a vehicle for dealing with a particular risk exposure. In this case, the risk exposure is if the individual loses some or all of his or her income due to a disability. If an individual or family has sufficient other resources such that the loss of one person's income does not create a serious financial problem, then this family probably does not need disability income insurance. For most individuals and families, this is not the case. One factor that lessens your need for disability income insurance is the amount of sick leave you have accrued at work. A person with a substantial amount of sick leave may be able to dispense with a short-term disability insurance policy, or at least use a long elimination period.

Another situation to consider is that if you were to be disabled for only a short amount of time, you probably would not want to file a claim. As with all insurance (with the obvious exception of life insurance), filing a claim increases the likelihood that the company will raise your premium the next time the policy comes up for renewal.

Many financial planners do not recommend disability income insurance for people who make less than $30,000 to $40,000 a year. In fact, some insurance companies won't offer coverage for people with incomes below $20,000. People employed in professions with high physical risk, such as oil-field workers, pilots, miners, and police officers, usually cannot buy these insurance policies.

Some employers offer disability income insurance as part of the employee benefits, while others pay for some of the premiums if the employee pays for the rest. In other cases, the employer offers the employee the opportunity to buy disability income insurance at group rates. All of these are good deals. If the employer pays the premium on the disability income insurance, then the income received under the policy is fully taxable. If the policy is purchased directly by the individual, then the income received on a claim is tax exempt.

The major problem with disability income insurance is that it is usually quite expensive compared to other forms of insurance.

Web Link 12.27

WHY WOULD SOCIAL SECURITY DISABILITY INCOME BENEFITS NOT BE SUFFICIENT?

Social Security also provides disability benefits to covered workers, but for several reasons these should not be considered the centerpiece of your disability income insurance program. First, the benefits are available only to covered workers, so it is possible you could lose your coverage. Second, the benefits do not start until you have been disabled for at least six months. Social Security's disability program assumes that families have access to other resources during short-term disabilities, including worker's compensation, insurance, savings, and investments. Third, Social Security's rules are incredibly strict as to what constitutes a disability. Social Security considers you disabled only if you are not able to do the work you did before the event that precipitated the disability. The Social Security administration reserves the right to decide if you could adjust to another, comparable line of work. Furthermore, the disability must last or be expected to last a year or to result in death.

Web Link 12.28

WHY WOULD WORKER'S COMPENSATION NOT BE SUFFICIENT?

Web Link 12.29
A key factor in determining the amount of disability income insurance needed is the **worker's compensation program** in that particular state.[4] A sufficiently generous worker's compensation program may greatly alleviate the need for disability income insurance. In general, benefits are paid whether the employee or the firm itself (as represented by other employees, managers, or general circumstances) is at fault for the accident. Worker's compensation operates on a "no-fault" basis; that is, the employer does not admit guilt and the employee does not have to sue for benefits. The exception to the "no-fault" concept is that if the accident results from horseplay, drunkenness, or illegal drugs, then the benefits are denied. Similarly, the disability may not arise from self-inflicted injuries, or from injuries incurred while a worker is off the job or violating company policy.

SUMMARY

➤ The six types of medical insurance are a basic policy, a major medical policy, an indemnity policy, a Medigap policy, a long-term care policy, and a group policy.

➤ The three major types of managed care plans are health maintenance organizations (HMOs), preferred provider organizations (PPOs), and point-of-service plans (POSs).

➤ The six choices for Medicare are Original Medicare Plan, Original Medicare Plan with a Supplemental Insurance Policy, Medicare Managed Care Plan, a private fee-for-service plan, Medicare Medical Savings Account Plan, and Religious Fraternal Benefit Society Plan.

➤ Medicare is a part of the Social Security program. Medicaid is an entitlement program for low-income and needy people.

KEY TERMS

coinsurance	cost-of-living adjustment option	deductible
elimination period	exclusive HMO	first dollar coverage
group plan	guaranteed future insurability	Health Care Financing Administration
health maintenance organization	hospital indemnity policy	individual practice association HMO
long-term care policies	major medical policy	Medigap policies
open enrollment period	point-of-service plans	pre-existing conditions
preferred provider organizations	primary care physician	reasonable and customary charges
replacement ratios	residual rider	worker's compensation program

[4]All states except Texas have a worker's compensation program.

PROBLEMS

12.1 Jim Hansen's doctor has just told him that he will need surgery costing $3,000. His insurance company defines the reasonable and customary charge for this procedure to be $2,500. Jim has not yet submitted a medical claim this year, so this will be his first. His fee-for-service policy has a 20 percent coinsurance provision and a $500 deductible. How much must Jim pay out of his own pocket?

12.2 Mary Wralston is reviewing the fee-for-service policy she receives through her employer. She has to pay part of the annual premium out of her paycheck. She has the choice of a $50 deductible with an annual premium of $1,500, or a $250 deductible with a $1,400 annual premium. Which is the better deal if she anticipates medical claims of $100 this year? $1,000 this year?

12.3 If you die before retiring, who benefits from the Medicare portion of the Social Security premiums you will have paid your entire working career?

12.4 If the data are available, determine what the Medicare copayment and deductibles are for 2002.

12.5 Obtain at least one quote for each of the following:

a. A short-term disability income insurance policy that pays $500 per month (which is less than 50 percent of take-home pay), has a two-week elimination period, and pays for up to two years.

b. A long-term care insurance policy that pays $150 per day, for up to three years.

REFERENCES

Web Link 12.30   Glossary of health insurance terms

WALL STREET JOURNAL RESOURCES

Web Link (WSJ) 12.31   "Health-Plan Changes Hit Workers," *The Wall Street Journal Interactive Edition*, November 7, 1999

For information that has changed since the book was written, for new information that pertains to this topic, and for some new web sites that pertain to the topic of this chapter, see **Web Link 12.32.**

PART IV

INVESTMENTS

CHAPTER 13

INTRODUCTION TO INVESTING AND FIXED RETURN INVESTMENTS

LEARNING OBJECTIVES

- Describe the two major philosophies of investing and the investment implications of each.
- Describe the features of a bond.
- Distinguish between agency, corporate, and municipal bonds.
- Describe how a bond call works and why it is bad for the investor.
- Discuss the various bond ratings and rating agencies.
- Compute the price of a bond.
- Compute the yield to maturity of a bond.
- Discuss how accrued interest is processed on bond trades.
- Explain the relationship between coupon yield, current yield, and yield to maturity, and indicate which an investor should use and when.
- Define "duration statistic."
- Describe how zero-coupon bonds and convertible bonds work.
- Obtain bond quotes.
- Explain how to get a quick reading on what the bond markets are doing.
- Describe some of the strategies to use when investing in bonds.

Web Link: www.wiley.com/college/woerheide

INTRODUCTION

The thought of investing money must be somewhat intimidating for a neophyte investor. There is a multitude of instruments from which to choose, including government bonds, corporate bonds, convertible bonds, common stock, preferred stock, rights, warrants, options, closed-end investment companies, mutual funds, REITs, and unit investment trusts. In addition to choosing among investment types, a new investor must select a broker or financial advisor. He or she must also clarify in his or her own mind the philosophy that will dictate how to make investment decisions.

In this chapter we will consider the case of Glenn Pettengill. Glenn has saved up a little money and has decided that now is the appropriate time to start his investment program. Glenn has not settled on an investment philosophy, but he knows he is interested in starting with fixed-return securities.

WHAT ARE THE TWO MAJOR INVESTING PHILOSOPHIES?

All investment strategies may be divided into two major philosophies. One is known as the **efficient market hypothesis (EMH)**, and the other, for lack of a better name, as the **inefficient market hypothesis (IMH)**. The EMH postulates that each security is fairly priced to provide an expected return commensurate with its riskiness. As an example, think of the market in terms of a horse race. If there are 10 horses in a race, and no one knows anything about the 10 horses (other than that they all have a head, four legs, and a tail), then each horse would be considered equally likely to win. That is, each horse would have a one-tenth or 10 percent probability of winning. Each horse would run at odds of 10 to 1, meaning that a better would receive $10 for every $1 bet on that horse if that horse wins.

However, the scenario changes when some people gain some knowledge about the horses. Let us say they learn about the times the horses have achieved in past races, as well as where each horse placed in each of its races. They learn the names and records of the jockeys on each horse and how the horses have done in their workouts since their last races. Based on this information, these people will recognize that at odds of 10 to 1, some horses are excellent bets while others are extremely poor bets. These knowledgeable betters will then begin betting money on the undervalued horses, causing those expected payoffs to fall. They will continue to bet money until such time that the expected payoffs of each horse reflect the probability of each horse winning.

Does *every better* need to be knowledgeable for the odds to reflect the probability of winning, or just a critical percentage of them? The latter generally appears to hold true.

Once the knowledgeable betters have placed their bets, then the expected payoffs for each horse will reflect the risk associated with betting on that horse. The horse with the lowest odds will have the highest probability of winning. Betting on this horse is considered a relatively "safe" bet. Safe bets provide a relatively low expected payoff per bet. The horse with the highest odds, say 99 to 1, will have the lowest probability of winning. Betting on this horse is considered quite risky, almost like throwing your money away. However, every now and then a long-shot horse does win a race, granting a fabulous payoff to those who bet on it.

Investments operate the same way. Some investments are incredibly safe, but provide a relatively low profit. Others are so risky that acquiring them might be like throwing your money away, except that every now and then a risky investment pays off big. The menu of investments available to an investor today includes everything from the risk-free to pure gambles.

To repeat, the key point about the EMH is its assumption that each investment will be priced so expected returns are commensurate with riskiness.

The IMH contradicts the EMH. Formal statements elaborating on the EMH philosophy are provided at **Web Link 13.1**. There are no formal statements about the IMH, as it is essentially just the position of those who reject the EMH.

Web Link 13.1

What Forms Does the EMH Take?

The EMH actually comes in three versions, known as forms. The first is the **weak form**, a statement that historical price information is useless in predicting future stock returns. This means that if you had some sort of chart with past prices for a security, no matter how much time you studied it you would learn nothing that would improve the quality of your investment decisions.

The **semi-strong form** of the EMH states that publicly available information is useless in predicting stock returns. This means that anything you read in the paper, in a company's annual or quarterly reports, see on the Internet, or otherwise find in the public domain, is of no value in helping you to make better decisions about buying and selling securities.

The third form of the EMH is the **strong form,** which states that even if you knew something important that no one else knew about a company, that information would still be of no value in predicting future stock returns.

WHAT ARE THE INVESTMENT IMPLICATIONS OF THE EMH AND THE IMH?

The two investment philosophies have radically different implications with respect to how one should manage one's investment portfolio. Thus, before you undertake an investment program, you must choose which of these two investment philosophies you believe to be more accurate.

If you believe the IMH—that the market is not efficient—then you should spend a great deal of time investigating investment opportunities until you find the opportunity you think will provide the biggest expected profit. A believer in the IMH should either make searching for investment opportunities his or her primary hobby, or should hire a professional to manage his or her portfolio.

A person who believes that the market is efficient does not worry about trying to buy underpriced securities and sell overpriced securities. He or she treats all prices as unbiased approximations of what they should be. Such a person will spend more time worrying about whether the portfolio has the correct amount of risk or whether it is adequately diversified. When such a person starts to build a portfolio, he or she may initially buy such securities as index funds (see Chapter 15). As his or her portfolio grows, individual securities will be added and index funds phased out. Eventually, such a person will worry primarily about finding securities that enhance the diversification of his or her portfolio. If you believe the market is efficient, why spend huge amounts of time researching investments?

Students often ask which theory of the market is correct. The truth is that the EMH can never be proved, it can only be disproved. Thus, there will never be an absolutely certain answer to this question. Each person must decide which theory he or she wants to follow, and then follow it diligently. This may sound a little bit like religion; the analogy is apt.

Nonetheless, much evidence shows that the market is much closer to being efficient than to being inefficient. For this reason, the individual is usually better off acting as if the market were efficient.

WHAT IS THE BEST WAY TO ACCUMULATE WEALTH OVER TIME?

For people who want to become wealthy over their lifetime, the single most important activity is to invest, not necessarily to find the absolute best investments. Consider the following example:

> Glenn Pettengill is 25 years old. He has just started his first full-time job, having obtained his bachelor's degree and his MBA. Glenn would like to really start to enjoy some of his income after living as a student for many years. However, he remembers the importance of the time value of money from his finance course in graduate school. Glenn is considering four strategies in saving for retirement. He would like to accumulate $1,000,000 by the time he retires in 40 years. The first strategy would be to save $200 per month ($2,400 per year). Setting aside this money in the next few years would really cut into Glenn's projected lifestyle. The second strategy would be to start saving $300 per month ($3,600 per year), beginning in 10 years. However, this is about the time Glenn anticipates starting his family. Glenn thinks he is more likely to be able to set aside $500 per month ($6,000 per year) if he starts his investment program in 25 years, once his kids are about to graduate from high school. This would be the third strategy. The fourth and final investment strategy would be to wait until his kids finish college. Glenn anticipates this would be in about 30 years, and at that time he could save $750 per month ($9,000 per year). Which strategy will produce the highest accumulation at retirement if Glenn is able to earn an average of 10 percent per year on his investments?

Web Link 13.2

The first strategy will produce a final wealth figure of $1,264,815.92. The second through fourth strategies will produce final wealth figures of $678,146.38, $207,235.17, and $153,633.73. The first strategy would be the only one in which Glenn would achieve his goal.

This example illustrates how setting aside some money now can be much more effective than setting aside more money later. Saving at a lower rate now is even more effective than waiting and investing at a higher rate. Consider the following extension of the previous example:

> Glenn believes that if he starts his investment program later, he will be able to spend more time in selecting securities, and that this additional time will result in higher rates of return. Thus, if he implements the second strategy he believes he can earn a rate of return of 11 percent, and with strategies three and four, 12 and 13 percent, respectively. At these higher rates, are any of the alternative strategies now better than the first strategy?

If you calculate Glenn's earnings, you would find that the answer is no.

These examples illustrate the single most important feature about accumulating wealth: Start saving sooner rather, allowing the investments as much time as possible to grow. Put another way, time matters more than how much you set aside or what interest rate you earn.

WHAT IS THE MOST IMPORTANT INVESTMENT DECISION A PERSON HAS TO MAKE?

Once you have committed to investing, you must make the single most important decision of the investment process. That decision is *not* what particular security to buy, but rather the **capital allocation decision.** The capital allocation decision identifies the percentage amounts of the portfolio allocated to each type of investment. That is, when the investor selects major types of investments such as money market investments, bonds, and stocks, he or she should then specify what percentage of his or her portfolio should be in each of these categories. Within each category, the investor may do some additional fine-tuning. For example, the category of bonds may be divided into government bonds, corporate bonds, and foreign bonds. The category of stocks may be divided into income-oriented stocks, growth stocks, and foreign stocks. Once the investor is comfortable with the different types of securities he or she wants in his or her portfolio and how much money will be placed into each type of investment, then the investor is ready to start selecting the actual securities. This is known as the **security selection decision.** The capital allocation decision tends to have much more impact on the portfolio over the years than does the security selection decision. Be cautious of any investment advisor who starts the investment discussion by focusing on the security selection decision rather than the capital allocation decision.

WHAT ARE BONDS?

When you buy a bond, you are effectively making a loan to the issuer of that bond. All bonds must have a maturity or due date when the loan will be paid off. The amount to be paid off on the maturity date, written on the face of the bond, is referred to as par value. Most bonds have a par value of $1,000. Bonds with a par value less than $1,000 are known as **baby bonds.** The maturity of bonds is almost never more than 30 years. However, recent years have seen bond issues with maturities of up to 100 years.

Most bonds pay interest semiannually. The interest is frequently referred to as the coupon payment. The annual interest paid on a bond divided by its par value is known as the **coupon rate,** nominal rate, or coupon yield of the bond. Thus, a bond that pays interest of $80 per year (in two six-month installments) has a coupon rate of 8 percent ($80 / $1,000). The coupon rate can never change over the life of the bond. Just as you may not inform a bank you want to pay a lower interest rate on your auto loan, a bond issuer may not inform its lenders (i.e., the bondholders) that it is lowering the interest rate it is paying. Bonds that pay no interest are referred to as **zero-coupon bonds.**

Bonds are most frequently categorized by the issuer. They may be classified as government (or Treasury) bonds, corporate bonds, municipal bonds, agency bonds, etc. Corporate bonds may also be described in terms of the collateral the issuer pledges or some special feature of the bond. Thus, corporate bonds may be classified as debentures, mortgage bonds, collateral trust bonds, convertible bonds, refunding bonds, etc. They may also be defined in terms of special features, such as convertibility. Each of these types of bonds will be discussed in more detail later in the chapter.

Web Link (WSJ) 13.3

What Risks Are Associated with Investing in Bonds?

Bonds contain two types of risk. The first is default risk, or the risk that the issuer will fail to make the promised payments. Default risk includes delinquency risk, in which the issuer makes the promised payments, but at a later date. If a payment is missed, investors always hope that the omission is a case of delinquency and not default, although it is not always clear at the time. As the financial strength of a company deteriorates, the prices of its bonds decline as the possibility of default grows more significant. This process also works in reverse. If a company grows stronger financially, then the prices of its bonds rise to reflect the reduced likelihood of default.

The second type of risk is interest rate risk. This is the variability in returns associated with changes in the level of market interest rates. An increase in the general level of interest rates is both good news and bad news for an investor. An increase in interest rates usually means that the prices of any bonds currently owned have declined. The larger the increase in rates, the greater the decline in prices. However, an increase in rates also means that any future investments in bonds will provide higher rates of return than they otherwise would have.

WHAT IS AGENCY DEBT?

In Chapter 5, we discussed the securities issued directly by the U.S. government known as Treasury bills, notes, and bonds. The payment of the interest and principal at maturity on these bonds is a direct obligation of the U.S. Treasury. Here we will discuss another type of bond in which the U.S. Treasury's obligation is indirect.

To accomplish its economic objectives, Congress over the years has established various federal agencies. These agencies are then authorized to issue bonds to finance their activities. The major agencies that issue bonds include: Federal Home Loan Banks, Federal Home Loan Mortgage Corporation, Federal National Mortgage Association, Farm Credit System, Student Loan Marketing Association, and the Tennessee Valley Authority. In some cases, the U.S. government guarantees agency debt. In other cases, many people treat agency debt as if the Treasury guaranteed it. Agency debt typically trades at prices just slightly lower than the prices at which comparable Treasury securities of the same maturities and coupon rates would trade. These slightly lower prices mean they provide rates of return just slightly higher than rates of return on comparable Treasury securities. The magnitude of agency bonds currently outstanding, by agency, may be found at **Web**

Web Link 13.4   **Link 13.4.** At the time of writing, there was about $1.3 trillion in agency debt outstanding. The two largest issuers were the Federal National Mortgage Association (FNMA) at $475.4 billion and the Federal Home Loan Banks at $402.4 billion.

Web Link 13.5   An overview of FNMA may be found at **Web Link 13.5.** Information on FNMA's
Web Link 13.5a   bonds may be found at **Web Link 13.5a.** Information on the Federal Home Loan Bank
Web Link 13.6   System is provided in **Web Link 13.6.**

WHAT ARE CORPORATE BONDS?

Corporate bonds are a major source of financing for many corporations. Corporate bonds have delinquency/default risk that ranges from minimal to extreme. Most corporate bond issues are not large enough to generate a substantial amount of daily trading activity. Thus, many corporate bonds may not be traded on a given day, and some corporate bond issues may have only one trade on a particular day. Hence, it is usually difficult to obtain quotes on corporate bonds.

Corporate bonds vary according to what kind of collateral is offered as security to the bondholder. The most basic collateral is a corporation's promise to pay principal and interest when due. Where no specific property or assets are pledged as collateral, such bonds are referred to as **debentures.** Holders of debentures would be general creditors if the company declared bankruptcy.

Bonds may also have specific property pledged as collateral. The most common type of this bond is the **mortgage bond.** Mortgage bonds work much like other mortgages; if the company enters bankruptcy, the assets pledged as collateral are sold and the proceeds used to pay off the mortgage bondholders. If the cash thus generated is insufficient to pay everything owed the bondholders, then they would become general creditors for the remaining amount.

Some bonds are known as **collateral trust bonds.** These bonds have other securities pledged as collateral. For example, suppose Company X owns 1 million shares of stock in Company Y. The stock currently trades at a price of $50 per share, making the holding worth $50 million ($50 per share × 1 million shares). Company X might issue $25 million worth of collateral trust bonds, pledging Company Y's stock as collateral. If Company X were to enter bankruptcy, then the stock would be sold and used to pay off the bondholders.

Some corporate bonds are **convertible,** in which case the bonds can be converted into other securities, usually the common stock of the company that has issued the bonds. We will discuss the mathematics of convertible bonds later.

Every corporate bond issue has associated with it an **indenture** and a **trustee.** The indenture is the legal document (actually a book) that defines both the obligations of the firm issuing the bond and the protections given to the bondholders. For example, an indenture promises that the company will pay the interest and principal when due. If property is pledged as collateral, the indenture requires that the property will not be sold without paying off the bondholders. The indenture also contains promises that the company will be managed in a manner that preserves and protects the interests of the bondholders. The indenture offers the legal grounds under which bondholders could sue a company in the event of failure to pay interest or to otherwise act as promised.

Few bonds would be sold if every prospective bondholder had to actually read the indenture. In addition, if every bondholder had to act on his or her own in taking legal action against a company, there would be little incentive to buy bonds. For these reasons, Congress passed the Trust Indenture Act of 1939, which, among other things, requires each bond issue to have a trustee who protects the interests of its bondholders. The trustee is paid by the issuer to monitor it, assuring that the terms of the indenture are constantly met

Web Link 13.7 and that actions are taken on behalf of the bondholders in case those terms are violated.

HOW DOES A BOND CALL WORK?

Nearly all bonds are **callable,** which means the issuer can buy back the bond issue at a predetermined price, known as a **call price.** The call price consists of par plus a **call premium.** The most common reason to buy back a bond issue is that a new set of bonds can be issued with a substantially lower coupon rate. Thus, bonds are called in and new bonds sold when the issuer can save a substantial amount of money in interest expenses. This saving to the company is invariably an opportunity loss for the investor.

WHAT ARE BOND RATINGS?

All publicly issued bonds and some privately issued bonds must be **rated** as to their quality. Quality in this case refers to a bond's delinquency/default risk. Quality also refers to the protection afforded to the investors in a particular issue. In order to have a bond issue rated, the prospective issuer applies for a rating from one or more of the bond rating firms. Although the issuer pays for its rating, suggesting that bond ratings might be tilted in its favor, no evidence has ever surfaced that bond ratings are biased. Furthermore, strong evidence shows that bond ratings are internally consistent. For information on bond defaults, see **Web Link 13.8.**

Web Link 13.8

Web Link 13.9

Web Link 13.10

The four well-established bond-rating firms in the United States are Standard & Poor's (S&P), Moody's, Duff & Phelps, and Fitch IBCA. Each rating agency has its own set of ratings, but let us focus on those issued by the largest two agencies, Moody's and S&P.

S&P's top rating is AAA. This rating means there is virtually no doubt that a firm will pay its obligations when due. The lower ratings are AA, A, BBB, BB, B, CCC, CC, C, and D. The CC rating signifies great uncertainty as to the continuation of payments. The C rating is used only in special situations. The D rating is used for firms who have missed one or more payments or are in bankruptcy. The exception to the assignment of a D for a missed payment is if the firm is still within the grace period allowed under its indenture and S&P believes the payment will be made. The BBB rating represents what is considered adequate investor protection. Ratings worse than BBB are considered speculative. S&P also adds a plus sign (+) or a minus sign (–) to ratings from AA to CCC to indicate ranking within the general category. Thus, there would be much less difference in quality between a B- bond and a CCC+ bond, than between a B and a CCC bond. Duff and Phelps uses the same scheme as S&P.

Web Link (WSJ) 13.11

Moody's ratings employ a slightly different coding scheme. The highest rating Moody's gives is Aaa. Its lowest rating is C. The dividing line between investment grade bonds and speculative bonds is Baa. Instead of pluses and minuses, Moody's adds the numbers 1, 2, or 3 within each rating category. For example, a bond rated Baa1 is considered among the strongest bonds within the Baa category. A chart comparing the ratings of different agencies is provided at **Web Link (WSJ) 13.11.**

SHOULD AN INVESTOR RELY ON BOND RATINGS?

For investors planning to acquire bonds, it is important to understand what bond ratings do and don't provide. Bond ratings do provide an excellent indication of default risk. However, just as the financial strength of a company can change over time for better or worse, so can its bond ratings change. Rating agencies raise or lower bond ratings as they see fit. However, research has shown that changes in bond ratings follow price changes rather than precede them. Thus, if a company's financial strength has deteriorated, the prices of its bonds will usually have already fallen to reflect the new rating at the time the change is formally announced. In other words, announcements of bond rating changes are like announcing that a barn door gate is open after the horse has run off.

Occasionally, the ratings agencies' estimates do not concur. Thus, S&P might rate a bond as BBB while Moody's gives it an A rating. Such ratings differences are relatively rare, but they do occur.

HOW CAN INVESTORS LEARN THE RATING OF A PARTICULAR BOND ISSUE?

To obtain a particular bond rating, you usually must go to a library and look up a company ratings manual at the reference desk because most of the rating agencies currently do not provide ratings over the Internet. The exception is Duff & Phelps. Consider the following example:

> Glenn Pettengill is thinking about buying some General Motors bonds. He would like an indication of their rating. How might he obtain such a rating?

Web Link 13.12

Glenn should go to Duff & Phelps' website at **Web Link 13.12,** where he can enter the company name of General Motors and click on *search.* At the time of writing, four choices appeared, one of which is General Motors Corporation. If Glenn clicks on the GM link, he will find that its notes/debentures have been rated A– since December 20, 1991. Although this is not the greatest rating in the world, it is still a solid investment grade rating.

WHAT DETERMINES THE PRICE OF A BOND?

A bond typically consists of two sets of cash flows. The first is the series of interest or coupon payments. These payments constitute an annuity. For example, consider a bond that has a 10 percent coupon rate, matures in 12 years, and pays interest semiannually. The interest payments are providing a 24-period $50 annuity, where a period lasts six months.

The second cash flow is the principal that is paid at maturity. In the previous example, the principal would be $1,000, due in 12 years. To price the bond, a person would need to decide what rate of return would be appropriate to justify investment in that bond. The rate of return that would be required includes compensation for the bond's level of risk.

To price the bond, compute the present value of the coupon payments and the present value of the principal repayment, using the required rate of return as the discount rate.

Then add these two answers together to produce what you believe the value of the bond to be. This figure is the maximum price you would pay for this bond.

Web Link 13.13a

In equation format:

$$P_B = \text{Coupon Payment} \times \text{PVIFA}_{r,n} + \text{Par} \times \text{PVIF}_{r,n} \qquad (13\text{-}1)$$

where

P_B = price of the bond today based on the investor's estimate of r

r = the required rate of return based on the investor's estimate of the bond's riskiness

Par = Maturity value of the bond (e.g., $1,000 usually)

$\text{PVIFA}_{r,n}$ = present value interest factor of annuity based on r and n

$\text{PVIF}_{r,n}$ = present value factor based on r and n

n = maturity of the bond

Consider the following example:

> *Glenn Pettengill is considering buying some bonds of the LDP Corporation to help finance his children's education. The bonds have a $1,000 par value, mature exactly 15 years from today, and have an 8 percent coupon rate with interest paid semiannually. He would require at least a 10 percent rate of return to buy these bonds. How much would he be willing to pay for each bond?*

Using the above equation:

$$P_B = \$80 \times \text{PVIFA}_{r,n} + \$1,000 \times \text{PVIF}_{r,n}$$

Before you find the solution, note that this equation is slightly misleading. Virtually all bonds pay interest semiannually rather than annually. Therefore, the annuity represented by the coupon in this example is actually a $40 annuity that runs for 30 periods, where a period is six months. Thus, the discount rate should be the six-month rate rather than the annual rate. If you solve the problem using the $80 annuity payment, the 10 percent discount rate, and a time horizon of 15 periods, you will obtain a slightly incorrect answer. Nearly all the calculators on the Internet automatically take this adjustment into consideration. In fact, some of the bond-pricing calculators actually ask the user to specify whether the interest is paid annually or semiannually. For simplicity's sake, we will discuss bonds as if interest is paid annually, but do the calculations using the semiannual assumption.

Web Link 13.13

The correct answer (with semiannual interest payments) is $846. Note that if you use any of the "calcbuilder" links, then enter both the *yield to maturity* and *today's market rate* as 10 percent, the *coupon rate* as 8 percent, the *face value* (i.e., par) as $1,000, and the *months until maturity* as 180 (i.e., 15 years). Note the payment frequency as semiannual, and click *results*. The answer is shown as dollars per $100 of par value. For simplicity, just think of the answer as if it were a percentage of par, even though it is shown in dollar terms rather than percentage terms.

WHAT IS THE "YIELD TO MATURITY"?

In the example above, the term **yield to maturity** was used in lieu of the term "required rate of return," but technically these two terms are not the same. The required rate of return, as described in the previous section, is the minimum rate an investor believes he or she must achieve to justify investing in that security. It is thus used as a discount rate to ascertain the maximum price the investor would pay for that security. In equilibrium, the required rate of return equals the yield to maturity, so many people use the terms interchangeably. The yield to maturity is the rate of return an investor could expect if he or she bought a bond at today's price, held it to maturity, and the company paid all promised payments when due. If the yield to maturity is 9 percent and the required rate of return is 8 percent, then the bond is a good deal, because it promises a higher rate of return than the investor requires. Conversely, if the yield to maturity is 7 percent and the required rate of return is 8 percent, then the bond is a poor investment. For a discussion about the relationship between a bond's price and its yield to maturity, see **Web Link (WSJ) 13.14.**

Web Link (WSJ) 13.14

HOW DO INVESTORS DETERMINE THE YIELD TO MATURITY ON A PARTICULAR BOND?

The yield to maturity number can be found using equation 13-1, except that now we know the price of the bond and we want to find the discount rate. In mathematical terms (i.e., substituting the mathematical expression for the present value terms), we would need to solve the following equation for r:[1]

$$P_B = \text{Coupon Payment} \times [(1 - (1 / (1 + r)^n)) / r] + \text{Par} \times [1 / (1 + r)^n] \qquad (13\text{-}2)$$

In the case of the bond used in the previous example, we could substitute the following known values:

$$\$846.28 = \$80 \times [(1 - (1 / (1 + r)^{15})) / r] + \$1{,}000 \times [1 / (1 + r)^{15}] \qquad (13\text{-}2)$$

This equation cannot be explicitly solved for r. Thus, any calculator solution is based on a trial and error process. To show how this works, let's take the previous problem and work it in reverse:

> *Glenn Pettengill is considering buying some bonds of the LDP Corporation to help finance his children's education. The bonds have a $1,000 par value, mature exactly 15 years from today, and have an 8 percent coupon rate with interest paid semiannually. They trade at a price of $846.28. What is the yield to maturity on these bonds?*

Web Link 13.15

By using any of the calculators at **Web Link 13.15,** we find the solution is 10 percent.

[1]Keep in mind that this equation is presented in terms of annual coupon payments for simplicity's sake, even though bond interest is paid semiannually.

HOW IS THE ACCRUED INTEREST ON BONDS COMPUTED?

When bonds are traded, prices are simplified by adjusting for accrued interest. If bonds were not traded with accrued interest, each time a bond's issuer paid a semiannual interest payment, the price of the bond would decline dramatically, presumably equal to the amount of interest paid. Bond investors would need to know the interest payment dates of the bonds in which they were investing.

The accrued interest payment included in bond trades is based on a pro-rating of the semiannual interest payment. Consider the following example:

> *Glenn Pettengill is considering buying some bonds of the LDP Corporation to help finance his children's education. The bonds have a $1,000 par value, mature on October 1, 2020, and have an 8 percent coupon rate with interest paid semiannually. If today's date is August 14, 2001, how much accrued interest will Glenn owe if he buys the bond today?*

The interest payment dates are normally set at six-month intervals, with the last interest payment being paid on the day a bond matures. Thus, if the LDP bond matures on October 1, then the other interest payment date is April 1. There are 183 days from April 1 to October 1, inclusive. In nonleap years there are 182 days between October 2 and April 1. August 14 is the 135th day after April 1. The coupon payment on October 1 would be $40 (i.e., one-half the annual coupon payment of $80). Thus, Glenn would owe accrued interest of $29.51 ($40 × [135 / 183]). If Glenn still owns this bond on October 1, he will receive the full $40 coupon payment. Of this, $29.51 reimburses him for the accrued interest he paid when he bought the bond, and the remaining $10.49 ($40 – $29.51) is the interest he has earned between August 14 and October 1. The accrued interest calculation is made by the exchange where the bond is traded.

Web Link 13.16

If a company is delinquent on its interest payments, then the accrued interest adjustment is not used. In fact, when a bond trades without accrued interest, it is said to be trading flat. Newspaper quotations for such a bond usually carry the letter *f* next to the company's name.

HOW DO INVESTORS DETERMINE THE CURRENT YIELD ON A BOND?

The current yield on a bond is the annual interest payment divided by the current market price of the bond. As the annual interest payment does not change (unless the company defaults on an interest payment), any changes in the current yield on a bond would be due to changes in the market price. Consider the following example:

> *Glenn Pettengill is considering buying some LDP bonds. The bonds have a $1,000 par value, mature in 15 years, and have an 8 percent coupon rate with interest paid semiannually. If the current price of the bond is $846.28, what is its current yield?*

Web Link 13.17   The current yield is 9.45 percent ($80 / $846.28).

WHAT IS THE RELATIONSHIP BETWEEN COUPON YIELD, CURRENT YIELD, AND YIELD TO MATURITY?

We have now discussed three different measures of yields on a bond. The coupon yield is a purely descriptive measure that equals the annual interest payment divided by the par value of the bond. The current yield is more meaningful, in that it reveals the relationship between the promised coupon payment and the current price. The current yield would be an investor's rate of return if the price of the bond were not to change. However, bond prices do change, usually every trading day. The yield to maturity reflects the effective rate of return an investor would receive if the bond were bought at today's price and held until maturity.

The coupon yield is independent of the price of the bond. If a bond trades at a **discount** (i.e., at a price less than par), then the yield to maturity is greater than the current yield, which in turn is greater than the coupon yield. If a bond trades at a premium, then the coupon yield is greater than the current yield, which in turn is greater than the yield to maturity. If the bond trades at a price equal to par, then all three of these yields are equal. To see an example of these relationships, consider the following:

> *Glenn is thinking about purchasing some LDP bonds. Glenn is interested in what the various yields on these bonds would be if the market rate of interest on comparable bonds (i.e., the appropriate discount rate) were 6 percent, 8 percent, and 10 percent. These bonds have an 8 percent coupon rate and 15 years to maturity.*

Web Link 13.13

Regardless of the market rate, the coupon yield is, of course, 8 percent. The market rate of interest is, by definition, the yield to maturity. To obtain the current yields, we need to compute the price of the bonds under each of the three yields to maturity. Using any of the calculators at **Web Link 13.13,** we obtain prices of $1,196.30, $1,000, and $846.80. These prices produce current yields of 6.69 percent ($80 / $1,196.30), 8 percent ($80 / $1,000), and 9.45 percent ($80 / $846.80). Thus, when this bond trades at a discount (i.e., at a price of 84.68), the yield to maturity (10 percent) is greater than the current yield (9.45 percent), which in turn is greater than the coupon yield (8 percent). When this bond trades at a premium (e.g., 119.63), the coupon yield (8 percent) is greater than the current yield (6.69 percent), which in turn is greater than the yield to maturity (6 percent). When the bond trades at par (e.g., 100), all three yields are the same (8 percent).

WHICH YIELD SHOULD AN INVESTOR USE IN DECIDING TO BUY OR SELL A BOND?

At this point, it is appropriate to stop and ponder the question of which yield an investor should primarily focus on when making decisions about buying and selling bonds. With a few exceptions, the most important yield to an investor is the yield to maturity. This is the most comprehensive measure of the prospective rate of return, and also the least speculative.

Sometimes the current yield is useful, such as when the investor is using a portfolio to pay for current living expenses and wants to be assured of a fixed amount of income without having to sell any securities. He or she might want the portfolio to provide a minimum current yield. Consider the following example:

> *Glenn Pettengill is 75 years old. He has social security income of $1,500 per month and pension income of $1,000 per month. He wants another $2,500 per month in income. He has $600,000 in an investment portfolio that he wants to invest in bonds. What is the minimum current yield he needs from this portfolio?*

First, the monthly income needed must be converted to an annual figure. In this case, the $2,500 per month equates to $30,000 ($2,500 × 12) per year. If we divide the $30,000 in minimum income needed by the $600,000 in his investment portfolio, we find that the portfolio needs to provide a current yield of at least 5 percent ($2,500 / $50,000). This does not mean that every single bond must have a current yield of 5 percent, but that the weighted average of the current yields must be 5 percent, where the weights are based on market values. In this situation, Glenn would clearly prefer to buy bonds with the highest possible yield to maturity, so long as the portfolio maintains a current yield of at least 5 percent and the bonds do not exceed appropriate risk levels.

HOW WILL INTEREST RATE CHANGES AFFECT MY BOND'S CURRENT VALUE?

A major concern of bond investors is interest rate risk. Whenever the general level of interest rates change, the prices of most bonds adjust accordingly. If interest rates fall, bond prices rise, and if interest rates rise, bond prices fall. Although this formulation sounds like a cause and effect statement, it is actually a tautology, because bond prices are defined by interest rates and interest rates are defined by bond prices.

Previous sections of this chapter showed how to compute a bond price by selecting an appropriate discount rate. Next, given a bond price, yield to maturity was determined. When we talk about interest rates, we are talking about yields to maturity. Thus, when one says interest rates have gone up, one is simultaneously saying that bond prices have gone down and vice versa. Likewise, when one says bond prices have gone up, one is simultaneously saying that interest rates have gone down and vice versa. A change in the bond prices caused by a change in the level of interest rates is known as **price risk.**

Having said this, let us note that not all bond prices change by the same dollar amount or percentage amount when interest rates change. That is, price risk varies among bonds. Thus, when an investor looks to buy a bond, although it is important to focus on expected return (i.e., the yield to maturity) and default risk (a bond's rating), it is also important to understand a bond's price risk. One way to think about price risk is to measure how much a bond's price changes when interest rates change. Consider the following example:

> *Glenn is looking at two corporate bonds. Both have an 8 percent coupon rate, a yield to maturity of 8 percent, both are rated BBB (or Baa), and both have a par value of $1,000. The only significant difference among the bonds is that the first has a five-year maturity and the other has a 25-year maturity. Glenn would like to get a sense of the price risk exposure of the two bonds. That is, if interest rates were to rise or fall by one percentage point (i.e., up to 9 percent or down to 7 percent), what would be the percentage price change of each bond?*

The first step is to compute the current prices of both bonds. In this case, no calculations are necessary because one of the first rules of bond pricing is that whenever the coupon rate equals the yield to maturity, the price of the bond will equal par regardless of any other features of the bond. Thus, both bonds must have a current price of $1,000. Using the calculators at **Web Link 13.13** to find the other four prices, we find:

	Term to Maturity	
	5 yrs.	25 yrs.
YTM = 7%	104.27	111.70
YTM = 9%	95.96	90.15

Because the current price of both bonds is 100, we can easily compute the percentage change in the prices of the bonds if interest rates change by one percentage point. The price of the five-year bond goes up 4.27 percent and down 4.04 percent if interest rates (i.e., the yields to maturity on comparable bonds) fall or rise by one percentage point. For the 25-year bond, the percentage changes in the bond price are plus 11.70 percent and minus 9.85 percent. In effect, the 25-year bond has slightly more than double the price risk exposure than the 5-year bond.

WHAT IS THE DURATION STATISTIC FOR A PARTICULAR BOND?

Computing the sensitivity to changes in interest rates is clearly important, but it is also cumbersome if the investor has to compute the prospective percentage price changes for each bond. A statistic useful in describing a bond's exposure to price risk is known as the **duration statistic.** The duration statistic is beyond the scope of this discussion, but an excellent introduction to it may be found at **Web Link 13.20.** The derivation of the duration statistic may be found at **Web Link 13.21.**

Web Link 13.20
Web Link 13.21

The duration statistic can be thought of as an *index* of potential bond price changes. The larger the duration statistic, the more a bond's price will fluctuate as interest rates change. Thus, if one bond has a duration statistic of 6.0 and another bond has a duration statistic of 3.0, the first will undergo roughly double the percentage change in its price when interest rates change. The point here is that just as you can check out a bond's default risk by looking up its quality rating, you can check its price risk by looking up its duration.

WHAT IS A ZERO-COUPON BOND?

Web Link 13.22

One choice available to bond investors today is known as **zero-coupon bonds.** These bonds literally have no coupon payment. They are bought at a discount from par and the investor receives par at maturity. The U.S. Treasury, governmental agencies, municipalities, and corporations issue zero-coupon bonds. In addition, some investment firms will acquire normal coupon-paying Treasury bonds and separate the coupon payments from the bond itself. They sell one set of receipts that are claims on the par value of the bonds, and another set of receipts that are claims on the coupon payments. The receipts for the par values are for all practical purposes zero-coupon Treasury bonds.

A tricky aspect to investing in a zero-coupon bond is that each year the investor still technically receives interest, known as **imputed interest.** Imputed interest is an interest expense the issuing corporation is allowed to take, and the bond investor is required to report, even though no cash actually changes hands.

Zero-coupon bonds have two disadvantages. First, imputed interest income must be declared as taxable income each year, but the investor receives no cash with which to pay the taxes. For this reason, many investors buy zero-coupon bonds only in tax-sheltered accounts such as IRAs (these are discussed in Chapter 17). The second major disadvantage of zero-coupon bonds is that these bonds have the maximum amount of price risk for bonds of comparable maturity. The duration statistic for a zero-coupon bond is equal to its maturity. Thus, the duration statistic for a 15-year zero-coupon bond is 15. The duration statistic for a 30-year bond with a 6 percent coupon rate, annual interest payments, and a 6 percent yield to maturity is 14.59. In other words, a 15-year zero-coupon bond has more price risk than a 30-year coupon bond! Normally, the longer the term to maturity, the larger the duration statistic and the higher the price risk is.

However, zero-coupon Treasury securities have one major advantage. If the investor plans to hold these bonds to maturity, he or she has perfect certainty as to the maturity value. Consider the following example:

Glenn Pettengill has a 3-year-old daughter. He would like to guarantee that some cash is available to help pay for her college education in 15 years. He could buy a $10,000 par value zero-coupon Treasury bond. The yield to maturity is 8 percent. How much would Glenn have to pay for the bond today, and how much cash would he have at maturity?

Web Link 13.23

The price he would have to pay is the present value of $10,000 in 15 years, discounted at 8 percent, or $3,152. In 15 years, Glenn's daughter could be perfectly certain of having $10,000 to help fund her college expenses.

WHAT ARE CONVERTIBLE BONDS?

Convertible bonds are bonds that can be exchanged into other securities, usually common stock. The exchange is always at the request of the bondholder. The number of shares of common stock that will be received upon exchange is called the **conversion ratio,** which is defined in the indenture when the firm initially issues the bonds. At any point in time, multiplying the current price of the firm's common stock by the conversion ratio gives you the **conversion value.**

The market price of a convertible bond will never be lower than its conversion value; otherwise, investors would immediately convert their bonds, sell the stock, and then use the proceeds to buy more of these bonds—a process that would continue until the stock price fell or the bond price at least equaled the conversion value. Because the interest income on a convertible bond is normally greater than the dividend income that would be derived from holding the shares received upon conversion, the convertible bond, with rare exceptions, trades at a premium to the conversion value. The difference between the price of a convertible bond and its conversion value is known as the **conversion premium.** If this difference is divided by the conversion value, the ratio is known as the **conversion premium percentage.**

Some sources of information on bonds provide not the conversion ratio but another number known as the **conversion price.** The conversion price is the dollar's worth of par the investor must give up for each share of stock received upon conversion. The conversion ratio and the conversion price are two different ways of saying the same thing. In equation form:

$$\text{Conversion price} = \text{Par} / \text{Conversion ratio, and}$$

$$\text{Conversion ratio} = \text{Par} / \text{Conversion price.}$$

Consider the following example:

> *Glenn Pettengill is looking at the Hilton Hotel convertible bond. The coupon rate is 5 percent, the bond matures in the year 2006, and it has a par value of $1,000. The bond converts into 45.1154 shares of common stock. On October 27, 1999, the common stock closed at $8.75 and the bond closed at a price of $77.316 (i.e., $773.16). What are its conversion price, conversion value, conversion premium, and conversion premium percentage?*

The conversion price is $22.16 $\frac{1}{2}$ ($1,000 par value / 45.1154 conversion ratio). The conversion value is $394.76 (45.1154 conversion ratio × $8.75 price of common stock). The conversion premium is $378.40 ($773.16 price of bond – $394.76 conversion value). The conversion premium percentage is 95.86 percent ($378.40 conversion premium / $394.76 conversion value). [See **Web Link 13.24** for the current price of this bond.]

Web Link 13.24

In this example, the conversion premium percentage of 95.86 tells us that the price of the common stock would have to rise by 95.86 percent to have the conversion value equal the price of the bond—an extremely large rise. Therefore, the conversion feature in this bond currently carries little value for the investor. The bond's attractiveness lies primarily in the coupon payments and the par value at maturity.

It is important to think about how convertible bonds would fit into an investor's portfolio. On average, convertible bonds provide rates of return greater than those provided by **straight** bonds from the same firms. A straight bond is any bond without the convertibility feature. However, on average convertible bonds provide investors with lower rates of return than what they could get by owning the common stocks of the same firms. Convertible bonds are less risky than owning common stock, but more risky than owning straight bonds from the same firms, an attractive feature for someone who wants less risk than that of common stocks, but who does not want to add straight bonds to his or her portfolio.

Web Link 13.25

WHAT ARE MUNICIPAL BONDS?

In the bond markets, the term **municipal bond** is used to describe any bond issued by a government or governmental agency other than the federal government and its agencies. Thus, a city, county, state, park district, and so on could issue a municipal bond. The key feature to *all* bonds issued by any government entity is that they are exempt from taxation by higher or lower government entities. For example, the interest income from bonds issued by the federal government (e.g., Treasury securities and savings bonds) is exempt from taxation by state and local governments. Likewise, the interest income from municipal bonds is exempt from federal taxation. Because federal income taxes are substantially greater than state and local income taxes, it is municipal bonds that are referred to as **tax exempt.**

Of course, municipal governments may tax the interest income on their own bonds (although many do not), and the federal government certainly taxes the interest income on its own bonds. Municipalities also tax each other's interest income. Thus, a resident of New York who owns a bond issued by the state of New York is exempt from both federal and state income taxes on its interest. However, if that resident moves to New Jersey, then the interest on the New York bonds suddenly becomes taxable income on the state of New Jersey tax return. Tax exemption applies only to the interest income from these bonds; any capital gains achieved when these bonds are sold are taxed by all tax authorities.

There are two general types of municipal bonds: **general obligation bonds** (GOs) and **revenue bonds.** The full taxing authority of whatever municipality issued the bond supports a general obligation bond. Thus, a state of New York GO bond is supported by the ability of the New York state government to tax the citizens of New York whatever is necessary to assure that the interest and principal payments are paid. A revenue bond is issued to finance a particular project. The revenues from the project are pledged to guarantee payment of interest and principal. For example, if the state were to build a toll road and finance it with revenue bonds, then the tolls collected are pledged as collateral for the bonds. In most circumstances, GOs are much less risky than revenue bonds. As such, GOs

Web Link 13.26

typically have lower yields than do revenue bonds.

Because of the tax-exempt feature on municipals, investors interested in bonds need to choose between taxable and tax-exempt bonds. This decision makes sense only if the bonds are considered of equal riskiness. Thus, a comparison of the income from a taxable Treasury bond with the income from a revenue bond where the underlying project is in financial difficulty is misleading at best, if not downright fraudulent. The basic formula for

Web Link 13.27

comparing taxable and tax-exempt bonds is either to convert the taxable interest to an after-tax value, or to convert the tax-exempt interest to a pre-tax equivalent. Let us use the first approach. The after-tax value of taxable interest is the coupon rate times one minus the federal tax rate. Consider the following example:

Glenn Pettengill is looking to buy either a 10-year Treasury bond with a coupon rate of 8 percent, or a 5.5 percent GO municipal bond issued by the State of Kansas. As Kansas enjoys an AAA rating, Glenn considers the risks of the bonds to be equal. Both bonds trade at par value. Glenn is in the 28 percent federal tax bracket. Which bond should he buy?

On an after-tax basis, the federal government bond is paying 5.76 percent ($8\% \times [1 - .28]$). This is still more than the municipal bond, which pays 5.5 percent. Hence, in this example the Treasury bond is preferable. Note that we have implicitly assumed in this problem that the interest income on both bonds is treated identically on Glenn's state tax return. If this were not the case, then another computation would be necessary.

WHERE CAN I OBTAIN QUOTES ON BONDS?

Bond quotes are more difficult to obtain than stock quotes on the Internet because most corporate bond issues do not have enough bonds outstanding to assure steady and active trading in them. In addition, bond investors are not as likely to want frequent access to prices as are stock investors. Nonetheless, some bond quotes are available on the Internet.

Web Link 13.27a
Web Link (WSJ) 13.28

A list of the previous day's prices on Treasury notes and bonds may be found at **Web Link (WSJ) 13.28.** See Figure 13.1. The first column provides the coupon rate for each bond. The second column provides the month and year of maturity for each bond. Where there is an *n* following the year of maturity, the security being quoted is technically a note rather than a bond. As was discussed in Chapter 5, there is no practical significance between a Treasury note and a Treasury bond. Some notes and bonds mature in the same month and year but this does not necessarily mean they mature on the same day. Nearly all bond issues mature on either the first, the fifteenth, or the last day of the month—information not listed here. An investor wanting to know the specific day an issue matures would have to use other resources. The next two columns are the bid and asked prices. As will be discussed in more detail in Chapter 16, the bid price is what an investor could get if he or she wanted to sell the bond, and the asked price is what he or she would have to pay to buy it. As with all bond quotations, the price should be viewed as a percentage of par. The part after the colon symbol stands for 32nds. Hence, the first asked price in Figure 13.1, 100:02, should be read as 100 and $2/32$ percent of par. If par were $1,000, then

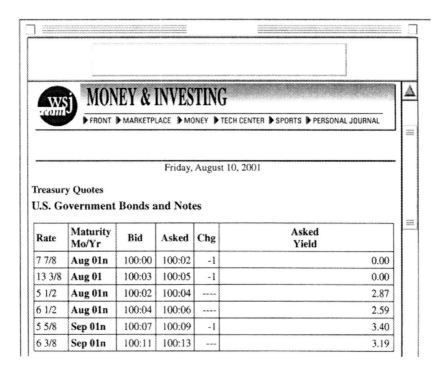

Rate	Maturity Mo/Yr	Bid	Asked	Chg	Asked Yield
7 7/8	Aug 01n	100:00	100:02	-1	0.00
13 3/8	Aug 01	100:03	100:05	-1	0.00
5 1/2	Aug 01n	100:02	100:04	----	2.87
6 1/2	Aug 01n	100:04	100:06	----	2.59
5 5/8	Sep 01n	100:07	100:09	-1	3.40
6 3/8	Sep 01n	100:11	100:13	---	3.19

FIGURE 13-1 Treasury Quotations

the actual asked price of this bond would be $1,000.625 (100 $^2/_{32}$ × $1,000). The next to last column shows how much the asked price changed since the previous trading day. For the first bond listed in Figure 13.1, there was no change in the closing asked price from the previous day. The last column shows an approximation of the yield to maturity for each bond based on the asked price.

If you look down the Change column, you will notice that direction of most of the changes in asked prices is the same. In Figure 13.1, most of the price changes are positive, which indicates that on this day bond prices were up and thus interest rates were down. When most or all of the changes are negative, bond prices have dropped and thus interest rates have risen.

Web Link 13.28a
Web Link 13.29
An alternative set of closing price quotations for all of the Treasury notes and bonds (as well as STRIPS) is at **Web Link 13.28a.** The advantage of this site over the *Wall Street Journal* site is that it includes the day of the month in which the various bonds mature.

Instead of looking at all the quotes, an investor may want to focus on a few bonds that meet one or more specific criteria. Consider the following problem:

> *Glenn Pettengill is interested in buying some Treasury bonds. He would like to obtain some price quotes and yields to maturity. He wants bonds with maturities of no less than 10 years and no more than 30 years. He would like a coupon rate of not less than 7 percent, and a yield to maturity of not less than 6 percent. As he is seeking a bond with a coupon rate greater than the desired yield to maturity, he knows such a bond will trade at a premium. Thus, he is willing to pay a price of at least 100 ($1,000). How many bonds meet these criteria?*

Web Link 13.30
A visit to **Web Link 13.30** turns up a list of 35 Treasury bonds that meet these criteria at the time of writing. On the selection table, you may enter only those values noted in the problem. Thus, for coupon rate, enter a minimum value of 7 percent, as a maximum value is optional.

Web Link 13.31
To obtain quotes on corporate bonds that meet specific criteria, use **Web Link 13.31.** Consider the following example:

> *Glenn Pettengill is interested in buying some corporate bonds. He would like to obtain some price quotes and yields to maturity. He wants bonds with maturities of no less than 10 years and no more than 30 years. He prefers a minimum rating of BB (a.k.a. Ba) and a maximum rating of A. He would like a coupon rate of not less than 7 percent, and a yield to maturity of not less than 6 percent. As he is seeking a bond with a coupon rate greater than the desired yield to maturity, he knows such a bond will trade at a premium. Thus, he is willing to pay a price of at least 100 ($1,000). He has no preference as to industry group, except that he is not interested in government agency bonds. How many bonds meet these criteria?*

At the time of this writing, 62 bonds were listed that met these criteria. If the user clicks on the company name for any of these bonds, additional details for that issue can be seen. At **Web Link 13.31,** you may also obtain bond quotes on municipal and zero-coupon Treasury bonds.

HOW CAN I GET A QUICK
GLANCE AT THE BOND MARKET?

**Web Link
(WSJ) 13.32**

Two techniques can help you get a general feel for what is happening in the bond market. One is just to look at how some of the bond indices are doing, and the other is to look at what is happening to yields on selected securities. Let's consider each of these.

Web Link (WSJ) 13.32 provides six Treasury bond indices, five corporate bond indices, four municipal bond indices, four indices for mortgage-backed securities, and two broad market indices. Information from this site is provided in Figure 13.2. Multiple bond indices exist for several reasons. First, there can be differences in what is happening in each of the various bond markets. Second, although all bond prices tend to move together, not all bond prices move in perfect synchronization. Credit markets are generally divided into three broad ranges based on maturities: short-term, intermediate-term, and long-term bonds. Short-term means one year or less, intermediate-term generally ranges anywhere from one to ten years, and long-term is considered more than ten years. Often, bond prices in one of these markets may move one direction while those in the other markets remain unchanged or move in the other direction. To truly follow bond prices, you need all of these indices to get a complete sense of what is happening.

**Web Link
(WSJ) 13.33**

Yields on selected securities may be found at **Web Link (WSJ) 13.33.** Tables such as these give a quick overview, but obviously will lack the detail that looking at a variety of bond indices will provide.

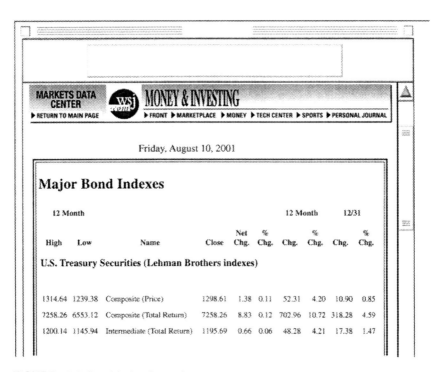

FIGURE 13-2 Bond Index Quotations

WHAT ARE SOME STRATEGIES FOR INVESTING IN BONDS?

Investors who wish to hold all or a significant part of their investment portfolios in bonds can choose from a variety of strategies depending on the goal sought. For example, if an investor desires a high degree of liquidity, then the optimal strategy is to buy mostly short-term and intermediate-term Treasury notes and bonds. If the investment objective is to escape high rates of taxation, then the investor should focus primarily on acquiring tax-exempt bonds. If corporate bonds are to be a part of the portfolio, then the investor must decide how much of a default risk he or she can tolerate in the portfolio. If the objective of the bond portfolio were to provide cash at specific points of time in the future, then zero-coupon bonds would be highly desirable.

Because maturity is the primary factor in price risk (which is best measured by the duration statistic, described earlier), an investor needs to keep it in mind. The maturity of bonds in a portfolio always contains an implicit bet on the direction of future interest rates. For example, if an investor believes interest rates will fall, then the maximum price appreciation comes from holding bonds with long maturities (i.e., large durations). Conversely, if the investor believes interest rates are going to rise, then the least loss would be from bonds with short maturities (i.e., small durations).

A neutral strategy regarding future interest rate movements is a **bond ladder,** in which the bond maturities are evenly spaced out over some selected time horizon. Consider the following example:

> *Glenn Pettengill has $200,000 to invest in bonds. He does not want to bet incorrectly on interest rate movements, so he would like to take a neutral position. At this time, he does not want the maturity of any bonds to exceed 20 years. How can he evenly distribute the maturity allocation of his portfolio?*

In this case, a bond ladder is clearly appropriate. Several bond ladders could be constructed. The simplest one would be to divide his portfolio into 20 segments with maturities spread equally over the 20 years. Thus, he could put $10,000 into bonds that mature in one year, another $10,000 into bonds that mature in two years, and so forth. The final $10,000 would be placed in bonds that mature in 20 years. As each segment matures, it could be reinvested in a new segment of 20-year bonds. In this way, the bond portfolio is kept evenly spread over a 20-year period horizon.

Another bond ladder would be to divide the portfolio into 10 segments and invest in bond maturities based on two-year intervals. Thus, the first $20,000 would be invested in 2-year bonds, the next $20,000 in 4-year bonds, and the last $20,000 in 20-year bonds. The intervals could also be 4 years, 5 years, and 10 years. All of these ladder portfolios take a neutral position, in effect saying, "I will accept whatever happens to interest rates." If rates go up, the investor can be glad when the first segment of the portfolio matures, because this cash can be reinvested at higher rates. If rates go down, the investor can be glad about the part of the portfolio that was invested in long-term bonds.

Bond investments lend themselves well to a process known as **tax swaps.** In a tax swap, an investor sells an investment on which he or she has sustained a loss so that the loss can be recognized for tax purposes, and buys another investment of nearly identical characteristics. Consider the following example:

Glenn Pettengill would like to own a long-term Treasury bond. He finds a bond that matures in May 2021 with a coupon rate of 8 ⅛ percent. He notes another Treasury bond that matures in August 2021 with a coupon rate of 8 ⅛ percent. The former has an asked price of 118:19 and the latter an asked price of 118:21. Both have an approximate yield to maturity of 6.51 percent. Suppose Glenn buys $10,000 worth of par of the first bond. If in the next few months interest rates rise sharply and the price on this bond falls to 90, what would be the savings to Glenn from a tax swap? Assume that short-term capital losses would be taxed at Glenn's marginal federal tax rate of 28 percent.

The asking price of 118:19 means that Glenn will have to pay $11,859.38 for $10,000 worth of par. If the price later falls to 90, then Glenn will receive only $9,000 for these bonds. This would mean a loss of $2,859.38 ($11,859.38 – $9,000). With a 28 percent tax bracket, Glenn would save $800.63 ($2,859.38 × 28%) on his federal tax return. In addition, the August bonds will presumably have fallen to almost exactly the same price because these two bonds are nearly identical. Glenn can take the proceeds from the sale and buy the August bonds. His coupon rate will be unaltered (as both carry the same coupon rate), as will his risk exposure because both bonds are Treasuries with almost identical maturities). In addition, Glenn has an $800 tax refund to spend as he sees fit. Discussions of tax swaps are provided at **Web Link 13.34.**

Web Link 13.34

You may wonder why Glenn doesn't just buy back the same bonds. The reason is what is known as the **wash rule.** The wash rule says that if the exact same security is repurchased within 30 days, the IRS treats it as if no sale had taken place. Thus, Glenn can recognize the loss for tax purposes only if he waits at least 30 days to repurchase the bonds—a risky move, because during that 30-day period the price of the bonds could rebound substantially, causing Glenn to lose in price appreciation what he gained in tax savings.

SUMMARY

➤ The two major philosophies of investing are the EMH and IMH. The major implication of the former is that investors should focus on the capital allocation decision and the appropriateness of a security for his or her portfolio. The major implication of the latter is that investors should focus on the security selection decision.

➤ The two major features of a bond are the par value that is paid to the bondholder at maturity, and the coupon payments provided every six months.

➤ Agency bonds are issued by federal agencies, corporate bonds by corporations, and municipal bonds by any governmental unit that is not federal.

➤ A bond call allows the issuer to buy back the bond at the call price, which equals par plus a call premium. Bond calls usually mean investors wish to reinvest their money at lower interest rates.

➤ The four major bond rating agencies are Standard & Poor's, Moody's, Duff & Phelps, and Fitch. The ratings give an unbiased opinion of the likelihood of delinquency or default on a bond.

➤ Accrued interest is based on the semiannual coupon payment and the number of days since the last coupon payment was made.

➤ The coupon rate is irrelevant to an investor. The current yield is of some importance to investors focusing on income, and the yield to maturity is the most important yield on a bond.

➤ The duration statistic is an index of a bond's price volatility.

➤ Zero-coupon bonds provide investors only with the par value at maturity. Zeros carry imputed interest income that could complicate your tax return. Convertible bonds can usually be converted into a company's common stock at the conversion ratio.

➤ Bond quotes are less widely available than stock quotes, but a few sites provide a number of quotations.

➤ The current performance of the bond markets (and, inversely, interest rates) can be gauged from bond indices or from looking at the net change in the prices of selected bonds.

➤ Bond investments lend themselves well to establishing precise guidelines of price risk (as measured via duration) and default risk (as measured by ratings). They also facilitate tax swaps.

KEY TERMS

baby bond	bond ladder	callable
call premium	call price	capital allocation decision
collateral trust bond	conversion premium	conversion premium percentage
conversion price	conversion ratio	conversion value
convertible	coupon rate	debenture
discount	duration statistic	efficient market hypothesis
flat	general obligation bond	imputed interest
indenture	inefficient market hypothesis	mortgage bond
municipal bond	price risk	rated
revenue bond	security selection decision	semi-strong form
straight	strong form	tax exempt
tax swap	trustee	wash rule
weak form	yield to maturity	zero-coupon bond

PROBLEMS

13.1 Rachel is 22 years old. She has started thinking about how she will plan for retirement. Most of her friends tell her she is silly to start saving now, as she has plenty of time later. Her friends say current contributions would be too small to be meaningful at retirement. She is thinking about investing $100 per month into a stock mutual fund. An alternative strategy is to wait 10 years and then invest $200 every month, or to wait 20 years and invest $400 every month. If she plans to retire at age 67 and she expects to be able to average a return of 9 percent over any investment period, which strategy will produce the largest portfolio at retirement?

13.2 Locate three bonds issued by three different government agencies. Compare their yields to maturity with those of three Treasury bonds of comparable maturities.

13.3 Obtain the names of three companies that currently have AAA bonds outstanding. What are the coupon rates, term to maturity, and yield to maturity of at least one bond issued by each company? Repeat the process using bonds that are rated BB are worse.

13.4 Compute the current yield and price for the following three bonds:
   a. a 10-year, 7 percent coupon bond with a yield to maturity of 5 percent.
   b. a 10-year, 7 percent coupon bond with a yield to maturity of 7 percent.
   c. a 10-year, 7 percent coupon bond with a yield to maturity of 9 percent.

13.5 Compute the current yield and the yield to maturity for the following three bonds:
   a. a 10-year, 7 percent coupon bond with a price of 80 (i.e., $800).
   b. a 10-year, 7 percent coupon bond with a price of 100 (i.e., $1,000).
   c. a 10-year, 7 percent coupon bond with a price of 120 (i.e., $1,200).

13.6 The IJK bond has an annual coupon rate of 9 percent. The bond currently trades for 85 (i.e., $850) and the last coupon payment was two months ago. If the brokerage commission were $10, how much would you have to pay out of pocket to buy the bond today?

13.7 R.J. sees some zero-coupon bonds that are trading for 20 (i.e., $200). They mature in 25 years. If he buys them today, what is his yield to maturity?

13.8 The LMN Corporation has outstanding some convertible bonds with a coupon rate of 7 percent, a term to maturity of 20 years, and a conversion price of $50. The market price of the common stock is $30 per share. The bonds trade at a price of 70 (i.e., $700). Compute the following values for the bond:
   a. conversion ratio
   b. conversion value
   c. conversion premium
   d. conversion premium percentage
   e. current yield
   f. yield to maturity

13.9 Using as a reference the closing prices on the day before your next class meeting, indicate what happened in the bond markets and provide some evidence to support your conclusions.

13.10 Alex would like to own a long-term Treasury bond. He finds a bond that matures in March 2025 with a coupon rate of 8 percent. He notes that there is another Treasury that matures in September 2025 with a coupon of 8 $\frac{1}{8}$ percent. The former has an asked price of 118:22 and the latter an asked price of 119:12. Suppose Alex buys $10,000 worth of par of the first bond. If in the next few months interest rates rise sharply and the price on this bond falls to 85, what would savings could Alex gain from a tax swap? Assume that short-term capital losses would be taxed at Alex's marginal federal tax rate of 28 percent.

REFERENCES

Web Link 13.35 FAQs for bonds
Web Link 13.36 Pointer sites for bonds
Web Link 13.37 Calculators for the holding period yield on a bond
Web Link 13.38 Calculators for the yield to call on a bond
Web Link 13.39 Inflation-indexed Treasury bonds
Web Link 13.40 Mortgage-backed securities
Web Link 13.41 Collateralized Mortgage Obligations

WALL STREET JOURNAL RESOURCES

Web Link (WSJ) 13.42   Where can I obtain current commentary on the bond market?

Web Link (WSJ) 13.43   Where are some glossaries on bond issues?

Web Link (WSJ) 13.44   A calculator that converts bond yields to prices and prices to bond yields

Web Link (WSJ) 13.45   "Bond-Market Diversification Is an Option for 'Chickens'," *The Wall Street Journal Interactive Edition,* July 24, 2001

For information that has changed since the book was written, for new information that pertains to this topic, and for some new web sites that pertain to the topic of this chapter, see **Web Link 13.46.**

CHAPTER 14

COMMON STOCK AND RELATED SECURITIES

LEARNING OBJECTIVES

- Explain what common stock represents
- Describe the role of a Board of Directors
- Discuss the voting process at an annual meeting
- Explain why the payment of dividends is not crucial to an investor
- Indicate why forward and reverse stock splits and stock dividends are usually meaningless
- Value a share of stock using a simple dividend growth model
- Find information about a stock's value and information about a company on the Internet
- Evaluate tolerance for risk
- Compute the degree of diversification of a portfolio
- Define a methodology for selecting stocks in which to invest
- Understand what is meant by the different types of stocks
- Describe the concept of classes of stock
- Define the differences between preferred and common stock
- Describe rights, warrants, and put and call options

Web Link: www.wiley.com/college/woerheide

INTRODUCTION

The most basic of all investments is common stock. Its value can be complicated to estimate, but it is a relatively simple instrument in terms of its features and benefits. For many people, investing means nothing more than buying common stocks. Common stock is a risky security. In this chapter, we will follow Dick Dowen, who is interested in buying some shares of stock, as he attempts to acquire information about them and to better understand what it means to own common stock. We will also take a brief look at securities closely related to common stock, which include preferred stocks, rights, warrants, and options.

HOW DOES COMMON STOCK REPRESENT OWNERSHIP OF A CORPORATION?

Common stock is the security that represents ownership of a corporation. Think of the following scenario. Dick Dowen wants to start a business. He starts it as a **sole proprietorship,** which means he has exclusive ownership of his business. As his business grows, he becomes concerned about the personal legal liability associated with his business operations, so he decides to incorporate. Incorporation allows him to draw a line between his business assets and his personal assets. As part of the incorporation, he issues himself shares of common stock. These shares of common stock now represent his ownership.

As Dick's business grows even more, he finds it needs more cash to support this growth. However, either he personally does not have the additional cash to invest in the firm, or he does not want to further commit his own personal wealth. Dick turns to other people, some of whom are willing to invest some cash in his firm, but only under the condition that they receive partial ownership of the firm. Dick then agrees to have the firm sell them some newly created shares of common stock in exchange for the cash they are investing in the firm. Now the firm has many owners, each with varying amounts of common stock. Each investor is a part owner of the firm, entitled to have his or her say at shareholder meetings.

When a corporation becomes large enough to have tens of thousands of shareholders, it becomes impractical for each shareholder to say something on every issue. But even in the largest corporations today, any shareholder has the right to place an issue on the agenda of the annual meeting so that it can be voted upon by all of the shareholders.

Web Link 14.1

WHAT IS A BOARD OF DIRECTORS?

Corporations must hold at least one annual meeting of the shareholders, although additional meetings may be called if needed. Each year the shareholders elect a **Board of Directors.** As it is cumbersome for the shareholders of corporations to meet regularly to handle corporate business, the shareholders elect a Board of Directors to represent the shareholders' interest in overseeing the activities of the firm.

Compensation for directors is usually depends on the size of the firm. Someone serving on the Board of Directors of a Fortune 500 company[1] may receive a compensation package of $10,000 to $20,000 a month. The Board of Directors is responsible for developing a slate of nominees each year, although the Board's slate consists primarily of the existing Board and it wins the election virtually all of the time. It is not uncommon for an entire Board to stand for reelection for many years in a row. Some members have served on their Boards for 30 years or more.

New people tend to be added in only one of three circumstances. The first is when the Board member is an officer of the corporation. For example, if the company president, who always serves on the Board, were to leave the firm, he or she would almost certainly also resign from his or her Board membership and be replaced by the new company president. The second way in which a Board vacancy develops is when someone retires, and the third is when a Board member dies.

[1]The largest 500 firms in the country are often referred to as the Fortune 500. This list is named for *Fortune* magazine, which annually updates and publishes it.

When vacancies appear on a Board, larger companies sometimes use recruiting agencies to seek out new people. Smaller companies tend to either use a nominating committee or accept the suggestions of the president of the company. Although the basic role of the Board of Directors is to represent the interest of the shareholders who elect it, a Board can be a great resource for the company. An ideal Board brings together people who can provide information and resources useful for the various deliberations a Board performs. The Board should consist of people who are knowledgeable about the firm's business and industry, as well as people familiar with how corporations need to be run.

A director's position is known as a **seat.** Directors can be classified as either **inside directors** or **outside directors.** An inside director is a person otherwise employed by the company. Inside directors usually consist of the top officers of the firm. Outside directors are people not otherwise employed by the company. Usually the distinction is clear-cut, but there can be overlap. For example, it is not completely clear that a retired company president is an outside director. In general, the more outside directors on a Board, the higher the price of the company's stock.

The Board must elect a **Chair of the Board of Directors,** who is technically the most powerful person in the firm, as the Board of Directors hires (and fires) the firm's officers. Thus, if the Board of Directors becomes dissatisfied with the company president, it may terminate his or her employment contract.

Web Link 14.2

HOW DOES VOTING TAKE PLACE AT A SHAREHOLDERS' ANNUAL MEETING?

According to the most common voting procedure, each share entitles its holder to one vote, and all issues are decided by a majority vote. The election of the Board of Directors in a majority system works the same as any other majority voting system. If there are five seats open on the Board of Directors, an investor who owns 100 shares could cast 100 votes for each of five people. Thus, an investor can vote for as many people as there are seats available. In this system, anyone who owns or controls at least 50 percent of the shares outstanding (actually, 50 percent plus one) would effectively control both the Board of Directors and all meetings of the shareholders. Most corporations use this method of voting.

An alternative voting system is the cumulative system, which allows an investor to accumulate his or her votes. Thus, if there were five seats open on the Board of Directors, an investor with 100 shares could cast 500 votes for one person. This system guarantees that any individual or group of individuals with a significant minority ownership of shares could acquire a position on the Board of Directors. Consider the following example.

> *Dick Dowen owns 18,000 shares of common stock in the Northern Illinois Widget Corporation. There are a total of 100,000 shares outstanding. At the upcoming annual meeting, all five seats on the Board of Directors are up for election and the company uses a cumulative voting system. Dick is not currently on the Board, but would like to take a position on the Board. Does he have enough shares to guarantee his election?*

As there are five seats to be elected, Dick has a total of 90,000 votes (5 seats × 18,000 shares). The owners of the other 82,000 shares have 410,000 votes (5 seats × 82,000 shares). If the other shareholders cash their votes equally among five candidates, each of their candidates will receive 82,000 votes (410,000 votes / 5 candidates). Thus, Dick finishes first with his 90,000 votes, and the other five candidates are tied for second. The remaining five candidates would most likely have to have a runoff to determine which would not serve. The other shareholders can shift their votes around to give 90,001 votes to their preferred candidates, but this will not keep Dick off the Board. If the other shareholders give 90,001 votes to each of four candidates, then they will have only 49,996 votes left for their fifth candidate (410,000 – 4 × 90,001). Thus, Dick is again guaranteed election to the Board, as he will finish fifth. Cumulative voting has the potential of increasing the diversity of interests on a company's Board, but it also has the potential of creating a Board that has difficulty working together.

Web Link 14.3

WHY DON'T ALL CORPORATIONS PAY DIVIDENDS?

One of the actions that Boards of Directors may undertake is to declare a dividend. A company typically computes its net income or net profits each quarter. The Board of Directors may decide to declare a dividend based on these profits. Thus, if a corporation has a net profit of, say, $500,000 and has 1,000,000 shares outstanding, then it has an **earnings per share** (EPS) of $.50 ($500,000 net profit / 1,000,000 shares). A Board might decide to declare a dividend of, say, $.20 per share to be paid to the common stockholders. The firm retains what is not paid out as dividends.

A student of investments will quickly note that many firms pay no dividends. There are several reasons for this. First, some companies are faced with so many exciting investment opportunities that the Board believes the shareholders will be better off if all of the earnings are invested in them. If dividends were paid, some potential investments would have to be delayed or foregone.

If a Board elects not to declare a dividend and the investment opportunities perform as envisioned, then the price of the firm's stock will typically go up by an amount at least equal to what the dividend would have been. The investor thus receives his or her profits in the form of greater stock price appreciation in lieu of a lesser price appreciation and a little dividend income. Because dividends are taxed as ordinary income and price appreciation is taxed as a capital gain only when the stock is sold, many investors actually prefer to own stocks of companies that pay no dividends.

Another reason a firm might pay dividends is if it lacks cash or is having financial difficulty. Thus, the failure to pay a dividend may be a good sign (indicating that the Board wants to keep the cash for attractive investments) or a bad sign (suggesting that the Board cannot afford to give up the cash).

HOW ARE DIVIDENDS PAID?

Dividends can only be declared by the Board of Directors, and must be declared by the Board each and every time they are paid. Even though many firms declare the same dividend quarter after quarter, nonetheless each dividend declaration must be voted on separately by the Board. Four key dates are associated with the payment of a dividend. The first is when the Board votes to approve a dividend payment, which is known as the **declaration date.** At this time, the Board also sets the other dates.

Next comes the **record date,** the date by which an investor must own stock in order to receive the dividend. Most trades take three business days to be finalized. Thus, if an investor buys a stock on a Monday, then he or she will receive legal ownership of it on Thursday and pays for it then. Monday would count as the **trade date,** and Thursday as the **settlement date.** Thus, to be the owner of stock on a record date, you must have bought the stock at least three business days beforehand. The date two business days prior to the record date is known as the **ex-dividend date.** Anyone buying a stock on or after an ex-dividend date will not receive that particular dividend. Anyone selling a stock on or after an ex-dividend date will receive that dividend, even though he or she would not actually own the stock at the time the dividend is paid.

It is quite common for a share of stock to open trading on the ex-dividend date at a price that is lower than its closing price the day before by an amount equal to the declared dividend. That is, if a company declares a dividend of $.50 per share and the stock closed at $28.25 on the third day prior to the record date, then it will most likely open at $27.75 ($28.25 − $.50) on the ex-dividend date.

The final key date in the dividend process is the **payment date,** when the company pays the dividend. The declaration, record, and payment dates may be separated by as little as a few weeks, or as long as a month or two.

**Web Link
(WSJ) 14.4**

Dividends that are declared each day are reported in the financial press, as shown in **Web Link (WSJ) 14.4** and in Figure 14.1. The first listings in Figure 14.1 are noted as

MONEY & INVESTING
▶ FRONT ▶ MARKETPLACE ▶ MONEY ▶ TECH CENTER ▶ SPORTS ▶ PERSONAL JOURNAL

Thursday, August 9, 2001

Dividends Reported August 9

Company	Period	Amount	Payable	Record
Regular				
Allegheny Tech	Q	.20	9/11/01	8/27
Amer Business Fin	Q	.08	8/31/01	8/20
CPAC Inc	Q	.07	9/21/01	8/24
Cndn Natural Res	Q	b.10	10/ 1/01	9/14
Community Bkshrs Va	Q	.20	9/14/01	8/31
Delta&PineLand	Q	.04	9/12/01	8/31
Fidelity Bancorp	Q	.10	8/31/01	8/15
1st St Bncp NM	Q	.09	9/12/01	8/15
Liberty Finl Cos	Q	.10	9/ 5/01	8/21
Magna Intl clA	Q	b.34	9/17/01	8/31

FIGURE 14-1 Dividends Reported for August 9, 2001

regular dividends. A regular dividend means that the company is declaring the same dollar amount per share dividend as its previous dividend, and it is following a set pattern. In other words, the dividend is what you would expect given the pattern the company has established. The company name is followed by a letter indicating the period represented by the dividend. Because most companies pay dividends on a quarterly basis, most of the periods are marked as "Q." Some companies pay dividends on a monthly (M), semiannual (S), or annual (A) basis. The next item shown in Figure 14.1 is the dollar amount of the dividend, and the final two columns are its payable and record dates.

After noting the regular dividends, the listing at **Web Link (WSJ) 14.4** then provides notice of **irregular dividends**—payments that follow no pattern. Next are the listings of dividend payments for mutual funds, real estate investment trusts (REITs), closed-end funds, and limited partnerships (LPs) (most of these entities are discussed in Chapter 15). Other categories of reported dividends include increased dividends, reduced dividends, foreign companies, and initial dividends. There is even a category for companies that have omitted making their regular dividend payment.

If you follow a firm's dividend payments over time, you usually observe that the payment dates follow an extremely consistent pattern. If a company pays a dividend on the last day of a certain quarter (say March 31), then it will likely pay dividends on the last day of every quarter (i.e., June 30, September 30, and December 31). This pattern would be broken up only when those dates fall on holidays or weekends.

The key point here is that although dividends must be declared each and every time they are paid, they are highly predictable in nature, and rarely offer any surprises.

Web Link 14.5

DO STOCK DIVIDENDS AND STOCK SPLITS HAVE ANY VALUE?

In addition to paying cash dividends, companies will sometimes declare **stock dividends** and **stock splits.** A stock dividend might work in the following manner. If a company declares a 5 percent stock dividend and an investor owns 100 shares, the company will give the investor 5 additional shares. In a stock split, if a company declares a two for one (2×1) stock split and an investor owns 100 shares, the investor turns in his or her 100 shares for 200 new shares. The new shares will be different than the old shares. Most stocks have a **par value,** a number with little significant meaning, except that after a stock splits old and new shares are distinguishable by their differing par values. Suppose a company's stock had a par of $10 per share prior to the split. With a two for one split, the new par value would be $5 per share.

Research has shown that stock dividends and splits have no economic value. When there is a stock dividend, the price of the stock declines on the ex-dividend date by the percentage amount of the stock dividend. For example, if a company declared a 5 percent stock dividend, the price of its stock drops by approximately 5 percent on the ex-dividend date. The same adjustment occurs with stock splits. In a two for one split the new shares trade at one-half the value of the old shares. A useful analogy for understanding stock splits and stock dividends is the cutting of a pie, where the size of the pie represents the value of the company. Normally, we might cut a pie into eight pieces. If we cut a pie into 16 pieces and gave everyone two pieces, would each person be better off? Of course not!

Some people argue that if stock splits and dividends were of no economic value, why would companies do them? There are several answers to this question. First, some investors feel they are getting something of value, and Boards of Directors like to be appreciated, even if they know nothing of value was given.

Second, some people think that the price of a stock will return to its pre-split level automatically. This might be true if most investors focused only on a stock's price, and not its price to earnings ratio, dividend yield, and so on. Sometimes companies have 2 for 1 splits and the stock does return relatively quickly to the old level, but in these circumstances the stock price would likely have doubled even without a split. In many cases, a company's stock price immediately drops after a split.

Finally, companies declare stock splits and stock dividends because they are certain of one economic consequence: the number of shareholders will ultimately increase. A company with 4,000 shareholders today that declares a stock split may have 5,000 to 6,000 shareholders within a few years. The reason is that many investors prefer to buy at least 100 shares, or a **round lot,** when they buy a stock. If a stock has a price of, say, $120 per share, a round lot would cost $12,000. Most people don't have $12,000 to make a single purchase, but many of these same investors might be willing to put $3,000 into this stock. So if the stock is trading at $120 per share, a company might declare a four for one split to encourage the typical investor to buy a round lot at the new price of $30 per share. In other words, more people are willing to trade in stocks with lower prices, and this leads to a greater number of shareholders.

Web Link 14.6
Web Link 14.7

DOES A REVERSE SPLIT HURT ME?

A split that increases the number of shares outstanding is known as a **forward split.** The most common forward split is two for one. Companies can also reduce the number of shares outstanding through a process known as a **reverse split.** For example, a company might declare a 1 for 10 reverse split. If you had 100 shares prior to this reverse split, you would end up with 10 new shares. As the par value will also be adjusted, you will not be able to pass off the old shares as the new shares! If your shares were trading at a price of $2 each prior to the reverse split, they will be trading at $20 per share after the 1 for 10 reverse split.

As with forward splits, there is no definitive economic value to a reverse split. Sometimes reverse splits are created just to enhance the image of a stock, since any company would prefer a stock price of $5 per share over $.50 per share. Also, some exchanges set minimum nominal stock prices, so if a company's stock falls below this minimum, the company uses a reverse split to solve the problem.[2] A reverse split in this circumstance causes no harm to the investor.

---

[2]Exchanges also have a minimum number of shares outstanding as a listing requirement. Thus, the use of a reverse split that puts the number of shares outstanding below this value will not work.

WHAT DETERMINES THE VALUE OF A SHARE OF COMMON STOCK?

Like any asset, financial or real, the value of stock is based on the benefits it is expected to provide to the owner. Although there may be intangible benefits to owning stock, such as the satisfaction that comes from saying one is a part owner of a certain company, no one would assign any monetary value to these intangible benefits. The only real benefits are the tangible ones: expected cash dividends and the selling price received when a stock is sold. According to the most common valuation model, the price of a share of common stock is the present value of the dividends owners expect to receive plus the present value of the expected selling price. These expected benefits are discounted at an appropriate discount rate. The expected selling price will itself be a function of the dividends that subsequent owners of the stock expect to receive.

WHAT IS THE CONSTANT DIVIDEND GROWTH MODEL OF VALUATION?

The valuation model suggested above is insufficient to quantitatively estimate the value of a share of stock without using some simplifying assumptions. The first of these is that dividends will grow at a constant rate forever. When one makes this assumption, the valuation model reduces to the following equation:

$$V_0 = D_1 / (r - g) \tag{14.1}$$

where

V_0 = value of the stock today (at time zero)

D_1 = value of the dividend expected to be paid in the coming year

r = appropriate risk-adjusted discount rate

g = rate at which dividends are expected to grow in the future

This more detailed model is simple enough to be easily understood and used, yet complex enough to reasonably reflect reality. Consider the following example:

Dick Dowen wants to buy some stock in the local utility company, DeKalb Electric. The company just paid a dividend of $2.10 for the last year. Dick believes the company's sales, earnings, and dividends will grow at a rate of about 4 percent in the future. As the company is a pretty low-risk operation, he believes he could expect (and require) an 8 percent rate of return. What is the most Dick would want to pay for the stock given these expectations?

We can solve this problem using equation 14.1. The numerator in this equation is *next* year's dividend, but the problem only reveals last year's dividend of $2.10. However, because dividends are expected to grow at a rate of 4 percent, we can calculate next year's expected dividend as $2.184 ($2.10 × [1 + .04]). The denominator is the difference between the required rate of return (8 percent) and the expected growth rate (4 percent). Hence, the DeKalb Electric stock value is

$$V_0 = \$2.18 \,/\, (.08 - .04) = \$54.60.$$

If Dick can buy the stock for less than $54.60, then he is getting a good deal. If he can buy it for exactly this price, then he is getting a fair deal. If the stock trades for more than this price, then Dick should forget about it as an investment, as it appears to be overpriced.

WHERE CAN I LEARN ESTIMATES OF A STOCK'S VALUE?

The entire security analyst industry has been built around the task of estimating the prices of each company's stock. While security analysts frequently pick a target price to which they think a stock will move, they rarely share the details of how they make these calculations, which can be arrived at using many different models. The constant growth rate model discussed in the previous section is just one of these. Each model carries with it certain assumptions that affect the validity of the model and its forecast. If the assumptions are ill-considered, then the stock price prediction generated by that model is unlikely to be of value.

Many times analysts do not forecast actual prices for a stock, but simply post their opinions as to whether the stock is a "buy," "hold," or "sell." Every potential investor needs to be aware of the bias in these recommendations. Analysts rarely post a sell recommendation for a stock, because they obtain much of their information from company officers who usually prefer not to share information with people who have suggested their companies' stock is overvalued (i.e., the stock should be sold). One of the goals of a company president is to keep the price of the stock going up. Consider what would happen if an analyst who had recently posted a sell recommendation on a stock called to ask the president of that company for information so that he or she can update his or her report. The president is likely to be suspicious if not downright angry, and in fact may not even talk to the analyst. Information posted by analysts is thus skewed due to their desire not to offend companies with negative evaluations that could cost the analysts access to valuable information.

Buy recommendations can also be biased. Analysts' reports are intended to be used by brokers and portfolio managers. Analysts usually work for brokerage houses, where stockbrokers make money only when an investor first buys and then later sells a security. Brokers, whose income is the commission on each trade, need security analysis reports that provide buy recommendations if they are to convince customers to buy a stock or to sell one stock and buy another. Recommendations that say hold or sell do not encourage an investor to buy a stock, so buy recommendations are always in greater demand.

The result of all of these pressures is that (1) buy recommendations are plentiful, (2) a downgrade in a recommendation from buy to hold is actually a recommendation to sell, and (3) a sell recommendation means that the analyst either strongly believes the stock is overpriced or has a grudge against that company.

Consider the following:

Dick Dowen has some extra cash he would like to invest and is thinking about buying some stock. His broker recommends Safeguard Scientific (SFE). Dick would like to find out what the analysts are saying about the company. Specifically, he would like to find out how many buy, hold, and sell recommendations are currently outstanding on the company.

Web Link 14.8

At the time of this writing, a listing of these recommendations, which may be found at any of the sites at **Web Link 14.8,** were

Strong buy	5
Moderate buy	5
Hold	1
Moderate sell	0
Strong sell	0

The weighted recommendation score (where strong buy = 1 and strong sell = 5) is a 1.6. In other words, the analysts like the company.

WHERE CAN I OBTAIN SOME GENERAL INFORMATION AND RESEARCH DISCUSSIONS ABOUT A COMPANY?

Web Link 14.9
Web Link 14.10
Web Link 14.10a

An investor usually wants to know more about a company than just a summary of analysts' recommendations. Sources of information for companies are located at **Web Link 14.9.** Copies of a company's recent filings with the SEC may be obtained at **Web Link 14.10.** Copies of a company's annual report may be obtained at **Web Link 14.10a, Web Link 14.10b,** and **Web Link 14.10c.**

HOW IMPORTANT ARE THE NEXT PERIOD'S EARNINGS OF A COMPANY?

In the constant dividend growth model, we saw that the growth rate of future dividends was of critical importance. Even if you do not have a good idea of what that growth rate should be, you could still make some good decisions about a stock if you knew how that growth rate was changing. For example, if you sensed that the estimated growth rate in dividends used by most of the investors for a particular stock were increasing, then you could guess that it is quite likely that the price of the stock would increase. It doesn't matter if that increase is from 1 percent to 2 percent or 10 percent to 15 percent; so long as the projected growth rate in dividends increases, the price of the stock has to go up in the constant dividend growth rate model. This is because the denominator equals the discount rate minus the growth rate, so when the growth rate increases, the denominator becomes smaller and the stock price larger.

One of the single most important pieces of information used to adjust estimates of future growth rates in dividends is the next period's earnings report. Every quarter, publicly traded companies announce their quarterly earnings per share—the net income of the firm for the quarter divided by the number of shares of common stock outstanding.

The investment community always projects in advance what this number will be. If the actual earnings per share announced is higher than what the investment community was expecting, then investors will start thinking that the company is doing better than had previously been thought and bid up the stock price, expecting the growth rate in dividends to be higher as well. If the actual earnings per share announced is lower than what the investment community was expecting, the opposite is true.

Almost every day, a company announces *higher* earnings per share than the same quarter for the prior year and the stock price *drops;* or a company announces *lower* earnings per share and the stock price *rises.* This tells you that the investment community is reacting based on how the announced earnings per share compares to what was expected. For example, let's say everyone knows that a particular company is going through a difficult period and that its expected earnings per share are $1.50 (down from $2.00 in the same quarter for the prior year). If the company announces its quarterly earnings to be $1.75, then investors will react quite positively to this news, most likely bidding the stock up.

Anyone who can make superior predictions of a company's earnings can consistently outperform the market, so it is important to know what to expect in terms of earnings per share for a company.

Web Link 14.11
Web Link 14.12

HOW USEFUL IS A CHART OF RECENT STOCK PRICE MOVEMENTS?

Charts of a company's stock price covering a multitude of different periods are readily available on the Internet. But is it worth your time to look at them? People who use charts as their primary source of information to decide when to buy or sell a stock are known as **chartists.** There are a variety of ways to construct a chart. The most common method (particularly over the Internet) is by using a bar chart. Consider the following example:

Dick Dowen is giving serious consideration to buying shares of Safeguard Scientific. Its ticker symbol is SFE. Dick would like to look at the chart of the recent price movement, because he expects it to clearly predict future movement. Is Dick correct in this assumption?

Web Link
(WSJ) 14.13

Dick can find such a chart at **Web Link (WSJ) 14.13.** The default option on these charts is a one-year time horizon, using closing daily prices. With this type of chart, a single point represents the closing price each day, forming a line that moves up and down over time. The default option also includes a 200-day moving average. To observe the traditional bar chart, click on the price display option described as *Candlestick.* A candlestick chart has a vertical line that connects the high and low price of the stock for each day of trading.

Web Link 14.14

Although many people base their trading primarily on it, and many others use it to supplement other forms of analysis, charting has never been proven by any solid research to be of any value. One argument why this should be the case is as follows. Given the simplicity of creating charts, everyone could easily have access to them. So if a chart signaled that a stock price was definitely about to go up by three dollars, then everyone would want to buy that stock, and no one would want to sell it—resulting in a price that would immediately be $3 higher. Because the price jump would already have occurred, the chart's prediction that the price will jump $3 would no longer have any value.

Even though charts have no predictive value, they may still tell a potential investor what type of situation he or she is getting into. If the chart shows the price to have increased substantially in recent months, the investor should wonder if his or her reasons for buying the stock have already been incorporated into the price. For example, if you heard that a drug company had developed a new medication that will do wonders for a particular illness, you might want to buy stock in that company. However, if the chart shows that the price of the stock has doubled in the last two months, you might well conclude that the effect of the information you heard has already been incorporated into the price of the stock.

Another potential scenario is if the stock's price has fallen in recent months. In this case, the company could be considered a turn-around situation. A lot of money can be made in turn-around situations, *if* the company turns around. Just because a company's stock has fallen from $20 to $10 does not mean that it is a good deal. It could still fall from $10 to $5, or even fall from $10 to zero if the company declares bankruptcy.

Once an investor buys a stock, looking at the chart can be a source of great joy if the stock price subsequently rises (regardless of what it did prior to the purchase). Conversely, looking at the chart can be a source of much sadness and regret if the price subsequently declines.

WHAT SHOULD BE THE INVESTMENT GOALS OF A BELIEVER IN THE EMH?

In the previous chapter, we discussed the efficient market hypothesis, or EMH. If an investor believes in the semi-strong hypothesis, then his or her primary objective would be to make sure that his or her portfolio conforms to his or her desired *level of risk*. The second objective would be to make sure that his or her portfolio is as adequately *diversified* as possible. The third objective would be to minimize the various *transaction fees*. Let us discuss each of these three objectives.

What Is My Tolerance for Risk?

One of the most fundamental paradigms that most investments professionals agree on is the positive relationship between the riskiness and the expected return of any investment. Most professionals also agree that this positive relationship is linear. Thus, on a graph with expected return on the vertical axis and risk on the horizontal axis, the world of investments would lie on a line starting on the vertical axis at the risk-free rate of return, and proceeding upward and to the right. The most important task for any investor is to figure out how far up that line he or she wants to be.

Some companies have developed questionnaires regarding the willingness of an individual to handle risk. There are no right or wrong answers to these questions, except that individuals should know and mark their own true feelings. The questionnaires are then scored and matched with the optimal portfolio for the individual. This portfolio is defined not by specific securities but by asset categories. Thus, someone who scores as highly risk averse may be recommended to hold a portfolio that consists of 40 percent Treasury bills, 20 percent Treasury bonds, 20 percent corporate bonds, and 20 percent stock. A person who scores as highly aggressive with regard to risk may be recommended to hold a portfolio that is 75 percent stocks, 25 percent corporate bonds.

What Is an Adequate Amount of Diversification in a Portfolio?

One of the more difficult questions for investors to decide is how much to diversify. Although this question sounds simple, it is quite complex.

First, adequate diversification depends on how you define your assets. The biggest single asset most people own is what is sometimes referred to as **human capital.** Human capital (discussed in Chapter 2) is measured as the present value of each person's future income stream. A recent college graduate may have a human capital value of from $500,000 to $1 million or more. Let's say that this graduate decides to buy $2,000 worth of one company's stock. If we define this graduate's portfolio as consisting of just the financial assets, the portfolio has absolutely no diversification. If we define the relevant portfolio as including both human capital and financial assets, the portfolio still lacks adequate diversification—but not because of the stock investment. In this case, the lack of diversification comes from the fact that at the start of your working career, the value of your human capital outweighs any investment so much that you cannot diversify away from it.

As you grow older, though, the value of your human capital eventually starts to diminish as the number of remaining years of work declines. At that time, the content of the financial portfolio becomes more important. During retirement the degree of diversification among a person's financial assets becomes extremely critical.

However, for now let us consider just the diversification of a financial portfolio. The need for diversification depends in part on how risky the portfolio is. A person who has, say, 95 percent of his or her portfolio invested in Treasury bills has such a safe portfolio that even if the remaining 5 percent of the portfolio is invested in only one highly speculative security, this person is adequately diversified.

Next, some securities come with a high degree of diversification built in. For example, mutual fund shares (see Chapter 15) represent claims on portfolios that typically contain several hundred securities. Thus, if a person's investment portfolio were divided among, say, four mutual funds, each with different objectives, then this would probably constitute more than adequate diversification.

Suppose a person's financial portfolio consists only of common stocks. If the portfolio is approximately evenly distributed among 15 companies in unrelated industries, then this too is usually considered a good degree of diversification. However, suppose that five of the stocks in the portfolio were companies closely tied to the auto industry. Then the fact that approximately one-third of the portfolio was auto industry related would mean this portfolio had lost a substantial degree of its diversification value.

There is a formula that can help decipher the extent to which a portfolio is diversified. Called the Woerheide-Persson diversification index,[3] it is computed by first calculating the percentage of the portfolio invested in each security. The second step is to square these weights. The third step is to sum these squared terms, and the final step is to subtract this sum from one. Consider the following example:

[3]"An Index of Portfolio Diversification" by Walt Woerheide and Don Persson. *Financial Services Review*, Vol. 2, No. 2 (1993), pp. 73–85.

Dick Dowen is looking over his portfolio and wondering how diversified he really is. He holds seven securities, broken down as follows:

Company	Value of Holding	Percentage Weight
Stock A	$45,000	45%
Stock B	20,000	20
Stock C	15,000	15
Stock D	8,000	8
Stock E	5,000	5
Stock F	5,000	5
Stock G	2,000	2
Totals	$100,000	100%

How diversified is his portfolio?

To compute diversification using the index, we first convert all of the holdings into decimal form and square these numbers. Thus, 45 percent would become $.45^2$, or .2025. Converting the other weights to decimals and squaring them produces the values of .04, .0225, .0064, .0025, .0025, and .0004. The sum of these squared terms is .2768. When we subtract this number from one, we obtain .7232. Now, what does this diversification number mean? For that, we have to consult Table 14.1, which displays the index values of truly diversified portfolios categorized by how many securities each has. For example, an index value of .5 would indicate that the portfolio in question has as much diversification as a portfolio of two securities each containing 50 percent of the portfolio's value. A diversification index of .667 indicates the portfolio in question has as much diversification as a portfolio of three securities each containing one-third of the value of the portfolio. The

Table 14.1
Woerheide-Persson Portfolio Diversification Index Values

Index value	# of securities in equivalent, equally distributed portfolio
.500	2
.667	3
.750	4
.800	5
.834	6
.857	7
.875	8
.889	9
.900	10
.917	12
.934	15
.950	20

underlying relationship is that a portfolio containing n securities equally balanced will produce an index value of $1 - 1 / n$. Thus, a portfolio containing four securities, with each one containing one-fourth of the portfolio's value, will produce a diversification index of .75 $(1 - \frac{1}{4})$. In the above example, the computed index value of .7232 is between .667 and .75. Thus, we can say it is slightly more diversified than a portfolio with three securities equally distributed, but less diversified than a portfolio with four securities equally distributed. Dick Dowen's portfolio is unquestionably poorly diversified. His seven-security portfolio is more like a portfolio with three to four securities. If a minimally diversified portfolio contains 15 securities, then an investor would want a diversification index value of at least .934. Index values of .95 or higher (corresponding to at least 20 equally held securities in the portfolio) would clearly represent ample diversification.

How Do I Measure the Impact of Transaction Fees?

The two primary transaction fees that an investor pays over the course of a year are trading commissions and capital gains taxes. The growth in Internet-based trading is driving commission levels down to almost trivial values. Furthermore, capital gains taxes are at extremely low levels compared to where they have been during the twentieth century. However, just because these transaction fees are low does not mean they will be trivial. There are several direct and indirect ways to measure the impact of these various fees. For an investor who manages his or her own portfolio, it is important to see the impact of these fees on his or her decisions. Likewise, an investor who lets someone else manage his or her portfolio should regularly assess the impact of these trading fees as well.

Web Link (WSJ) 14.15a

For one thing, the person managing the portfolio may do so with less than total honesty. If the person managing a portfolio is also the one who executes the buy and sell orders, he or she is receiving the commission income from his or her own orders—a practice, when done for no other reason than to pad one's income, known as **churning.**

Investors should also measure trading activity. An easy way is to use what is known as a **portfolio turnover ratio.** This ratio takes the sum of the lesser of all purchases or all sales within the portfolio for the last 12 months and divides it by the average total assets in the account for the year. Another way to measure trading activity is to compute the brokerage commissions paid as a percentage of the average assets in the account. This ratio is known as the **brokerage ratio.** Consider the following example:

Dick Dowen reviewed his brokerage account statements for the last 12 months and noted the following information:

Month	Total Assets	Securities Sold	Securities Bought	Commissions Paid
April	126,814	0	0	0
May	130,580	0	0	0
June	136,103	0	0	0
July	146,017	10,000	0	0
August	143,008	0	11,397	59.90
September	140,974	0	0	0

Month	Total Assets	Securities Sold	Securities Bought	Commissions Paid
October	141,305	0	0	0
November	155,334	7,694	7,842	59.90
December	162,386	0	0	0
January	160,528	14,911	0	39.00
February	155,649	0	16,299	149.75
March	149,761	0	0	0

How aggressively is Dick's account being traded?

To determine the level of trading activity in Dick's account, we need to compute the average value of the assets in the account and the sum of sales, purchases, and commissions paid over the last 12 months. The average of the net assets in Dick's account over this period is $145,705. The total of securities sold is $32,605, the total of securities purchased is $35,538, and the total brokerage commissions paid is $309. The $32,605 of securities sold is smaller than the amount of securities purchased, so we divide this number by the average net assets to obtain a portfolio turnover ratio of 22.38 percent ($32,605 / $145,705). The brokerage ratio is the sum of commissions paid divided by average net assets, or .21 percent ($309 / $145,705). Next we must interpret these values.

It is not uncommon for professional portfolio managers to have portfolio turnover ratios of about 100 percent, meaning that on average they are selling and replacing each security in their portfolio once per year. Turnover ratios consistently in excess of 100 percent would serve as a warning of possible churning. A ratio in excess of 200 percent for two years in a row is an even stronger warning, and if you see a ratio in excess of 400 percent at any point in time you had better call your broker. With a portfolio turnover ratio of 22.38 percent, the level of trading activity in Dick's account is quite reasonable.

The advent of Internet-based trading has given birth to a new breed of investor: the **day-trader**. A day-trader is a person who constantly trades, seeking to profit from short-term price movements and holding positions from only a few minutes to a few hours. Day-traders may well convert their portfolios to cash at the end of the trading day and may negotiate special commission arrangements with some of the brokerage firms. It would not surprise a day-trader to learn that his or her portfolio turnover ratios average out to 100 percent or more per day! The news media occasionally run stories on day-traders who have had a string of luck. Sometimes they will pick up a story on a day-trader who has gone broke. There is not a lot of solid data on how day-traders are doing in the aggregate, but what little evidence there is suggests that few make money at it consistently and most lose substantial money over time.

A brokerage ratio tells the investor what percentage of his or her account is being paid out to the brokerage firm each year. A brokerage ratio of 1 percent would suggest that the trades the investor is making would need to generate at least an extra 1-percent per year in returns just to cover the cost of those trades. Dick's brokerage ratio of one-fifth of 1 percent tells him that transaction expenses are eating up a relatively small portion of his return.

HOW DO I SELECT STOCKS?

The investor who disbelieves the efficient market hypothesis (EMH) clearly wants to hunt for undervalued stocks. Investors who do believe in the EMH will not make finding an undervalued stock their top priority, although they would always prefer an undervalued stock to a fairly valued or overvalued one. We discussed earlier the concept of how stocks are valued, so now we are ready to turn to the question of how to attempt to pick out undervalued stocks, or at least to pick stocks that fit some set of criteria.

There is no guaranteed way to pick stocks. Although the universe of stocks in which a person might invest is finite, there are so many to choose from that you might as well consider the number of available stocks to be infinite. One criterion sometimes used to select investments is to identify those companies whose products you particularly approve of. A second criterion might be to find companies in industries about which you are knowledgeable, although the drawback here is that if you are only knowledgeable about a few industries, your portfolio will lack diversification.

Another way to approach the selection of stocks is to seek out sources of investment advice. One source that is well respected is *Value Line,* a weekly publication found in most libraries. Many active investors like to use *Investor's Business Daily* and *Barron's.* Business publications with more general news stories that may direct you toward a particular company would include *Wall Street Journal, Forbes, Fortune, Business Week,* and *U.S. News & World Report,* among others.

Web Link 14.16

Web Link 14.17

In general, there is no lack of resources willing to suggest how a person might go about trying to get started in investing.

HOW CAN I NARROW DOWN MY SEARCH?

If you can specify some criteria about the characteristics of the company in which you would like to invest, you can use several stock screening programs on the Internet. Of course, no known set of criteria will enable the investor to consistently outperform the market; nonetheless, some tested criteria can help you identify stocks you wish to examine more closely. Consider the following example:

> *Dick Dowen is reviewing his small portfolio and concludes that he would like to add to it a regional bank company. In addition, he would like the company to have a price-earnings (PE) ratio of between 10 and 20, a dividend yield between 1 and 2 percent, and a stock price between $20 and $50 per share.*

Web Link 14.18

Web Link 14.18 provides a fairly comprehensive stock screen. In this particular case, click on *Regional Bank* in the Industry Class menu, enter the minimum and maximum PE ratios and dividend yields in the Valuation section, and enter $20 and $50 in the Price & Share Info Section. At the time of writing, these criteria produced a list of 36 companies from which to choose. Clicking on any company's ticker symbol brings up additional information on that company.

Web Link 14.19
Web Link 14.20

WHAT WILL BE MY RATE OF RETURN IF I SELL NOW?

Everyone is at least occasionally curious as to how well they have done on a particular investment. In the case of a stock that has paid no cash dividends between the original purchase date and the present, the rate of return is simply the discount rate that equates the present value of the stock to the original purchase price. Consider the following simple example:

> *Dick Dowen bought 200 shares of MFA Company stock five years ago (i.e., 60 months) at a price of $30 per share. The stock has paid no dividends during this time period and trades at a price of $36 per share today. Dick's long-term capital gains tax is 20 percent, and he pays a commission of $29 for each trade. What would be his rate of return if he sold his stock today?*

In this example, Dick's stock is worth $7,200 ($36 × 200) today, and he paid $6,000 for the stock ($30 × 200). However, his cost basis would include the commission, and thus is actually $6,029. His net proceeds today would be the stock's value less the commission and capital gains tax. The net proceeds after commission would be $7,171 ($7,200 − $29). His long-term capital gain would be $1,142 ($7,171 − $6,029), and so his capital gains tax would be $228.40 ($1,142 × 20%). Thus, Dick's net proceeds come out to $6,942.60 ($7,200 − $29 − $228.40). The final step is to find the discount rate that equates the present value of this figure, over five years, to the original cost. In equation form this would be

$$\$6,029 = \$6,942.60 \, / \, (1 + r)^5$$

Web Link 14.22 The value of r turns out to be 2.86 percent. This solution may be found on any of the calculators at **Web Link 14.22,** although the answers on some of these calculators are rounded up to the nearest whole number value of 3 percent.

If dividends are paid, then solving for the exact rate of return one has earned gets more complicated. The various calculators available make an approximation of this number. Consider the following example:

> *Everything is the same as in the previous example, except that the company has paid a dividend of $.25 per share every quarter that Dick has owned the stock. Thus, his average quarterly dividend income has been $50 ($.25 × 200). If Dick has spent this income within two months of receipt, how will this have affected his rate of return on the stock?*

We can again use the calculators at Web Link 14.22, except that we now have to add the dividend information. The rate of return from the investment is now (as measured by the internal rate of return) 7 percent. In this case, the dividends are clearly a nontrivial portion of the return on the investment.

WHAT IS MY CURRENT YIELD FROM DIVIDENDS?

The annual rate of return from holding common stock can be divided into two components, the **dividend yield** and the **capital gain yield.** The dividend yield is that portion of the rate of return attributable to the dividend income, and the capital gain yield is that portion of the rate of return attributable to price appreciation. As rates of return should always be expressed on an annualized basis, the dividend and capital gains yields should only be measured over 12-month intervals. The formula for the annual rate of return on a stock is

$$r = \frac{D_1}{P_0} + (\frac{P_1 - P_0}{P_0})$$

where

$$r = \text{annual rate of return}$$

$$D_1 = \text{dividends paid during the year}$$

$$P_0 = \text{price at the start of the year}$$

$$P_1 = \text{price at the end of the year}$$

Consider the following example:

> *Dick Dowen noticed that at the start of the year MFA stock traded at a price of $30. During the year he received $3 in dividends. The price of the stock at the end of the year was $31. What were Dick's annual rate of return, his dividend yield, and his capital gain yield?*

The dividend yield was $3 divided by $30, or 10 percent. The capital gain yield was $1 ($31 – $30) divided by $30, or 3.33 percent. Thus, his total rate of return was 13.33 percent. These rates of returns are all pretax numbers. Each of them could be converted to an after-tax equivalent by multiplying them by an amount equal to one minus the appropriate marginal tax rate. The pretax and after-tax dividend yields can be computed at **Web Link 14.23.** Consider the following example:

Web Link 14.23

> *Dick Dowen had 100 shares of stock worth $60 at the start of the year. He received $2.40 in dividends during the year. His federal and state marginal tax rates are 15 and 10 percent. What are his pretax and after-tax dividend yields?*

The pretax dividend yield is 4 percent ($2.40 / $60). The after-tax dividend yield is 4 percent times 75 percent (1 – .15 – .10), or 3 percent.

DO THE DIFFERENT CATEGORIES OF STOCKS MATTER?

Many people like to classify stock into unique categories. Some of the more commonly used classification names include: *blue chip* stocks, *growth* stocks, *value* stocks, *income* stocks, *cyclical* stocks, *defensive* stocks, *speculative* stocks, and *penny ante* stocks. These classification schemes may help an investor evaluate different types of companies, but in truth, these schemes are somewhat misleading.

For one thing, there are no universally accepted definitions as to what these terms mean. Researching the definitions of these terms, you might find some commonality of themes—for example, blue chip stocks are usually described as those of large companies that are financially strong and safe investments, and growth stocks are sometimes described as those whose price is expected to grow faster than the market in general. However, the technically correct definition of a growth stock is one whose company *earnings* are expected to grow at a rate faster than the economy. Growth stocks are known for paying few or no dividends. A value stock is one where the price of the stock is low relative to the earnings of the company (i.e., the company has a low price-earnings ratio). An income stock provides a high dividend yield but is expected to provide little price appreciation. A cyclical stock is one whose company earnings are expected to fluctuate with business cycles in the economy, but again the price of the stock may or may not fluctuate at all. A defensive stock is one whose company earnings would be expected to be relatively unaffected, or even positively affected, by a recession. A speculative stock is one where there is great uncertainty about what is going to happen to a company. For example, if there are rumors that a tender offer is about to be made for a company, then its stock becomes a speculative stock. Finally, a penny ante stock has an unusually low price, perhaps no more than a few pennies per share. Penny ante stocks are usually companies whose ongoing existence is in question.

Although these descriptions would seem to be clear categories, in fact it is quite easy for different people to label the same stock differently. This is not to say that using such labels is bad, so long as you use them only to sort out a company's key characteristics. But keep in mind that just because someone calls a stock a blue chip company does not mean it is a blue chip company. The label only tells you what that person thinks, not whether his

Web Link 14.24

or her reasons for doing so are good ones.

WHAT ARE CLASSES OF COMMON STOCK?

Some corporations issue what are known as classes of common stock, usually distinguished by names such as Class A and Class B shares. Sometimes companies will use other letters, such as in the case of General Motors, which has a Class H common stock. There is no overriding definition as to what the different classes represent. Thus, when a shareholder is looking at a company that has multiple classes of common stock, the share-

Web Link 14.25

holder needs to find out specifically what the differences between the classes are. For example, Berkshire Hathaway has Class A and B shares of common stock. Class A common stock is convertible at the option of the holder into 30 shares of Class B common stock, but Class B common stock is not convertible into shares of Class A common stock.

WHAT IS PREFERRED STOCK?

Some companies issue preferred stock in addition to common stock. Preferred stock is usually similar to a bond, but it does share several features with common stock. Neither has a maturity date. In both cases, the distribution of profits is known as dividends and all dividend payments must be declared by the Board of Directors each time they are to be paid. The major difference between preferred and common stock is that the dividend rate on preferred stock is a promised rate, normally printed on the face of the security itself. Thus, if a company issues a $50 par value preferred stock with a promised dividend rate of $3 per share, then it is committing to a dividend of $.75 per share per quarter ($3/4) to the preferred shareholders. This rate is promised, not guaranteed. If the Board of Directors feels the company does not have the cash to make the quarterly dividend payment when it comes due, it may omit the dividend.

Sometimes preferred stock has the additional feature of being convertible into common stock. The conversion ratio will have been fixed when the preferred stock was issued. The conversion process for convertible preferred stock is the same as for convertible bonds.

For individuals, nonconvertible preferred stock is an extremely inappropriate investment. The reason for this lies in the corporate tax structure. When a corporation owns stock in another corporation, dividends are normally 70 percent tax-exempt. When a corporation wants to invest in another corporation, it has a strong preference to buy preferred stock instead of bonds because the interest income on bonds is taxed in full. As a result, the dividend yield on the preferred stock of a particular company will be *lower* than the current yield for that same company's bond, despite the fact that the preferred stock is a riskier security than the bonds.

Web Link 14.26

WHAT ARE RIGHTS TO BUY SHARES?

One method that companies have of raising new money is called a **rights offering.** In a rights offering, the company selects what is known as a subscription price and a subscription ratio. Based on the subscription ratio, securities known as rights are distributed to the current shareholders. The rights have an expiration date that makes them short-lived. The shareholders must either exercise their rights to buy the new shares that the company is issuing, or sell them in the market. They have a third option of letting the rights expire unused, but that means throwing money away. Consider the following example:

> *Dick Dowen has just been notified that the DeKalb Electric Company has issued him some rights. The DeKalb stock trades at $60 per share. The rights allow the holder to buy the stock at $40 per share (i.e., the subscription price is $40). However, 10 rights are required to buy each new share of common stock that the company is selling (i.e., the subscription ratio is 10 to 1). The rights expire in three weeks. What is the minimum value of the rights?*

Note that the rights allow a person to buy a stock at a price that is $20 less than the current market price. Because 10 rights are required to buy each new share of stock being sold by the company, the savings of $20 must be spread across all 10 rights. Thus, each right would have a minimum value of $2 ([$60 – $40]/10).

If Dick had owned 100 shares of DeKalb stock, he would have received 100 rights, as rights offerings are usually made in the ratio of one right per each share owned. Hence, Dick could buy up to 10 new shares of stock in the company at a total cost of $400 ($20 subscription price × 10 new shares). If Dick exercises the rights, he will end up owning 110 shares of stock. As an alternative, Dick could sell his rights in the market. He would likely receive a price of at least $2 per right, or $200 total ($2 per right × 100 rights owned), less commission. If Dick does nothing, his rights will expire and be worthless. Dick will have sustained an economic loss of $200. Whether Dick would be better off exercising or selling the rights depends on whether Dick would like to increase or reduce his investment in the company.

WHAT ARE WARRANTS?

Warrants are similar to rights in that they allow an investor to buy new shares of a company's stock at a fixed price. The primary difference between warrants and rights is how they come into existence. Rights are issued on a one-for-one basis to all existing common stockholders whenever the company wants to use this method to sell new common stock. Warrants usually come into existence when a company is attempting to borrow money. The loan may be directly from a lender such as a bank or a private investor, or through the issuance of bonds. As a part of the loan deal, the company might provide the lender with warrants in exchange for the lender accepting a lower interest rate.

Unlike rights, warrants tend to have long lives, such as five to ten years or longer. Some warrants have no expiration date. Also, the subscription ratio on warrants tends to be much lower than the subscription ratio for rights. Many warrants have subscription ratios on the order of one-to-one.

WHAT ARE OPTIONS?

The two basic types of options are the **call option** and the **put option.** A call option gives the holder the privilege of *buying* a fixed number of shares of a security at a fixed price (i.e., the subscription or exercise price) on or before a fixed expiration date. A put option gives the holder the privilege of *selling* a fixed number of shares of a security at a fixed price (i.e., the subscription or exercise price) on or before a fixed expiration date. These two options are precisely identical except for one key element: The owner of the call option pays for the privilege of buying shares from someone else, and the owner of the put pays for the privilege of selling shares to someone else. In both cases, the other party has no choice if the option holder elects to make the deal.

Rights and warrants are versions of a call option. The major difference is that rights and warrants involve the sale of newly created securities by a company for the purpose of raising new money, whereas call options are like bets between two investors regarding the future price of a company's stock. When a call option is exercised, no new stock is created. The owner of the call is buying existing stock from the person who has sold the call option. The company is not involved in the trading or exercise of call options.

There is one exception to the above observation. Companies frequently give stock options to some of their employees as part of the employee's compensation package. These stock options cannot be sold. When an employee exercises these options, the company is selling newly created stock. When the news media reports that certain employees have received unusually large compensations (such as several million dollars or more), the bulk of that compensation is usually in the form of the exercise of stock options granted at an earlier date. It is possible that these options could have ended up worthless.

SUMMARY

➤ Common stock is the basic instrument of ownership of a corporation.

➤ The key element of governance in a corporation is the Board of Directors, which is elected by the shareholders at the annual meeting.

➤ Voting at an annual meeting may be based on a simple majority system, or on a cumulative basis.

➤ Although the value of common stock is ultimately derived from the distribution of dividends to the owners, the payment of dividends in the current time period may actually be detrimental to the value of the company if dividends are a significant source of funds to finance growth.

➤ The simple growth model is $V_0 = D_1 / (r - g)$.

➤ The degree of diversification in a portfolio may be measured with the Woerheide-Persson Index.

➤ The Internet offers investors recommendations on various investments, as well as information about particular companies, and even stock screening calculators for identifying prospective companies to invest in.

➤ There are many different categories of companies, but assigning classifications is subjective.

➤ Some companies have several classes of common stock with differing terms on each class.

➤ Related securities include preferred stock, rights, warrants, and put and call options.

KEY TERMS

blue chip	Board of Directors	brokerage ratio
call option	capital gain yield	chair of the Board of Directors
chartists	churning	day-trader
declaration date	dividend yield	earnings per share
ex-dividend date	forward split	human capital
inside director	irregular dividend	outside director
par value	payment date	portfolio turnover ratio
put option	record date	regular dividends
reverse split	rights offering	round lot
seat	settlement date	sole proprietorship
stock dividend	stock split	trade date
warrants		

PROBLEMS

14.1 Obtain the listing of the members of a Board of Directors for a company of your choice.

14.2 Assume a company's Board consists of nine members or seats and that the company uses a cumulative voting process. If there are 1 million shares outstanding and you wanted to guarantee your election to this Board, how many shares would you have to own or control for voting purposes? How many shares would you need if the voting were on a majority basis?

14.3 Using the *Wall Street Journal,* determine how many companies declared a regular dividend. Which company declared the largest dividend per share? How many companies declared an irregular dividend? How many companies increased their dividends? How many companies declared an initial dividend?

14.4 For the same *Wall Street Journal* edition you used in Problem 3, determine how many companies declared a stock split on this date. Which company had the largest percentage increase in shares outstanding? How many reverse splits were there?

14.5 A company has just paid a dividend of $1.50 (i.e., $D_0 = \$1.50$). If you would require a 10 percent rate of return to invest in this company's stock, and if you expect dividends to grow at an annual rate of 3 percent forever, what is the most you would be willing to pay for this company's stock?

14.6 For a company of your choice, obtain a set of analysts' recommendations for buying, holding, or selling this company's stock.

14.7 For the company you selected in Problem 6, ascertain some of the current estimates for its earnings per share for the coming year.

14.8 Your portfolio has five different stocks with the following worths: $50,000, $30,000, $10,000, $5,000, and $5,000. Use the Woerheide-Persson Diversification Index to determine the diversification equivalency of this index value.

14.9 Use one of the stock screens on the Internet to select a list of stocks from which you might pick your next investment. Specify any criteria you would like, but make sure your list contains at least three stocks but not more than 10 stocks.

14.10 You bought some stock in the IJK company last year for $20 per share. During the year you received dividends totaling $.50 per share. The stock closed the year at $22 per share. What was your dividend yield, your capital gain yield, and your annual rate of return?

REFERENCES

Web Link 14.27 What are some sites with glossaries?
Web Link 14.28 What are some FAQ sites?
Web Link 14.29 What are some pointer sites?
Web Link 14.30 Where can I get some information on American Depository Receipts?

WALL STREET JOURNAL RESOURCES

Web Link (WSJ) 14.31   "Dividends, Not Growth, May Be Wave of Future," *The Wall Street Journal Interactive Edition,* August 21, 2001

Web Link (WSJ) 14.32   "The Best in Street-Speak: Market Chatter Offers Clues," *The Wall Street Journal Interactive Edition,* July 3, 2001

Web Link (WSJ) 14.33   "Seven Guidelines in the Midst of Market Turmoil," *The Wall Street Journal Interactive Edition,* September 17, 2001

Web Link (WSJ) 14.34   A quick overview on how to meet your investing needs online. From the book *Online Investing,* by the reporters and editors of WSJ.com

For information that has changed since the book was written, for new information that pertains to this topic, and for some new web sites that pertain to the topic of this chapter, see **Web Link 14.35.**

CHAPTER 15

INVESTMENT COMPANIES: MUTUAL FUNDS, CLOSED-END FUNDS, UNIT INVESTMENT TRUSTS, AND INVESTMENT CLUBS

LEARNING OBJECTIVES

- Distinguish between the different types of investment companies
- Explain the different types of fees and charges associated with investment companies
- Compute the net asset value per share
- Explain the source of dividend and capital gain distributions
- Analyze how various fees affect one's rate of return
- Decide which of two funds to purchase
- Compute the capital gain or loss on the sale of any mutual fund shares
- Discuss various criteria for selecting a mutual fund
- Describe an index fund and explain its advantages
- Obtain the current price or recent information on a mutual fund.
- Analyze a prospectus
- Distinguish between closed-end funds, unit investment trusts, and DPICs

Web Link: www.wiley.com/college/woerheide

INTRODUCTION

An **investment company** is an organization in which a group of people pool their money for the purpose of making investments. The degree of formality in the organization and the processes by which certain important steps are accomplished differentiate the multitude of investment companies. The simplest type of investment company is an **investment club,** in which friends, co-workers, or acquaintances pool their money and make investment decisions. Such clubs tend to have a small number of investors. At the other extreme are mutual funds having a million or more investors. In this chapter we will discuss mutual funds (known as open-end investment companies) first because they are the most typical type of investment company. We then look at closed-end investment companies. Open-end and closed-end funds differ primarily in how shares are sold to investors. A less common form of investment company, the unit investment trust, is then reviewed. The chapter ends by returning to investment clubs, which are some people's first exposure to investing (including this author, who formed his first investment club during his freshman year in college).

Throughout the chapter, we will consider the situation of Bruce and Barbara Oliver. The Olivers want to start saving some money toward their retirement years. They feel that an investment company would provide a much safer and surer route to accumulating wealth than investing directly in the stocks and bonds discussed in the two previous chapters.

Web Link 15.1

WHAT BASIC FEATURES ARE COMMON TO ALL INVESTMENT COMPANIES?

An investment company is formed for the purpose of investing in various securities. That is, an investment company is like any other corporation, in that it obtains money by selling shares of its own stock to investors. Let us suppose a new investment company, the AJJ Investment Company, sells 1,000,000 shares of its stock to various investors at a price of, say, $10 per share. The AJJ Company would then have raised $10,000,000 in cash. Its balance sheet would appear as follows:

Asset	**Net Worth**	
Cash $10,000,000	Common Stock (1 million shares)	$10,000,000

Like any other corporation, AJJ is governed by a Board of Directors, elected by the shareholders. The Board appoints a **management company** to oversee daily operations and a **portfolio manager** who is charged with investing the cash, overseeing the portfolio on a daily basis, and making trades.

Every investment company has its own well-defined investment objective. The portfolio manager must make sure that the portfolio and every investment in it conform to the company's unique **investment objective.** The investment objective typically consists of two elements: the major type of security the company seeks to hold and a subset of that type. The three major types of securities that investment companies hold are stocks, bonds, and money market instruments. Subsets of stocks, for example, include aggressive growth, long-term growth, income, large cap, small cap, foreign, and international. (*Cap* is used to stand for *capitalization.*) Although the foreign and international categories sound similar, they may be quite different; a foreign investment company invests *only* in securities issued outside of the United States, while an international investment company will hold both foreign and domestic issued securities. At times, an international investment company may go with nearly all foreign or nearly all domestic securities, a mix usually determined by the portfolio manager. A large cap investment company invests only in stocks of companies that have a large market value. Conversely, a small cap investment company invests only in the stocks of companies with relatively small market values.

Web Link 15.2

Web Link (WSJ) 15.3

Several of the better-known organizations that provide investors with information on investment companies include *Morningstar, Lipper,* and *Arnold Wiesenberger.* In addition, financial publications such as the *Wall Street Journal, Business Week, Barron's, Smart-Money,* and *Forbes* regularly evaluate the performance of investment companies and run steady streams of articles about mutual funds.

Such services categorize the investment companies by investment objective. Unfortunately for neophyte investors, these categories are not universally agreed upon! Thus, one service may identify a particular investment company as international, a second may

Web Link
(WSJ) 15.4

declare it an aggressive growth stock fund, and a third may label it a small cap company. The investor needs to look beyond these labels and focus on the portfolio itself. The *Wall Street Journal's* mutual fund classifications may be found in Figure 15.1. The site shown in this figure currently uses three broad categories of funds: equity, debt, and municipal debt. Within each of these broad categories are a large number of subcategories.

For their services, investment companies charge a **management fee** against the assets of the investment company, thus compensating the management firm and the portfolio manager. For example, if the assets of an investment company have a market value of $68,500,000 and if the management fee were 1 percent of the assets, then the management firm would charge the company $685,000 that year for its services.

For any investment company, one may compute what is known as a **net asset value (NAV)** per share. The NAV is the market value of the assets of the company less its liabilities, divided by the number of its shares of common stock. Consider again the company whose assets have a market value of $68,500,000 at the end of a trading day. Let's assume the liabilities of the company are $500,000. If the company has outstanding 7,542,293 shares of common stock, then the NAV at that point in time would be $9.02 ([$68,500,000 − $500,000] / 7,542,293). This company's NAV would likely change every day as the market value of its assets changes. Public quotations of the NAV are always rounded to the nearest penny. When investors buy or sell shares, the NAV is computed out to three or sometimes four decimal places for accounting purposes.

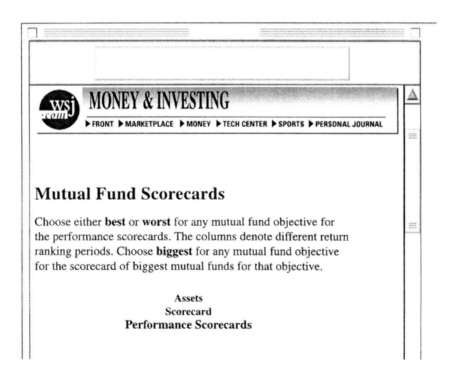

FIGURE 15-1 Mutual Fund Classifications Used by WSJ Interactive

Like any investor, investment companies make trades during the year. The quantity of trading they do and the cost of that trading are measured by the **portfolio turnover ratio** and the **brokerage commission ratio.** The portfolio turnover ratio is the lesser of the total sales or total purchases of securities in the portfolio, divided by the average total assets during the year.[1] The brokerage commission ratio is the annual commissions paid by the investment company, divided by average total assets.

HOW DO INVESTMENT COMPANIES DIFFER?

The primary differentiating characteristic among investment companies is whether they issue new shares on a daily basis. Investment companies are either **open-end** or **closed-end.** Open-end companies are known more commonly as **mutual funds.** Mutual funds stand ready at any time to sell shares to new investors or buy back shares from current investors. The buy-back process is referred to as a **redemption** of shares. In fact, a mutual fund investor can only acquire shares directly from the mutual fund company and can only sell the shares back to it. There is *no* trading among investors in the shares of mutual fund companies. Because the investor is limited only to buying from and selling to the fund itself, share prices are always based on the NAV.

Closed-end funds typically make an initial offering of shares to the public when the fund is being created.[2] All subsequent trades are in the secondary market, just like any other corporation. Occasionally, a closed-end fund may make an additional primary offering to obtain cash for new investments, but such cases are rare. In the secondary market, closed-end fund share prices are determined the same way other stock prices are set, namely the interaction of supply and demand at any point in time. Both the buyers and the sellers of the shares of a closed-end fund may ascertain the current NAV for those shares, which are printed in papers such as the *Wall Street Journal* and are available on the Internet. However, unlike in open-end funds, trades are not required to occur at the NAV and rarely do. The majority of closed-end funds actually trade at discounts to the NAV! This phenomenon will be discussed later.

Web Link (WSJ) 15.5

Variations to the closed-end fund structure include unit investment trusts, dual-purpose investment companies, and real estate investment trusts. We will discuss these later in the chapter.

HOW DO MUTUAL FUNDS DIFFER?

Web Link 15.6

The most common method for distinguishing among mutual funds is by categorizing them according to how their shares are sold to the public. Many years ago, all mutual funds used

---

[1]Many people assume incorrectly that the portfolio turnover ratio is measured by taking the average of the portfolio's sales and purchases, rather than the smaller number of the two. Using the average may be misleading for the following reason. Assume a new fund starts up and raises $100 million in the sale of new shares. The full $100 million is then spent on new investments, and none of these holdings are sold during the year. At the end of the year, the portfolio turnover ratio would be zero using the correct definition, and 50 percent using the incorrect definition. In reality, there was *no* turnover in the portfolio.

[2]Some closed-end funds come into existence when an open-end fund decides to close itself to any and all new investment. Similarly, there have been occasions when closed-end funds have converted to open-end status.

to be neatly categorized as **load** or **no-load funds.** The word "load" is industry jargon for commission. The maximum load is 8.5 percent of what the customer invests. Thus, if an investor puts $1,000 in a fund with an 8.5 percent load, then $85 would pay for the load and $915 would go toward the purchase of shares. As a result, one could also describe the load charge as equaling 9.29 percent ($85 / $915) of the money actually invested.

Load funds are sold through a sales force. A true no-load fund carries no sales commission whatsoever. These funds use direct advertising and rely on investors who contact them to purchase new shares.

In recent years, the distribution process has changed in many ways. First, there came the growth of funds known as **low-loads,** characterized by commission rates of 2 percent or less. Next emerged funds with **back-end loads** rather than the traditional **front-end load.** A back-end load is a commission charged at the time an investor redeems his or her shares in a fund. In fact, some of the funds with back-end loads reduce or eliminate load charges, depending on how long investors own their shares. Thus, the classification of these funds according to load charges depends on a person's intended holding period. Funds with back-end loads usually refer to themselves as no-load funds.

A recent innovation has been **12b-1 charges,** fees that the fund imposes on its assets (and thus the investor) to support the sales of new shares. The growth of assets generated by these monies supposedly allows the shareholder ultimately to be charged less in the way of management fees. 12b-1 charges also allow sales commission to be spread over the life of the investment, rather than imposed solely at the time of purchase. However, research has shown that the reduction in management fees generated by the expenditure of the monies collected as 12b-1 fees is small. For example, an investor may pay a 12b-1 fee of .25 percent per year and receive a reduction in the management fee of .05 percent!

Some funds have created **classes of shares,** where each class represents a different combination of load fees and 12b-1 charges. If you intend to hold a fund for a relatively short period of time, you would opt for as low a load as possible and be willing to incur a 12b-1 fee; if you expect a lengthy holding period, you would pay a higher load fee in exchange for as low a 12b-1 fee as possible. These different classes of shares are usually designated with letters, such as Class A, Class B, etc. Consider the following example:

> *Bruce and Barbara Oliver are considering buying $1,000 worth of QED Mutual Fund. The NAV of the shares is $10. Class A shares come with a 4 percent front-end load, but no 12b-1 charges. Class B shares are sold without a load charge, but have a .25 percent per year 12b-1 charge. Which class of share is the better deal if the Olivers plan to hold the investment for five years?*

In this case, Bruce is paying an extra 4 percent up front to avoid an annual fee of .25 percent. In five years, the annual fee will accumulate to approximately $1\frac{1}{4}$ percent ($5 \times .25\%$). Paying 4 percent to save $1\frac{1}{4}$ percent is unwise, so Bruce should focus on the Class B shares.

Web Link 15.7

DOES THE PURCHASE OR REDEMPTION
OF SHARES AFFECT THE NAV?

In almost all cases, the purchase of new shares or the redemption of existing shares in a mutual fund does not affect the fund's NAV. Let us consider the earlier example in which we computed an NAV of $9.02 per share. To buy 100 new shares in the fund, you would have to pay $902.00 (100 shares × $9.02 NAV). The assets of the fund would increase by $902 when the payment was added to the cash account of the fund, and the number of shares outstanding would increase by 100. Thus, in the formula for determining the NAV the numerator increases by $902 and the denominator increases by 100 shares. Because the ratio of the changes in the numerator and the denominator exactly equals the value of the ratio before the sale of the new shares, the ratio will be unchanged.[3]

The same argument applies when shares are redeemed; the portfolio pays cash to the investor and cancels the redeemed shares, so the numerator of the NAV formula declines by the amount paid out, and the denominator declines by the number of shares. Because the ratio of cash paid out to the number of shares redeemed equals the value of the NAV, it will not change.

HOW DO INVESTORS RECEIVE PROFITS FROM MUTUAL FUND INVESTMENTS?

On a monthly, quarterly, or even semiannual basis, mutual funds provide their shareholders with dividend distributions. For a fund that distributes these dividends quarterly, the dividends and/or interest are accumulated until the end of the quarter, divided by the number of fund shares, and distributed. Because the dividends on individual holdings tend to be stable, these **regular dividend distributions** are fairly predictable for a fund. For tax purposes, the treatment of the mutual fund dividends is identical to the tax treatment of the income generating the dividends. Thus, if a mutual fund held only common stock, the regular dividend distribution would be taxed as a common stock dividend. If the mutual fund held taxable bonds, the regular dividend would be taxed as interest income, not dividend income. If the mutual fund held municipal bonds, then the mutual fund dividends would be treated as municipal bond interest income to the investor.

At least once a year, a fund will make a **capital gain distribution** if necessary. A fund tracks its various capital gains and losses, during the year, and if the gains exceed the losses, the difference must be distributed.[4] The investor is also advised as to how much of the capital gains distribution is short-term gain and how much is long-term. An investor must declare these short-term and long-term capital gains on his or her tax return, just as if they were achieved on a direct investment.[5]

A few years ago, Congress required capital gains distributions to be paid in January for the preceding 12 months, and investors must report these gains when filing their returns for the prior calendar year. January payments create an awkward situation, in that taxpayers may not know their taxable income until January 31 of the following year. If the capital gain distribution is substantial, a taxpayer may withhold less than the necessary amount

---

[3]Another way to think about it is if you had a room full of people whose average height was 5 feet, 10 inches. If a person whose height is exactly 5 feet, 10 inches enters the room, the average height of people in the room does not change.

[4]If the capital losses exceed the gains, then the mutual fund simply records the difference and uses it to offset capital gains in subsequent years. There is no immediate tax benefit to the fund's investors from this net capital loss.

[5]Capital gain distributions are noted on Schedule D of the federal tax return.

of taxes during the preceding year, and then find that it is now too late to make that up. To avoid this problem, if you believe you might receive a substantial capital gain distribution in January, you should contact the fund in December or early January to obtain an estimate of it.

Ironically, a mutual fund that has been successful and has a portfolio whose market value substantially exceeds its cost basis is less attractive from a tax perspective than one that has performed poorly and whose portfolio's market value is below its cost basis. This is because the successful fund will eventually recognize its gains by selling its appreciated securities, distribute those gains to the shareholders, thus forcing shareholders to pay taxes on them. Even if you buy the mutual fund shares just before a capital gain distribution and thus did not own the shares when the appreciation occurred, you are still obligated to declare the capital gains on your taxes. A fund with substantial capital losses may be able to deduct them against future capital gains, thus providing its investors with an indirect tax shield.

HOW DOES THE REINVESTMENT PROCESS WORK?

Virtually all mutual funds allow investors to reinvest both the regular dividends and the capital gain distributions, although reinvestment does not allow the investor to escape paying taxes on the income. Nevertheless, reinvestment is one of the most convenient ways for investors to build up their portfolios.

The reinvestment process has one drawback. The investor must keep good records about the cost of each purchase of new shares. When the shares are eventually sold, the investor is obligated to declare as capital gains the difference between the proceeds from selling the shares and the cost basis. Shares whose dividends and capital gain distributions have been reinvested continually over long periods of time (10 or 20 years or more) will usually have substantially appreciated from the original purchase price. A significant portion of this appreciation may be represented by the cost basis of the shares purchased through reinvestment. Good record keeping may save an investor several thousand dollars in needless taxes.[6]

Web Link 15.8   We will look at an example of this record keeping process later in the chapter.

HOW MUCH DO FEES AFFECT MY RETURN?

One of the major drawbacks to investing in mutual funds as opposed to buying stocks and bonds directly is the abovementioned fees and charges. An investor's return from a mutual fund equals the rate of return earned by the portfolio less the fees and charges paid. When you consider a mutual fund, it is extremely important that you understand the impact of these fees, particularly if you are comparing funds whose fees and charges differ. Determining the exact rate of return can be quite complex. In addition to the problem of the timing of dividend and capital gains distribution payments, various fees paid each year are a function of the total assets during that year. Thus, even if you had two mutual funds with

---

[6]Most mutual funds will provide the investor with a copy of all the transactions in his or her account, but may charge a fee, which could be quite high if the time period is long. Also, as funds merge or otherwise go out of business, chances increase that an investor's records could be lost.

the same NAV in 1995 and then the same NAV again in 2005, these NAVs would have followed different paths and would have different rates of return after fees. The calculation of the impact of fees is always at best an approximation. Consider the following example:

Five years ago Bruce and Barbara Oliver bought 58.37 shares of a mutual fund at a price of about $34.26 per share. They have made no additional investment in the fund. The shares currently sell for $82.63. The fund had a 4 percent front-end load, but no deferred sales fee, exit fee, or back-end load. There has been a 1.25 percent annual management fee, and a .25 percent 12b-1 charge. The Olivers' marginal federal and state tax rates are 28 and 7 percent, and the long-term capital gains rate is 20 percent. What has been their rate of return before and after the impact of the fees and charges?

Web Link 15.9 Calculators that approximate the answer to this question may be found on any of the sites at **Web Link 15.9.** The approximate answer in this example is rate of return before fees and charges of 14 percent, whereas net of fees and charges equals a rate of return of 12 percent. Thus, the fees and charges reduce the annual rate of return by about 2 percent.

A quick way to visualize this answer is to think about the annual 1.25 percent management fee and .25 percent 12b-1 fee, which combine to cost the investor 1.50 percent per year. To complete this problem, the front-end load charge must be converted into an equivalent annual fee, easily done by dividing the load by the number of years the investment has been held. In this case, dividing the 4 percent load fee by the five-year holding period produces an approximate annual equivalent fee of .8 percent. When combined with the first two fees, this equals approximately 2.30 percent per year the investor has paid in fees.

HOW CAN I CHOOSE BETWEEN FUNDS?

No two funds have the same exact schedule of fees and charges, the same dividend policy, the same expected growth rate of the NAV, and the same amount of accumulated capital gains per share at the time of purchase. Thus, in choosing between two funds, an investor may have to make tradeoffs between important features. For example, the fund with the higher expected growth rate in NAV might have a lower level of dividend distributions. One fund may have a high front-end load and no 12b-1 fee. Another may have a low front-end load but no 12b-1 fee. Let us consider an example of this decision process:

Bruce and Barbara Oliver are trying to decide between the XYZ Rapid Growth Stock Fund, and the IJK Income Fund. Both funds currently sell at $40 per share, and the Olivers would purchase 50 shares of either. They also intend to invest an additional $100 per month in the fund they select. They plan to hold this investment for five years. Their marginal federal and state tax rates are 28 and 7 percent, and their long-term capital gains tax rate is 20 percent. All dividends would be spent at the time of receipt. The price of the XYZ fund is expected to grow at a 10 percent annual rate, and the price of the IJK fund is expected to grow at a 1 percent annual rate. The dividends of the XYZ fund are expected to grow at an 8 percent rate, and the dividends of the IJK fund are expected to grow at a 2 percent rate. The XYZ fund has a 4 percent front-end load, but the IJK fund has only a 2 percent front-end load. The XYZ fund has a 1.5 percent annual management fee, and the IJK fund has a .5 percent annual management fee. Neither fund has a back-end load charge. The initial long-

term capital gain distributions are $1.60 per share for XYZ, and $.40 per share for IJK. The initial short-term capital gain distributions are $.20 per share for both XYZ and IJK. The quarterly regular dividends are $.40 per share for XYZ, and $1.50 for IJK, all fully taxable. Which fund should the Olivers select?

Web Link 15.10 The solution to this problem may be found at any of the sites at **Web Link 15.10.** The XYZ fund provides a 10 percent pretax rate of return, and a 7 percent after-tax rate of return. The IJK fund provides a pretax return of 12 percent, and an after-tax return of 8 percent. Although both pre- and after-tax numbers favor the IJK fund, it is the *after-tax* rate of return that counts, not the pretax number. Thus, based on the above expectations the Olivers should buy the IJK fund.

HOW CAN I COMPUTE THE CAPITAL GAINS AND LOSSES ON THE SALE OF MUTUAL FUND SHARES?

If an investor simply buys some shares and sells them before any of the dividends or distributions are reinvested, then computation of the capital gains or losses is the same as with any other investment, as discussed in Chapter 3. However, tax computations in the sale of mutual fund shares are complicated by the reinvestment process and the fact that many people frequently do not sell all their shares at one time. Consider the following example:

Bruce and Barbara Oliver buy 58.370 shares of a mutual fund at a price of $34.26 per share. The fund distributes regular dividends semiannually, and capital gains annually. The Olivers elected to reinvest all distributions. Their first dividend distribution was $50. At the time of the distribution the NAV was $36.10, so this bought 1.385 new shares ($50 / $36.10). The second dividend distribution was $51.10, and as the NAV at that time was $35.12, this bought 1.455 shares. Finally, their capital gains distribution was $314.76, and as the NAV at that time was also $35.12, this bought 8.962 shares. The fund now trades at $37.22 per share, and the Olivers own 70.172 shares (58.370 + 1.385 + 1.455 + 8.962). If the Olivers sell 12 shares, what is their capital gain?

There are several approaches to this problem. The IRS allows investors to use an average cost basis. Another approach, and one more desirable when markets are generally rising, is what is known as **LIFO.** LIFO stands for last in, first out. The LIFO method of determining the cost basis of the shares sold assumes that these 12 shares were the last 12 purchased. In the above example, what is being sold is the 8.962 shares that were purchased with the capital gains distribution, the 1.455 shares bought with the last dividend distribution, the 1.385 shares bought with the first dividend distribution, and .615 shares of the original purchase. The LIFO cost basis would be computed as

$$8.962 \times \$35.12 = \$314.76$$
$$1.455 \times 35.12 = 51.10$$
$$1.385 \times 36.10 = 50.00$$
$$.615 \times 34.26 = \underline{21.07}$$
$$\$436.93$$

Note that if you use a **FIFO** system—or first in, first out—you would consider the 12 shares sold as having come from the first 12 shares purchased, providing a cost basis of $411.12 (12 × $34.26). Thus, determining which 12 shares were sold changes the cost basis by over $25. Clearly, accurate record keeping is critical if you elect to reinvest dividends or capital gains distributions.

WHAT CRITERIA SHOULD I USE TO SELECT A MUTUAL FUND?

In the previous section we considered the various attributes of investment companies in general and mutual funds in particular. The number of mutual funds is huge—about twice as large as the number of stocks on the New York Stock Exchange! If you have decided to invest in one or more mutual funds, then the really critical task is to decide which funds to study in detail, and ultimately, which funds to invest in. General guidelines for selecting investments within your risk-expected return framework were discussed in Chapter 13. To review, you should select funds that you believe will provide the highest after-tax return over the projected holding period, for your desired level of risk.

One of the traditional advantages of mutual funds is the professional portfolio management they offer. On the other hand, the majority of mutual funds provide the same or lower rates of return than market indices of the types of securities within those funds. How could this be? Three answers to this question can help you best select mutual funds in which to invest.

The simplest answer is that funds have expenses. Thus, even if a manager's portfolio earns a rate of return higher than market averages, expenses might well cause the **net return** (i.e., gross return less expenses) to fall below market averages. Consider a mutual fund with a management fee of 1.25 percent and a 12b-1 fee of .25 percent. The manager of this fund must consistently outperform the market by more than 1.50 percent to cover these expenses and still provide the fund's shareholders a higher rate of return than that of the market. In fact, most research shows that on average, mutual funds underperform market averages by the amount of the management fee.[7]

A second reason why funds underperform market averages is that mutual fund managers must do far more than simply manage a broad selection of securities. Managers have to worry about their cash positions. The sale of new shares of the fund, dividends, and the proceeds of the sale of portfolio holdings bring in new cash every business day, some of which goes toward the redemption of shares and the occasional payment of dividends or capital gains distributions to shareholders. On some days, cash inflows exceed outflows, but on other days, outflows exceed inflows. Thus, a mutual fund portfolio manager is sometimes forced to sell portfolio holdings to meet share redemptions even when he or she believes all of the portfolio's investments are attractive holdings. Likewise, heavy cash inflows may force a manager to buy stocks at times he or she would prefer not to, due to restrictions on the amount of cash the portfolio may hold.

Finally, funds underperform market averages because trades by mutual funds may be partially self-defeating. Funds tend to hold relatively large positions in many companies;

---

[7]"Stock Funds Just Don't Measure Up," Jonathan Clements. *The Wall Street Journal,* October 5, 1999, page C1.

holdings of 10,000 to 50,000 shares and up are common. When a fund wants to sell such a large block of shares, the price may drop before the sale can be completed. The same applies to purchases. When a portfolio manager believes a stock is a particularly attractive investment, he or she might well wish to purchase a large number of shares, driving up the price before the entire purchase has been completed.

Based on the above arguments, your selection of funds ought to take into consideration funds characterized by

1. few expenses,
2. little variation in fund sales and redemptions, and
3. relatively infrequent trading.

The biggest single expense of a fund is often the load. Does that mean you should avoid load funds, especially if two funds look similar except that one is a load fund and the other no-load? You might think the obvious choice would always be the no-load fund—but in some cases you might be wrong! Most of the time, investors should choose the no-load fund, but if the load fund has a substantially lower annual management fee, has no 12b-1 charges, and does little trading, the no-load has a high annual management fee, large 12b-1 charges, and active portfolio trading, then the cost of the load may be more than offset by the savings on the other expenses in later years.

Furthermore, for an investor with little knowledge or sophistication, the payment of a load charge may well be worth the price. Because load funds are sold through a sales force, investors have someone with whom they can discuss the investment process and the selection of particular investments. Salespeople deserve to be compensated for working with investors. A naive investor fearful of load funds who ends up making either no investment or one that is inappropriate for his or her investment objectives would have been better off to pay the load and get the money invested effectively.

Note that none of the above mutual fund selection criteria mentioned past performance. A multitude of web sites list historical rates of return for funds and will rank funds within any objective by their performance for various periods. A good example is the *Wall Street Journal* site at **Web Link (WSJ) 15.11.** For any designated investment objective category, the site will provide the top 15 best and 10 worst performers for the last 52 weeks. Another approach may be found at **Web Link (WSJ) 15.12.** Here, the user may identify any of 6 different time periods over which to measure performance, as well as 20 different fund objectives to consider (including the category *All*). Consider the following example:

Web Link (WSJ) 15.11

Web Link (WSJ) 15.12

> *Bruce Oliver would like to know which mutual fund specializing in companies involved in gold had the best performance over the last five years.*

At the time of writing, the top-performing gold fund was Oppenheimer Gold. It had a five-year annual return of −7.3 percent. (Although it is a little unusual to have the *best*-performing fund in a category have a negative return, it is obviously not impossible. As this was the best-performing fund in this category, just imagine how some of the poorer-performing funds did!) Other sites that allow you to analyze and rank funds based on past performance may be found at **Web Link 15.13.** Sites that provide information on how a fund has performed recently, without comparisons, may be found at **Web Link (WSJ) 15.14.**

Web Link 15.13

Web Link (WSJ) 15.14

Although it is fun to look at who the best performers are and how well they have done, ample evidence shows that past performance is no predictor of future performance! It may sound intuitively obvious to say that you should select a fund that has performed well recently, but it is also wrong. Nonetheless such lists do offer some benefits. While being ranked on a top-performance list is not a recommendation to buy, being ranked on a poor-performance list may be a recommendation *not* to buy! A fund that has performed poorly may very well continue to do so, if, for example, it has unduly high management fees.

WHAT IS A FAMILY OF FUNDS?

A mutual fund's membership in a **family of funds** is usually a positive attribute. A family of funds is where one management company manages more than one fund. Currently, the largest family of funds is the Fidelity Group. Most fund families allow **switching,** which is to move some or all of one's investment from one fund in the family into any other fund with just a phone call. Most families of funds tend to waive the load fee on switches, unless you are switching from a no-load to a load. Switching is the best opportunity in the marketplace to move substantial amounts of money from one investment objective to another quickly and at little or no cost. Thus, if you awoke one morning and decided to move $50,000 from a high-risk stock fund into a money market fund, you most likely would be

Web Link 15.15   able to do so.[8]

HOW CAN I NARROW DOWN MY SEARCH FOR MUTUAL FUNDS?

One of the great investment tools on the Internet is the screening page, which lets you specify criteria for selecting a mutual fund and then displays funds that meet them. If your criteria are too restrictive, the screen may produce no funds that meet all of them; conversely, setting the screens too loosely may result in a large and thus meaningless number of selections. Set your screening criteria as narrowly as possible initially, continually relaxing the least important until you identify a reasonable number of funds to investigate further. Screening pages should not be used to make the final selection of a fund in which to invest, but to reduce the number of funds to be seriously investigated from several hundred or even several thousand to maybe five or ten. Consider the following example:

> *Bruce and Barbara Oliver would like to invest in a mutual fund. After much research, they have decided to buy a fund that has earned an annualized rate of return of at least 10 percent over the last five years, has a SmartMoney grade of at least a B, and has a beta of between 1 and 2. They also want this to be an equity fund (that is, a fund of common stocks) with assets between $50 million and $50 billion, and a portfolio turnover ratio between 50 percent and 200 percent. They want a maximum load of 1 percent, no redemption fee, a maximum 12b-1 fee of .25 percent, an expense*

[8]Mutual funds execute all sales of new shares and redemptions after the close of trading. Frequently, orders to buy or redeem must be placed at least a half-hour before the close of the markets on that same day, if not earlier. So a person who decides in the morning to request a switch must actually wait until the end of the day for the transaction to take place.

ratio of less than 1 percent, and an initial purchase between $50 and $1,000. They have no preferences as to which family the fund is from, but they are not interested in closed-end funds. How many funds meet these objectives?

Web Link (WSJ) 15.16

Web Link 15.17

At the time of this writing, the WSJ search screen, located at **Web Link (WSJ) 15.16** found three funds that met all of these criteria. Other search calculators may be found at **Web Link 15.17.** Keep in mind that each specifies search criteria differently, so no two calculators will produce the exact same list of funds. You therefore should try several search calculators before moving on to further research.

WHICH LINKS DISPLAY SPECIFIC TYPES OF MUTUAL FUNDS?

The screening programs discussed above may not be the best place for every investor to begin identifying of funds for further consideration. Suppose you are interested in funds with a particular objective that is not listed in any of the screening programs. For example, you might be looking for funds that meet the narrowly defined objective of *socially responsible investing.* Most fund categories are based on the portfolio's type of securities and their price risk exposure. Funds that focus on socially responsible investing would be classified not by the characteristics of securities, but by the philosophical bent of the managements of the companies in which they invest. An investor desiring to invest only in

Web Link 15.18

socially responsible funds would do well to visit **Web Link 15.18.**

Based on the above commentary that a good screening criterion might be the lowest level of expenses, you might want to begin there—a quite reasonable strategy. A list of

Web Link 15.19

funds with the lowest costs may be found at **Web Link 15.19.**

As the largest single expense may be the load—which can be as much as 8.5 percent of the proceeds paid to acquire a fund—another way to start a search is to seek out the no-load funds. An investor must select no-load funds cautiously though, because low-load funds and back-end load funds tend to be called no-loads. A list of funds described as no-

Web Link 15.20

load may be found at **Web Link 15.20.**

WHAT IS AN INDEX FUND?

A special type of mutual fund is the **index fund.** The goal of an index fund is to match a particular type of index. (Several stock market indices are discussed in Chapter 16.) A common index that is emulated is the Standard & Poor 500 index. Thus, a fund following the S&P 500 will try to hold the same 500 stocks held in the S&P 500 index, with the same weightings used to compute it.

Because the sole objective of an index fund is to match a target index's performance by holding the same securities as that index, these funds will typically have extremely low portfolio turnover ratios. Their turnover ratios will be greater than zero only due to variations in the sales and redemptions of shares in the fund and to index composition changes, in which the index fund must sell shares of companies dropped from the index or must buy

Web Link 15.21
Web Link 15.22

shares of those added.[9] Index funds typically have extremely low management expense ratios and small or no loads. Thus, they are great investments for individuals who want a passive investment with minimal fees and a high degree of diversification.

WHERE CAN I OBTAIN THE CURRENT PRICE OF A MUTUAL FUND?

If you already own a fund, you might be interested in its current price, which tells you whether you have made or lost money on it.

Most of the sites identified in Chapter 14 as providing price quotes on common stocks also provide quotes on mutual funds. If you are seeking to buy a fund, its current price is irrelevant. This is because funds are sold in fractional shares. If you were to send in a check for $1,000 to buy shares in a no-load fund, and the current asset NAV were, say, $28.32, then your account would be issued 35.3107 shares.[10] The number of shares is computed by dividing the total dollar purchase by the NAV (in this case, 35.3107 shares = $1,000 / $28.32). If the fund is a load fund, the computation occurs after deduction of the load charge. Assume a 5 percent front-end load in the previous example. If you send a check for $1,000, then $50 would be deducted as the load, and the remaining $950 would buy you 33.5452 shares ($950 / $28.32).

Web Link
(WSJ) 15.23
Web Link 15.24

WHAT IS A PROSPECTUS?

When an investor is ready to buy a mutual fund, then under the Securities Act of 1933 he or she must receive a prospectus from the fund. A prospectus contains all sorts of useful information, including a description of all the fund's fees and charges. Prospectuses can be obtained from many of the sites of the individual funds or at Web Link 15.25.

Web Link 15.25

HOW DO I EVALUATE A MUTUAL FUND PROSPECTUS?

The Securities and Exchange Commission has well-defined rules as to what a prospectus should contain. It must provide some historical rates of return information, including how well a $10,000 investment would have performed over the last 10 years in both that fund and a market index such as the Standard & Poor's 500. It should include a statement of the fund's investment objective and information on the funds' largest holdings. It should include a listing of every security held in the fund's portfolio, the number of shares, and the current market value, as well as a balance sheet, an income statement, a statement of changes in net assets, and financial highlights (including various expense ratios and the portfolio turnover ratio for each year reported). To evaluate the prospectus, you should

---

[9]In recent years, advance knowledge of changes in the compositions of some of the indices (such as the Dow Jones Industrial Average) could have netted substantial profits for an investor.

[10]Some funds round the number of shares to three decimal places, and others to four.

1. Make sure the fund objective is consistent with the type of portfolio you want to hold and that the fund's securities match its stated objective.[11]

2. Make sure you are comfortable with at least the five largest holdings in the portfolio.

3. Use the balance sheet to compare the portfolio's current market value to its cost basis. If the market value exceeds the cost basis substantially, you might soon owe substantial capital gains taxes if the fund sells the securities with the larger accumulated gains and makes a capital gains distribution.

4. Examine the consistency of the various expense ratios over time, as well as that of the portfolio turnover ratio, comparing them to those of other funds.

Web Link 15.26

5. Review the footnotes for any unusual information, such as pending litigation.

WHAT ARE CLOSED-END FUNDS?

Web Link 15.27

As mentioned at the start of the chapter, all trading after the initial sale in closed-end funds is among investors, so no formula can determine the price for the shares. The NAV is still published for closed-end funds, as it is for mutual funds, but trading may take place at, above, or below the NAV since only supply of and demand for the shares determine their actual prices. In practice, the majority of closed-end funds trade at prices lower than their NAVs. This is referred to as **trading at a discount,** and occurs for several reasons.

First, closed-end funds include a potential tax liability when the market value of their portfolio exceeds the cost basis of their portfolio. Second, closed-end funds might invest in some securities for which there are not active markets, meaning that the prices used to compute the NAV may at best be guesses. Third, these funds have operating fees, resulting in lower returns to the investor than the overall return on the portfolio. A discount in the share price compensates for this. Finally, active trading by portfolio managers creates the capital gains distributions that require investors to pay capital gains taxes, which they might have avoided had the portfolio followed a buy and hold strategy.

All of these arguments also apply to open-end funds. However, the constant growth of open-end funds resulting from net new purchases of shares by investors means that these reasons do not seem to affect investors when they are evaluating open-end funds. In fact, one of the mysteries of modern finance is why closed-end funds so often trade at discounts when the sales of open-end funds are booming.

Web Link 15.28
Web Link (WSJ) 15.29

WHY DO CLOSED-END FUNDS HAVE TWO RATES OF RETURN NUMBERS?

Two rates of return numbers are often provided in describing the performance for closed-end funds. One measures the rate of return on the stock itself. The other measures the rate of return on the NAV of the fund. In theory, these two numbers should always be the same,

---

[11]An example when this was not the case is described in "Excuse Me, Sir! But There Are Tech Stocks in My Bond Fund," Pui-Wing Tam, *The Wall Street Journal,* February 14, 2000, page C1.

but in practice, they virtually never are, and sometimes the differences can be dramatic. For example, a fund's NAV might be down 5 percent for the year, and yet its stock could be up 15 percent. Over long periods of time, one should expect some reasonable correlation between these two series of numbers.

HOW CAN I NARROW DOWN MY SEARCH FOR CLOSED-END FUNDS?

Like the screening sites that facilitate the selection of mutual funds, at least one site screens closed-end funds. Consider the following example:

> *Bruce and Barbara Oliver would like to buy a closed-end fund, but they have not yet chosen an objective. They will consider only funds with a five-star Morningstar rating and any premium or discount. They only want to consider funds that have earned an average annual rate of return of at least 1 percent over the last three years on both the NAV and the market rate of return.*

Web Link 15.30   The site listed in **Web Link 15.30** provided 15 matches.

WHAT ARE UNIT INVESTMENT TRUSTS?

Unit investment trusts (UITs) are self-liquidating, closed-end investment companies. UITs typically invest in bond portfolios, although stock UITs do exist. UITs come into existence via the sale of shares to the public. The proceeds of the sale are then invested in securities that have been identified for the portfolio. If it is a bond portfolio, then as the bonds mature the principal is distributed to the shareholders along with the interest income. When the last bond in the portfolio matures, the UIT is considered liquidated. Little trading occurs in the portfolios of UITs, except for the replacement of bonds that are in default. There are secondary markets on the shares of UITs, but trading is minimal. Investors in a UIT should intend to hold their shares until the portfolio is liquidated.

Stock UITs are dedicated to a particular investment strategy. For example, in recent years many investors have become intrigued by what is known as the "dogs of the Dow" investment strategy. This is based on the belief that at any point in time, the 10 stocks in the Dow Jones Industrial Average with the highest dividend yields will as a group outperform both the rest of the Dow and the broader market averages for the next 12 months. A brokerage firm will set up stock UITs to invest in these 10 securities. One year from the

Web Link 15.31   creation of each UIT, that UIT is liquidated. Investors can have their money back, or can
Web Link 15.32   roll the proceeds into the next year's UIT.

WHAT ARE SPDRS, WEBS, AND DIAMONDS?

The term SPDR (known as "Spider") stands for Standard & Poor's Depositary Receipt. These receipts are based on the S&P 500 Composite Stock Index, discussed in Chapter 16. The SPDR Trust is a UIT that holds shares of all the companies in the S&P 500 and closely

Web Link 15.33

tracks its price performance and dividend yield. SPDRs, just like any other stock, trade continuously throughout the trading day. SPDRs represent an excellent opportunity for an investor who wants to buy a broad-based portfolio and hold it, as well as for an investor who wants the ability to quickly get into and out of a market index.

The term WEB stands for World Equity Benchmark. These are UITs designed to mimic the price movement of the Morgan Stanley Capital International (MSCI) index for a particular country. At this time, 17 different WEBs are being traded for countries such as Australia and the United Kingdom. WEBs give an investor the ability to immediately invest in a broad distribution of shares of companies based in a particular country. WEBs are an effective vehicle for those who want to achieve international diversification with relatively small amounts of cash.

Web Link 15.34

Finally, DIAMONDs are UITs based on the Dow Jones Industrial Average. As this average is the most commonly quoted and popular of all of the stock market indices, this investment represents a unique opportunity to hold exactly this portfolio.

Web Link 15.35

WHAT ARE REAL ESTATE INVESTMENT TRUSTS?

Web Link 15.36

A **real estate investment trust** (REIT) is a closed-end fund that participates in the real estate sector in some manner. A REIT that holds mortgages on commercial or industrial properties is known as an income REIT. A REIT that holds ownership positions in real estate projects is known as an equity REIT. Other REITs may do some of both.

WHAT ARE DUAL PURPOSE INVESTMENT COMPANIES?

Dual-purpose investment companies (DPICs) are closed-end funds with two classes of shares. One is the **income share,** and the other is the **capital appreciation share.** The income share is like a preferred stock with a maturity date. It promises a fixed rate of return, and then par value back at maturity. The capital appreciation share promises no dividends during the life of the income shares. At the maturity of the income shares, the fund can take several options with the capital appreciation shares. It may liquidate its entire portfolio, in which case the capital appreciation shareholders are paid whatever is left over after the income shareholders are paid off. If the fund has performed well, capital appreciation shareholders would do quite well. If the fund has done poorly, the income shareholders may end up with the better rate of return. If the fund has inadequate assets to pay the income shareholders in full when the income shares reach maturity, then the capital appreciation shares would be worthless. An alternative to liquidating the capital appreciation shares at the maturity of the income shares is to convert them into a mutual fund or a closed-end company with only one class of shares outstanding.

As there is not a lot of trading activity in the shares of DPICs, it is difficult to obtain quotes. Furthermore, few analysts are interested in following these companies.

WHAT ARE INVESTMENT CLUBS AND HOW CAN I GET INFORMATION ON THEM?

At this point, it is worth returning to the subject of investment clubs. The formal investment company structures discussed in this chapter offer nothing that individuals cannot duplicate themselves with an investment club. An investment club is an informal organization of two or more people who come together to pool their cash and make investment decisions. The key to making an investment club work is to define its processes carefully. That is, policies should specify how the finances are handled when a person enters the club, when a person leaves the club, and how differences in contributions are treated to assure equitable distributions of the club's income. The process for making the various investment decisions should also be well defined, as well as the characteristics of the portfolio the club intends to maintain. Several organizations dedicated to supporting investment clubs may be found at **Web Link 15.37.** Help with setting up and running an investment club may be found at **Web Link 15.38.**

Web Link 15.37
Web Link 15.38

The easiest way to keep records in an investment club is to treat the club as if it were an open-end investment company (which it actually is). In effect, the club should create (on paper) the concept of stock in the investment club. Thus, each time anyone contributes money toward the club's portfolio, that person should be assigned additional shares in the investment club based on the NAV of the portfolio at that time.

One advantage of this approach to record keeping is that the rate of return on the club's portfolio can then be computed as the percentage change in the NAV of the club. In many instances, clubs have confounded the contribution of new capital with the performance of the existing portfolio. Probably the most famous instance of this happening is the book entitled *Beardstown Ladies' Common-Sense Investment Guide: How We Beat the Stock Market—And How You Can, Too.* The Beardstown ladies were a group of housewives who formed an investment club and over a period of many years saw their portfolio grow dramatically in value. They wrote a book describing their apparent success in substantially outperforming the stock market, appeared on many talk shows, and were the envy of investors for a period of time. Their fame came to a grinding halt when their investment results were formally audited; it was discovered that they had included their contributions of new cash in measuring their rates of return. Once the rates of return were adjusted to reflect only the performance of the stocks in their portfolio, it turned out that they actually *underperformed* the stock market, and by several percentage points. The publicity surrounding their book died immediately.

Consider the following example:

Bruce Oliver and 19 other friends decided to form an investment club, known as the Sanhedron. They agreed to each contribute $1,000 to start the club and to meet on the last Saturday of each month to make new contributions to the portfolio and to make their various investment decisions. At their first meeting they reached agreement on what stocks to buy. By their second meeting, the portfolio, including some uninvested cash, was worth $21,500. At this second meeting, some of the members brought an additional $1,000 to invest, others brought $500, and the remaining members opted not to add to their investments. If the club decided to set the initial NAV for the shares in the club at $10 per share, how many shares were assigned to each member after the first meeting? How many additional shares were assigned to those investing $1,000 at the second meeting? $500 at the second meeting?

At the time of the first meeting, the members will have contributed $20,000 (20 members × $1,000 each). If the NAV of the club's shares were set at $10, then each member would be assigned 100 shares ($1,000 contribution / $10 NAV). Because there are 20 members, the club will have assigned a total of 2,000 shares (100 shares to each member × 20 members). Hence, at the time of the second meeting, the NAV of the club's shares will equal $10.75 ($21,500 portfolio value / 2,000 shares).

Based on this value, each person contributing an additional $1,000 will be assigned an additional 93.0233 shares ($1,000 contribution / $10.75 NAV). Each person contributing an additional $500 will be assigned an additional 46.5116 shares ($500 contribution / $10.75 NAV). Each person contributing nothing will be assigned no new shares. By assigning shares and computing the NAV at each meeting, the club can now easily accommodate current members who wish to cash out, new members who might want to join, and the fact that some people may want to invest different amounts than others.

SUMMARY

> The two major categories of investment companies are open-end (mutual funds) and closed-end. Other variations include REITs, UITs, and DPICs.

> Major fees include the load (front-end and back-end), the management fee, and 12b-1 charges. An implicit fee is the brokerage ratio.

> The net asset value (NAV) of a fund equals the market value of the assets, less any liabilities, divided by the number of shares of the fund outstanding.

> Mutual funds pass through their interest and dividend income as dividend distribution, and at least once per year make a capital gain distribution if they have any trading profits.

> The selection of a particular fund may require an analysis of the trade-offs between one-time charges (such as a load) and on-going fees such as the management fee.

> The most important criterion for selecting a mutual fund is the investment objective of your portfolio. Next, you should seek to minimize the total impact of all the fees and charges.

> If you reinvest either the dividend distributions or the capital gain distributions, keep good records to avoid paying excess capital gains taxes when you finally sell the holding.

> Index funds seek to match the performance of a particular stock index. Low management fees, low or no loads, no 12b-1 charges, and low portfolio turnover ratios characterize them.

KEY TERMS

12b-1 charges	back-end load	brokerage commission ratio
capital appreciation share	capital gain distribution	classes of shares
closed-end	dual-purpose investment companies	family of funds
FIFO	front-end loads	income share
index fund	investment club	investment company
investment objective	LIFO	load
low-load	management company	management fee
mutual fund	net asset value	net return

no-load fund	open-end	portfolio manager
portfolio turnover ratio	real estate investment trust	redemption
regular dividend distribution	switching	trading at a discount
unit investment trust		

PROBLEMS

15.1 Using any of the Internet screening pages, identify a set of criteria that produce a list of no fewer than three and no more than ten mutual funds in which you would consider investing some money. Assume your investment objective is to start a portfolio that will provide income during your retirement years.

15.2 Using one of the funds you identified in problem 1, determine the load charge (or it is a no-load fund). Also determine last year's management fee, portfolio turnover ratio, and 12b-1 charges. What is the current NAV of this fund? (If this fund has multiple classes of shares, determine these characteristics only for the Class A shares.)

15.3 The Knock-em-dead Mutual Fund has a 5 percent front-end load charge. The current NAV is $18.23. How many shares could you buy if you invested $10,000? (Assume shareholdings are computed to the third decimal place.)

15.4 You bought 500 shares in the We're Great Mutual Fund last year. At the time of purchase, you requested that all capital gain distributions and all dividend distributions be automatically reinvested. The current NAV is $22.76. The fund just declared a capital gain distribution of $2.17 per share, and a dividend distribution of $.56 per share. How many shares will you own as a result of your reinvestment?

15.5 Identify three index funds and which index each one is intended to track.

15.6 Using any of the Internet screening pages, identify a set of criteria that produce a list of no fewer than three and no more than ten closed-end funds in which you would consider investing some money. Assume your investment objective is to start a portfolio that will provide income during your retirement years.

15.7 For each of the closed-end funds you identified in problem 6, determine the current market price, NAV, and percentage premium or discount of the market price relative to the NAV. Based on these numbers, which of the funds would you be most intrigued in and would consider purchasing?

REFERENCES

Web Link 15.39 Miscellaneous sites for investment company information
Web Link 15.40 FAQ sites
Web Link 15.41 Pointer sites for mutual fund information
Web Link 15.42 General news stories on mutual funds
Web Link 15.43 General news on closed-end funds
Web Link 15.44 Issues in the taxation of mutual fund investments
Web Link 15.45 Calculators for measuring mutual fund performance
Web Link 15.46 Links to a large number of funds

Web Link 15.47 Sites that provide price charts on mutual funds
Web Link 15.48 Additional information on a fund
Web Link 15.49 Sites providing ticker symbols for mutual funds

WALL STREET JOURNAL RESOURCES

Web Link (WSJ) 15.51 Mutual Fund Quarterly Reports: Complete coverage of mutual funds in the U.S., Europe and Asia

Web Link (WSJ) 15.52 "Fund Companies Pump Out Sector Funds Despite Risks," *The Wall Street Journal Interactive Edition,* August 14, 2001

For information that has changed since the book was written, for new information that pertains to this topic, and for some new web sites that pertain to the topic of this chapter, see **Web Link 15.53.**

CHAPTER 16

SECURITIES MARKETS AND MARKET MECHANICS

LEARNING OBJECTIVES

- Discuss why financial markets exist and what benefit they provide to society
- Explain the difference between the primary and secondary market
- Describe the IPO process and the role of DPOs
- Describe the different securities trading locations, methods, and listing standards
- Name several common stock market indices
- Distinguish between the types of brokers and brokerage firms
- Decide whether to order out stock or leave it in street name
- Analyze the benefits of DPPs and DRIPs
- Define the most common types of trading orders and explain the advantages and disadvantages of each
- Describe how buying on margin works
- Explain the process of selling short
- Describe how dollar cost averaging works
- Describe how to experiment in the market without actually investing cash
- Discuss the protections available to an investor
- Describe pyramid and Ponzi schemes

Web Link: www.wiley.com/college/woerheide

INTRODUCTION

The last three chapters covered the three primary types of investment securities: bonds, stocks, and mutual funds. In this chapter, we turn our focus to the investment markets and the mechanics involved in the trading process. Once you conclude that you want to buy some stock, you must figure out how to select a broker, type of account, and type of order. In this chapter, we will consider Susan Jordan's assessment of various investment strategies.

WHY DO THE FINANCIAL MARKETS EXIST?

Financial markets exist for a simple reason. Although everyone needs money, not everyone wants to spend all of his or her money today. Some people want to spend more money today than what they have, while others want to set aside money today in order to have more of it in the future. For example, a corporation may want to raise $50,000,000 to finance the construction of a new facility. On the same day, 5,000 families, each of whom has $10,000, may want to save for some future need such as the purchase of a car, house, or payments for college. It takes well-functioning financial markets and reasonable financial securities to facilitate the smooth transfer of the money from the families to the firm. Without financial markets, there would be little economic growth, and little opportunity for people to save effectively.

WHAT IS THE DIFFERENCE BETWEEN THE PRIMARY AND SECONDARY MARKET?

Financial markets can be characterized by distinguishing between the **primary** and **secondary markets.** The primary market is the sale of new securities. If a company wanting to raise $50,000,000 sells bonds, the sale is a primary market sale. In the primary market, the issuer of the securities receives the proceeds from the sale of the securities. After securities have been sold in the primary market, any subsequent trades involving these securities are trades in the secondary market. Trades in the secondary market occur between two investors; the issuing company is not involved.[1]

WHAT IS AN IPO?

When a corporation sells its stock to the public for the first time, the process is known as an **initial public offering,** or IPO. To facilitate such a sale, the corporation normally hires an **investment banker** who, ironically, is neither an investor nor a banker! The term refers to a firm that specializes in helping other firms raise money. The sale of new securities is covered by the **Securities Act of 1933,** which requires that all investors in a public offering be given a **prospectus.** The prospectus contains basic information about the company, audited financial statements, a description of how the money raised will be used, and the characteristics of the securities being sold. The **Securities and Exchange Commission** (SEC) reviews the prospectus, and, upon its approval, the company may proceed to offer the securities.[2] During the SEC review, the unapproved copy may be distributed to prospective investors in order to start drumming up interest. This unapproved copy has a paragraph printed in bright red on the front page notifying the reader that while approval

---

[1] An exception to this rule occurs when the issuers of securities enter the secondary market to buy back some of their own securities. For example, corporations are always buying back shares of their stock for various reasons; such trades count as secondary market transactions.

[2] The SEC was established under the **Securities Exchange Act of 1934,** which is focused on the secondary market.

Web Link 16.1

is pending, the document does not constitute a solicitation to sell the security. This preliminary document is known as a **red herring.** If all goes well, the SEC approves the proposed prospectus, the investment banker proceeds with the offering, and the company acquires the money it seeks.

Buying an IPO offers two benefits to investors. First, the investment banker pays the commission to the broker, not the individual investor. In fact, the commission rate on IPOs is usually substantially larger than that on normal trades. For this reason, most investors will find their stockbrokers more than delighted to have them participate in an IPO. The second is that IPOs, on average, are sold at a price that the investment banker believes is slightly below the market price that will emerge once the security starts trading in the secondary market. This process, referred to as **underpricing,** is usually on the order of 5 to 10 percent. However, IPO offerings have been known to double or even triple on the day of the offering, particularly when the industry is considered "hot." In the 1990s, companies whose operations were related to the Internet were deemed "hot." A list of companies that have recently had IPOs or are scheduled for an IPO in the near future may be found at **Web Link (WSJ) 16.2.** An example of the *Wall Street Journal*'s watch list is provided in Figure 16.1. Pointer sites for IPO offerings are at **Web Link 16.2a.** Some research suggests that after the initial underpricing windfall has corrected itself, companies with IPOs tend to underperform the market on average over the next five years. A discussion of this point may be found at **Web Link 16.3.**

**Web Link
(WSJ) 16.2**

Web Link 16.2a

Web Link 16.3

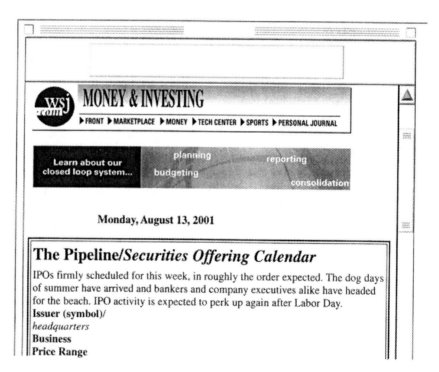

FIGURE 16-1 Prospective IPOs Listed in the WSJ

Just because a security is offered through an IPO and promoted by one or more well-known investment bankers does not always mean it is a good investment. Some offerings involve securities from companies engaged in highly risky business activities. The issuance of a prospectus is only meant to guarantee that the prospective investor cannot say he or she was not fully informed of the riskiness of the securities. If you buy an IPO without reading the prospectus and particularly its discussion of the risks facing the company, you are not being a good steward of your money.

Web Link 16.4

WHAT IS A DPO?

Although the IPO market works extremely well for large companies, it will not work for "small" companies. First, a small company's offering typically would not be large enough to justify hiring an investment-banking firm. A traditional alternative way small firms raise capital is by finding a **venture capital firm.** Unfortunately, the venture capital firm will want a significant portion of the stock (and thus ownership) of the firm, and entrepreneurs are usually hesitant to give up a large share of control of the company. The arrival of the Internet has greatly facilitated the ability of firms to sell offerings of stock directly to the public. Such offerings are known as **direct public offerings,** or DPOs. A DPO is an IPO without the middleman. Although DPOs must still meet the same regulatory constraints as IPOs do, the small size of the firm and the absence of scrutiny by an experienced investment banker can make DPOs quite risky.

Web Link 16.5
Web Link 16.6

WHERE ARE STOCKS TRADED?

The secondary market is made up of several exchanges and markets. An exchange is characterized as national or regional, depending on its listing requirements and the nature of the companies included. The largest exchange in the world is the **New York Stock Exchange** (NYSE), located in New York City. For a company to have its stock traded on the NYSE, it must apply to the NYSE and meet the current listing standards. If approved, the company then pays an initial listing fee and an annual fee to remain listed (assuming it continues to meet the listing standards).

The only other national exchange in the United States is the **American Stock Exchange,** or AMEX. The AMEX, once independent, recently merged with the National Association of Securities Dealers Automated Quotations, or NASDAQ. The two largest U.S. regional exchanges are the Chicago Stock Exchange (CSE) and the Pacific Coast Stock Exchange (PCSE). Others include the Boston Stock Exchange (BSE) and the Philadelphia stock exchange (PHLX). Other countries also have their own national stock exchanges, such as the Hong Kong Stock Exchange (Figure 16.2).

Web Link 16.7
Web Link 16.8
Web Link
(WSJ) 16.8a

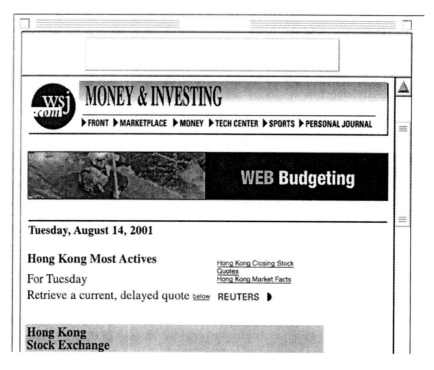

FIGURE 16-2 Hong Kong Most Active

An exchange does not necessarily have to have a physical location. The fastest growing market is the over-the-counter (OTC) market, a huge market made up of many people connected via computers. The OTC market is formally known as the NASDAQ, whose home page is the same as that of AMEX since their merger.

Web Link 16.9

There are also exchanges for trading securities other than common stock. Most bond trading is done in the OTC market, although the NYSE and AMEX sponsor trading in some corporate bonds. Options are traded on several exchanges, the biggest being the Chicago Board of Options Exchange (CBOE), the AMEX, and the PHLX. Futures contracts are traded on the Chicago Board of Trade (CBOT) and the Chicago Mercantile Exchange (CME), among others.

Web Link 16.10

WHAT LISTING STANDARDS AND FEES EXIST?

All of the exchanges discussed in the previous section are member-owned. Membership is referred to as a **seat** on the exchange. A seat allows a person to trade securities on that exchange. Seats are actively traded just like any other security. In many cases, a seat on the exchange is a better investment than the securities traded on the exchange!

An exchange is only interested in listing securities that will generate enough trading volume to allow its members to make a profit (from commissions) in trading it. Hence, the central requirement for a company to be listed on an exchange is a certain quantity of trading. Let's consider some of the listing criteria for two exchanges.

Web Link 16.11

The listing criteria for the NYSE can be found at **Web Link 16.11.** At the time of writing, the first listing criterion involved meeting any one of several different standards, including:

- At least 2,000 round lot holders in the United States
- At least 2,200 total shareholders, together with an average monthly trading volume for the most recent six months of 100,000 shares
- At least 500 total shareholders together with an average monthly trading volume for the most recent 12 months of 1,000,000 shares

The second listing criterion required at least 1,100,000 shares to be outstanding. The remaining criteria deal with a company's market value, earnings, sales, cash flows, and total assets. To compare the NYSE with a regional exchange, consider the BSE, whose initial listing requirements include having at least 600 shareholders and at least 750,000 shares outstanding but do not mandate the number of shareholders with round lots or average trading volume over a recent time period.

Web Link 16.12

A company that lists on the NYSE incurs an initial listing fee of $36,800. The company must then also pay annual fees based on its number of shares outstanding. For the first million shares outstanding, the NYSE charges an annual fee of $14,750. An additional fee is charged based on how many additional shares are outstanding. The BSE has a $250 application fee, a $7,500 per issue initial listing fee, and a $750 annual fee. It is clearly a lot less expensive to be traded on a regional exchange than the NYSE.

Web Link 16.13

For all of the fees involved, one has to ponder if it is worth the cost to a company and its shareholders to be listed on the NYSE. Research tends to suggest that listings benefit a company's officers more than its shareholders.

Web Link 16.14

In recent years new types of trading entities have come into existence. These include the Arizona Stock Exchange (AZX), Instinet, and Posit. In the AZX market, all participants are connected to a computer in Phoenix. An official exchange auctioneer calls out a trial price for each security to determine the amount of buying and selling interest at that price. The price is then adjusted appropriately until buying and selling interests are balanced. Trades are then executed at this price. The ASX is currently limited to institutional investors and broker-dealers looking to enter transactions in government debt instruments and U.S. corporate debt and equity securities.

Web Link 16.15

Instinet and Posit are trading organizations that simply seek to match large orders. They do not engage in price discovery activity itself. Instinet has been in existence since about 1969, and Posit since about 1988.

Web Link 16.16

Similar to the AZX, the Cincinnati Stock Exchange has changed from a traditional regional exchange format to an electronic exchange without a trading floor. Contrary to its name, the Cincinnati Exchange is headquartered in Chicago.

Web Link 16.17

HOW DOES TRADING WORK?

Trading is performed on the various exchanges and markets according to two methods. The NYSE uses what is known as a specialist system, which assigns a specialist (technically, his or her firm) to each stock. The specialist is obligated to assure a fair and orderly

Web Link 16.18 market for each stock assigned to him or her. The specialist must therefore be available to trade with anyone at any time the exchange is open and must assure that prices are reasonably continuous. These tasks are accomplished by the continuous posting of **bid** and **asked prices.** A bid price is the price at which the specialist will buy a security from an investor wanting to sell; the asked price is the price at which the specialist will sell a security to an investor wanting to buy. Consider the following example:

> *Susan Jordan is thinking about buying 100 shares of Exxon. In talking to her broker, she learns that the most recent trade of the stock was at $75.15. The current bid and asked prices are $75.10 and $75.20. What would it cost her to buy the stock?*

The specialist is willing to sell the stock at $75.20 per share. It is possible that when Susan's order gets to the floor of the stock exchange, a better price might be available. It is also possible that by the time the order arrives at the floor of the exchange, the specialist may have changed his or her prices. Having noted all of this, Susan acknowledges that she most likely will have to pay $75.20 per share, plus commission.

The second method of trading is a dealer system. In a dealer system—the one used in the OTC market—one or more brokers opt to act as dealers in a particular stock. Each dealer then sets his or her own bid and asked prices. When a broker places a customer's order in such a stock, the broker should then seek to direct the trade to the dealer offering the best quote.

In both systems, the difference between the bid and asked prices is known as the **bid-asked spread.** Unlike brokerage commissions, this spread is a cost of trading securities that most investors do not see. The bid-asked spread is just as real a cost as the brokerage commission, it just doesn't show up anywhere explicitly in the numbers provided to an investor.

WHAT IS A STOCK MARKET INDEX?

People want to know how "the market" is doing for several reasons. First, by knowing how "the market" is doing in general, you can infer how your own portfolio is doing without having to look up every item in it. Furthermore, you can benchmark your portfolio's performance in comparison to the overall market. If "the market" went up 10 percent in the last six months and your portfolio went up 12 percent, then you have reason to be pleased with its performance.

However, there is no true measure of "the market" because there are too many unanswerable questions to define the term. For example, should "the market" include preferred stocks, bonds, rights, warrants, options, and futures contracts, as well as common stocks? Should it include securities listed on only one exchange, or securities from many exchanges and markets? Should it include only securities listed on U.S.-based exchanges, or securities from around the world?

Over the years, different measures of "the market," known as stock market indices, have therefore evolved. Each index is unique in terms of what securities are included, how many are included, and the mathematics of how the index is constructed, so no two stock market indices move in perfect synchronization. On a day-to-day basis, stock market Web Link 16.19 indices can differ dramatically in their performance.

WHAT IS THE DJIA?

Web Link
(WSJ) 16.20

Web Link
(WSJ) 16.20a

Web Link 16.20b

Web Link 16.20c

The most quoted stock market index is the **Dow Jones Industrial Average** (DJIA), which is owned by the Dow Jones Corporation. Its current value may be found at **Web Link (WSJ) 16.20.** To obtain a list of the 30 stocks that currently make up the average, go to **Web Link (WSJ) 16.20a.** When the DJIA was originally created, it contained only 12 stocks (listed at **Web Link 16.20b**); membership was expanded to 30 in 1928. High, low, close, and component listings of the DJIA for any day since May 26, 1896 (when it was first published), are at **Web Link 16.20c.**

The DJIA was originally computed by adding up the prices and dividing the total by twelve. This process created two minor problems in interpreting the index. The first was that it omitted dividends. If the average dividend yield in the DJIA were, say, 3 percent, then using the index to estimate the rate of return on the market would understate that return by 3 percent per year. This dividend omission is still a problem today in interpreting the index.

The second problem was that whenever a stock in the index split, the index would show a substantial drop even when the value of the company had not changed. This problem has since been resolved by adjusting the denominator to offset any stock splits and dividends that occur. Thus, the denominator at the time of writing is not 30, but 0.2252. To get today's DJIA value, add up the prices of the 30 stocks in the average and divide by 0.2252 (i.e., by the current denominator).

Every few years, the Dow Jones Company opts to change one or more of the stocks in the DJIA. If it were to delete a stock whose price at the time was, say, $10, and replace it with a stock whose price was $90, the DJIA could substantially jump without any real change in value having occurred. This problem is also solved by adjustments to the denominator.

Because of the way the index is computed, it is known as a **dollar-weighted index,** meaning that the highest-priced stocks dominate it. Despite DJIA's popularity, it is truly a terrible index with which to follow the broad market. The population of the index is small compared to other averages, cash dividends are not incorporated, and it is biased toward its higher-priced stocks.

Web Link 16.21

Other Dow Jones indices include the Dow Jones Transportation Average (DJTA), which has 20 stocks, the Dow Jones Utility Average (DJUA), which has 15 stocks, and the Dow Jones Composite Average (DJCA), which has 65 stocks and which combines the stocks in the other three averages.

Web Link
(WSJ) 16.22

WHAT OTHER MARKET INDICES EXIST?

The most common alternative stock market index is the S&P 500, compiled by the Standard & Poor's Corporation. As the name suggests, it contains 500 stocks. The S&P 500 is computed in a completely different manner than the DJIA. Like the DJIA, the S&P 500 does not include dividends in its computation. However, because of the way it is computed, it is impervious to any impact from stock dividends or stock splits. The index is based on the market value of the companies included in the index compared to their market value on a base date. A company's market value is its price per share times the number of shares

Web Link 16.23
Web Link 16.24

outstanding. The S&P 500 is known as a **value-weighted index.** The stocks in the index are chosen for market size, liquidity, and industry group representation. Standard & Poor's also publishes other indices, but the S&P 500 has the greatest fame.

In addition to the DJIA and the S&P 500, hundreds of other indices exist, including the NYSE Composite Index, the NASDAQ Composite Index, the Frank Russell 3000 Index, and the Wilshire 5000. The NYSE Composite Index includes all of the stocks on that exchange and is computed in the same manner as the S&P 500. As stocks are listed or unlisted on the exchange, they are added to or removed from this index.

Web Link 16.25
Web Link 16.26
Web Link 16.27
Web Link 16.28
Web Link 16.29

The NASDAQ Composite Index includes all NASDAQ domestic and non-U.S. based common stocks listed on the NASDAQ Market. This index is also value-weighted. At the time of writing, there were 4,841 companies in this index. A smaller version of this composite index is the NASDAQ 100.

Web Link 16.30

The Frank Russell 3000 Index measures the performance of the 3,000 largest U.S. companies based on total market capitalization. At the current time, these represent approximately 98 percent of the market value of the publicly traded U.S. equity market.

Probably the broadest stock market index in popular use is the Wilshire 5000. Its name is somewhat misleading, because more than 7,000 stocks are currently included in this index, although there were 5,000 stocks when the index was established.

Web Link 16.31
Web Link 16.32
Web Link
(WSJ) 16.33
Web Link 16.34

Additional details and descriptive information on some of the market indices discussed above may be found at **Web Link 16.32.** To obtain current quotes on many of these various indices, the reader may use **Web Link (WSJ) 16.33.** A pointer site for links to sites providing comprehensive quotes is at **Web Link 16.34.**

SHOULD I USE A FULL-SERVICE BROKER OR A DISCOUNT BROKER?

The brokerage industry can be divided into two general groups: **full-service brokers** and **discount brokers.** In full-service brokerage firms, a specific individual handles each account. The emphasis is on personalized service, including investment research advice. Full-service brokers will contact their customers to suggest trades. In some cases, these brokers will actually encourage their customers to open **discretionary accounts,** an arrangement by which the holder of the account gives written power-of-attorney to someone else, often a broker, to buy and sell without prior approval of the holder. These accounts are also known as managed accounts or controlled accounts. There are generally two rationales for opening a discretionary account. One is that the investor can continue to be the primary decision maker without missing an attractive trading opportunity when the broker cannot reach him or her in a timely manner; the broker can place orders at his or her own discretion. The other rationale for a discretionary account is that the investor is asking the broker to act as the portfolio manager and to make the trades that he or she deems appropriate for the account. Examples of what can go wrong with a discretionary

Web Link 16.35

account may be found at **Web Link 16.35.**

Stockbrokers who work at a full-service brokerage firm are paid solely with the commissions they generate. The commission income the investor pays is split between the firm and the broker. Generally, the higher the broker's total annual commissions, the higher the percentage of those commissions the broker gets to keep.

In a discount brokerage firm, on the other hand, accounts are with the firm, not a specific broker. Thus, customers simply place an order with the firm and not a specific broker. A discount broker never calls a customer to initiate a trade.[3] Accounts at discount brokerage firms are for investors who really want to manage their own account and seek to minimize the cost of maintaining an account.

Until a few years ago, these distinctions between a full-service broker and a discount broker were more clearly delineated; in recent years they have blurred. Many traditional full-service brokerage firms are implementing discount service operations for customers who want substantially discounted commissions, while many discount brokerage firms are seeking ways to provide higher levels of service for customers who want more personalized contact.[4] Nonetheless, the general guidelines still hold true and are worth considering when you decide which type of brokerage you want.

Web Link 16.36

HOW SHOULD I SELECT A BROKER AND A BROKERAGE FIRM?

If you choose to go with a full-service brokerage firm, you will then need to select the particular broker with whom you will open an account. It is highly recommended that you interview and otherwise evaluate your broker before handing over thousands, tens of thousands, or even hundreds of thousands of dollars to him or her. Start by asking for the broker's professional credentials, educational training, and background. Assess the broker's investment philosophy and style, particularly his or her attitude toward risk and skill in dealing with risk. What is ultimately important is whether the broker will manage the account in a manner consistent with your client's objectives. Finally, it is important to understand in detail how the broker will be compensated. Particularly with discretionary accounts, some brokers will charge a fee based on a percentage of the assets. If a broker is going to actively trade an account, this might work out to be a better deal than paying a commission on every trade.

Web Link 16.37

Your first concern in selecting a brokerage firm should be its insurance coverage. Each firm should at a minimum provide **Securities Investor Protection Corporation** (SIPC) insurance coverage. The SIPC is a nonprofit federally chartered private corporation funded by the brokers and dealers to whom it provides insurance. The current minimum insurance coverage is $500,000, with cash in the account covered only up to $100,000. Consider the following example:

> Susan Jordan just sold several stocks that she has held for many years. She left the cash in her account while deciding which new investments she wanted to acquire. Her account was worth $720,000, of which $120,000 was in cash. Her broker files for bankruptcy. What is her SIPC protection?

The first step of the SIPC would be to attempt to arrange a merger so that Susan's account would be left intact. In this situation, Susan would lose nothing. Failing this, the firm

---

[3]There are exceptions to this statement. If any broker discovers an illegal or inappropriate position in an account, then he or she will contact the customer to correct the situation.

[4]It should be noted that to receive more personalized service at a discount brokerage firm, you might need to have at least $500,000 or $1 million in assets in your account.

would be liquidated and the assets of the customers returned to them (or transferred to new accounts they have specified). If Susan's account were worth $720,000 with $120,000 in cash, then the securities were worth $600,000. Susan would be guaranteed to get back at a minimum $100,000 in cash and $400,000 worth of securities. If the liquidation process went well, Susan might receive back her entire holdings.

If the SIPC cannot find the securities that were supposed to be in Susan's account, then she would receive cash for them.[5] The SIPC sets what is known as a **value date**— usually the date on which the SIPC initiated legal action against the failed brokerage firm. Susan would receive the market value of her securities as of that date. Note that receiving this cash equivalent constitutes a sale of these securities for tax purposes. Still, a de facto sale is much better than total loss of value.

Web Link 16.38

If an investor's account holds well under $500,000, then SIPC insurance is adequate. Many brokerage firms buy additional insurance protection, sometimes for up to $2 million or more.

Your second concern in selecting a brokerage firm should be whether that firm can meet all of your needs. Not all firms provide all potential services. A third concern is the quality of service. Everyone would like to pay the cheapest commissions possible, but beware of firms that do not provide an adequate number of phone lines or employ an adequate number of people to handle all calls at all times.

The fourth concern somewhat contradicts the third concern. Just because a broker offers better service and more features does not mean it is necessarily worth paying extra commissions for them. Consider the following example:

> Susan Jordan wants to set up an IRA account. She is considering two brokerage firms. The first firm charges a $20 annual custodian fee and $25 commission per trade. The second firm waives the annual custodian fee, but charges $30 per trade. The two firms appear identical in all other respects. Which firm should Susan select?

The answer clearly depends on how many trades Susan expects to make in the account per year. If she goes with the second firm, she is paying an extra $5 per trade in commission to save a $20 fee. If she expects to average three trades or fewer per year, she should go with the second firm, but if five or more, the first. If she expects to average four trades per year, the two firms really are basically identical.

A fifth concern in choosing a brokerage firm is hidden charges. Most brokerage firms advertise primarily one price: the commission cost on a simple stock transaction. The commission on bond trades is most likely different, so an investor who does a lot of bond trades will want to check on this detail. Brokerage firms will usually charge for wire transfers (typically $25 or more), and these rates vary. Some brokers charge for closing out an account (sometimes $50 or more!), so if you become disenchanted with your service you actually have to pay a fee to move your account.

Finally, you should take into account the quality of the monthly and year-end summary statements. Even this author has found the statements of some brokerage firms to be

---

[5]Securities may "disappear" either through criminal activity or incompetence. For example, the brokerage firm may never have bought them, or the broker may have pocketed the cash and sent the customer a fictitious confirmation. Or, if the brokerage firm failed to maintain its records properly, it might simply be unable to identify or otherwise locate those securities.

Web Link 16.39

nearly incomprehensible. A comprehensible monthly statement and a clear and concise year-end statement are valuable benefits. The year-end statement, known as Form 1099, is critical for obtaining tax return information.

WHICH STOCK BROKERAGE
FIRMS PROVIDE INTERNET ACCESS?

Web Link 16.40
Web Link 16.41

Before the dramatic growth of the Internet in the 1990s, brokerage firms attracted customers via name recognition and "bricks and mortar" location. Many investors like to physically visit their broker's office. The Internet allows firms with little in the way of physical office space to compete effectively for a national array of customers. We appear to be in a period of rapid proliferation of brokerage firms, all competing to establish themselves through the Internet. At some point, some clear leaders will emerge, and there will be a general industry shakeout. Internet access to brokerage firms may be found at **Web Link 16.40. Web Link 16.41** provides pointer sites for finding brokerage firms on the Internet.

Web Link 16.42

Several sites on the Internet attempt to rate various brokerage firms'. As discussed earlier, no absolute measure of quality exists, because different firms offer different combinations of services and prices. Nonetheless, the reader may find some of these opinions at **Web Link 16.42.**

Web Link 16.43
Web Link 16.43a

Some firms post their commission schedules beside those of other firms. Naturally, when comparisons are offered, each firm picks the type of trade and a set of competitors that make them look best.

SHOULD I ORDER OUT STOCK
OR LEAVE IT IN STREET NAME?

When an investor buys a security such as stock, one of the choices to make is whether to **order out** the stock certificate or to leave it in **street name.** The majority of investors choose to do the latter, but the first option also has advantages.

Ordering out means having the certificate mailed to you. In this case, your name and address show up on the company's books as one of the owners of the company.[6] This enables the company to contact you directly. For instance, if the company mails out dividend checks, then each investor's check would go directly to his or her mailing address, as would mailings such as annual reports, quarterly reports, proxy ballots, and any special press releases. Some companies send new investors or even current investors promotional items such as discount coupons for the company's products or free samples of them.

However, there are three major drawbacks to ordering out a stock certificate. The first is that if it becomes lost or destroyed, the replacement process is cumbersome. Each year, approximately $5 billion worth of securities are misplaced, stolen, or lost in the mail. This is not a trivial problem. Second, when the investor wants to sell the stock certificate, he or she will have to arrange for delivery of the certificate to the brokerage firm, unless

---

[6]Technically, the investor's name would be recorded on the books of the transfer agent for the stock, rather than the actual company's books.

the investor were able to sell the certificate on his or her own. (Any two people can purchase stock from one to another, just as with any asset, such as a car or a house.) The third drawback to ordering out is that collecting tax information at the end of the year becomes more cumbersome.

Leaving a certificate in street name just means leaving it in one's account at the brokerage firm. On the books of the company whose stock has been purchased, the brokerage firm is the owner of the stock. The investor's ownership is shown through the trade confirmation sent to the investor when the stock is purchased, and through the monthly statements issued to the investor. Thus, the company mails out dividend checks to the brokerage firm, not the individual investor. Each investor should specify when opening an account how the brokerage firm is to treat these dividend checks. You may request that these checks be forwarded to you. (It is always fun to receive a dividend check in the mail.) More often, cash from the dividends sits in the account until the investor provides specific instructions. Mailings are likewise sent to the brokerage firm, which arranges to have them forwarded to the investor. The major disadvantages to leaving certificates in street name are the potential delay in receiving dividends and other information from the company, and the risk that the brokerage firm may close. The brokerage firm's insurance coverage mitigates the second risk, but it is still an inconvenience to have one's assets tied up while the receiver sorts everything out.

Web Link 16.44

HOW DO I BUY STOCK DIRECTLY FROM A COMPANY?

One way to invest in stocks and keep the transaction costs low is to buy stock directly from a company. Many companies allow you to open an account through the Internet for just this purpose. These are known as **direct purchase programs,** or DPPs. In some cases, the company may actually provide the stock at a price slightly lower then the current market price! The advantages of buying stock directly are the waiver of commission and a possible discount. The main disadvantage of such a purchase is that one must leave the security on deposit with the company. Thus, you could not accumulate these stocks into one portfolio located with one broker. To sell some or all of the shares acquired through a DPP, the investor places an order to sell, and the order is executed at the leisure of the firm holding your stock, usually either at the end of the trading day or at the end of the month.

Additional commentary on direct purchase plans may be found at **Web Link 16.45.**
Web Link 16.45   Directories of companies that provide these direct stock purchase programs may be found
Web Link 16.45a   at **Web Link 16.45a.**

WHAT ARE DRIPS?

DRIPs are **dividend reinvestment programs.** Investors who already own stock in a company, whether purchased through a broker or directly from the company, may be able to start a dividend reinvestment program. In this program, the company uses the dividend it would normally send you to purchase additional shares. Sometimes there is a small transaction fee, and sometimes the purchase may be at slightly less than the current market price. Remember, even if you do not receive the cash dividend, you still must declare it as taxable income at the end of the year. The investor who participates in a DRIP needs to keep appropriate records, as each dividend reinvested becomes the cost basis for the stock so purchased.

Dividend reinvestment plans have several major advantages. First, DRIPs are one of the few ways of instantaneously investing small amounts of cash. Normally, a $20 or $30 dividend check (or even a $200 or $300 dividend check) is not easily invested into anything other than a money market account. Second, dividend reinvestment programs automatically provide a form of dollar cost averaging (to be discussed later). Many dividend reinvestment programs also allow the investor the benefit of purchasing additional shares directly from the company.

If the original investment in a company is through a direct purchase plan, then setting up a dividend reinvestment plan is almost automatic. If the original investment was purchased through a stockbroker, then the companies will usually require you to deposit your shares in an account with them—a reasonable request, as they need to be able to verify that you are the current owner of the shares whose dividends are being reinvested. Thus, an investor would have to order out his or her stock certificate, and then forward it to the company for deposit in a DRIP account.

Some brokerage firms also offer DRIPs for securities that are in street name. In some cases, the brokerage firm may just set up an account with the company and act as an agent for the investor. In other cases, the brokerage firm creates a simulated DRIP plan. That is, they aggregate all dividends being reinvested in a company by all of the customers who own that company through the brokerage firm and use the combined cash to buy new shares. These shares are then assigned to the various accounts as if the purchase were a DRIP plan. Unless their commission fees are excessive, simulated DRIP plans have all the benefits of DRIP plans, while customers have the convenience of keeping their securities in street name.

DRIPs' only potential disadvantage is increased concentration of a limited number of stocks in the portfolio, because the reinvestment is (by definition) only in stocks you already have.

Web Link 16.46

WHAT DIFFERENT TYPES OF ORDERS CAN BE PLACED?

When it comes time to buy a stock, an investor actually has a choice as to the type of order that can be placed. Although a large variety of orders exists, only two types are used by all but the most sophisticated traders; the **market order** and the **limit order.** A market order directs that the security be bought (or sold) at the best available price as soon as the order reaches the appropriate trading location. When you place a market order, you are absolutely guaranteed that the trade will occur immediately. You have some uncertainty only as to price. In this case, the term *immediately* means typically a few seconds, and at most one or two minutes. If you know the bid and asked prices on the security just before placing a market order, you are very likely to find the actual price someplace within this spread. Stock prices could conceivably move several points between the moment quotes are obtained and the time the order is delivered, but such an event is rare.

In a limit order, the order to buy specifies the maximum price the investor is willing to pay. In a limit order to sell, the investor specifies the minimum price he or she will accept. With limit orders, you have some confidence of the price at which the trade might occur, but no guarantee the trade will take place. Consider the following example:

Susan Jordan is thinking about buying some stock in the Andrew Corporation. The current quotes are 17.25 bid and 17.50 asked. She would like to buy the stock for no more than 17.25. She places a limit buy at 17.25. What will happen?

One of two things will happen. The first is that the bid and asked prices could decline to the point that Susan is able to buy the stock at her designated price. The second is that the bid and asked prices could stay at the current price range or move up, in which case, no purchase will occur unless Susan modifies her order.

When limit orders are placed, some time specification must be noted. It is certainly possible to make the order **good till cancelled** (GTC). The most common alternative is the **day order,** which is canceled by the end of the day if not executed. Other time specifications are also possible.

Limit orders can be quite effective in saving an investor $25, $50, $100, or more on a trade; however, they can cause an investor to miss out on thousands of dollars in investment gains. Imagine that in the above example the stock of Andrew Corporation went from 17.25 bid, 17.50 asked to 35.25 bid, 35.50 asked over the next few days, without the asked price ever dropping to the 17.25 level. In this case, Susan would have missed out on doubling her money in this investment by trying to save an extra $.25 per share. Limit orders are sometimes referred to as "penny wise and pound foolish."

Web Link 16.47

WHAT IS BUYING ON MARGIN?

Buying on margin refers to borrowing part of the money to pay for the purchase of a security. Thus, if an investor wants to buy 100 shares of a stock trading at $30 per share, the total cost of the purchase, before commissions, would be $3,000. Margin refers to how much of that the investor pays with his or her own cash. Thus, with an initial margin rate of 60 percent, the investor would be required to pay at least $1,800 ($3,000 × 60%). The rest, up to $1,200 in this case, is usually borrowed from the investor's broker. The primary advantage of buying on margin is that for a given amount of money you acquire more shares. If the price of the security increases at a rate greater than the interest rate on the loan, you make greater profits (both in dollar terms and in percentage terms) than if you strictly paid cash. Consider the following example:

Susan Jordan has $6,000 with which to invest in stocks. She sees a stock trading for $60 per share and she thinks this stock will increase to $80 in a year's time. Susan can pay cash for the stock, or she can combine her cash with a loan from the broker. How much would she make in dollar terms and percentage terms under each strategy? Assume a 60 percent margin rate and ignore commissions.

If Susan pays cash, she will be able to buy 100 shares ($6,000 / $60). If the price goes to $80, she would have a $2,000 profit in dollar terms. In percentage terms, she would have a $33\frac{1}{3}$ percent profit ($2,000 / $6,000).

If Susan buys on margin (i.e., with borrowed money), then we first have to ascertain the maximum amount she can borrow. The maximum amount she can pay for the stock multiplied by the margin rate must not exceed the amount of cash she has. Thus, we can set up the following equation:

Maximum amount purchased × 60% = Investor's own cash.

Susan's own cash is $6,000, so the maximum amount she can purchase is $6,000 divided by the 60 percent margin rate, or $10,000 worth of stock. In other words, Susan can borrow a maximum of $4,000 ($10,000 − $6,000). At a price of $60 per share, this means Susan could buy a total of 166⅔ shares. Although one cannot buy a fraction of a share in a stock purchase, we will use the fractional share purchase just to keep the example simple. If the price goes up by $20 per share, Susan will have a dollar profit of $3,333.34 (166⅔ shares × $20 per share). To determine her profit in percentage terms, we have to divide her profit by the amount of her own money she invested, not the amount she paid for the stock. Thus, her percentage rate of return is now 55.56 percent ($3,333.34 / $6,000).

The above numbers would all have to be adjusted for the interest that would be charged on the margin loan. (Stockbrokers do not loan money for free!) Let's say that Susan's broker charges a current interest rate of 8 percent. At the end of the first month, Susan would owe one month's interest, or $26.67 ($4,000 × 8% × $1/12$). Susan could either pay this interest or add it to the balance she owes the broker. Let's assume that she pays the interest in cash. At the end of the year, Susan would have paid $320 total in interest ($4,000 × 8%). Her dollar profits from buying on margin would be reduced by this amount, and her percentage rate of return would also be reduced.

The effect of buying on margin can be expressed in a simple formula. Let ROA equal the percentage rate of return an investor would receive if he or she paid all cash for the investment. Let m = the percentage of the purchase price that the investor actually pays from his or her own pocket. If we define ROE as the investor's percentage rate of return when he or she buys on margin, it turns out that ROE = ROA / m. If m equals one (i.e., the investor pays all cash), then ROE = ROA. If m equals 50 percent (i.e., the investor borrows one-half of the purchase price), then ROE = ROA / .5 = 2 × ROA. In other words, you double whatever the percentage gain or loss would have been on an all cash purchase.

When the interest expense of borrowing is introduced into the equation, it would be modified as follows:

$$ROE = \frac{ROA}{m} - I$$

where I equals the interest rate for the time period of the investment.

Therefore, if an investor buys on 75 percent margin (m = .75), pays an annual interest rate of 10 percent, and in six months the stock goes up 50 percent, then that investor's rate of return for the six-month period would be

$$61.67\% = \frac{50\%}{.75} - .05$$

Note that a margin loan has no maturity to it. The investor must pay it off if he or she sells the security that is pledged as collateral against the loans. The investor may pay it off any time he or she has the cash and would like to reduce his or her indebtedness. Finally, the investor must pay off part or all of the loan if the equity value of the portfolio falls below what is known as the **maintenance margin rate.** The equity value of the portfolio is the market value of the assets less any margin loans. If the maintenance margin rate were, say, 30 percent, then as long as the equity value is at least 30 percent of the market value of the assets, the investor would be safe. If the equity value were to fall to less than 30 percent, then the investor would receive what is known as a **margin call** from his or her broker. The margin call is a request to either pay down some of the loan with new cash or sell some of the securities to pay off some or all of the loan. Receiving a margin call will ruin the day of any investor! Consider the following example:

> *Susan Jordan recently bought 100 shares of Bergen Brunswig at $30 per share. At the time, she put down 50 percent of the purchase (i.e., $1,500) and borrowed the balance (i.e., $1,500). The price of the stock has just fallen to $20 per share. If the maintenance margin rate is 30 percent, how much equity (i.e., cash) will Susan be asked to provide?*

If the maintenance margin rate is 30 percent, then the loan cannot exceed 70 percent of the market value of the stock. In this case, the loan is $1,500 ($3,000 × [1 − .50]). So, if we divide the $1,500 loan by the 70 percent maximum value of the loan, the market value of the stock cannot be less than $2,142.86 ($1,500 / [1 − .30]). As the actual market value of the stock is $2,000 ($20 × 100 shares), Susan will be asked to send in a check for the difference, or $142.86.

The interest rate on margin loans is never a fixed rate. Stockbrokers borrow from banks the money that they lend to their customers. The interest rate charged by the banks is known as the **call money rate.**[7] Stockbrokers charge their customers this rate plus a markup. The call money rate is a variable rate that banks can and do change at any time. As soon as the lending bank changes its call money rate, the stockbroker changes the rate it is charging its customers. It is certainly possible that the interest rate an investor pays on a margin loan could change four, five, or more times in a month, although most of the time, **Web Link 16.48**   it is fairly stable.

Web Link 16.49

The Federal Reserve Board (often referred to as the Fed) sets the minimum values of the initial margin rate and the maintenance margin rate. The authority to set these rates is provided in Regulation T (which can be accessed in **Web Link 16.49**). Currently, the minimum initial margin rate is 50 percent, and the minimum maintenance margin rate is 25 percent. Individual brokers can always set higher margin rates if they so desire. The Fed also reserves the right to set higher margin rates for particular securities. In fact, the Fed **Web Link 16.50**   sometimes forbids the use of margin for purchasing some securities.

Buying on margin provides the opportunity for investors to increase their wealth much more rapidly than would otherwise be the case, but it also creates the potential to be wiped out much more quickly if things go wrong.

---

[7]For purposes of comparison, the call money rate is sometimes 100 basis points or more below the prime rate. For current rates, see **Web Link (WSJ) 5.31.**

HOW CAN I TAKE ADVANTAGE OF EXPECTED PRICE DECLINES?

Most people think of the investing process as one in which an investor buys a stock, hopes the price goes up, and then sells the stock later at presumably a higher price. The investor's profit is then the price appreciation on the stock, plus any dividends received during the time the stock was owned. This process is referred to as "going long" the stock. Being long means one is the owner, one owns the security.

Our markets allow this process to be reversed for many securities. That is, an investor can "sell" a stock he or she doesn't own but thinks will go down. If the investor is correct and the price goes down, then he or she later buys the stock. This process is referred to as "going short." Being short means one has sold something one did not own. The person who has gone short has an obligation to buy it back later.

To facilitate a short sale, the broker for the seller must borrow from someone the security that is being shorted. Thus, the person with whom the seller completes the short sale (i.e., the buyer) receives the stock, having no idea that it was borrowed. When the short-seller buys the stock back, it must be returned to the person from whom it was borrowed.

When a person shorts a security, the seller is not allowed to hold the cash from the transaction. The broker holds the cash. In addition, the seller must also post additional margin. For example, assume the initial margin requirement on short sales is 50 percent, and an investor wants to sell short 100 shares of a stock at $100 per share. The stockbroker would hold the $10,000 (100 shares × $100) proceeds from the sale and the investor would have to provide an additional $5,000.[8] When the short seller later reverses the transaction by buying new shares to replace the borrowed ones, the stockbroker returns whatever cash is left over after the purchase. For example, suppose in this case the investor is able to buy the 100 shares of stock back a few weeks later at $80 per share. The cost of these replacement shares is $8,000 (100 shares × $80 per share). The broker would then return to the investor $7,000 cash—the $5,000 margin deposit and $2,000 profit.

When you go short some stock, your losses are potentially unlimited. Suppose you go short 1,000 shares of a company's stock at, say, $20 per share. Just think what would happen if overnight the company announced that it had developed a cure for cancer. That stock could open trading the next morning at a price of $1,000 per share! You would have sustained a loss of $980,000 overnight! In other words, because the potential loss from a short sale is unlimited, most people try not to remain in a short position for an extended period of time.

When most people first hear about the concept of selling short, it sounds like fraud! In reality, it is an important aspect of market pricing. The price of a security should at all times reflect the best estimate of its true value. Short-selling allows investors who have a strong negative opinion on a stock to attempt to profit from that feeling. If such investors are correct, then they also do a service by helping to lower a stock's price to where it should be sooner than would otherwise be the case. In summary, selling short is truly only for the brave (or foolish).

Web Link 16.51
Web Link 16.52

---

[8]In practice, the investor would only need to post $5,000 in assets, not necessarily cash specifically.

WHAT IS DOLLAR COST AVERAGING?

In dollar cost averaging, instead of purchasing an investment at one time, purchases are spread out over time. The purest form of dollar cost averaging would involve equal dollar purchases made over equal intervals of time. For example, you might purchase $1,000 worth of a security on the first of every month. In practice, perfect dollar cost averaging is difficult, because the amount you have to invest may not be exactly divisible by the value of a whole number of shares plus the commission cost. It is more easily done with a mutual fund.

Dollar cost averaging may be strategic, or it may be done out of necessity. For example, an investor who has $6,000 cash in hand may opt as a formal choice to invest $1,000 on the first of each month for the next six months, instead of investing the entire $6,000 today. Alternatively, if the money for the investment is coming out of this investor's paycheck, he or she might have to make the purchases in monthly intervals only because of the lack of cash to make the full purchase today.

To fully understand the dollar cost averaging process, let us look at Table 16.1. The first column of this table represents the first day of the month for each of the next six months. Four scenarios represent a variety of possible changes in the price of a stock over time. In the first scenario, the stock price rises steadily. In the second, it rises in a series of up and down jumps. The third and fourth scenarios are similar, except the price ends up lower.

In all four cases, $6,000 was invested. Had all of the stock been purchased on the first day of the first month, the investor would have bought 300 shares ($6,000 / $20 per share). In the first two scenarios, the ending value of these 300 shares would have been $9,000. In the last two scenarios, the ending value would have been $3,000.

Table 16.1
The Impact of Dollar Cost Averaging Under Various Stock Price Scenarios
Assuming $1,000 Is Invested Each Period

	Scenario 1		Scenario 2		Scenario 3		Scenario 4	
Time	Price	Number of shares bought	Price	Number of shares bought	Price	Number of shares bought	Price	Number of shares bought
1	20	50	20	50	20	50	20	50
2	22	45.45	16	62.5	18	55.55	24	41.67
3	24	41.67	24	41.67	16	62.50	16	62.50
4	26	38.46	18	55.55	14	71.43	22	45.45
5	28	35.71	28	35.71	12	83.33	12	83.33
6	30	33.33	30	33.33	10	100.00	10	100.00
Ending holdings		244.62		278.76		422.81		382.95
Value of holdings		$7,338.60		$8,362.80		$4,228.10		$3,829.50

The dollar cost averaging table illustrates the following two points. First, if the price of the investment is going to go up, an investor is usually better off to invest the full cash on the first day. Second, if the price is going to go down, the investor is better off with dollar cost averaging.

Although the potential effects of dollar cost averaging are clear-cut, they don't really tell you whether you should engage in it. Some guidelines, however, do exist. First, if you are forced to choose between dollar cost averaging and not investing at all (because you can only set aside a little money each month to invest), then you should dollar cost average. Second, if you truly are faced with a choice of whether to invest all of some cash today or to dollar cost average, the answer depends on your personality. Many investors are faced with a paralysis of action, for fear that they will regret any action that results in their losing money, leading them to delay investing their money in case the market goes down that day and to wait hopefully for a better deal tomorrow. Such fear easily leads to the money never being invested. If these fearful investors were to set up a dollar cost averaging process, they could get their money invested while minimizing the likelihood they would feel regret. Consider the following example:

> Susan Jordan has just retired from her job. She has the option of cashing out her pension and moving the assets into an IRA account she has already set up. If she does this, she will add $150,000 in cash to her IRA account. She is now faced with the task of investing this money. What are her choices in terms of the timing of investing this money?

Her first choice is to identify one or more stocks in which she would like to invest, and then to place orders to invest all of this money on the first day it is available. However, if Susan is like most people, she would freeze at the thought of investing this money all at once. An alternative is to commit to a dollar cost averaging plan. She could pick one investment and once per month invest something like $5,000 or $10,000 in it. If the investment goes up that month, she can be pleased at her profit; if it goes down, she can console herself that she can get a better deal when she makes her purchases next month. Still another strategy is to buy not one but a variety of securities in order to obtain diversification. Susan might still use dollar cost averaging by allocating, say, $5,000 to each purchase, limiting herself to one purchase per day, week, or month. Although this would not be pure dollar cost averaging, it is nonetheless a form of it, to the extent that most security prices move in the same direction.

Web Link 16.53

HOW CAN I EXPERIMENT IN THE MARKET WITHOUT ACTUALLY INVESTING CASH?

For those who have never invested or are timid about buying stocks, there is an easy way to develop a comfort level with the stock market. A common piece of advice for neophyte investors is to invest "on paper." You might find this interesting for a day or two, but most people usually lose interest after awhile because of the paperwork associated with constantly looking up quotes, multiplying the quotes by the number of shares purchased in each company, and then adding up the value of all the holdings. Fortunately, you can do all of this on the Internet! The opportunity to construct imagined portfolios and follow

**Web Link
(WSJ) 16.54**

Web Link 16.54a

Web Link 16.55

Web Link 16.55a

them is offered at **Web Link (WSJ) 16.54.** This format is shown in Figure 16.3. A pointer site for portfolio tracking sites may be found at **Web Link 16.54a.** Some sites allow the investor not only to create, monitor, and edit a portfolio over time but to do so in the form of a game. Some of the games are for fun (see **Web Link 16.55**), and some are for actual prizes (including cash). Examples of stock market games with cash prizes are provided at **Web Link 16.55a.**

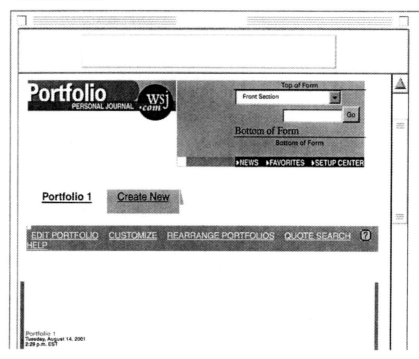

FIGURE 16-3 Creation of a Personalized Portfolio

WHAT PROTECTIONS DO INVESTORS HAVE?

Unfortunately, not all investment experiences lead to satisfactory results. If you select your own investments, place those orders with a broker, and lose some or all of your money, then that is simply a misfortune that sometimes happens. No one would be to blame. We have already discussed the protection provided to the investor through the SIPC if the brokerage firm fails. However, in the investment process, lots of things can and do go wrong, and sometimes it does happen that someone can be held at fault for breaking rules or guidelines, or for engaging in actual criminal activity. Exchanges all attempt to minimize the risk of inappropriate and illegal activity. In addition, investors who believe they have been wronged may turn to several regulatory bodies, including the National Association of Securities Dealers, or NASD (an industry organization), and the Securities and Exchange Commission, or SEC (a federal government agency).

Web Link 16.56

WHAT ARE PONZI AND PYRAMID SCHEMES?

A **Ponzi scheme** is an illegal investment method named after Charles Ponzi, who operated in Boston in the 1920s. He was by no means the first person to create a Ponzi scheme, but he made it famous. A Ponzi scheme is characterized by using the money from new investors to pay returns to old investors. For example, a con artist starts a Ponzi scheme by offering to pay 20 percent interest *every three months* for money invested. Now, 20 percent compounded every three months is the same as 207.36 percent (i.e., $[1 + .20]^4 - 1$) per year. If \$10,000 were invested initially, then at the end of *three months,* the "investor" would be owed a whopping \$2,000 in interest. Let's assume that during that three-month period, others hear about this fantastic rate of return and invest \$30,000 of new money with the con artist. The original investors would be unlikely to have taken their money out, as an annual rate of return of 207.36 percent is really nice. Even if the original investors take the interest but leave their original money, the con artist would have taken in \$40,000 in cash, and only paid out \$2,000. At the end of the second three-month period, he would owe at most \$8,000 (\$40,000 × 20%), but he would have all of the principal that was "invested" plus any new monies brought in from more new investors who heard about this great investment scheme. All Ponzi-type schemes eventually collapse.

A pyramid scheme works on the same principle as a Ponzi scheme. Let's say a promoter sells distributorships for \$1,000, each giving the buyer the right to sell additional distributorships also at \$1,000 each. Proceeds from all sales are split between the original promoter and the distributor who sells them. If the promoter sells four distributorships in the first month, he would take in \$4,000. If each of those distributors sells four distributorships, then the promoter would have taken in \$8,000 in the second month, while each of the first round distributors would have taken in \$2,000 each. Let's assume that the next month each of the 16 distributorships sells another four distributorships. The original promoter now receives \$32,000, and each of the distributors receives \$2,000. This sounds great, particularly for the promoter. However, for this process to continue, within a relatively short period of time everyone in the world would have to have bought a distributorship. In other words, like Ponzi schemes, pyramid schemes will also eventually collapse.

Web Link 16.57

SUMMARY

> Financial markets exist to allow people with more cash than they want to spend today to get together with other people who want to spend more cash than they have available.

> The primary market is the initial sale of securities by a firm for the purpose of raising cash. The secondary market is the subsequent trading of securities between any two investors.

> When a company is selling its stock to the public for the first time through an investment banker, the process is referred to as an IPO. Small companies may sell securities directly to investors through a process known as a DPO.

> The secondary market is made up of trading on national and regional exchanges, as well as the computerized OTC market. Each exchange has its own standards for listing a particular company. Trading is accomplished either with market makers or dealers.

> The most popular index is the DJIA. Other major indices include the S&P 500 and the NASDAQ Index.

> ➤ When opening an account for trading, an investor needs to decide between a full-service broker and a discount broker.

> ➤ Once a security is purchased, an investor then needs to decide if that security should be held in street name or ordered out.

> ➤ A particularly convenient way to buy stocks is through a DPP or a DRIP.

> ➤ The most common orders are a market order and a limit order.

> ➤ Buying on margin means borrowing money to buy an investment, usually magnifying the investor's percentage gain or loss.

> ➤ Dollar cost averaging means spreading one's purchases out over time. Some investors may utilize this strategy out of necessity, but others do it by choice.

> ➤ The Internet provides substantial opportunities to create imaginary portfolios to practice investing.

> ➤ An investor's main protections are SIPC and the filing of complaints with either the NASD or the SEC.

> ➤ Investors should always be on the lookout for scams such as Ponzi schemes and pyramid schemes.

KEY TERMS

American Stock Exchange	asked price	bid-asked spread
bid price	buying on margin	call money rate
day order	direct public offering	direct purchase programs
discount brokers	discretionary account	dividend reinvestment programs
dollar-weighted index	Dow Jones Industrial Average	full-service brokers
good till cancelled	initial margin rate	initial public offering
investment banker	limit order	maintenance margin rate
margin call	market order	National Association of Securities Dealers Automated Quotations
New York Stock Exchange	order out	over-the-counter market
Ponzi scheme	primary market	prospectus
red herring	seat	secondary market
Securities Act of 1933	Securities and Exchange Commission	Securities Exchange Act of 1934
Securities Investor Protection Corporation	street name	underpricing
value date	value-weighted index	venture capital firm

PROBLEMS

16.1 You want to buy 100 shares of WW stock at a price of $50. The initial margin rate is 60 percent and the maintenance margin rate is 40 percent. Ignore transaction fees and taxes.

    a. How much cash must you put up to buy the stock if you provide the minimum initial cash?

    b. If the stock goes to $70 by year-end and the average interest rate on margin loans during the year is 10 percent, what are the return on the stock (ROA), and the return on your investment (ROE)?

    c. If the stock goes to $70 by year-end and you wanted to take some cash out of the account, how much cash could you withdraw?

    d. If the stock goes to $70 by year-end and you wanted to buy as many additional shares of WW as possible without posting any more cash, how many shares could you buy?

    e. If the stock fell during the course of the year, what is the lowest price the stock could reach before you became eligible for a margin call?

16.2 You plan to buy some stock under a DPP. The stock currently trades at $50 per share, and you open the account with a $500 investment. On the last day of each month, you will have $100 withdrawn from your account and used to buy additional shares. Shares are computed out to the third decimal place. Over the next 12 months the stock price closes at $48, $45, $42, $40, $41, $47, $55, $60, $58, $60, $57, and $53. (Ignore transaction fees and taxes.)

    a. How many shares will you own 12 months from now and what will be the value of your account?

    b. If you had taken the entire amount you spent on buying the shares during the year and invested that in one lump sum at the start of the year, how many shares would you have bought and what would have been the value of your account at the end of the year?

    c. Reverse the order of prices over the next 12 months (i.e., assume that the prices had appeared as $53, $57,..., $48). Repeat questions a and b.

16.3 Submit the details of a DPP/DRIP program for a company of your choice.

REFERENCES

Web Link 16.58   Discussion about insider trading
Web Link 16.59   Glossaries of investment-related terms
Web Link 16.60   FAQ sites for direct stock purchase and dividend reinvestment programs
Web Link 16.61   Pointer sites for investment-related topics
Web Link 16.62   Miscellaneous sites

WALL STREET JOURNAL RESOURCES

Web Link (WSJ) 16.63   Discussion of online trading
Web Link (WSJ) 16.64   Information on filing a complaint in each state

For information that has changed since the book was written, for new information that pertains to this topic, and for some new web sites that pertain to the topic of this chapter, see **Web Link 16.65.**

PART V

PLANNING FOR RETIREMENT AND DEATH

CHAPTER 17

PLANNING FOR RETIREMENT, PART I: SOCIAL SECURITY AND PENSIONS

LEARNING OBJECTIVES

- Describe the basic features of Social Security
- Compute the Social Security taxes for any paycheck
- Describe who qualifies for various Social Security benefits
- Compute a Social Security retirement benefit
- Describe how a spouse's Social Security retirement benefits are determined
- Compare and contrast the two major types of pension programs
- Estimate a person's pension benefit from each program
- Explain the importance and limitations of PBGC for people with DB pensions

Web Link: www.wiley.com/college/woerheide

INTRODUCTION

For many people, saving for retirement is a major objective in financial planning. Nobody wants to find him- or herself 80 years old and broke! An unusually conservative person might be tempted to simply say he or she will save aggressively every year of his or her life to assure adequate funding for the retirement years (i.e., the annual saver discussed in Chapter 1). Although this goal is admirable, it is not necessarily how most people really want to live their lives. Financial planning always involves choices. Amply funding your retirement years normally means giving up doing things today that are important and meaningful. Taking your family to Disney World today may be much more important than setting aside that money to fund three trips to Disney World when you and your spouse are in your eighties and your children have little interest in going to Disney World with you! The point is that although you should save for retirement, doing so at the expense of enjoying life today is an unwise gamble. Remember, some people do not live long enough to retire and some die shortly after retiring.

In this chapter, we will focus on Dan O'Neill as he starts to think about his retirement years. The mechanics of retirement planning are simple; figuring out the appropriate numbers to use is more of a challenge. First, decide how much income you would be comfortable living on during your retirement years. Second, project your income from the four primary sources of retirement income: Social Security; pension benefits; tax-favored retirement programs such as IRAs, 401(k)s, 403(b)s, and annuities; and personal savings.

If the income from these four sources matches or exceeds what you would like to have during retirement, then you are set. Most people come up with a shortfall, which must be made up with income from personal investments. Next, ascertain how many assets you need to provide the desired income. Finally, think about the impact of inflation during the retirement years. To the extent that your projected retirement income will be fixed, a serious bout of inflation would do serious damage to your standard of living, especially in your later years of retirement.

This chapter looks at the first two sources of retirement income, namely Social Security and pensions. In the next chapter, we will discuss tax-favored savings programs, along with some basic examples of the retirement planning model. These models can help you design a savings program today that will round out projected retirement income to your desired level.

Web Link 17.1

WHAT ARE THE BASIC FEATURES OF SOCIAL SECURITY?

Web Link 17.1a

Social Security started out as a simple program. Over the years, Congress has expanded it in a variety of ways, so that now it is a multifaceted program. Most people probably think of Social Security as simply a retirement program, probably because most public discussion about Social Security centers around this. However, Social Security also provides disability income and survivor's benefits, as well as Medicare (see Chapter 12). Most of the web sites that provide information on Social Security focus primarily on its retirement program, so this chapter will do so also. The reader is asked to remember its other elements.[1] Because Social Security taxes and Social Security benefits affect virtually everyone, each of us should understand how Social Security taxes are determined and how retirement benefits work.

Web Link 17.1b

As we review the basics of the program, keep in mind two key points. First, Social Security was never intended as an investment program, but as a program of social insurance. Thus, some of its features may not seem "fair" if viewed as an investment program. However, understood as a broad safety net for many people, Social Security does make sense. Second, Social Security was never intended to provide all the income you need for a comfortable retirement, but is intended to supplement other sources of retirement income. Probably one of the luckiest beneficiaries of the Social Security retirement program was Ida Fuller, the first person to receive a Social Security retirement check. Ida had paid a total of $44 in Social Security taxes over her working life before retiring in 1940. During retirement, she received total benefits of $20,885 before dying in 1975.

HOW ARE SOCIAL SECURITY TAXES DETERMINED?

Social Security taxes are structured as a **regressive tax.** A regressive tax is one in which lower-income people pay a higher percentage of their income than higher-income people

---

[1]For a discussion of Social Security's survivor's benefits, see Chapter 11.

do. There are two key elements of the Social Security tax: the tax rate, and the maximum amount of income to which this tax applies. Let us consider each of these elements.

Web Link 17.2

The Social Security tax rate for employees is the sum of two numbers: currently, a 6.20 percent rate for OASDI (the traditional Social Security programs) and a 1.45 percent rate for HI (the Medicare Hospital Insurance program). Since 1990, the sum of these two numbers has been 7.65 percent. However, one of the catches to Social Security taxes is that the effective tax rate is nearly double the stated rate, because employers are required by law to match the Social Security taxes their employees pay. For self-employed individuals, the tax rates are exactly double those of employees. Thus, self-employed individuals pay a Social Security tax of 15.30 percent, which is the sum of 12.4 percent for the OASDI programs and 2.9 percent for the Medicare program. To put this in perspective, consider that when Social Security taxes were first collected in 1937, the rate was 1 percent and applied only to the OASDI program.

Web Link 17.2a

There is an upper limit (found at **Web Link 17.2a**) to the amount of income to which the OASDI tax applies. For 2001, this limit was $80,400. Until 1990, the HI tax applied to the same income limit as did the OASDI tax. For comparison purposes, the limit in 1937 was $3,000, so the most a person paid in Social Security taxes then was 1 percent of $3,000, or $30.

The last year the amount of income on which one paid HI taxes was limited was 1994. For that year, it was $60,600 for the OASDI tax, and $135,000 for the HI tax. Beginning in 1995, the ceiling was eliminated for the HI tax. Thus, no matter how much you earn in wage income, you (and your employer) will each pay the 1.45 percent HI tax. The ceiling for the OASDI is set by formula, and increases each year. As soon as your wage or salary income exceeds this limit, the OASDI tax is no longer deducted from your paycheck (which can be like getting a raise during the year). If you work two jobs and your combined wages exceed the tax limit, you cannot request a waiver from this tax. Rather, you would apply the excess Social Security tax to your federal income taxes. Consider the following example:

> *In 1999, Dan O'Neill worked two jobs. On one job he earned $60,000 and on the other he earned $50,000. On the first job, he had $4,590 ($60,000 × 7.65%) in Social Security taxes withheld from his paycheck. On the second job he had $3,825 ($50,000 × 7.65%) in Social Security taxes withheld. How will this affect his federal income tax return?*

Dan's combined taxable income was $110,000 ($60,000 + $50,000), and his combined Social Security taxes were $8,415 ($4,590 + $3,825). In 1999 only the first $72,600 of income was subject to the OASDI, although the full pay was subject to the HI tax. Thus, the actual Social Security taxes Dan owes would be computed as follows:

$$\text{OASDI Tax: } \$72,600 \times 6.20\% = \$4,501.20$$

$$\text{HI Tax: } 110,000 \times 1.45\% = \underline{1,595.00}$$

$$\text{Total Due } 7,096.20$$

Thus, Dan could apply the extra $1,318.80 ($8,415 − $7,096.20) he paid in Social Security taxes to his federal income tax bill. Note that Dan's overpayment would seem to imply that one or both of his employers should also be entitled to share in a $1,318.80 refund, as they matched his contributions. However, this is one of the quirks in the Social Security tax system; neither employer in this case would be entitled to a refund of their overpayments of Dan's Social Security taxes.

Some special situations apply to the payment of Social Security taxes. One deals with domestic employees (e.g., maids or butlers). Up until 1993, neither the domestic employee nor the employer had to pay Social Security taxes if the total amount paid each quarter was less than $50. In 1993, President Clinton had two disastrous nominations for Attorney General who foundered on the problem that neither nominee had paid Social Security taxes for her domestic employees. This led Congress to reconsider the minimum amount a domestic employee had to earn to be covered by Social Security taxes. In 1994 Congress raised this minimum to $1,000 per year and set a formula in place to provide subsequent increases; it went up in 1998 to $1,100 per year.

Web Link 17.3
Web Link 17.3a

WHAT DOES IT TAKE TO QUALIFY FOR SOCIAL SECURITY BENEFITS?

Qualification for Social Security benefits is based on a **quarters of coverage** system. The maximum number of quarters a person can earn in one year is four quarters. In 2001, a quarter of coverage is earned for each $830 earned during the year, regardless of when it was earned. Thus, anyone earning at least $3,320 (4 × $830) during the year would automatically earn four quarters of coverage.

Web Link 17.4

To receive retirement benefits, a person must have at least 40 quarters of coverage.[2] This means, of course, you must have 10 years of qualifying employment to be covered by Social Security. Having extra quarters of coverage provides no special benefits. Once a quarter of coverage is earned, it can never be taken away. Your family is also fully qualified for survivor's benefits after you have 40 quarters of coverage; depending on your age at the time of your death, fewer might be sufficient.

The number of quarters of coverage you need for disability benefits is much more complicated. If you are younger than age 24, you only need six quarters earned in the three-year period preceding the date of your disability. Between and including ages 24 and 30, you need to have earned one-half of the quarters that occurred between when you turned 21 and when you became disabled. For example, if you become disabled at age 29, you would need credit for four years of work (16 credits) out of the past eight years (between age 21 and age 29). Between and including the ages of 31 and 42, you need to have earned 20 quarters of coverage, of which all must have been during the 10 years prior to when you became disabled. If you are over 42, then you need 20 quarters plus one quarter for each year above the age of 42.[3] Thus, if you were 50 when you became disabled, then you would need 28 quarters of coverage, at least 20 of which must have been earned in the prior 10 years. At age 62 or above, you need the full 40 quarters of coverage to receive disability benefits.

---

[2]The rule of having 40 quarters of credit for retirement benefits applies only to those born in 1929 or later. People born in 1928 only need 39 quarters, in 1927, 38 quarters, and so on.

[3]The rules regarding quarters of credit for coverage for disability benefits are different for those born prior to 1929.

WHAT RETIREMENT AGE DOES SOCIAL SECURITY SPECIFY?

For nearly the entire life of the Social Security program, the normal retirement age has been 65.[4] Recent Social Security reforms have established a schedule increasing it in increments to age 67. The first adjustment will occur for individuals born in 1938, who will have a normal retirement age defined as 65 years and two months. The normal retirement age then increases by two months for each later year of birth up to 1943. For people born between 1943 and 1954, the normal retirement age is now 66. For those born from 1955 to 1959, the normal retirement age increases by two months for each year later one was born. For those born after 1960, the normal retirement age is 67. Of course, as with all the rules in the Social Security system, Congress could change these definitions at any time. However, moving up normal retirement ages is a sensitive and visible political issue, so it is doubtful that Congress will change these numbers anytime soon.

Web Link 17.6

Although the normal retirement ages have increased, the time frame in which people may draw Social Security retirement benefits has been broadened. Currently, the earliest you can draw retirement benefits is at age 62, and the latest is at age 70. If you draw retirement benefits before reaching your normal retirement age, those benefits are reduced; likewise, deferring the start of retirement benefits rewards you with incremental benefits.

HOW WILL MY SOCIAL SECURITY RETIREMENT BENEFITS BE COMPUTED?

Computation of Social Security retirement benefits is quite complex. A later section of this chapter describes easier ways to estimate benefits, but those students interested in learning how to compute benefits themselves may pursue the following set of computations. The first step is to index or adjust a person's Social Security income each year. Social Security income is defined as the maximum amount on which you pay Social Security taxes (OASDI). Thus, even if you earned $500,000 in 2001, you could only count $80,400 as your income for that year in the retirement benefit formula. The indexing process adjusts a person's Social Security income to account for changes in average wages since the year the earnings were received. The average wage rates used by the Social Security Administration may be found at **Web Link 17.7.** Next, the sum of the indexed earnings for a person's best 35 years of earnings is computed. If you have not paid 35 years of Social Security taxes, zeros are used for those remaining years. The sum of the 35 best years of income is divided by 420 (number of months in 35 years), producing the **average indexed monthly earnings.**

Web Link 17.7

The next step involves what are known as bend points. A bend point is the dollar value of average indexed monthly earnings where additional monthly income results in lower incremental retirement income. These bend points are provided at **Web Link 17.7a.** For 2001, the two bend points were $561 and $3,381. The monthly retirement figure equals the sum of 90 percent times the first $561 of average indexed monthly earnings, plus 32 percent times the next $2,820 (or, $3,381 – $561), plus 15 percent of any amount over

Web Link 17.7a

---

[4]For a discussion of how 65 came to be the age of normal retirement, see **Web Link 17.5.**

$3,381. That total is the **primary insurance amount** or PIA. Let's look at an example of how this works:

What would be Dan O'Neill's monthly retirement benefit at age 65 if his average monthly indexed earnings were $500, $3,000, and $5,000?

Web Link 17.7b

The answers appear in Table 17.1. A worksheet example of the computation of a person's retirement benefit may be found at **Web Link 17.7 b.** and Table 17.2.

Table 17.1

Computing Primary Insurance Amount Using Bend Points

Avg. Income	Up to first bend	Up to second bend	After second bend	Total
$1,000	90% × 561 = 504.90	32% × 439 = 140.48	–	$645
$3,000	90% × 561 = 504.90	32% × 2,439 = 780.48	–	1,285
$5,000	90% × 561 = 504.90	32% × 2,820 = 902.40	15% × 1,619 = 242.85	1,650

Table 17.2

Worksheet for Figuring Social Security Retirement Benefit for a Person Retiring in the Year 2000

Step 1: Using the table below, list in Column B the smaller of your wage income for each year or the amount shown in Column A. If you had no wage income in some of these years, enter zero.

Step 2: Compute your "indexed earnings" by multiplying the wage income figure in Column B by the "index factor" shown in Column C. Enter this result in Column D for each year. If the wage income for any year is zero, the indexed earnings will also be zero.

Step 3: Select from Column D the largest 35 years of indexed earnings, and add up these numbers. When fewer than 35 years of indexed earning exist, the remaining years are treated as zero income.

Step 4: Divide the total in Step 3 by 420 (the number of months in 35 years) to compute the average indexed monthly earnings, the figure used to determine a person's monthly retirement check.

Step 5: Using the bend points for the applicable year, multiply the components of the average indexed monthly earnings by the respective replacement ratios. For the year 2000, multiply the first $531 of average monthly income by 90 percent, the next $3,202 of average monthly income by 32 percent, and any income over this amount by 15 percent.

Step 6: Total the components from Step 5 and round down to the nearest dollar to determine a person's monthly retirement benefit if retirement occurs at the normal retirement age.

Step 7: Adjust the figure in Step 5 if a person retires earlier or later than the normal retirement age.

Year	A. Maximum Earnings	B. Actual Earnings	C. Index Factor	D. Indexed Earnings
1951	$3,600		10.31	
1952	3,600		9.71	
1953	3,600		9.19	
1954	3,600		9.15	
1955	4,200		8.74	
1956	4,200		8.17	
1957	4,200		7.93	

Year	A. Maximum Earnings	B. Actual Earnings	C. Index Factor	D. Indexed Earnings
1958	4,200		7.86	
1959	4,800		7.49	
1960	4,800		7.20	
1961	4,800		7.06	
1962	4,800		6.73	
1963	4,800		6.56	
1964	4,800		6.31	
1965	4,800		6.20	
1966	6,600		5.84	
1967	6,600		5.54	
1968	7,800		5.18	
1969	7,800		4.90	
1970	7,800		4.67	
1971	7,800		4.44	
1972	9,000		4.05	
1973	10,800		3.81	
1974	13,200		3.59	
1975	14,100		3.34	
1976	15,300		3.13	
1977	16,500		2.95	
1978	17,700		2.73	
1979	22,900		2.51	
1980	25,900		2.31	
1981	29,700		2.10	
1982	32,400		1.99	
1983	35,700		1.89	
1984	37,800		1.79	
1985	39,600		1.72	
1986	42,000		1.67	
1987	43,800		1.57	
1988	45,000		1.49	
1989	48,000		1.44	
1990	51,300		1.37	
1991	53,400		1.32	
1992	55,500		1.26	
1993	57,600		1.25	
1994	60,600		1.22	
1995	61,200		1.17	
1996	62,700		1.11	
1997	65,400		1.05	
1998	68,400		1.00	
1999	72,600		1.00	

Source: http://www.ssa.gov/pubs/10070.html, May 15, 2001.

The bend points, like most of the other factors in the Social Security formulas, are also indexed to the national average wage index, provided in Web Link 17.7c. The national average wage index is the average of wages reported to the Social Security administration by employers on Form W-2. To demonstrate this calculation, let's look at how the 2001 first bend point of $561 was computed. In 1977, the national average wage index was $9,779.44; in 1999 the index stood at $30,469.84. Because of a lag in the availability of data, adjustments in bend points are based on the index from two years before. So we must look at 1979, and we find that the first bend point then was $180. Next, find the ratio of the "current" wage index to the "base" wage index. Multiply it by the first bend point. Following these steps to determine the first bend point for 2001 we compute:

$$(\$30,469.84 \, / \, \$9,779.44) \times \$180 = \$561$$

with the answer rounded to the nearest dollar. To the extent that the national average wage rate reflects the inflation rate, one could say that the benefit formulas are inflation-adjusted.

The effect of this process is that a person with a low average Social Security income will have a relatively high **replacement ratio**—the percentage of Social Security retirement benefit received divided by pre-retirement salary. The replacement ratio for someone with a high average Social Security income will be low, although the actual dollar value of the retirement benefit will be greater than the actual dollar value of the retirement benefit for a low-income person. Consider the following example:

Using the Social Security benefit figures for Dan O'Neill from the previous example, what is Dan's replacement ratio if his average monthly indexed earnings were $500, $3,000, and $5,000?

His replacement ratios are 64.5 percent ($645 / $1,000), 42.83 percent ($1,285 / $3,000), and 33 percent ($1,650 / $5,000), respectively. Note how after the second bend point each $1,000 of incremental average monthly indexed earnings adds only $150 to Dan's benefit check. Thus, his replacement ratio will steadily decline toward 15 percent as his average monthly indexed earnings grows.

The PIA is the monthly retirement benefit a person receives by retiring at the normal retirement age. As mentioned above, you may start taking monthly retirement benefits anytime after you turn 62, but you incur a double penalty for doing so. First, people who retire at age 62 would not be able to use the Social Security income they would have earned during the last three years of their careers to calculate average monthly indexed earnings. If these income figures would have been higher than any of their best 35 years of Social Security income to date, then by retiring early they lose the benefit of increasing their average monthly income figure used in the formula to determine the PIA. The second penalty is that Social Security reduces the PIA figure by five-ninths of 1 percent for each month a person retires early. Thus, a person retiring at 62 whose normal retirement age is defined as 65 would have his or her PIA reduced by 20 percent ($5/9$ of $1\% \times 36$ months).

If you do not start to receive retirement benefit checks by age 65, you get a bonus for continuing to wait. This bonus is an increase in the PIA per month of deferral. The reward for postponement is good up to age 70. The amount of this reward has gone up over the years. For people born in 1943 or later, the value of postponement for each year is 8 percent (or $2/3$ of 1% per month). The value of postponement for people born before 1943

Web Link 17.8 may be found at **Web Link 17.8.** Furthermore, if you work during the period of postponement, your higher income earned may result in higher indexed earnings and thus an even higher PIA figure.

The constant value of postponement combined with the increase in normal retirement age means that at age 70 a retiree will be able to draw a smaller percentage of his or her PIA than would be the case if the normal retirement age had not changed. Consider the following example:

> *Dan O'Neill was born in 1947. He is planning on not starting to draw his Social Security retirement income until he reaches age 70. What percentage of his PIA will he be able to obtain?*

According to the retirement age adjustments discussed earlier, Dan's normal retirement age will be 66. He will be rewarded with an 8 percent per year increase in the PIA base amount for each year he defers starting his retirement benefits. The most he can defer is four years (from age 66 to age 70). Thus, if he waits the four years, his retirement benefit will be 132 percent of his PIA. People born in 1960 or later, whose normal retirement age will be 67, can defer only three years, so the most they can receive is 124 percent of the PIA.

Since 1975, retirement benefits each year have been increased with a **cost-of-living adjustment** (COLA). Eligibility for cost-of-living benefit increases begins at age 62 and applies even if the individual doesn't start taking the benefits until a later date, or even until age 70. COLAs for each year back to 1975, when they were first instituted, may be found Web Link 17.9 at **Web Link 17.9** Today COLAs are based on increases in the Consumer Price Index for Urban Wage Earners and Clerical Workers (CPI-W) from the third quarter of the prior year Web Link 17.10 to the corresponding quarter of the current year in which the COLA became effective.[5]

WHAT WILL MY CURRENT (OR EX-) SPOUSE'S RETIREMENT BENEFITS BE?

A person's current spouse is entitled to the larger of 50 percent of that person's retirement benefit, or the retirement benefit he or she has earned in his or her own name. To illustrate this point, let's consider two situations.

In the first, the husband has been the sole income earner for his family his entire life. If his PIA is $1,500, his wife is automatically entitled to $750 in retirement benefits even though she has never paid a penny of Social Security taxes herself. If the wife dies first, the husband continues to receive his $1,500 in benefits. If the husband dies first, then the wife begins to receive the husband's benefit amount.

In the second situation, both husband and wife work their entire careers and earn the same incomes. If their PIAs are each $1,500, each will receive that amount. Upon the death of either person, the spouse continues to receive only his or her own benefit check. Clearly, from an investment perspective Social Security is a better deal for a family in which only one spouse works. However, keep in mind that Social Security was set up as a program of social insurance, not an investment program.

---

[5]The CPI-W and the computation of inflation rates were discussed in Chapter 4.

In some situations, a spouse may be better off claiming only his or her spouse's share and not the benefit earned in his or her own right. Consider the following example:

Dan has applied for Social Security benefits and learned that his monthly check will be $2,000. His wife could claim a benefit check of $1,200 based on the Social Security taxes she paid over the years, or take the spousal check of $1,000 per month. Which should she claim?

Although it would seem obvious that she should prefer $1,200 to $1,000, there is a catch. If Dan dies first and she had selected the spousal check, she would then move up to the $2,000 monthly check. If she takes the $1,200 check, she is locked into that benefit amount until she dies. Before making this type of decision, she and Dan would do well to give some thought to their life expectancies, and consider whether the extra $200 per month today is worth giving up the extra $1,000 she would get after Dan's death if he predeceases her.

A divorced individual may be entitled to claim Social Security retirement benefits based on the ex-spouse's income. The marriage must have lasted at least 10 years and the couple must have been divorced at least two years. Also, both ex-spouses must be at least 62. Each ex-spouse is then entitled to the larger of the Social Security benefits earned in his or her own name, or 50 percent of the ex-spouse's benefit. The fact that a person's ex-spouse might be drawing retirement benefits based on the former marriage does not prevent that person's current spouse from also drawing retirement benefits. In fact, it is possible under these rules that a person could marry five times, have each of the first four marriages last at least 10 years before ending in divorce, and then have all five spouses receive the spousal retirement benefit!

WHAT IS THE EASIEST WAY TO ESTIMATE MY SOCIAL SECURITY RETIREMENT BENEFITS?

Fortunately, no one actually needs to undertake the complex task of computing his or her own retirement benefit. An estimate of your Social Security benefits may be obtained free of charge from the Social Security Administration (SSA). The official name of the projected benefits report is the **Personal Earnings and Benefit Estimate Statement** (PEBES). This report may be requested on the Internet at **Web Link 17.11.** Also, Congress has now mandated that taxpayers receive once per year a copy of their PEBES to better understand their Social Security benefits.

Web Link 17.11

The PEBES indicates your Social Security salary for each year in which you paid Social Security taxes. Remember that your Social Security salary is the lesser of your actual salary and the maximum income on which you pay Social Security taxes. The PEBES also lists your salary with respect to the Medicare tax, which, since 1994, had no upper limit. Thus, the Medicare tax since 1994 reports your actual salary for each year.

The PEBES provides best guesses as to your retirement benefits for different retirement ages, your disability benefits, and your survivor benefits. It also indicates whether or not you have enough quarters of credit to receive each of the different benefits. *Everyone who has ever paid a penny of Social Security taxes should make sure he or she receives a PEBES as least once every two years.* SSA occasionally makes mistakes in its record keeping, and you have a limited amount of time to correct such errors. No one wants to go into the SSA offices at age 70 only to find that his or her income has been understated over the years!

Another way to project your Social Security benefits is to download a program from the Social Security Administration that does this task. This program may be obtained at **Web Link 17.12.**

Web Link 17.12

DOES EARNING A SALARY DURING RETIREMENT AFFECT MY SOCIAL SECURITY RETIREMENT BENEFITS?

As a result of legislation passed in April 2000, the income limits after which you would start to lose some of your benefits if you are above your normal retirement age have been eliminated. However, if you are under your normal retirement age, there is a limit on how much income can be earned without losing some or all of one's retirement benefits. The maximum amount of income that early retirees may earn without losing any retirement benefits is a rather complicated figure to compute. For 2001, if your earnings exceed $10,680, then you risk losing some of your retirement benefits.

Web Link 17.13

The amount of benefit reduction is one dollar for every two dollars of salary income in excess of the applicable upper limit. Consider the following example:

> *Dan O'Neill is 63 years old. He started his Social Security retirement benefits as soon as he turned 62. In 2001 he had wage income of $11,000. How much of his benefits will he have to return?*

If we assume that the lower limit applies to Dan, then he would owe back one-half of the amount in excess of $10,680, or $160 ([$11,000 – $10,680] × .5). Keep in mind that Dan would still have to pay income tax on the money that he earned. This is such a steep tax rate that Dan would do well to consider terminating his retirement benefits until the excess income penalty is diminished or eliminated when Dan turns 70.

WILL SOCIAL SECURITY RETIREMENT BENEFITS BE THERE WHEN I AM READY TO RETIRE?

For many years there has been recurring debate about whether or when the Social Security system will go broke. Many younger workers simply do not believe that the money they paid into Social Security will guarantee them benefits when they get ready to retire. Let's consider for a moment how Social Security works. Social Security has always functioned as a "pay as you go" system. This means that the Social Security taxes that are collected each month are used to pay the current beneficiaries. Each year since the system was created, taxes collected have exceeded benefits. Four Social Security trust funds have come into existence to contain these surpluses. The first two trust funds are the OASI and DI Trust Funds. Retirement and survivor's benefits are paid from OASI and disability benefits from DI. The third trust fund is the HI Trust Fund, which pays hospital Medicare benefits. The fourth is the Supplemental Medical Insurance (SMI) Trust Fund.

The first two trust funds are funded by the OASI insurance premium, which was the 6.20 percent tax on the first $80,400 in wage income in 2001. The HI Trust Fund is funded by the Medicare Tax, which in 2001 is 1.45 percent of all wage income. The voluntary medical insurance fund premium is paid by those retirees who desire coverage, and the government matches all premiums paid. Each of the four funds has a separate financial status, although most attention to the financial health of Social Security focuses only on the OASI fund. According to the 1999 Trustees' report on the four funds, the OASI Fund can cover its projected expenses through 2034, the DI Fund is good until at least 2020, the HI Fund is good until 2015, and the SMI Fund is good indefinitely. Virtually all public debate focuses on the date at which the OASI Fund would be unable to cover expenses. The financial vitality of these funds is sensitive to the state of the economy. The strong economic performance of the economy in the 1990s pushed back default dates of these funds.

Web Link 17.14

Several steps can be taken between now and 2034 to protect the OASI Fund. One is to have the Treasury directly fund it (implying that federal income taxes would be used to pay Social Security benefits). Another is to increase again the Social Security taxes and/or the various hurdles to collecting benefits, such as the definition of the normal retirement age. Still another is to reduce the benefits, through such steps as reducing the percentage compensation rates in the formula for computing the PIA or reducing the bend points at which lower replacement ratios are applied. Increasing the amount of Social Security benefits subject to taxation is also an option—one that would cause some people to postpone collecting benefits. None of these steps are politically palatable to elected officials, but all of them are doable. It is highly likely that Congress will opt to do one or more of these adjustments before it ever reaches the point when it must announce to the voting public that the OASI Fund has gone bankrupt. In the meantime, everyone would do well to worry more about the DI and HI Funds, which face much earlier bankruptcy dates![6]

WHAT ARE PENSIONS?

For many people, the pensions they earn through their employers may be more significant in financial terms than Social Security. A pension is money contributed to an investment program that provides income after the employee retires. Be aware of the multitude of issues associated with pensions. First, when taking a job, you should not assume that the employer provides a pension. Many companies, particularly smaller ones, have no pension programs. A second issue is that not everyone is covered by a company's pension. New hires may be excluded for a specified period of time. The rules for who can legally be excluded are complicated, so do some research if you are told you are not allowed to participate in the company's pension program.

Pension contributions come out of the employee's paycheck, are paid by the company, or consist of some combination of the two. If the pension plan is registered as a **qualified pension plan,** the contributions from the employee's paycheck are tax-deductible, in the sense that the employee's taxable income reported on his or her W-4 form equals gross pay less the pension contributions. Thus, an employee who has gross pay of $50,000 for

---

[6]At the time of writing, President Bush is attempting to build support for a proposal that allows people to divert some of their Social Security taxes to special investment accounts, at the expense of reduced Social Security benefits.

the year and who contributes $5,000 to a qualified pension plan will have his or her taxable income reported to the IRS as $45,000. If the pension plan is a nonqualified plan, then there are no tax savings associated with the contributions (although such contributions may still be well worthwhile).

A critical feature of a pension plan is the **vesting** requirement. Vesting refers to an employee's right to claim the contributions made by his or her employer. An employee is always entitled to his or her own contributions. The law defines a choice of two upper limits on the vesting period an employer may establish, although an employer is free to use more generous standards (and many do). One legally mandated upper limit is that an employee must be 100 percent vested by the end of five years by the time he or she joined the pension plan. The other is that the employee must be at least 20 percent vested by the end of the third year, 40 percent vested by the fourth year, and so on to 100 percent by the end of the seventh year. Vesting is critical if a person leaves an employer before retirement. As most people work for multiple employers over their careers vesting rules may matter more than the rules as to how the retirement benefits are determined.

The mechanics of how the retirement benefit is determined vary substantially among employers. However, all plans fall into two broad categories: defined benefit and defined contribution. Historically, almost all plans were defined benefit plans, but today the vast majority of new plans are defined contribution plans. So the majority of assets held in pension plans are still in defined benefit plans, but the percentage of plans that are defined benefit plans is rapidly falling.

Web Link
(WSJ) 17.16

How Does a Defined Benefit Pension Plan Work?

A **defined benefit (DB) pension** plan is where the pension benefit itself is defined through some explicit formula. In the most common type of DB plan, the pension is defined as a fixed percentage per year worked times the number of years worked; this product is then multiplied with some salary number. Consider the following example:

> Dan O'Neill's employer provides a DB pension plan. The plan pays 1.5 percent per year worked times the employee's final salary. Dan started with the company when he was 35, and plans to retire at age 65. He projects his final salary to be $100,000. What will his company pension be?

Dan will have worked for the company for 30 years at the time of retirement. Multiplying 1.5 percent per year worked by 30, we obtain a pension percentage of 45 percent. This pension percentage is then multiplied by Dan's final salary of $100,000 to obtain an annual pension benefit of $45,000. If the pension were paid on a monthly basis, Dan would receive $3,750 per month ($45,000 / 12).

Although some pension plans do literally use the wage income during the last year of employment, most DB plans instead use a **final average salary** number. The number of years used to compute final average salary varies, but three years and five years are quite common. Some firms average the employee's salary over his or her entire career with the firm. An important factor is whether the formula includes overtime or bonus pay. When pensions allow the employee to count overtime pay in computing the average salary, employees have been known to volunteer for overtime virtually every week during their last few years. Such overtime not only increases the employee's pay, it also dramatically increases his or her pension benefits.

Some plans define the pension benefit in terms of dollars per year worked instead. For example, a pension could be defined as $125 per month for each year worked. If Dan's employer had used this formula in the above example, Dan would have the same pension at retirement, because $125 per month per year worked times 30 years equals $3,750. Defining a pension in terms of dollars per month per year worked is particularly common among unions.

How Does a Defined Contribution Plan Work?

In a **defined contribution (DC) pension** plan, the contributions are invested in one or more designated investment vehicles. Typically these are mutual funds. Some employers offer a menu of funds limited to the employer's stock, a money market fund, and one or two diversified common stock funds. Other employers will offer a large menu, including one or more large families of funds (mutual funds are discussed in Chapter 15).

The contributions are then used to purchase shares or units in the selected vehicles. Each person has his or her own account. For example, let's assume that the investment vehicle selected by a particular employee is the XYZ Mutual Fund. Each pay period a contribution is then sent to that employee's pension account at that fund. In terms of mechanics, this is no different than if the employee opened up an account at that fund on his or her own and sent in a saving contribution each month. However, two important differences exist for the employee. First, if the pension fund is a qualified fund, then all of the contributions by the employee are deducted from the amount of his or her taxable income reported to the IRS. Second, the dividends and capital gains earned by the account accrue tax-free, regardless of whether the pension fund is a qualified pension or a nonqualified pension.

Which Pension Plan is Better, a DB or a DC?

After learning the basics of the two types of pension programs, most people decide they would prefer a DB pension to a DC pension. However, both types of pensions have advantages and disadvantages.

The biggest disadvantage of a DC plan is, of course, that the rate of return on the pension account is not guaranteed. The biggest nightmare you could face would be to have a major market crash just before your planned retirement date. To minimize the potential impact of such an event, you can move your assets from aggressive investments toward more conservative ones as you approach retirement. Thus, at the start of your expected last year of employment, you might have 60 percent or more of your pension assets invested in conservative assets such as money market mutual funds and intermediate term government bond funds.

One major advantage of the DC plan is that you can directly observe the value of the account. Another advantage is that once an employee is vested, the value of the pension accrued to date will not drop as a result of changing jobs. Consider the following example:

Dan O'Neill has a DC pension and is fully vested. The current value of the account is $100,000. Dan's money is invested in a diversified common stock portfolio. He plans *to retire in 20 years, and he believes his pension account will earn an average annual rate of return of 10 percent. If he were to leave his job today, what would his account be worth upon his projected retirement date? If he believes his account will provide a monthly payment of one-half of 1 percent per month, what will his monthly benefit be from this account?*

Web Link 4.1   The answer to the first question is a simple future value calculation. If we go to **Web Link 4.1,** we will find the future value to be $672,750. If he draws one-half of 1 percent per month from this account, he will have a monthly pension of $3,363.75. If Dan's portfolio grows in value over time and Dan continues to withdraw one-half of 1 percent of its value each month, then Dan's income could actually grow during retirement.

With a DB pension, it is the obligation of the employer to provide whatever contributions are necessary to assure ultimately that the pensions are paid. Such an arrangement certainly makes it sound as if there were great safety and certainty in a DB pension. However, certain features mitigate this safety. The first and most common is that an employee will decide to move on to another job. Employees who are not vested will have a substantial loss of benefits. However, those who are vested still can incur substantial losses, because when it comes time to pay the pension, benefits will be based on the employee's salary at the time he or she left the job, not the actual salary at the time of retirement. Consider the following example:

Dan O'Neill worked for 20 years at a firm that paid a pension of 1½ percent per year worked, times the final salary. Dan was fully vested and his salary after 20 years was $50,000. Dan left that job and worked another 20 years at a second firm that paid the same type of pension. His final salary at that job was $100,000. How much will Dan's combined pensions from the two companies be? How much would his pension have been if he had stayed with the same company and had the same ending salary of $100,000?

Dan's annual pension from his first job will be $15,000 when he retires (1.5% × 20 × $50,000). His annual pension from the second job will be $30,000 upon retirement (1.5% × 20 × $100,000), so his combined pensions would be $45,000. Had he stayed at the original job and earned a final salary of $100,000, his pension would have been $60,000 (1.5% × 40 × $100,000). Thus, the job shift caused Dan to end up with only 75 percent of the pension he otherwise would have had. It is certainly possible that had he stayed at the original job, his final salary might not have been as high as what he had when he switched. Nonetheless, the example illustrates the potential high cost of changing jobs with DB pension plans.

To further illustrate this problem, Table 17.3 shows the ratios of combined pensions of someone who changes jobs compared with the final pension of someone who did not change jobs given various combinations of job changes and average annual salary growth rates over a 40-year career. For example, if you changed jobs three times over a 40-year career, you would have stayed in each job for 10 years. If your annual average salary growth rate were 5 percent (whether you stayed with one job or switched three times), then the ratio of the combined pensions to the single pension is 55.55 percent. In other words, you would have lost nearly half of your pension by job-switching. Two facts are clear from this table. First, the setback to pension income increases as the frequency of job changes increases. Second, the harm done is greater the higher the person's annual salary growth

Table 17.3
Ratio of New Pension Benefit to Old Pension Benefit for a Person Who Changes Jobs Many Times in 40 Years

Number of Job Changes	Salary Growth Rate			
	3.00%	5.00%	7.00%	9.00%
1	77.68%	68.84%	62.92%	58.92%
2	70.96%	59.80%	52.34%	47.25%
3	67.74%	55.55%	47.45%	41.91%
4	65.86%	53.10%	44.65%	38.87%
5	64.62%	51.50%	42.84%	36.92%
6	63.74%	50.37%	41.58%	35.57%
7	63.09%	49.54%	40.64%	34.57%

rate. The only way to mitigate this effect is to obtain a large enough salary increase each time a job change is made to offset the loss of pension benefits.[7]

So far, we have only considered the pension reduction of an employee who voluntarily changes jobs. If the employee is forced by various circumstances to change jobs, the impact is just as great or greater, because the employee probably will be unable to obtain salary increases sufficient to offset the harm to the pension.

Still another danger is that the employer will decide to terminate the DB pension plan. Many employers do exactly this. They terminate their DB pension plans, making arrangements to assure that the employees will be paid the pension they have earned to date, and then replace this with no pension or a DC pension. This elimination of the pension has the same disastrous effect as changing jobs.

Some DB pensions incorporate what is known as **integration** or Social Security offset into their benefits. This normally means that the dollar value of the employer's pension is reduced by the amount of Social Security benefits. Thus, the retirement benefit promised by the company includes both its own pension and the Social Security retirement income. Employees should be careful not to count Social Security twice in these situations.

Obviously, both types of pensions can leave great uncertainty as to what the benefits ultimately will be. It would be incorrect to say unequivocally that either type of pension plan is always better than the other. Much depends on the specific terms of the plan. For example, generous vesting terms make a big difference.

In general, the two broad types of pension plans follow four rules.[8] First, the higher your expected annual salary growth rate, the more likely a DB pension plan is to be desirable. Second, the higher the rate of inflation you expect over your career, the more desirable a DC pension is likely to be. Third, the older you are (and therefore the less remaining time you will work), the more desirable a DB pension is to be. Conversely, the longer you are likely to work, the more desirable the DC pension is likely to be.

[7]For additional discussion on this issue, see "The Pension Penalty Associated with Changing Employers," Walt Woerheide and Rich Fortner. *Financial Counseling and Planning*, Vol. 5 (1994), pp. 101–116.

[8]The proof for the following observations is provided in "The Impact of Salary Growth, Inflation, Employee Age, and Career Length on the Relative Desirability of Pension Fund Type," Walt Woerheide, *Financial Counseling and Planning*, Vol. 6 (1995), pp. 53–59.

HOW SAFE IS MY PENSION?

Web Link 17.17

The **Pension Benefit Guarantee Corporation** (PBGC) is a government agency created by the Employee Retirement Income Security Act of 1974. The PBGC charges premiums to employers that provide DB pensions in exchange for guaranteeing the promised pensions if the company or the pension fund itself fails. To protect itself from excessive generosity on the part of employers, the PBGC places an upper limit on the monthly pension benefit it will pay. The upper limit is a function of the year in which the employee's plan terminated. When the PBGC was first set up, this upper limit was $750. For 2001, the upper limit is $3,392.05 if the employee retires at age 65. Retirement at earlier ages lowers the limit on the maximum pension. For an employee retiring at age 55, the maximum monthly benefit is $1,526.42. For current or historical values of these upper limits, see **Web Link 17.17**.[9] These upper limits would not impose a loss of benefits from what had been promised by their plans for most employees covered by the PBGC. The upper limit could significantly cost high-income individuals.

Web Link 17.18

Although the number of workers covered by DB plans has increased from 38 million in 1985 to 42 million in 1999[10], the number of plans covered by the PBGC has declined from 114,000 in 1985 to 44,000 today. Most of this decline in plans has been at companies with fewer than 100 employees. Many factors explain this decline, of course, but the two primary reasons for it are the cost of the paperwork required from these insured plans and the steadily increasing cost of the premiums. In 1974, when Congress created the PBGC, the premium was $1 per participant for single-employer plans. Today, single-employer pension plans pay $19 per participant per year. An additional variable-rate charge must be paid by underfunded pension plans, those that have fewer assets than they need to finance earned pension benefits. The additional premium for unfunded vested benefits is $9 per $1,000 of unfunded vested benefits. Smaller, multi-employer pension programs pay a premium of $2.60 per participant per year.

The PBGC pays the monthly benefits to the employees for the pensions it has taken over out of two sources of income. The first is, of course, the premiums it charges the employers. The second is the income from the assets it has obtained from funds that failed. When a company or fund fails, the PBGC not only takes over the promised pension obligations (up to the maximum allowable), but also whatever assets the fund owed at the time of failure. Premium payments to PBGC go into what is known as the Revolving Funds. At the PBGC's fiscal year-end of September 30, 1998, this fund had $11.6 billion in assets. By law, this fund must invest all of its assets in fixed income securities. The assets received from the various terminated plans go into what is known as the Trust Funds. As of September 30, 1998, these assets stood at $6.5 billion. The PBGC has no control over what these assets will be when they are received. Most of the portfolio consists of what are considered blue-chip common stocks.

Web Link 17.19

As with any large program of this nature, some of the people who are entitled to pension benefits cannot be found. If you believe you or a relative may have a potential claim on a pension, then you can use the PBGC search program to look for your name on their list.

[9]For multi-employer plans, the upper limit is $16.25 per year worked under that particular plan.

[10]The 42 million covered workers include 33 million in single-employer defined benefit plans and 9 million multi-employer plans. Multi-employer plans are common in industries such as construction, where various employers hire workers through a common source such as a union.

As with most pension plans, the PBGC allows a recipient to select a joint survivorship option extending the pension to the spouse if the pension earner passes away first.

Does the PBGC Eliminate the Risks Associated with DB Pensions?

The PBGC clearly eliminates some of the risks associated with a DB pension plan. An employee need not worry about the total loss of pension benefits if his or her employer goes bankrupt. However, a substantial number of risks are still associated with DB plans. The PBGC does not protect against loss of benefits for employees who change jobs often or who are fired. It does not protect against the loss of benefits the employee incurs by the company's demise: if you have 10 years on a job when your company goes under, your final pension benefit is based on your salary when the company failed, not what your pension might have been had you kept working there until normal retirement age.

WHAT ARE A PENSION'S SPOUSAL CONSTRAINTS?

A retiring employee has several choices regarding the payment of a pension. Married employees must choose whether to take the pension as a joint and survivor pension or only for as long as the retired employee lives. The drawback to a joint and survivor pension is that the monthly payments will be lower. As part of the Retirement Equity Act of 1984, Congress required that all employees who refuse a joint and survivor payment must obtain the written permission of their spouses.

Many pensions allow a lump sum distribution from the pension upon retirement. If the lump-sum payment is greater than $3,500, the employee must again obtain the written permission of the spouse. Other activities involving spousal permission include starting the pension benefits prior to age 65 and waiving the cash value benefit to the survivor if the worker dies before retirement,

As the coverage and value of pensions have grown since the end of World War II, so has their role in divorce settlements. In fact, the PBGC actually provides information on QDROs (Qualified Domestic Relations Orders) at its web site to facilitate the drawing up of a specific agreement.

Web Link 17.20

SUMMARY

➢ Social Security provides not only a retirement program, but also a disability income program, income for dependent survivors, and Medicare.

➢ Social Security taxes are currently 7.65 per cent of the first $80,400 of wage income (for 2001), and then drop to 1.45 percent of all additional income.

➢ Qualification for various Social Security benefits is based on quarters of coverage. Retirement benefits are earned with 40 quarters of coverage.

➢ For people born before 1938, normal retirement age is 65. For people born after 1959, it is 67. For people born in between those years, it ranges between ages 65 and 67.

➤ Social Security retirement benefits are based on average monthly indexed wages based on the best 35 years. Bend points are then applied to this number to derive the actual retirement benefit.

➤ A current or ex-spouse may draw as benefits either one-half of the other spouse's benefit, or whatever was earned in his or her own name.

➤ Everyone should make sure to receive a PEBES at least once every two years.

➤ Retirement benefits may be reduced if you start receiving them before your normal retirement age. After the normal retirement age, there are no limits on earnings.

➤ At present, the Social Security system is destined to collapse. Fixing it will require a political solution.

➤ A defined benefit (DB) pension is based on a formula based on salary. A defined contribution (DC) pension is based on the performance of the securities acquired and held in the pension account. Both have advantages and disadvantages.

➤ The PBGC guarantees pensions in the event an employer with a DB pension plan goes bankrupt. It does not eliminate all the risks of such a pension system.

➤ Spouses have certain rights with regard to the drawing of pension benefits.

KEY TERMS

average indexed monthly earnings	bend points	cost-of-living adjustment
defined benefit (DB) pension	defined contribution (DC) pension	final average salary
integration	Pension Benefit Guarantee Corporation	Personal Earnings and Benefit Estimate Statement
primary insurance amount	qualified pension plan	quarters of coverage
replacement ratio	regressive tax	vesting

PROBLEMS

17.1 How much would you owe in Social Security taxes in the year 2001 if you had wage income of $50,000? $100,000? $200,000? How much would you pay in Social Security taxes as a percentage of your wage income at each of these incomes? What is the percentage you are effectively paying if the employer's contribution is included with your own contribution at each of these income levels?

17.2 What is the normal retirement age for someone born in 1937? 1947? 1957? 1967? What percentage increase in their primary insurance amounts would each of these people receive if they waited until age 70 to start drawing their Social Security benefits?

17.3 For each of the people in problem 2, approximately how long would each person have to draw Social Security benefits to justify waiting from their respective normal retirement ages until age 70 to draw their retirement benefits (ignoring time value of money considerations and COLAS)?

17.4 Compute the monthly Social Security retirement benefit for a person who retired in the year 2000 whose average monthly indexed earnings were $2,000? $4,000? $6,000? For each of these people, what is the ratio of their monthly retirement benefits to their average earnings (i.e., what are their replacement ratios)?

17.5 You are 27 years old and plan to retire when you are 67. You currently make $40,000 per year. You participate in a DB plan that pays 1.5 percent of your "final" salary per year worked. Assume final salary means your salary during the last year of employment. If you work with this same company the entire 40 years, and your salary grows at the rate of 3 percent per year for the remaining 39 years, what would be your pension income as a percentage of your last year's salary? What would be your pension income in dollars?

17.6 You are 27 years old and plan to retire when you are 67. You currently make $40,000 per year. You participate in a DC plan in which you pay 5 percent of your annual income, which your employer matches. Assume the contributions are paid at the end of each year and that you will earn an average rate of return of 8 percent on your pension monies. If you work with this same company the entire 40 years and your salary grows at 3 percent per year for the remaining 39 years, what would be your pension income as a percentage of your last year's salary? What would be your pension income in dollars? Assume you will draw 6 percent per year of whatever the value of your pension account is on the day you retire.

REFERENCES

Web Link 17.21   Glossaries for Social Security
Web Link 17.22   Sources for research on Social Security issues
Web Link 17.23   FAQs for Social Security
Web Link 17.24   Miscellaneous sites for Social Security

WALL STREET JOURNAL RESOURCES

Web Link (WSJ) 17.25   Recent articles on retirement planning
Web Link (WSJ) 17.26   Recent articles dealing with retirement topics
Web Link (WSJ) 17.27   "Companies Find Host of Ways to Pare Retirement Payouts," *The Wall Street Journal Interactive Edition*, July 27, 2000
Web Link (WSJ) 17.28   "Ready to Retire? Planners Say Start the Benefit Checks," *The Wall Street Journal Interactive Edition*, June 15, 2000
Web Link (WSJ) 17.29   "Older Workers Lose in New Pension Plan," *The Wall Street Journal Interactive Edition*, October 3, 1999
Web Link (WSJ) 17.30   "Pension Terminations Become Temptations for Some Employers," *The Wall Street Journal Interactive Edition*, June 15, 1999

For information that has changed since the book was written, for new information that pertains to this topic, and for some new web sites that pertain to the topic of this chapter, see **Web Link 17.31.**

CHAPTER 18

PLANNING FOR RETIREMENT, PART II: TAX-FAVORED PROGRAMS AND PERSONAL SAVINGS

LEARNING OBJECTIVES

- Define the characteristics of a tax-favored savings program
- Explain the key features of the different IRA programs
- Calculate whether a person should opt for a Roth or a traditional IRA
- Describe Keogh, 401(k), and 403(b) programs
- Describe an annuity
- Explain the various payout options on an annuity
- Distinguish between a fixed rate and variable rate annuity
- Choose among various annuity proposals
- Project retirement expenses
- Compute how long a portfolio can provide cash payments
- Estimate how much needs to be invested each month to support a retirement plan
- Construct a retirement plan

Web Link: www.wiley.com/college/woerheide

INTRODUCTION

In the previous chapter we looked at the primary building blocks of retirement planning, namely Social Security and pension programs. For many people, the income these two sources provide will just not be enough. Apparently, many in Congress have also felt this way, as over the years Congress has created tax-favored programs that allow individuals to save toward retirement or other goals such as housing and college educations for their children. In this chapter, we will continue to consider the case of Dan O'Neill as he ponders how to save money for retirement. We will look at various tax-favored savings programs, including annuities. We will then look at a general model of retirement planning. The chapter ends with a consideration of the problem of inflation during retirement.

WHAT TAX-FAVORED SAVINGS PROGRAMS EXIST?

A tax-favored savings program gives some sort of special tax break to the individual. Many exist, offering tax savings provisions in three ways. First, your contribution to such a program may be tax-deductible. Thus, if you contributed $1,000 to such a program and your marginal tax bracket were 28 percent, you could deduct from your taxes $280 ($1,000 × 28%). Second, the value of such assets sometimes grows tax-free. Thus, whether the income consists of interest, dividends, rent, or capital gains, you do not count it as taxable income in the year received. Finally, any withdrawals from such an account may be tax-exempt as well.

However, no single tax-favored savings program offers all three of these tax preference treatments (tax deduction, tax deferral, and tax exemption). Such a program would be in great demand by everyone! Most tax-favored programs usually combine two of the three features. The most common combinations are the first and second and the third and second.

HOW DOES A TRADITIONAL IRA WORK?

An Individual Retirement Account, or **IRA,** allows individuals to set aside money toward retirement. An IRA account can be applied to a variety of investment vehicles. For example, you can set up a passbook savings account as an IRA, buy certificates of deposits through an IRA account, invest in mutual fund shares in an IRA account, or even set up a self-directed account at a stock brokerage firm. In other words, *almost* any type of investment you can make in a personal account can be made through the vehicle of an IRA account. Restrictions as to what you can acquire through an IRA include such assets as jewelry, guns, stamps, and coins.

Under current regulations, an individual may contribute up to $2,000 per year to a new or existing IRA account. As long as the account is set up by December 31 of any one year, a person could contribute the $2,000 any time up until he or she files his or her tax return or April 15 of the following year, whichever comes earlier.[1]

Contributions to a traditional IRA can be made by any taxpayers under age $70\frac{1}{2}$ who have earned income. Even minors can set up their own regular IRA accounts, provided they have *earned* income. Year to year income in an IRA account is tax-deferred.

Contributions to a traditional IRA may be tax-deductible so long as the contributor is not participating in an employer-sponsored retirement plan. However, if the contributor does so participate, the IRA contribution may still be tax-deductible if the contributor's adjusted gross income is less than $32,000 if a single taxpayer or $52,000 if a married taxpayer filing jointly. These income levels are for 2000, and they are scheduled to increase to $50,000 for single tax payers by 2005, and to $80,000 for taxpayers filing jointly by 2007. The phase-in schedule of the income limits may be found at **Web Link 18.1.** If you have any question about the extent to which a traditional IRA contribution is deductible based on the pension fund status of either spouse or the income level of the family, see **Web Link 18.2.**

Web Link 18.1

Web Link 18.2

Regular withdrawals may begin as early as the year the account holder turns $59\frac{1}{2}$. Withdrawals made earlier than that might be subject to a 10 percent federal tax penalty as well as possible state penalties. The federal penalty tax is waived if the money taken out is used for the first-time purchase of a home (up to $10,000 lifetime limit) or spent on college-related expenses for the individual, spouse, or children. For additional information on

---

[1]Recall that anyone may file for an automatic four-month extension on his or her tax return. The tax return will include information about any IRA contribution. For people requesting the extension, the IRA contribution must still be completed by April 15.

traditional IRAs, see **Web Link 18.1.** Regardless of whether the withdrawal is subject to a penalty and regardless of what the withdrawal is used for, all withdrawals are treated as ordinary income for the year of the withdrawal. If most of the withdrawal comes from capital gains, then the account holder will end up paying more taxes on this profit than if he or she had invested the money directly in stock. Consider the following example:

> *Dan has $2,000 to invest. He intends to buy some nondividend paying stock. Dan is not eligible for a deductible IRA contribution. Dan's capital gains tax rate is 20 percent, and his marginal tax rate on ordinary income is 28 percent. He plans to hold the stock for 20 years, expects to earn an average rate of return of 10 percent, and intends to cash out the investment in one lump sum. How much will he end up with if he makes the investment through a nondeductible IRA account, and how much if he buys the stock directly?*

Web Link 4.1

First, let's figure the value of the stock after 20 years. This is a future value calculation, for which we can use **Web Link 4.1.** After 20 years, the stock will be worth $13,455. If Dan owned the stock directly, he would end up with $11,164. That is, he would pay a 20 percent capital gains tax on his accumulated profit of $11,455 ($13,455 – $2,000). The tax will be $2,291. Thus, he would have his original principal of $2,000 plus his after-tax capital gain of $9,164 ($11,455 – $2,291). If he owned the stock through an IRA account, he would have to pay a 28 percent marginal tax rate on his profits in the account, which comes to $3,207.40 (28% × [$13,455 – $2,000]), leaving him with $10,247.60 ($13,455 – $3,207). In this case, Dan would be better off by $916.40 if he owned the stock directly rather than through an IRA account.

HOW ARE WITHDRAWALS FROM A DEDUCTIBLE IRA TAXED?

If all of the contributions to an IRA were deductible, then all of the withdrawals are fully taxable as ordinary income. If some or all of the contributions were nondeductible, then a portion of each withdrawal is nontaxable. The nontaxable portion is basically the ratio of nondeductible contributions to the market value of the account at the time of withdrawal. Consider the following example:

> *Dan O'Neill has an IRA currently worth $80,000. Of this, $10,000 is from nondeductible contributions. Dan plans to take out $10,000 this year from the account. Let's assume that he does this and by next year the account grows back up to $75,000, at which time he withdraws another $10,000. How much of each withdrawal is tax-exempt?*

At the time of the first withdrawal, one-eighth of the account (i.e., $10,000 / $80,000) is from nondeductible contributions, so one-eighth of the withdrawal is tax exempt. One-eighth of the withdrawal is $1,250 ($\frac{1}{8}$ × $10,000). This reduces the nondeductible contributions in the account to $8,750 ($10,000 – $1,250). In the second year, if the value of the account has grown to $75,000, then the portion of the next withdrawal that is tax-exempt is based on the ratio of $8,750 to $75,000, or 11.670 percent. If $10,000 were again withdrawn, then 11.67 percent of this amount (i.e., $1,167) would be tax-exempt.

WHAT MINIMUM AMOUNT MUST BE WITHDRAWN FROM AN IRA?

Penalty-free withdrawals from an IRA account begin when you turn $59^1/_2$, but withdrawals are not mandatory until one year after you reach age $70^1/_2$. For example, a person who turns 70 on August 14, 2002, will turn $70^1/_2$ on February 14, 2003. This person must start withdrawing from the IRA account sometime in 2004, with the first withdrawal no later than April 1 and the second no later than December 31. Each year thereafter, this person has until December 31 to make the withdrawal. Once you are legally entitled to make withdrawals, you can take as much as you want, including closing out the entire account. However, if you take less than the minimum withdrawal required for a year, you must pay a 50 percent penalty tax on the difference between that minimum and what was actually taken.

The minimum withdrawal for each year is computed by dividing the account balance as of the previous December 31 by an IRS life expectancy figure. During the year after a person turns $70^1/_2$, the first minimum withdrawal is based on the account balance and life expectancy applicable to the previous year, the second is based on the current year's formula. Consider the following example:

> Dan O'Neill's IRA account balance was $200,000 at the close of trading for December 31, 2001, and $210,000 on December 31, 2002. Dan was born October 1, 1931. What are Dan's minimum required withdrawals in 2003?

Dan turned 70 on October 1, 2001, and so he turned $70^1/_2$ on April 1, 2002. Therefore he must make the two minimum withdrawals by April 1 and December 31 of 2003. To determine these minimums, we first look up Dan's life expectancy on December 31, 2001. On this date, Dan was 70 years old. Based on Appendix I for Single Life Expectancy in IRS **Web Link 18.3** Publication 590 (see **Web Link 18.3**), Dan should calculate using a life expectancy of 15.3 years. The minimum withdrawal by April 1, 2003, would be $200,000 divided by 15.3, or $13,072.

To determine the minimum withdrawal by December 31, Dan has two choices. Dan can simply subtract one from his 2001 life expectancy or else look up his life expectancy each year and use the IRS figure as the denominator. Let's assume he opts to use the method of subtracting one. In this case, subtract the first withdrawal of $13,072 from the ending account value of $210,000 on December 31, 2001, and divide the difference by 14.3. The difference is $196,928, and the quotient is $13,772. To determine the minimum withdrawal for the year 2004, Dan will take the value of the account on December 31, 2003, and divide this number by 13.3.

Web Link (WSJ) 18.4 The required minimum withdrawals may also be based on the joint life expectancy of the account holder and the beneficiary. Joint life expectancy tables are also provided in IRS Publication 590.

HOW DOES A SPOUSAL IRA WORK?

A **spousal IRA** is no different than a regular IRA in all ways but one. All you need to open a spousal IRA is a combined income of the spouses that equals or exceeds the amount contributed. Thus, if the husband were to have earned at least $4,000 during the year, both spouses could contribute up to $2,000 to their respective IRA accounts even if the wife had no income during the year. A spousal IRA may take the form of either a traditional IRA or a Roth IRA (see below).

Web Link 18.5

HOW DOES AN EDUCATIONAL IRA WORK?

An **educational IRA** is an IRA set up to finance a child's education. The maximum that can be contributed in a child's name in any one year is $500. Thus, two grandparents cannot both contribute $500 for the same grandchild, although they could each contribute $250. The contributor need not be related to the child for whom the contribution is made. The contributions are not deductible, but as with all IRAs, income is tax-deferred. Finally, if the withdrawals are used to pay for qualified educational expenses, they are tax-exempt. One of the drawbacks to an educational IRA is that in the year a student takes a tax-free distribution, the student cannot also take either the Hope Scholarship or Lifetime Learning Credits. If an IRA distribution does occur in the same year, then it must be treated as a fully taxable income.

There are income constraints on the person making the contribution to an educational IRA account. Single individuals with an adjusted gross income (AGI) of less than $95,000 may contribute up to the maximum, while single individuals with an AGI over $110,000 are not eligible to contribute. Single individuals with AGIs in between may make pro-rated contributions. The corresponding numbers for married couples filing jointly are $150,000 and $160,000. In addition, no contribution can be made for a child in the same year that anyone has contributed to a qualified state tuition program on behalf of that child. It should be noted that there is no minimum income requirement for anyone contributing to an educational IRA. Thus, someone with no taxable income (such as a child) could even contribute to this account. Educational IRAs are IRAs that do not require gross income of equal or greater value than the contribution.

Contributions to an educational IRA may be made until the date on which the beneficiary turns 18. The educational IRA must be closed out when the beneficiary turns 30, unless its assets are transferred to another family member, such as a brother or sister. Any distributions that are used for nonqualifying expenses (which could include the mandatory close-out "distribution" at age 30) not only count as ordinary income but incur a 10 percent penalty. Note that taxable distributions are taxed the same as those of nondeductible IRAs. That is, only the withdrawals in excess of the original contributions are subject to taxation. Qualifying expenses include any payments for tuition, fees, books, supplies, equipment, and certain room and board expenses relating to post-secondary education.

Web Link 18.6

HOW DOES A ROTH IRA WORK?

Roth IRAs are named for Senator William Roth from Delaware, who chaired the Congressional committee that initiated the legislation creating this vehicle. The Roth IRA's distinguishing characteristic is that contributions to it are nondeductible, but withdrawals are tax-exempt under certain conditions. As with the traditional and spousal IRAs, the maximum contribution to a Roth IRA is $2,000 per year.[2] However, to be eligible to contribute to a Roth IRA, one must have income at least equal to one's contribution. Also, AGI cannot exceed $150,000 for couples and $95,000 for singles to be eligible to contribute the full $2,000. With AGI between $150,000 and $160,000 for married couples and $95,000 and $110,000 for singles, a pro-rated contribution is allowed. Above those limits, contributions to Roth IRAs are not allowed.

So long as you have sufficient income and are not over the AGI limit, no age limit concludes the period in which you may make contributions to a Roth IRA.

To be eligible for a tax-free distribution, your contribution must remain in the Roth IRA for at least five years, and the holder of the account must be at least 59$^1/_2$ years old. However, if the account has been established for at least five years, then tax-free withdrawals are also permitted if the account holder has died, become disabled, or makes a first-time home purchase. Note that the first-time home purchase applies not only to the account owner, but also to the account owner's spouse, children, grandchildren, and even parents. There is, however, a $10,000 lifetime cap on taking out money for this purpose.

Nonqualified withdrawals are treated as ordinary income and incur a 10 percent penalty. However, this penalty is waived for direct transfers to a traditional IRA account, as well as in other conditions, including for medical expenses, certain qualified education expenses, and distributions for first-home purchases. Note that when a nonqualified withdrawal is made, it is treated as if the withdrawal comes first from contributions. Withdrawals of contributions are not taxable. Only when nonqualified withdrawals exceed the original contributions is there taxable income, and then the taxable income is only the amount in excess of the contributions.

Another major difference between a traditional IRA and a Roth IRA is that the latter has no minimum age at which you must begin withdrawing money from the account.

Web Link 18.6a
Web Link 18.7

For additional comments on a Roth IRA, see **Web Link 18.6a.** Tables providing comparisons of all three types of IRAs may be found at **Web Link 18.7.**

WHAT WILL THE FUTURE VALUE OF MY IRA BE?

Figuring the future value of an IRA is either a future value calculation if you plan not to make further contributions to it, or a future value of annuity calculation if you still plan to contribute a fixed amount every year. Consider the following problem:

> *Dan O'Neill is 25 years old. He is ready to set up an IRA account and plans to contribute $2,000 per year (at the start of each year) to it. He plans not to touch the account until he turns 65, and believes he can earn an average rate of return of 10 percent. How much will be in the account when he is ready to start withdrawals?*

Web Link 18.8

The solution may be found at **Web Link 18.8** (which is an annuity due calculator). In this case, Dan will have contributed a total of $80,000, and the account will be worth $973,704.

---

[2]If you contribute to both a traditional and a Roth IRA, your combined contributions cannot exceed $2,000 per person.

WHICH IS BETTER,
A TRADITIONAL OR A ROTH IRA?

If you are not qualified to make a tax-deductible contribution to a traditional IRA account, you should contribute to a Roth IRA account. If you are also ineligible to contribute to the Roth IRA account, then you should simply make a nondeductible contribution to a traditional IRA. A more interesting question arises when a person is eligible to make either a tax-deductible contribution to a traditional IRA account or to a Roth IRA account. Consider the following situation:

> *Dan O'Neill has an AGI of $45,000 per year. He is married and will contribute $2,000 per year to a retirement program for both himself and his wife.[3] He will make his contributions at the start of each year. Dan intends to invest conservatively, and believes he can earn 8 percent per year on his investments, both before and after retirement, and in either an IRA account or direct savings program. His combined federal and state tax bracket both now and after retirement is 35 percent. Dan is 25, and plans to start taking his withdrawals at age 60. He wants his funds to last at least until age 85, but has no desire to have any funds left at that point for his beneficiaries. If Dan's goal is to maximize his retirement income, should Dan invest his annual contributions in (1) a deductible IRA account, (2) a nondeductible IRA account, (3) a Roth IRA account, or (4) a direct savings program?*

Web Link 18.9   The solution may be found at **Web Link 18.9.** Key results are shown in Table 18.1.

Table 18.1
Comparison of IRAs with Direct Savings Account

	Deductible IRA	Nondeductible IRA	Roth IRA	Direct Savings
Pretax accumulation at retirement	$372,204	$241,933	$241,933	n.a.
After-tax accumulation at retirement	241,933	173,181	241,933	$128,762
After-tax monthly income	1,811	1,284	1,811	755

Note that the deductible IRA and the Roth IRA will provide identical after-tax monthly income. This is no coincidence. These amounts match because we need to reconcile the fact that a $2,000 contribution to a deductible IRA costs less than a $2,000 contribution to a Roth IRA. As Dan has a 35 percent marginal tax bracket, his contribution to the deductible IRA actually only costs him only $1,300 ($2,000 × [1 − .35]) out of pocket. Without some explicit consideration of how this $700 tax savings were allocated, it would be misleading to compare the monthly income generated from a deductible IRA with a Roth IRA. The easiest way to make this adjustment is just to assume that the Roth IRA contribution equals not $2,000, but whatever the after-tax contribution to the deductible IRA would have been. In this case, the Roth contribution is assumed to be $1,300, or 65 percent of the deductible IRA contribution. This same assumption is built into the nondeductible IRA contribution. Hence, it is easy to see why the pretax accumulation at

---

[3]The $2,000 figure in this example represents the pre-tax contribution. If the contribution is tax-deductible, the full $2,000 goes into the account. If the contribution were nondeductible, only the amount minus the taxes due on that income would be contributed.

retirement for the Roth IRA is 65 percent of the pretax accumulation of the deductible IRA (i.e., \$241,933 / \$372,204 = 65%). If the same marginal tax rate is then applied to the deductible IRA at retirement, then the after-tax accumulations of the two will be the same, as there is no tax due on the Roth IRA. Because the after-tax accumulations are the same, the after-tax monthly incomes will also be the same.

Now let's change some of the parameters in the above example. Suppose that at the time of retirement, Dan's marginal tax rate drops from 35 percent to 18 percent. If we then rerun the calculator changing the after-retirement marginal tax rate, we will see that the deductible IRA provides a monthly payment of \$2,284 while the Roth's payment remains at \$1,811. As the Roth's ending value is tax-exempt, it would be unaffected by the change in the after-retirement tax rate. The point here is that if an investor anticipates a lower marginal tax rate at the time of retirement, then the deductible IRA actually provides a better deal than the Roth IRA.

Finally, suppose that the investor believes his or her marginal tax rate will actually be higher in retirement. Let's say the investor anticipates a marginal tax rate at retirement of 40 percent. When we rerun the numbers, we see that the deductible IRA provides a monthly payment of \$1,671 compared to the Roth's monthly payment, which still stays at \$1,811.

The conclusion here is quite simple. If you have the opportunity to choose between a deductible IRA and a Roth IRA, the one that is best for you depends on whether your marginal tax bracket will go up or down at retirement.

It should be emphasized that many, many calculators on the Internet will assess whether a person should contribute to a deductible, nondeductible, or Roth IRA. Many of these calculators come up with different answers. The calculator used to do the above comparison assumes that the nondeductible IRA and the Roth contributions equal the after-tax equivalent of the deductible IRA contribution. Some calculators assume that the full \$2,000 goes into each account, regardless of whether the contribution is tax-deductible. Such assumptions will obviously produce a different answer. Other calculators assume that the tax savings from a deductible IRA are invested in a direct savings program. Various calculators also build in different assumptions about when the IRA contribution is made: the start of the year, end of the year, or pro-rated over 12 months. Each of these assumptions produces a different answer as to the value of the particular IRA.

Web Link 18.10

SHOULD I CONVERT MY TRADITIONAL IRA TO A ROTH IRA?

The previous section focused on which IRA to choose when starting out. But what if you already have a traditional IRA and are considering moving some or all of it into a Roth IRA? To qualify for a rollover, your AGI must be less than \$100,000 (prior to the transaction). The 10 percent early withdrawal penalty is waived in this case, but all money withdrawn must be treated as taxable income in the year of withdrawal. So the question becomes "Is it worth it to pay the extra taxes now in order to have all of the withdrawals be tax-free later?" Keep in mind that any rollovers must meet the standard requirements for a tax-free distribution from a Roth account. Let us consider the following example:

Dan O'Neill has $50,000 in a deductible IRA. Dan is 40 and plans on working at least until age 65. He is seriously considering rolling over the full $50,000 from his traditional IRA to a Roth IRA so that the money will be tax-free when it is distributed. As Dan would hold the exact same investments in the Roth that he held in the traditional account, his projected rates of return in both accounts are 8 percent. Dan's current tax rate is 34 percent; he anticipates it to be so at retirement as well. He plans no additional contributions to an IRA between now and retirement. Dan wants his distributions to last until he would turn 90. As the rollover does not incur the 10 percent fee, but does involve declaring the $50,000 as taxable income that year, Dan will owe additional income taxes. Assume Dan will pay the taxes from his transfer amount. Is this a good idea?

Web Link 18.11   The solution may be found at Web Link 18.11. If left untouched in the original IRA, the $50,000 would have grown to $342,424. When withdrawn at age 65, the amount would be reduced by payment of taxes to $226,000. From this, Dan could take a monthly benefit of $1,691. If Dan takes the $50,000 out of the traditional account, however, he will owe $17,000 in taxes now ($50,000 × 34%). By paying this out of the transfer amount, he is left with $33,000 to put into his Roth IRA. The $33,000 will grow to $226,000 by the time Dan reaches age 65. So Dan would still have a monthly income of $1,691. As we saw in the previous section, if the marginal tax rates during Dan's working years and at the time of retirement are the same, it will make no difference which strategy Dan follows as his monthly benefit will be the same.

Suppose, however, that Dan's marginal tax rate at the time of retirement is 18 percent and not the 34 percent it was during his working years. Dan's monthly benefit from his traditional IRA will now be $2,101, and his benefit from the Roth will of course remain unaltered at $1,691, as it is unaffected by taxes. A higher marginal tax rate at retirement would obviously tilt the process in favor of moving one's money to a Roth IRA. Another event that would tip the decision in favor of the rollover into the Roth IRA would be any delay in paying the income taxes due on the withdrawal from the traditional IRA. In our example above, a delay of eight months in paying the income taxes due would increase the monthly benefit under the Roth IRA by $43 to $1,735.

A more dramatic way to increase the monthly benefit from the transfer would be to pay the taxes out of spare cash and place the full $50,000 into the Roth IRA. When analyzed in this fashion, the monthly benefit from the Roth IRA becomes $2,563. This is a much more attractive number, but implicitly the investor has also increased his or her investment in the IRA account, having spent $17,000 out of pocket to facilitate the transfer.

As with deciding between a Roth IRA or a traditional IRA initially, rollover decisions can be assisted by means of many calculators on the Internet. Likewise, many of them will come up with different numbers, because they have different assumptions built
Web Link 18.12   into their models.

HOW DOES A KEOGH ACCOUNT WORK?

Keogh accounts are named for Eugene Keogh, the representative from New York who originally introduced the legislation authorizing them. A Keogh account is intended to serve as a pension fund for self-employed individuals. However, if a self-employed individual hires other workers, the Keogh plan must also cover them. Keogh accounts are similar to a traditional, deductible IRA account. A Keogh plan may be either a profit-sharing or a money purchase plan. In a profit-sharing plan, contributions are limited to 13.04 percent of a person's self-employment income, up to a maximum of $30,000 per year. The contribution percentage can be adjusted yearly. In a money purchase plan, a person can set aside up to 20 percent of his or her income, to a maximum of $30,000 per year. However, the percentage contribution can't change once it has been established. This $30,000 upper limit in both types of Keogh plans makes Keoghs the most attractive of all of the tax-favored savings programs, in terms of building a retirement nest egg as quickly as possible.

An individual may set up both types of plans. A special feature of Keogh plans is that the self-employment may be a second job, or even a hobby, of the individual. Thus, the contributor may have a regular job where he or she is fully vested in a generous pension plan. As long as all of the income from the second job is self-employment income, this person can still create a Keogh account. Basically, any sole proprietor who files a Schedule C with his or her tax return, or any partnership that files a Schedule E with each partner's tax return, is eligible to set up a Keogh plan.

A Keogh account must be set up by the end of a calendar year, although the creator has until his or her taxes are due (usually April 15) to make the full contribution. Contributions are fully deductible, and all withdrawals from a Keogh account are taxable as ordinary income.

Web Link 18.13

WHAT ARE 401(K)S AND 403(B)S?

401(k)s and **403(b)**s are essentially the same type of program, the former authorized for employees at for-profit businesses and the latter for employees at nonprofits and not-for-profits. These plans may serve as an employee's pension, or may supplement a regular pension program. The names of these accounts come from the section of the Internal Revenue Code in which they are defined.

401(k) and 403(b) plans typically function as a defined contribution type of account. The employee's contributions are fully deductible, and any contribution by the employer is not taxable to the employee. Employer contributions normally come in the form of cash, but some employers (at corporations) provide the contribution in the form of the company's stock. As these plans are covered by the Employee Retirement Income Security Act (ERISA), the assets in the accounts are protected from creditors and from being assigned to anyone else, except in the case of domestic relations court cases dealing with divorce decrees or child support orders.

Web Link 18.14
Web Link 18.15

Another feature of these plans that separates them from traditional pension programs is the limits on the amount that can be contributed in a year. The current maximum that an employee can contribute is $10,500 in pretax dollars.

WHAT ARE ANNUITIES?

A type of investment particularly well suited for retirement is a retirement annuity. An annuity may be designated as either qualified or nonqualified. A **qualified annuity** is one that is purchased through a tax-sheltered program such as a 401(k), a 403(b), or an IRA. The tax deductibility rules for these accounts still apply. Nonqualified annuities are the same investments as those that can be purchased in a qualified plan, but without the tax deductibility of contributions.

An annuity can be purchased with a single (obviously large) payment, or it can be purchased with premiums paid over time.[4] When the annuity is purchased with a single payment, it is usually an **immediate annuity,** meaning that the payments to the **annuitant** (i.e., the investor) start immediately. These are also called **income annuities.**

When the contributions are made over time, the annuity is analogous to any other type of pension plan, where the payments will be taken upon retirement. This type of annuity is usually referred to as a **deferred annuity,** or a **tax-deferred annuity.** A deferred annuity can be broken into two segments: the **accumulation phase** and the **payout phase.** The advantage of a deferred annuity is that the money in a person's account grows on a tax-deferred basis. Withdrawals from a tax-deferred annuity may start as early as age $59^1/_2$, but the annuitant may wait until age 85. If the annuitant dies before starting the withdrawals from the annuity, there is usually a guaranteed death benefit.

Web Link 18.16

Annuities are classified into four basic types:

1. SPDAs (Single Premium Deferred Annuities). A nonqualified SPDA is appropriate for someone who has suddenly come into a lot of money that he or she would like to apply toward retirement. The windfall cash might be from the sale of a home, an inheritance, and so on. A qualified SPDA would be ideal for an individual taking money from a pension plan, IRA, 401(k), or other tax-deferred savings program.

2. FPDAs (Flexible Premium Deferred Annuities). A nonqualified FPDA would be a form of savings program for retirement. Qualified FPDAs are used for IRAs, 401(k)s, and Teacher's Retirement Plans. FPDAs allow you to contribute on a monthly basis.

3. CD-type annuities. These are similar to SPDAs, but have guaranteed rates over selected periods of time.

4. SPIAs (Single Premium Immediate Annuity). Similar to an SPDA, the SPIA would be set up with a lump sum payment. It differs in that the benefit payments begin upon receipt of the single premium.

SPDAs and SPIAs allow an investor to save for retirement primarily in other forms and then, as the investor approaches retirement, move the money into an annuity program. For example, an individual who starts saving through an IRA account early in his or her career might well wish to continue saving through that account. Upon retirement, the money could then be moved into an annuity policy. The alternative is to place the contributions directly into the annuity over the working career (i.e., to buy an FPDA). The benefit of investing through something like an IRA initially is that you can have more direct control

---

[4]Most people should own both a life insurance policy and an annuity. The premiums on the life insurance policy are in case you die prematurely; premiums on the annuity are in case you live well beyond your life expectancy. Dying earlier or dying later than expected both cause financial problems, although most people would surely prefer the second of these problems!

over the investments made. Once the money is in an annuity policy, your choices are usually greatly limited; moving the money elsewhere may be difficult and costly.

HOW DO FIXED RATE AND VARIABLE RATE ANNUITIES DIFFER?

A critical feature of any annuity policy is the underlying investments associated with the policy. When the investor pays the premium, the insurance company then invests that premium on behalf of the investor. If the policy is a fixed rate policy, the company invests the premiums in mutual funds that are in turn invested in fixed rate securities such as government and corporate bonds. If the policy is a variable rate policy, then the premiums are invested in mutual funds that are invested in common stocks.

With a deferred annuity, the investor may choose one type of policy during the accumulation period and switch during the payout period. Frequently, people choose a variable annuity during the former and switch into a fixed rate annuity during the latter. In addition, the premiums do not have to be placed into only one policy; investors are usually allowed to split their contract between the two policies. Thus, one might put half of one's premium into a fixed rate policy and half into a variable annuity policy.

WHAT PAYOUT OPTIONS DO I HAVE WITH AN ANNUITY?

An annuitant may choose among five payout options. These include:

1. cash refund option,
2. installment refund option,
3. life with period certain,
4. life or straight life option, and
5. joint and survivor option.

With a deferred annuity, the annuitant does not have to select the payout option until the accumulation phase is complete. Obviously, with an immediate annuity, the payout option must be chosen when the policy is purchased. If the annuity is a fixed annuity, then the dollar amount of the payments are fixed in all scenarios, whereas, if the annuity is variable, the dollar amount of the payments will fluctuate with the value of the underlying portfolio.

All five options are known as life options because annuitants are guaranteed payments for as long as they live. The distinctions among these five options are the consequences upon the death of the annuitant. A cash refund option guarantees that any cash value present in the policy when the annuitant dies is immediately paid to the **contingent payee.** The contingent payee is analogous to a beneficiary. The second option, an installment refund, guarantees that this cash value will be paid to the contingent payee in installments equal to those the annuitant was receiving at the time of death.

The life with period certain option provides for a guaranteed minimum number of payments, even if the annuitant dies the day after purchasing the policy. Common periods of certainty include 5, 10, 15 and 20 years. The shorter the number of periods, the higher the payment per period.

The life or straight life option has no residual guarantee. Thus, if the annuitant dies the day after buying the policy, the annuity offers no residual value to the estate. Few straight life policies are sold, because most people don't want their beneficiaries to have to live with the regret of having paid for a policy that would become worthless when the annuitant dies shortly after taking it out.

The joint and survivor option makes a great deal of sense for a couple. The key decision in a joint and survivor option is how much of the annuity will continue once the first spouse dies. Common choices include 75 percent, $66^{2}/_{3}$ percent, and 50 percent. Reductions make good sense, since the cost of living for the surviving spouse will be lower. The lower the percentage that is continued after the death of the first spouse, the higher the initial payment amount will be.

The joint and survivor option can also be combined with any of the other life options. Thus, people frequently combine the period certain feature with the joint and survivor option. Purchasers must then choose how much of the annuity will be continued after the first spouse dies as well as how many years of certain payments are desired.

HOW ARE ANNUITY PAYMENTS TAXED?

If the annuity is part of a qualified plan, then the usual tax treatment applies—all of the payments during the payout period are fully taxable as ordinary income. This is because the premiums were tax-deductible and the taxation of the earnings in the account (i.e., interest, dividends, and capital gains) was deferred.

If the annuity is a nonqualified account, then a substantial portion of it may be tax-exempt. In this case, because the premium payments were made with after-tax dollars, part of each benefit payment is considered a return of the principal, and so that portion is tax-exempt. Let's consider a simple example. Suppose you paid $13,500 in premiums for a policy. When you are ready to start drawing monthly benefit payments, let's assume your life expectancy is 15 years (or 180 months). Let's also assume that the monthly benefit payment is $150. Over the next 15 years, you would be expected to receive $27,000 ($150/month × 180 months) in benefits. One-half of each payment would be tax-exempt and the other half would be taxed as ordinary income (because you paid $13,500 in premiums, or one-half of the $27,000 in expected benefits). A recent change in the federal tax code now requires that if the annuitant lives longer than the 15 years in this example, then the entire monthly benefit must be taxed as ordinary income.

Web Link 18.17

HOW SHOULD I SELECT A POLICY?

If you are buying an immediate annuity, then shopping for a policy is straightforward. Indicate how much you are willing to pay, which payout option you prefer, and your desired frequency of payments. For example, suppose a retired couple that had an extra $100,000 they wanted to put to use decided on a joint and survivorship fixed annuity policy with 10 years certain, with monthly payments. Each insurance company the couple contacts will then propose the monthly payment it would be willing to provide. Clearly, a company willing to pay $1,000 a month would be preferable over one willing to pay $900 a month. There is a catch: annuities are not insured or otherwise guaranteed by a federal agency, so if the insurance company paying the annuity fails, the annuitant could sustain a substantial loss. Such failures do happen, albeit rarely. Thus, you should investigate the insurance company that comes up with the best offer to validate its financial soundness.

Obviously, before you purchase an annuity, obtain proposals from several companies to make sure you are getting a relatively good deal. Whenever possible, approximate what the monthly payment might be. Consider the following example:

> *Dan O'Neill and his wife Sharon are considering the purchase of an immediate, joint and survivorship annuity with a 60 percent continuation. Dan was born on July 1, 1932, and Sharon was born on July 1, 1935. The valuation date for this purchase is July 1, 2002. The policy would provide a rate of return of 8 percent for the first 15 years, and then 6 percent thereafter. What would be an approximation of the O'Neill's monthly payment if the O'Neills have $100,000 available for the purchase?*

Web Link 18.18

The answer may be found at **Web Link 18.18** (be sure to enter that the annuity is payable for 100 years). In this case, the calculator produces an annuity factor of 9.8447. To convert this annuity factor into dollars and cents, multiply the factor by twelve and divide the product into the amount of money available for buying the annuity. For the above example, this works out to $846.50 ($100,000 / [9.8447 × 12]).

Web Link 18.19

If you are buying a deferred annuity, you have even more to consider when selecting a policy. First, the purchase of an annuity policy is a lot like buying a mutual fund. The investor is investing in portfolios managed by the insurance company. As with mutual funds, historical performance has little to do with future prospects, although it is best to avoid funds that have consistently performed poorly. A more important consideration would be fees. As with other insurance products, commission on the sale of the product itself usually applies. In addition, you must pay annual fees for managing the investments underlying the annuity and usually a **surrender charge** if it is terminated early.

In the case of fixed annuities, the insurance company will usually offer an initial interest rate that is guaranteed for a fixed number of years, after which the rate will be subject to market conditions. A company may place a **floor** (the lowest rate the company will guarantee to pay) or other constraints on how the rate will be determined. The higher the floor, the more attractive the policy. Usually, the longer the guarantee period, the higher the initial guaranteed interest rate. The longer guarantee period allows the company to invest the money in securities with longer maturities that generally provide higher yields.

Web Link 18.20
Web Link 18.21

The drawback here is that if the annuitant wants his or her money back during this guaranteed period, a high surrender charge is applied.

WHAT IS MY LIFE EXPECTANCY?

Chapter 17 and the bulk of this chapter have given you descriptions of the various traditional sources of income during a person's retirement years. These included Social Security benefits, pension benefits, and tax-favored savings programs such as IRAs, 401(k)s,

403(b)s, and annuities. Now you are ready to move into the heart of the retirement planning process.

Retirement planning would be extremely easy if we could know our date of death. Unless you are fortunate enough to experience a miraculous vision offering you this information, you may want to look up your expected date of death in a **life expectancy table.** A life expectancy table, however, can only tell you how long people who are your age and otherwise have your critical features such as gender are likely to live *on average*. Remember, roughly half of us will die prior to our expected age, while the other half will live beyond our expected age of death. Effective retirement planning should really assume that each of us will live to age 100 or even beyond. After all, it would be little consolation to know that you should have died at age 85 if you live to be 95 and are broke!

Having said this, it is still fun to have some idea of how long each of us is expected to live. Several tables or calculators on the Internet provide this information. Consider the following example:

> *Sharon O'Neill is a white female, age 48, who has never smoked. She is somewhat active, but not in tip-top athletic condition. Neither she nor her parents have any early health problems. She is 5' 4" tall, and weighs 165 pounds. What is her life expectancy?*

Web Link 18.22   Several calculators or tables that will answer this question may be found at **Web Link 18.22.**

WHAT WILL BE MY COST OF LIVING DURING RETIREMENT?

Everyone would love to have plenty of income during retirement. But as Chapter 17 made clear, a huge amount of retirement income could imply living a life of poverty prior to retirement. It is usually assumed that the typical person wants to strike some type of balance, aiming for a lifestyle during retirement that exactly matches his or her lifestyle before retirement. Two general approaches can determine the desired amount of retirement income.

The first is called a bottom-up calculation, where each person or family creates a budget projection, projecting the expenses likely to be incurred during an early year of retirement. The longer it is to retirement, the more difficult such an exercise becomes, especially because of the inflation factor and uncertainty about the manner of retirement lifestyle. For a family with small children, a large mortgage, auto loan payments, and college educations to fund, budgets are invariably tight. At retirement, the mortgage is usually small or has been paid off; cars have been paid off or purchased with cash, and the children have by then attended college and are out earning their own incomes. Many of us may be able to live more comfortably on less income during our retirement years. Nevertheless, such budget projections are highly speculative. Consider the following example:

> *The O'Neills are starting to think about retirement, even though it is still 10 years away. They have identified various major types of expenses. They group these expenses into two categories: costs that may decline at retirement and costs that may increase. For each of these expense categories, they identify their current monthly payments and what these payments would be today if they were retired today. These categories and projected values are*

Expense Category	Monthly Amounts Current	Estimated
Expenses that may fall		
Housing	$ 1,700	$ 300
Life Insurance	$ 100	$ 0
Transportation	$ 200	$ 100
Clothing	$ 250	$ 100
Debt Payments	$ 500	$ 0
Education	$ 1,500	$ 100
Other	$ 2,000	$1,500
Expenses that may rise		
Medical	$ 80	$ 200
Food	$ 400	$ 500
Recreation	$ 100	$ 300
Property Liability Insurance	$ 20	$ 30

The O'Neills believe that inflation will average 3 percent between now and retirement. What are the O'Neill's current level of expenses, what would be their total expenses if they were retired today, and what are these retirement expenses projected to be in 10 years when adjusted for inflation?

Web Link 18.23
Using any of the calculators at **Web Link 18.23,** the O'Neill's current monthly expenses turn out to be $6,850. If they were retired today, their expenses would be $3,130. In 10 Web Link 18.24 years, adjusted for a 3 percent annual inflation rate, their expenses would be $4,223.

The second way to project post-retirement income is to look at the rules of thumb suggested by various professionals. These rules are ostensibly based on the experiences of people who have retired. It would be really nice if everyone who has worked with the retired were able to report the same recommendation, but such is not the case. Generally, the rules of thumb for estimating post-retirement income vary from $66^2/_3$ to 80 percent of pre-retirement income as the optimal target. The most commonly suggested number is 80 percent.

Naturally, using this approach requires an estimate of what a person's salary will be at the time of retirement. One way to determine this number is to look at a person's current salary, ascertain how many more years this person will work, project this person's average annual salary increase between now and retirement,[5] and then compute the future value of his or her salary. Consider the following example:

Dan O'Neill is 25 years old. He currently earns $40,000. He believes his salary will grow at a rate of 3 percent per year, and he plans on working another 40 years. What will be Dan's salary at the time of retirement, and what would be his cost of living if he would need 80 percent of this amount?

Web Link 18.25
This problem may be solved with any of the calculators at **Web Link 18.25.** At retirement, Dan's salary will be $130,482. If he will need 80 percent of this amount to live on, he will have projected expenses of $104,386 (80% × $130,482)

---

[5]Technically, the annual average salary growth rate should be computed as the geometric mean of the annual salary increases between now and retirement. However, there most likely would be negligible difference between the geometric mean and the arithmetic average, and the latter is computationally easier and vastly better comprehended by most people.

HOW MUCH INCOME WILL MY PERSONAL ASSETS PROVIDE DURING RETIREMENT?

As described previously, income during retirement is generally categorized into the following four sources: Social Security retirement benefits, pension income, payments from tax-qualified plans, and cash withdrawals from personal assets. The income that can be derived from Social Security, pensions, and tax-qualified plans has been covered in the last chapter and earlier in this chapter. Let us now consider how much in cash withdrawals a person should expect from his or her personal assets (such as a portfolio consisting of stocks, bonds, and mutual funds).

How much cash you can withdraw is based upon how much you save between now and retirement, what rate of return you earn between now and retirement, and how long you expect to live after retirement. Keep in mind that cash withdrawals from personal assets are not necessarily the same as investment income on the portfolio. The reason is that as one approaches the end of one's life, it is certainly reasonable to consume part of the principal. Consider the following example:

> Dan and Sharon O'Neill have saved $5,000 to date for their retirement. They plan to add $3,000 per year ($250/month) for the next 40 years to their retirement portfolio. They believe they can earn 10 percent per year on their investments between now and retirement, at which time they will switch to more conservative investments. This move would reduce their rate of return to 8 percent. If they expect to live no more than 25 years after retirement, how much income per month will this savings program produce?

This problem can be solved in two steps. The first step is to figure out how much the O'Neills will have accumulated by the time they retire. This answer can be found at any of the links at **Web Link 18.26,** and turns out to be $1,613,883. The second step is to figure out how much could be withdrawn from this account on a regular basis. It turns out that the solution to this problem is identical to the solution of a problem in which the accumulated assets could be thought of as a loan that is taken out today, and the withdrawals are analogous to the monthly payments. Thus, if we use any of the calculators at **Web Link 18.27** and treat the accumulated assets of $1,613,883 as the loan balance and 8 percent as the interest rate on a loan that lasts for 25 years (i.e., 300 months), the monthly withdrawal is $12,456.20.

Some people may raise the question about the above scenario that it ignores the possibility of the O'Neills living beyond the projected 25 years. No one wants to take a substantial cut in income at the age of 90! This concern can be resolved in one of two ways. One is to use an incredibly high number as the projected life expectancy after retirement. In the above example, let us assume the O'Neills want their investment income to last 40 years rather than 25 (which would mean they would live to the age of 105). This extended life expectancy would mean they could withdraw no more than $11,221.50 per month from their portfolio.

The second way people deal with concerns about outliving their investment income is to set their withdrawal rate at a level below the rate of return they expect to achieve on their portfolio. Research has suggested that if you withdraw no more than .5% ($^1/_2$ of 1 percent) of the value of a stock portfolio at the start of each month, then it is a near certainty you will not exhaust your portfolio income. One-half percent per month is approximately

Web Link 18.26

Web Link 18.27

6 percent per year. In our above example, .5 percent per month would be $8,069.15. The drawback to this strategy is that it creates variability in a person's retirement income. But the simple truth is, no one can have both perfect certainty of income and inflation protection. Hence, everyone must accept one of these risk exposures.

FOR HOW LONG WILL I BE ABLE TO WITHDRAW MONEY FROM MY PORTFOLIO?

A variation on the above question is the time period for which a person can live off of a portfolio. For example, if you had a portfolio worth $500,000 and planned to withdraw $60,000 from it each year (i.e., $5,000 per month), you should want to know how long this portfolio would last. Many people would simply divide $500,000 by $60,000 and assume it would last 8.33 years. However, if the portfolio is invested and generates a positive rate of return, then the cash inflow from the portfolio will last substantially longer than eight years and four months, because after each withdrawal, the remaining assets continue to grow in value. Consider the following example:

> Dan and Sharon O'Neill project they will have a personal portfolio with $500,000 on the day they retire. They project they will want to withdraw $60,000 per year at the start of each year from this portfolio. They believe that during the retirement years they can generate an average annual rate of return of 8 percent. If that is the case, for how long can they draw out the $60,000 per year?

The answer is slightly over 13 years. To illustrate why this is so, remember that if they start with $500,000 and draw out $60,000 to start the year, they will still have $440,000 in the portfolio. Over the course of the next year, the portfolio should grow in value by $35,200.

Web Link 18.28

HOW MUCH DO I NEED TO SET ASIDE TO FUND MY RETIREMENT INCOME?

Ideally, after you have projected your retirement income and your retirement expenses, the first will equal or exceed the second! Most people find this not to be the case. Thus, the real question they face is not how much income their retirement portfolio will produce, but how much they will have to set aside to increase their retirement income to the desired level. The answer to this question is incredibly complex. Many assumptions must be made either explicitly or implicitly. Because of the variety of assumptions that must be made, and because of the variety of ways this problem can be approached, a large number of web site calculators are available, each producing different answers for a user. Some of the web sites take a fairly simple approach to the problem, and others incorporate many technical details. A simpler calculator might serve a user as well or better than a more complex one. Let's consider some of the simpler calculators first, and then turn to some of the more complex ones.

In a simple model, you start with the assumption of how much supplemental retirement income you will need. Supplemental retirement income is the difference between your projected expenses in retirement and your projected income from all other sources.

You would then solve for how much money you would need to save to meet this objective. Consider the following example:

Dan and Sharon O'Neill have decided they will need $40,000 in supplemental annual retirement income. They are 25 now, and plan to work 40 years. By investing in aggressive stock mutual funds, they believe they can earn an average rate of return of 10 percent. Finally, they believe that between them, they will live no more than 25 years after retirement. How much do they need to contribute to achieve this goal?

Web Link 18.29   The answer to the first question, found at **Web Link 18.29,** is $56.94 per month, or $820.35 on an annual basis.

In some cases, people may want to tackle the above problem in two steps. The first step would be to figure how much they would need to accumulate at retirement to generate a particular annual cash flow. If we change the question in the above problem to ask how much the O'Neills would need to accumulate to draw out $40,000 per year for 25 **Web Link 18.30**   years, then the answer, found at **Web Link 18.30,** is $399,389.

Although the above calculations are straightforward, and the problem sounds like a relevant one, it is also a misleading way to look at supplemental retirement income, because it ignores the impact of inflation. Most people think about retirement income in terms of the purchasing power of *today's* dollars, so when you say you want an additional $40,000 per year during retirement, you most likely mean you would like $40,000 of today's purchasing power per year. For example, rework the previous problem, taking into consideration an expected annual inflation rate of 3 percent between now and retirement. The necessary accumulated wealth increases from nearly $400,000 to $1,654,184.83. To understand this increase by a factor of four, consider that, given 3 percent inflation, in 40 years it will take $130,481 to provide the purchasing power of $40,000 today. The amount it is necessary to save each year also would be four times larger.

WHAT DOES A COMPREHENSIVE RETIREMENT PLAN LOOK LIKE?

In the previous section, we considered only the case of the individual deciding how much additional income he or she would desire during retirement and then solved for the savings necessary. A comprehensive retirement plan looks at a person's retirement income from a multitude of sources, projects that person's retirement expenses, and then suggests some solutions for meeting any shortfalls. Comprehensive retirement plans require an extremely large number of assumptions. Many of the calculators on the Internet will incorporate some of their own assumptions without informing you what they are. More than ever, using different calculators will produce different solutions, so use several before making a firm commitment to a financial plan. In addition, use comprehensive retirement calculators about once a year to track how you are progressing toward retirement. Doing so is like timing your laps early in a long-distance race to see if you are running too fast or too slowly; you will find it is much easier to make adjustments earlier than at the end!

Consider the following comprehensive example:

Dan and Sharon O'Neill are both 25. Dan earns $38,000 per year, and Sharon is a full-time homemaker. They both plan to retire when they turn 65. They believe inflation will average out to 3 percent per annum, and that Dan's salary will grow at the average annual rate of 3 percent. Neither expects to live beyond the age of 90. They would like to leave $100,000 in their estate at the time of death (to cover funeral expenses, the costs of settling their estates, and a little something for their beneficiaries). They believe their effective federal and state marginal tax rates will be 28 and 7 percent, both now and during retirement. In terms of today's dollars, they would like to provide for monthly living expenses of $4,000 per month for the first 15 years of retirement, then $3,500 per month thereafter. They will let the calculator estimate Social Security income based on the assumption that they will both start drawing benefits when Dan turns 65.

Dan projects he will have a $1,000 monthly pension, and that he will receive this for the next 25 years after retirement. The first payment will not be adjusted for inflation. The O'Neills are planning no special one-time investments, and do not have a savings program outside of their pension and supplemental retirement programs. Dan has a current balance in his 401k plan of $3,500. He currently adds $60 per month to this program, and his employer adds $120 per month. Dan has a traditional IRA account containing $6,300, but no further additions to it are planned. Beginning today, Dan will put $167 per month into a Roth IRA account. On both IRA accounts and the 401k, the O'Neills believe they will earn an average of 10 percent per year between now and retirement on this money, and average 8 percent after retirement. Do the O'Neills need to make any adjustments to cover their retirement years?

Web Link 18.31   Solve this problem using several of the calculators at **Web Link 18.31**. It turns out that the O'Neills will need to make some substantial adjustments if they want to achieve their retirement goals. This is because the plan outlined above will fund the O'Neills' living expenses only until they are 75 years old. Thereafter, their income from Social Security and Dan's pension will cover only 56 percent of their living expenses. In this case, they would have the following choices:[6]

1. increase their current savings by $1,088 per month,
2. reduce their projected retirement income by $966 per month,
3. work an additional nine years before retiring,
4. work the first five years of retirement to earn $8,995 per month,
5. invest at a higher rate of return,
6. shift more investments into tax-deferred accounts, or
7. decrease the amount of wealth to be left at the time of death.

Web Link 18.32   Naturally, the O'Neills may engage in some combination of the above choices. The Inter-
Web Link 18.33   net-based calculators are ideal for fine-tuning your assumptions.

---

[6]The recommended solutions are from a run of the calculator at www.calcbuilder.com/cgi-bin/calcs/RET2.cgi/usatoday.

SUMMARY

> A tax-favored savings program either allows the contributions to be an adjustment to income, the interest and dividends to accumulate tax-free, the withdrawals to be tax exempt, or some combination of the above.

> The major IRA programs are the traditional, Roth, and the educational. Only contributions to the traditional may be an adjustment to income. Interest and dividends accumulate tax-free in all of them, and only withdrawals from the Roth have the possibility of being completely tax-exempt.

> The decision of whether to contribute to a traditional or Roth IRA depends most critically on how one's marginal tax rate today will compare to one's marginal tax rate during retirement.

> Keogh, 401(k), and 403(b) plans function like traditional IRAs wherein the contributions are an adjustment to income.

> A traditional annuity provides periodic income until a person dies.

> The five payout options for an annuity are cash refund, installment refund, life with period certain, straight life, and joint and survivor option.

> A fixed rate annuity provides constant payments, and a variable rate annuity's payments are dependent upon the investment performance of an underlying portfolio.

> Retirement expenses can be built on a bottom-up basis in which future expenses are projected, or a top-down basis in which one projects income at the time of retirement and takes a percentage of that number.

KEY TERMS

401(k)	403(b)	accumulation phase
annuitant	contingent payee	deferred annuity
educational IRA	floor	immediate annuity
income annuities	IRA	Keogh accounts
life expectancy table	payout phase	qualified annuity
spousal IRA	surrender charge	tax-deferred annuity

PROBLEMS

18.1 Josiah is 16 years old. He has earned enough to put $2,000 into a Roth IRA. He figures he doesn't really need to start saving for retirement until around 35. If he contributes the full $2,000 to a Roth IRA, and does so every year for the next 50 years, what will be the value of his account if he earns an average rate of return of 6 percent? 8 percent? 10 percent?

18.2 Shaq James has $30,000 in a deductible IRA. As Shaq is 36 and plans on working at least until age 66, he is giving serious consideration to rolling over the full $30,000 from his traditional IRA to a Roth IRA so that the money will be tax-free when distributed. As Shaq would hold the same investments in the IRA account he held in the traditional account, his projected rates of return in both are 9 percent. His current tax rate is 28 percent, and his tax rate during retirement is anticipated to be 15 percent. He plans no additional contributions to an IRA between now and retirement. Shaq wants his distributions to last until he would turn 90. As the rollover does not incur the 10 percent fee, but does involve declaring the $30,000 as taxable income that year, Shaq will owe additional income taxes. Assume Shaq will pay the taxes from his transfer amount. Is this a good idea?

18.3 John and Hazel Weatherby project they will have a personal portfolio with $1,000,000 on the day they retire. They project they will want to withdraw $100,000 per year at the start of each year from this portfolio. They believe that during retirement they can generate an 8 percent average annual rate of return. If that is the case, for how long can they draw out the $100,000 per year?

18.4 Brad and Nancy Foster have decided they will need $50,000 in annual retirement income from their personal assets. They are 30 now, and plan to work 36 more years. By investing in conservative stock mutual funds, they believe they can earn an average rate of return of 9 percent. Finally, they both expect to live no more than 25 years after retirement. How much do they need to contribute to achieve this goal?

18.5 Using one of the retirement planning calculators on the Internet, develop your own retirement plan projection. Make whatever assumptions seem appropriate for your situation.

REFERENCES

Web Link 18.34 FAQs for IRAs
Web Link 18.35 Pointer sites for information on IRAs
Web Link 18.36 Miscellaneous sites for IRAs
Web Link 18.37 FAQs for annuities
Web Link 18.38 Miscellaneous sites for retirement planning
Web Link 18.39 Glossaries of retirement planning terms

WALL STREET JOURNAL RESOURCES

Web Link (WSJ) 18.40 Calculator for retirement planning
Web Link (WSJ) 18.41 Recent articles on estate planning
Web Link (WSJ) 18.42 Recent articles dealing with estate planning topics
Web Link (WSJ) 18.43 "Retirement Models That Let Reality Bite," *The Wall Street Journal Interactive Edition,* February 20, 2001
Web Link (WSJ) 18.44 "Taxpayers Have Trouble Understanding IRS Plan Designed to Simplify IRA Rules," The *Wall Street Journal Interactive Edition,* February 18, 2001
Web Link (WSJ) 18.45 "Proposed 401(k) Law Would Allow Investors to Sock Away $15,000," *The Wall Street Journal Interactive Edition,* February 5, 2001
Web Link (WSJ) 18.46 "Investors Should Use Caution When Buying IRAs Online," *The Wall Street Journal Interactive Edition,* March 19, 2000
Web Link (WSJ) 18.47 "Don't Wait to Start Saving If You Want to Retire Early," *The Wall Street Journal Interactive Edition,* February 13, 2000
Web Link (WSJ) 18.48 "Calculating Retirement? It's No Simple Equation," *The Wall Street Journal Interactive Edition,* February 7, 2000

Web Link (WSJ) 18.49   "Retirement Optimists Often Forget to Factor Inflation into Portfolio," *The Wall Street Journal Interactive Edition,* January 30, 2000

Web Link (WSJ) 18.50   "The Web's for Everything, Right? Not for Selling Variable Annuities," *The Wall Street Journal Interactive Edition,* January 10, 2000

For information that has changed since the book was written, for new information that pertains to this topic, and for some new web sites that pertain to the topic of this chapter, see **Web Link 18.51.**

CHAPTER 19

PREPARING FOR DEATH: WILLS, TRUSTS, GIFT AND ESTATE TAXES

LEARNING OBJECTIVES

- Explain why it is important to have a will
- Distinguish between a will and a letter of last instructions
- Describe the key features of a will
- Explain the advantages of a codicil
- Describe the probate process
- Show how to avoid probate
- Discuss how to select an executor
- List the duties of an executor
- Describe what a living will accomplishes
- Explain the concept of guardianship
- Define a trust
- Describe various trusts, including a revocable living trust, a bypass or AB Trust, and a life insurance trust
- Outline the basic rules of estate and gift taxation
- Explain the value of the projected increases in the unified tax credit
- Compute an estate tax liability
- Ascertain if your state has inheritance taxes
- Describe the history of gift and estate taxes

Web Link: www.wiley.com/college/woerheide

INTRODUCTION

The final aspect of personal finance is the issue of dealing with the expectation of death. In Chapter 11 we dealt with the personal finance issues associated with *premature* death. Now we need to delve into the topics associated with the *eventuality* of death.

Some people take a flip attitude in dealing with death. After all, once they are dead, why should they care what happens? For two reasons, however, they really should care. The first is that many people have to deal with the financial issues associated with the death of their parents. We can frequently save ourselves much potential grief if we understand how to help our own parents plan for the financial consequences of their own deaths.

Second, by planning for the financial consequences of our own demise we may substantially increase how much our dependents will inherit and reduce the amount taken by estate taxes, inheritance taxes, and gift taxes. Such planning will reduce the grief and aggravation our dependents have to go through in wrapping up our estates. Newspapers regularly report stories of families that have come apart after feuding over the assets of an estate. One of the greatest gifts a person can provide to his or her family is a clean, clear estate planning process.

In this chapter, we will focus on the case of Meroune Lakehal-Ayat. Meroune has become a member of the "between" generation. His parents are in ailing health, and as the only son he wants to be sure that their finances are sorted out and their wishes clearly noted. Meroune is also reaching the age where the growth of his and his wife's assets, combined with the need to provide for three young children, means that he can no longer put off developing plans for handling his assets at his own demise.

DO I REALLY NEED TO WRITE A WILL?

About one-half of the U.S. population dies without a will, which is referred to as dying **intestate.** It is neither difficult nor expensive to make a simple will, so why do so many of us fail to do so? One possible answer is that the process of writing a will causes people to focus on their own death, an unpleasant thought for many. Some people think subconsciously, or even consciously, that writing a will invites death. If they postpone writing a will, perhaps they will postpone death by being unprepared for it! Some people don't fully appreciate the value to their family of having a will at the time of death. For example, they don't think they have enough assets to justify writing a will and are unaware of some of the other benefits of doing so. Finally, some people think paying for a will is a waste of money until they reach an age where death is likely. Unfortunately, anyone reading the obituary page will quickly note that people (and even children) of all ages die. There is no one age at which a person moves from unlikely to die to likely to die, although each year the older we get, the more likely we are to die than the previous year. A legal will can be written by anyone who is 18 or older and is mentally capable.

**Web Link
(WSJ) 19.1**

Wills can do more than just pass on property. In this chapter, we will look first at the question of what happens if a person dies intestate. We will review the probate process, and consider the selection and role of an executor. We will look at living wills. Next, we examine trusts, an alternative way to pass on some or all of a person's assets. Finally, we look at the taxes that can apply upon a person's death.

SHOULD I WRITE A LETTER OF LAST INSTRUCTIONS?

A will should not be confused with a **letter of last instructions,** a letter that should be written at the same time as the will and updated regularly. Remember that a will may not be read until after the funeral, particularly if it has been kept in the safe of the attorney of the deceased. Imagine how a family would feel if they had cremated the deceased, only to arrive for the reading of the will to hear that under no circumstances should their loved one be cremated. A letter of last instructions should provide any information immediately pertinent once the person has died, such as preferences regarding funeral arrangements, type and location of assets owned, and names and contact information of key people or next of kin. No **executor,** the person designated as legal authority over the deceased's assets, wants to miss including something in an estate out of unawareness of its existence. In many circumstances, a letter of last instructions may be more important than the will itself.

WHAT HAPPENS IF I DIE INTESTATE?

Whether you know it or not, you already have a will! State laws that apply to any person dying intestate determine how that person's belongings will be handled. However, no universal rules govern how your estate would be handled if you die intestate. Despite variations from state to state, some common themes exist. Generally, a spouse and children will receive a majority if not all of the estate, although the ways the estate is split between them can vary greatly.

Some states place constraints on your will that prohibit certain actions. For example, in some states you may not completely disinherit a spouse or a child even if you wanted to. If you die intestate and no relatives can be found, your assets will be turned over to the state. If you have children who are minors and your spouse is declared unfit or cannot be found, the state will appoint a guardian for your children.

Wills not only pass on assets, but name the executor of your estate and the guardian of any minor children. They can outline your preferences in case of certain events, such as a primary beneficiary dying before you do or you and your spouse dying "simultaneously."

About the only people who do not need wills are minor children and single people who absolutely do not care what happens to their body, assets, or dependents after their death. Everyone else who is 18 or older and mentally competent should most likely have a will.

Web Link 19.2
Web Link 19.3

COULDN'T I SAVE MONEY BY BUYING A DO-IT-YOURSELF WILL?

It is tempting to write a do-it-yourself will. Anyone can sit down and do so using do-it-yourself kits available at book or stationery stores. Such an approach unquestionably will save on the cost of writing the will itself. However, such wills may contain errors and critical omissions. For example, if you specified that your spouse will serve as guardian of minor children but neglect to indicate that he or she need not post a bond or provide reports to the court, you could be creating substantial expense and hassle for your spouse and children. Furthermore, if anyone were unhappy with your will (e.g., a relative who was not named a beneficiary), any errors in a do-it-yourself will would make it easier to overturn.

A single person or a couple whose members are naming each other as sole beneficiaries, and who have a relatively simple estate and no relatives, are good candidates for a do-it-yourself will. Also, you might want to draft a do-it-yourself will in order to think through the variety of decisions that must be made in a will before you visit a lawyer. In fact, asking a lawyer to review a do-it-yourself will might be cheaper than having the lawyer draw up the will from scratch. Therefore, some do-it-yourself wills are appropriate.

Web Link 19.4
Web Link 19.5

WHAT MAKES A WILL LEGITIMATE?

To pass legal scrutiny, a will must be written in a way that will convince a court that it is the expression of the testator's wishes at the time of death, and that the testator knew full well what he or she was doing at the time the will was written and signed. (A **testator** is the person for whom a will is written and by whom a will is signed.) In order to establish these facts, wills usually state them explicitly, using language that names the document as the **last will and testament** of the individual, and making clear that any prior wills are invalid. Such a statement will normally be included even in the first will a person writes.

Testamentary capacity requires that the testator be fully cognizant of his or her actions at the time the will was written and signed. A will's declaration that the testator is of sound mind usually establishes this. Note that being of sound mind does not mean that the deceased was fully knowledgeable. The testator may well have been unaware of many legal and tax issues that he or she should have known about or at least considered. The testator may even have been given poor or incorrect legal advice. Also, being of sound mind does not mean that the testator necessarily has any sense of fairness. If someone can demonstrate that the testator was not of sound mind or was **unduly influenced,** then a will can be overturned. When a will is overturned, the estate is treated as if the testator had died intestate. However, courts are quite hesitant to overturn a will. To overturn a will, it takes more than proving that the testator behaved unusually at the time of death or that the will is inherently unfair.

If a will is typed, then typically two independent witnesses must sign it. If the will is properly signed and notarized, then it should be *self-proving,* which means that no additional documentation is necessary to have the will be accepted as valid. Some states accept a **holographic,** or handwritten, will. Witnesses are not required for a holographic will. Holographic wills are usually do-it-yourself wills, and carry the advantages and disadvantages discussed above.

Web Link 19.7
Web Link 19.8

Consider the following situation:

> *Meroune, at the age of 45, has decided to have his will prepared for the first time. He discussed with his attorney all the details of what he would like written, and he incorporated many of the attorney's suggestions to cover situations Meroune had not considered. Meroune has stopped by the attorney's office to sign his will, but it is lengthy and he is in a rush. Should he sign it without reading it?*

The answer is an absolute no. As wills tend to follow standard formats, attorneys will tend to copy an example of a previously drawn will or edit a standard will form to meet Meroune's wishes. Errors can easily occur in this process, so Meroune should not sign this document until he has gone over every paragraph to make sure each section meets his intent. If necessary, Meroune should take a copy of the will with him and return at a later time to sign it.

WHAT ARE COMMON FEATURES OF WILLS?

Web Link 19.6

To review, the most critical features of a will are that testamentary capacity has been established, that it is the last will, that it has been properly witnessed, and that it appoints an executor. The remaining features of a will establish how the testator wants his or her estate distributed, and make any necessary appointments. The estate is defined as everything a decedent owned, including personal and real property. A **beneficiary** is a person named in a will to receive personal property or other benefits. An **heir** is a person entitled to receive property when a decedent dies intestate. Because virtually all intestate succession laws include only relatives, heirs must be relatives of the deceased. A beneficiary need not be related to the deceased, although few people leave assets to anyone other than family.

The gift of personal property in a will is called a **bequest** or **legacy.** The receiver is known as a **legatee.** The gift of real estate in a will is called a **devise,** and the recipient is referred to as the **devisee.** Personal property in an estate includes financial assets such as stocks, bonds, or bank accounts, and tangible property, such as furniture, automobiles, and jewelry.

If the decedent has dependents, such as children, then a **guardian** must be named. A guardian is the person legally entrusted with the care of a minor child. The definition of *minor* varies by state, but for all states the **legal age of majority** is between 16 and 18 years of age. At the legal age of majority, a child is considered **emancipated,** that is, an adult for legal purposes. Guardians of minor children are, of course, usually the spouse of the deceased. Guardians may be required to post a bond with the court and regularly report on monies spent on the children. Normally, testators ask that the bond be waived and no reporting be required. This places no restraints on the surviving spouse in taking care of the children as he or she sees fit. If the testator is a single parent with no ex-spouse or if the ex-spouse is considered to be an unacceptable parent (e.g., is in jail), then a will's appointment of a guardian becomes crucial. No one would want his or her children left standing at the end of the funeral service with no one to take them home.

In cases of divorce where the decedent has sole custody of the children, a guardian other than the children's natural, surviving parent is sometimes designated. The courts have set aside these requests in cases where the ex-spouse can meet five conditions:

- proof of a long marriage,
- evidence that the ex-spouse has remained active in the children's lives,
- desire of the children to be with the ex-spouse,
- evidence that it is in the children's best interest to go to the ex-spouse, and
- evidence that the ex-spouse can financially support the children.

Web Link 19.9

A testator may give the executor the **power of appointment.** A general power of appointment allows the executor to distribute the estate as he sees fit. A limited or special power of appointment places some restrictions on what the executor may do. Wills cannot do or require anyone to engage in illegal activities. Any such provisions are automatically set aside.

WHAT UNUSUAL SITUATIONS CAN DEVELOP WITH WILLS?

There have surely been bizarre wills and bizarre circumstances surrounding wills as long as people have been drafting them. The oldest known still dates from 2548 B.C. and could almost pass for its modern-day equivalent. The shortest will on record is just 10 words long: "Being of sound mind and body, I spent it all."

Some wills are noteworthy for their meanness. One probated will reads as follows:

To my wife, I leave her lover and the knowledge I wasn't the fool she thought I was. To my son, I leave the pleasure of earning a living. For 25 years he thought the pleasure was mine. He was mistaken. To my daughter I leave $100,000. She will need it. The only good piece of business her husband ever did was to marry her. To my partner, I leave the suggestion that he take some other clever man in with him at once if he expects to do any profitable business.

Another documented case involved a will in which a fellow left everything to his girlfriend. She refused to pay for the funeral expenses. The decedent's daughter ended up picking up the tab, and that was all she inherited from her father.

Finally, an urban legend relates a similar twist on a will. The story usually involves a person who sees a newspaper advertisement offering to sell a late-model, deluxe car for some ridiculous price such as $25. When the prospective buyer shows up, the woman selling the car supposedly explains that she is the executor of her late husband's estate, and

Web Link 19.10   that his will asks that the car be sold and the proceeds be given to his girlfriend.

WHAT IS A CODICIL?

Sometimes a testator would like to make a small change to his or her will. Rewriting a will every time this happens would clearly become expensive and time-consuming, so you may add what is called a **codicil,** a short amendment to a will. Codicils are meant as additions

Web Link 19.11   or clarifications, not fundamental changes. If many arise, then rewriting the will would
Web Link 19.12   become worthwhile. Codicils must be witnessed and signed with all the formalities of an
Web Link 19.13   actual will.

WHAT DOES PROBATE INVOLVE?

Probate refers to the process in which a will is presented to the Probate Court and validated. Once probated, the will becomes a public document. Legal authority is granted to the **executor** or **executrix** named in the will to distribute the assets according to the terms of the will. It is debatable whether probating a will serves any useful purpose for most estates, other than to provide a steady source of income for lawyers. Nonetheless, it is not an option for most estates.

Probate must occur in the county in which the deceased resided at the time of death. The first step in the probate process is for the executor, or other interested party, to file the original copy of the will with the court, along with a copy of the death certificate. We will assume in this discussion that it is the executor who files. The executor may do this much on his own, but because a lawyer is usually needed later in the process, many people use one for this first step. If no will exists, then either someone may volunteer to serve as an **administrator,** or the court will appoint one. It is also possible that every potential executor named in the will has died before the decedent did, in which case an administrator is again needed.

Once the court is satisfied as to the validity of the will, it is admitted to probate. As part of this process, potential beneficiaries and other interested parties are informed of the probate process and of the pending appointment of an executor. A deadline is established for filing any protests. If any interested parties have concerns about the legitimacy of the will or the individuals who will be put in charge of the estate, they may at this time file a claim. Once any such claims have been resolved, the executor is then given legal authority to handle all assets of the estate. This legal authority is established with the issuance of what are known as **letters testamentary** or **letters of administration.**

Web Link 19.14
Web Link 19.15

CAN I AVOID PROBATE?

Web Link 19.18

People seek to avoid probate for three reasons. First, it is time consuming, sometimes tying up assets for a year or longer. Second, attorney's fees may take 5 percent or more of the estate. Hence, even if probate cannot be avoided, it may be beneficial to substantially reduce the amount of assets that are included in the probate estate. Third, people like privacy as to what they own.

You can avoid probate in several ways. Most states set a minimum value of an estate below which it is not necessary to probate it. For example, in California estates below $100,000 need not be probated. They can be probated if the executor so decides or if circumstances render it appropriate, but it is not mandatory.

Web Link 19.16

Another way is to ensure that some of the assets are held in accounts with designated beneficiaries and thus are not part of the probate estate. The simplest way to do this is to establish a **payable-on-death** (POD) account (see **Web Link 19.16**) that names one or more beneficiaries. Under FDIC rules, currently eligible as beneficiaries on POD accounts are one's spouse, children, grandchildren, parents, and siblings. POD accounts may be set up at any depository institution, such as a bank, savings and loan, or credit union. A POD brokerage account may be established in the 29 states that have enacted the Uniform Transfer-on-Death Securities Registration Act. However, brokerage accounts with this provision are known as transfer-on-death (TOD) accounts.[1] In a POD or TOD type account, the beneficiary must appear at the financial institution and present evidence of the death of the account holder (usually a death certificate) and proof of his or her own identity.

Web Link 19.17

Another primary example of assets that would bypass probate is those held in **joint accounts with right of survivorship** (JTWROS). Note that some states use the term **tenancy by the entirety** rather than JTWROS. Tenancy by the entirety is limited to married couples, but as a practical matter, they are the same thing. It is an entirely different matter if the joint account carries the title of **tenants in common** (TIC). If one of the owners of a TIC account dies, then his or her ownership of one-half of the account passes to his or her beneficiary, who may not be the other tenant.

IRA accounts, Keogh plans, 401(k) plans, pension accounts, and savings bonds are other examples of assets that may be able to bypass the probate process. In general, any

---

[1]TOD accounts are restricted to brokerage accounts with one small exception. California and Missouri currently allow TOD registration for automobiles. It is likely that TOD brokerage accounts will eventually spread to all 50 states, and that more states will approve TOD auto registrations.

account in which the owner may specify a beneficiary is eligible to bypass probate. Naturally, if the account owner does not specify a beneficiary or specifies his or her own estate, then the assets will end up as part of the probate estate. Life insurance proceeds are also payable directly to the named beneficiaries (except when the estate itself is the named beneficiary). You can also set up trusts and make other financial arrangements so that the dollar amounts of assets that are transferred by your will are minimal.

There are, of course, still other ways to avoid having specific assets or the entire estate go through probate, but remember that this avoidance process is not cost-free. For some, the avoidance process may be worse than the alternative. For example, if you give away your assets prior to death, you could avoid probate—but die a pauper!

Some states are known as **community property** states.[2] The community property process works similarly in all states. All property owned by one spouse is automatically owned by the other, unless the spouses sign an agreement stating otherwise. An exception to this rule involves inherited assets. However, if the inherited assets are mixed with other community assets to the point that they become indistinguishable, they can be community property. In most community property states, community assets are treated as JTWROS and are exempted from probate.

Web Link 19.19

WHOM SHOULD I CHOOSE TO BE MY EXECUTOR?

Certain guidelines can help testators choose an executor. First, the testator should verify that the person so named is willing to serve. Anyone is free to renounce an appointment to serve as an executor, and many do. Second, it would help if the person named had the knowledge, insight, time, interest, and resources necessary to do the job. Some states require that some or all of the executors be residents of the state. Executors may be paid or may be asked to serve without payment. Also, executors may decline payment. A common reason for declining payment is that the executor may be the sole or primary beneficiary, and a payment would count as taxable income for the executor. If the payment of an executor's fee results in savings on the estate tax that outweigh the personal income taxes paid, then drawing a fee would make financial sense. However, if little or no estate tax is due (as with the majority of estates), then the payment of an executor's fee accomplishes nothing except the enrichment of the United States Treasury.

A testator might also consider appointing co-executors who could share the work burden. Also, this provides protection if one of the executors renounces the role or dies before or simultaneously with the testator. Frequently, an institution such as a bank trust department or a law firm is named as a co-executor. An institutional or corporate executor should bring substantial knowledge and experience to the process, but can also bring an expensive fee. Finally, a testator should name an alternate executor, in case none of the named executors are available to serve.

Some states require that executors post a bond. If the testator thinks this may be appropriate, he or she may require it in the will. Most testators do not wish to place this

---

[2]Currently, these are Alaska, Arizona, California, Idaho, Louisiana, Nevada, New Mexico, Texas, Washington, and Wisconsin.

Web Link 19.20

burden and expense on their executors, and so include a provision in the will explicitly exempting the executor from posting a bond.

WHAT ARE THE RESPONSIBILITIES OF AN EXECUTOR?

The executor named in the will will normally be the person to probate the will, and then will be given letters testamentary or letters of administration. The next steps are to reconcile all money owed to and by the deceased, to identify and inventory the deceased person's property, to obtain appraisals on it where appropriate, and to liquidate such assets as appropriate. Once the executor is confident that all assets are under control, he then pays off all debts and taxes due (which usually includes filing one or more tax returns). The next step is to distribute the remaining cash and property to the beneficiaries as the will directs. Finally, the executor informs the court that all of the above steps have in fact occurred. To do so, the executor may well ask the beneficiaries to sign statements acknowledging receipt of assets from the estate. Once the paperwork has been filed and the court finds everything in order, the executor is discharged.

Web Link 19.21
Web Link 19.22

WHAT IS A LIVING WILL AND HOW DO I OBTAIN ONE?

A living will is somewhat of a misnomer. It has nothing to do with a traditional will that settles an estate. A living will is a legally binding statement about your desired medical treatment should you become unable to give such instructions. Simply put, it is a statement that you wish no extraordinary means to be used to keep you alive when the chance of a recovery is virtually nonexistent. Living wills are designed to avoid huge medical expenses that would serve no real or useful purposes when quality of life has deteriorated to the point where you will cause only hardship for your family. Living wills are not permission to commit euthanasia, which would be proactively terminating the life of a critically ill person. Rather, living wills are authorization to withhold treatment even if the known consequence of doing so is death. Living wills are meant to alleviate the financial and emotional costs to the family and friends of observing a terminally ill person linger.

There are different levels of permission in living wills. The least permissive is one that allows only extraordinary means of medical treatment to be withheld, usually respirator care. More extensive levels of permission would include the withholding of artificial nutrition, and even the withholding of hydration.

Some people have religious objections to such withholding of treatment. Others may not want treatment withheld even if there is only a one in ten million chance of recovery. Still, everyone age 18 or older should at least consider having a living will.

Web Link 19.23
Web Link 19.24

WHAT IS GUARDIANSHIP?

The appointment of a guardian is not limited to wills. Guardianships may be established on behalf of anyone who is deemed incapacitated. Thus, if you believe your parents have reached a stage in life where they are incapable of making rational, appropriate decisions, and they refuse to accept guidance, you may move to establish guardianship. State guardianship laws[3] protect the personal and property rights of people who are incapacitated. Guardianship cases usually start when someone files a **petition to determine capacity** along with an application for appointment as guardian with a state circuit court. A guardian must be at least 18 years of age and have an interest in the protection of both the personal and property rights of the incapacitated person. Once a hearing is scheduled, a notice is provided to the alleged incapacitated person as well as to the known next of kin. The court then appoints a committee of doctors to examine the alleged incapacitated person, and will appoint an attorney to represent this person if he or she does not have one. A hearing is then held and a decision rendered. If the person is declared incapacitated, a guardian is appointed, and in some cases two, one for property and one for the person himself or herself.

The guardian must then file an **initial guardianship report** that details the plan of how the **ward** will be taken care of. Next, the guardian must file **annual guardianship reports** documenting that care. Guardianship can be limited to certain aspects of a ward's life. If the ward is deemed to be able to make reasonable decisions in some aspects of his or her life, he or she is supposed to be left free to do so.

Web Link 19.25

Some alternatives to guardianship exist. One is establishment of a **representative** or **protective payee,** who is authorized to receive certain income on behalf of the incapacitated person. A second alternative is a **conservatorship,** a voluntary proceeding in which the **conservatee** asks the Probate Court to appoint a conservator to manage the conservatee's estate. The court must find the conservatee incapable of managing his or her own financial affairs, but capable of choosing a conservator to do so. The most formal alternative is to establish a **power of attorney,** in which one individual simply gives another individual the authority to make binding decisions and otherwise represent his or her own interests. Anyone can give a power of attorney to anyone else. Power of attorney should only be extended where a strong bond of trust exists. In many cases on record, someone befriends an elderly or incapacitated person, convinces that person to assign them power of attorney, and then runs off with his or her financial assets, never to be seen again.

WHAT ARE TRUSTS?

Trusts come in a multitude of forms, depending upon the asset being passed, the arrangement of the trust, and the intent of the trust. A trust could complement a will and serve as the primary means for passing on your assets, although it should never be an alternative to a will. However, trusts may be used for many purposes and should not be viewed solely as vehicles for passing on your estate.

---

[3]This discussion is based on the guardianship process for the state of Florida. Florida's disproportionately large number of elderly makes it a particularly important state in terms of guardianship laws.

The basic parties to a trust are the **grantor,** the **trustee,** and the **beneficiary.** The grantor is the person who places the assets in the trust. The trustee is the person who manages the assets in the trust. The beneficiary is the person who receives the financial benefits of the trust. Sometimes one person takes all three roles, but more often several people are involved. The grantor may be a couple, or even relatives such as siblings. The trustee may be a corporate entity such as a bank trust department or a law office. The beneficiary could include an **income beneficiary,** who receives the income from the trust during the life of the trust, and a **remainderman,** who receives the assets of the trust when it is liquidated. The assets in the trust are known as the **principal** or **corpus.**

A trust may be described as either **inter vivos** or **testamentary.** The former, also known as a **living trust,** is created and funded during a person's lifetime. The latter is created through the terms of a will. Trusts can also be classified as either revocable or irrevocable.

A trust may offer an opportunity to save on estate and/or income taxes. It may allow one individual to pass to another the task of managing his or her assets without giving up the income from those assets. It may allow an individual to give up the income from assets without giving up the assets themselves. A trust may be established to protect assets from creditors, and even from a spouse or soon-to-be ex-spouse. Trusts may also provide privacy that will not exist for the probate estate. Probate fees (such as those charged by lawyers to probate an estate) are based on a percentage of assets, so assets in a trust (and not the probate estate) do not count in the computation of these fees. To delve extensively into all types of trusts would go beyond the scope of this chapter. However, as trusts can complement a will, some basic information about them is useful when financially preparing for death.

Web Link 19.26

WHAT ARE THE ADVANTAGES OF A REVOCABLE LIVING TRUST?

The most common form of trust is the revocable living trust, which can, by definition, be revoked at any time. Simple revocable living trusts that stay in the control of the grantor provide no savings whatsoever on income taxes. Any income on the assets in the trust (be it dividends, interest, capital gains, rent, etc.) is taxed exactly the same as if it were income to the individual. The only savings from a simple, revocable living trust is on probate costs, particularly the legal fees that will be based on the size of the probate estate.

At the death of the grantor, a revocable living trust obviously becomes irrevocable. If the grantor was serving as trustee, there must be a provision for a successor trustee. With a copy of the death certificate and a certified copy of the trust agreement, the new trustee can take control of the trust assets and begin distribution of them to the designated beneficiaries if necessary. Thus, a trustee could begin distributing assets within weeks after the death of the grantor, as opposed to the months or even years that would be required before an executor or administrator could begin to distribute proceeds of the will.

A revocable living trust should always be accompanied with a will and never be a substitute for it. For one thing, not all of the grantor's assets may be in the trust at the time of death. Many people intend at the time of death to have all remaining assets transferred to the trust via the will. Such a will is called a **pour-over will.** Second, as we saw earlier, a will is more than just the distribution of assets, but also the appointment of an executor or guardian and directions for paying all debts and taxes owed by the decedent. Without an executor, there is no one to transfer any designated assets to the trust!

Drawbacks to using a living trust include the expense of drawing up the agreement, a fee that could easily exceed $1,000. If a person's estate is small, the money spent to create a living trust may well exceed the probate expenses that would have been due without the trust. Spending $1,000 today to save your beneficiaries $500 in 20 years doesn't make a lot of sense! Another drawback is the paperwork hassle associated with the creation of a new form of ownership for some of your assets. Finally, the alternative methods to avoid probate, discussed previously, may adequately cover your assets, so if the primary goal of creating a trust is to avoid probate, you can find simpler and cheaper ways of doing it.

Web Link 19.27

Web Link 19.28

Web Link 19.29

WHAT IS A BYPASS OR AB TRUST?

Consider the following situation:

Meroune and his wife would like to assure a speedy distribution of assets to their children after they both are gone. Their current assets total $2 million. Meroune is concerned that a trust would be dissolved and assets distributed to the children after the first of them dies, leaving the surviving spouse with a substantially reduced income. Also, Meroune fears that if death occurred while his children were still minors that they would come into control of substantial monies before they had the maturity to handle it. What should Meroune do?

The above situation is ideal for what is known as a bypass or AB Trust. In an AB Trust, when either parent dies, the assets in part A are willed to the children, while the income from these assets goes to the surviving spouse. When the surviving spouse dies, all of the assets go to the children. This is advantageous from an estate tax exemption perspective (discussed in full later in the chapter). A bypass trust allows both the husband's and wife's exemptions to be applied to the assets; without the trust, if all assets are left to the spouse, only the remaining spouse's estate tax exemption can be used when passing assets to the children. A bypass or AB Trust saves a substantial amount of estate taxes, assures that assets do not pass prematurely to the children, and keeps the income from the assets for the surviving spouse. In such a situation, the Lakehal-Ayats need only assure that a successor trustee is appointed upon the death of the second spouse, and that the trust matures when the children reach a certain age.

As the Lakehal-Ayats have more than one child, they must decide whether the trust should be maintained as a single entity or split into separate trusts for each child upon the death of the remaining spouse. Many parents use the former approach, which allows flexibility in dealing with emergencies—such as if one child turns out to have special needs, the principal of the trust can be used to help this one child. For example, if one child were in an auto accident that resulted in permanent disabilities and extensive medical care while the other child wound up a successful surgeon, most parents would like to have a way to leave more to the debilitated child.

Still another decision the Lakehal-Ayats must make is when the trust's assets will be distributed to the beneficiaries. Distribution upon the death of the grantor might not be appropriate if the beneficiaries are still children at that time. They might choose either a specific date for distribution, such as July 1, 2015, or a birth date for each child, such as each child's 25th birthday.

Such trusts have some restrictions. For example, once the first spouse dies and the trust becomes irrevocable, the assets must eventually go to the children. The second spouse is no longer free to use the assets as he or she sees fit. For example, if the surviving spouse remarried and wanted to liquidate some of the assets to finance activities of a second marriage, he or she would not be free to do so. In particular, the surviving spouse could not will the assets that were put in the trust to his or her own surviving spouse from a second marriage. A bypass or AB trust absolutely prevents a surviving spouse from disinheriting his or her children from the first marriage.

Web Link 19.30

WHAT ARE IRREVOCABLE LIVING TRUSTS?

As the name implies, an irrevocable living trust cannot be altered once it has been created. Thus, if a person names his or her children as the beneficiaries of an irrevocable living trust and then later wishes to disinherit them, he or she cannot do so. The major advantage of an irrevocable living trust is that the assets are effectively removed from the grantor's (or settler's) estate, so a substantial amount of estate taxes may be avoided. Again, some restrictions apply.

First, the grantor must not be a beneficiary of the trust. Hence, the grantor irrevocably gives up not only the assets, but also any income from them. Second, transfers to an irrevocable trust could be subject to a gift tax at the time of transfer. (Gift and estate taxes will be discussed later in the chapter.) However, a key feature of gifts is that each person has a $10,000 annual exemption on gifts per person. Thus, a person with three children could give each of them $10,000 per year as gifts without fear of any tax consequences. A husband and wife together could give to three children a total of $60,000 per year without concern about gift taxes. Thus, an irrevocable trust would work best if it were set up early enough so that annual gifts of $10,000 per year could be used for most or all of the contributions to the trust.

Irrevocable trusts are frequently used to support incapacitated family members, to establish education funds for children or grandchildren, and to fund charitable remainder and life insurance trusts.

Web Link 19.31

WHAT IS A CHARITABLE REMAINDER TRUST?

In a charitable remainder trust, a charity is specified as a beneficiary. A charity could be designated the recipient of income during the life of the trust, with the trust assets going to a different party (such as one's children) at its termination. The opposite and more common arrangement is for the income from the trust to go to the grantor or the grantor's children until the death of the last income beneficiary, after which the assets go to the charity originally designated by the grantor. Income from the trust can be specified as a set percentage, which fluctuates with the trust's market value. Part of the market value of the assets contributed to a charitable trust counts as an itemized tax deduction, so long as the trust is irrevocable. Usually, charitable trusts are funded with appreciated assets such as securities. The creation of the trust allows the grantor to escape the capital gains taxes that would be due on the sale of the donated assets. It also allows the grantor to take a large income tax deduction now, rather than as a credit on his or her estate taxes. Despite all these advantages, the ultimate motive in setting up a charitable trust has to be the altruistic desire to give some of one's wealth to one or more charities.

The exact value of the income tax deduction will vary, based on the expected value of the charitable contribution at the time the trust is created. The higher the annual income that is provided to the income beneficiaries during their lives, the lower the tax deduction. In addition, the IRS uses a published discount rate to compute the value of the contribution. The higher the published rate, the lower the contribution value of the assets used to set up the trust. Finally, the younger the grantor, the lower the value. Consider the following example:

> Meroune and his wife would like to give $100,000 to their alma mater. They could give the cash directly, but their tax advisor has suggested a charitable remainder trust. Based on their current ages and the discount rate used by the IRS, they would receive a $40,000 tax deduction if they set up and fund the trust this year. They also note that they have some highly appreciated stock. They could give $100,000 worth of shares in Exxon Mobil. Their cost basis in this stock is $1,500. What are the tax consequences if they fund the charitable trust through a gift of stock if the capital gains tax rate is 20 percent and the marginal rate on ordinary income is 35 percent? Also, assume the marginal tax rate on their estate would be 55 percent.

If the capital gains tax rate is 20 percent, then selling the stock would cost the couple $19,700 ([$100,000 – $1,500] × 20%) in taxes. The $40,000 charitable tax deduction is worth $14,000 ($40,000 × 35%) in tax savings. In addition, if the couple were to die tomorrow with the $100,000 worth of stock in their estate, they would owe $55,000 ($100,000 × 55%) in incremental estate taxes. However, if they die owning the stock, they will owe no capital gains tax (a topic to be discussed later).

Web Link 19.32

WHAT IS A RESIDENCE TRUST?

A residence trust is designed to remove the market value of your residence from your estate. Essentially, you transfer ownership of your property to a trust, and when it expires ownership of the property reverts to the remaindermen (e.g., your children). The point of a residence trust is that it fixes the value of the residence for estate tax purposes. The value of the residence would always be at most the property's market value at the time of the contribution. Sometimes an even lower valuation will be applied. Once property is in the trust, it is excluded from the estate, its price cannot appreciate, and the trust itself is not subject to gift taxes.

Residence trusts do involve risk. First, if the grantor fails to outlive the residence trust, then the whole trust is moot. Second, after the trust expires, the remaindermen truly own the house. The beneficiaries would have the right to ask the occupant to vacate the property; in other words, the children could throw their parents out of the parents' home.

Web Link 19.33

WHAT IS A LIFE INSURANCE TRUST?

A life insurance trust is usually set up to pay federal estate taxes. The purpose of buying this life insurance through a trust is to keep the death benefit out of the grantor's estate. This can be done in a two-step process. First, the grantor establishes the trust with enough cash to pay the first year's premium. Second, the trust buys the life insurance policy, naming itself the beneficiary on the policy.

To appreciate how this sequence avoids all estate taxes, consider what would happen if the two steps were reversed. If the policy were bought before the trust was created, then the grantor is personally buying the policy. Upon creation of the trust, the contribution of the policy into the trust is a gift. Gifts made within three years of a person's death are normally treated as part of a person's estate. Thus, if the policy is bought directly by the grantor rather than through the trust and the grantor dies before the three years is up, then Web Link 19.38 the trust has failed to provide protection from estate taxes. The policy will be treated as if Web Link 19.38a the grantor owned it and the death benefit added to the value of the estate.

WHAT OTHER TYPES OF TRUSTS EXIST?

The charitable remainder trust, the residence trust, and the life insurance trust are not the only types of trusts. Trusts can be created for a wide variety of purposes and with a wide variety Web Link 19.34 of terms. Although we will not go into detail, a few additional common trusts include:

Web Link 19.34a
- The Crummey Trust: designed to obtain the annual $10,000 gift exemption without actually giving control of the gift to the beneficiary

Web Link 19.34b
- The Qualified Terminable Interest in Property (QTIP) Trust: designed to assure that assets go to children without the surviving spouse losing the income from the assets

Web Link 19.34c
- The Family Limited Partnership (FLP) Trust: designed for families where the primary asset consists of real estate or a family business

Web Link 19.34d
- The Grantor Retained Annuity Trust (GRAT): designed to eventually pass assets to children and to provide an income to the grantor for a specified number of years

Web Link 19.34e
- The Generation-Skipping Trust: designed to avoid estate taxes on up to one million dollars, while at the same time providing income to one's children

SHOULD I CONSIDER A CORPORATE TRUSTEE?

Just as there are valid reasons for appointing an institutional or corporate executor or co-executor in one's will, there are similar reasons to consider a corporate entity such as a bank trust department or a law firm as a trustee or co-trustee for a trust. A corporate trustee brings many potential advantages, such as knowledge, experience, and—in the case of Web Link 19.35 trusts involving multiple family members—impartiality. Many families have been irrevo- Web Link 19.36 cably split by disagreements or suspicions over the fairness in the handling of estates and Web Link 19.37 trusts. The major disadvantage to a corporate trustee is that the cost can be substantive.

WHAT RULES COVER ESTATE AND GIFT TAXATION?

The basic rules of gift and estate taxes are few and simple. First, any gift or inheritance given to a spouse is tax exempt.[4] Second, gifts and bequests given to a charitable organization are exempt from all gift and estate taxes. Third, a gift to a noncharitable organization or an individual may require the payment of gift taxes. A person may give tax-free up to $10,000 per year to any individual. Thus, someone who gives $10,000 to each of 10 people during one year would have given away $100,000 but would owe no taxes, whereas if this same person gave the whole $100,000 to one individual—some lucky soul!—the giver could owe substantial taxes on that gift. A married couple together can give $20,000 per individual per year tax-free, even if only one of the spouses actually provides the gift. Giving money away in yearly installments of $10,000 (or $20,000 if you are married) is about the simplest way to minimize your probate estate and avoid gift and estate taxes. Beyond that limit the giver must file a form with his or her tax return that reports the tax consequences of this gift.

Everyone has what is known as a one-time-only unified tax credit. In 2001, this unified tax credit was $220,550. This means that after you compute the taxes you owe on a gift, you may offset these taxes up to the amount of your unified tax credit. For example, if you give someone (other than your spouse) a gift of $15,000 during a year, you would owe gift taxes on $5,000. The tax rate on this $5,000 is 18 percent (the marginal rates will be discussed later), so your gift tax liability would be $900 ($5,000 × 18%). You could then reduce your unified tax credit by $900 (to $219,650). Eventually, your estate would end up paying $900 more in estate taxes than would otherwise have been the case, assuming of course that your estate would owe at least $900 in estate taxes.

Web Link 19.50

If you make no taxable gifts during your lifetime, as is the case for most people, then the entire unified tax credit would be available for your estate. For the year 2001, the unified tax credit exactly offsets the estate taxes on the first $675,000 of one's taxable estate. Hence, in estate planning for the year 2001, no one would need to worry about estate taxes for estates of less than $675,000. This would not mean you do not need to engage in estate planning, just that estate taxes are not an issue for you.

Web Link 19.40

IN VIEW OF THE MARITAL DEDUCTION, WHY NOT JUST LEAVE EVERYTHING TO MY SPOUSE?

The exemption of gifts and inheritances transferred to one's spouse from gift and estate taxation is known as the **marital deduction**.[5] A person with an estate of $2,000,000 who left everything to his or her spouse would owe no estate taxes. If the surviving spouse remarries and leaves everything to his or her spouse in turn, estate taxes are still avoided. Theoretically, as long as surviving spouses continued to remarry and leave everything to the new spouses, estate taxes could be forever avoided, but as a practical matter, the surviving spouse usually leaves everything to the children. In another scenario, the surviving

---

[4]If securities are given as a gift, the cost basis remains unchanged. If securities are received as a bequest, then the cost basis is usually adjusted to the market value at the time of death of the decedent. In certain circumstances, the market value six months later can be used as the cost basis.

spouse could avoid estate taxes by spending most of the marital assets before dying. However, in many cases the inherited assets actually grow in value before the surviving spouse leaves everything to the children. The surviving spouse's unified tax credit will save some estate taxes, but a substantial portion of estate taxes could still be due. Had the spouse who died first left some of the assets to the children (or at least placed them in a trust with the children as the remaindermen), then his or her own unified tax credit could have been used. Although the assets going directly to the surviving spouse would be fewer, the estate taxes eventually owed on these assets would be less. The surviving spouse must be a citizen of the United States, by the way, or tax-exempt distributions are more constrained.

Web Link 19.41

WILL THE UNIFIED TAX CREDIT ALWAYS EXEMPT $675,000 IN TAXABLE ESTATE?

For many years up until 1997, the unified tax credit was $192,800. This effectively exempted the first $600,000 of taxable estate from estate taxes. The Taxpayer Relief Act of 1997 authorized increases in the unified tax credit to $202,050 in 1998 and steadily increasing to $345,800 in 2006. So while in 1998 the first $625,000 of the taxable estate was exempted, by 2006 the first $1,000,000 of taxable estate will be. Table 19.1 displays the value of the unified tax credit for each year and the amount of estate that this will exempt.

Web Link 19.42

Table 19.1
Unified Tax Credits and Exempt Assets

Calendar Year	Estate Tax Credit	Amount of Transfer Exempted
2000–2001	$220,550	$675,000
2002–2003	$229,800	$700,000
2004	$287,300	$850,000
2005	$326,300	$950,000
2006 or later	$345,800	$1,000,000

Source: http://www.irs.ustreas.gov/plain/forms_pubs/pubs/p95003.htm, May 15, 2001.

Two exceptions to the unified tax credit are family-owned businesses and farms. Currently, estates holding either of these are allowed a combined exemption of $1,300,000. The standard exemption applies to all of the rest of the net estate, and the difference between the standard exemption and $1,300,000 applies to the farm or family business. For example, in 2001 when the standard exemption is $675,000, an additional $625,000 exemption can be applied to family-owned businesses and farms. Restrictions on what constitutes a family-owned business or farm may be found at Web Link 19.42a.

Web Link 19.42a

[5]For many years the marital deduction was limited to the greater of one-half of the estate or $250,000.

WHAT IS THE TAX SCHEDULE FOR ESTATES?

The schedule for taxes on gifts and estates can be presented in two ways. Gifts and estates are taxed under the same schedule because if the taxes on gifts were lower than those on estates, everyone would give their estate away as they lay dying.[6] If the taxes on estates were lower than the taxes on gifts, people would give fewer gifts.

Under the IRS Code for 2001, if none of the unified tax credit has been used for gift taxes, then the first $675,000 of taxable estate is exempt from taxation. Estates valued between $675,000 and $750,000 are taxed at 37 percent of the amount over $675,000. Thus, an estate of $700,000 would owe estate taxes of $9,250 (37% × [$700,000 – $675,000]). An estate worth exactly $750,000 would owe estate taxes of $27,750 (37% × [$750,000 – $675,000]). Estates worth more than $750,000 but not more than $1,000,000 would owe taxes of $27,750 plus 39 percent of the amount over $750,000. This $27,750 fixed amount represents the portion of the estate between $675,000 and $750,000 being taxed at 37 percent. Thus, an estate of $850,000 would owe estate taxes of $66,750 ($27,750 + 39% × [$850,000 – $750,000]). Once an estate exceeds $50,000,000 the estate tax equals $27,500,000 plus 55 percent of the amount over $50,000,000. The good news is that most of us will not have to worry about having an estate of this size!

Web Link 19.43
Web Link 19.44

The tax schedule for estate taxation may be found at **Web Links 19.43** and **19.44**. **Web Link 19.43** does not incorporate the unified tax credit. Thus, this format computes the estate tax due on the entire estate, and then deducts the unified credit or whatever credit is left if some of the credit had been previously applied to gifts to determine if any net estate tax is due. Note that at this link the lowest tax rate is 18 percent, and it is applied to the first $10,000 of taxable estate. Thus, although it is technically correct to say that estate taxes run from an initial marginal rate of 18 percent to a final marginal rate of 55 percent, it is also misleading. Because of the unified tax credit, the first marginal rate that becomes an effective rate is 37 percent. Hence, it would be more accurate to say that marginal gift and estate tax rates run from 37 percent to 55 percent. Consider the following example:

> *Meroune's father, Rajiv, is a widower who plans to leave all his assets to his children. His estate totals $1,600,000. How much will his children receive net of federal estate taxes? Assume he has not used up any of his unified tax credit.*

The tax on a $1,500,000 estate is $555,800. The marginal tax rate between $1.5 million and $2 million is 45 percent, so Rajiv's estate would owe another $45,000 on the last $100,000 of his estate. Hence, his total tax bill before the unified credit is applied is $600,800. If Rajiv dies in the year 2001, his net estate tax due would be the difference between the $600,800 total tax and the $220,550 unified credit, or $380,250.

The sites listed at **Web Link 19.44** already incorporate the unified tax credit. Hence, they provide the tax rates for that portion of the estate that exceeds the exempt amount.

Naturally, some calculators available will compute your estate tax directly, rather than just providing a table of the estate tax rates. Some of these calculators ask for a detailed listing of the assets that will be included in the estate. These calculator sites are

---

[6]The IRS used to views all gifts made within three years of one's death as gifts made in anticipation of death, and may therefore declare these gifts as part of the estate. Now, only the gifts of life insurance and a few other items could be moved from gift to estate if they happen within three years of one's death.

Web Link 19.45 provided at **Web Link 19.45.** Caution must be exercised in using these sites because some of them fail to update the unified tax credit each year as it changes.

WHAT DOES MY TAXABLE ESTATE CONSIST OF?

The value of the taxable estate for most people would equal the net worth of their personal balance sheet, as discussed in Chapter 2. However, a few adjustments would be necessary. The formula for computing the taxable estate, also known as the **adjusted gross estate** (AGE), is

$$\text{Gross Estate} - \text{Allowable Deductions} = \text{Net Taxable Estate}$$

The gross estate includes all of the typical assets of a household, such as cash, securities, real estate, and personal property. Some other items that would be included are

1. dividends and interest owed to a decedent at the time of death,
2. the death benefit (less any policy loans outstanding) of life insurance policies owned by the decedent,
3. the value of any qualified retirement plans and IRAs,
4. Uniform Gifts to Minors Act (UGMA) accounts and Uniform Transfer to Minors Act (UTMA) accounts set up and controlled by the decedent, and
5. the value of any annuities that do not terminate with the death of the decedent.

Allowable deductions include all debts and taxes owed by the decedent at the time of death. Presumably, the executor will pay all of these obligations with cash generated by the estate. Four additional items are included in allowable deductions:

1. the marital deduction, to the extent that it is used,
2. the charitable deduction, to the extent that the will leaves gifts to qualified charities,
3. "final expenses," a euphemism for the cost of the funeral, and
4. administrative expenses.

Estate taxes are due nine months after the date of death. Because an executor cannot allow the estate to come up short in its obligations to pay debts, income taxes, administrative expenses, and estate taxes, it is appropriate to withhold all distribution of assets until these items have been paid in full. For this reason, distribution of assets from estates normally takes at least a year.

If an estate tax return is to be filed, then the executor has the option of valuing the estate at market value either at the time of death or six months after death. If the latter is chosen and any assets are sold during the six-month period, those assets are valued at the sale price. If no estate tax return is due, then the valuation date must be the date of death.

Selecting the valuation date is not so simple as it seems at first glance. It is true that the date that provides the lower valuation will minimize the estate taxes due. However, keep in mind that the valuation of assets for the estate also sets their value for beneficiaries. Let's say the estate includes 1,000 shares of Global Crossing stock whose price is $35 on the date of death and $45 after the six-month interval. Valuation at the date of death will obviously minimize the estate tax; however, it also means that the beneficiary will have to note the cost basis as $35 per share rather than $45 per share, creating a difference of $10,000 ([$45 − $35] × 1,000 shares) in capital gains when the stock is eventually sold. Thus, determination of the valuation date will affect whether the estate pays now in the form of estate taxes or the beneficiary pays later in the form of capital gains taxes. At the present time, the marginal tax rates on estates are substantially higher than the marginal tax rates on capital gains, so it would make sense to minimize the estate's tax bill. Furthermore, the beneficiary might never sell the stock, donating it to charity or leaving it to **Web Link 19.46** his or her own beneficiaries, in which case, the cost basis would become irrelevant.

WHICH STATES HAVE DEATH (OR INHERITANCE) TAXES?

So far, we have focused exclusively on the federal estate tax. Some states also tax estates. To avoid confusion, these taxes are usually referred to either as inheritance taxes or death taxes. The states that currently have them are Connecticut (to be phased out by 2005), Delaware, Indiana, Iowa, Kansas, Kentucky, Louisiana, Maryland, Michigan, Montana, Nebraska, New Hampshire, New Jersey, North Carolina, Pennsylvania, South Dakota, and **Web Link 19.47** Tennessee.

Web Link 19.48 An example of New Jersey's schedule of state inheritance taxes may be found at **Web Link 19.48.** In this case, the marital exemption is applied. Bequests to parents, grandparents, and children are also exempted from taxation. Bequests to siblings and in-laws are taxed starting at a rate of 11 percent on amounts over $25,000. Bequests to anyone else are taxed starting at a rate of 15 percent on amounts over $500.

HOW MIGHT I REDUCE MY ESTATE TAXES?

Once a person discovers that his or her estate will owe estate taxes, it is natural to turn one's thoughts to how to reduce or avoid them. Remember, one of the reasons Congress inserts techniques for reducing or eliminating taxes into the tax code is to encourage people to engage in them. It is wrong to *cheat* on taxes, but it is perfectly appropriate and desirable to use legal, recommended techniques to reduce one's taxes. Tax avoidance is good for society; tax evasion is immoral and illegal.

Let us review the primary techniques for reducing estate taxes. The most common techniques for reducing estate taxes have already been mentioned—namely the 100 percent marital deduction and the $10,000 per person per year exemption on gifts to an individual (or the $20,000 per person per year exemptions on gifts by a married couple). Another technique is simply to give some of your estate to charity. If you own your life insurance policies (i.e., you bought the policy and you pay the premium on the policy) then your estate includes the life insurance proceeds regardless of who the stated beneficiary is. So another technique to reduce estate taxes is to transfer ownership of the policy to someone else, such as the beneficiary. The life insurance proceeds then pass outside of your estate. More complicated techniques involve the creation of various types of trusts as discussed earlier in the chapter.

Web Link 19.49

HOW HAVE THE GIFT AND ESTATE TAXES EVOLVED OVER TIME?

The modern version of the federal estate tax was put into effect in 1916 to help with the funding of World War I. After the war, it was continued to prevent an increase in the concentration of wealth. The tax was to be applied to that value of estates that exceeded a $50,000 exemption. The marginal tax rates ranged from 1 percent to 10 percent, but the 10 percent rate only applied to that portion of estates over $10 million. Naturally, people attempted to avoid this tax, and they found they could do so by simply giving away that portion of their assets above the exemption. (Remember, in 1920, $50,000 had the same purchasing power as about $1,000,000 today.) Congress directly attacked this avoidance process by placing a tax on gifts in 1924. From 1943 to 1976, the dollar exemptions and marginal tax rates for the gift and estate taxes had stabilized. The estate tax exemption stood at $60,000, and the gift tax exemption stood at $30,000 for the lifetime exemption and $3,000 per recipient per year. The marginal estate tax rates at this time ranged from 3 percent to 77 percent, but the gift taxes were set at two-thirds the value of the estate taxes. Hence, the system still strongly encouraged people to give away as much of their estates as possible.

The fundamental structure of the federal estate and gift tax laws changed with the passage of the Tax Reform Act (TRA) of 1976 and the Economic Recovery Tax Act of 1981 (ERTA). Unfortunately, the marginal tax rates for gift taxes were increased to equal those of the estate tax rates, discouraging giving. However, these acts also brought substantial relief from taxation for many. The top marginal tax rate was scaled back to 55 percent and the annual exclusion from the gift tax was increased to $10,000. In addition, the amount of the estate exempt from taxation was increased to $600,000. In the Taxpayer Relief Act of 1997, provisions were made to increase the exemption on estates to $1,000,000 by the year 2006.[7] Currently, estate and gift taxes account for about one percent of federal revenues. The cost of collecting this revenue approximately equals the amount of revenue collected. In September of 1999, Congress actually voted to repeal the estate tax, but President Clinton vetoed this legislation. For additional discussion of the history of gift and estate taxes, see **Web Link 19.51**.

Web Link 19.51

Estate taxes were one of the topics of debate in the presidential election of 2000. President Bush campaigned on the proposal to eliminate estate taxes. What was not clear is whether such elimination would also eliminate the opportunity to step up the cost bases for all inherited taxes. If the step-up in cost bases is eliminated, then many estates would actually owe more in income taxes upon liquidation of the estate than they would have owed under current estate taxes rules. It is highly likely that estate taxes will be changed

---

[7]The Taxpayer Relief Act of 1997 also established special exclusions for qualified family-owned businesses.

in some way during President Bush's administration; it is just not terribly clear what that change will be.

SUMMARY

➤ It is important to have a will even if you have few assets, because a will handles many other eventualities.

➤ Critical information should be left in a letter of last instructions.

➤ A codicil is an addendum to a will and saves you from rewriting an entire will for minor changes or additions.

➤ The probate process involves presenting a will in Probate Court and having it validated as a public document.

➤ Probate can be avoided for small estates and by structuring your assets so that many pass outside of the estate.

➤ A living will is simply an instruction not to use heroic means to keep a person alive.

➤ Guardians should be named in wills, although anyone may be placed in guardianship.

➤ The universe of trusts allows you to transfer wealth over time. The key parties to a trust are always the grantor, the trustee, and the beneficiary.

➤ Trusts include a revocable living trust, a bypass or AB Trust, and a life insurance trust.

➤ You may give away $10,000 per year per person (or $20,000 per couple) without incurring gift taxes.

➤ All estates are subject to a unified gift and estate tax credit, currently allowing $675,000 of net estates to avoid estate taxes.

➤ Some states have death or inheritance taxes, which can be a substantial portion of the estate.

KEY TERMS

AB Trust	adjusted gross estate	administrator
annual guardianship report	beneficiary	bequest
bypass trust	codicil	community property
conservatee	conservatorship	corpus
devise	devisee	emancipated
executor	executrix	grantor
guardian	holographic	heir
income beneficiary	inter vivos	initial guardianship report
intestate	joint accounts with right of survivorship	last will and testament
legacy	legal age of majority	legatee
letters of administration	letter of last instructions	letters testamentary
living trust	marital deduction	payable-on-death
power of appointment	petition to determine capacity	pour-over will

power of attorney	principal	protective payee
remainderman	representative	tenancy by the entirety
tenants in common	testamentary	testamentary capacity
testator	trustee	unduly influenced
ward		

PROBLEMS

19.1 Using a sample will from the Internet, write a will for yourself.

19.2 What would be the estate tax on a $1,000,000 net estate for each year from 2001 to 2006. What is the estate tax as a percentage of the estate in each year?

19.3 Using one of the Internet calculators, compute the size of a taxable estate for a well-to-do individual. Make whatever assumptions you would like.

REFERENCES

Web Link 19.52   Miscellaneous sites
Web Link 19.53   FAQ sites
Web Link 19.54   Pointer sites
Web Link 19.55   Miscellaneous sites relating to wills and trusts
Web Link 19.56   FAQ sites relating to wills and trusts
Web Link 19.57   Glossary sites
Web Link 19.58   Pointer sites

WALL STREET JOURNAL RESOURCES

Web Link (WSJ) 19.59   Recent articles on retirement planning
Web Link (WSJ) 19.60   Recent articles dealing with retirement topics
Web Link (WSJ) 19.61   "Wait to Do Estate Planning Until the Rules Are No Longer in Limbo," *The Wall Street Journal Interactive Edition,* January 28, 2001
Web Link (WSJ) 19.62   "Death, Taxes and Philanthropy," *The Wall Street Journal Interactive Edition,* December 18, 2000
Web Link (WSJ) 19.63   "Who Gets What? Mistakes Can Ruin Estate Plans," *The Wall Street Journal Interactive Edition,* September 11, 2000
Web Link (WSJ) 19.64   "Living Trusts Are Usually Unnecessary for Those without a Large Estate," *The Wall Street Journal Interactive Edition,* June 19, 2000
Web Link (WSJ) 19.65   "Estate-Planning Web Sites Provide Direction on Wills, Taxes and More," *The Wall Street Journal Interactive Edition,* April 30, 2000
Web Link (WSJ) 19.66   "The Rich and Famous Use Trusts to Hide Ownership of Property," *The Wall Street Journal Interactive Edition,* November 27, 1998

For information that has changed since the book was written, for new information that pertains to this topic, and for some new web sites that pertain to the topic of this chapter, see **Web Link 19.67.**

APPENDIX

Appendix A.1
Future Value Interest Factors

Interest Rates

Time	1%	2%	3%	4%	5%	6%	7%	8%	9%	10%	11%	12%
1	1.0100	1.0200	1.0300	1.0400	1.0500	1.0600	1.0700	1.0800	1.0900	1.1000	1.1100	1.1200
2	1.0201	1.0404	1.0609	1.0816	1.1025	1.1236	1.1449	1.1664	1.1881	1.2100	1.2321	1.2544
3	1.0303	1.0612	1.0927	1.1249	1.1576	1.1910	1.2250	1.2597	1.2950	1.3310	1.3676	1.4049
4	1.0406	1.0824	1.1255	1.1699	1.2155	1.2625	1.3108	1.3605	1.4116	1.4641	1.5181	1.5735
5	1.0510	1.1041	1.1593	1.2167	1.2763	1.3382	1.4026	1.4693	1.5386	1.6105	1.6851	1.7623
6	1.0615	1.1262	1.1941	1.2653	1.3401	1.4185	1.5007	1.5869	1.6771	1.7716	1.8704	1.9738
7	1.0721	1.1487	1.2299	1.3159	1.4071	1.5036	1.6058	1.7138	1.8280	1.9487	2.0762	2.2107
8	1.0829	1.1717	1.2668	1.3686	1.4775	1.5938	1.7182	1.8509	1.9926	2.1436	2.3045	2.4760
9	1.0937	1.1951	1.3048	1.4233	1.5513	1.6895	1.8385	1.9990	2.1719	2.3579	2.5580	2.7731
10	1.1046	1.2190	1.3439	1.4802	1.6289	1.7908	1.9672	2.1589	2.3674	2.5937	2.8394	3.1058
11	1.1157	1.2434	1.3842	1.5395	1.7103	1.8983	2.1049	2.3316	2.5804	2.8531	3.1518	3.4785
12	1.1268	1.2682	1.4258	1.6010	1.7959	2.0122	2.2522	2.5182	2.8127	3.1384	3.4985	3.8960
13	1.1381	1.2936	1.4685	1.6651	1.8856	2.1329	2.4098	2.7196	3.0658	3.4523	3.8833	4.3635
14	1.1495	1.3195	1.5126	1.7317	1.9799	2.2609	2.5785	2.9372	3.3417	3.7975	4.3104	4.8871
15	1.1610	1.3459	1.5580	1.8009	2.0789	2.3966	2.7590	3.1722	3.6425	4.1772	4.7846	5.4736
16	1.1726	1.3728	1.6047	1.8730	2.1829	2.5404	2.9522	3.4259	3.9703	4.5950	5.3109	6.1304
17	1.1843	1.4002	1.6528	1.9479	2.2920	2.6928	3.1588	3.7000	4.3276	5.0545	5.8951	6.8660
18	1.1961	1.4282	1.7024	2.0258	2.4066	2.8543	3.3799	3.9960	4.7171	5.5599	6.5436	7.6900
19	1.2081	1.4568	1.7535	2.1068	2.5270	3.0256	3.6165	4.3157	5.1417	6.1159	7.2633	8.6128
20	1.2202	1.4859	1.8061	2.1911	2.6533	3.2071	3.8697	4.6610	5.6044	6.7275	8.0623	9.6463
21	1.2324	1.5157	1.8603	2.2788	2.7860	3.3996	4.1406	5.0338	6.1088	7.4002	8.9492	10.8038
22	1.2447	1.5460	1.9161	2.3699	2.9253	3.6035	4.4304	5.4365	6.6586	8.1403	9.9336	12.1003
23	1.2572	1.5769	1.9736	2.4647	3.0715	3.8197	4.7405	5.8715	7.2579	8.9543	11.0263	13.5523
24	1.2697	1.6084	2.0328	2.5633	3.2251	4.0489	5.0724	6.3412	7.9111	9.8497	12.2392	15.1786
25	1.2824	1.6406	2.0938	2.6658	3.3864	4.2919	5.4274	6.8485	8.6231	10.8347	13.5855	17.0001

Appendix A.2
Present Value Interest Factors

Interest Rates

Time	1%	2%	3%	4%	5%	6%	7%	8%	9%	10%	11%	12%
1	0.9901	0.9804	0.9709	0.9615	0.9524	0.9434	0.9346	0.9259	0.9174	0.9091	0.9009	0.8929
2	0.9803	0.9612	0.9426	0.9246	0.9070	0.8900	0.8734	0.8573	0.8417	0.8264	0.8116	0.7972
3	0.9706	0.9423	0.9151	0.8890	0.8638	0.8396	0.8163	0.7938	0.7722	0.7513	0.7312	0.7118
4	0.9610	0.9238	0.8885	0.8548	0.8227	0.7921	0.7629	0.7350	0.7084	0.6830	0.6587	0.6355
5	0.9515	0.9057	0.8626	0.8219	0.7835	0.7473	0.7130	0.6806	0.6499	0.6209	0.5935	0.5674
6	0.9420	0.8880	0.8375	0.7903	0.7462	0.7050	0.6663	0.6302	0.5963	0.5645	0.5346	0.5066
7	0.9327	0.8706	0.8131	0.7599	0.7107	0.6651	0.6227	0.5835	0.5470	0.5132	0.4817	0.4523
8	0.9235	0.8535	0.7894	0.7307	0.6768	0.6274	0.5820	0.5403	0.5019	0.4665	0.4339	0.4039
9	0.9143	0.8368	0.7664	0.7026	0.6446	0.5919	0.5439	0.5002	0.4604	0.4241	0.3909	0.3606
10	0.9053	0.8203	0.7441	0.6756	0.6139	0.5584	0.5083	0.4632	0.4224	0.3855	0.3522	0.3220
11	0.8963	0.8043	0.7224	0.6496	0.5847	0.5268	0.4751	0.4289	0.3875	0.3505	0.3173	0.2875
12	0.8874	0.7885	0.7014	0.6246	0.5568	0.4970	0.4440	0.3971	0.3555	0.3186	0.2858	0.2567
13	0.8787	0.7730	0.6810	0.6006	0.5303	0.4688	0.4150	0.3677	0.3262	0.2897	0.2575	0.2292
14	0.8700	0.7579	0.6611	0.5775	0.5051	0.4423	0.3878	0.3405	0.2992	0.2633	0.2320	0.2046
15	0.8613	0.7430	0.6419	0.5553	0.4810	0.4173	0.3624	0.3152	0.2745	0.2394	0.2090	0.1827
16	0.8528	0.7284	0.6232	0.5339	0.4581	0.3936	0.3387	0.2919	0.2519	0.2176	0.1883	0.1631
17	0.8444	0.7142	0.6050	0.5134	0.4363	0.3714	0.3166	0.2703	0.2311	0.1978	0.1696	0.1456
18	0.8360	0.7002	0.5874	0.4936	0.4155	0.3503	0.2959	0.2502	0.2120	0.1799	0.1528	0.1300
19	0.8277	0.6864	0.5703	0.4746	0.3957	0.3305	0.2765	0.2317	0.1945	0.1635	0.1377	0.1161
20	0.8195	0.6730	0.5537	0.4564	0.3769	0.3118	0.2584	0.2145	0.1784	0.1486	0.1240	0.1037
21	0.8114	0.6598	0.5375	0.4388	0.3589	0.2942	0.2415	0.1987	0.1637	0.1351	0.1117	0.0926
22	0.8034	0.6468	0.5219	0.4220	0.3418	0.2775	0.2257	0.1839	0.1502	0.1228	0.1007	0.0826
23	0.7954	0.6342	0.5067	0.4057	0.3256	0.2618	0.2109	0.1703	0.1378	0.1117	0.0907	0.0738
24	0.7876	0.6217	0.4919	0.3901	0.3101	0.2470	0.1971	0.1577	0.1264	0.1015	0.0817	0.0659
25	0.7798	0.6095	0.4776	0.3751	0.2953	0.2330	0.1842	0.1460	0.1160	0.0923	0.0736	0.0588

Appendix A.3
Future Value Interest Factor for an Annuity

Interest Rates

Time	1%	2%	3%	4%	5%	6%	7%	8%	9%	10%	11%	12%
1	1.0000	1.0000	1.0000	1.0000	1.0000	1.0000	1.0000	1.0000	1.0000	1.0000	1.0000	1.0000
2	2.0100	2.0200	2.0300	2.0400	2.0500	2.0600	2.0700	2.0800	2.0900	2.1000	2.1100	2.1200
3	3.0301	3.0604	3.0909	3.1216	3.1525	3.1836	3.2149	3.2464	3.2781	3.3100	3.3421	3.3744
4	4.0604	4.1216	4.1836	4.2465	4.3101	4.3746	4.4399	4.5061	4.5731	4.6410	4.7097	4.7793
5	5.1010	5.2040	5.3091	5.4163	5.5256	5.6371	5.7507	5.8666	5.9847	6.1051	6.2278	6.3528
6	6.1520	6.3081	6.4684	6.6330	6.8019	6.9753	7.1533	7.3359	7.5233	7.7156	7.9129	8.1152
7	7.2135	7.4343	7.6625	7.8983	8.1420	8.3938	8.6540	8.9228	9.2004	9.4872	9.7833	10.0890
8	8.2857	8.5830	8.8923	9.2142	9.5491	9.8975	10.2598	10.6366	11.0285	11.4359	11.8594	12.2997
9	9.3685	9.7546	10.1591	10.5828	11.0266	11.4913	11.9780	12.4876	13.0210	13.5795	14.1640	14.7757
10	10.4622	10.9497	11.4639	12.0061	12.5779	13.1808	13.8164	14.4866	15.1929	15.9374	16.7220	17.5487
11	11.5668	12.1687	12.8078	13.4864	14.2068	14.9716	15.7836	16.6455	17.5603	18.5312	19.5614	20.6546
12	12.6825	13.4121	14.1920	15.0258	15.9171	16.8699	17.8885	18.9771	20.1407	21.3843	22.7132	24.1331
13	13.8093	14.6803	15.6178	16.6268	17.7130	18.8821	20.1406	21.4953	22.9534	24.5227	26.2116	28.0291
14	14.9474	15.9739	17.0863	18.2919	19.5986	21.0151	22.5505	24.2149	26.0192	27.9750	30.0949	32.3926
15	16.0969	17.2934	18.5989	20.0236	21.5786	23.2760	25.1290	27.1521	29.3609	31.7725	34.4054	37.2797
16	17.2579	18.6393	20.1569	21.8245	23.6575	25.6725	27.8881	30.3243	33.0034	35.9497	39.1899	42.7533
17	18.4304	20.0121	21.7616	23.6975	25.8404	28.2129	30.8402	33.7502	36.9737	40.5447	44.5008	48.8837
18	19.6147	21.4123	23.4144	25.6454	28.1324	30.9057	33.9990	37.4502	41.3013	45.5992	50.3959	55.7497
19	20.8109	22.8406	25.1169	27.6712	30.5390	33.7600	37.3790	41.4463	46.0185	51.1591	56.9395	63.4397
20	22.0190	24.2974	26.8704	29.7781	33.0660	36.7856	40.9955	45.7620	51.1601	57.2750	64.2028	72.0524
21	23.2392	25.7833	28.6765	31.9692	35.7193	39.9927	44.8652	50.4229	56.7645	64.0025	72.2651	81.6987
22	24.4716	27.2990	30.5368	34.2480	38.5052	43.3923	49.0057	55.4568	62.8733	71.4027	81.2143	92.5026
23	25.7163	28.8450	32.4529	36.6179	41.4305	46.9958	53.4361	60.8933	69.5319	79.5430	91.1479	104.6029
24	26.9735	30.4219	34.4265	39.0826	44.5020	50.8156	58.1767	66.7648	76.7898	88.4973	102.1742	118.1552
25	28.2432	32.0303	36.4593	41.6459	47.7271	54.8645	63.2490	73.1059	84.7009	98.3471	114.4133	133.3339

Present Value Interest Factor for an Annuity

Interest Rates

Time	1%	2%	3%	4%	5%	6%	7%	8%	9%	10%	11%	12%
1	0.9901	0.9804	0.9709	0.9615	0.9524	0.9434	0.9346	0.9259	0.9174	0.9091	0.9009	0.8929
2	1.9704	1.9416	1.9135	1.8861	1.8594	1.8334	1.8080	1.7833	1.7591	1.7355	1.7125	1.6901
3	2.9410	2.8839	2.8286	2.7751	2.7232	2.6730	2.6243	2.5771	2.5313	2.4869	2.4437	2.4018
4	3.9020	3.8077	3.7171	3.6299	3.5460	3.4651	3.3872	3.3121	3.2397	3.1699	3.1024	3.0373
5	4.8534	4.7135	4.5797	4.4518	4.3295	4.2124	4.1002	3.9927	3.8897	3.7908	3.6959	3.6048
6	5.7955	5.6014	5.4172	5.2421	5.0757	4.9173	4.7665	4.6229	4.4859	4.3553	4.2305	4.1114
7	6.7282	6.4720	6.2303	6.0021	5.7864	5.5824	5.3893	5.2064	5.0330	4.8684	4.7122	4.5638
8	7.6517	7.3255	7.0197	6.7327	6.4632	6.2098	5.9713	5.7466	5.5348	5.3349	5.1461	4.9676
9	8.5660	8.1622	7.7861	7.4353	7.1078	6.8017	6.5152	6.2469	5.9952	5.7590	5.5370	5.3282
10	9.4713	8.9826	8.5302	8.1109	7.7217	7.3601	7.0236	6.7101	6.4177	6.1446	5.8892	5.6502
11	10.3676	9.7868	9.2526	8.7605	8.3064	7.8869	7.4987	7.1390	6.8052	6.4951	6.2065	5.9377
12	11.2551	10.5753	9.9540	9.3851	8.8633	8.3838	7.9427	7.5361	7.1607	6.8137	6.4924	6.1944
13	12.1337	11.3484	10.6350	9.9856	9.3936	8.8527	8.3577	7.9038	7.4869	7.1034	6.7499	6.4235
14	13.0037	12.1062	11.2961	10.5631	9.8986	9.2950	8.7455	8.2442	7.7862	7.3667	6.9819	6.6282
15	13.8651	12.8493	11.9379	11.1184	10.3797	9.7122	9.1079	8.5595	8.0607	7.6061	7.1909	6.8109
16	14.7179	13.5777	12.5611	11.6523	10.8378	10.1059	9.4466	8.8514	8.3126	7.8237	7.3792	6.9740
17	15.5623	14.2919	13.1661	12.1657	11.2741	10.4773	9.7632	9.1216	8.5436	8.0216	7.5488	7.1196
18	16.3983	14.9920	13.7535	12.6593	11.6896	10.8276	10.0591	9.3719	8.7556	8.2014	7.7016	7.2497
19	17.2260	15.6785	14.3238	13.1339	12.0853	11.1581	10.3356	9.6036	8.9501	8.3649	7.8393	7.3658
20	18.0456	16.3514	14.8775	13.5903	12.4622	11.4699	10.5940	9.8181	9.1285	8.5136	7.9633	7.4694
21	18.8570	17.0112	15.4150	14.0292	12.8212	11.7641	10.8355	10.0168	9.2922	8.6487	8.0751	7.5620
22	19.6604	17.6580	15.9369	14.4511	13.1630	12.0416	11.0612	10.2007	9.4424	8.7715	8.1757	7.6446
23	20.4558	18.2922	16.4436	14.8568	13.4886	12.3034	11.2722	10.3711	9.5802	8.8832	8.2664	7.7184
24	21.2434	18.9139	16.9355	15.2470	13.7986	12.5504	11.4693	10.5288	9.7066	8.9847	8.3481	7.7843
25	22.0232	19.5235	17.4131	15.6221	14.0939	12.7834	11.6536	10.6748	9.8226	9.0770	8.4217	7.8431

INDEX

fn indicates entry found in footnote

Printed in the United States
96513LV00005B/4/A

9 780471 465447